SOCIAL CHANGE IN WESTERN EUROPE

SOCIAL CHANGE IN WESTERN EUROPE

COLIN CROUCH

OXFORD

UNIVERSITY PRESS

OXFORD
UNIVERSITY PRESS

Great Clarendon Street, Oxford OX2 6DP

Oxford University Press is a department of the University of Oxford.
It furthers the University's objective of excellence in research, scholarship,
and education by publishing worldwide in

Oxford New York

Athens Auckland Bangkok Bogotá Buenos Aires Calcutta
Cape Town Chennai Dar es Salaam Delhi Florence Hong Kong Istanbul
Karachi Kuala Lumpur Madrid Melbourne Mexico City Mumbai
Nairobi Paris São Paulo Singapore Taipei Tokyo Toronto Warsaw

and associated companies in Berlin Ibadan

Published in the United States
by Oxford University Press Inc., New York

British Library Cataloguing in Publication Data

Data available

Library of Congress Cataloging-in-Publication Data
Crouch, Colin, 1944–
Social change in Western Europe / Colin Crouch.
Includes bibliographical references and index.
1. Social change—Europe, Western. 2. Europe, Western—Social
conditions—20th century. I. Title.
HN373.5.C78   1999   303.4'094—dc21   99–32731
ISBN 0–19–874275–4
ISBN 0–19–878068–0 (pbk)

1 3 5 7 9 10 8 6 4 2

Typeset by BookMan Services
Printed in Great Britain
on acid-free paper by
T.J. International
Padstow, Cornwall

For Joan, Daniel, and Benjamin

European Societies

Series Editor: Colin Crouch

Very few of the existing sociological texts which compare different European societies on specific topics are accessible to a broad range of scholars and students. The *European Societies* series will help fill this gap in the literature, and attempts to answer questions such as: Is there really such a thing as a 'European model' of society? Do the economic and political integration processes of the European Union also imply convergence in more general aspects of social life, like family or religious behaviour? What do the societies of Western Europe have in common with those further to the east?

The series will cover the main social institutions, although not every author will cover the full range of European countries. As well as surveying existing knowledge in a way that will be useful to students, each book will also seek to contribute to our growing knowledge of what remains in many respects a sociologically unknown continent.

Forthcoming titles in the series:

Religion in Europe
Grace Davie

European Cities
Patrick Le Galès

Education in Europe
Walter Müller, Reinhart Schneider, and Suzanne Steinmann

Ethnic Minorities in Europe
Carl-Ulrik Schierup

CONTENTS

PREFACE

The arrival of the single European currency, other developments in increasing European integration, and the frequent reference in much political and economic discussion to a 'European model' of society are enough to justify writing a general sociology of contemporary Western Europe. Is there such a thing as a Western European social form? And where would such a form fit into more general patterns of social change in advanced societies? These are the questions I have tried to answer in these pages.

The initial decision to undertake such a task is straightforward; but the choices that then have to be made if this is to be a single-volume, single-person study completed in a reasonable number of years are troublesome. First, is one to write generally about the European population, in the way that a US American sociologist would write a sociology of the USA without constantly working round state by state? Or ought one deliberately keep the nation states as the essential units? Or should one refuse to accept the boundaries of states as necessarily being social boundaries and try to accumulate data at lower geographical levels, determining in the light of those what geographical social entities actually exist? These decisions are in fact made for one by some very practical considerations. Very little statistical data and even less sociological research exist at the level of a generalized Europe; it is also clear after the most elementary study that Western Europe is far too heterogeneous a place to make a generalized study legitimate even if it were possible. The ideal choice would be the third one, building up from local data, to see if nation states really are social units. Unfortunately, two further practical considerations rule this out. First, too much statistical material is available at national but not lower levels; and the sub-national geographical coverage of research findings is very patchy indeed. Second, the criterion of the single-volume, single-person study completed in a reasonable number of years could not possibly be met. *Faute de mieux*, the study becomes one of nation states. Just occasionally one can move to a lower level; frequently one can aggregate nation states into groups of countries; but most of the time one pretends that nation states are societies. This is not a principled decision that I defend, though as will emerge from several chapters, there are reasons for believing that nation states have a particularly important formative influence. The state does shape many social institutions; how many and how much are questions which I should like to submit to sustained empirical test, but that will have to be a different project.

This issue raises further interesting methodological questions for the comparative study of societies. We tend to see individual societies as a series of examples of more or less the same thing, being made up of similar components, albeit of different shapes and sizes—just as we might see a group of dogs as all being individual examples of the same basic item. But to the extent that societies are related to each other through trade, each having different comparative advantages and therefore trading asymmetrically, they are not a series of examples of similar systems, but components of a wider system, the world order. In this respect societies are more like bees in a hive than a group of dogs; what we learn about a drone will tell us little about a worker bee, let alone a queen. To some extent this issue is discussed in the following chapters, but I cannot claim to have treated it at all adequately, and this remains a serious deficiency. To do so would have required sustained analysis of Europe's relations with other parts of the world, both today and in former colonial times.

A second troublesome set of decisions has concerned which national societies should be included. A frequent solution is to concentrate on those with the largest populations: France, Germany, Italy, Spain, the UK. However, not only does this leave out a good deal of the population of Western Europe, but it would also ignore some very interesting social forms. Often precisely because their populations are not large and diversified in several different ways, the smaller European countries exhibit particularly clearly certain characteristics shared by larger ones but less distinctly. However, there has to be a limit. Some of the very small countries (like San Marino, Monaco, or Liechtenstein) are little more than small cities, heavily dependent on surrounding larger societies for many institutions, while collecting material on them can be just as time-consuming as doing the same for societies of several million persons. I therefore decided not to include any countries which had populations smaller than one million. This means that one Member State of the European Union (Luxembourg) is excluded from consideration as well as the even smaller ones. The smallest country fully included is Ireland. This leaves us with 16 cases: the 15 current Member States of the European Union, less Luxembourg but plus Norway and Switzerland.

A similarly pragmatic decision led to the focus solely on the western subcontinent and not on Europe as a whole, or even that extension to the east which would have brought in Poland, the Czech Republic, and Hungary—all relatively soon to join the European Union. The Central European countries have had a shared history with the western lands for most of the past millennium, except for the interlude of soviet communism from the end of the Second World War to the end of the 1980s. Unfortunately, however, it was during that period that much of the sociological material on which this book depends was gathered. Not enough reliable research was carried out in those countries in those years to make it easy to bring them into comparisons. This is not true for all areas of research, and these countries had particularly strong sociological achievements in some. My decision to exclude them is therefore open to fair criticism. However, with an agenda already over full with my existing choice of cases, I have been easy prey to any arguments for exclusion.

The problem of country coverage goes further than what to include within Europe. One of the core questions in this book is the extent to which there might be such a thing as a distinctive Western European form of society. This can only be addressed if the European cohort is compared with some non-European cases. However, this must be done in a way which does not overwhelm the primary European focus of the study. I therefore decided to take basic data from the two largest advanced societies outside Europe: Japan and the USA, two countries which have the added advantage of being very different from each other. Some discussion of these will be found in each chapter, but its role is to help us gain a perspective on the European cases, not to learn much about Japan or the USA in themselves.

A third set of questions concerns the kind of evidence that should be used. Here there are two principal constraints that help one make the decision. First, any data used should help us to compare countries; second, they must be capable of being treated in a way which helps us with the central difficulty of this project—keeping a study of 16 countries down to a manageable size. Both criteria dictate a strong emphasis on quant-itative material. Where good statistics can be found, countries can be very succinctly compared, especially if diagrams can be formed from the statistics. Therefore most chapters are equipped with a heavy statistical apparatus. This itself has usually been confined to the book's Statistical Appendix, only figures based on these appearing in the chapters. The comparisons with Japan and the USA have also been largely confined to these statistical parts of the discussion.

A major problem with statistics is that they are often not truly comparable. Usually one is dependent on data collected by national authorities, and although there have in recent years been some attempts to standardize definitions and other elements to ensure comparability, these have not advanced very far. Readers will find in most chap-ters reservations about the reliance that can be placed on the statistics used because of variability in definitions and methods of collection, and sometimes whole countries have to be left out of discussions because of the unavailability of relevant statistics. These problems are particularly important with the earlier period discussed in most of the book, the 1960s.

The numerical analyses are supplemented by discussions of the existing sociological literature. This greatly enriches our accounts beyond the bare bones of the statistics, but brings considerable problems of comparability. There are today some excellent examples of multi-country studies, particularly on such issues as the family, education, social mobility, and industrial relations, and readers will see how dependent I have been on these. However, one also needs to make much use of restricted two- or three-country studies, or even more often of studies of just one country or a few places within it. There is no way that we can extend the findings of these to countries not included, so necessarily the discussions acquire an anecdotal, haphazard character.

While at times my central problem has been a lack of research findings on a par-ticular item of importance, clearly the opposite problem of too much material for a single-volume study has loomed larger. One basic decision I took in order to simplify this was to concentrate on studies of action and institutions rather than attitudes and beliefs. A large amount of sociological research is concerned with the latter: what do people believe to be their social class (rather than how we can best analyse their social class)? How unequal do they think their societies are (rather than how unequal do we find their societies to be)? Do they believe that husbands and wives should equally share domestic tasks (rather than what their actual division of labour proves to be)? To add discussion of these findings to those of the actual behaviour concerned would add enormously to the questions that need to be addressed. Also, research findings on attitudes can be very speculative, especially when they concern questions that the respondents may not have thought about before the survey took place. For practical reasons of the manageability of the material I therefore decided to concentrate almost solely on action and institutions and to ignore attitudes and beliefs. This breaks down at some points. To take a couple of examples: I am more interested in whether people go to church than in whether they believe in the Devil; or in whether they postpone having children until a convenient point in mothers' working lives than in whether they think that married women ought to have careers; but I cannot ignore the relation-ship between the attitudes and the behaviour in these cases. The study is therefore one which is overwhelmingly but not solely concerned with action as opposed to attitudes.

A fourth issue for me has been the style of presentation, and this is the one point where I have not been governed by the rule of seeking maximum economy of language. There would have been two ways of submitting to that rule. I could write a book for specialists, in which shorthand terms were used and few concepts explained; or I could write a textbook for students that did not go beyond exposition of the literature. Perhaps foolishly, I have instead tried to have the best of both worlds. I am trying here to address specialists on a number of theses about the character of the societies of Western Europe and the ways in which they are changing. But I also want second- and third-year undergraduates and masters course students to be able to make use of the book for their course work. I am therefore trying both to advance new arguments and to explain matters in as jargon-free a manner as is possible. One means that I have used to make the work accessible is to avoid endnotes. These have been used for two purposes only: to explain questions of methodology and the use of statistical sources; and to make occasional points about countries other than Western European ones. Everything else has been included in the main text.

A fifth set of choices concerned which aspects of social life to study. Here at last is an area where my decisions have been guided by theoretical principle and not expediency. As readers will quickly learn, the argument of the book centres on a theory of what I call the mid-century social compromise, which relates to four institutional areas: industrialism, capitalism, traditional community, and citizenship. Those aspects of social life are discussed which fit readily into an account of those areas and the relations between them. How this is done is spelt out at the end of Chapter 1. Sadly some important institutions were difficult to fit into the resulting scheme, in particular the question of the geography of human settlement (the sociology of towns, cities, villages, etc), and of criminal and deviant behaviour. The former topic makes some appearance in Chapter 14, but in general these areas have had to be sacrificed.

A final area of choice has been time period. My general concept of the advanced societies sees them as subject to constant change; as I say in Chapter 15, if they have points of equilibrium, they are like those of someone riding a bicycle, not of a static object. Therefore any piece of evidence about a particular society leads me to ask: 'When was this?' For example, the statement that Swedish women tend to have more children than Italian ones is true for the 1990s, but not at all for previous decades. A fuller comparison of the childbearing habits of Swedish and Italian women should give an account of how these have changed over a number of decades. But it is very difficult to present evidence and information in a form of this kind, demonstrating constant change, when one is discussing 16 countries. I have therefore had recourse to the 'snapshot' technique that I have used before (Crouch 1993) and concentrated on two moments in time. For reasons that will become apparent in Chapter 1, these are the early 1960s and the mid-1990s. A starting date of 1960 takes us past the years of recovery from the disruption of the Second World War and close to the peak of industrialization in many of our countries. Most of my statistical material concentrates on these two points. Like all simplifying devices, this has its costs, as it cannot show the details of intermediate change. Where this has seemed particularly important (as with patterns of welfare state expenditure) I have given some interim statistics too, and often the narrative discussion tries to fill the space between my two time points, especially when there have been changes which have reversed direction during the period (e.g. the distribution of income in many countries).

Nevertheless there will remain many points where readers will wish that I had filled in more detail of the period between my starting and end points, or moved back to an earlier start. I can only plead that they would have found themselves bogged down in the complexity of the resulting narrative. I have however made one major attempt to locate contemporary Western Europe in a much wider historical perspective. Artificial though calendar numbers may be, writing a book at the very end of the 1990s about the subcontinent which dominated the world for much of the preceding thousand years and whose major church numbered our years in the first place has made it impossible to ignore the end of the second Christian millennium. Writing the book at Florence, the city where, at the very mid-point of that millennium, thinkers and artists gave birth to much of what we still today perceive as the 'modern', proved a further temptation to indulge in a far longer historical perspective than those in which sociologists, creatures of the nineteenth and twentieth centuries, usually attempt. I therefore start the book with a sociological look back at that millennium, extending my snapshot technique to leaps of 250 years and taking in at each point the same themes that later form the subject matter of the remaining chapters.

C.C.

Fiesole, Florence
December 1998

ACKNOWLEDGEMENTS

I could not have written this book had I not been fortunate enough to be appointed to a chair in the Department of Social and Political Sciences at the European University Institute at Florence in January 1995. Being surrounded by colleagues, both other professors and students, virtually all of whom are concerned with comprehending some aspect or other of individual European societies or the process of Europeanization in general, has provided the ideal context for an attempt to write a general sociology of Western Europe. Since my own work had previously concentrated on issues of industrial relations, I have been very dependent on colleagues for guidance on subjects outside this range. I presented early versions of most of the chapters at my regular student seminar, and in addition to the helpful discussion I unfailingly received, barely a week passed without someone sending me an e-mail or coming to see me to suggest an article I ought to read or an argument that I ought to pursue or clarify. Discussions of a number of the Institute's doctoral theses and the books of professorial colleagues have also found their way into various chapters. I owe a special thanks to those students who worked as my research students during the course of the project: Bernd Baumgartl, Isabelle van de Gejuchte, Harald Wydra, and Valérie de Campos Mello.

Also vital has been Eva Breivik, who has provided me with such superb administrative support over the years.

Outside the Institute, detailed and very helpful comments were made on earlier drafts of the book by a number of sociological colleagues: Jelle Visser (Amsterdam), Chelly Halsey (Oxford), Carlo Trigilia (Florence), Peter Hall (Harvard), and Göran Therborn (Stockholm). Other people read various chapters to help me make my sociologized English more generally accessible: Joan Crouch, Ben Crouch, and Mari Prichard. I am of course responsible where I have failed to take their advice, or tried to take it but still got things wrong.

Thanks are also due to Tim Barton at Oxford University Press, who persuaded me to write the book in the first place.

The author and publisher are grateful to the following for permission to reprint copyright material: page 127: Table 5.1, taken from E. O. Wright (1995), *Classes* (London: Verso), reprinted by permission of Verso Publishers. Page 164: Table 5.3, taken from OECD (1997), *Employment Outlook* (Paris: OECD), reprinted by permission of the OECD. Page 317 and pages 322–4: Table 11.2 (reprinted with some modification) and Table 11.3, taken from J.-E. Lane and S. O. Ersson (1987), *Politics and Society in Western Europe* (London: Sage), by permission of Sage Publishers.

LIST OF FIGURES

LIST OF TABLES

LIST OF APPENDIX TABLES

ABBREVIATIONS

The following abbreviations are used to indicate various countries in some of the tables and figures:

A   Austria
B   Belgium
CH   Switzerland
D   Germany (the former West Germany)
DK   Denmark
E   Spain
F   France
GR   Greece
I   Italy
IRL   Ireland
JAP   Japan
Lux   Luxembourg
N   Norway
NL   Netherlands
P   Portugal
S   Sweden
SF   Finland
UK   United Kingdom
USA   United States of America

Other abbreviations used in the text:

EU   European Union
ILO   International Labour Office
OECD   Organization for Economic Co-operation and Development

INTRODUCTIONS

PROLOGUE: THE END OF THE EUROPEAN MILLENNIUM

In most of this book we shall be concerned with very recent developments in European societies; we shall rarely look back before the 1960s, and we shall come as far into the 1990s as sources of data and research material permit. But whenever one starts an account of human development one is interrupting a story that has already begun. It is not possible to understand the past thirty or forty years without some knowledge of what went before. In the case of Europe—what Italians call *il vecchio continente*, the old continent—matters have been 'going before' for a very long time. Often a remote past has surprising continuing effects. I shall therefore begin what will be primarily a socio-logical account of contemporary society with a brief look back at a far longer period: the thousand years which, according to inaccurate medieval calendar calculations of the birth of Jesus Christ, end in the year 2000. From about halfway through that millen-nium one could say that Europe, or at least its western part, had become one of the two or three core civilizations of the world. Before then Western Europe had either been, during the first half-millennium after Christ's birth, one part of the Roman Mediter-ranean world or, in the first few centuries following the collapse of Rome, just a rather backward zone (Davies 1997: ch. 4). During the second half of this millennium Europe, or rather some of its constituent political powers, rose through military conquest to become the dominant, ruling continent of the world. Then, during the final half century it declined again to a more junior role. The second half of the second Christian millennium has therefore been *the* European period of history, and it is a period that has now closed.

EUROPE AT THE START OF THE MILLENNIUM

If we were able to examine with modern sociological analysis the human communities that occupied the western part of the European land mass around the year 1000, we should observe societies which were both more uniform and more diverse than their geographical successors today. Virtually all economic activity took the form of culti-vating the land and raising animals—for food, clothing, fuel, and the construction of buildings—using equipment universally simple and labour-intensive. On the other hand, the forms of agriculture varied considerably, being heavily determined by climate and the character of the terrain. The difference between hunting or gathering people and settled farmers, which, at earlier periods of European history and far more recently in parts of Africa and Asia, had been a difference with massive implications for social organization, was almost gone from the western parts of Europe by 1000. However, there remained other important differences. For example, where the main labour was cultivation of crops and domesticated cattle and the subsequent preparation of food-stuffs, men and women alike were usually engaged in the activities. Where hunting was still important, women were likely to play a more domestic role—though that domest-icity included many operations, such as producing flour from wheat, which several centuries later started to take place in specialized factories.

The fact that women were involved in what later came to be seen as non-domestic work activities does not mean that these societies lacked gender differences. Two facts tended to assert a distinct gender order. These were violent times with little settled authority. At one extreme, great invasions of whole peoples—usually moving from east to west, later also from north to south—meant that entire populations could be trans-planted and resettled through acts of war. At the other extreme, there was often nothing resembling a modern police force and system of justice to resolve small disputes over the ownership of land and property. People often had recourse to violence to defend or usurp rights. Being in general physically stronger gave men distinct advantages in these activities. Second, childbirth was (and was long to remain) both a very dangerous activity and one that people had only rudimentary means of controlling. However dif-ferent organizations of agricultural activity might divide up the work of the genders, women were likely to be in subordinate positions to a prevailing patriarchy.

Most of this economic activity was for subsistence: families used the soil, plants, and animals to which they had access to provide their own food, clothing, and shelter. Very little was marketed, though not long after this date the great urban fairs, at which luxuries and other non-local products could be bought, had started. These took place only occasionally, sometimes annually. There were few shops in the sense we now understand, and as had been understood during the more developed period of the Roman Empire. There was little or no distinction as we now know it between work as employment in a formal economy and domestic work for the family. There was con-sequently for most people no concept of having a 'job', or of types of employment relations. This does not mean that Europe comprised a mass of independent peasants. The relationship people had to the land varied in many different ways, but the eco-nomic aspects of this relationship were part of a wider politics. Most of the cultivable land mass was owned by families who tried to assert a hereditary right to it, which they maintained by such law as was enforceable and by more or less autonomous armed force. They then parcelled out this land to various ranks of tenants and subtenants, the direct cultivators of the soil being either those who rented a piece of land of their own (the true peasants) or landless labourers who worked for either these peasants or for tenants higher up the scale who themselves did little or no work but lived on the pro-duce of the labourers' travails. These labourers were remunerated with food and other products of cultivation. In a sense they were the forerunners of the concept of the 'employee', but no one understood such an idea at that time.

The area of cultivable land in the Western European land mass was considerably smaller than that which we have known for the past few centuries. Much of it was swamp, marsh, impenetrable forest, or inhabited by fierce beasts who resisted human incursion. Only very slowly, using very simple, inefficient tools, powered by human or other mammal power with no mechanical assistance, did people chip away at the en-veloping wilderness and extend the area of cultivation. For the same reason communi-cation between places of human settlement was extremely difficult; there were very few things that could be called roads, and they were mere tracks. The most efficient means of communication, hazardous though it was, was by sea. The sea journeys attempted were remarkable; for example, goods were brought from Persia to Ireland at this time. However, most people were unlikely to meet strangers very often; customs, language, modes of eating and dress, varied across what we would today regard as very short distances, especially in mountainous, marshy, or other geographically difficult terrain. This was one of the sources of great diversity—far greater than that possessed by modern Europe—amid the monotony of subsistence, poverty, and constant fear of famine and disease.

FAMILIES AND COMMUNITIES

There were however towns, concentrations of buildings, the inhabitants of which had by and large left direct agricultural production and were engaged in various forms of craft (usually making implements for agricultural work or simple domestic equipment) or in the few non-manual occupations of the time (such as law and the church). Many of the towns or cities already established by that time continue, more or less in the same place, today. Some, such as Athens, Rome, Naples, Marseille, Syracuse, Florence had already seen many more centuries pass before the year 1000 than they were to see between 1000 and 2000.

Mention of this point reminds us that, were we to take our story back another half, or even whole, millennium, we should have a far richer story of urban life and communications to tell. From various dates between the seventh century BC and AD 500 the city of Rome had become a major metropolis, with around a million inhabitants, many of them served by recognizable modern urban facilities of water supply, street lighting, maintained roads, and regular markets, and a set of more or less implemented, codified laws. That model then spread to many other places in Europe, as far as the boundaries of the Danube and the Rhine and including parts of the British Isles. Something similar was achieved on the southern and eastern shores of the Mediterranean too; the Roman Empire was a Mediterranean and only partly a European world.

In those parts of Europe that had once been reached by the Roman power, life around the year 1000 was in most senses less organized and structured than it had been 500 and 1,000 years previously. The elites of the time knew this and constantly looked back to Rome, its language, its laws, and its institutions of government as the way in which things ought to be done, if only it could be achieved. Alongside this, in northern parts of Europe old Germanic ideas of warrior kingship survived. Groups of male warriors were sworn to the defence of their ruler in the many battles with other similar groups that took place. Eventually this became an important strand of the feudal form of a whole social order, though initially its activities were limited to warfare.

In the absence of large-scale institutional structures, much weight rested with family and immediate neighbourhood. To displease other members of one's family and village to the point where one was expelled from them meant almost certain death, as one would have to subsist in the dangerous wilderness, unless one could somehow make one's way to a neighbouring countryside or town and seek a very meagre living as a landless labourer. Family and community therefore provided the source of virtually all security and the satisfaction of needs. Considerable power could be exercised by those who occupied dominant positions in those institutions—primarily the oldest able-bodied males. The family principle (heredity) and that of dominance by the leading males in the family (patriarchy) therefore informed all loyalties. Whether as holders of small plots of land, as urban craftsmen, or as rulers over vast tracts of territory, people saw it as their duty to establish what they had as family property to be passed on to their sons. Both the *residuum* of Roman law that survived and the customs of the many tribes which had come together over centuries to form the medieval European population conveyed this message.

This does not mean that life acquired a settled continuity with more and more property and rights increasingly becoming family acquisitions. Men contested each other's claims violently; living conditions were poor, disease rife. Life expectancy was very low; one could congratulate oneself on having survived quite well if one passed a thirtieth birthday. Couples produced large numbers of babies; in societies where the family was about the only institution protecting the individual from hostile natural and human forces, extra people in the family meant extra help with work tasks, and extra sources of security in times of adversity and old age. But several of these children would die, and mothers often died in childbirth. Plague, natural disaster, and warfare would often render whole communities homeless, enforcing desperate searches for a means of survival in some remote place.

THE CHRISTIAN CHURCH

Important though family and community were to the maintenance of human society and survival, the most extensive and successful institution—and indeed the one which sustained the rules of family formation and conduct—was the one which made no use of family and which partly owed its very success to this fact. This was the Christian Church. Partly because its rulers and authorities were required to be celibate, the Church did not experience constant hiving off as did private, family property in its attempts to develop an essentially public, collective institution. Thus, it had become virtually the only enduring public institution above the very local level in post-Roman society. It had received its initial implantation within European societies from the Roman Empire early in the third century when the emperor Constantine had adopted it as the official imperial religion, whereupon it set about the task of extirpating all other religions from imperial territory, including in particular those of Rome itself which had in their turn tried to extirpate Christians and Christianity. The Church managed to outlive classical Rome, and through a combination of negotiations with whomever held military and political power over a particular territory—together with skilful deployment of its claims to speak ultimate truths about a superior world—it had managed to push its conquests into northern Germany, by the end of the first millennium gaining a toehold in southern Scandinavia, and eastwards into the most westerly of the countries of the Slav peoples. All these were areas which Rome had never penetrated. In Ireland, the furthest western shores of the Empire, an autonomous Christianity also survived, and sent its missionaries abroad earlier than those of the Roman Catholic Church, only gradually being absorbed into that dominated by the Vatican.

The conversions it effected would mainly be of local chiefs and rulers, who would then lend their power to that of the Church in persuading the common people to give up the gods of their forefathers and accept the story of Jesus Christ. In so doing the

Church also made serious compromises with local religions, adapting their festivals to its own calendar in a process of syncretism. Apart from a few secret pagan survivals, there were only two important exceptions to the Christian triumph, and both belonged to the same basic family of religions. The Jews, according to Christian doctrine God's chosen people until the time of Christ, were settled in small groups in various parts of southern Europe, where they had lived since scattered from their original territory in Israel by Rome in the first century AD. As both God's original people, but as putative accomplices in the murder of Christ who resolutely refused to accept the Church but sustained their own communities, their position within Christian Europe was ambiguous and difficult. It was to become increasingly precarious in various subsequent centuries, though none as appallingly so as the first half of the twentieth.

Most of the Iberian peninsula was settled and ruled over by followers of Islam, the principal religion of the Arab lands south of the Mediterranean for the previous 300 years—a faith which saw itself building on Christianity in the way that the latter believed it had built on Judaism. Moslem settlements had been expelled from southern France in AD 972, but Sicily remained under Islamic rule until 1072. Around the year 1000 Islamic civilization dwarfed that of Christendom in its capacity for military and political organization, urban development, and cultivation of science and arts. Although Christian Europe resented the Islamic presence in Spain, and even more that in Israel, the Holy Land of Christ itself, not much could be done about it.

With these exceptions the Christian Church provided the main, indeed the only, force imparting some social meaning to the concept of Europe. It was also the force that enabled ordinary people to relate their lives—otherwise totally bound by the exigencies of survival and the difficulty of moving more than a small distance from their village or town—to a wider social frame of meaning; in aspiration to an ultimate, infinite meaning. Although its rituals varied in detail from place to place and although centralized control was difficult to maintain given the state of communications, religious authorities based in Rome had sustained since the fourth century a set of beliefs, certain symbols (mainly the cross), specific rituals, and a hierarchy of priestly authority. Given the importance of cultural symbols and texts to the religion, this also made possible the spread of certain Europe-wide, though locally nuanced, forms of expression in writing, music, and pictorial representation. In particular it sustained the languages of the old Empire as Europe-wide languages of spiritual and intellectual discourse: Latin in the West, Greek in the East.

This was not achieved without frequent local rebellions, usually based on some arcane principle of doctrine but in reality expressing some local drive for autonomy or expression of social discontent. Virtually all these were defined as heresy by Church authorities and put down violently in order to maintain the unity of the Church. One such break however, occurring just after the turn of the millennium, could not be contained. This was the split in 1054 between the churches based on Rome and those based on Constantinople. In principle the dispute was on a question of doctrine—the relative precedence of Christ within the Holy Trinity—but behind the division lay wider social and cultural antagonisms, not least the difficulties of running a single organization from two geographical centres. Although Rome was the acknowledged centre of the religion, there was no important political authority corresponding to that territory which could sustain its claim under challenge. Constantinople, which had been made the capital of the Empire in place of Rome by Constantine, still remained the political centre of the so-called Roman Empire, holding effective authority over an extensive territory but excluding Italy and the rest of the former western and primarily European Empire.

There had been frequent rifts between these two geographical wings of Christianity in the past, division between the Greek and Latin languages being another source of tension, and the eventual schism was probably inevitable. When religious authorities in territories under the control of the secular power in Constantinople challenged Roman interpretations of Church teaching, the Pope and other authorities could not call on a local military power to deal with them as it could within the western territories. The religion therefore split into the eastern (Orthodox) and western (Roman Catholic) churches, and subsequent attempts at reconciliation always failed.

The boundary established between the zones of these two forms of Christianity fitted awkwardly across existing divisions. While most Slav-speaking people were to the east, those in the territories now known as Poland, Czechoslovakia, Croatia, and the non-Slav groups in Hungary became Catholics.

While the Church in Rome was at a disadvantage in its struggle with Constantinople in not being linked to a specific significant secular power, it was to turn this characteristic into a major advantage over subsequent centuries, producing thereby an abiding and highly important distinction between the western and eastern churches and indeed western and eastern societies. The Church—or eventually churches—in the East became tied to specific rulers and had little freedom from them. The Roman Church in contrast maintained autonomy from secular powers and had a relationship of political bargaining with, rather than subservience to, them. Secular and religious authorities had different tasks but, except during their frequent conflicts and wars, each side supported the authority of the other. The sentence attributed to Christ: 'Render unto Caesar the things which are Caesar's; and unto God the things that are God's' (Matthew 22: 21) legitimated this division of labour. This established something of very wide sociological importance: the idea of a tolerated separation between different, highly organized and important institutions. As we shall see at various points in this book, this was to become a fundamental and distinctive point of European social organization. Such a recognition of relative separateness was very different from the position in, say, Islamic societies, where no such distinction between the sacred and a legitimate secular was recognized; or in Japan, where the emperor was not appointed by God but a god himself.

INSTRUMENTS OF GOVERNMENT

There was in principle a successor empire to Rome within the western part of Europe. It had been established 200 years before by Charlemagne, based on his territories around what we would today regard as the Franco-German border, but extending to include most of modern Western Europe apart from Scandinavia, Iberia, and the British Isles. To Charlemagne and his associates this at last promised to be the restoration of the Roman Empire; they described themselves thus; and the Pope was prepared to bless them and recognize this new *imperium* as the secular arm of God on earth. However, making that claim good in practical political terms was far more difficult. Lower levels of more or less hereditary kings, dukes, occasionally bishops of the church, rarely needed to give more than ritual acknowledgement to the emperor. Effective political authority was difficult to stabilize. The extent of the territories ruled over by particular families not only changed shape from time to time, but were often not contiguous. For common people therefore there was no sense that membership of a particular geographical area of rule conferred some kind of affective identity, as with a modern nation state. Rulers had to be obeyed and deferred to because they could wield coercive and violent power; they might well come from a very different ethnic group and culture from oneself. The term nation was in use, but it referred to areas that we would today regard as local regions. These would be areas—often defined by some geographical barrier like a river or range of hills—within which people more or less shared a language or dialect, various social customs and traditions of dress and eating. People from outside the group were 'strangers'.

In any case most common people had no political rights at all. Politics was a matter for those landowners whose holdings gave them some capacity to raise military strength and who were therefore men to be bargained with (or fought against) by anyone trying to establish some sphere of effective control over a territory. There was no citizenship, not even the rudimentary rights the Roman Empire had extended to many of the peoples it conquered. There were no social entitlements; sickness, infirmity, and other forms of incapacity had to be dealt with within the limits of family and community resources. For most people these were barely enough for the subsistence of the able-bodied, though a general claim for mercy and charitable aid could be made to churches. Apart from the Church and groups of armed retainers gathered around men of power, there were no recognizable organizations of interests.

One can hardly call eleventh-century European societies rigid or static, as so much in life was uncertain and constantly subject to instability. There was not yet a settled order of social rank, and in some regions (such as Scandinavia) there was little structure to the social order beyond some local military chieftains and groups of farming families more or less dependent on them. However, in the areas that had enjoyed some continuity since, or at least had a memory of, the Roman period, there was a clearer continuation of the Roman concept of strongly demarcated ranks of hereditary militarized land-ownership. Especially in the territories of northern France, spreading to England following the Norman conquest of that region in 1066, the vague outline of ranks of deference and rules of obligation based on hierarchies of such persons was creating the beginnings of the feudal status order.

EUROPEAN SOCIETIES AROUND 1250

If we now move forward by a quarter of a millennium to the years around 1250 we see certain important points of change, though for much of the population daily life was not very different. Only a few technological developments had eased the back-breaking task of cultivating the soil. However, much more of the wilderness had been cleared, so the area of cultivation was greater, matching the gradually growing population. The inhabitants of the Rhine and Somme estuaries, the Dutch and the Flemish people, had some time before started the project of draining their territory, part of which lay below sea level, and had travelled widely within Europe practising the skills they had developed to clear other wetlands.

Employment contracts, if we can call them that, had become more varied and had moved in conflicting directions. In some areas powerful landowners had accumulated enough territory to re-establish the Roman *latifundium*, vast plantations where a servile, virtually slave, population was engaged, not exactly as wage labour, for they were usually paid in food, but certainly as a form of employee. This was mainly concentrated in southern Italy and parts of Spain. In other places the tenant system described above had continued to develop in great complexity, with property and landless labour rented out through chains of agreements. Throughout most of the western part of the continent and in much of England this was the economic or agricultural end of a chain of ties, the other end of which was the pattern of feudal politico-military obligations. In a few areas free tenants not owing any allegiance to a lord managed to survive. The great programme of land clearance had increased the possibilities of such settlements, since it sometimes created a surplus of land and a labour shortage. People would move to the new areas of free settlement, founding new towns and avoiding domination at least for some time. Meanwhile the consequent labour shortages on existing land led landlords to ease conditions for those left behind. Such grim features of life as recurrent plague also contributed to labour shortages by wiping out large numbers of the economically active. This would often be good news for those who survived. (As Phelps Brown and Hopkins (1955, 1956) once demonstrated, the real incomes of English building workers reached a peak in the wake of the Black Death of the 1340s that was not equalled for another five centuries.)

Economic conditions for ordinary people could therefore vary quite considerably. Meanwhile, at the higher levels of society the armed landowning class was turning itself into an aristocracy, developing a rich array of symbols to demonstrate social superiority that, while starting from Roman rudiments, was also highly innovative. Although life remained subject to many hazards, a settled hereditary status and class order, with barriers of entry to newcomers, was emerging. It was most prominent in France, where monarchic and aristocratic court life was developing apace, but similar phenomena could be found in England and Spain and the smaller units of Italian, German, and Flemish society.

FAMILY, CHURCH, AND EMPIRE

Below all these developments family life continued as before, unless disrupted by disasters, wars, and disease. Throughout the continent a patriarchal model of the family was in place, though the form varied. In north-western areas the two-generation nuclear family living apart from wider kin, characteristic of 'modern' societies, was already in place. To the east and south extended patterns could be found, with three generations and ranges of cousins living together. Everywhere people's dependence on their family remained strong, and family obligations beyond the nucleus were recognized as important. Birth and death rates remained high; population grew very slowly. Family continued to be the main principle for allocating roles through hereditary succession, at all levels of society. If anything its grip had been tightened with the stabilization of aristocratic rank.

The Church too had grown in influence as a social organization, being an important constitutive component of the growing towns as well as spreading to virtually every rural area of habitation. It continued to press its influence, aided by secular powers. The Moslems had been driven out of all Spain in the previous century, except for the area around Granada where a small Islamic kingdom, with a well integrated Jewish minority, remained. Christianity also spread further north into the sparsely populated wastes of Scandinavia and Finland, but it was the spread of Eastern Orthodoxy based on Constantinople rather than Roman Catholicism that converted the easterly Slav territories. Cathedrals were beginning to be the central landmark of the cities that developed as the European economy improved, and bishops often became local rulers, presiding over both a city and its surrounding countryside; Cologne was a particularly strong example. The papacy in Rome was only the largest single example of a more general phenomenon.

In various regions—especially France, Spain, England, and Scandinavia, where monarchies were established, as well as in areas of powerful duchies who formally continued to owe allegiance to the emperor, important bases of secular authority had become established. These kingdoms and duchies did not constitute nations; as in the earlier period, there was little notion of the identity between ruler, population, and territory that the concept of nation conveys to modern ears; and although there would usually be a core territory that gave its name to the rule, a given ruler's domains were still very scattered. Kings and dukes received legitimation from the Church, the authority of which was far more strongly entrenched among the people than the idea of nation.

The potential challenge these growing secular authorities might have posed to the continent-wide rule of the Church was limited by the fact that they often made alliances with the Pope in their shared concern to limit the power of the Empire. By 1250 it had become clear that this last had failed in its mission to fill the shoes of its Roman predecessor and had to content itself with presiding over the duchies, counties, free towns, and bishoprics that in practice ruled Germany and northern Italy.

At times all three powers of Christendom—Church, Empire, and local rulers—joined forces against their defined common enemy, the Moslems, primarily in a series of largely unsuccessful wars to gain control of the Holy Land. In some way this period represented a kind of peak of a united Western European Christendom, as the authority of the Pope in Rome was now recognized by all rulers from Ireland to the kingdom of Poland and from most of Sweden to all but the southern tip of Spain. There was no concept of Western Europe, but there certainly was one of Western Christendom, which was by that point almost coterminous with what we today understand as Western *and Central* Europe. Western Christendom both covered the whole of this territory and was limited to it, forming a geographical cultural whole. It is essential to note that this European unity was defined by religion and those many aspects of culture which at that point flowed from religion; it was not a political or military unity, nor a social one in those elements of social life that escaped a religious influence. For example, secular music took instantly recognizable local forms, while Church music, following strict rules, had similar qualities wherever it was composed.

In Western Christendom there now began the detailed intellectual study of the holy writings, including pre-Christian Greek and Roman philosophy which had been co-opted into the Christian corpus. In this intellectualism the Western Church resembled

Judaism but became sharply distinguished from its Eastern counterpart which concentrated almost solely on ritual and liturgy. These studies took place in the great monasteries that were themselves important economic institutions throughout Western Europe, and in the universities which, beginning with Bologna, Paris, and Oxford in the eleventh and twelfth centuries, started to spring up in important towns. Scholars began to teach an intellectualized, rationalistic approach to the study and justification of the Christian faith which eventually developed the temper of scientific enquiry that spread to other branches of knowledge over successive centuries. It was in this way that European knowledge began to build on its Greco-Roman legacy and slowly to overtake that of the Arab world. In so doing, however, it eventually sowed the seeds of a critical, scientific enquiry that would be turned against religion itself with devastating effect in the eighteenth and nineteenth centuries. Other cultural developments in the growing new atmosphere of the Italian cities were preparing the way for changes that we shall encounter 250 years later in the Florentine Renaissance.

THE EMERGING CITY BELT

It continues to be pointless to discuss political and citizenship rights for the common people, though polities of a more or less stable kind were developing around the courts of medieval rulers, sometimes including assemblies of various ranks of people that became the prototype of parliaments. Also, and in some ways more directly antecedent to twentieth-century concepts, were the ideas of urban governance and citizenship beginning to develop in the growing city belt.

New cities had been established during the preceding 250 years. The most important were those that combined position on major trade routes (mainly navigable coastal areas and river valleys), autonomy from aggressive territory-based powers (and therefore mainly in the lands of the Empire, where effective powers were on a more local scale than in the growing monarchies), and a lengthy history of established power. In general this produced a belt of mutually interacting and trading cities spreading east and south from southern England, down through the Low Countries, western parts of Germany, eastern France and Switzerland, and into northern Italy.

The rivalry between Church and Empire had also been at the heart of this urban growth. It had burst into armed hostilities that continued for most of the thirteenth century, devastating many territories, destroying many local rulers, weakening the Empire to a cipher and reducing populations to the miseries of looting, maiming, and being rendered homeless. It was within the interstices of this ravaged political structure that the towns often appeared as tough little units that could withstand the disaster, often having no effective claim made over them by aristocratic power. Their populations grew and so did their wealth, the latter being reflected in the appearance of more solid and lasting buildings. Most prominent among these were churches and cathedrals, structures which for the first time enabled medieval people to feel they were approaching the scale of the Roman-built environment. Most significant of all, the distinct urban social order of guilds, corporations, and local government by elders, just about perceptible around 1000, was developing in certain parts of Europe. This was a non-aristocratic order preoccupied with matters of trade, handicrafts, and even certain basic social infrastructure and welfare functions necessitated by the collective conditions of urban life (Black 1984; Reynolds 1997). It contrasted sharply with the military and agricultural concerns of the landed aristocracy. Drawing on the common Franco-German word for town, *bourg* (the English borough), this phenomenon gave rise to the French concept of the *bourgeois* (Italian *borghese*, German *Bürger*), which was later to denote a whole rival class order to the aristocratic one, based on urban wealth (capital) rather than rural (land). (*Bürger* was also to become a word for citizen. Languages deriving from Latin (which here includes English) turned to the Latin for city, *civitas*, to derive such words as citizen, *citoyen*, *cittadino*.)

These autonomous cities often received guarantees of their liberties in the shape of formal charters and effective protection from kings in exchange for money. City growth of this politically significant kind was an almost exclusively Western European phenomenon. It was to be an extremely important development. It created the possibility of handicraft production and inter-city trade, especially textiles and small wooden and metal goods, between centres. It signalled a model of political development different from that of the aristocratically ruled countryside. It also expressed the concept of long-term co-existence of rival and antagonistic organized forces mentioned above as one of the legacies of the complex relationship between Church and Empire, and which became the hallmark of a distinctive Western European form of social organization.

EUROPEAN SOCIETIES AROUND 1500

By the mid-point of the millennium there had again been major changes, though life for the great majority of people continued to be a matter of three or four decades spent gaining subsistence from the soil. There were some improvements in technology to ease the burden, and the area of cultivable land had now become very extensive. Perhaps the most striking innovation during the century to come was the arrival of new foodstuffs, such as tomatoes and potatoes, representing some of the results of the great sea voyages of discovery, plunder, massacre, colonization, and economic development that European people began to practise from the late fifteenth century until the twentieth in other parts of the globe. In some parts of Western Europe—especially England—we begin now to see the growth of wage labour, the beginnings of a recognizable form of employment contract, and an important cash economy both in agriculture and above all in the still growing urban economy. Since elsewhere such forms as *latifundium* servitude and feudal bonds continued, the diversity of work arrangements became very extensive.

Trade had been growing strongly, and this required in turn the growing importance of cash. As Georg Simmel first analysed in his *Philosophie des Geldes* (1900), money both required and made possible major social innovations. Something like a stable governing authority able to issue coins that people were willing to trust had to exist (paper money, requiring far more trust, came much later); then, once that had happened, the use of money made possible transactions between strangers which in the past were possible only among people who more or less knew each other. If one could trust the means of exchange, one did not need so much to trust the purchaser. Banks developed in the wake of the growth of money. These started in the cities, where wealth was more likely to be held in cash form than in the countryside, where it took the form of land.

This was the original source of the great wealth of the Medici family of Florence, and the Florentine currency—the florin—became a widely used and accepted currency in many parts of Europe.

The growth of rural wage labour in England and elsewhere affected family life, reinforcing the division of labour between men and women and producing the model of a 'breadwinner' male who went off to work each day within the formal cash economy and the domestic wife who concentrated on home-making, though at this stage home-making continued to include certain stages in the preparation of food and clothing that in later centuries would be removed to factories.

Starting at some point around the fifteenth century a further change had begun to affect the family: beginning in the north-west (England, the Low Countries, much of France, the western parts of Germany, northern Italy) people began to marry older than they had in the past, as late as their mid- or late-twenties (Hajnal 1965). A move to high rates of bachelorhood and spinsterhood accompanied this change. Very gradually over several centuries the pattern began to spread east and south within Europe and also to some other parts of the world. The fascinating reasons why this occurred need not concern us here, but they probably had something to do with attempts at achieving economic security in advance of family formation and therefore represented a kind of subordination of the desire to form family unions to considerations of acquiring property and occupational positions. They may therefore have been related to the growth of wage labour and associated rise of the cash economy, which started in much the same region.

THE REFORMATION

Even more momentous changes were affecting the world of religion, again giving a distinct character to the north-western corner of the continent. In 1492 the final expulsion of the Moors (and along with them the Jews) from Spain marked the complete triumph of the Church of Rome over Western Europe. In preceding centuries the conversions of the Nordic territories had been completed. Apart from recurrent movements of dissent within the Church, some small Jewish communities, and the dominance of the Orthodox Church in Greece, the entire territory covered by this volume can be described as Catholic, in addition to some Slav lands to the East. It was however to be a short-lived dominance, since by 1521 the religious struggles known as the Reformation had begun, eventually to produce, in the Protestant churches, forms of Christianity which did not recognize the authority of Rome and—sociologically very important— which did not make as extensive a claim on other social institutions as did Catholicism. As Hervieu-Léger has argued (1994), it is not a capacity to escape religion that is characteristically modern—many societies have developed means by which individuals can do that—but the branding as illegitimate religion's claims to a wider social authority.

The pragmatic formula which initially emerged as the solution to the religious wars provoked by the Reformation was that the religion chosen by the ruler of a territory would be the religion of everyone in that territory (summed up neatly in the Latin formula *cuius regio, huius religio*). This re-established the concept of a division of labour within a European political community that was henceforth to be riven by major religious cleavages, but at the same time it indicated how limited was the extension of liberty to the private lives of citizens: one did not have the right to practise a religion different from that of one's prince. By thus reasserting the communal nature of religion, that is as something that all the people living within a certain territory and united by its political and administrative institutions ought to hold in common, the formula rejected the individualistic approach that had been developed by Protestantism itself, and which was to return at many lesser moments of schism over the coming centuries. During the Reformation it had been common for individuals or groups of people to reach the grave conclusion that they disagreed with a major element of church teaching, and to be sufficiently confident in the correctness of their position to risk appalling punishments both this side of and beyond the grave, taking their dissent to the point of founding new religious institutions based on the new teaching.

Revolt against Roman Catholic doctrines had happened often before in the history of Christianity. On nearly every occasion the rebels had either been branded as heretics and destroyed (usually physically, with the help of the secular authorities), or persuaded to modify their disagreements into a matter of emphasis and become a monastic order within a rule authorized by and agreed with the Pope. The Reformation split unleashed a far greater diversity of approaches to religious life, principally because one of the fundamental tenets of many of the Protestant reformers was that man could approach God directly and did not require the medium of a church. The doctrine of *nulla salvatio sine ecclesia* (no salvation outside the church) had established the Catholic Church as the sole route through which God could be approached and thereby reinforced, politically the authority structure, sociologically the community structure, of Christians. Protestantism, by regarding every person as capable of direct communion with God, considerably weakened the strength of this claim to unity. Although Protestant churches quickly established the importance of the authority of their ministers, of secular rulers, and of local community pressure over those who radically questioned particular teachings, there was always potential for new division. This was most likely to happen in territories where Catholics and Protestants were co-existing and trying to develop some kind of *modus vivendi*; once this was done space might be found for other variants of Protestantism. In this way a new refinement of liberalism was developed: not just an agreed combination of autonomy and interdependence between religious and other institutions, but one among different religions—or at least denominations of Christianity—themselves.

Religion remained the principal cradle—and frequently cage—of knowledge and culture. Schools and universities were virtually always under church control and sponsorship. While this limited enquiry, it was within this framework that scholars developed further the legacy of rational enquiry that was in the coming two centuries to unleash the first great confrontation between religious and scientific certainties. Art and music were also about to open new avenues of human expression. Starting principally in Florence and other Italian cities, the movement known as the Renaissance was combining a rediscovery of classical Greek and Roman culture with a new inventiveness that would fuel creative work for the whole of the second half of the millennium. The church continued to form the framework within which much or even most of this work was done, but purely secular art forms now began to flourish as never before during the Christian period. In several countries too Latin was abandoned as the means of instruction in universities, and vernacular languages developed as capable of sophisticated means of expression in the manner pioneered for Italian 200 years before by Dante Aligheri.

THE NATION STATE

The concept of *cuius regio, huius religio* suggests some development in relations between rulers and ruled. Of course, local rulers had always been concerned to have obedience and lack of trouble from the people from whom they extracted rents or labour services, but now, at least in relation to the prosperous *bourgeois* and middle ranks of non-aristocratic farmers, there was a need to think a little more about shared bodies of values, though this was not enough to produce anything that we would today recognize as national identification, except at times of clear military threat from a people speaking a different language or being in some other way culturally distinct. In fact, the Reformation coincided with, or was part of the same general set of movements as, a drive for more autonomy from Church and Empire among lower levels of rulers. And although these were still societies in which ordinary people had few rights, there was a growing bourgeoisie and there was more concern than in the past that the people living in the territories ruled over by a particular king or duke should somehow have a particular set of characteristics, perhaps a language, a cultural style, or a particular branch of Christianity. The development of printing in Mainz in Germany in 1450 had not only provided the first example of industrial mass production, but made possible a spread of literacy and literature that was to assist the great flowering of writing in vernacular languages mentioned above.

The monarchies of France, Spain, Portugal, England, Scotland, Scandinavia were well embedded now, though the Empire and Papacy between them continued to make a claim over German and Italian lands that inhibited the rise of anything beyond dukedoms and city states there. Further important forces at work were the voyages of discovery and foreign conquest. These not only produced great wealth and new opportunities for wars against each other for the European monarchies, but also engineered a major shift in the geographical orientation of the continent. At the very time when the Florentine Renaissance was celebrating the continuing leadership of the Mediterranean as the post-Roman cultural heartland of the West, the voyages were bringing a decisive advantage to countries of the Atlantic seaboard: England, Spain, Portugal, France, the Netherlands. Within another three centuries this was to produce a complete reversal of the earlier concept of centre and periphery within Europe, combined with, but by no means overlapping, the northern Protestant defection.

The city belts had continued to grow and flourish, and around 1500 the great Italian city states, like Florence and Venice, continued to play a military, diplomatic, and cultural role at least equal to that of France or England. The continuing growth of cities meant that some—in particular Paris—now exceeded ancient Rome in size, though in other parts of the globe settlements of that kind were also known. As noted, cities became increasingly important centres of wealth and culture, the urban form of governance continued to develop and to spread throughout the region, and many street plans and buildings that are still visible today took shape.

The city state form was however nearing its peak. Before the end of the sixteenth century France had defeated Florence in war, though it was to be a further two centuries before Austria did the same to Venice. Elsewhere city walls were beginning to be dismantled, not so much because it was now safe to dispense with them, but because kings saw them as a challenge to their rule. This too was a long process; it was not until the late seventeenth century that Louis XIV symbolically entered rebellious Marseille through a hole his troops had blasted in the city wall rather than through the gate.

CONSOLIDATION OF THE STATUS ORDER

Despite all this change, we still see no fundamental shifts in citizenship and political life for the common people. The position of representative assemblies, parliaments, of higher-order *bourgeois* became consolidated in some places, but since this process ran alongside and was part of the consolidation of patterns of rule by kings, what was gained by parliaments in constitutional form was probably lost in effective power. The class structure based on the hierarchy of armed rural lords was similarly consolidated into a more rigid and codified set of ranks, with the aristocracy surrendering its right to bear autonomous arms in exchange for the promise of royal support for its authority over the peasant majority.

One aspect of these processes was often a codification of different status orders, including for example different courts for different designated classes, and sumptuary laws that forbade the wearing of certain kinds of garment by non-aristocratic classes or Jews. These laws gave the consolidated post-feudal social order an impression of rigidity and clarity that influenced all subsequent thinking about class structure, right up to modern sociological theory. It is therefore important to note that in important respects this codification was defensive. Sumptuary laws were only needed if lower classes (in particular the urban *bourgeoisie*) were beginning to be able to *afford* the lifestyle of the nobility. To preserve the distinctiveness of the lifestyle it was necessary to proscribe its imitation by outsiders.

Overall, the unity and singularity of Western European Christendom observable in 1250 was about to fragment, in two directions. The Reformation was about to divide the subcontinent along the very dimension which had shaped and defined its unity, while the imperial conquests of European powers were about to end the unique identity of Christendom with Europe. In both cases the rise of European nation states was to be at the expense of the idea of Europe itself, though without that rise Europe would itself have been unlikely to develop into the dominant global force that, both together and against each other, for good and for ill, its constituent parts became.

EUROPEAN SOCIETIES AROUND 1750

If we now return after a further 250 years, we find ourselves on the very eve of two massive changes that were to produce the Europe finally recognizable to those living at the end of the millennium. These were the Industrial Revolution that developed, initially in England and Scotland, from the middle of the century, and the French political revolution of 1789. Even before these events, important divergences in levels of development had become apparent. Incipient differences between north-west Europe and elsewhere, already visible in 1500 in the spread of the wage system, had become far more important. Particularly in Britain and the Netherlands there was extensive wage labour, partly in agriculture but also in the towns which continued to be the centres of a growing proportion of economic activity. There had also been a considerable growth of the characteristic urban professions, such as law and medicine, as well as of capitalist commercial activity (shopkeeping and the management of trading enterprises). These latter included multinational English and Dutch companies that grew in the wake of imperial conquests. A greatly expanded bourgeois class developed. The range of occupational types had grown extensively with both more sophisticated agriculture and the growth of urban crafts.

Further north, east, and south more traditional occupational patterns continued. Scandinavian rural workers continued to be either independent small farmers or tied labourers; only in Denmark was there much development of an urban bourgeoisie and modern activities. In the eastern parts of Germany most rural workers were *Untertanen*, virtually serfs tied to the land of their aristocratic masters. And in the south, in southern Italy, Portugal, and Spain, the large *latifundium* form of plantation agriculture survived alongside other complex forms of landed tenure.

A capitalist mode of production was clearly gaining in dominance in Britain and the Netherlands, especially the former. Money and the banking system had continued to advance, and systems of bookkeeping and the maintenance of proper business accounts had developed. As Max Weber later showed (1922), these enabled businessmen to keep track of their affairs, to calculate profit and loss, and—perhaps even more important— to separate their working from their private lives, in ways that had not been possible before. Wealthy families from outside the ranks of the landed aristocracy had been developing in England for several centuries as the volume of trade and commercial activity grew. At mid-century these groups stood on the threshold of as yet unimagined possibilities of advance through the chances of investment in industrialization.

It was however not in England but in France that the strains of relations between aristocracy and bourgeoisie finally boiled over into the momentous events of the Revolution. Those events, combined with the implications of industrialism, were about to dislodge landed aristocracy from the position of real and symbolic dominance which that kind of social group—hereditary, landed, arms-bearing—had held in Western and Central Europe since the original Roman republic. The period of bourgeois capitalist dominance was beginning. Units of capital, beginning as extensions of bourgeois family property, were to develop into the large impersonal joint stock companies of the late twentieth century, with increasingly complex and rapidly changing patterns of ownership. A mass of managerial occupations then developed to mediate between the function of capitalist ownership and the actual work tasks of the organizations that produced the wealth.

CHANGES IN THE FAMILY

Family relations were changed by the growth of wage labour, in that this was more likely to lead to a breadwinner model. With the spread of crafts and the rise of the cash economy, many productive tasks were removed from the home and transferred to specialized factory buildings. Women were about to become 'housewives' in the modern sense—though in the early factories both they and also very young children were likely to be employed. In any case, the changes did not affect the vast areas of continuing peasant agriculture, where women still worked within an undifferentiated economy that did not distinguish between work for the household and some work for the external economy.

The family was also at the centre of a very gradual erosion of community ties that, at least in parts of England and France, began to develop alongside economic change. Principles of reciprocity, which constituted the strength of traditional community-based society, become problematic as pure markets develop. These latter require exchanges to be precise and calculated, so that they can be carried out efficiently, so that profit can be extracted from them, and so that the relative prices of different transactions may be known. Therefore the initial impact of the spread of the market economy within a society is hostile to networks of reciprocity. At the same time however such networks are useful. As the Scottish economist Adam Smith first pointed out during the mid-eighteenth century itself, and as Fred Hirsch more recently explored in depth (1977), market exchanges depend on much taken-for-granted social behaviour. It is also useful to actors within a market economy not to have to pay for everything: in particular, not to have to purchase the initial socialization of children into accepting the importance of obedience and order; or the feeding, clothing, resting, and reproduction of the workforce. Families, households, and some other institutions (like churches) have therefore been useful to markets, despite the problems they create (Polanyi 1957). In general, where an activity could be usefully taken over by the market for processes of efficient resource allocation and the extraction of profit (such as the production of goods in family workshops), it was largely though not entirely removed from the control of the family and entered the market. Where such a process was more difficult, such as the care of very small children, the activity remained in the family.

Families, local communities, and churches thus evolved in this period as welfare societies protecting those with little chance of securing vital needs through the market. They provided not only childcare, but also care for the aged and infirm, and support for those unable to find work.

RELIGION AND TOLERANCE

Communities of trust were often based on religion; one felt less able to trust and to relax with members of groups who drew their sense of mankind's ultimate meaning from a different source. Most important of all, members of a religion would strive to ensure that their young people found their friends and associates from within the community of believers; otherwise the risk appeared of marriage to someone from a different faith and very major difficulties over the religious identity of the next generation. These communities did not however necessarily live in geographically distinct parts of a country or even a city, or work for different employers; and often they would have to share the government of their district. In some parts of Europe—again mainly in Britain and the Netherlands—an institutional basis had been established for tolerance of this kind.

It involved a certain combination of separateness and cooperation, and developed in its purest form in the Netherlands, where a tradition of religious tolerance eventually permitted the co-existence of a reformed, Calvinist Church, a small, more fundamentalist Calvinist breakaway from this, and a continuing large Catholic minority (Bax 1990: chs.

4, 5). This last in particular, which suffered various exclusions from full participation in national life, organized itself as a separate, strong community, and the same process was then followed by the others in slightly weaker form. The segregation extended to most areas of life, being most rigid of course at the core of religious activity itself, and becoming gradually more flexible as it moved out towards more secular areas of life (Kruijt 1958). Later, in the nineteenth century, when first liberal and then socialist forms of secular, non- or even anti-religious ideas developed, groups around these organized themselves in a similar way. The important point is that the groups, while building very separate lives, continued to act as parts of the same interdependent wider society (Daalder 1971, 1974). They came to see the different groups as different pillars or columns (in Dutch *zuilen*) which together, though separate, supported the overall edifice of Dutch society in general—just as wooden pillars driven deep into the polder supported (and still support) the buildings of the great Dutch cities and prevented them from sinking into the mud of the reclaimed land on which parts of the country were constructed. As we shall see in subsequent chapters, diluted versions of such forms became very important devices for managing social compromises during the twentieth century.

By 1750 religion in Europe was generally enjoying one of its rare peaceful phases. The upheavals of the Reformation had continued in France, Germany, Britain, Ireland, and the Netherlands throughout the seventeenth century, but eventually new accommodations had been reached, even if not usually as elaborately as in the Netherlands. These accommodations continued to mean difficulties and subordination for Catholic minorities in England and Scotland, the Netherlands, and Germany, and for the Catholic majority in Ireland (ruled over by Protestant England). Protestant minorities barely existed in Catholic lands, where in earlier centuries the Church had not been prepared to tolerate even their survival. The peace was however only a lull, as the French Revolution was to unleash anti-clerical forces which, while initially limited to that country, would later spread to many parts of Europe. It combined with a growing intellectual willingness to challenge and dispute Christian teachings.

In many countries there was also a temporary peace between religion and the pursuit of knowledge. The Church had come to terms with the challenge posed by seventeenth-century physical science to its Aristotelian inheritance; the far more severe challenge to be posed to biblical teaching itself by biological science in the nineteenth still lay in the future. The greatest tensions at this period were between the Catholic Church and major secular, sometimes explicitly anti-religious, developments taking place in philosophy, especially in France where *les philosophes* challenged Christian accounts of morality and the meaning of human life. While the physical sciences were more or less at peace with religion, it was developments within them which were preparing the way for the great changes of the next two centuries: the steam engine, electricity, the blast furnace, eventually the internal combustion engine.

THE FRENCH REVOLUTION AND MODERN POLITICS

The French Revolution would also see the start of a real sense of national consciousness in many parts of Europe. The post-revolutionary French republic saw itself as the representative of a modern, rational France set down within a *congeries* of traditional polyglot, culturally diverse local societies. France was to be constructed as a nation state by this republic within a geographical terrain called France, but whose residents did not yet constitute Frenchmen and Frenchwomen, but Bretons, Burgundians, Provençales, etc. These 'provincial' identities were traditional, local, small, and not associated with modernization. Building from them to construct a large modernizing nation state could be presented as a rationalizing task.

However, although the Revolution initiated for the first time the concept of a general democratic citizenship (for males), and beyond Europe the newly independent society of the United States of America was also about to embark on a more or less democratic approach to government, for the most part societies remained without these attributes, except for the citizenship of tiny numbers of aristocrats and leading bourgeois. Different though French and US American societies were and are, they share two important criteria: first, the rejection of any single national church (though in very different circumstances); second, a project of nation building that saw itself as conquering certain forms of pre-modern, more local, rival loyalties (Bourdieu 1993). Both became important symbols of modernity and of the paradoxical though central position of the concept of the nation state within that modernity.

Citizenship in the urban form of participation in organized interests had continued to grow alongside the continuing development of towns and cities, which was closely associated with the rise of commercial capitalism. In the mid-eighteenth century the main European cities were largely the same ones which had been important 250 years before, though there had been a major shift in the centre of gravity of development. The partly aristocratic, partly bourgeois cities of northern Italy, Flanders, and elsewhere which had represented the peak of urban cultural achievement in the sixteenth century had stagnated as the focus of European development shifted to the Atlantic seaboard, to commerce, and to monarchies. In France a monarchical strategy of concentrating all important business on the palace of Versailles and neighbouring Paris had led to the decline of such cities as Lyon and Marseille, while London and Amsterdam also became great centres.

Industrialism was about to produce a completely different type of urban growth. More city walls were stripped down in the face of the need to herd masses of people together in factory forms of employment. In some cases totally new cities were to develop in this way. No longer would the city be primarily a place of closely shared urban governance and small crafts and commerce, but the location of large industrial buildings and tenement blocks where large numbers of people, flowing in from the surrounding countryside and eventually from far beyond, would work and live. In 1750 this still lay in the future, and the places that were to embody this new meaning of city—Manchester, Birmingham, and other cities of northern England, or those of the Ruhr valley in Germany—were but small towns or even villages. Others, such as Glasgow or Vienna, were to be transformed from medieval into industrial cities.

The classic form of Western European urban government, with its structure of craft guilds, was already well past its peak. The two most advanced powers of the day, France and Britain, would both finally suppress this form of social participation in the early nineteenth century; only in 'backward' Prussia were they developed and encouraged and incorporated within a model of modernization. The early stages of the development of capitalist society were producing an increase in opportunities for participation through the market, but sometimes at the cost of more direct participation.

The status of Western Europe as some kind of social whole was now becoming ambiguous. On the one hand, at the level of political and cultural elites, advances in transport and written communication made it even easier to sustain the extensive networks across the subcontinent that had existed for many centuries. Monarchies routinely intermarried, though virtually never with anyone outside Europe: the colonies had not yet produced families of adequate status, while the rest of the world was non-Christian. Artists and musicians inhabited even more than before a cross-European world. For example, even though Wolfgang Amadeus Mozart died at the age of 35, he had visited and performed in many of the major cities of Germany, France, Italy, and England. Since the development of a great court at St Petersburg at the western rim of the growing Russian empire, the elite circle was no longer confined to Western and Central Europe, but crossed the old divide between Catholic and Orthodox. On the other hand, ordinary people were increasingly being oriented towards the nation state as a focus of loyalty and cultural identity, especially in Protestant areas, obscuring the European identification which, albeit implicitly, had been embodied in earlier concepts of Christendom. Christendom itself had now become considerably more extensive than Europe, having conquered the entire American continent, with enclaves in other parts of the world. However, while its European content had become diluted in this way, Christendom expressed a European domination of the world. Until the American Revolution in 1775, all parts of the world where Christianity had spread were ruled over by powers based somewhere between Stockholm and Madrid, London and Vienna—or, if we include Eastern Europe, St Petersburg.

FROM 1750 TO 1950

Over the following two centuries a transformation took place in the working lives of European people unlike anything else that had occurred in the past. Work on the land, the dominant form of human labour since the beginning of human society, became a residual minority activity. Millions of people learned the new ways of working associated with factory life, acquired new and often changing mechanical skills, or took on posts of administration and management of a kind not known before. This process was highly uneven in its impact. In England already by 1850 more people were working in industry than in agriculture, a situation that would be reached in southern Europe, including France, only a century later. By that time industrial employment itself was declining, to be replaced by new forms of work. This brings us to the period when sociology began to develop as a subject in its own right, a development which was itself largely a response to an awareness of massive changes in social arrangements.

Our next 250-year episode, the state of society at the very end of the millennium, is the subject of the remaining chapters of this book. The changes between 1750 and now have been so extensive that, to bring us to that point, I need to abandon the 'snapshot' approach I have been using so far and summarize briefly the processes of change in that intervening period.

Within peasant economies there is little need for precision in the definition of either occupational statuses or different non-working roles and categories of person. People carry out a diffuse set of jobs, some perhaps for wage labour but others just as part of their family contribution. Whether digging up potatoes, most of which will be taken to market but some of which will be consumed by the family, counts as having a 'job' as potato digger or as helping to get the family's dinner is not a relevant question to ask.

Similarly, there is in peasant economies no such thing as 'unemployment' as we have come to know it in industrial societies. There may well be underemployment if there are more people in the family than its plot of land and local casual job opportunities can really use, with the result that there are literally too many mouths to feed; but this is different from the situation typical of urban industrial societies where—unless one is a housewife or a member of a clearly defined dependent category—to have no formal job places one in a distinct and unattractive category. The decision whether or not to work, or to try to seek work, can be much more complex than the simple dichotomy between employment and unemployment, invented for the benefit of official statistics, suggests. The issue of when married women with dependent children are to be counted as unemployed has raised this issue acutely in many societies, but it can then be extended to men too (Dex 1985: ch. 3).

THE NEW OCCUPATIONAL STRUCTURE OF INDUSTRIAL SOCIETY

Industrialization brought work in factories and eventually large offices; travel by railway at previously unimaginable speeds, followed by motorized road transport, steam-powered ships, and finally the aeroplane. In the twentieth century the speed and forms of communication were changed utterly by the invention of radio, then television, and finally the computer-based interactions of electronic mail and information networks. The sheer range of goods produced increased, and cheap materials made it possible for even poor people to equip their homes with a growing range of products. By the early twentieth century the US motor manufacturing factory of Henry Ford had initiated a process of mass-production and mass-consumption that interacted with each other, unleashing a spiral of goods acquisition. In the Ford factories highly efficient forms of organization made it possible for low-skilled workers to produce goods of high value. This enabled them to earn higher wages, which enabled them to buy more products. This increased demand in turn made it possible for other industries to use mass-production methods, and so on and so on. It took some time for this pattern to spread and to cross to Europe. By 1940 it was still possible for the English writer George Orwell to write that most British people owned only a few clothes and sticks of furniture; this could also have been said of their ancestors in 1750. It could no longer be said of their own children by 1970; but that is the story of our remaining chapters.

The growth of new occupations in the course of industrialization led, among many other things, to a need for new ways of defining what work people were doing. Since this had been, and continued to be, a vital component of the ways in which people were classified, ranked, and hierarchically ordered, new schemes of stratification were devised. Although there were important national variations, in general the new occupational system of manufacturing industry developed the following kind of scheme; the main changes occurred at varying points in the nineteenth century, depending on the timing of industrialization, but they will be described here as part of a trajectory lasting until deep into the twentieth century.

Initially, there is a division between those concerned with exercising authority and monitoring the work done and those actually engaged in production; the latter tasks have been conceived as manual work, the former defined residually as non-manual. This became a fundamental division; it marked off those exercising authority from those receiving orders; those who worked in clean offices with pieces of paper, from those who got dirty at work in factories and used muscular power; those, therefore, with a higher education from those with a lower. (For major studies of the historical distinctiveness of non-manual, office work, see Kocka 1981 and Lockwood 1989.) There were also major implications for levels of earnings.

Next, there have been further divisions within each of these groups, corresponding to subdivisions of authority and skill. Contrary to the expectations of Karl Marx, who foresaw a radical simplification of relations between owners and manual workers, the history of capitalism has been one of growing complexity and subdivision of these differences as the result of four processes.

First, the range of skills has increased as a result of growing technical sophistication. Among manual workers there have been divisions of skill, sometimes demarcated very clearly through the formalization of qualifications, with further divisions based on the need for some authority functions to be exercised within the manual group itself.

Second, managerial hierarchies have lengthened as firms have grown in size. Management itself became an occupation, a distinctive skill rather than just an extension of the power of ownership.

Third, major divisions appeared within non-manual work as a large number of very routine occupations developed, supporting managerial tasks. Although these staff themselves had no authority, they were seen as being more trusted than the manual workers, worked in the office rather than the factory, and could be entrusted with secrets (many of them being called secret-aries). The ranks of the junior levels of these staff grew considerably and, during the course of the twentieth century, have almost everywhere become primarily female.

Fourth, firms made use of advanced non-manual skills for such complex tasks as product and process design, building design, the management of accounts, relations with the legal system. In so doing they established relations with a completely different class of occupations, the origins of several of which entirely pre-date the growth of industrial society: the professions. These are occupations which have managed, by a combination of the sheer level of knowledge required for their work plus political agility, to establish organizations which control the definitions of their skills and have responsibility for overseeing the training of new entrants and the conduct of existing practitioners (Burrage and Torstendahl 1990; Torstendahl and Burrage 1990). Often they have succeeded in securing some state guarantee of their position, whether through legal imposition of the monopoly of practice, through state maintenance of their training schemes, or through the state itself having initiated them in the first place. Often originally organized as independent practitioners of their skills, many members of professions gradually found themselves as employees of either capitalist enterprises or state organizations. Others continued in private practice, being used as consultants instead of direct employees by firms. As time has passed, so the range of occupations seeking recognition of professional status has grown, with varying levels of success.

Manufacturing industry, especially as it developed within a capitalist context, therefore produced the following array of occupations: a mix of relatively small numbers of owners and managers (with spans of control of very varied length, from top positions in giant enterprises to either junior managerial positions or top positions in very small firms); a small number of members of various professions, sometimes working within the firms, sometimes not; larger numbers of various 'routine' office workers; and a large force of manual workers divided by various levels of recognized skill.

Several of these distinctions between types of occupations often became embedded in law through the recognition of different levels of rights and responsibilities. This was particularly important for the professions; the special rights of owners were of course also recognized through property law. The generally poor conditions of manual workers in the nineteenth-century factory led to special legislation protecting their health and safety; and in many countries occupational groups were identified as the appropriate targets for the provision of social insurance and other aspects of the emerging welfare state. In these ways the distinctions became cemented in time and in social consciousness, even if sometimes the social reality was changing as forms of work developed that could not be readily fitted to them. Occupations themselves often formed associations—trade unions—to defend their interests. These usually found it easier to spread from one occupation to another within these heavily defined categories than to move within a single employing organization to other types and levels of worker. The professions had often done this before the arrival of industrialization; certain kinds of skilled manual groups, operating in a similar way to the professions, followed.

THE EMERGENCE OF THE INDUSTRIAL URBAN FAMILY

Although the initial implications of amassing people in new urban concentrations around factories were disastrous for human welfare, eventually the growth in wealth and availability of new products through the factory process led to gradual improvements in health. The industrialization of cotton production made it possible for ordinary working people to wear clothes made of these fibres—easily washed and therefore able to be kept clean—instead of the traditional wool—difficult to wash and often dirty. The quality and quantity of food gradually improved with rising wealth, after the initial decline associated with the growth of city populations unable to cultivate their own soil. These changes in clothing and diet began to improve life long before modern medicine began to make its contribution. People began to live longer; the population level began to rise rapidly. However, the capacity of Western Europeans to develop distinctive demographic patterns—already seen in the delayed marriage system—now produced a response in reduced fertility. This process, known as the demographic transition, has since been seen in many other parts of the world. It seems that at a certain moment in the process of modernization mortality rates, especially among young children, decline; after an interval fertility rates decline too (Chesnais 1992). This leads to the modern pattern of low death rates and low birth rates. Such a process began in most of Western Europe in the late nineteenth century, gradually spreading from northern Europe to southern, and from wealthier groups to poorer. (However, the first case of the demographic transition, in France, began a full century earlier than this, well before industrialization, though at the same time as the wider political and cultural changes associated with the French Revolution.)

Families began to be less important institutions for their members, as not only the world of work opened up new possibilities of activities remoter from family control, but the general range of social institutions both increased in number and in their mutual separation. One element of the growth of new forms of work was a need for more systematic approaches to the education of populations; before the period of industrial development social elites had little interest in the intellectual capabilities of primarily peasant populations. Until the development of modern school systems the ordinary mass of people had relied largely for their education on their families and on what churches chose to provide. The relative roles of State and Church in education were fought out as a central social political issue in nearly all countries in the late nineteenth century and the first half of this. Especially in Roman Catholic lands, the Church had seen its control of education as fundamental to its ideological power. The determination of states to establish their own systems—sometimes in direct ideological rivalry with the Church, sometimes for more technical purposes of looking to the skill needs of an industrial economy—produced considerable social conflict in late nineteenth-century Europe. Its eventual settlement saw a dominance of state education with a certain space given to church schools and sometimes (as, for example, in Italy and the UK, but certainly not in France) a guaranteed minimal space for religious worship within the state's own schools. These settlements had usually been reached by the end of the Second World War, even if aspects of the conflict rumbled on to the end of the twentieth century.

By the late nineteenth century a number of European states had introduced systems of compulsory education for young children. Slowly, over the next century this pattern spread to remaining countries of the region (mainly in the south), and the age at which young people left the education system rose. This brought literacy and formal knowledge to millions of people whose parents and grandparents had known very little beyond their own immediate life experience and what they learned in church, transforming cultural perspectives as well as imparting vocationally useful skills.

RELIGION AND THE CHALLENGE OF SECULARIZATION

The churches faced many challenges over the final 250 years of the millennium in which they had for the most part been such a dominant institution. However, for much of the earlier part of the period between 1750 and 1950 the main development was a growth of new and enthusiastic forms of Protestant Christianity.

A central doctrinal division of the Reformation had been the insistence of the reformers that priests were not necessary to the direct relationship between God and man, and that every individual was responsible for his or her own conscience before Him. This became inconvenient as reformers set about organizing new church structures, ensuring each church's dominance within the ruler's territory, insisting on obedience and discouraging heterodox opinions. Successor generations of Protestants were expected by their parents to inherit the faith, even if the idea of personal conversion was sustained through the ritual of confirmation (as it was even in the Catholic Church), or in some cases even of adult baptism. Protestant churches therefore became the focus of communities as had the Catholic Church, and came to interpret the aspirations of communities, and not just of collections of personally converted individuals.

However, there were fairly indelible differences. First, an aspect of the Reformation had been a desire to reduce the imagery and obscurity that characterized Catholic practice. Parts of this process, such as performing religious services in the local language rather than Latin, or basing hymns on the strophic patterns of popular song, clearly strengthened the role of religion as community expression. But the general decline in the use of symbol reduced the saliency, the tangibility of the faith. Second, the stress on the individual in direct communion with God, however compromised by subsequent insistence on the importance of church attendance and deference to ministers and (in some churches) bishops, reduced the element of public and communal display in worship. Religious practice became more private. These characteristics produced differences in the social structure of Protestantism which, as the centuries passed, influenced a wide range of quite secular social institutions.

A third characteristic was that, Protestantism having emphasized the individual's conscience, it was always vulnerable to further divisions. For many years these could be dealt with in the same way as in Catholic lands: ostracism from the local community and, if matters got out of hand, intervention by the secular authorities. However, as general concepts of individual liberty and rights spread (more quickly in Protestant than in Catholic countries), the punishments for non-conformists weakened and, especially in the nineteenth century, a variety of other forms of Protestantism began to grow. Where established churches had become remote from some sections of the population—those in new social classes produced by modernization, those in remote areas, or sometimes those in modern urban areas where the national church remained rural in emphasis—great waves of religious enthusiasm resembling the Reformation itself would sweep through whole territories (McLeod 1997). Often these were rooted in little sects originating from the seventeenth and eighteenth centuries. New churches would be formed and would become the representative expression of communities that had felt themselves to be excluded from access to symbols of shared meaning by the state church.

These new Protestant sects were most easily able to establish themselves where secular authorities were already trying to balance more than one faith: in the Netherlands, where a reform Calvinist group became very important; in the UK where, after the union between England and Scotland, the state had to recognize an Anglican state church in England but a Calvinist one north of the border. Something different happened in Denmark, which country's Lutheranism henceforth became different from that in the rest of Scandinavia. The state church extended its scope to welcome all kinds of Protestant expression. As a result there was little need to form new sects, though at the expense partly of any subsequent unified authority; continuing conflicts between more conservative and more liberal strands led at times to a form of pillarization within the one church structure (Riis 1994). In Switzerland too, where different churches cross-cut quite separate distinctions between German-, French-, and Italian-speaking communities, Protestantism became very diverse.

As Brown (1992) has shown in the case of Britain (both England and Wales, and Scotland), in the wake of the rise of these more popularly responsive denominations, religious adherence and church attendance grew considerably in the second part of the nineteenth century, peaking in the early twentieth and declining as these particular denominations also declined—growing therefore during the climactic years of British industrialization and urbanization.

Behind this growth, Christianity was in fact entering a crisis, produced by scientific and political challenges. Theories of biological evolution, particularly the works of Charles Darwin, led to radical questioning, not only of the biblical account of creation, but more seriously of Christian concepts of the uniqueness of human beings as a species. Psychology also disturbed Christian concepts of the human spirit and its relationship to the body. Only an intellectual few were deeply affected by these challenges, and churches eventually learned to redefine their claims; but permanent damage had been done to the awe and mystery surrounding the Christian definition of human identity and destiny.

The political challenge was more immediately serious, especially the impact of *laïcisation*. This French word should not be translated as secularization (noting a mere decline of religion); nor is it even easily translated as laicization, which refers to a mere social process; nor again should it be confused with atheism or agnosticism, since it is possible to be a believer and also support a *laïcisation* project. It refers to a drive to expel religious institutions from public life, in particular from entanglement with the state, its symbolism, and the education system. It is therefore a version of liberalism. Among the countries with which we are concerned, *laïcisation* has been mainly a French phenomenon (Willaime 1994: 156). Starting with the revolution of 1789, and then again a century later during the Third Republic, republican political interests were determined to separate the Catholic Church completely from any involvement with national public life. Since the majority of French people during this period were practising Catholics and since the Catholic Church is accustomed to being strongly associated with public life, this was often a matter for great and sometimes bloody conflict. By the beginning of the twentieth century a kind of rapprochement had been reached whereby the church remained content with a major place in the lives of French people, but not in the symbolism of the French republic (ibid.: 154). It could also organize its own sector of education, but its symbols could not enter the schools of the republic.

Nowhere else in Western Europe do we find such a rigid separation of Church and State and exclusion of the Church from formal public life at the national level (Davie 1994: 60). Whether in Protestant or other Catholic countries there is always one or a small number of churches which have a special status as the official national religion. In Protestant cases (as in the Nordic countries or the UK) there is often a designated official state church. Even in Italy, where the Church initially opposed the creation of a secular national state in the 1870s, by the time a settled democratic republic was established after the Second World War Christian Democratic forces had achieved a political ascendancy and had restored the church to its national pre-eminence though without a formal role in public affairs.

THE MODERN STATE

The post-revolutionary French republic saw a need to modernize France by breaking down local and religious loyalties. Germany and Italy were built out of a mass of more local polities as part of a self-conscious process of economic and political modernization in the late nineteenth century. Further east the opposite process occurred. After the collapse of the Austro-Hungarian Empire at the end of the First World War, the various nationalities that comprised it (including Czechs and Slovaks, Hungarians, some Poles, Yugoslavs) were granted statehood by the victorious powers. Modernization and rationalism were held to mean that self-conscious nations should be self-governing and not ruled over by others. The same concepts governed the liberation of the territories of the British, French, Belgian, Dutch, and later Portuguese empires in the mid-twentieth century.

Within Western Europe we think mainly of nation-state building in terms of the erection by the French, British, German, Italian, and Spanish states of national loyalties transcending and replacing various lower level identities. However, the story of Ireland's separation from the UK, of Norway's from Sweden, and of Finland from Russia all took place during the twentieth century, as did the dismemberment of the short-lived Nazi German *imperium* over large parts of the continent.

In all these cases, whether nation states were being built up from smaller units or constructed from parts of a dissolving empire, a process of nation building was introduced by governing elites: national loyalty was demanded; flags and other symbols became objects of respect; children were taught to love their country beyond all others. If the potential nation shared a language, this became a national symbol; if it did not, elites set about constructing one. If the territory had enjoyed some historical continuity as a shared area of rule, this would be celebrated even if, as in the case of Italy, this meant reaching back over several centuries. A particularly important task had been to try to inculcate this sense of nation in groups who had been included within a nation-state boundary but whose loyalties seemed more likely to belong within a neighbouring state (for example: Catholics in Northern Ireland; Catalans in France; Alsatians in France or Germany, depending on who was ruling them at the time) or in a potential state that was not permitted to exist at all (Ireland until 1921; the Basque country; Burgundy; Scotland).

Various means were used by states to fashion these national identities—not always consciously (Cotts Watkins 1991). Railway and road networks would link provinces to each other and, particularly important, to the capital city; they usually become much thinner at boundaries. (During the nineteenth century and until 1945 this would have been partly for military motives within Western Europe: invading troops and equipment could move by train and road.) Postal and later telephone networks were more concerned to link the nation across its internal provincial borders than to link with foreigners across national ones. Newspapers, later radio and television, tended to serve both local and national audiences, but not beyond. National education systems were established which usually imposed the official national language or dominant dialect, and encouraged young people to identify with their nation. The great processes of urbanization and industrialization meant that people moved from rural areas to state capitals and industrializing towns, where they met and mixed with others from different parts of countries. These places often became national rather than regional cities. States extended the legal structures that would enable people easily to buy, sell, and save within a nation. This, combined with the communications networks, made possible the extension of national markets; Paris fashions replaced traditional provincial dress in remote parts of France; regional cuisines could be extended beyond the region to the whole nation. However, until the formation of the European Economic Communities there were trade barriers that partly protected these national markets from international influence.

THE DIFFICULT BIRTH OF MODERN CITIZENSHIP

While a major implication of industrialization was the rise of capitalist against aristocratic predominance, in the longer run there were also important changes in the position of ordinary working people. Not all the new factory population comprised an undifferentiated proletarian mass. Industrial activities required new skills, and the workers who practised the trades that used these skills could, especially if they organized themselves in trade unions, try to exercise leverage in bargaining with their employers. Furthermore, the urban masses presented challenges to social order of an unprecedented kind. The combinations of Church, community pressure, and local lords which had stamped heavily on social dissent in rural society were absent from the new urban agglomerations, which brought people together in unprecedented numbers and with pressing needs for collective facilities to combat disease, squalor, and difficulties of transportation.

Working people began to organize themselves to make demands for improvements in their lives, often first joining in with bourgeois challenges to the aristocratic monopoly of power, but eventually seeing the bourgeoisie as their own principal political enemy and confronting them alone or sometimes even in a new alliance with church and other traditional social groups engaged in their own battles with the new phenomenon of industrial capitalism. The ensuing struggles were often violent and bitter. For the first time politics had to adjust to attempts at participation by masses of people. There were demands for democracy and the formation of mass political parties to represent the new interests. By the late twentieth century it was possible in retrospect to see these developments as leading gradually to the creation of certain distinctive new institutions: trade unions and a general system of democratic interest representation; welfare states to cope with many of the problems of collective living and demand for an amelioration of the logic of capitalism; political parties trying in different degrees to represent ordinary people and competing in elections to win control of the levers of government which for so many centuries had been the family possessions of ruling dynasties. But such a view of a peaceful, logical evolution would be mistaken. At every point trade unions, the welfare state, and challenges to capitalism have been at the heart of controversy and continuing social struggle—a set of conflicts which then acquired a new virulence at the very end of the millennium.

By the early twentieth century two particularly distinctive responses to new mass demands had emerged (both starting in Germany) which, in different ways, combined acceptance of mass involvement with the suppression of democratic participation. Both drew support from the chaos induced in Europe by the disastrous First World War of 1914–18.

The first of these was a Communist movement which claimed directly to represent the industrial working class against capitalism, but which did so by insisting on a particular interpretation of the class's interests, which precluded direct and open participation in shaping policies and ideas. Communists sought power through revolution, and succeeded in making one in the most populous and geographically largest but most backward of all European powers, Russia, in 1917. They established a pro-proletarian, anti-capitalist but non-democratic dictatorship which was eventually able to spread its power to the entire Slav area of Europe as well as Hungary and part of Germany by the end of the Second World War in 1945. Communist regimes finally collapsed in a context of economic decline and inability to resist demands for democracy at the end of the 1980s. This marked yet another stage in the separation of the histories of the eastern and western part of the continent. Since the terrain of this book is defined in terms of Western Europe, the details of the Communist system in Europe do not concern us here, though the existence of this particular form of society had implications for the behaviour of Western Europeans.

The second form of anti-democratic mass society took the form of a series of highly nationalistic movements known as Fascist or national socialist which spread, mainly in southern Europe and in Germany and Austria but with echoes throughout Europe, in the wake of the dislocations of the First World War and other crises of the growth of mass society. While they differed considerably in programme from each other, these movements sought to deflect the attention of the masses from their demands for democracy and for reforms to capitalism by directing their resentments against foreigners of various kinds; in Germany and Austria particularly against the Jews. Traditional elites, often despairing how to sustain order in mass society, stood aside to enable these movements to rule in Italy and Portugal in the 1920s, in Germany, Austria, and Spain in the 1930s. In Germany and Italy, especially the former, the logic of hostility to foreigners led these forces to embark on military campaigns that led quickly to global war by 1939, a war which ended in their total defeat.

THE END OF THE EUROPEAN MILLENNIUM

Important to the rise of the Fascist movements was the strong sense of national, ethnic identity that had been developed among many European populations, which then reacted violently when their own life chances seemed problematic while their societies had been entered by minorities of different ethnicity. Paradoxically, while the nineteenth century saw a consolidation of the nation state, it also witnessed the beginnings of something that was to become a major feature of late twentieth-century society: the migration of large numbers of people from outside the European region. Particularly large waves of intra-European immigration took place as some parts of Europe industrialized in advance of others (Castles and Miller 1993: 53–8). These usually occurred between countries adjacent to each other and are difficult to distinguish entirely from rural–urban migrations taking place within countries. Irish migration to England and Scotland took the form of internal migration at that time, though the cultural gap was larger than that experienced by Belgians and Frenchmen moving to each other's countries, or Italians and other southern Europeans moving to France. Poles also moved to Germany, usually under officially sponsored temporary labour schemes. Czechs, Slovenians, and Hungarians went to Vienna. Many members of all these groups intermarried and assimilated.

The disruptions of the First World War produced further movements, but the economic depression and mass unemployment that characterized most of the inter-war years led to a considerable reduction in intra-European migration, except in France where a long-run demographic stagnation continued to provide opportunities for many southern Europeans as it had done in the nineteenth century (Castles and Miller 1993: 59–61; Limousin 1988).

But the most important contribution of the 1930s to the record of European ethnic minorities, and probably the single most significant episode of that entire record, was the systematic genocide of Jews, gypsies, and some other minorities by the German Nazi state and its allies. Between five and six million Jews were rounded up throughout the territories of Europe controlled by Germany, worked as slaves and then slaughtered in death camps in horrifying circumstances. Since the mid-nineteenth century most Western (though not Eastern) European Jews had moved out of ghetto segregation and had integrated or completely assimilated in the societies around them. However, even the latter condition did not protect them from a genocide based solely on biological criteria. This slaughter reduced the six million continental European Jewish population to a few hundred thousand. It also had enduring implications for sensitivities to ethnic intolerance and to the treatment of minorities in Germany, the rest of Europe, the USA, and other parts of the world.

In the wake of the Second World War there were further major disruptions as Germans were driven out of lands in eastern and south-eastern Europe that had been conquered by the Soviet Union and its allies. About 12 million of these various groups of German expellees entered the war-devastated territory of western Germany between 1945 and 1950.

Since 1914 Europe had been an arena of extraordinary destruction and violent death. The rivalries of the various nation states which had played their part in asserting the overall world dominance of Western European rule had finally put an end to that dominance. Exhausted and bankrupt by war, in 1945 Western Europeans had to look to two external powers—the USA and the Soviet Union—to conclude their peace. The former sustained and defended a capitalist system of economic organization; the latter a state socialist one. This East–West division did not correspond to the thousand-year-old split between Orthodox East and Catholic West, though it embodied much of it. Countries that had been part of the religious west but now found themselves part of the east included Czechoslovakia, Estonia, Latvia, Lithuania, Hungary, Poland, as well as the eastern parts of Germany. One of the neutral countries that served as a buffer between the new zones of Europe, Yugoslavia, incorporated not only both Catholic and Orthodox regions, but also Islamic ones. Greece, though Orthodox, found itself allied to the West, though only after a bitter civil war. Oddly, this new East/West division did correspond more closely to the much older division between the Slav and other language groups. No Slav country became part of the Western bloc; East Germany was the only Western-language country within the Eastern. (Romanian was the only Latin-based language within the realm of the Orthodox Church. The distinctive Finno-Ugrian group (Estonian, Finnish, and Hungarian) does not belong clearly to East or West, and Greek is a case by itself.)

The European millennium had ended with half a century still to run, and world leadership passed to the USA, a secondary European society in that its dominant ethnic groups were of European origin. In the rest of this book we shall therefore be concerned with a period when Europe had lost its dominant place in the world; when the diversities and rivalries that had made it such a complex and antagonistic place for so many centuries had passed their culmination; and when new attempts at a kind of European unity were being started—not by a crusading Christianity, nor by military aggression, but for the first time ever by peaceful means, by the intergovernmental agreements and bureaucratic co-ordination of the European Community and European Union.

But the Western European recovery from destruction was remarkably rapid. By 1960 the economies of virtually the whole subcontinent except for the Iberian peninsula were showing extraordinary dynamism, nowhere more than in defeated Germany. The level of mass prosperity rose and, again with the exception of Iberia, democratic citizenship became the normal form of governance. To explore these developments and their subsequent changes further is the task of the rest of this book.

Chapter 1

THE MAKING OF
CONTEMPORARY EUROPE

The Europe that emerged devastated by the Second World War comprised a very diverse set of countries. Some had long been established as primarily industrial, their populations specializing in manufacturing a wide range of goods in factories: the United Kingdom, Belgium, Czechoslovakia, Switzerland. Others were on the way to that position, but still had large agricultural sectors: France, Sweden, the Netherlands, Germany (which was also suffering from the destruction of its industrial base in the defeat of the war). Others again were still primarily agricultural, with just small industrial sectors and most of their farms comprising small-scale peasant plots: nearly all of southern and eastern Europe. Although for most of the first part of this century industrial might already lay at the root of national success, and although the momentous process of change from a society based on farm and village to one based on factory and city had already been written about for over a century, for much of the population of Europe personal experience of that change still lay in the future. It was however to be the very near future; fifty years later only small minorities of the population of all countries in at least the western part of the European continent are still rooted in the land.

In labelling a society 'industrial', whether 'capitalist industrial' or 'state socialist industrial' we might be thought to imply that everything that takes place in that society is oriented towards its economic characteristics. In practice no society really does this, though they do vary in the extent to which they depart from the concept. Here we shall consider four sets of institutions in modern societies which exist as a kind of quadrilateral of forces; interdependent but potentially hostile, they exist in a state of tension but also with a certain hierarchy. They are:

- the *economic activities* whereby people overcome the problem of scarcity and meet their needs and desires for food, goods, and services;
- the system of *ownership and control* of resources within which these activities are embedded;
- and the world of non-economic matters, which may be divided again into two: *community* and *political society*. The former of these relates to questions of identity and affective solidarity (principally family, religion, ethnicity, and nation); the latter to political structures, the organization of interests, and the rights of citizenship. It will be noted that nation and political identity overlap the boundaries of each of these two categories.

In European history this quadrilateral has been the site of massive struggles. The French Revolution had set citizenship and community against each other; the Industrial Revolution had pitted the economy against both, and had raised major questions over the relationship of the organization of work to the manner in which it was owned and controlled: the fundamental intra-national political division of the twentieth century. There were also tensions between institutions within individual sides of the quadrilateral: among nation, church, family; or between the politics of parties and that of organized interests. And of course there were conflicts within individual instances of particular institutions: between churches, between families, and many others. European history has been particularly rich in forging divisions of this kind, as parts of the rapid review of the past millennium in the Prologue have shown. As Göran Therborn (1995: 356) put the same point in his study of *The Future of European Modernity*, civil war has been somehow endemic to the European approach to modernity, with what he calls its 'ism-ic' features, 'its clear and rigid divisions into warring, principled camps, slugging out all the issues about and around modernity among themselves, in civil wars'. Or, as Mendras (1991: 15) describes the phenomenon in a different, more specific, context:

In 1914, French society was divided into four great social groups, each of which had its own particular characteristics: the peasants, the bourgeoisie, the proletariat and the 'middle classes'. The peasants represented the most important numerical group, but were themselves divided into countless independent local communities and for that reason remained relatively isolated from the rest of society. Each region spoke its own language and guarded itself against the intrusion of outside forces, especially the state.

By the second half of the present century, after Europe's final exhaustion in war, most of these conflicts had more or less changed into a form of structured tolerance. Typically, people would be organized around one of the great divisions, and from that vantage point would at best pursue an active cooperation with old enemies, at worst accept an armistice across the lines. Workers and employers, having organized themselves for industrial conflict, used their organizations to make deals with each other. Different religious denominations, while remaining proud of the distinctive beliefs and practices defended by their particular organizations, then set up various types of cooperation with other, theoretically rival denominations. Political parties cooperated in government, or at least in sustaining democracy; nation states which had defined themselves against each other and set up state machines for making war against each other, now used those same machines to launch an ambitious movement for a European economic community.

One can see this mutual tolerance as a form of *liberalism*, but not in the loose sense of 'live and let live'. Liberalism is a much abused idea. Its original use referred to the Church and the court leaving other institutions (including each other) alone and not seeking to exercise control over their internal workings. This says nothing about how life is organized *within* the institutions in question, which could be highly authoritarian. This survives today in the notion of economic liberalism, which means releasing economic transactions and market forces from government intervention, but which is quite compatible with firms themselves exercising very strict authority over their employees. It is this sense that I want to retain here: liberalism as forbearance or tolerance *between* institutions, but not necessarily *within* them. A 'liberal' approach to the family by the state, for example, means the state not interfering with the internal conduct of families—which might well include not protecting children from being beaten by their parents. Of particular interest to us here is not economic liberalism (based on market forces) or the political doctrine of liberalism, but a form of cooperation among institutions based essentially on organization to avoid potential hostility, a structured sociological liberalism.

Its immediate roots lay in Dutch and, less formally, English and Scottish religious tolerance after the Reformation, as highly organized, rival forms of Christianity came to accept that they had to cooperate with each other rather than strive for mutual elimination. This was discussed in relation to the Dutch case in the Prologue with reference to the process of *verzuiling* or pillarization. While these Dutch institutions were very specific, in some respects *verzuiling* also stands as a kind of type for the entire concept of sociological liberalism. The essential points are the subtle mix of separation and cooperation; and the fact that what seems to be a matter of ideas and values is in reality embedded in firm structures of social relations. Within the individual pillars life could be highly hierarchical: a pillar is after all a vertical structure.

Much further back one can see a preparation for this model in the recognized division of labour between Church and Empire. When, for example, Giddens (1990: 56) speaks of the economy in capitalist societies being 'insulated' from other institutions, in particular the political, he is pointing to an important legacy of institutional separation from the remote pre-capitalist past.

In advanced societies sociological liberalism has mainly been a process whereby parts of traditional society were protected and given space within modernization. It is not necessarily concerned with democracy or equality. To consider these we need a further concept. Societies differ in the extent to which everyone living within them is able to enjoy what might be described as rights of membership, including rights of political participation, legal protection and assurances of certain standards of welfare. I shall call this dimension that of citizenship. Here there was also considerable diversity in past European experience at the dawn of the post-war peace. No countries had a lengthy experience of more than a small number of items within it. The Scandinavian countries and possibly the UK had probably moved furthest towards a combination of political democracy and welfare citizenship, but even their developments were in their infancy. Austria and Germany had pioneered the rudiments of welfare citizenship since the late nineteenth century, but without a democratic context, and then one interrupted by the Nazi period. French developments had been the other way round (strong democracy; weak welfare). Outside these, whether countries had experienced inter-war Fascism or not, their past records contained little.

Again, however, over the coming decades all Western European countries were to witness major changes towards the construction of mass democratic welfare citizenship as here defined. For a lengthy period such a pattern remained strongest where it had started (Scandinavia, the Netherlands, the UK), while in southern Europe it did not develop until the 1970s; there continued to be diversity within the framework of the uniform march.

THE MID-CENTURY SOCIAL COMPROMISE

We can summarize the overall shape of convergent change in the post-war decades as follows:

1. Nearly every one of these societies had either already become or now seriously started to become *industrial* rather than agricultural in its occupational structure and economic output.

2. Every society in Western Europe had a primarily *capitalist* framework of property ownership (the central defining contrast with Eastern and Central Europe).

3. In the wake of the defeat of Fascism and the rejection of Communism, most of these societies had a *sociologically liberal* institutional structure in relation to traditional community institutions.

4. It also became widely accepted that nearly every adult living in these societies possessed certain rights of membership, of *citizenship*.

The general idea of a balance among these characteristics constituted the distinctive social form of the mid-century social compromise that was a shared inheritance of most of the countries of Western Europe, the USA, and some other countries. The scope for variation in the particular shape of the balance produced a diversity among them.

The degree of unity that existed in pursuit of the social compromise model is easily taken for granted fifty years later, and we may not see the considerable tensions, almost contradictions, that exist among certain elements of the package. Full maximization of the potentialities of capitalist industrialism would involve the subordination of all other institutions to its requirements, which would compromise the autonomy principle of liberalism. (For example, imagine a society where families and churches were required to follow company law and market principles in transactions among their members.) Similarly, the inequalities inherent in capitalist property ownership are difficult to reconcile with the idea of equality of rights embedded in the concept of mass citizenship. The ways in which societies found various resolutions to these conflicts become sources of continuing diversity within the overall uniformity; continuing instabilities in and disturbances to these resolutions became sources of social change.

One such resolution is of course for one or other of the four elements to lose in a conflict with the logic of another. For example, the claims of citizenship might simply be defeated by those of the requirements of capitalism. Alternatively, different elements might be segregated from one another, each affecting different sections of the population or different social roles. Sociologists and political scientists have long been aware of the role of segregations in limiting and channelling conflict: the concept of the institutionalization of conflict is particularly useful. The central concept here is of conflicts being insulated from each other by institutional structures, so that they did not overflow into each other and create uncontrollable civil warfare. The idea of electrical insulation, preventing charged electrical wires from crossing and causing dangerous short circuits, is useful to an understanding of this. Certain institutions can perform such a task for social conflicts, preventing for example industrial conflict and religious conflict from combining with each other.

The concept was initially developed by various North American observers of post-war societies, trying in particular to understand why certain societies (mainly the UK and the USA) had been able to accommodate social struggles of the inter-war years while others (especially Germany) had not. The best sustained theoretical elaboration of the theme was by the German sociologist Ralf Dahrendorf, initially in *Class and Class Conflict in Industrial Societies* (1957, 1959); but far more recently and with more attention to the subsequent development of post-war societies in *The Modern Social Conflict* (1988). Central to Dahrendorf's ideas is that conflict becomes damaging to the wider society not only if it is not subject to institutionalization, but also if it is suppressed. A strong society is therefore one in which conflicts are expressed and played out, but do not become mingled.

These ideas are included in my concept of sociological liberalism, though I intend something wider than the channelling of conflict, rather the more general framework of mutual respect of each other's autonomy by diverse institutions.

FORDISM

Recently the most dominant strand within sociological theory for expressing this point has, rather oddly, been that associated with the idea of 'Fordism'. The origins of the term are obviously in the history of the Ford Motor Company and of the mass-production method of industrial manufacture, mentioned in the Prologue. We must explore this further.

In Ford's Detroit factory of the early twentieth century, the task of production was stripped down to its simplest component parts and arranged on a sequential production line so that a workforce of low skills and considerable cultural, linguistic, and ethnic heterogeneity (and therefore capable of only a minimum level of cooperation) could produce cars with unrivalled efficiency. These work methods were pioneered by the industrial engineer Frederick Taylor, and are often by themselves labelled in the literature 'Taylorist', but the concept of Fordism itself goes beyond the method of production. Because the workers were efficient, they could earn considerably higher wages than normally available to semi-skilled manual workers. Furthermore, these work methods benefited from considerable economies of scale: the more that could be produced, the cheaper the cost of an individual unit; and the cheaper the individual unit, the more could be sold. Gradually, as the logic of mass production became extended to an increasing number of firms and types of good, a powerful process was launched. Sophisticated goods like motor cars came within the purchasing power of people on modest wages; and if these people were themselves working in mass-production industry, their wages were less modest than in the past.

The concept was seen as potentially denoting a whole new form of the capitalist economy by Antonio Gramsci, the inter-war leader of the Italian Communist Party who made major contributions to modern social thought while languishing in prison during the Fascist regime. Although the Ford factories began to operate in their distinctive way in the early years of the present century, it was much later that such a system became generally embedded in Europe. It was only in the 1970s, when the system seemed to be coming to an end, that it was taken up again in serious analysis, initially in the work of the French *régulationiste* school, who see Fordism as one of the modes of organization of capitalist economies (e.g. Boyer and Saillard 1995; Coriat 1979). (Although the French word *régulation* seems easily translated as regulation, it really has a more extended meaning, referring to the whole way in which something is organized and not just the way in which it is regulated in the sense of the English word.) One of the leading *régulationiste* economists, Robert Boyer (1988: 11) uses 'Taylorist' to describe the wage/labour relations that began to develop from the nineteenth century onwards, and 'Fordist' to denote the period 1945 to 1973—that is, the years of virtually uninterrupted economic growth among Western European nations, the USA, and Japan between the end of the Second World War and the first oil shock.

For the first time in history there was then a real possibility of mass prosperity. In the past the production of goods, despite important progress which came with the Industrial Revolution, had been limited to simple items for the masses of the poor and luxury goods for a small rich elite. This did not offer much scope for expanding incomes for producers. In the agricultural sector sales and earnings were even more constrained by the vagaries of weather and natural disasters. The prospects of a rapid improvement in the standard of living of the poor were limited. The difficulty in envisaging a rapid growth in overall wealth was an important factor in creating resistance to social reform and the extension of democracy and citizenship among the wealthy classes of pre-industrial and early industrial societies, explaining part of the support they gave to Fascist and Nazi movements during the tumultuous years after the First World War and the Russian Revolution. After the Second World War the prospects of rapidly advancing productivity and a mutually sustaining spiral of increasing production and rising real wages helped give them confidence that mass prosperity might advance at little or no cost to their own comforts. They looked to the USA to try to understand how that country had managed to sustain both mass citizenship and a highly inegalitarian capitalist distribution of wealth and income. One lesson they learned was that of Fordist mass production.

By itself Fordism as such was not adequate for self-sustaining mass prosperity; after all, the USA had suffered a terrible recession during the late 1920s and 1930s with a rise in mass unemployment, mass poverty, and even some de-industrialization as desperate people left the workless cities to try to return to scraping a living from the soil. Since those years ideas had been circulating among economists about how governments might manage their own revenue-collecting and expenditure to smooth out the sharp economic cycles that plagued capitalist economies. The name most powerfully associated with these plans was that of an Englishman, John Maynard Keynes, though similar ideas were developed, in company with Keynes, by such Swedish political economists as Ernst Wigforss and (later) Rudolf Meidner and Gösta Rehn; plans for government demand management were first introduced in Scandinavia during the 1930s. Certain forms of these ideas were built into the post-war package of economic reforms introduced by several Western governments and supported by such international agencies as the Organization for European Economic Co-operation (OEEC; later Organization for Economic Co-operation and Development, OECD). This had been established primarily by the USA and the UK to oversee the new politico-economic order being erected in Western Europe as an alternative to both the defeated Fascism of the immediate European past and the threatening Communism of the East.

Keynesian economic management was consistent with Fordist production, as it stabilized the economic cycle and gave confidence, both to business firms that they could invest in expensive mass-production technology, and to ordinary working people to buy the goods and thereby stimulate more production. Furthermore, Keynesian policy required governments to run large budgets, so that their actions in either stimulating or curtailing demand would be sufficiently powerful to affect a whole economy. But previously governments had maintained budgets of that size only during periods of war; in peacetime their revenue-raising and expenditure returned to low levels. It was in fact during the Second World War and as a result of its enormous expenditure that political and business elites had an initial opportunity to witness Keynes's ideas being implemented; and indeed, the rise in mass prosperity in Nazi Germany as the regime spent vast sums on armaments during the 1930s had given an even earlier glimpse. This could be sustained in peacetime only with different kinds of expenditure.

(However, the state of permanently high levels of increasingly expensive armaments occasioned by the Cold War between the West and the Soviet East from 1947 to 1989 enabled warfare to maintain more of its contribution during peacetime than usual.) The Scandinavian experiments of the 1930s, and some more limited action in the USA at the same time, had pointed the way to alternative possibilities: a high level of government revenue-raising and expenditure on public welfare: health, education, social insurance. Thus, the welfare state, itself one of the principal embodiments of the concept of mass citizenship, became also one of the major ways in which economic stability and prosperity could be guaranteed, and politico-economic elites thereby re-assured that the potential tensions of the social compromise model could be sustained.

Political economists and sociologists of the Fordist school have therefore embraced within their concept both Keynesian demand management and the modern welfare state, so that Fordism becomes a description of an entire politico-economic order and not just a method of production of motor cars. To this, some accounts of Fordism have incorporated trade unionism. Especially in the traditions that developed in the USA (and to a lesser extent the UK) trade unions came to represent the limited and narrow concerns with wages and conditions of manual workers within the context of the segmented, low-skilled workforces of the Fordist factory. Widespread unionism also represented another achievement of mass citizenship.

The Fordists have then gone further. The essential principle of Fordist or Taylorist production was the breakdown of work tasks to highly specialized roles carried out under the close control of a business management. The organization of human welfare by the bureaucracies characteristic of welfare states can be seen as an extension of this process. Just as Fordist motor-car production was more efficient than earlier craft pro-duction, so welfare tasks are performed more efficiently by these specialized organiza-tions than by the small organizations that would otherwise take charge of them—that is, families and voluntary societies. Families do not however become redundant, but, true to the Fordist model, specialize in the functions that they can perform best (which may be defined as either the maintenance and repair of the workforce during non-working hours, or as the provision of love and affection). One thus sees references to the 'Fordist family' (Böckler 1999: 328 ff.).

Fordism has therefore been used to describe an entire *social* order. This is confusing. Taylorist production methods, Keynesian economics, the welfare state, and the trade unionism of semi-skilled workers may turn out to have complemented each other, but it is misleading to see them as belonging to a constructed whole meriting the name of an 'ism', which implies some kind of deliberate conceptual or ideological unity. In practice, the US business elites who are the groups most obviously evoked by the term Fordism have been probably the most vociferous and successful opponents of the welfare state and trade unions in the post-war Western world; in recent decades they have also taken the lead in a successful attack on Keynesian demand management too. Furthermore, use of 'Fordism' implies that the framework of post-war Western polit-ical economy was essentially American in origin. While this is true for some elements of the so-called Fordist package, it is not valid for all; certainly the origins of the welfare state require a different interpretation. One might in particular note that several of the characteristics incorporated within Fordism describe those large-scale organizations that result from the attempt at organizing work in the most rationally efficient, precisely goal-oriented and hierarchically controlled manner possible; a concept developed by Max Weber in the early years of this century to describe modern state and business bureaucracy. In many respects Taylorism was the extension of Weber's concept from the office to the factory.

Finally, extension of the Fordist concept to define family structure makes very challengeable assumptions about the power of industrial organization to shape other institutions. If taken seriously, it must imply that the organization of the family was primarily determined by the productive system and therefore possessed no autonomy. This leaves out the possibility that certain stubborn realities of family structure might have shaped the behaviour of the productive system. Similarly, it might be argued that, because the Taylorist/Fordist production system developed within the context of considerable ethnic heterogeneity, a situation of ethnic pluralism is somehow 'Fordist'. In reality, the production system adapted to the social reality it found around itself. It then adjusted the shape of that reality; but the essential point is that there is a mutual interaction between society and productive system. Use of the term Fordism seems to prejudge and oversimplify that relationship.

The interconnections and institutional relationships identified for us by the Fordist school have been invaluable to social analysis, and I shall make considerable use of them in the following chapters. Because of its deficiencies, however, I shall not use the term itself, but instead the more general one of mid-century compromise society as defined in terms of the quadrilateral discussed above, the detailed characteristics of which will be completed as we proceed.

POST-INDUSTRIAL, POST-FORDIST, POSTMODERN?

The question must arise whether, nearly half a century later, we are still living in a society with these characteristics, and the tendency of much recent literature has been to argue that we do not. For nearly thirty years now sociologists and others have been speaking of 'post-industrial society'. One also finds references to 'post-capitalism'. The Fordist writers came into existence at a point when they regarded the political economy they were defining as being transcended: their main concern is to tell us about 'post-Fordist' society. 'Post-liberal' writing certainly exists, but largely within political thought. 'Post-citizenship' or 'post-democratic' I have not encountered. There is clearly therefore some unevenness in the perception of the redundancy or transcendence of the mid-century themes. Most fundamentally, widespread use is made of the idea of 'postmodernity' in both sociological and cultural debate, as though the entire modernization process of the move from traditional and rural society is being replaced by something new. As 'post-' concepts, these new ideas define the new models they are describing in very negative terms. Such concepts say: something has changed (or is changing) and is (or is about to be) no more; the character of what has come (or is coming) into existence is not yet clear.

POST-INDUSTRIALISM

The central idea of post-industrial theory (see especially Bell 1974) has been that, as economies develop, so the workforce moves from employment in manufacturing industry to what are known as the 'service occupations', and that therefore being 'industrial' no longer characterizes the societies in which we live. If true, this has considerable implications for the analysis of contemporary European societies as social compromise societies, because a central component of that definition was industrialism. In particular, the thesis predicts the decline of the most significant (though never majority) category of person in industrial society: manual workers in manufacturing industry. These are, at least in Bell's view, being replaced by a more skilled, considerably better educated scientific workforce.

The French sociologist Alain Touraine (1971) also used the concept of post-industrialism with the meaning of a more skilled, intellectual workforce in the services sectors, but, coming from a Marxist background, saw their role differently. These new educated groups—who in the future would be the people who had been radical students in their youth—would challenge capitalist domination of the economic system. They would become a kind of new proletariat, but better equipped than their industrial working-class predecessors to raise effective political challenges.

POST-FORDISM

Post-Fordism also takes up the possibility of a collapse of industrialism, certainly of the mass-production methods associated with Fordism. There is however some division in the literature over what is held to be replacing this model of employment. Some writers, similarly to Bell, saw a move to a better and more flexibly skilled workforce, returning to some extent to the pre-Fordist model of craft autonomy though with modern educational and technological standards (among many examples, see Hirst and Zeitlin 1990; Kern and Schumann 1987; Mathews 1989; Piore and Sabel 1984). The Fordist hierarchy, necessary to maintain an extreme division of labour and specialization among an unskilled workforce, was no longer necessary. Work organizations therefore change their structure considerably. Other writers, on the other hand, while agreeing that a new flexibility would replace the unusually high degree of stability and predictability of Fordism, saw this flexibility taking the form of increased insecurity among a workforce that is deprived of the certainties of the Fordist hierarchy and its associated trade unions, Keynesian demand management, and welfare state (Böckler 1991; Jessop et al. 1991). The new flexibility then results, not so much from increased skill levels, as from great insecurity in the global economy and rapid change in production methods that have undermined the basis of post-war economic stability. If the former school saw post-Fordism bringing an enhanced citizenship through a population better equipped to participate in public life, the latter saw a decline in citizenship as the securities of the Keynesian welfare state diminish.

POSTMODERNITY

Both forms of post-Fordism see a fragmentation of the large, regimented and segregated groups of the Fordist model of industrial society, and it is this quality of fragmentation and accompanying loss of structure and settled characteristics that is particularly implied by the idea of postmodernity. The original references here are cultural, in particular architectural, rather than sociological, though the core ideas are then extended, sometimes by analogy, across a wide range. The modernist style of architecture that was initiated in the early twentieth century concentrated on clear, clean, undecorated lines. Its development in the early years of this century runs historically parallel to both Weber's concept of bureaucracy and the development of the Fordist/Taylorist production system. Among its central characteristics were functionalism and an avoidance of redundant detail. It was indeed particularly well equipped for the accommodation of bureaucracies (office blocks) and large factories. More generally, modernity as a cultural term refers in the same way to functionalism and rationality. Sociologically the process of modernization describes the movement from traditionalism (in which religion, ascribed status, locally rooted and small-scale, culturally specific communities predominate) to rationalism (science, achieved status, convergent, large-scale organization, and cosmopolitan urban societies).

Postmodernist architecture constitutes a revolt against what came to be seen as the dreary, massive, expressionless functionalism of modernist built forms, in favour partly of a return to older, more decorative styles, but in particular to the idea of a fragmented, more or less arbitrary and ahistorical simultaneous combination of several styles, a deliberate abandonment of the idea of overall unity of form which was at the heart of both modernity and the styles it replaced which had developed from the Renaissance onwards. The themes of fragmentation and arbitrariness have carried over into the general cultural stance that calls itself postmodernist. Theories of society affected by postmodernist ideas stress the breakdown of former social forms (for example, classes, the family, gender roles and relations), an increased heterogeneity (produced by intensified communications and in particular the rise of multi-ethnic societies), and the fragmentation of organizations: the word 'disorganized' appears frequently in postmodernist sociology (e.g. Offe 1985; Lash and Urry 1987).

To address this issue adequately requires us to retrace our steps and examine more closely the idea of modernity itself, in relation to which postmodernist theorists claim to have produced such a large trend break. Therborn (1995: 4) works from within a long and strong tradition of Western thought when he defines modernity in terms of orientation to the future, as 'an epoch turned to the future'. This distinguishes it clearly from its main point of contrast, traditional society, which saw the future only as a repetition of the past. It also helpfully distinguishes it from postmodernity which, Therborn says, has lost all sense of time direction, the original meaning of postmodernism in the cultural and architectural context and one that can be transferred to sociology. Viewed in this way, modernity appears as an essentially *cultural* concept. It consists in a particular approach to action: one which involves constantly reappraising institutions and ways of acting in order to determine whether they are the most efficient possible means of achieving their ends. (Max Weber's discussion of *Zweckrationalität* (1922) is the *locus classicus* for this phenomenon; he too was primarily contrasting this 'goal rationality' with traditional action.) Asked why she acts the way she does, the truly modern person replies: 'I do things this way because at present it seems to be the most efficient means of achieving my ends; but I keep reappraising the situation in the light of all available information and new developments, and this might require change at any time.'

This can be contrasted with traditional action, where it is considered right to do things the way they have been done since a remote past, without sustained enquiry into their efficiency. Asked why he acts the way he does, the traditionalist replies: 'We [he is more likely to say we than I] do it this way because it has always been done this way.'

Defined in this way modernity has no *content*; it is all process. It is easier to put content into the idea of 'modernization', which can be seen as those actions and institutions produced by people as they have historically set about the task of becoming modern. By the nature of the process, this content is constantly changing. There is a rich sociology of modernization, but not much on modernity. We can however treat modernity as a historical period as well as a set of cultural values applied to a process of social construction. A period of modernity is that during which modernizing forces, as defined, are the most powerful ones shaping institutions, and the *ensemble* of institutions and other social products they produce constitutes the modern period.

This period is now a long one. Modernity has been a force at work for at least 400 years in some parts of Europe, and, precisely because it is about constant change and re-examination, the institutional forms associated with it keep changing. It is not therefore easy to study 'modern society' *in toto*. Therefore in this book I have tried to take the form of modern institutions at a particular moment in time, what I call the mid-century, when a certain set of social problems demanded institutional re-design in a number of societies, and to consider the subsequent moves until the present time in modernity's continuing process of adjustment. This happens to bring us into a period when doubt is being cast on whether the concept of modernity should be used, or whether we have entered a moment of decisive break and an end to modernity as such.

It is here that the idea of postmodernity enters the frame as a claim that somehow this entire historical trajectory since the Renaissance has now been changed and checked, and that we live in a time of radical departure from the modern. The successor period, the postmodern, implies a fragmentation of forms rather than rational directedness, randomness, chaotic variety, an end to the unidirectional nature of 'progress' and (as part of this) a *rapprochement* between the modern and the traditional. In architecture this is easy to achieve by mixing historical styles and by ornamenting in a very heterogeneous way. Sociologically it would be necessary to find institutional forms that correlate with such an idea. These would then constitute postmodernity. Several social changes relevant to the themes of this book are discussed in this context: for example, the collapse of the strongly articulated structures and apparently fixed identities of the mid-century period, the rise of multiculturalism, the rise of fringe, magic-based religious cults.

These are very interesting questions. Disintegration and loss of form are attributes *of the process of change* as such, even changes that lead from one solid state to another. (For example, nineteenth-century sociologists, seeing the social dislocation involved in the large-scale movement of people from the countryside to the towns, assumed that dislocation was an aspect of life in industrial cities, rather than of the change process of urbanization.) Our own period embodies some similarities. The process of de-industrialization which has taken place as old industries have been run down strengthens the impression of a moving away from something known into a future of varied and uncertain possibilities. If contemporary society is described in terms of such phenomena as the fragmentation of occupational identities, or of cultures, or the breakdown of organizations, is this a description of the characteristics of the social institutions that are being created for a world in which major change is endemic, or of the loss of distinct form that *temporarily* accompanies change?

REFLEXIVE MODERNITY, RISK SOCIETY, AND GLOBALIZATION

More specifically, it can be contended that these disintegrative trends do not presage a move to a new form of society, but are signs of increasing difficulty and crisis in the management of the tensions that we have above analysed as endemic to the social compromise model. This has been argued by those critics of postmodernist theory who speak instead of 'reflexive modernity' (Giddens 1990: 36 ff.) or the 'risk society' (Beck 1986).

Reflexive Modernity
The first of these unusual phrases refers to the essential characteristic of modern scientific thought of reflecting back on itself and constantly changing its conclusions. This imparts an uncertainty, not so much because there is no stable social world to know (as postmodernist interpretations would have it), 'but that knowledge of that world contributes to its unstable or mutable character' (Giddens 1990: 45). This is embedded in the whole scientific temper from the Enlightenment period on and is therefore neither specific to the current period nor a departure from modernity. As anthropologists will remind us, we should not confuse the extreme margins of scientific method for the way ordinary people conduct their everyday lives, where often much of traditionalism survives. However, it is likely that, with an increasing proportion of the population taking education to higher levels than in the past, something of the scientific temper moves deeper into everyday life. For Giddens this is far from being a change of direction as 'postmodernity' implies, but a process whereby 'the consequences of modernity are becoming more radicalised and universalised than before' (1990: 3).

Risk Society
The second phrase, 'risk society', embodies two important points. Clearly, in speaking of contemporary society as embodying risk, Ulrich Beck (the German sociologist who has popularized this phrase) is not arguing that life was risk-free in earlier societies. Rather, he is contrasting risk with danger, the former implying a measured approach to the calculation of probabilities. Instead of a fatalism that sees life as vulnerable to any number of disasters, the modern temper seeks to identify and calculate risks, then makes reasoned judgements about probability. Second, Beck is considering a number of risks that have developed within advanced societies (for example, environmental damage, rising crime, the spread of HIV-related diseases); the mid-century compromises had not taken account of these and they therefore cannot be fitted into its terms and the institutions it erected for dealing with anticipated problems.

Globalization
Since the early 1980s social scientists and others have erected a further new concept within which some of these themes have been integrated: globalization. This conveys a sense of the interdependence of the entire world, and of the interchangeability of many elements in it. Exposure to extra-European social and economic forces is no novelty to Europe. The Roman Empire itself straddled Europe and the Middle and Near East. Trade in silk, spices, and other largely luxury products with lands to the east of

Europe reaching as far as China was part of European life in both Roman times and again from the Middle Ages onwards. Europeans initiated a new stage in global development through their voyages of discovery from the fifteenth century onwards.

If globalization at the end of the twentieth century has any distinctive qualities apart from a sheer extension of scale they consist in two phenomena. First, the changes in the global location of production activities exceed any capacity of state regulation. Production processes can be moved from continent to continent, countries lose control to rapidly moving financial markets; the post-war international regulatory order has collapsed and is being replaced by little more than the regulation of deregulation (Michie and Grieve Smith 1995). Second, after at least two centuries when Europeans experienced a net balance of outward migration, Europe has become a major target of inward population movements. These changes have considerable importance for our themes at a number of points. They have exacerbated some aspects of change in economic structure and have therefore been implicated in post-industrialism. They have disturbed the balance of relationships between capitalism and other social forces. They have produced an internal cultural heterogeneity that is one component of post-modernity. We shall investigate these questions in subsequent chapters.

ANALYSING THE PROCESSES OF CHANGE

If some of the fixed points of the mid-century social compromise model have begun to unravel, are we yet able to discern the characteristics of a new model? Or are we entering a period of social development in which no particular models seem applicable? Can we see beyond a process of change? Are the changes tending to make our societies converge, or are there different paths through post-industrialism and postmodernity? If so, which countries form groups together, and why? Are there any distinctive 'European' solutions to these issues, not shared by American and Japanese societies? The following chapters will attempt to answer these questions by examining different institutions within the framework of the social compromise model.

A similar task has been carried out by Kaelble (1987), using the same set of countries as those studied here, and comparing them with the USA (though not with Japan). Whereas I shall trace change over the relatively brief period from what I regard as the height of the mid-century model (around 1960), his study has the advantage of going back further in time, to 1880, in order to capture to what extent there really was a break in the trajectory of European societies in 1945. I have, on the other hand, tried to be more systematic in my treatment of the different countries, only permitting myself Europe-wide generalizations if these cover almost all sixteen cases. Kaelble's methodology is explicitly different, since he seeks only majority tendencies (1987: ch. 1). In fact, as we shall have occasion to note at certain points, he sometimes permits a 'European' generalization provided a point holds for some northern European cases.

Therborn (1995), also attempting a survey of the current state of European societies, shares my view that the period since the early 1960s constitutes a turning point:

With some international variation of timing, the period from the early 1960s to the early 1980s was an amazing concentration of social historical turns. Immigration began to outpace out-migration. Secularization jumped forward. Women turned from the married kitchen to the labour market and to individual emancipation. Labour demands expanded and contracted. Industrial employment peaked and descended. The working class reached its strongest position ever, and soon lost it. The boom culminated and went into its first crises. Socialist radicalism exploded and imploded. Post-war right-wing liberalism and moderate conservatism were discredited by the left, and re-emerged, invigorated, in a much more militant form.   (1995: 351)

These institutions that we must study are interactive, and their relative weight in the interaction is a matter to be discovered, if possible, rather than assumed from the outset. This can easily be presented graphically, when we can simultaneously depict a series of arrows, headed at either end, linking the institutions in a way that criss-crosses the diagram. However, when we come to description we cannot avoid the linear character of human speech and writing; some things will have to be discussed before others, even though the impact on the former of the latter will have to be presented before the latter have been properly introduced. This is unavoidable, but I have tried to adopt an order of presentation that leaves fewer questions begged or waiting for later resolution.

The relationship between a graphical presentation and my chapter order is displayed in Figure 1.1. If we start at the left-hand side with the fundamental question of human labour, we instantly confront the major division between work in the formal occupational system and work within the family, an issue mediated through the gender division of labour. This division immediately takes us in two different kinds of direction. Here I shall follow first (in Part I) that which runs through the formal occupational system. We shall consider (in Chapter 2) the organization of employment which enables us to address the fundamental questions of the move from industrialism to a possible post-industrialism, and then the related issues of different forms of work (Chapter 3) and economic sectors (Chapter 4). Together these constitute the first master theme, economic activity and industrialism.

In discussing occupational forms and types we shall have considered the inequalities of rank that distinguish these from each other. This leads us naturally to the second master theme (Part II), the ownership and control of the economy and capitalism. This divides into two questions: capitalism as a structure of inequality (Chapter 5), but also capitalism as a phenomenon that takes a number of different forms (Chapter 6).

At this point we return to the alternative direction we might have followed from consideration of the world of work, through the family and on to a related set of issues concerning human community (Part III). This is where the theme of sociological liberalism becomes significant for the analysis of the mid-century social compromise. After the family itself (Chapter 7) we look at the way in which it plays a fundamental role as the channel through which certain social forms are perpetuated over time (Chapter 8). By taking us to consider the inheritance of capital this links us back to consideration of capitalism; in considering cultural capital through the question of education we confront the link between family, culture, back to the occupational system for which education is a preparation, and on to the welfare state (to be considered fully in Chapter 13) since education is one of the main components of twentieth-century social citizenship. Education as a cultural theme can however also take us to other aspects of culture: religion (Chapter 9), and its ambiguous ally and enemy, the nation state (Chapter 10), which also enables us to consider the cultural themes of nationality and ethnicity.

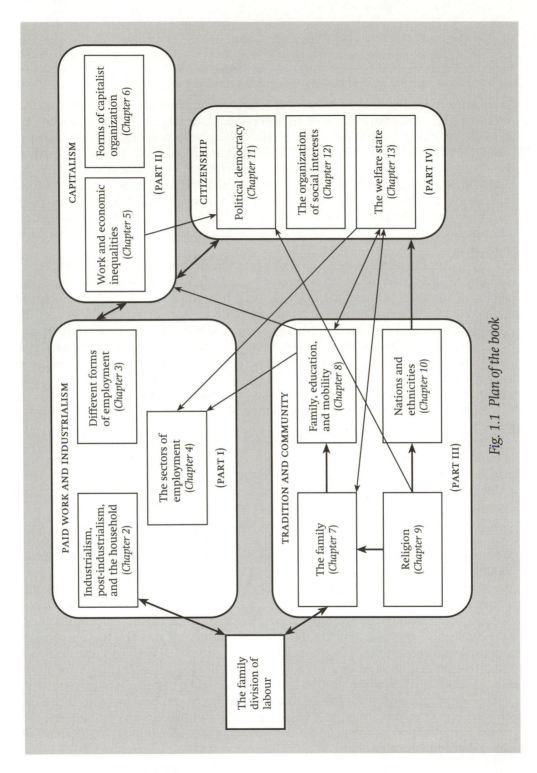

Fig. 1.1 Plan of the book

Consideration of the nation state leads necessarily to the institutions of political society, the theme of citizenship in the structure of the mid-century compromise. In this final part (Part IV) we examine the key institutions of mass citizenship: parties in Chapter 11 (and here we link back to both the social classes produced by capitalism and to religion and ethnicity as major sources of political allegiance); organized interests in Chapter 12 (and since we are focusing on economic interests this returns us to the themes of Parts I and II again); and the welfare state in Chapter 13.

Finally the interrelationship of all these topics will come together in two Conclusions. The first tries to summarize both the extent to which there is such a thing as European society, and the second considers the character of the societies which are replacing those of the mid-century compromise.

Although I have reviewed above a number of theories and models of contemporary societies, in the following chapters I shall be concentrating on a small number of themes. If we start with the assumption that there was something resembling the mid-century compromise in a number of countries, certain themes acquire particular importance. One is the question of post-industrialism, since mid-century society is strongly defined in terms of having become industrial. How useful is the concept of post-industrialism in identifying what comes afterwards? There are then often two branches of post-industrial theory: a kind of benign form, which sees societies which have transcended the main conflicts and power struggles of the industrial period; and a pessimistic form, which sees either a continuity of old capitalist antagonisms or the birth of new ones. Where relevant, which of these two versions of post-industrial theory is a more useful guide to understanding Western European societies at the end of the second millennium?

These two forms of post-industrial theory are particularly helpful with Parts I, II, and aspects of IV. For Part III, other aspects of IV, and certain elements of I and II, ideas of postmodernity have more to contribute. In addition to debate about whether there is a discontinuity between modernity and postmodernity or merely the continuing unravelling of the former, we can again distinguish between optimistic forms, which see the decline of the strong structures associated with modernity as a form of human liberation, and darker visions which see deceptive new forms of domination, or even disguised continuities of old ones.

In the final Chapter (15) we shall consider the relative usefulness of each of these approaches to understanding the topics we have reviewed throughout the book, often finding the results to vary from subject to subject.

Part I

THE FATE OF INDUSTRIALISM: INDUSTRIALIZING, INDUSTRIAL, OR POST-INDUSTRIAL SOCIETIES?

In comparison with rural societies, the organization of work in those that have been industrialized is a highly elaborate process involving complex and frequently changing arrangements of both occupations themselves and of the organizations within which they come together to fulfil their tasks. Discussion of this more or less formal occupational structure will occupy most of the next few chapters. However, by no means all work goes in specialized occupations and organizations; their emergence and elaboration is itself a variable element in social development. We therefore need some preliminary consideration of what we mean by 'work', and where and when we regard it as taking place.

At its most general the word is used to describe any human activity which requires effort. For Mingione (1991: 72) the crucial criterion is that the activity contribute to material survival, though this would seem to leave out large non-material areas of activity, especially in advanced economies that have gone far beyond the mere assurance of survival. In practice however we are unlikely to use it to describe activity undertaken solely for individual consumption by the person doing the work. While it is possible to say that someone 'worked hard' at eating his dinner, or at choosing which television programmes she would watch, that usage would almost certainly be ironic. We might be willing to describe someone as 'working' at a hobby if practising a musical instrument, cultivating the garden, or cleaning the flat, even if he never played in public, allowed other people to see the garden, or lived alone in the flat; but we might also regard this as an extreme case of use of the term, whereas we would have no such difficulties if the musician were preparing to play in even an amateur concert, or the garden would be enjoyed by a circle of friends, or a family lived in the flat; once the effort is done by one person or group on behalf of others a division between production and consumption appears.

Work requires effort and is normally carried out at least potentially for the benefit of individuals other than the one performing the work. Does an activity become more obviously 'work' if it is carried out as a person's *principal* form of effort, and/or if it is carried out for reward? These are very important questions for considering the emergence of work into modern occupational structure. When these two conditions come together we describe a person doing the work in question as having a 'job', and we shall probably go so far as to *describe* her as being the performer of the tasks: not just someone who plays an instrument, cultivates a garden, or cleans a flat, but musician, gardener, cleaner. The two conditions—doing the work as principal form of activity and doing it for reward—do not necessarily go together, though if the former applies but not the latter the person in question must have other answers as to how she receives the resources necessary to sustain life. If we produce for another's consumption, it must (perhaps outside the important limiting case of slavery) be in exchange for something—otherwise we should not ourselves have opportunities for consumption and, where some items of consumption are concerned, would as a result be incapable of producing any more.

It is important therefore to have in mind a continuum of specificity for the institution of human work. At one extreme we have simply a mass of undifferentiated activity; at the other we have extrinsically oriented, specifically defined, organized, and remunerated occupations, the performance of tasks within which is strictly demarcated from other aspects of life. Many human activities come somewhere between these extremes, having the characteristics of earning money but not the formal, bounded concept of the job. This was very typical of work in pre-industrial societies; and, as we shall discuss in Chapter 3, it returned to be an important aspect of work 'flexibility' at the end of the twentieth century.

Not all human beings are capable of work or even of ensuring their own survival: small children, the very old, and persons suffering from certain disabilities. There are in principle and in practice various ways in which the problems of the helpless can be tackled, including the use of the formal occupational system to provide for the work of 'caring', but at least part of this work is carried out by persons either biologically related to those requiring care or recognizing particularly strong obligations to them. Even people fully engaged in formal occupations and in principle capable of caring for all aspects of their own survival (either by their own efforts or by purchasing specialized services from others) in practice acquire many of the services and some of the goods they need from work offered to them by persons within these confines of biological and other human closeness.

This may seem a very roundabout way of saying that people live in families. The point of putting it like this is to relate family and work, and to locate family in the process of human goal-seeking and need fulfilment. In particular we can see that, in the continuum of work from undifferentiated activity to specific occupations, the family occupies a very important place towards the former end. It has a strong claim to be considered prior to the formal occupational system in the analysis of work. It is historically prior, in that familial arrangements of various kinds pre-date the development of the modern occupational system; and it remains temporally prior in the life experience of human individuals. The main work that humans encounter in their early years is that performed by the families around them—usually their mothers. And when they start to carry out work tasks themselves it is usually within the family.

The ancient Greek word *oikos*, from which we derive the word 'economics', meant 'household'. Such a breadth of meaning was possible within the peasant economy of ancient Greece, where work was far less separated from the context of family than in modern societies. Since then, family and economy have become more specialized institutions, and households have lost their original connection with the word 'economy'; indeed, we are likely to use 'family' and 'economy' as contrasting terms. When therefore we need to interpret the family's role in work, should we analyse it as part of 'normal' modern economic organization, that is, as a kind of firm existing within the market? From the point of view of a strictly economic approach to society, all human activity is seen in terms of exchange, and the most rational and efficient exchanges are those where there is a purchase of clearly defined goods and services. The diffuse web of barely considered exchanges that exists within families therefore presents a problem. Some economists (notably Becker 1974) have therefore tried to view the family as though it were a clear exchange process, and to explain such phenomena as female subordination in these terms, regarding women as more dependent on the existence of the family unit than men because of their position as the mothers of helpless infants.

Marxist analyses approach the family rather similarly, though for different reasons. Marxism explains society through the system of production, and all institutions are explained in terms of their contribution to a particular set of production relations that in turn sustain a particular set of class relations. Thus, the worker *qua* worker is seen as a contributor to the production process. Human labour differs from plant and equipment in that the capitalist does not have to pay directly for its maintenance and repair; in a conventional male-dominated society this task is carried out for the worker at home where he is fed, rested, and cared for by a wife. The worker's wage is then seen as the means to support both him and his wifely servicing agent, and also any children—viewed in the theory as the reproduction of the next generation of labour.

While these approaches may well have something to contribute to the analysis of the family—and we shall return to them in a later chapter—it would be misleading to ignore the many ways in which work as carried on in families differs from the way in which it is carried on in the formal occupational system: the definition of work roles, the character of the obligation to perform them, the relationship between effort and reward. We need to bear in mind both that work can take place in families and other informal contexts as well as in the formal occupations and firms that are familiar to us, but we need also to recognize the differences in the way that work is conceived within them.

In Chapter 2 we consider the allocation of work between these different contexts within which it is carried out, looking at both differences among societies and at changes which may have taken place between the hypothesized high point of mid-century industrial society in the early 1960s, and the possibly post-industrial society of the *fin de siècle*.

A central aspect of the mid-century model of employment was a certain formality and rigidity of the occupational system and its boundaries with other institutions. The claim that this characteristic has been changing is central to post-Fordist and postmodernist analyses. In what ways can we assess the validity and meaning of this claim? In what ways do countries differ on this variable? What are the implications of what we find for the mid-century model? Do the changes we observe enable us to characterize a type of society that might be replacing it? Can these changes be fitted into a general scheme of modernization as either postmodernism or reflexive modernism? A fragmentation of the structures of the first three decades of post-war industrial society becomes evident, and in Chapter 3 we consider questions of types of paid work and the issue of security and flexibility.

Presentation of the thesis of post-industrial society and of alternative theses of differential productivity and of the international division of labour requires a detailed analysis of the sectors of employment and production, going beyond the standard discussion of three sectors on which we rely in Chapter 2: primary (agriculture and mining), secondary (manufacturing industry, public utilities, and construction), tertiary (services). The three-sector theory claims to serve as an evolutionary as well as a classificatory scheme, and attempts at improving it will need to match this characteristic. A six-sector model developed by Joachim Singelmann (1978) is used in Chapter 4 for this purpose, and applied to all countries in the study. It further demonstrates the relevance of the gender structure of employment, in particular for employment in social and community services. This raises further interesting implications for the mid-century model, as much employment in this area has developed within the welfare state, and thus to serve the mass citizenship aspect of mid-century society. The complex implications of this for post-Fordist and post-modernist theories will be addressed.

The educational backgrounds and occupational statuses of persons working in the different sectors are also analysed as a test of Bell's (1974) hypothesis concerning the character of work in post-industrial society, and of rival hypotheses concerning the implications of post-Fordist flexibility. The results of this are complex, and while they support the general thrust of arguments about an increasingly educated workforce, they also contain some evidence of an opposite kind. The general theme of a fragmentation of the occupational structures of mid-century industrial society is reinforced.

Chapter 2

WORK, HOUSEHOLDS, AND OCCUPATIONS

We are here at one of the points heralded in the introductory chapter where a potential conflict between the criteria governing the formal economy and those governing another institution, in this case the family, is in the ideal type of the mid-century social compromise resolved by a segregation rule, by specialization and by specificity. Mid-century society, with its emphasis on the efficient pursuit of industrialism alongside the liberal principle of leaving separate spheres to themselves, requires institutions that keep family and work apart. The world of the family needs to be kept separate from that of formally defined work, partly because many of the rules that govern the two are different. For example, family members are not expected to calculate their relations with each other in strict exchange terms as they would do in business relations, buying and selling, but on the basis of the diffuse, affective ties that we usually call 'love'; it might be thought wrong were they to calculate their exchanges very precisely. Equally, within the world of formally defined work, the economy, it is in most modern societies considered wrong to act on the basis of affective ties rather than precise calculation and the application of objective criteria. For example, to appoint someone to a job because he is one's nephew, literally nepotism, is often seen as improper, even illegal. On the other hand, the same rule does not normally apply if one owns the firm in question, since this is seen as being part of private property which, according to the conventions of Western societies, can be inherited. People are expected to know when they should recognize a family obligation and when to act on the criteria of the formal outside world. To make a mistake in either direction is to court criticism. (This is not a characteristic unique to modern societies; one of the central themes of Greek tragedy concerned the dilemmas experienced by characters whose sense of family obligations led them to break the rules of the political units of the newly emerging city state. An example is the case of Antigone, torn between carrying out her family duty to perform funeral rites for her dead brother and obeying the law of her city, which regards him an enemy and refuses to allow his body to be buried.)

As we saw in the Prologue, an important segregation of work and family was gradually achieved in industrial societies by the withdrawal of all but a tiny number of married women from the workplace. The few who did work were in very specific activities, usually doing things related to the female family role (such as housekeeping, making garments, nursing the sick, or teaching the young; that is, domestic service, the textile and clothing industry, nursing, and schoolteaching). Stereotypes of male and female personalities, produced through differences in their upbringing as children, reinforced the process. In this way the rules of family, rooted in affective ties, and those of work, rooted in calculated exchange, could be separated and protected from one another through the work, behaviour, and indeed expected character traits of the two genders. Women looked after the world of reciprocity (the family, community, the soft, diffuse exchanges of kin and friends), while men entered the calculating world of the market—coming home in the evening to be soothed from the strain of it all.

This relates to a further profound process in the development of modern societies which we noted in the Prologue and which will return to our attention in several chapters. The Italian sociologist Enzo Mingione distinguishes (1991: 24–9) between markets and relations of either informal reciprocity or formal associations. These last (associations) will be discussed in Chapter 12. Reciprocity however is of immediate importance as it refers to the diffuse, uncalculated mass of exchanges that take place among people operating for long periods in close contact. Under the principles of reciprocity, people may well be trying to advance and protect their own interests, but they do so without frequent, explicit calculation; they find themselves within relationships where they are often asked to give to or do favours for someone else, and they frequently receive such services from others. Apart from moments of crisis, they do not keep stopping to add up their balance of gains and losses; they live in a world of repeated, uncalculated give and take. Families, households, and other institutions of community are important examples of institutions which work this way (Trigilia 1991).

Families sustain various non-contributing members: those too young, too old, too infirm to participate in either paid work or housework; and also those participating in full-time education who may be regarded as investing in an occupational future. An important source of diversity within industrial economies is the extent to which the tasks of looking after these various non-working people is left to the household, probably therefore to the houseworking wife. An alternative that has very different implications is to have such tasks assumed by specialized agencies. If the family is not the centre of work organization, and therefore has few means of securing income as a joint enterprise rather than through the occupations of its individual members, various means can be devised for providing resources for certain categories of dependent persons not in gainful employment in the formal economy. This is sometimes done through the state, sometimes through insurance policies of employers or of individuals themselves. This was another element of mid-century societies as defined in the previous chapter: based on work within formal organizations, but giving guarantees of near-universal citizenship, these societies needed to provide means of underwriting the welfare of persons not formally employed in ways which did not interfere with the business of organized, remunerated work. It was therefore necessary for these 'non-working' persons to be classified and categorized, like the employed population, so that resources might be directed at them. Examples of such statuses are: elderliness, sickness, lack of employment, motherhood of small children, participation in full-time education. While in peasant society there is no reason to decide whether a supernumerary son is a family worker, a dependent, or an unemployed person, in modern economies with formal rules these categories must be defined. Whether we are considering the existence of specialized agencies to care for these designated groups, or the provision of special money payments for them, we are entering territory usually occupied by the welfare state—a specific institution of the mid-century compromise that will be examined further in Chapter 13.

These processes of the formalization of work, its differentiation from family, and the formalization of welfare for non-workers reached their climax in the mid-century com-promise, an important part of which involved capitalism having to come to terms with subsistence needs that could not be met in the labour market. This form of society therefore sees both an extreme gender-role segregation and the establishment of a full welfare state. In this chapter we concentrate on the former. However, there is a poten-tial tension between women being outside the formal economy and the development of the welfare state, which we shall encounter in a number of subsequent chapters (especially Chapter 4).

All theories that claim that the mid-century model has now been transcended—that is, all 'post' theories—should anticipate major changes in these characteristics. Optim-istic theories should predict the fragmentation of rigid boundaries and the growth of new flexibilities; pessimists will see an attack on the family by economic forces.

We can test these arguments in the following way. Mid-century society should have seen most men who were capable of working in the role of full-time employees, and most women as housewives. In a postmodern economy there should be a greater divers-ity of employment forms and an erosion of gender differences. In this chapter we shall concentrate on gender, in the next on employment forms. First, however, something must be said about the idea of a standard employment form.

Official statistics recognize three types of employment: family workers, the self-employed, and the employed (more clumsily but more accurately, those in dependent employment). The first of these describes people who, although working within the market rather than the household economy, do so as part of their diffuse family ob-ligations and are not normally paid an individual wage; they simply live as part of the family, sharing its food, shelter, and belongings. This is interesting, as it forms a clear part-way position between two types of economy that we are distinguishing in this chapter. These family workers, normally found in the traditional rural economy, were inconsistent with the central concepts of the mid-century economy. As we shall see, they also present other difficulties.

The self-employed are also a complex case. A major characteristic of all national oc-cupational statistics is a distinction between people who work for themselves (perhaps employing other people too) and those who work for another person, a firm, a govern-ment, or some other organization as an employee. Sociological theories often place considerable importance on this distinction too; it is for example at the heart of the Marxist distinction between the bourgeoisie and the working class, that Marxist theory holds to be the basis of class structure in capitalist societies. More modern, non-Marxist theories of class still place considerable weight on the variable; as we shall see in Chap-ter 5, some of the most dominant theories of social stratification and mobility in con-temporary society consider that self-employment immediately places the practitioners of an occupation in a different class from those doing similar work as dependent em-ployees. Also, national statistics vary in the extent to which they differentiate between employers as such and people working for themselves. Meanwhile, and on the other hand, many owners of businesses, especially large ones, often have the status of an employee of the firm for national taxation and statistical purposes. Further, and in contrast to these points, firms sometimes require the people working for them to have the status of self-employed because it limits their liability to them, even though to all intents and purposes they are as much under the control of that firm as any employee.

The legal category of self-employment may therefore tell us little about its sociological reality.

For present purposes a more significant characteristic of the self-employed is that the group includes (though is not coterminous with) people for whom there is little clear separation between home and work: the proprietors of businesses who do not distinguish between their homes, family members, and personal property and finance, on the one hand, and business premises, staff, and company property, on the other. In true mid-century society the separation of work from other areas of life was signified by the establishment of work organizations as separate institutions with their own institutional and legal personality, separated from the persons who either owned or worked in them. Potentially therefore the self-employed are also an anomalous group within such a society.

Finally, we need to consider persons whose position in the workforce is partial, that is whose lives cross the family/work division, even if they are also employers or self-employed. Everybody employed in the formal system does this to the extent that they go home from work and have aspects of life separate from it: at most full-time means work for about 60 of the 112 hours in a week for which most adults are awake; more normally about 40 hours (Gershuny 1993). Research suggests not only that those women who work in modern industrial societies may have approaches to their work very similar to those of men, but also that men are rather more oriented to the relevance of their work to their lives as family members than the stereotype suggests (Dex 1985: 41–4).

People working less than a certain number of hours are considered to be 'part-time' workers. As a partial category they are problematic for the concept of the mid-century workforce.

TESTING THEORIES OF TYPES OF SOCIETY

We can use this approach to test the applicability to the societies of the early 1960s of certain elements of the mid-century social compromise, and to see which theories of subsequent change seem most consistent with the available evidence. In the light of the above discussion we can broadly identify the following different roles of family members in modern societies (individuals might simultaneously occupy two of these roles, but it would be rare for anyone to occupy three):

(1) those unable to look after themselves. I define as those over 80 and those aged 15 and under. I call these the 'dependent', and always use that word with this meaning and not to mean all family 'dependents' or in the economist's sense of 'dependent' labour (i.e. employees rather than self-employed). Age 80 is an artificial cut-off point for those regarded as too old to look after themselves or to be of much use for work around the house. Many people continue to be active some time after they reach 80, while others become infirm at an earlier age; there is no way of reaching a more accurate assessment. Similarly, there is no way of estimating those who are infirm despite being of working age. Those aged under 15 includes both infants and the majority of young people in education. For our present purposes there is no need to separate these groups; any people in employment in this age range have been excluded from these figures and added to those in the workforce;

(2) those in full-time education. I define these as all those over 15 and in full-time education; for these purposes apprenticeships count as full-time education;

(3) those working within the family. These are here called the 'domestic' labour force. It is impossible to establish from national statistics whether able-bodied people not in the labour force do in fact participate in domestic tasks. Here the category is a residual one: it is *assumed* that everyone between the ages of 15 and 80 who is in neither paid employment nor registered as unemployed, nor in full-time education participates in domestic work. The assumption almost certainly exaggerates, in particular, the number of men who engage in domestic work. On the other hand, some unemployed people will be mainly part of the domestic labour force;

(4) those seeking access to the external economy (the unemployed);

(5) those working in the external economy, subdivided in terms of: (*a*) family workers; (*b*) the self-employed; (*c*) part-time workers of various kinds;[1] and (*d*) full-time employees.

THE 1960S: HIGH-WATER MARK OF THE MID-CENTURY SOCIAL COMPROMISE WORKFORCE?

In the ideal typical mid-century society there is a distinctive pattern to the allocation of persons to the above roles. There is a sharp gender difference: adult men of working age will be found primarily in the full-time workforce; married women will be engaged within the family. Children and the elderly of both genders will be at home; and there will be a certain number engaged in education to prepare for their place at work. Given the role of education in preparing for occupations, more young males than young females will be in education after the compulsory school-leaving age. Most people (men) who are at work will be in modern formal work organizations and therefore will have the status of employees, though a small number will be self-employed. There will be very little part-time work as this interferes with the division between work and family.

The full statistics upon which the following argument is based will be found in Table A.2.1 in the Appendix, but Figure 2.1 summarizes the most important data. At the simplest level it enables us to consider what proportion of the non-dependent population were working in the remunerated sector. The range was from something over one-half to two-thirds, but higher in Japan and Austria. But there are strong gender differences. Male working was very high and the differences among countries far narrower (between 80% and 95%). In general therefore men in the 1960s worked in the remunerated economy, with little divergence within or between countries. Unemployment rates were generally very low, and most non-working will be accounted for by those over 60 or 65 leaving the workforce. There is much more variety among women: nowhere does the proportion in work exceed 57% (Austria), and it falls as low as 18% (Portugal and Spain). It is notable that three countries (Austria, Finland, and Japan) have a higher female working rate than the others; this factor will be considered in more detail below.

In all societies the thesis of role segregation embedded in the model of the mid-century compromise is effective at its simplest and most obvious task of predicting a strong male/female segregation, with women far more likely to be in the domestic

---

[1] Data are not available on part-timers for 1960. The earliest attempts at cross-national comparison date from the early 1970s. I have therefore assumed that between 1960 and 1970 part-time employment grew at the same rate that it did from 1970 to 1990.

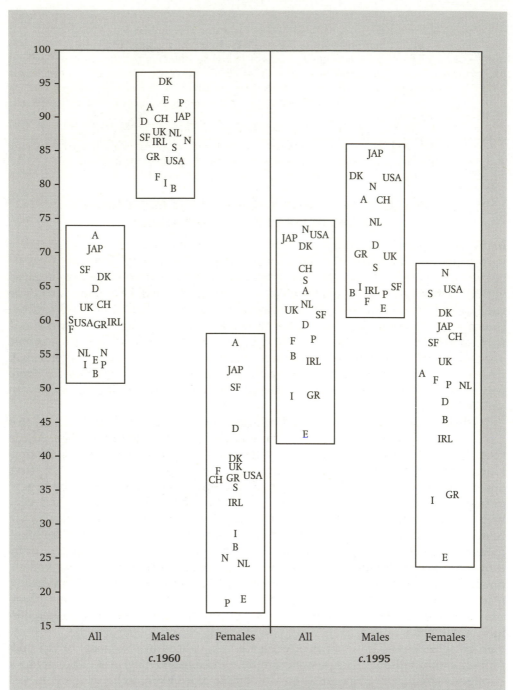

Fig. 2.1 *Percentages of non-dependent populations in paid employment,*
c.1960 and c.1995, 18 countries

economy than men. If we subtract the number of women in remunerated work of all kinds from the number of men in such work we have the male–female differential statistic given for each country in Appendix Table A.2.1. The differences range from 34.73% (Austria) to 73.71% (Portugal). However, the differences in the proportions of the two genders engaged in full-time employee status—the core form of mid-century employment—are not so large as those for total work (from 22.19% in Greece to 55.56% in the UK). In only 4 of the 18 countries (Austria, Germany, Japan, and the UK) was the gap larger. This to some extent contradicts the model of male employment being the essential form of full-time employee status. (This will be discussed in more detail in Chapter 3.)

Can we explain the diversity in proportions of the population engaged in paid work or differences between the genders by any general theories of modernization? The theory of the mid-century economy should predict that the growth of modern industrial employment will be accompanied by an increase in the proportion of the population engaged in full-time employee status, and that this will be particularly seen in the case of men. In testing this we shall want to be sure (i) that it is full-time employee status that is being explained and not just paid work in general; and (ii) that it is industrialization as such that explains any differences rather than some other index of modernization.

We can easily consider (i) by examining data on total work as well as full-time employee status. We can test (ii) in a number of ways, but each of these involves some anticipation of the argument of later chapters. I shall therefore here introduce them briefly, postponing full discussion until the more appropriate place. If we want to test the simple industrialization hypothesis, the best test will be the proportion of the total workforce engaged in manufacturing industry, as this is the most straightforward indicator of the rise in the industrial economy. If we want to test instead some idea of the 'modernization' of economies rather than just industrialization, we can best do a negative test, measuring modernization in terms of the decline of the agricultural sector, and making the assumption that agriculture is always a 'traditional' sector. Third, we might make an early test of the post-industrial thesis by checking differences in working patterns against the size of the services sector, defining this in terms of the main kinds of service discussed in the post-industrial thesis: business services, and community, social, and personal services.[2] Finally, anticipating discussions in Chapters 9 and 13, we should consider the fact that, with the exception of Austria and Germany, all countries in which the Roman Catholic Church exercised considerable political influence at that period had lower levels of female working (other than as family workers) than Protestant or secularized countries (with the exception of Norway). The former are Belgium, Ireland, Italy, Netherlands, Portugal, and Spain. The latter are Denmark, Finland, Switzerland, the UK, Japan, and the USA.

In addition, we can test the gender segregation thesis by considering not only whether male working is better explained than total working by the explanatory variables, but also whether they explain differences in the proportion of women in the domestic role.

---

[2] Although we are not led by the theories of post-industrial society to expect to see evidence of this kind as early as 1960, it will be valuable to examine the evidence for that period now, in order to compare it later with that for 1990, when the thesis is considered to apply. The definitions of sectors and the considerable problems that attach to several of them will be further discussed in Chapter 4.

Table 2.1 Associations between employment and indicators of modernization, c.1960

Dependent variable	Independent variable	Sign	F-statistic	Significance level
Total work	Agricultural employment Manufacturing employment 'Services' employment			
Total full-time employment	Agricultural employment Manufacturing employment 'Services' employment	– + +	14.40 19.14 6.99	0.00160 0.00047 0.01770
Male work	Agricultural employment Manufacturing employment 'Services' employment			
Male full-time employment	Agricultural employment Manufacturing employment 'Services' employment	– + +	20.74 26.07 10.11	0.00030 0.00010 0.00580
Female domestic	Agricultural employment Manufacturing employment 'Services' employment			

Only results with significance levels above 5% confidence level are displayed.

Table 2.1 summarizes the results of testing these hypotheses.[3] None of the cited factors vary significantly with the size of the total workforce at all; this remains true whether we consider total work, just male work or female domesticity as the dependent variable. However, when we consider not all remunerated work, but the proportion of the total non-dependent population in *full-time employee status* we have a significant result. This is the real test of the mid-century social compromise model, since this is the form of work most strongly embodied by it and by the concept of Fordism. This proportion varies significantly and inversely with the relative size of the agricultural workforce and significantly and directly with both the manufacturing and service sector workforces, especially the former. The situation is similar when the dependent variable is male full-time employment only, and the significance levels in this case are considerably higher.

At this broad statistical level, therefore, the thesis of mid-century society is vindicated: industrialization is associated with a rise in the proportion of the working population, and in particular the male population, engaged in full-time employee status; and it is industrialization rather than other indicators of modernization that seems to be the most significant variable. Beyond that, and more difficult to quantify, is the question mentioned above of influence on social policy of the Roman Catholic Church

---

[3] Appendix Table A.2.2 presents the data necessary for making the calculations.

in certain countries. This leads us to discussions which we shall pursue further in a number of later chapters, and reminds us of the way in which family structure, religion, politics, and the welfare state are bound up together in these phenomena.

Variations among types of countries do not seem particularly relevant in modifying these generalizations. We can test this by examining the strongest relationships examined here, and seeing which countries do not seem to conform to them. This can be established objectively through the statistical technique known as standardizing the residuals, and considering as outliers all cases where the actual value on the dependent variable deviates from the predicted value by more than 1.5 times the standard deviation of the equation. This procedure shows Greece to have had a smaller number of full-time employees (both total and male) than the size of its services sector should suggest. On the male measurement Ireland joins Greece, while Switzerland had a larger proportion of total full-time employees than expected by the size of its services sector.

These are the only major differences; they indicate the strength of the self-employment sector in Greece, but that country's exceptional situation is not very surprising given its marginal position at that period within Europe. It is interesting to note that Japan and the USA do not appear as outliers in these statistical patterns formed primarily by Western European cases. It is only when considering the data on total work that an interesting peculiarity that has already been mentioned appears: the high level of female work in agriculture in Austria, Finland, and Japan. This is consistent with the general argument that it is the rise of *industrial* employment which sees the big decline in female work; for example, in France the lowest point in female employment during the twentieth century was the period 1962–5 (Mendras 1991: 166). However, by no means all societies with large agricultural sectors saw large numbers of women working in them. (See Spain for a particularly strong reverse example.) This is a useful reminder of the diversity of forms of agriculture and patterns of work within it in traditional societies. It is beyond the scope of this book to examine this in detail, but it will return later in this chapter and in Chapter 4 when we examine changes in the patterns of female work in other sectors of the economy, as well as the question of whether modernization produces greater or smaller differences in work behaviour than earlier forms of economy. It is also worth noting that these are three very diverse societies in many other respects.

WORK IN THE 1990S

The question now is how societies have changed between what we suspect may have been some kind of high point of industrial society to something that might be post-industrial. We move forward to the mid-1990s and consider the same basic data as before, presented in detail in Appendix Table A.2.3, with the most salient findings reported again in Figure 2.1, where they can easily be compared with those for the earlier period. The overall level of participation among the non-dependent population in remunerated work is much the same as before (between 43% and 73%), though there is diversity in the experience of individual countries. In Austria, Finland, Germany, Greece, Ireland, Italy, and Spain there have been net declines in employment. These are—along with Portugal, the employment experience of which has been very different—the countries where in the 1960s agricultural employment was highest. Another group has been more or less stable (Belgium, France, Japan, the UK), while another has seen rises (the three Scandinavian countries (Denmark, Norway, Sweden), the Netherlands, Portugal, Switzerland, and the USA).

These aggregate developments cannot be understood without paying attention to the remarkably different experiences of the genders during these three decades. Although there is still a difference between male and female participation in the employee role, the gap has shrunk considerably in nearly all societies. In *all* countries male employment has declined. We must remember that the proportion of the population engaged in education has been removed from these data, so no explanation can be found there. It is true that life expectancy has improved, and that more men have been living past formal retirement age into those years *up to* age 80 that we are considering here as potential members of the domestic or remunerated workforce, and this will explain some of the male decline. It will not however explain it all, and we must therefore assume that many men have left the workforce younger than they did in the past. Some have been affected by the universal increases in unemployment since 1960, as will be seen in the next chapter. However, the table also shows that many of them must be regarded as having become part of the 'domestic' workforce; in what ways they might perform in that capacity we shall examine in Chapter 7 when we consider the family.

Where male employment is concerned, Japan now does seem in a class of its own as a high-employment country; it has experienced the universal drop in male working, but by only a small proportion. Although the USA's position is little different from the leading European countries, the *majority* of European countries do 'work less' than either of the extra-European comparators. The range of male employment levels is now greater than in the 1960s (between 61% (Spain) and 84% (Japan)).

Although women have been even more affected than men by the increase in longevity, their labour-force participation has increased very significantly in nearly all societies. The only exceptions are Austria and Greece, the former of which in 1960 had the highest proportion of female workers, largely as we saw because of the high number of women in agriculture. However, the other two countries with this characteristic in the 1960s (Finland and Japan) have remained high on the scale of female working even after the transformation of their rural economies. It is notable that female participation is highest in Scandinavia, the USA, and Japan, leaving continental Europe some considerable way behind.

Portugal had one of the very lowest female participation rates in 1960, but had leapt to a middle position by 1990. (The change is attributed by observers to the impact of the temporary Marxist revolution of 1974, which liberated Portuguese women from their previous position in a very rural, Catholic society governed by a conservative dictatorship (Chagas Lopes, Ferreira, and Perista 1991: 7).) It is notable that its Iberian neighbour, Spain, which shared many characteristics in the 1960s and which also had a major but gentler political revolution in the mid-1970s, has experienced nothing like the same change.

Table 2.2 reports the results of the same analysis of work data for the mid-1990s as was done for 1960 in Table 2.1.[4] This time it has been possible to include a test of the

---

4 Appendix Table A.2.4 presents the data necessary for making the calculations.

Table 2.2 *Associations between employment and indicators of modernization, mid-1990s*

Dependent variable	No. of cases	Independent variable	Sign	F-statistic	Significance level
Total work	18	Agricultural employment	–	3.23	0.0900
	18	Manufacturing employment	+	0.10	0.7500
	18	*'Services' employment*	+	*4.91*	*0.0400*
	15	GDP p.c.	+	1.90	0.1914
Total full-time employment	**17**	**Agricultural employment**	–	**9.50**	**0.0076**
	17	Manufacturing employment	+	1.02	0.3280
	17	*'Services' employment*	+	*5.71*	*0.0305*
	14	GDP p.c.	+	2.66	0.1288
Male work	18	Agricultural employment	–	0.08	0.7700
	18	Manufacturing employment	+	1.49	0.2300
	18	'Services' employment	–	0.46	0.5000
	15	GDP p.c.	+	0.76	0.3980
	18	Female domestic			
Male full-time employment	**17**	**Agricultural employment**	–	**17.33**	**0.0008**
	17	Manufacturing employment	+	3.47	0.0824
	17	'Services' employment	+	3.04	0.1015
	17	*Female domestic*	–	*6.95*	*0.0187*
	14	GDP p.c.	+	4.07	0.0666
Female domestic	18	Agricultural employment	+	4.26	0.0556
	18	Manufacturing employment	+	0.24	0.6258
	18	**'Services' employment**	–	**18.85**	**0.0005**
	15	GDP p.c.	–	1.16	0.3026

Note: **Bold** entries indicate significance levels above 1% confidence level.
Italicized entries indicate significance levels above 5% confidence level.
GDP p.c. = per capita gross domestic product.

significance for employment patterns of another potential indicator of modernization: the relative wealth of the different countries.[5]

One remarkable fact is that, across the 18 countries, the number of women in the domestic workforce correlates *inversely* with the number of men in full-time employment, to a degree significant at the 5% level. We might well have expected the opposite, for men's presence in the core labour force to vary positively with women staying at home. It is clear that women's entry into the labour force has not been at the expense of men's. Clearly far more important than any potential effect of that kind has been the tendency for some societies to generate more work for men and women alike than

[5] This has been established by calculating per capita gross domestic product, expressed in US dollars at purchasing power parity rates. Adequate comparable data were not available for more than a few countries for the 1960 period, and even in 1990 it has been necessary to exclude Belgium, Greece, and Ireland from consideration as some necessary statistics are not provided.

others. That this would seem to be associated with an overall 'modernization' variable is supported by the fact that the relationship only holds between female domesticity and male full-time employment; there is no relationship at all between the former and male work in general.

As in 1960, neither agricultural nor manufacturing employment help explain the total proportion of the non-dependent population in remunerated work, and neither these variables nor service sector employment explain male work. However, there is some significant positive association between service sector employment and *total* work. This demonstrates the importance of female work in services in determining the differences between work levels in different countries. The proportion of women in the domestic labour force also varies highly significantly but negatively with the size of the services workforce. Manufacturing employment is not associated with significant differences on this variable, but there is a slight positive association between female domesticity and agricultural employment. There is therefore some support here for a certain form of the post-industrial thesis that sees work in the services sector as a key defining characteristic of a new stage of modernization, provided such theories stress the role of female work in this. The tests of these variables concerning work and domesticity against estimates of per capita GDP for 15 of our countries fail to show any significance.

The relationship to the potential explanatory variables of total non-dependent population in full-time employee status has changed since 1960.[6] It continues to vary significantly and inversely with the relative size of the agricultural workforce and significantly but directly with service sector employment, but no longer varies at all significantly with the manufacturing workforce. Only the negative relationship with agricultural employment has significance when we consider male full-time employment alone, and the relationship with services sector employment is here the weakest of the three. This confirms the evidence that it is female employment in services which has become the main source of growth in remunerated work, even full-time employee status work.

The theses of mid-century society and those of its possible transcendence under post-industrialism emerge in a complex form from these general tests. Employment in manufacturing has ceased to be associated with any particular development of work patterns, that role now being played by the services sector. The rise in female employment is the main factor associated with this. There is therefore a clear decline of mid-century society on two points: the priority of industrialism and the segregation of gender roles between remunerated and domestic work—the latter being broken down both by the rise of female employment and by women's combination of domestic and remunerated work roles through part-time employment. As we shall see in Chapters 3 and 4, in some respects men remain the gender of the mid-century compromise—more likely to be in full-time employment in manufacturing—while women are the gender of the *fin de siècle* economy, working part-time in services. However, the particularly heavy concentration of women in employee (albeit part-time) status dilutes the impact of this generalization, as do some other aspects of their employment that we shall discuss in the following chapters.

---

[6] Unfortunately some data for the more recent year are not yet available for Switzerland, so the following analysis and those of other specific forms of work considered below are based on 17 countries only.

There are more cases of individual countries being outliers from the observed associations than in the 1960s. Again we shall concentrate on cases that deviate by at least 1.5 standard deviations from the strongest associations. I shall consider only issues that concern the size of the services sector and ignore agriculture, given that the latter is now a small sector in most of our countries and interest focuses strongly on services. Japan is unusual in a number of respects, but I shall concentrate here on the European countries.[7] As in 1960, the position of full-time employment status is weak in Greece, both total and male levels being lower than the size of the services sector would suggest. Spain also occupies such a position for total work. More surprisingly perhaps, the Netherlands shares Greece's position where total (but not male) full-time employment is concerned, and it is notable that both this country and its Belgian neighbour have higher levels of female domesticity than the size of their services sector would lead us to expect. Finland has fewer part-time workers than we would expect on the basis of its service sector size, which is particularly remarkable given the large size of the female labour force in that country.

Although analysis of these aggregate figures is very useful in looking at major trends, it can also somewhat exaggerate the degree of similarity among countries. In particular there are differences in the age profiles of workforces. A recent comparison of two European countries (Germany and the Netherlands) with the USA concentrates on changes in age cohorts (those born in different years between 1945 and 1965) in the proportions in employment of young men and women aged between 15 and 19 years and between 20 and 24 years (Sanders 1993). In the European countries the study shows a tendency for workforce participation among the younger group to fall from those born in the mid-1950s onwards (in the Netherlands boys' participation drops among those born in the mid-1940s onwards). Among the 20–24 year-olds, male participation dips among those born by the mid-1950s, but women's remains stable in Germany and even climbs in the Netherlands, until it stabilizes at a level slightly below the men's among those born at the end of the 1950s. The US pattern is different; participation by both female groups rises until stabilizing among those born in the latter 1950s; and male participation remains remarkably stable, with only a slight decline.

Sanders explains the European patterns in terms of a theory of generations. Those born in the latter part of the period constitute what is often called 'the lost generation', those who experienced the initial economic uncertainties and downturns of risk society in the early 1970s. They chose to remain in education for longer than their predecessors of the 'protest generation', for whom there were many opportunities. The women's pattern works somewhat differently from men's. As we would expect from the above discussion, initially their labour-force participation is considerably lower than men's. However, as educational participation in general began to increase, so more young women wanted to make use of their education to enter the workforce, their confidence in doing this resisting for a while the general pessimism of the period. It is only when their aggregate level of workforce engagement approaches that of men that

7 We have already picked Japan out as having a particularly large working population. In particular, it has more people in total work, more men in full-time employment, fewer women outside the remunerated labour force, and more people (largely women) in part-time work than we should expect on the basis of services sector size, the main engine of employment (and particularly female employment) among the other countries. We shall be able to explore this in more detail in Chapter 4.

they begin to be affected by the mood and start to *prolong* their education—this re-placing domesticity as the reason for their absence from the labour force.[8]

This explanation of gender differences concentrates on the supply side: young women choose whether to be domestic, to study, or to work; young men whether to study or to work. However, the demand side must also be considered. What kinds of work opportunities have been available to people in recent decades, and how have opportunities varied between men and women?

There is considerable evidence that the supply of female labour is culturally contingent. For example, in the Nordic countries there has been a long-standing tradition of female independence and equality that led to their early acquiring political and economic rights (Knudsen 1991: 24). Knudsen points out paradoxical aspects of this. The greater activity of women in the public sphere seems to have been associated with their playing a smaller role than in many other societies in sustaining the strength of family links; in consequence the extended family became weak, and people could not look to their wider families for help as they might in southern Europe. This might be expected to have rebounded by making it more difficult for mothers to organize childcare while they worked, but instead the result was an early development of the welfare state—which in turn became a major employer of female labour. There is then a further paradox in that this employment seems to mark a departure from a mid-century employment pattern (conceived as primarily industrial and male), while in reality it is a further extension of the segregations associated with this pattern—a subject which we shall take up again in a number of later chapters.

An imaginative piece of work conducted in Denmark suggests that women there, who have pioneered much social change in the issues covered by this chapter, may also have borne the brunt of many of its costs. Based on research carried out in 1986, Hansen (1993: 140–7) argues that, since the 1970s, real incomes for Danish women have diminished and they consider that their working conditions have worsened (increase in mentally exhausting work, increased exposure to accidents, more high-speed monotonous work). These declines were mostly experienced by younger women (ibid. 142); they were worse in the public sector (where female employment is concentrated) than in the private (ibid. 147); and they were not paralleled in male experience. The more highly educated that these young women were, the more pessimistic they felt about the future of their work, especially schoolteachers and nurses (ibid. 151).

In contrast with the Danish evidence, a survey of the Austrian population carried out in the mid-1980s suggests that Austrian women in paid employment were more content with their work than men (Cyba 1987: 73). It is interesting that the majority of these Austrian working women nevertheless thought it better if women did *not* work (ibid. 90); that fewer women in Austria are in the paid labour force than in Denmark; and that Austria is the only country to have experienced a decline in female labour-force participation.

In general southern, Catholic Europe has low levels of female involvement in paid employment, but there are important internal differences. France is a marginal case

---

[8] The US exception is explained by the author as possibly because it is more common in that country to combine study and paid employment—partly, one might add, because student financial support is more difficult to find there, and partly because the greater flexibility of US labour markets compared with much of northern Europe makes it possible for young people to combine certain kinds of low skilled work with study.

for being considered 'southern', and has a relatively high female labour-force participation. A further puzzle is presented by Germany, where female participation in paid work is higher in southern than in northern *Länder*, though it is the former which are, in general, Catholic. Particularly interesting here is the fact that these regional differences seem to have held constant for at least a century (Sackmann and Häussermann 1994).

CONCLUSIONS: TRANSCENDING THE MID-CENTURY EMPLOYMENT PATTERN OR EXTENDING IT?

We can summarize the discussion of this chapter by concluding, first and unsurprisingly, that total engagement in formally defined work increases as the agricultural sector becomes smaller. This is consistent with our finding earlier that work becomes more formally defined outside the world of agriculture, as part of the developing segregation process. Second, however, there is a check to and an ambiguity within this pattern in straightforward industrial societies with large manufacturing sectors. The check is the low level of female participation.

In some respects the post-industrial development can be seen as a break with the segregation of genders characteristic of the mid-century social compromise, confirming hypotheses that post-industrialism transcends that society. Seen differently, however, it is simply taking that segregation in new directions. Much service activity as defined here is of a *household-replacing* kind: caring and domestic activities that might be carried on within the home by family members are moved into the formal occupational sphere. In this sense, the process of moving work away from the family, central to the social compromise, is *continued* and indeed taken to new heights in post-industrial society. Also, while there is a kind of breach with mid-century principles in the increase in female participation in paid work, women are overwhelmingly represented in that part of the remunerated workforce that carries out the caring and formerly domestic tasks—the segregations of the social compromise are reproduced but at a different institutional location.

In that sense, we are seeing, not a transcendence of mid-century principles of social organization, but their extension—an extension that requires some reorganization of the gender division of labour and the position of the family. This happens, not at a peak of industrial, let alone manufacturing, employment as such, but with the post-industrial development of certain services sectors. It is therefore essentially a feature of modernism, if that phenomenon needs to be distinguished from industrialism. To consider these issues further we need to consider in more detail the organization of working life that lies behind the broad statistics that we have considered so far, and also a more detailed analysis of the areas of economic activity in which work takes place. The following two chapters will be devoted to these questions.

Chapter 3

THE ORGANIZATION OF WORKING LIFE: BETWEEN STABILITY AND FLEXIBILITY

According to the theory of the mid-century social compromise, men (who constitute the majority of the workforce) should obtain full-time employment in a firm or other organization and either remain there or move to one or more similar organizations, for a large part of their lives, both in terms of hours within the year and years within their lives. Unemployment should be a rare, brief experience; governments should manage the economy so that major recessions, throwing people out of work as they did in earlier periods of capitalism, do not occur. These elements of the model can be derived from the Fordist or bureaucratic model of work and from the idea of welfare citizenship. For the advanced industrial economies of Western Europe and elsewhere actual experience of the post-war years corresponded to the theory until around 1973. Since then complex and contradictory changes have taken place. We saw in Chapter 2 that between 1960 and the 1990s there was a decline in the proportion of men and a rise in that of women engaged in the paid workforce; but a large proportion of these women worked part-time, that is divided their lives between the paid and the domestic workforces. Unemployment has returned to levels similar to those of the pre-war, pre-compromise period, and there has been a growth of various forms of insecure work. As Mingione points out (1991: 162):

informal activities are one of the consequences of the employment crisis, in the context of which unemployment and non-employment increase without a parallel decrease in the cost of reproduction of guaranteed labour. Availability for informal work thus increases and, at the same time, the cost of reproducing this type of labour decreases, for the very reason that the increase in self-provisioning and domestic work resulting from the crisis involves above all informal work.

The various theories of 'post-' society, which largely agreed on the broad trends discussed in Chapter 2, start to diverge when they attempt to interpret these changes. Early post-industrial theorists (e.g. Bell 1974) did *not* envisage change in the employment form, Bell's post-industrialism involving work in large scientific, educational, and other largely public service organizations. Postmodernists and post-Fordists do expect a fragmentation of stable employment, but there are various interpretations of what is happening.

Optimists in both schools see people being liberated from standard employment in large structures and able to pursue a diversity of careers, sometimes as self-employed entrepreneurs or franchisees, sometimes taking their advanced skills to various kinds of flexible firms, either as temporary employees or as subcontractors. For optimistic postmodernists this is an aspect of the collapse of the single form of rationalist organizational development, bringing with it something of a return to the complex diversity of pre-modern work organization. Optimistic post-Fordists are more likely to stress the plurality of modern production methods and their ability to avoid the rigid production lines and regimented semi-skilled manual or clerical workers of the Fordist period.

More pessimistic theorists see a new insecurity, produced partly by economic globalization, partly by technological change. As a result of these developments they see a new unpredictability in the economy and a resurgence of the ability of employers to determine working conditions, both leading to an increasing insecurity in workers' lives, a greater risk of unemployment, and the rise of precarious kinds of work.

For a full exploration of these issues we need to consider the sectoral changes that have taken place: the decline of agriculture and industry and the rise of various kinds of services employment. This is the task of Chapter 4. For other aspects we need to consider changes in the character of contemporary capitalism; this is the task of Part II. First, we shall look in detail at overall changes in forms of work and worklessness: unemployment, part-time work, atypical and precarious employment. Within each of these categories we shall look at change over time and see to what extent we can find evidence of an initial mid-century form, how we might define changes that have taken place, and the degree of diversity among the countries in which we are interested.

THE RISE IN UNEMPLOYMENT

In the previous chapter we concentrated on the simple issue of whether people worked or not, irrespective of whether non-working counted as unemployment. The idea of unemployment is not straightforward. It is partly an economic idea, referring to those people who are theoretically in the labour market, that is potentially competing for jobs and thus affecting the price of labour, but who do not actually have jobs; they constitute excess demand for work. Alternatively unemployment is a social policy concept, defining categories of entitlement to benefit. The latter is vulnerable to variation as governments change entitlement rules. This makes it difficult to track changes over time or to compare countries. Attempts have been made to cope with this problem by using standardized international surveys of the population in which people are asked if they have worked in recent weeks or if they have sought a job. This solves some problems, and in this discussion I shall use statistics gathered on this basis as far as possible. However, there are still difficulties. In some countries, but not others, people do not consider they have worked unless it has been in a 'real' job with security; also, people working in the black economy while also drawing benefit are unlikely to tell an official survey that they have been working.

The rise of women's paid employment has made these problems of definition far more significant than they were before, since women's tendency to regard themselves as unemployed or as actively seeking work will vary in more complex ways than men's, the legacy of the mid-century model still making them more likely to define themselves as housewives, mothers, or other categories outside the labour market. In general therefore I prefer to consider the aggregate figure for what I defined in the previous chapter as the domestic non-dependent population plus the registered unemployed as the true size of the *potential* labour force. However, in considering the contemporary instability of the labour market it is important that we now confront one of the biggest differences between the workforces of 1960 and the 1990s: the considerable rise in nearly all countries of unemployment, that is of the number of people stating that they wish to work but are unable to find a job.

From the perspective of the 1990s, unemployment in 1960 was extraordinarily low: nowhere in Western Europe or Japan was it above about 3%, and even in the USA it was no more than 5% (Figure 3.1).[1] These low levels are fully in line with the expectations of the mid-century compromise thesis. The change since that time in virtually every country is one of the most remarkable social changes between the two periods; there has also been a reversal of the situation in which unemployment tended to be higher in the USA than in most Western European countries. The rise seems difficult to reconcile with the fact that a higher proportion of the population is working than in 1960, despite the fact that young people are staying longer in education and older people tending in most though not all countries to leave the workforce earlier. There is of course an obvious answer to the paradox: the rise in participation has been solely among women, while that of men has declined. However, this only opens new paradoxes. As we have seen, although women's employment has risen steadily alongside rising unemployment, there is little evidence that women's employment increases *at the expense* of men's—rather the reverse.

Also, at least among countries in the EU, the increase in female employment has largely taken place among married women returning to the labour force after some years of absence with young children, rather than either new labour or the unemployed (Meulders, Plasman, and Vander Stricht 1993: 33). The experience of these latter women has been similar to that of men—except that women's unemployment is often not concentrated among the less well educated but the reverse (ibid. 135). Also, although women's employment has grown and men's declined, in most countries a higher proportion of women in the formal labour force are unemployed than men.

Most of the national groupings with which we have been familiar from the previous chapter no longer seem to apply. The 'high employment' Scandinavian group is scattered throughout the list, having (in 1995) some of the higher (Finland, Sweden) and the lower (Norway) unemployment levels. (This is a very recent experience. Until the early 1990s there was low unemployment in all Scandinavian countries, except Denmark. The Finnish case can be partly explained in terms of the collapse of the country's main trading partner, the Soviet Union, in 1989.) The low-work southern European group also disappears, with Spain having particularly high unemployment, Portugal very low.

Male unemployment has risen virtually everywhere, but in the mid-1990s remained low in Austria, Japan, Portugal, and Switzerland, though this can give a misleading impression that these countries have in no way been touched by the experience. For example, even though Austrian unemployment in the mid-1980s was very low, 16.4% of men and 14.6% of women had experienced it over the past five years (Cyba 1987: 47). The experience was concentrated among less-skilled workers, but 27% of the apprenticeship-trained skilled workers had also had the experience, concentrated in

---

[1] This figure, like all others in this chapter (except 3.2, 3.3, and 3.5), is based on the detailed data which will be found in the Appendix in Table A.3.1.

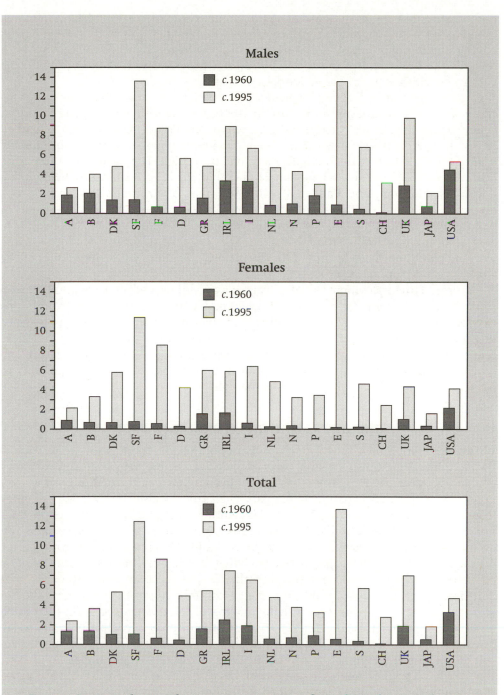

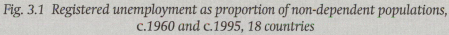

Fig. 3.1 Registered unemployment as proportion of non-dependent populations,
c.1960 and c.1995, 18 countries

the construction industry. Male unemployment was particularly high in Finland, Ireland, and Spain—significantly all countries which had very recently emerged from having a high proportion of their workforce in agriculture. Japan and the USA are both towards the lower end of the range, but do not provide any real exceptions to the pattern established by the varied European experience.

Female experience of unemployment was rather similar, and, despite or rather because of women's increasing entry into the labour force since 1960, has generally risen faster than men's. It was particularly large in Finland, France, and Spain. It remained lowest in the countries of low male unemployment, together with the interesting case of the UK where male unemployment had been high. The UK has for some time been unusual as a country where female unemployment is considerably below male (Meulders, Plasman, and Vander Stricht 1993: 130). Throughout southern Europe (including France) it is young women—often educated ones—who bear the brunt of unemployment (ibid. 135). In Germany the increase in unemployment has been concentrated among certain groups—women, the less skilled, foreign workers—while working conditions have improved for the majority, leading to a segmentation of the workforce (Glatzer *et al.* 1992: ch. 4.1).

Patterns of unemployment therefore vary in ways not immediately apparent in overall statistics. In general, for example, US unemployment takes the form of short bursts experienced by a relatively high proportion of the workforce; in European countries unemployment is concentrated among a smaller proportion of the workforce, but these remain unemployed for long periods. In both cases the mid-century compromise employment form is clearly under severe challenge, with the changes corresponding to the expectations of the more pessimistic theories.

THE ORGANIZATION OF WORKING TIME

Within the compromise model, only a minority of the adult population worked (able-bodied males), but did so for large parts of their lives. There have been contradictory changes in these patterns. There has overall been a downward trend in both weekly hours and length of occupational life spans. The latter is caused by both delayed entry (education) and earlier leaving. The trend is common to both men and women, so does not explain the feminization of the labour force. At least among European societies, an age band (roughly between 20 or 25 and 50) is coming to replace gender as a basis for distinguishing the domestic population from that in paid work (see Figure 3.2). In many countries, but especially Denmark, Netherlands, and the USA, many students hold part-time jobs (OECD 1996: table 4.10). The US combination of the young and the old participating in the labour force, usually in parts of the services sector, has led some observers to argue that the higher level of labour-force participation that today distinguishes the USA (and Canada) from much of Western Europe is in fact the result of growing employment in low-productivity sectors (Noll and Langlois 1994; Petit 1990 (for a particular analysis of the French case)). There is some truth in this, as we shall see in the following chapter when we examine sectors of employment. This is perhaps emerging as an American–European difference; the welfare states of many European societies both increase the cost to businesses of employing low-productivity workers and make people less dependent on finding work at any price. If so, one

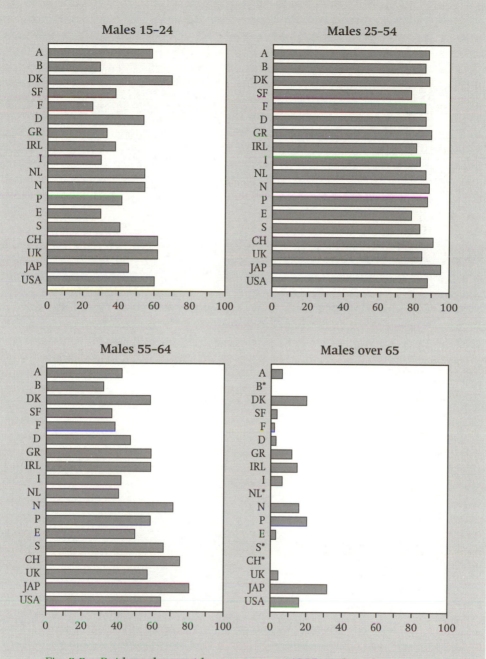

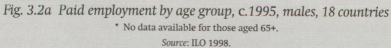

Fig. 3.2a Paid employment by age group, c.1995, males, 18 countries

* No data available for those aged 65+.

Source: ILO 1998.

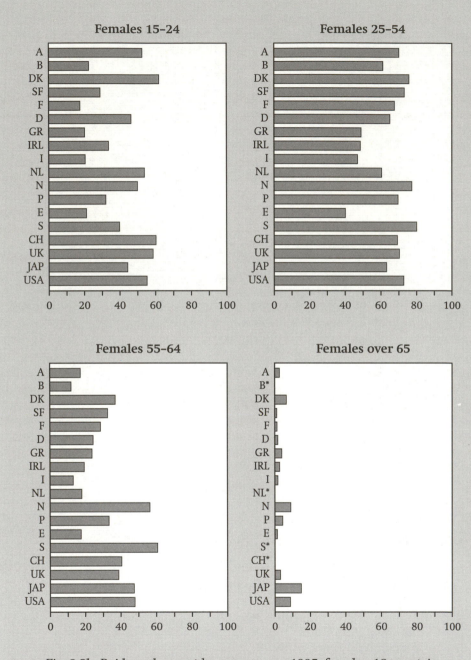

Fig. 3.2b Paid employment by age group, c.1995, females, 18 countries

* No data available for those aged 65+.

Source: ILO 1998.

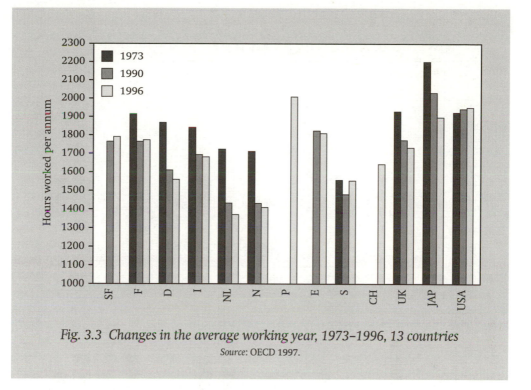

Fig. 3.3 Changes in the average working year, 1973–1996, 13 countries
Source: OECD 1997.

ironical consequence of the welfare state might have been to improve productivity and efficiency but reduce employment opportunities.

Today far more people work than in earlier periods of industrial society, including the early 1960s, but for shorter periods of their lives. The decline in the working year that has taken place in virtually all countries—except the USA—at the same time strengthens this same tendency (see Figure 3.3). Postmodern theories expect work to play a smaller part in people's lives as these become more varied, and this evidence is consistent with them. However, there must be some surprise at US exceptionalism here. Within Europe the lowest hours are worked in the most 'advanced' economies of the north, which is what might be expected. Japan and the USA however stand outside that range.

Central to working hours is the question of part-time work. Figure 3.4 plots changes in the distribution of this since the early 1960s.[2] There is little doubt that part-time work has risen over the period, except in Denmark, Sweden, and the USA. It remains relatively low in southern Europe. The most important variable determining the distribution

---

[2] In fact, the earliest collections of comparable cross-national data on part-time work did not start until 1970. In constructing a figure for 1960 I have therefore assumed a similar growth rate between 1960 and 1970 as that for the subsequent 20 years. This certainly underestimates the contrast between the two dates, as in most countries most of the acceleration took place in the latter part of the period. However, since I am drawing attention to the degree of change, it is better that I underestimate its extent. A second problem with these data is that for the earlier period one cannot be certain what is understood by part-time work. For the 1990s however we have data based on a standard definition of 30 hours per week or less.

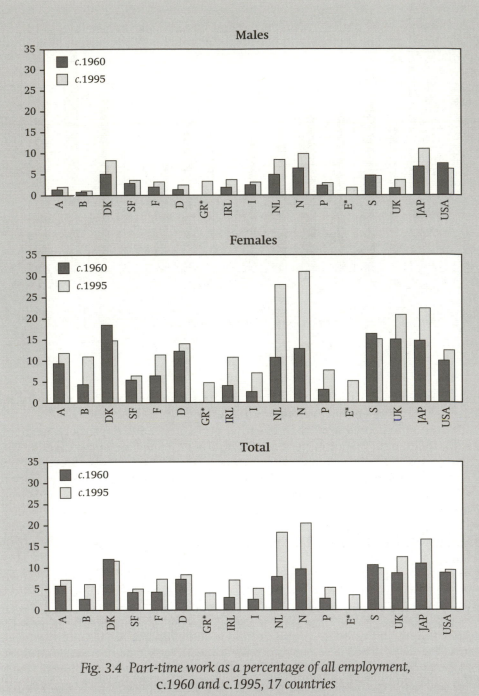

Fig. 3.4 Part-time work as a percentage of all employment,
c.1960 and c.1995, 17 countries
* No data available for earlier year.

of part-time work is gender, it being overwhelmingly women who are involved. Among men it is concentrated among the young (under 24) and elderly (over 55); among women the age-related differences are less clear and are inverted, part-time work being concentrated in the middle (child-rearing) years (Meulders, Plasman, and Vander Stricht 1993: 85).

In general, male part-time employment, such as it is, tends to be found in the same countries as female (Delsen 1998). In only 4 countries (Denmark, the Netherlands, Norway, Japan) does the level of male part-time employment exceed 5% of the male workforce. In fact the Netherlands has become in recent years a case of its own in this respect, with a rapid rise in male part-time working.[3] As Visser and Hemerijck (1997) comment, this has become a particular form taken by work-time reduction. Whereas Dutch trade unions, like their counterparts in several other countries, have had their campaign for a shorter working week checked by employer resistance, Dutch employers have been happy to initiate part-time working. One might summarize the difference between the two by saying that the former embodies the security guarantees associated with the mid-century model, while the latter brings with it flexibility and insecurity associated with pessimistic post-Fordist theories: employment rights of part-time workers are nearly always inferior to those of full-timers. On the other hand, the recent Dutch experiments have forged a kind of compromise between the two models, by negotiating inferior but established rights for part-timers (ibid.).

The uncertainties of this point have created considerable dispute in the literature over the significance of this kind of work (see especially Blossfeld and Hakim 1997; O'Reilly and Fagan 1998). Drewes Nielsen (1991) has analysed part-time female work among the small high-tech firms of certain regional labour markets in Denmark, and found considerable dissatisfaction with it. Some have argued that, since employers tend to provide only part-time work for women, women have been unable to join the full-time labour force to the extent they would ideally want. Others argue that differences in the level of part-time work result from differences in levels of childcare facilities that might enable women to work full time, though the limited amount of OECD data available suggest no correlation with this variable (OECD 1995). A more profound approach has been explored by Pfau-Effinger in comparisons between Germany and Finland (1993) and those countries and the Netherlands (1998). (While, as we saw above, neither Finland nor Germany rates as a high part-time country, Finland has a particularly low rate of such work for a country with such a high level of female employment.) She argues that the differences between these two countries largely represent different trajectories of modernization. German industrialization moved through a period of intense urbanization that dissolved traditional family structures and imposed a gender division of labour of the kind established as the core pattern in theories being discussed in this book. Finland, on the other hand, moved rapidly from a rural society of isolated families with little cultural or occupational segregation of genders into the period of late twentieth-century employment patterns.

A particular contrast that emerges from many studies is that between British and

[3] One possible explanation may be that at least Dutch males regard being trainees as being part-time; 75% of Dutch males under 25 (i.e. 53% of male part-timers) gave training as the reason for their being part-time (Plantenga 1991: 36). It is difficult to distinguish from this group students who take on part-time work to help them through their studies.

French women (Coutrot *et al.* 1997; Burchell *et al.* 1997; Hakim 1997; Hantrais 1985; O'Reilly 1994), many of the former working part time and seeming very content with the arrangement, while in France few women work part time (many more are full-time workers) and where neither employers nor employees seem to want it. O'Reilly (ibid.) examined this contrast within the banking sector, but her conclusions may be more generally applicable. Not only was part-time work more closely regulated in France (which reduced employers' incentive to use it), but French women had better access to professional childcare than their British counterparts and could therefore more easily work full time. Perhaps most interesting, French women tended to have higher educational levels and to be more committed to work as a career, which led them to dislike the unambitious character of part-time work.

We can perhaps regard part-time female employment as smoothing the transition from the mid-century model and the uncertain social forms that are developing from its partial collapse: the gender-role divisions of the former are moderated *but* both the full-time male employment model and (as we shall see in Chapter 7) the female family role are somehow kept intact. Arguing on similar lines, Hirdmann (1988) and O'Reilly and Fagan (1998) talk of the renegotiation of the 'gender contract'—a contract which in terms of the thesis of this book should be seen as having taken a certain form at the heart of the mid-century compromise and therefore clearly being renegotiated at the present time. These authors cut through much of the polemic over the attractiveness or otherwise of part-time work by pointing out that, if part-timers are able to have access to pension and other rights associated with 'normal' work, then it might well be not only an entirely viable form of occupational organization, but also facilitate the integration between home and work that seems to be central to the achievement of a new social compromise.

ATYPICAL EMPLOYMENT

In addition to unemployment and part-time work, changes have been taking place in a number of work forms other than the straightforward employment contract typical of the compromise model.

FLEXIBILITY

A key term in this discussion is the idea of 'flexible' employment. At least two different models are embodied in this concept (Nielsen 1991). First, it can mean making employees more disposable, in the senses of: easier and cheaper to dismiss; less covered by constraining agreements and regulations over the conditions in which they can be required to work; less protections offered to their health, safety, and security; less controls on the extent to which they can be ordered to take on different kinds of work. This is generally known as 'numerical' flexibility because it takes as its most important component the capacity to vary either the number of workers or the amount of labour time.

Closely related to it is the idea of *pay* flexibility. Wages can include large profit-, productivity-, or sales-related components, so that an employee's pay varies widely from week to week, in step with the progress of the business and therefore not imposing fixed costs on employers. A similar effect might be achieved by varying the number of hours an employee works according to fluctuation in levels of business; wages fluctuate accordingly. Numerical and pay flexibility can both be called 'neo-liberal' flexibility, as they are guided by neo-liberal economic theory, which stresses the efficiency gains that come from making the costs of factors of production as flexibly responsive as possible to market pressures.

In contrast, flexibility can refer to workers being equipped with a variety of advanced skills that enable them to tackle a variety of tasks (an attribute called polyvalency in German industry) (Kern and Schumann 1987); it may also refer to organizational designs that stress teamwork and cooperation at the expense of hierarchy and command. This is usually referred to as 'functional' flexibility (Hirst and Zeitlin 1990).

The two concepts are not mutually contradictory. As O'Reilly (1992) points out on the basis of an examination of flexible employment strategies in banking in Britain and France, employers do not necessarily have a preference for one or other of these notions when they reach out for such devices as temporary work, subcontracting, or part-time work to solve their personnel problems. Common to both numerical and functional flexibility is the idea of workers being able to take on a diversity of tasks, though numerical flexibility stresses management's unfettered ability to order them to change tasks, while functional flexibility stresses the workers' own capacity to tackle them. The emphasis on workers' skills tends to lead in a very different direction from that on workers' responding to commands (Johnson and Lundvall 1991). Both models contrast with the rigid specialization of Fordism, though numerical flexibility shares with Fordism a concern with hierarchical command, and functional flexibility shares with certain approaches to Fordism the idea of worker security.

To the extent that either is relevant to the notion of post-industrialism, numerical flexibility is closer to some of the components of the services sector—for example hived-off business services and many personal services—but not with most of the employment found in social and community services (Drewes Nielsen 1991). The high skills stressed by functional flexibility will be found in business and social (and community) services, but not in most personal services. Numerical flexibility threatens the mid-century social compromise insofar as it challenges the employment guarantees that are a component of the model, but it is fully compatible with the capitalist character of the economy. It is therefore consistent with pessimistic versions of post-Fordist theories. Functional flexibility, on the other hand, is anticipated by optimistic postmodern theories.

UNUSUAL EMPLOYMENT FORMS

Flexibility can also take the form of forms of employment relationship which differ from the mid-century employed status. Part-time working is sometimes an example of this, reflecting firms' needs for more precisely measured, less committed amounts of work, though within the framework of its stipulated hours part-time work can be highly stable, normal employment. Other changes have different implications.

Particularly important is the growth of temporary or limited-contract work. One way in which employers can ensure numerical flexibility is by committing themselves to employing individuals for a limited period of time only. This enables unsatisfactory or inconvenient individuals to be easily disposed of rather than improved; it might also enable the firm to adjust quickly to fluctuating demand by varying the total number of persons it employs; very commonly also employees' rights are related to length of service, and temporary employees accumulate only limited rights.

Calculations of the level of temporary working in EC countries plus Japan and the USA in 1991 are given in Figure 3.5. With the exceptions of France and Spain there is no evidence here of a major rise in temporary working, and in most countries there have been either very small rises or even small decreases. Like statistics on unemployment and part-time working, these data depend on self-descriptions; people are asked in surveys whether they regard their current job as being temporary. Also, the meaning of temporariness can vary; there is considerable difference between a temporary contract lasting a decade and one lasting six months.

Nevertheless, the evidence must be taken as implying that much recent discussion has exaggerated any rises in temporary work. One explanation might be that it has been rising in areas of work or among age groups where it has in the past been rare, concealing a decline in other areas or among other age groups. For example, it is possible that many young people seeking permanent jobs are finding that they can only obtain temporary ones, while elderly people who used to do much temporary work are finding it more difficult to obtain. (As early as 1988, 21% of working people in Germany aged under 25 were in posts with fixed-term contracts; on average, far more men were in this situation than women, but women's contracts tended to be shorter (FORSA 1987). Overall, 7.4% of Germans were in such contracts in 1988; there was virtually no difference between German and foreign workers in this respect (Glatzer *et al.* 1992: 161). By far the highest relative incidences of these contracts were in regional administrative bodes and social insurance agencies; they were also important in non-profit organizations and private households, miscellaneous services and agriculture—not in manufacturing (ibid.).) Alternatively, as the OECD (1997) has suggested, people may *feel* more temporary even though the formal conditions of their contracts have not changed, because they know that redundancy and unemployment are more likely today than in the past.

Temporary work is concentrated among women (Figure 3.5a). Only in Greece and Spain (two recently industrialized countries) were much less than 50% of all temporary employees women. Temporary working is also far more likely to be found among part-timers than full-timers (Figure 3.5b; see also Meulders, Plasman, and Vander Stricht 1993: 87–92). Only in Germany (where levels of both part-time and temporary working are low) was there not a large differential between the proportions of full- and part-time workers with temporary status. Among part-timers men were in all countries more likely to be temporary (ibid.). This reflects the unusual nature of male part-time work in most countries.

The statistical evidence therefore suggests that in Western Europe the mid-century model of employment has not yet been disrupted in a major way by temporary working. Such inroads that have taken place have largely been confined to female workers and (partly the same phenomenon) have also mainly affected the part of the workforce already marginalized through part-time status. Full-time, relatively secure *male* employment has been undermined by unemployment and early withdrawal from the

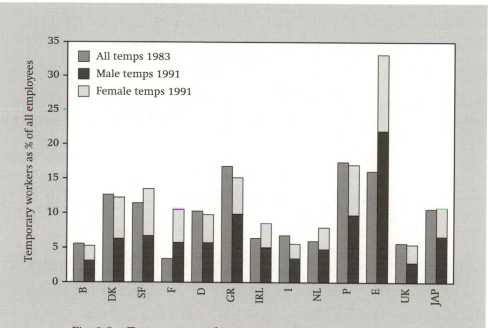

Fig. 3.5a *Temporary working, 1983 and 1991, 13 countries*

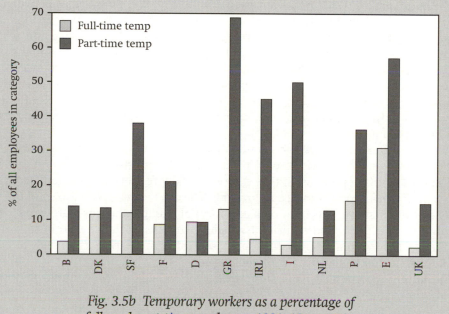

Fig. 3.5b *Temporary workers as a percentage of
full- and part-time employees, 1991, 12 countries*
Source: OECD 1995.

labour force, but not by unusual time patterns or insecure forms of employment. In the USA both genders have been more likely to follow the European 'female' pattern, and where part-time working is concerned this is also happening in the Netherlands. Looking at the same evidence from the opposite direction, the flexibility of many women and some men has enabled them to find places in the labour force by sacrificing the security and full-time nature of the mid-century model of employment. This is entirely consistent with postmodern theories of development; whether it is more consistent with optimistic or pessimistic versions depends very much on evaluation and on which parts of the labour market one observes.

SELF-EMPLOYMENT

For many years self-employment declined throughout the industrial world as large, rationalized corporations seemed to absorb small businesses and partnerships. This is consistent with the mid-century model and with theories of Fordism. Looking at the whole 1960–1995 period, self-employment declined everywhere except Portugal and the UK, being more or less stable in Italy, Sweden, Switzerland, and the USA (see Figure 3.6). The biggest declines were in Denmark, Greece, Ireland, and Norway.

Self-employment is primarily a male phenomenon, as Figure 3.6 shows, though the very large gender gap has narrowed somewhat in nearly all countries since the early 1960s. Among men it is only in the UK that there has been an increase, while among women small increases have been widespread.

More recently, however, there has been a more general change, and self-employment has been increasing. Within the European Community it grew by 22.4% between 1975 and 1989, against a growth in dependent employment of only 8.9% (Meager 1993: 15). It remains low, ranging from 5% to 20% of the workforce, and all European countries with more than 10% are those with large 'traditional' sectors: Spain, Greece, Ireland, Italy, Portugal (Heidenreich 1997: 295–6). Japan has 10.3%, but this is also a country with a large traditional sector. In a long-term perspective, self-employment is associated with indicators of economic 'backwardness'. This suggests either that the recent rise is a wayward variation, or that some major change in the character of work organization may be occurring.

Two very different explanations dominate discussion of the latter possibility. One is that self-employment is evidence of a new level of entrepreneurship and initiative-taking by a working population that is moving away from the dependent security of mid-century social compromise employment. The other that it is an aspect of the flexibility discussed above; it is then seen as a form of fragmented, insecure work, where people lose the rights and security associated with the social compromise, without gaining real entrepreneurial status. This kind of fragmentation as a *return* to earlier work forms is postmodernity with a vengeance.

The latter hypothesis is consistent with the findings of Boegenhold and Staber (1991), whose study of self-employment in eight OECD countries suggested that the rise has been the result of a decline in the chances of achieving stable dependent employment. They note that the rise coincided with the onset of the period of economic stress in the mid-1970s (ibid. 227), and that self-employment is associated with a high business failure rate and therefore with considerable insecurity. It is also relevant that

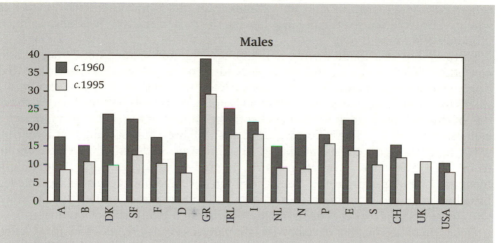

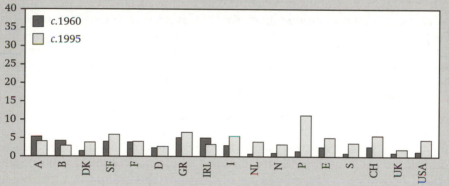

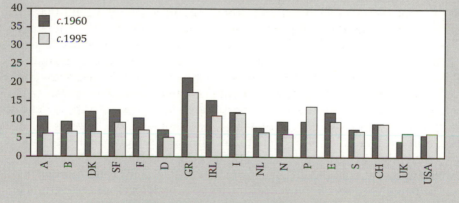

Fig. 3.6 *Self-employment as a percentage of all employment,*
c.1960 and c.1995, 17 countries

self-employment is predominant among immigrant and ethnic minority communities, who usually experience difficulty in achieving the most attractive positions within an economy (Haller 1997: 390).

Furthermore, it is found mainly in marginal economic sectors, not dynamic ones; and often tends in practice to be very dependent on large corporations rather than being genuine self-employed activity as such. In true self-employment the person works for a large number of customers and is not in hierarchical subordination to any one of them. Once a single customer becomes so important that the business would collapse if it withdrew its trade, a degree of subordination approaching that associated with employee status comes into being. In some cases, such self-employment results from a desire by large corporations to rid themselves of the inflexibility of commitment to dependent employees. They thereby reduce the obligations that employers usually have towards employees; but they then so constrain the contract that they have with these persons that they are in no less dependent a position than employees.

One form of this that has developed very rapidly in recent years is franchising. A firm contracts with a group of people that they will run a business on behalf of the firm, usually a shop or restaurant in which the firm's products will be sold. Although in principle the people are running their own shop, in practice they come under the rules and codes of the firm just as much as if they were its employees. For example, much of the work called self-employment in the UK comprises what is known as 'lump labour' in the construction industry. These are large numbers of workers who are not given employee status because that enables the employer to avoid certain social security, safety and other liabilities towards them, while in all other respects they are employees, working under orders and in no sense having businesses of their own.[4] In a similar situation are other categories who seem to have the dependency of employees but without their rights, mainly freelancers and homeworkers, who work from their own homes and have self-employed status, but all of whose work is done for one purchasing company. According to Boegenhold and Staber (1991) this group constitute the largest number of the self-employed, ranging from 46% in Germany to 80% in the USA, and is rising fast in several other countries.

We cannot therefore deduce merely from a rise in self-employment that there has been a rise in entrepreneurship, or in small businesses, or in entry to the *petite bourgeoisie*. In a recent study of self-employment in the European community, Meager (1993: 11) makes this argument, and also demonstrates the great variety of kinds of work embraced by this heading: farmers, practitioners of the free professions, craftsmen, outworkers, workers on their 'own account'. Our analysis above suggests that a high proportion of self-employed working is associated primarily with some indicators of economic backwardness and traditionalism, not a move into a new kind of dynamic innovation. Meager (ibid. 18–21) found that, although self-employment tended to be particularly high in agriculture, and although the relative size of agriculture varies very widely, these variations do not explain the considerable diversity found in the size of the self-employed sector. Indeed, countries with high levels of agricultural employment have high levels of self-employment in their *non*-agricultural sectors. This is largely

---

4 UK official statistics are unusual in not distinguishing this form of self-employment from small businesses (Assimakopoulou 1998).

but not solely explained by a negative relationship between both large agricultural sectors and self-employment, on the one hand, and *per capita* income, on the other.

When discussing variations in overall participation in the paid workforce in the previous chapter, we found that practices associated with the agricultural sector tended to carry over into other sectors in those societies in which agriculture continues to have a large share of total employment, and perhaps where industrialization has been recent. The same phenomenon may well be at work when it comes to self-employment, which would reinforce the argument that self-employment is characteristic of pre-'modern' economies. In fact, although it has grown in all sectors of the economy, it is found more strongly in both agriculture and services than in manufacturing—in other words, more strongly in *both* pre- and post-industrial employment systems. This suggests a U-form curve of development and also certain similarities between the forms of occupational system either side of the mid-century model of industrial work.

Consistent with the view that self-employment is associated with pre-modern work forms is the evidence that in societies with still large agricultural sectors the mid-century concept of the occupation is not clearly established. For example, in Italian agriculture it is often difficult to classify workers as self-employed, family workers, or employees, since they often occupy all these categories in different jobs that they do (Altieri and Villa 1991: 39). A similar point is true of Portugal and Spain (Meulders, Plasman, and Vander Stricht 1993: 41), and most of all in Greece. For example, about 63% of farmers in eastern Macedonia and Thraki earn income from multiple sources, while 60% of those working in industry also work in agriculture and another 10% in tourism (Hadjimichalis and Vaiou 1990). Ethnic membership provides an important basis for differentiation.

On a different point but also consistent with this interpretation is the finding (Meager 1993: 36–40) that married men and women are more likely to be self-employed than are single, widowed, or divorced persons, with the widowed being the second most likely. This suggests that self-employment is a form of work that depends on, or is at least assisted by, systems of extended family support, the decline of which was associated with the rise of the mid-century economy. This way of putting together bundles of small jobs to make a full-time working life is now expanding within the USA, and more surprisingly perhaps in Germany: already in 1984 20.3% of working Germans under 20 had second jobs, and 13.9% of those aged between 21 and 25 (Merz and Wolff 1986).

One factor facilitating the spread of self-employment in the more advanced countries has been the growth of early retirement and redundancy schemes. Employers shedding labour have often offered employees who leave their service an early start to the payment of retirement pensions, though usually at a reduced rate. These people are often still young enough to work, and now have the buttress of at least some stable income through their early pension. They are therefore available for work in a self-employed capacity.

With the exception of Germany, the unemployed are a major source of the self-employed; this association is seen particularly strongly in the UK and Greece (Meager 1993: 84). Meager has devoted some care to an analysis of the major difference between Germany and the UK on this variable (ibid.; and Meager, Kaiser, and Dietrich 1992). The issue of flexibility seems to be central. In the UK it is easy to set up a business without prior qualifications or training, and relatively easy to acquire short-term bank credit;

in Germany the opposite applies. On the other hand, the flexibility operates in both directions: British small businesses have a particularly high failure rate and the self-employed are likely to return to unemployment. In comparison with Germany, there is less chance of support from others in the business community (united in Germany through common background in apprenticeship and training), and the bank credit that was advanced on easy terms in the UK is likely to be withdrawn easily too. In this way differences in employment systems can be related to differences in the overall organization of the economy—an issue which we shall explore further in Part II.

While this evidence seems to support the hypothesis that the rise of self-employment is an indicator of the weakness of labour markets rather than of the strength of entrepreneurship, its growth has been fastest in the sectors of growing employment and low unemployment levels (Humphries and Rubery 1991). However, there is evidence from at least some countries (e.g. Germany and Italy) that self-employed women tend to have lower educational qualifications and incomes than those in dependent employment (Meulders, Plasman, and Vander Stricht 1993: 75–6).

An interesting indicator here is whether the self-employed have employees of their own; if they do, they are less likely to be in 'false' self-employment and more likely to be entrepreneurs. Here there is a considerable division between northern and southern Europe (Meager 1993: 50–3), with the self-employed in the former being considerably more likely to have employees than the latter. For these purposes Ireland and, to a lesser extent, Belgium behave more like southern Europe than northern. Ireland shares important characteristics with southern Europe: low incomes, high level of agriculture, dominance of the Catholic religion; Belgium shares only the Catholicism. Self-employment without employees has had a mixed development. Declining alongside declines in agricultural employment, it began to increase among women in the Netherlands, Italy, and the UK, particularly in services (Meulders, Plasman, and Vander Stricht 1993: 75).

Taking all this evidence, including the two-country comparison between Germany and the UK, we can perhaps draw the following conclusion. As we have already noted, a relative rigidity characterized employment in the mid-century social compromise: the rigidity of security and predictability. The end of the overall economic conditions that supported these qualities leads to the rise of new forms of flexibility in working arrangements that, while dealing with a new situation, also share features with a more or less agricultural past. Hence the observed U-curve. These findings are clearly more in line with postmodern than with earlier post-industrial interpretations of contemporary change. It is difficult to conclude on the basis of the evidence reviewed here whether optimistic or pessimistic versions of these theories are better supported, and whether we are witnessing a genuine new diversity of post-rationalist work types or simply the logic of capitalism working out its highly rational interests through different forms. For this we need the evidence of the analysis of capitalism in Part II.

THE INFORMAL ECONOMY

To the extent that the rise in self-employment can be interpreted as part of flexibilization, it can be located within the general category of the *informal economy*. This term has been given various meanings, usually including both illegal activities as well as perfectly legal ones that are simply not normally counted as constituting economic trans-actions (Mevissen and Renooy 1987; Sandwijk and van Waveren 1987; Pahl 1988; Kiely and O'Raw 1994). The illegality of the former case may refer to criminal activities as such, including the handling of stolen goods or trade in such illegal substances as dangerous drugs; or it might mean that activities, legal in themselves, are being carried on in secret in order to avoid taxation. What brings all informal economy transactions together, whether they comprise a cocaine smuggling ring or a woman looking after a friend's children in exchange for gifts, is that they are not counted in official estimates of economic activity—these often being made on the basis of taxation returns. Seen in these terms the concept is disappointingly bureaucratic and relatively meaningless for the sociology of work. However, it is almost always accompanied by the sociologically more substantive characteristic that the people performing these tasks are not seen to have, and probably do not see themselves as having, a 'job' in the formal, clearly delineated sense of the mid-century economy.

The biggest single issue raised by this is of course one considered in the previous chapter: whether the work carried out by family members for each other, that is house-work and house maintenance, counts as part of the informal economy. It is work which is, with the exception of certain house-maintenance tasks, carried out by women. Presvelou (1994) suggests that this sector would, if able to be counted, add between 35% to 50% to estimates of the gross national product for most societies. She bases this on a number of estimates made in the 1970s and 1980s in Belgium, France, and the Netherlands. She also finds that such a figure matches a 1950s estimate for the UK; estimates from the USA and Sweden for various years before the Second World War suggest a lower figure, c.25% (ibid. 27).

Once the question of counting domestic work has been raised, the issue of whether voluntary work of various kinds should also count as the informal economy has to be considered (Defourny 1994). Kiely and O'Raw (1994: 97) list the following forms of informal transactions: (i) transactions within the household (e.g. housework); (ii) transactions between families and relatives (e.g. care for the young and old); (iii) transactions between friends; (iv) community service; (v) individuals (i.e. voluntary and informal services to persons other than friends); (vi) institutions (educational and other services provided without charge and on an informal basis). Presvelou (1994) has an alternative list, covering domestic work, charitable and voluntary activity (bénévolat), the black economy, the rendering of services in kind (and therefore not measured through financial accounting systems), and criminal business. Similarly, Mingione (1991: 80) has a continuum running from formal, legal, monetary, and public activity, gradually dropping these to become informal, illegal (or, differently, not provided by law), non-monetary, and private. This takes him from (i) the pure formal economy; through (ii) mixed formal and informal activities such as partial 'black' (undeclared) payment; (iii) jobs that elude fiscal, social security, or labour legislation; (iv) criminal activities; (v) transactions not provided for in law (such as informal barter); (vi) reciprocal or voluntary unpaid activities; and (vii) self-provisioning within the household; to (viii) normal domestic work. It is notable that most of the items in all these lists are concentrated at the diffuse, non-standard end of the original work continuum considered in Chapter 2.

In some societies, accounts of the informal sector concentrate on family and small enterprises, or homeworkers; in others (e.g. Belgium and the Netherlands) there is interest also in the role of the voluntary or charitable sector (Defourny 1994; de Hoog 1994)—6% of the total of informal work, according to the Dutch research in 1988. The informal sector is very large in Italy, where it includes both 'genuine' small enterprises (Bagnasco 1977, 1988; Beccatini 1987; Trigilia 1986) and a large criminal sector, with the distinction between the two not being absolute. In Greece, where self-employment is particularly high, it was estimated in the early 1980s that the informal economy was equal to 2% of the GDP (Delivanis-Negreponti 1981).

In the Netherlands women carry twice as much as men of the total burden of informal work (housework, shopping, childcare, charity, etc.) (de Hoog 1994: 60). In Portugal the informal economy is officially calculated to represent about 22% of GDP (Lopes 1994). The main part of this is carried out by women, in a society where a large number of women work either as residential domestic servants to the wealthy, or as cleaners, etc. to less wealthy families. As elsewhere in modern society, an increasing number of Portuguese women are part of the normal paid workforce, though the evidence is that they continue to bear the greatest share of family housekeeping too. As Lopes puts it, other forms of exchange than the dominant monetary one affect the way that society operates. She also calculates (ibid. 77) that in Portugal domestic production not counted as part of the money economy has a value of about one-third of household income—rather more in families on modest incomes. Meanwhile, Déchaux's (1994) calculation for France suggests as much as two-thirds for the informal economy overall (including the criminal sector), and between 31% and 44% for the domestic sector.

There has been some rise in precarious employment in Germany, but it is still very small (Büchtemann and Quack 1989; Glatzer *et al.* 1992: ch. 4.3). Estimates of the size of the German informal economy vary widely and have been put at anything from 10% to 35% of GDP; it certainly seems to have grown since the early 1970s (Glatzer *et al.* 1992: ch. 12.2; Wagner *et al.* 1989; Schäfer 1984). Estimates of the value of household production vary from 23% to 68% of GDP (Glatzer *et al.* 1992: 424). With estimates so diverse we can only conclude that little is really known.

FAMILY WORKERS

The 'family worker' category is the form of informal economic activity most easily recognized by official statistics, but it can conceal a considerable amount of activity that is unrewarded by money income. For example, in rural Greece it is estimated that female 'family workers' work up to 19 hours a day during certain seasons (Pavelle 1994). Pavelle estimates that about one-third of the value of the GDP of Greece is constituted by this labour. Greece also provides interesting examples of the use of rural traditions within industrialization (mainly food, textiles, and clothing). In northern Greece (Hadjimichalis and Vaiou 1990) firms distinguish between a core and a periphery workforce; the latter tend to be classified as semi-skilled, have either unstable or no formal contracts, and are often engaged as home workers. They have minimal rights and low wages. Many of them are women.

Family work, however, has become a very minor aspect of the economy of the advanced societies for both men and women (see Figure 3.7), its decline correlating very closely with its level in 1960—evidence of true convergence. While we note evidence of some decline in orthodox 'mid-century' employment and a rise in female labour-force

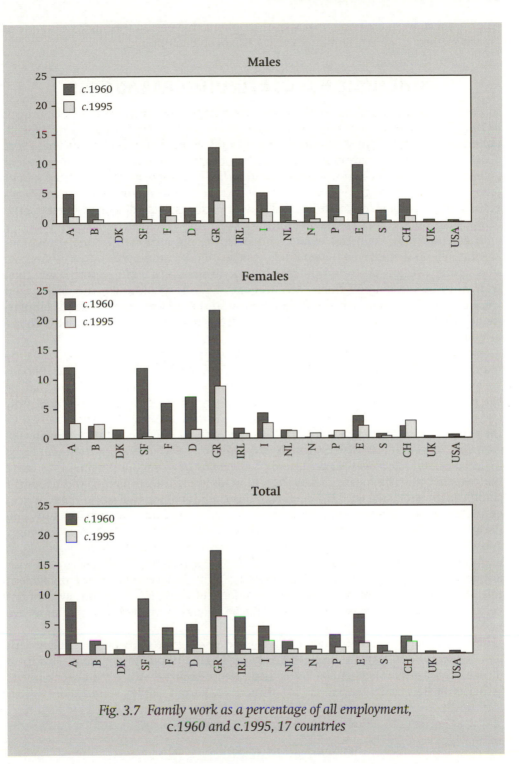

Fig. 3.7 Family work as a percentage of all employment,
c.1960 and c.1995, 17 countries

participation, we must remember that throughout this period this major example of an earlier form of largely female work has also been declining.

CONCLUSIONS: CONTINUING PARADOXES

In view of this last point, it is perhaps not surprising that we find overall no decline but indeed a small rise in the fundamental mid-century work category of full-time dependent employment, as Figure 3.8 shows. The paradox is that this rise consists entirely of a rise in *female* participation in this category—despite women seeming to represent a challenge to the mid-century pattern and to be in many ways the marginal labour force. This is surprising: the gender, whose entry into the labour force in many ways embodies the postmodern shift in employment patterns, has in fact sustained the stability of the mid-century employment form.

In general in all countries women tended to be proportionately (and sometimes absolutely) more employed in two kinds of non-full-time employee statuses than men —as family workers or as part-timers—but men were considerably more likely than women to be working on their 'own account'. Therefore, although in general men were clearly the gender who conformed more to the mid-century model of employment, women were relatively less likely than they to diverge from the model in the direction of self-employment.

Statistical analyses similar to those carried out in the previous chapter[5] and summarized in Tables 2.1 and 2.2 can be carried out for both the early 1960s and mid-1990s periods. The results are presented in Tables 3.1 and 3.2, respectively. They show that, by the mid-1990s the proportion of the total workforce engaged as family workers (now very small almost everywhere) continued as in 1960 to vary strongly and positively with the proportion engaged in agriculture. This was particularly true of the proportions of women engaged. It also varied strongly and negatively with the proportion employed in services, but there was no association with manufacturing employment, as there had been in 1960. This means that by the mid-1990s industrialism as such was no longer significantly associated with the decline of this traditional form of work; only services employment stood here as an indicator of modernity. Working 'on own account' similarly correlated very strongly and positively with agricultural employment, strongly and negatively with services employment, but no longer at all with employment in manufacturing. This would suggest that self-employment is not associated overall with any postmodern or post-Fordist collapse of mid-century social compromise employment relations, but remains primarily a traditional form of work. However, our evidence of very recent change suggests that this might be changing in the U-curve manner we have described.

Part-time work was, on the other hand, associated significantly and positively with services sector employment and negatively with agricultural employment. This form of non-standard employment—closely associated of course with female working—is associated with post-industrialism, but primarily as part of employee status, not any return to self-employment. Men are far more likely than women to be in self-employment, and women far more likely than men to be in part-time *employee* status. Further, as

---

5 Again based on Appendix Tables A.2.2 and A.2.4.

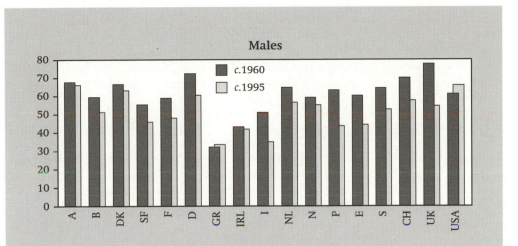

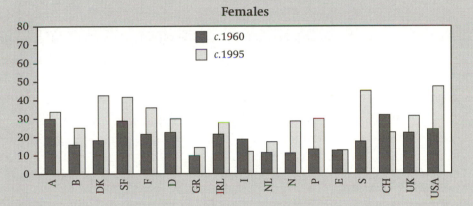

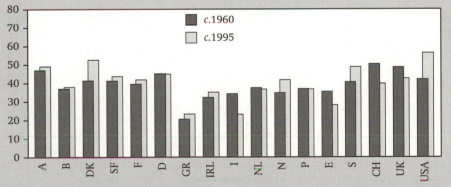

Fig. 3.8 Full-time paid employee status work as a percentage of non-dependent
populations, c.1960 and c.1995, 17 countries

Table 3.1 Associations between atypical work forms and indicators of modernization, c.1960

Dependent variable	Independent variable	Sign	F-statistic	Significance level
Part-time working	Agricultural employment			
	Manufacturing employment	+	11.50	0.00370
	'Services' employment	+	6.16	0.02460
Family workers	Agricultural employment	+	22.96	0.00010
	Manufacturing employment	–	11.50	0.00370
	'Services' employment	–	20.44	0.00030
Own account workers	Agricultural employment	+	40.63	0.00000
	Manufacturing employment	–	24.87	0.00010
	'Services' employment	–	18.18	0.00060

Table 3.2 Associations between atypical work forms and indicators of modernization, mid-1990s

Dependent variable	No. of cases	Independent variable	Sign	F-statistic	Significance level
Part-time working	17	*Agricultural employment*	–	*6.40*	*0.0231*
	17	Manufacturing employment	–	0.36	0.5564
	17	**'Services' employment**	**+**	**15.87**	**0.0012**
	14	GDP p.c.	+	2.59	0.1336
Family workers	**17**	**Agricultural employment**	**+**	**20.41**	**0.0004**
	17	Manufacturing employment	+	0.36	0.5595
	17	**'Services' employment**	**–**	**16.07**	**0.0011**
	14	GDP p.c.	–	0.26	0.6117
Own account workers	**17**	**Agricultural employment**	**+**	**14.12**	**0.0000**
	17	Manufacturing employment	–	0.74	0.4024
	17	**'Services' employment**	**–**	**18.37**	**0.0006**
	14	GDP p.c.	–	1.16	0.3026

Note: **Bold** entries indicate significance levels above 1% confidence level.
Italicized entries indicate significance levels above 5% confidence level.
GDP p.c. = per capita gross domestic product.

Gallie *et al.* (1998) found in the UK, the new insecurities often run along old class lines, reducing any novelty.

Finally, we should consider the tests against the per capita GDP variable for which we do not have comparable information from 1960. At only one point did this variable achieve significance. There is no evidence that a collapse of employee status (the work form most associated with the mid-century pattern) in favour of self-employment is a concomitant of development 'beyond industrialism', but there is clearly a move towards the part-time form of that status.

Can we reach any conclusions on whether the changes discussed here are part of an increasing postmodern diversity in economic forms, or in contrast the enhanced rationalism of a capitalism released from some of the constraints of the mid-century compromise? While we shall be unable to reach any firm position on this until we have considered many other aspects of the theme, some interesting contributions to this process emerge from the current discussion.

Kiely and O'Raw (1994) found that in Ireland participation in the informal economy seemed to *increase* with higher levels of disposable income and of employment, and this despite the historically important role of informal services within families and communities among the poor of rural Ireland. This is an example of a familiar but cruel paradox caused by the odd relationship between *dependence on* a form of service and *capacity to obtain* it.

We can represent this paradox as in Figure 3.9. Among poor communities and families there may be very heavy dependence for survival on informal services produced within the local community, following from the sheer absence of resources and the gains that can therefore flow from pooling and sharing them in the manner made possible by informal as opposed to money exchange. However, the same sheer absence of resources may also mean that there is simply very little to share; the number of different tasks that can be mutually provided by a community that does little other than grow potatoes is very restricted. As wealth grows, so the capacity to produce informal services within the community grows simply because there are more things that can be done and therefore more scope for interdependence. However, in the normal case, dependence on such services then declines, because people are able to obtain their wants and needs from the formal market economy.

Both extreme situations are unstable, because of the paradoxical character of the relationship. Sheer poverty cannot support communities; the individuals concerned either die or move away. Those poor traditional societies that were able to survive and therefore leave behind the historical record of poor *communities* were able to do so because their resources and therefore capacity to generate and obtain services were somewhat better than zero and they made use of what they had. We see these societies as the epitome of informal economies, not so much because they had so much that they shared, but because the poor amount that they did share constitutes a high proportion of their total assets.

Except among wealthy groups who *choose* to sustain communities, the opposite extreme is likely to be unstable because, with very low mutual dependence, utilization of community exchange is likely to decline, leading to a decline in the availability of

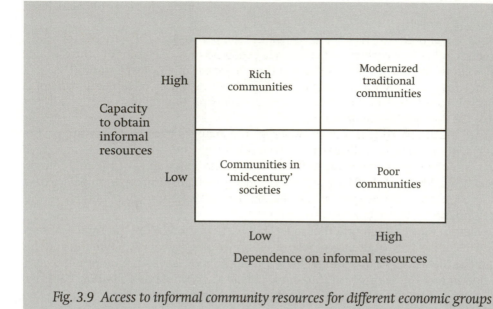

Fig. 3.9 *Access to informal community resources for different economic groups*

the informal resources themselves; there will therefore be a strong tendency for such societies to move to the bottom left-hand corner, which is the classic situation of mid-century industrial societies. In these cases, a certain combination of market economy and welfare state replaces the informal resources. Very wealthy groups may be better able to withstand the collapse, since their wealth enables them to afford both community and its replacements.

Finally, there is the top right-hand possibility of retaining a real dependence on informal resources alongside a capacity to obtain and generate them, which though highly stable and satisfactory is slightly puzzling. It can occur if the supply of informal goods and services is more reliable or ample than the equivalent in the formal market or welfare state. The main European examples of such economies are to be found in central Italy, where a high level of prosperity has been achieved by communities which prefer to maintain a local scale of activities and personal rather than bureaucratic relationships (e.g. the area is characterized by small family firms) (Bagnasco 1977, 1988; Beccatini 1987; Trigilia 1986). Whether one speaks of mid-century economies as having a community deficit, or of these high/high societies as having a *formal* system deficit is a complex issue and an unavoidably normative one. What we can notice here is the viability of alternative possibilities. This is consistent with our earlier hypothesis that the return of the informal economy (and other aspects of flexibility) in contemporary societies results from the growing uncertainty of the formal economy and reductions in the welfare state—key characteristics of the mid-century compromise. A revival of family solidarity (Déchaux 1994) or female informal economic activity in general (de Hoog 1994) may develop as alternatives to the welfare state; but by no means all communities will be capable of generating these resources, having lost them in earlier periods of modernization that had little use for them.

To look at the matter differently, one result of changes in the field of work at a time of growing insecurity will be a tendency for groups which have established some position of security and strength to keep trying to stabilize that position even further, leading possibly to growing segmentation of the workforce between those who have won security and those who remain marginal. Some years ago Berger and Piore (1980) suggested that a fundamental change was taking place in the acquisition of security, leading to a dualistic division of the labour force between those possessing stability and those in various of the marginal positions that we have discussed above. Since then many other authors have contributed to the analysis, moving from the simple dualism of Berger and Piore to elaborate a more detailed model of 'segmentation'.

Divisions of this kind between insiders and outsiders explain much of the unevenness of unemployment patterns. At a time of employment insecurity, those with jobs find ways of protecting themselves, often at the expense of those seeking to enter work. Hence, unemployment tends to be concentrated among the young, women, and immigrant groups. At the same time, when the employment which the insiders sought to protect was doomed—as had become the case in a number of manufacturing industries by the 1980s—those excluded from such employment were often better able to find work in growing new sectors—though it often remained very insecure.

It is notable that, as we discussed briefly in Chapter 1, some observers have seen the most recent developments in late industrial societies as constituting the coming of 'risk society' (most notably, Beck 1986; Giddens 1990). Included in this must be the rise of new risks within populations which have over several decades taken steps to protect themselves from risk—at the very time when some of the institutions that they had created for such protection are undergoing crisis. Within the field of employment, these risks often differed very much by economic sector, the analysis of which is the subject of the next chapter.

Chapter 4

THE SECTORS OF EMPLOYMENT

We must now consider in more detail the different kinds of activities that constitute human work in the formal occupational system. We have already made use of the idea of different sectors of employment, and have referred to the familiar distinctions between primary (*extractive* activities: agriculture and mining), secondary (*productive* activities: manufacturing, construction, utilities), and tertiary (*services*) sectors. These categories refer to the distinctions among: extracting resources directly from nature; processing what has been wrought from nature in order to produce material goods; and providing services, activities distinguished from the other sectors in that what is provided is direct human labour, not a material product. Therefore, as one moves from primary to secondary to tertiary, one moves away from nature and objects towards more completely human activity. As such the concept is highly suggestive, embodying a sense of evolutionary progress as well as a kind of hierarchy. It has been used in this way to great effect to analyse a process of change to which all societies seem subject as they advance and become richer. Work first done by Colin Clark and others in the 1930s (Clark 1940) identified a historical shift of this kind. Its most immediately interesting implication is what happens to employment in manufacturing industry during economic growth. First, it rises strongly as agricultural employment gives way to it. Then, as the tertiary sector rises, it begins to fall again. So, according to this thesis, a country having a high proportion of persons employed in the secondary sector is associated with an intermediate stage of modernization.

As we have already noted in Chapter 2, these sectoral differences are relevant to the concept of a putative rise and fall of the mid-century social compromise, but in a problematic way. The society of the compromise, it will be recalled, is not just industrial society in general, but a specific form of it with advanced democratic citizenship rights. The latter involve a high level of employment in the welfare state, delivering citizenship *services*. The more extended formulations of the Fordist model similarly assume an extensive welfare state. To some extent the segregations and specializations that both models imply suggest the delegation to professional services of a number of welfare functions, though in the male employment predominance assumed by both theories these functions are shared in an unspecified way with women in the domestic labour force. These forms of industrial society therefore occupy an uncomfortable, loosely specified, partial position within the theory of sectoral change. The process of a shift from the secondary to the tertiary sector has begun, but is in its early stages. Theories of post-industrial society take us into a world in which the balance between secondary and tertiary has slipped still further towards the latter but again in awkwardly unspecified ways, as we shall see.

So powerful has the three-sector concept been that it is used almost universally in discussions of economic change. It is however problematic, in particular because the tertiary sector, which is fundamental to contemporary employment development, is defined residually. It covers all those human work activities that do not involve the extraction or production of material objects. Although a growth of the tertiary sector is associated with an 'advance' beyond industrialism, in terms of both historical succession and the sophistication of some of the activities pursued within it, many very ancient (e.g. priests, merchants, teachers) and also some very menial (e.g. cleaners, waiters, domestic servants) tasks are included. Furthermore, while some services are very remote from the production of material goods (say, occupations in education and religion), others are very close to it (e.g. the transport of goods).

There have therefore been several attempts at further defining the services sector. Katzovien (1970) suggested distinguishing between services complementary to industry, 'new' services such as the welfare state and leisure, and 'old', mainly domestic services. Singer (1971) made a similar proposal, but replaced the distinction between old and new by one between 'collective' and 'personal'. Others similarly tried to add quaternary and quinary and further sectors to the tertiary. Finally, the German sociologist Joachim Singelmann (1978) suggested the six-sector model which will be used here. This and the other new models have mainly kept to the original idea of moving away from nature to humanity and from concrete to abstract. Sector I remains agriculture and extractive industry, and Sector II manufacturing, construction, and utilities. The tertiary sector (Sector III) strictly defined then becomes a matter of the movement and transport of physical goods, seen as just one step removed from their actual production. This covers all *distributive* activities, both the transport and sale of goods. Unfortunately, because of the ways in which national statistics are collected, it is impossible properly to separate these. Data on transport will include the movement of persons as well as goods; these in turn are difficult to separate from postal services, which are often included with telecommunications.

A quaternary sector (Sector IV) is then defined to cover the next stage back from production: like the distributive sector, these are services related to the production of goods, but they do not involve handling them directly. These are the *business services*: the financial sector of banking, insurance, accountancy, and management of the ownership of companies; legal services; design services such as architecture or engineering design. Here again, the nature of statistical sources disappoints any attempt at fully analysing occupations in this way. Much of telecommunications should really be included here rather than under transport, while it is impossible to separate out which aspects of financial, legal, and design services are ancillary to the business sector rather than to ultimate consumers.

An important additional problem encountered here, and to a lesser extent in other of these sectoral divisions, is the difficulty of defining whether certain employments are located in this sector or in the secondary. The sectors of occupations are usually classified according to the principal business of the employing organization. Thus, if a manufacturing concern employs its own designers these will be counted within the secondary sector. If however it has identical tasks carried out by consultants from specialist design firms, these will be counted under the business services sector. Singelmann (1978) drew attention to the arbitrariness of this, making a particular point concerning comparisons between Germany and the USA. The former country is often considered to have a less advanced economy than the latter because it has a relatively large manufacturing sector. Singelmann pointed out however that it was common practice in German firms to keep many business services in-house, while US corporations preferred to use external consultant firms; this increased the relative size of the business services sector in the USA, without any difference at all in activities being undertaken (for a more recent, similar argument, see Stille 1990: 109). Similarly, Cohen and Zysman (1987) have pointed out the many tight linkages between a broad core of services and manufacturing.

Next, the quinary sector (Sector V) moves further from contact with material goods to cover certain services rendered directly to persons: *social and community services*, including all public administration. This includes the welfare state sector which, alongside industrialism, is a major constituent part of the mid-century compromise model. Although in practice much employment in this sector is in public ownership, this is not a defining characteristic, and private sectors of, for example, health and education are included here. Again, there is unavoidable overlap with other sectors: some elements of telecommunications, legal, and other services ought really to be counted here if we could get data sufficiently sophisticated; and some education is clearly a service to business.

Some models of occupational structure, including some still used by certain international and national statistical services, include in this quinary sector all personal and domestic services, but there has been considerable dissatisfaction with this, again initially articulated by Singelmann (1978). At issue is the distinction between the social and the personal. The former will broadly embrace services which are provided to the general collectivity (such as defence or the maintenance of order), or which, even if delivered to individuals, are generally regarded as providing some collective good as well (such as education services, which sustain the overall cultural level of the society and, presumably, its economic capacities; or health services, much of which are concerned with protecting public health or with sustaining the physical capacity of the workforce). While there can always be disagreement about what constitute collective goods, in practice there is reasonable agreement about which services should be defined under this category and most national statistical services now present data organized in this way. The fact that such services are often at least in part provided by the state or some other public agency is an indication of their collective, public status, even if they can in practice also be provided through market mechanisms. Some idea of moving progressively away from assistance with the productive process within the analysis of the services sectors is retained by listing this one the fifth.

The sixth category (Sector VI) therefore defines *personal* services, those services which are provided purely to individuals without an associated collective or social good. Here will be included all services that are ultimate services to persons, serving no further instrumental end. Examples are all domestic service, and by extension the services of restaurants and hotels, which have to be removed from the distributive sector where they might otherwise be located. The provision of leisure, recreation, culture, the arts, and sport will also be included. This raises some severe definitional difficulties, as it is impossible to distinguish certain activities carried on as education from those defined as culture, or body care (beauticians, hairdressers) from health services. (In several countries the red and white pole still sometimes seen outside barbers' shops, symbolizing a bandaged bleeding arm, reminds us that medical and hairdressing services were once combined in the role of the barber-surgeon.) However, not only would an attempt at redefining this boundary create new problems, but few countries collect their oc-cupational data in a manner that would enable one to make practical use of such a distinction in analysis. Fortunately, the numbers of persons involved in such work are very small. Problems of overlap also continue: cleaning services, for example, are normally considered as an aspect of hygienic and sanitary activities, and hence within Sector V, though they also include the clear domestic service of house cleaning (Sector VI), and also a considerable amount of cleaning of business premises (Sector IV).

It is doubtful whether we have reached a final point in the question of the definition and analysis of economic sectors. Singelmann's is the most sophisticated yet, but is per-haps too concerned with a contemporary set of debates and controversies to endure. However, the debates with which it is concerned—the question of an evolutionary progression after the rise of industrialism; the character of the work being carried out in different sectors—are particularly relevant to the concerns of this book. In this chap-ter therefore we shall use his definitions of six employment sectors, accepting that the allocation of occupations to sectors will always include inaccuracies and inappropriate generalizations.

POST-INDUSTRIAL SOCIETY?

It is the idea of a progression through economic sectors that makes evolutionary theories of 'post-industrial society' so attractive, as the march from primary through secondary and on into the different services sectors is seen as a progression in the advancement of human needs and desires. One reason why Daniel Bell's (1974) version of the thesis has been particularly powerful is that it sees the move from industrial society as the result of a constant advance in the role of knowledge. Other approaches, particularly those associated with Ronald Inglehart (1990, 1997) go even further and relate economic change to a presumed evolution of human needs; humans are con-sidered to need first to satisfy their basic physiological needs before they can move on to higher matters, in particular knowledge and culture (which we might allocate here to Sectors V and VI).

This is attractive but unconvincing. Two very common characteristics of human life challenge it. First, there is considerable evidence that poor, even primitive, groups and societies do devote themselves to non-material pursuits. Indeed, art and religion—often very much combined—occupied a considerably higher proportion of the activ-ities and artefacts of pre-modern and primitive societies than they do of advanced ones; they probably did so in compensation for the absence of material resources. One needs only to consider the beautiful and complex designs that craftsmen in virtually all prim-itive cultures, operating with crude and difficult tools, worked into the objects they produced. Whether the motive was aesthetic or religious is unimportant here; both motivations are non-material. Second, the idea that material appetite reaches a kind of ceiling, beyond which people turn to cultivating the non-material, is contradicted by the evidence of the behaviour of very wealthy people, whether in contemporary so-cieties or earlier. They have demonstrated a truly extraordinary capacity for finding new objects of material expenditure and ever higher frontiers for quantities of physical gratification.

Bell's arguments, concentrating on the rise of knowledge, correspond more securely to the many traditions of social thought which identify the modernization process with mankind's growing rational control over both its own thought processes and its environment. Society's growth from material to non-material is seen in the gradual shifts in employment as the sectors, from primary to quinary, rise and fall. This is, further, not just a question of consumption, but of production. As we move through the sectors away from the primary, so the knowledge content in the provision of the goods or services that are the sector's output increases, culminating again in the education system, where knowledge is itself the product. Bell demonstrates how, in the United States, which he sees as the world's most advanced society, the proportion of people employed in educational and scientific activities has risen steadily. If the key figure in pre-industrial society was the peasant and the key institution the farm, and the equivalents in industrial society were the industrial worker and the factory, for Bell the key images of post-industrial society are the scientist and the university.

Two decades ago the British sociologist Jonathan Gershuny (1978) challenged the notion that with progress we move from consuming goods to consuming services, pointed to several examples of exactly the opposite, in particular to the decline of domestic service as an occupation. For many centuries even only modestly wealthy families in much of Europe employed some paid help to wash clothes, clean the house, and sometimes to cook food. Their place has been taken by washing machines, vacuum cleaners, food processing equipment—the products of pure secondary sector metal-manufacturing industries! Similar arguments apply to the replacement of live entertainment by manufactured audio- and televisual equipment, of public transport by private cars, and of house building and decorating firms by 'do-it-yourself' activities using purchased tools. Far from there having been a replacement of goods by services, he argued, there has been the opposite. Gershuny classifies much of this as the 'self-service society'. We purchase goods from the manufacturing sector in order to engage in service activities that are carried on in the domestic, not the formal, economy, and which are therefore not recognized in accounts of economic activity but return us to the unclear boundaries around paid work and family work that we discussed in Chapters 2 and 3.

However, developments since the 1970s throw some doubt on both Bell's and Gershuny's arguments. Much recent growth in employment has been in Sector VI, personal services, requiring, as we shall see below, very little in the way of science and education, and in many cases taking the form of a *return* to forms of domestic or quasi-domestic service.

Gershuny's 1970s case remains valid in that a central error of the post-industrialism thesis was to equate consumption within a particular society with production measured in manpower input within that same society. There are in fact two errors here. First, in mistaking labour input for physical output, the thesis overlooks the highly differential impact of productivity improvements. Within both agriculture and manufacturing there are both continuous minor improvements in productivity as methods and labour practices develop, and also occasional qualitative improvements when major technological advances are made. For many years work in the services sectors was less affected by anything other than minor changes of this kind; and health and education were perhaps affected least of all. If an occupation exists to provide a person-to-person service, rather than to use machinery in order to produce physical objects, there are clear limits

THE SECTORS OF EMPLOYMENT   101

on how far the human labour input can be reduced before the provision of the service itself is adversely affected. This helps explain why there has been a shift in employment patterns from the direct production sectors (I and II) to many of the services sectors; it is not that we actually consume less material goods—rather the reverse. (Economic theory recognizes this problem as an aspect of the 'Baumol effect'. Baumol (1967) showed that, as a result of greater capacity for productivity improvements in manufacturing, services were likely to become relatively more expensive over time.)

This period may be coming to an end, as we are in the midst of a technological revolution that has implications for employment in services just as strong as automation did for goods production. When automation began in a major way, during the 1950s, there was considerable debate over whether this would lead to uncontrollable unemployment—the Industrial Revolution itself had led to similar fears, stimulating, among other things, Luddism and machine-wrecking. In the event it did not happen. Automation made production cheaper and therefore stimulated demand. Technological advance also increased the range of products that could be made, so further people were employed in the manufacture of these new goods. In most industrial societies employment in manufacturing industries continued to rise until the beginning of the 1970s. By then perhaps the accumulated impact of automation had begun to have an effect. Initially the great growth of other sectors was also in progress and there was still no widespread joblessness, but ever-improving productivity and technological innovation had by the 1980s produced massive job losses in most of the industries that had been the core employers of industrial society. For some countries, especially in southern Europe, including France, this loss of industrial employment occurred while the last stages of agricultural decline were also in progress.

We are now experiencing the new wave of innovation in information technologies, which has implications for services sectors as well as for manufacturing: handling information was the main defining characteristic of Bell's optimistic vision of service sector employment, but machines can do much of that work more quickly and efficiently than human employees. Initially, as with automation, there was an *expansion* in demand for labour as declining costs led to falls in relative prices and thus enough increase in demand to compensate for the technological replacement of labour. But this eventually peaked, to be followed by a decline in employment. This has been seen in the 1990s in several industries (banks are an important example) where not only are clerical workers displaced by information technology, but whole layers of management become redundant as senior levels can carry out their work of middle-order supervision by monitoring computerized data flows. Will new forms of work develop to employ the people who would otherwise have worked in these sectors, as the services themselves expanded to meet the release of workers from the land and the factory? We do not yet know, and both pessimistic and optimistic forecasts are made.

The second error is that, by failing to distinguish between production and consumption, most post-industrialism theories ignore exports and imports. It is perhaps significant that the Bell thesis comes from the USA, where foreign trade is a much smaller proportion of total trade than in European countries. We often find that a reason why employment in a particular sector has declined in a society is that people have started to purchase the output of that sector from abroad. Agriculture is the most obvious case, but it now applies to many parts of the manufacturing sector and an increasing number of services too as part of the globalization process described in earlier chapters. It is also important to remember that globalization is not a one-way process whereby jobs and production capacities move from the existing industrial countries in Europe, North America, and Japan to the new industrializers as though they were disappearing into a hole in the ground. A growth in employment in the new economies leads to growing purchasing power there too, much of which is used to buy goods and some services from the existing industrial countries. Pascal Petit and Terry Ward (1995) have shown that, while South-East Asian manufacturers increased their share of third-country imports into the then European Community area from 12% to 18% between 1985 and 1992, their share of exports from the Community to third countries increased from 8% to 13% over the same period. Although conventional wisdom maintains that globalization threatens the industries of the advanced world, the majority of countries in the European Union consistently maintain trade surpluses in manufacturing trade with the great majority of newly industrializing countries (OECD 1997: 104). (Only Norway, the Netherlands, and the UK have deficits in this manufacturing trade; Italy and Sweden have particularly large surpluses. Japan runs a very large surplus indeed with the industrializing countries, but the USA a large deficit (ibid.). Of course, this does not necessarily mean that employment in manufacturing is being sustained at high levels. Often European countries have achieved their competitive strength by auto-mating production and moving out of labour-intensive industries—therefore reducing labour.) Living standards in the new industrializing countries eventually rise, leading to both a reduction in the gap in labour costs and a rise in trade opportunities for the advanced countries as much as for themselves.

These factors remind us of a point made in the Preface: should we see individual societies as a series of examples of more or less the same thing, or as components of a wider system? The theory of sectors in the post-industrial thesis is one point where this distinction has to be made or we shall make major errors. For example, Germany now has more people working in, and has a larger share of its gross domestic product in, the manufacturing sector than almost any other society being considered in this book. Does this mean that Germany is somehow becoming backward, or that it has a sustain-able comparative advantage in manufacturing?

We cannot answer these questions here, but in the light of this background we can at least examine what sectoral changes have taken place in various economies in order to consider their sociological implications.

SECTORAL CHANGE OVER TIME

An ideal-typical society of the mid-century social compromise should have twin peaks in its sectoral occupational structure. The principal peak should be Sector II, because this is primarily an industrial society form. The subsidiary peak should be Sector V, because the mid-century compromise model is not one of pure industrialism, but one which incorporates developments in social citizenship. Theories of post-industrial society envisage this pattern changing as Sector II declines and V grows, becoming the primary peak. Growth will also be envisaged in Sector IV. Little is said about Sector III, which primarily serves industry.

It is unfortunately not possible here to follow our preferred pattern of comparing the early 1960s with the 1990s, because too few countries produced data in the earlier period which made possible an adequate breakdown of the various services sectors. Attention will therefore have to concentrate on the more recent period. We can how-ever gain some impression of overall trends from partial studies of longer periods. Figure 4.1 presents the findings of Castells (1996) on how employment across the six sectors has changed in the main Western European countries, the USA, and Japan since the 1920s, looking at data from the immediate post-war years and the early 1970s as well as the most recent available. The extractive sector (Figure 4.1a) has declined steadily and steeply in all. Figure 4.1b demonstrates the rise and fall of manufac-turing. Note how recent the decline is. Only in the USA did manufacturing peak before 1970 (around 1960). Japan's growth until that time is remarkably strong. In that context, there does seem to be a distinct 'European' experience of a gently growing industrial workforce until decline in the past twenty years. Only the UK departs slightly from this, being closer to the US pattern. The distributive sector has been relatively stable (Figure 4.1c). Although normally regarded as part of the services sector, the distributive trades lack many of the characteristics of other services, and have not shared in their growth. Business services (Figure 4.1d) have clearly increased rapidly over time, especially in more recent decades, but remain small. Social and community services (Figure 4.1e) have also grown considerably and have become very large employers. Finally, private services are seen to have had a varying growth pattern (Figure 4.1f).

Esping-Andersen, Assimakopoulou, and Van Kersbergen (1993: 37–9) have made calcu-lations comparing change across similarly defined sectors, mainly between the 1960s and the 1980s, for 6 countries (Germany, Norway, Sweden, Canada, the USA, and the UK).[1] The result is shown in Table 4.1. We can see the following as in Castells's list: overall decline and convergence in the goods-producing Sectors I and II; stability in III and VI; and considerable growth, but no real cross-national convergence, in Sectors IV and V. We can also see that in the early 1960s Sector V had not yet established itself as a clear second peak; at least in terms of persons employed, the citizenship component of the mid-century compromise had not advanced as far as our core theses would expect. This is a matter for further discussion in Part IV.

At the simplest level the Bell thesis of a shift to post-industrialism is confirmed on the grounds of the strong growth of Sector V, his key sector, for these important coun-tries at least—even if we discount Sectors III and IV as being *ancillary to* industrialism rather than as coming 'after' it, and Sector VI as being ambiguous. As suggested at the start of this chapter, a change of this kind constitutes a readjustment within the terms of the mid-century social compromise model—a decline in Sector II and a rise in Sector V. To what extent do these changes also constitute a 'Bell' shift to up-market, skilled, scientific employment? What has happened to the gender segregations that were central to the mid-century model? What variations do we find among countries? We

---

[1] Esping-Andersen, Assimakopoulou, and Van Kersbergen (1993) separate 'government' employment from social and community services, but if we reincorporate government within the latter we can reconstitute Sector V. They also amalgamate some of the categories (I, II, and III versus IV, V (minus government service), and VI) in order to contrast the size of what they term the Fordist and post-industrial sectors. The value of doing this will be discussed below.

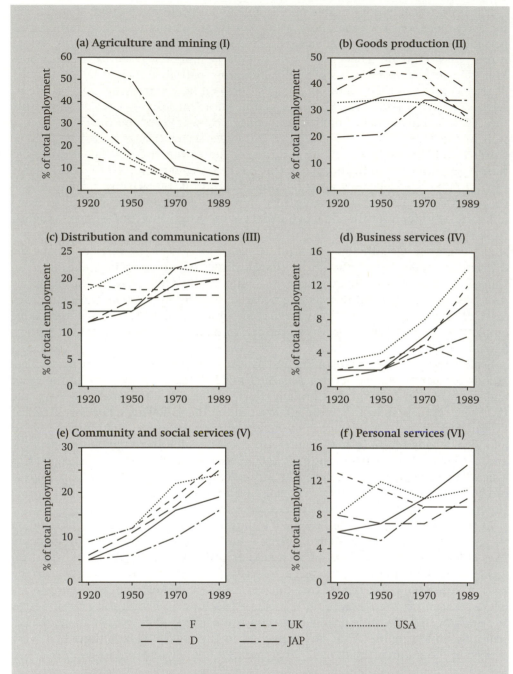

Fig. 4.1 *Sectoral employment changes, 1920–1989, 5 countries*

Note: In 1970 and 1989 'Germany' is the former western Federal Republic.

Source: Castells (1996).

Table 4.1 Sectoral change since 1960 in 6 countries (Esping-Andersen's model)

Sector	Germany			Norway			Sweden		
	1960	1985	change	1960	1985	change	1960	1985	change
I	14.2	4.9	−9.30	20.5	7.6	−12.90	14.1	6.5	−7.60
II	48.5	39.7	−8.80	33.3	26.6	−6.70	42.4	28.5	−13.70
III	18.7	20.7	2.00	26	23.8	−2.20	20.2	19.2	−1.00
IV	3.4	7.8	4.40	1.9	7.2	5.30	2.9	7.3	4.40
V	9.4	19.8	10.40	10.4	29.3	18.90	12.2	33.2	21.00
VI	5.8	6.4	0.60	6.9	5.6	−1.30	8.2	5.4	−2.80

Sector	Canada			United States			United Kingdom		
	1960	1981	change	1960	1988	change	1971	1981	change
I	12.2	5.4	−6.80	7.4	3.1	−4.30	2.6	2.2	−0.40
II	31.7	27.2	−4.50	35.3	25.4	−9.90	44.3	37.1	−7.20
III	26	24.6	−1.40	23.1	22.7	−0.40	21.1	22.2	1.10
IV	5.5	11.6	6.10	6.8	11.2	4.40	6.4	8.3	1.90
V	15.6	22.7	7.10	16.3	25.7	9.40	16.8	21.1	4.30
VI	9	8.7	−0.30	11.4	11.9	0.50	8.9	9.2	0.30

Source: Adapted from Esping-Andersen, Assimakopoulou, and Van Kersbergen 1993: 39–40.

shall look first at overall employment in the sectors by gender, and then consider the educational structure of the sectors.

SECTORAL EMPLOYMENT IN THE 1990S

If we now concentrate the analysis on the recent past (i.e. the years around 1990) alone, rather than being concerned with trends, we find data more readily available from national statistical offices for nearly all the countries with which we are concerned.[2] Unfortunately it is not possible to get data for all countries at the level of detail needed for a date later than 1990 or 1991. These statistics only become available in national censuses, which are carried out every ten years. It must be borne in mind that almost a decade has passed since the last census, and that it has been a decade of rapid change

[2] Cases with values outside the range plus or minus 1.5 standard deviations are regarded as outliers. It has not been possible to include data for Portugal or Switzerland. For Belgium and Finland it has not been possible easily to distinguish Sector VI, most of which is amalgamated with Sector V, with restaurants being included in Sector III. This affects the treatment of three out of six sectors in these countries, so they have to be treated apart.

on these dimensions. The relevant figures are presented in the Appendix in Table A.4.1, which shows overall employment by gender across the six sectors—together with information carried over from Chapter 2 on the domestic and unemployed populations in order to sustain our concern not to separate the study of paid work from unpaid. As in that chapter, we concentrate here on what I have defined as the 'non-dependent population', that is, all persons not in full-time education, not below school age, and below the age of 80. We shall consider each of the sectors in turn, the appropriate material from Table A.4.1 being presented graphically in each case.

SECTOR ZERO: UNPAID DOMESTIC LABOUR

Figure 4.2 starts with what we might regard as 'Sector Zero': the unpaid domestic sector (including unemployment). This is everywhere the largest single category, in most countries occupying between 35% and 45% of the non-dependent population. Below this range are Scandinavia (Denmark, Norway, Sweden) and the two non-European countries (Japan and the USA). There are however no true outliers. It is a category divided strongly by gender, as we saw in Chapter 2: in most countries, between 20% and 30% of all people in the age category are women in this domestic sector; only from 12%

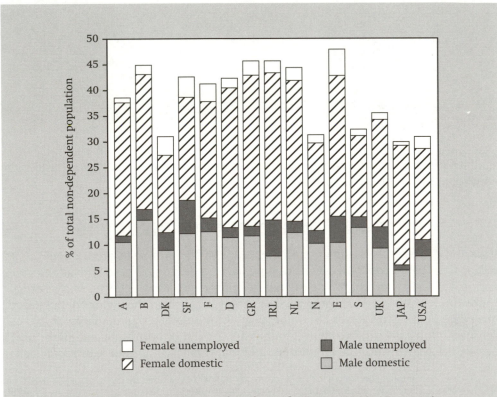

Fig. 4.2 Domestic and unemployed populations, c.1990, 15 countries

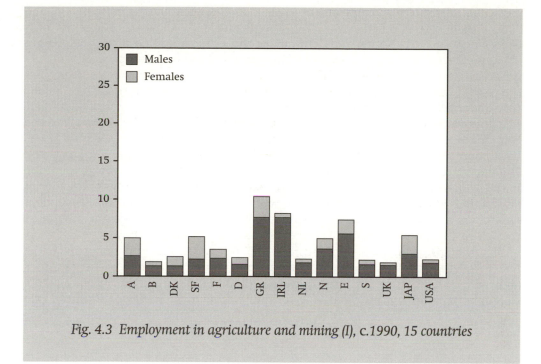

Fig. 4.3 Employment in agriculture and mining (I), c.1990, 15 countries

to 18% are men. While there are no upper outliers, at the extremes of this range for women are geographical groups: the southern European countries (Greece and Spain) plus Ireland have a higher proportion of their population as women in this category, while the Scandinavian countries have fewer, with Sweden being an outlier, and the USA on the margin. Among men the only low outliers are the two extra-European countries, while the only upper outlier is Finland.

SECTOR I: AGRICULTURE AND MINING

The primary sector (I: agriculture plus mining and other forms of mineral extraction) has everywhere become very small (see Figure 4.3), Figure 4.1 having already shown the sweep of that decline during the century in the largest countries. Only some southern European countries (Greece, Spain) and Ireland now have more than 5% of their core populations in this sector, though Finland and Japan come close. Belgium and the UK have even fewer than 2%. It is a sector that usually employs more men than women, though the proportions are fairly even in Austria, Denmark, and Japan, and there is a female majority in Finland. Only in Ireland, the UK, and the USA is the male dominance strong.

SECTOR II: GOODS PRODUCTION

The secondary sector (II: manufacturing along with construction and the generation and distribution of gas, electricity, and water) remains the largest or second largest individual sector of paid employment in all countries, most having between 15% and 20% of their core population working here (Figure 4.4). Below this range are only Greece and (just) the Netherlands. Overall, countries' positions do not correspond to obvious categories: nothing is explained by north and south of Europe, early and late industrializers, different sides of the Atlantic. The size of the secondary sector, once the central defining characteristic of a modernizing society, seems to have become a very under-determined variable.

It is everywhere a predominantly male sector, at a ratio of between 2.5 : 1 and 4.5 : 1 for most countries. At even higher ratios than that are the Netherlands and Spain, both countries with relatively small sectors. Lower than this range are Japan and Finland—interestingly two of the four countries where there was an even gender ratio in the primary sector. (The secondary sector ratio for Denmark, another of the four, is also rather low.) In most countries between 12% and 15% of the non-dependent population are men in this sector, overall the biggest single gender-sector sub-group, though rivalled in some individual cases by women in Sector V. Only Greece is a low outlier, though Spain, the Netherlands, and the USA are low—an interesting mix of the industrializing and the post-industrializing. Upper outliers are those countries associated with specialism in advanced industrial production during the 1980s—Austria, Germany, Japan. Very few women today find employment in Sector II: only Japan stands above a range of from 2% to 6% of the core population being women working here.

SECTOR III: DISTRIBUTION AND COMMUNICATIONS

The tertiary sector (III: distribution (wholesale and retail) as well as transport and communications (movement of persons, goods, and electronic messages))[3] is of all the sectors probably the least discussed in the literature, and as we have seen, its relative size (though not the contents of its internal composition) have changed relatively little during the twentieth century. It is a 'services' sector, and employment in it is interpreted by cruder indices as being part of post-industrial employment, but in reality much of it is very close to manufacturing in that physical goods are moved around. Given its stability in the face of the decline of Sector II, it is today not greatly smaller than that sector, employing almost everywhere something within the tight range of between 10% and 15% of the non-dependent population (see Figure 4.5). The outliers to this are few and clear: the two non-European countries stand well above the general European level.

The internal changes include the decline of transport (buses, trains, etc.) and the rise of telecommunications, but also considerable change and growth within the distributive sector following the expansion in many countries of shopping and of various kinds of food outlets. This is in fact a very dynamic sector at the present time, despite its static appearance.

It is largely a male dominant sector, but by only small margins; in only Greece and to some extent the Netherlands is the male preponderance strong; in Finland there is even a female majority. Overall, this is a sector that gives us one of our few European

---

[3] This is an example of a sector where data on Belgium and Finland are not comparable with the rest (see note 2), being exaggerated by the inclusion of restaurants and hotels.

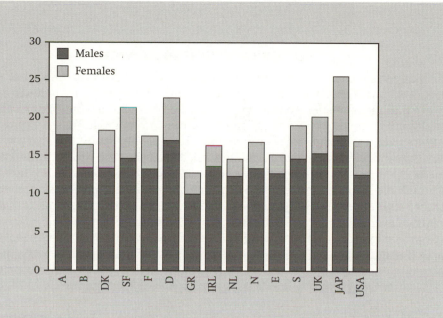

Fig. 4.4 Employment in goods production (II), c.1990, 15 countries

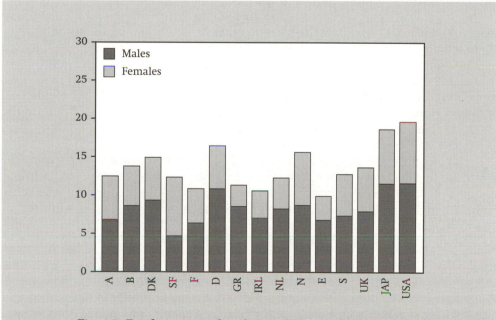

Fig. 4.5 Employment in distribution (III), c.1990, 15 countries

generalizations: compared with both Japan and the USA fewer Europeans, north or south, work at distributing and transporting goods or communicating messages.

SECTOR IV: BUSINESS SERVICES

The quaternary sector (IV: business services) is everywhere very small, but growing rapidly. As noted above, it is not easy to disentangle all of its components from others within national statistics, so the figures discussed here are to some extent estimates. Employing in general between 3% and 7% of the core population (see Figure 4.6), its outliers from that range are clearly defined: below, only Spain, but also low are two other late industrializers, Greece and Ireland; above, the USA—with the neighbouring cluster of Denmark, Germany, the Netherlands, and the UK also high. It is notable that, although the sector has developed a good deal in very recent years, its numbers of employees still reflect the historical dominance of Dutch, British, and American banking.

It is an evenly balanced sector in terms of gender, with a small male predominance everywhere except Ireland (slight female predominance) and Spain (heavy male dominance). It is among women that Spain and the USA obtain their opposite outlier positions.

SECTOR V: COMMUNITY AND SOCIAL SERVICES

Far larger proportions of people, and far more diversity among countries, are found in the quinary sector (V: social and community services) (see Figure 4.7),[4] with a very broad range of 10% to 20% of the core population working in this sector, Spain is a low outlier, primarily because of the low number of males in the sector; Sweden is an opposite outlier, because of its large number of females.

This is the first sector we have encountered where there is in general a female dominance, and a strong one; only Greece is an outright exception; Japan has only a very slight female majority. To understand fully both this sector and female employment in general we need to await our chapters on the family, the welfare state, and religion; but to anticipate those discussions, one might make the empirical observation that, as we move from high female to high male dominance, we move from all four secularized Lutheran Nordic countries, through the religiously pluralist Anglo-Americans, to the partly Catholic countries of core Western continental Europe, Shinto-Buddhist Japan, and Orthodox Greece.

In this sector there is both apparent pattern and considerable range, the latter mainly affecting the female population. The broad range of 5% to 15% of core population does not quite capture the full variation of female participation in this sector. Other countries with high female ratios also have high absolute numbers of women in this sector. The range among men is far narrower, one set between 4% and 7% of the core population catching all except Spain (below).

SECTOR VI: PERSONAL SERVICES

The sixth sector (VI: personal services) is everywhere small, similar in size to Sector IV (see Figure 4.8). A tight range of 4% to 7% of the core population excludes only France,

---

4 Again Belgium and Finland cannot be easily compared with the rest, as much of Sector VI is included here in their national statistics.

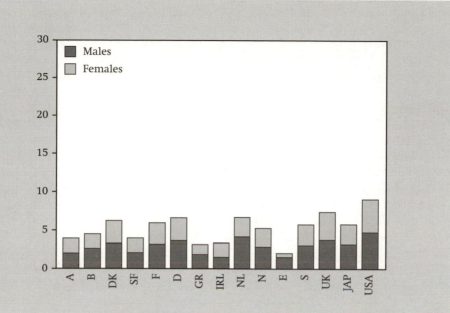

Fig. 4.6 Employment in business services (IV), c.1990, 15 countries

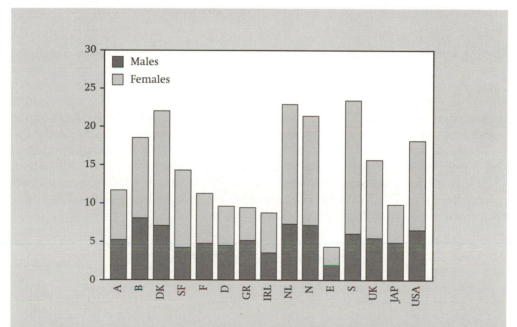

Fig. 4.7 Employment in social etc. services (V), c.1990, 15 countries

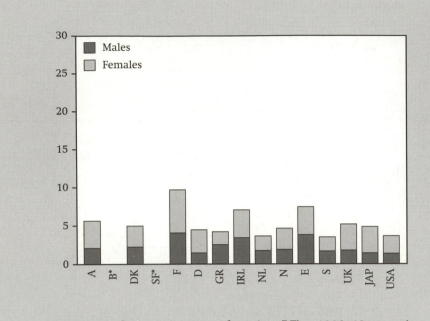

Fig. 4.8 Employment in personal services (VI), c.1990, 13 countries
* Data not available.

the only true upper outlier. There are some problems of definitions of what is included here rather than in Sectors III and V, and it is likely that some reorganization of categories would reduce France's score while raising it for Sector III; not too much should therefore be made of that country's relatively low ranking on III or high ranking here. Like Sector V, this is predominantly a female sector, with Greece and to a lesser extent Spain being exceptions. It is particularly female in Germany, the UK, and Japan, to some extent also in Austria and the USA. Overall, between 2% and 4% of the non-dependent population are women working in this sector. It is notable that, of the three countries coming below that level, two (Greece and the Netherlands) are cases where female participation is generally low, but the other is Sweden, where female participation in general is particularly high.

THE EMERGENCE OF THE BICEPHALOUS
GENDERED OCCUPATION STRUCTURE

We can now consider the implications of these findings. Our results have confirmed the basic outline of theses of post-industrialism, but with an important addition: in general, *men continue to be the population of industrial society* and, to a lesser extent, of the distributive sector adjacent to it. Women are filling relatively more places in the newly growing sectors, very predominantly in the clearly post-industrial case of Sector V, but also in Sector IV and the non-industrial (rather than post-industrial) Sector VI. Within the two peaks of mid-century compromise society (Sectors II and V), men specialize in the former and women in the latter. This is not however true of internal differences within Germany, where female employment is highest in southern regions with relatively low service-employment growth and strong industrial employment, of which women are part (Sackmann and Häussermann 1994). The feminization of the labour force that has taken place in nearly all countries is heavily associated with this factor. The combined impact of differential sectoral improvements in labour productivity and the growing impact of the citizenship component of the model in welfare state employment produced this bicephalously gendered occupational structure that distinguishes the current *fin de siècle* as a sub-species of industrial society. The segregation process, which in the initial (until 1960s) period took the form of a male population mainly engaged in manufacture and a married female one working on domestic tasks, is being replaced by a gender division of these two sectors, II and V.

We know that the predominantly male Sector II has been declining in size for some time and will probably continue to do so; we also know that the size of the *male* domestic and unemployed sector is increasing. Breadwinner industrial man is in decline. Meanwhile, dual-burden post-industrial woman is under some stress: Sector V employment may have peaked, at least to the extent that it is dependent on state-financed employment; and there is tension between women's domestic work and their paid work (the dual burden). These are some of the key tensions emerging as the stability once afforded to the mid-century compromise employment system by a certain balance between Sector II and Sector V shifts quite radically. It is difficult to see this current phase of post-industrial society as anything other than a temporary one in a constantly shifting disequilibrium. We shall encounter other ramifications of this tension in several later chapters.

Sector V is the key component of the services sectors, and indeed of the whole economy, for grasping both the character of change and the nature of cross-country differences. The proportions of non-dependent women engaged in other sectors apart from the domestic one are low and do not vary in very systematic ways; in Sector V the variation is large and seems to embody an embryonic pattern of country types. Furthermore, it is difference in this female Sector V population that accounts for most cross-national differences in general.

Esping-Andersen (1993*a*) goes so far as to argue that two distinct class structures are developing within this gender segregation of economic activity. Unlike many authors, he recognizes the importance of the distinction between social and community (Sector V) and personal (Sector VI) services. He therefore sees two types of post-industrial society emerging, leaning towards either a Scandinavian concentration on Sector V or what he sees as an American leaning towards Sector VI. The above analysis has not confirmed the latter part of this expectation. The USA scored highly on Sector V; this will often have been through employment in privately provided social and community services, but that distinction is not our focus here. More important, it did not score at all highly for Sector VI—though it is a sector undergoing considerable growth in that country (OECD 1994*a*). More support for Esping-Andersen's argument will be found if it is phrased in terms of high US—and also Japanese—activity in Sector III, though female predominance was not particularly striking there, and it is not a sector in which post-industrial theories are interested.[5] This was the most clear country-group finding of our survey other than those relating to Sector V.[6]

Singelmann (1978: ch. 5) argued that only the Western European countries fitted the original Clark model of a transition from agriculture through manufacturing to services. In North America services had begun to grow earlier, manufacturing industry never reaching the point of dominance it did in (northern) Europe. In Japan there had initially been a shift from agriculture into services, with the growth of industry following later. A major explanation for this could be the fact that neither the USA nor Japan required to have such a high proportion of their product traded internationally as the European countries—a factor that correlates highly with the size of the industrial sector (ibid., ch. 4).

THE EDUCATIONAL STRUCTURE OF DIFFERENT SECTORS

A central component of the post-industrial society hypothesis is that the move from the productive to the services sectors is part of a shift to a knowledge-based society. We can test this by comparing the educational level of the workforce in different sectors of the economy. If the simplest forms of the 'shift to services' thesis are right, we should see higher educational levels in Sectors III to VI than in I and II. However, if we take account of the refinements of sectoral divisions discussed above, we might doubt whether Sectors III and IV can so easily be distinguished from II, and whether Sector VI is really part of any move to post-industrialism. This would leave us predicting Sector V to have a significantly stronger educational profile than all the others. This would also be the expectation if the Bell thesis in its full form is right, it being within this sector that Bell's 'knowledge-based' occupations in education and medicine are concentrated.

Appendix Table A.4.2 presents material relevant for all countries in our group for which such data are available. It shows the numbers of persons in the two genders of different educational levels employed in the different sectors expressed *as percentages of the total paid workforce*.[7] For each country I have, where possible, distinguished five levels of educational achievement in order to give some graded estimate of the diversity of educational qualifications without becoming lost in too much detail. However, it must be noted that this enables us to make comparisons *within* countries, not between them, because *there is no assumption whatsoever* that level 1 in country A means the same as level 1 in country B, as countries present these statistics in very different ways. For example, a country with a high proportion of people who have attended only primary school (say Portugal) will include this category (or even those with no schooling at all) as its initial

---

[5] It is interesting that it takes two very different, though possibly convergent, forms. In the USA it is often the large numbers of part-time students and elderly workers who provide this large number of services ancillary to the distribution of goods, as part of a general societal emphasis on sales and marketing; in Japan its origins are more in aristocratic notions of large numbers of servants.

[6] Have these sectors been appropriately defined, or should we try to discern certain kinds of service being provided in both Sectors III and VI that should be linked together rather than with their company in their current sector? For example, shop assistants are here grouped in Sector III alongside telecommunications operators, waitresses in Sector VI alongside footballers. This raises issues going beyond our current concerns.

[7] It is not possible to calculate the educational level of those in unpaid domestic work.

educational category; a country which has had compulsory secondary education for most of the twentieth century (say Germany) will have its lowest category pitched at a considerably higher level. We cannot therefore use these data to draw such conclusions as 'Industrial workers in Portugal are better educated than those in Germany, because a smaller proportion of them finished education at level 1'. What we may do is to note if in a particular country the men and/or women of a particular sector have an unusually high (or low) educational level *relative to the rest of the country's own workforce* than elsewhere, but that is all. Therefore, in Appendix Table A.4.3 I have presented for each country the proportions of men and women of different educational levels working within a sector expressed in relation to the proportion of the total workforce at that level. Therefore, if 30% of a total workforce in a country is at educational level 4, but only 5% of men (or women) in Sector I is at that level, the appropriate figure for that level in that sector is −25.

It has not been possible to collect data on education by sector for Finland, Greece, Ireland, Switzerland, Japan, or the USA, and these therefore cannot be included in this discussion.

In examining the educational level of a workforce we are assuming that educational level achieved corresponds in some way to the level of education required by the work being done. This assumption may be false in a number of directions and in random ways, but two systematic sources of error in the assumption need to be considered in particular.

First, since educational levels have risen steadily in all countries over the past few decades, younger age cohorts have on average higher levels than their predecessors. If different sectors have recruited the bulk of their workforce at different periods of time, there will be a tendency for 'younger' sectors to have more highly educated workforces than 'older' ones merely as a result of this fact. There is clear evidence that such a periodization of recruitment has indeed taken place; as we have already seen, agriculture long since ceased recruiting large numbers of new workers; manufacturing industry ceased doing so more recently; business services and community and social services have grown very rapidly, the former since the 1980s, the latter from the 1970s until some time in the 1980s. We should therefore expect, *ceteris paribus*, that people working in these two sectors will have a higher educational level than those working in industry, irrespective of the use being made of these educational levels. Of course, it may well be the case that this extended education makes it possible for work processes in these sectors to tackle more complex tasks than if they had an older force. Nevertheless, conclusions we draw about the educational level of sectors have to bear this process in mind.

Second, it is sometimes argued that women tend to be employed at levels below their educational level; it is the 'price' that has to be paid for either part-time work or re-entry into the labour force following some years at home looking after children. This does not necessarily mean that use is not made of their educational level, merely that this level is not recognized. (For example, many women employed as secretaries carry out managerial or professional functions.) However, it does mean that evidence that women with a certain educational level are working in a sector does not necessarily tell us much about the level at which they are employed. But it is not our immediate concern here to examine levels of work; that is a task for Chapter 5. In general, for those countries that provide separate male and female data, women in the paid workforce have a lower educational level than men, but this often needs to be qualified by the observation that women are less likely to be at *either the highest or the lowest* educational levels. While women's relative absence from the highest levels might be explained by the fact that, in nearly all countries, their educational achievements have in the past been lower than men's (see Chapter 8), we can perhaps explain their relative absence from the lowest levels by the hypothesis that women with low education are less likely to enter the paid workforce at all. Female workers seem to lag educationally behind males particularly in Austria, Denmark, the UK, and Japan; less so in Belgium, Germany, Greece, Netherlands, Spain, and Sweden. In France and Norway it is not clear that they can be described as being behind at all; and in Belgium, Netherlands, and Sweden it is only at the very highest levels that they are so. No patterns at all seem to be revealed by these differences. This may be because they are mere artefacts of the different systems of calculation; however, some more interesting analysis is possible when we examine individual sectors.

SECTOR I

Almost everywhere Sector I has the lowest levels of education, meaning very high concentrations of people completing education at the lowest levels, small concentrations of those at the highest levels, and a strong taper between these extremes. Norway seems to be an exception, but we must remember that the primary sector here includes the large, modern, and recent industry of North Sea oil exploration. The French and German primary sectors also seem relatively well educated; in the German case this may simply be an artefact of the disaggregated character of the educational statistics.

The low position of the primary sector is largely accounted for by the position of women within it (working in agriculture, there being very few women in mining); male workers did not diverge so far from the national cross-sector average.

SECTOR II

Without exception Sector II had a weak educational profile in all countries for which we have data. It is always stronger than Sector I.

As we have already seen, few women work in this sector. Those who do have different educational profiles from their male colleagues, but in different patterns. In Austria, Germany, Sweden, the UK, and to some extent Denmark, Italy, and Spain, they are found predominantly at lower levels. In France they are *less* likely than men to be found in either the lowest or the highest educational categories. In Belgium and Spain there is a variant from this latter pattern in that relatively similar proportions of them as of men are found at the very highest levels.

SECTOR III

Sector III had in general a profile similar to that of Sector II, but at a somewhat higher overall level of education; in the theory underlying the concepts of the sectors, this is the one that stands closest to manufacturing. As we saw above, a major difference between the two is that far more women are employed in Sector III, and the gender breakdown of educational levels shows us that it is the female participation that pushes the sector above Sector II, though again women were less likely than men to be at either the lowest or the highest educational levels. Since overall numbers are far greater at lower levels than at higher, the former effect has the larger overall impact on the educational profile of the sector. There is no real gender difference in Italy and the UK, while in Denmark women's educational position seems low. It is notable that the Nordic countries, which often appear so similar in analyses of gender workforce participation, here have contrasting profiles.

SECTOR IV

The small Sector IV had everywhere a very high educational base, usually having the second biggest concentrations of workers from the highest educational levels. There are no exceptions to this pattern. Also, in every case the educational level of the relatively large number of women in the sector was considerably lower than that of the men, though in some cases the now familiar tendency for men to congregate disproportionately at the very lowest levels can also be seen; Austria showed this tendency for women to be grouped in the middle of the educational hierarchy particularly clearly. In general women's low position is explained by the fact that they are under-represented at the top one or two grades. This generalization applies equally to countries with high levels of female participation as to those with low; if anything, it is seen most strongly in those, like the Scandinavian cases, with high female participation.

SECTOR V

Sector V is the heartland of the Bell post-industrial thesis, and fully confirms his predictions. Its overall educational level is always very high, particularly large proportions and indeed absolute numbers of persons from the very highest educational levels being found in it. Concomitantly, there are fewer people from the lowest educational levels than in most other sectors. Even in Belgium, where our data for Sector V are 'diluted' by those from Sector VI, the effect of the community and social services component is sufficiently dominant to prevent any exception. Apart from France, where Sector IV had slightly more top-weighted profiles, it is always the sector with the biggest concentrations of highly educated personnel, most of them found in the education and health services.

This is the sector which is today dominated numerically by women, but they dominate it at the lower (though not the lowest) educational levels. This largely female employment sector has a predominance of males at its highest—though also its lowest—levels. The biggest educational gender gaps are found in the Netherlands and Norway—both being countries with particularly high employment in the sector. France and Germany again appear with a relatively narrow gender gap, as does Spain (where the sector is less well developed). The gender gap is usually less wide than in Sector IV.

SECTOR VI

Finally, Sector VI is shown to be one of poor educational qualifications. In some cases (Denmark, the Netherlands, and the UK) it resembles Sector I in its low overall educational level. In some other cases it is slightly higher overall than Sector I, resembling Sectors II and III. In France and Spain, on the other hand, the sector does not appear especially low. In both those countries there are, among men, surprising concentrations at the highest levels.

It is again a sector where women tend to be concentrated at low levels, in some cases at the very lowest (Austria, Germany, and the UK).

In educational profile, though not in gender, this sector resembles the 'pre-services economy' sectors I and II more than it does the services sectors IV and V. Although it is part of the overall growth of services so widely remarked, it shares few of the characteristics stereotypically associated with that growth, being associated with neither strong knowledge bases nor high technology. This was anticipated by our earlier argument that this sector was not *post*-industrial. By separating Sectors V and VI we can see that both Bell and his critics were right. In all countries *both* knowledge-based service sector jobs and low-paid, poor-quality jobs have grown. (The latter is of course also closely associated with the issues of temporary work discussed in the previous chapter. The simultaneous growth of high- and poor-quality employment raises questions of potential polarization and segmentation to which we shall return in Chapter 5.) It is Sectors IV and V (business, and community and social services) which fit the model of the services economy as a knowledge-based economy; Sector III only matches the theory to the limited extent that it usually has a slightly higher educational profile than Sector II; Sector VI does not fit the theory at all. Singelmann's account of the sectors, which rejects the common assumption that the different services sectors are somehow closer to each other than any of them is to the non-service sectors, is a more reliable guide than the conventional three-sector model. It enables us to see Sector III as being close to Sector II, and Sector VI if anything close to Sector I as a sector descending in essentials from traditional society. As we noted at the start of the chapter, many services occupations are of ancient origin; many, or their modern equivalents, are concentrated in Sector VI.

AN ALTERNATIVE SECTORAL CLASSIFICATION

If the knowledge base of economic sectors is seen as relevant to their designation as modern or advanced, we can suggest the following schema of ascending levels of advanced status, which, *mutatis mutandis*, fits nearly all our countries:

> Level 1: Sectors I and VI (agricultural and extractive activities and personal services);
> Level 2: Sectors II and III (goods production and related physical services);
> Level 3: Sectors IV and V (business, and social and community, services).

Each of these levels has a distinctive gender mix. The pair in the first level both have reasonably high concentrations of women (VI considerably more than I), and both have particular concentrations of women at the very lowest levels. With the exception of mining and some forms of wage-labour agriculture (in other words with the exception of its non-traditional component), this sector tends to conform to the concept of historical economies before the characteristic gendered distinction of later industrial society between paid and domestic work became fully established. To the extent that a growth of service sector employment takes the form of an increase in Sector VI, it is only partly related to a growth of the 'knowledge' economy and partly the reverse—a dualism which Appelbaum and Albin (1990) noted with respect to the USA some years ago.

Sectors II and III are the sectors of industrial society, with a relatively low overall educational level and a sharp gender segregation, though the distribution and transport of goods, together with communications, involve less exclusion of women from the paid workforce than does their manufacture. And it is the women in Sector III who primarily raise its overall educational level above that of Sector II.

Sectors IV and V emerge as the embodiments of the knowledge-based economy. However, there remains a problem in defining Sector IV as being particularly 'post-industrial', since (it will be recalled) it partly comprises services ancillary to productive industry, services which might in fact sometimes be carried on within firms belonging to Sector II. This leaves Sector V as the only quintessentially post-industrial case; as such the post-industrialism thesis becomes primarily one about the growth of social welfare. These two sectors together have the highest concentration of female participants and therefore involve the biggest break with the gender assumptions of industrial society —including its mid-century compromise form, though the growth of the welfare state which has generated the female employment of Sector VI is itself part of that form.

However, as we saw, both Sectors IV and V incorporate strong internal gender divisions through their highly contrasted gender education profiles—and, in general, the larger these sectors (or at least Sector V) are in a country, the bigger is its educational gender gap. This brings us to another paradoxical conclusion. Analysis of the overall gender structure of workforces showed, for virtually every country, smaller gender gaps than for any individual sector. The reason for this is that, although women are at considerably lower levels than men in Sectors V and VI, these sectors are overall at higher educational levels than the other sectors, and women are concentrated particularly heavily within them. A comparison of gender concentrations and educational levels in the two biggest sectors, II and V, establishes this particularly clearly. Gender segregation in no way ends with post-industrialism; but it does take new forms.

We should again query the status of the sectors. This chapter has treated them as social realities, as life worlds which people working in them inhabit. But they are in the first instance abstract constructions of statisticians, economists, and sociologists. To what extent do they have a social reality, demarcating a way of life, in the way that the agricultural component of the primary sector clearly does or did? In many respects far stronger divisions of that kind exist within sectors, or even within their component industries—for example, the division between manual and some kinds of non-manual work might divide a factory worker from an office worker within the same Sector II industry, but unite the former with a railway worker from Sector III. A particular question is raised over Sector IV: although closely allied to the work carried out in Sector II, it comprises a separation of a primarily non-manual and professional component of the work being carried out in the latter sector, leading the distinction between the two to start to resemble the difference between life worlds.

The issue here is one of organizational boundaries. As was discussed earlier in this chapter, whether or not a particular task is counted as belonging to a specific sector (and especially the boundaries between Sectors II, III, and IV) depends on the overall character of the employing organization; an accountant working for an engineering firm works in Sector II; if he sets up his own business but continues working as a consultant to the same engineering firm, he is transferred to Sector IV. The practices and strategies of organizations therefore play a part in the shaping of economy and society quite separate from processes of industrialization and de-industrialization. This is true of many other aspects of society too. We therefore need to continue our analysis within a different framework. The primary agency of such organization in modern society has been capitalism. This has been a further limb of mid-century compromise society, and in Part II we turn to consider it.

Meanwhile, we must bear in mind the main directions in which the world of work and the division of labour seem to be moving as we enter the new millennium: bread-winner, manual-working manufacturing man no longer dominates the occupational landscape and will never do so again; post-industrial woman remains under some stress from her dual-burden; the public social sector of employment which has powered most post-industrial, highly skilled, and also female employment has ceased to grow. Bell and his pessimistic critics seem both to be right: there is a large upward shift in the educational levels of the workforce, particularly in some service sectors; but much mass employment growth seems surprisingly dependent on rather low-skilled jobs in the distributive sector.

Part II

CHANGES AND DIVERSITY IN THE CHARACTER OF CAPITALISM

So far we have primarily considered work as an activity performed by people in different kinds of process and in various relationships to households. But work also takes place within a structure of organizations, and in all the societies with which we are here concerned the primary organizational form has been the capitalist firm. Consideration of work organization therefore brings us to the second master principle of operation of societies of the kind we are discussing.

Capitalist work organization in advanced industrial societies is based on three principles.

First, work is typically carried out within entities that are privately owned, owners having the legal right to take the profits that arise from the activity in question.

Second, labour itself, and the goods, materials, and services which it both uses in its activity and produces as the result of that activity, are allocated according to market processes; that is, they are bought and sold according to prices that purchasers are able and willing to pay.

Third, the typical capitalist enterprise constitutes a hierarchy or authority structure; when someone goes to work for an organization, he or she does not just exchange his or her labour power for a wage or salary, but also accepts subordination to a chain of command.

Not all work in the societies we are studying follows all these principles. First, not all work organizations are privately owned; there has been considerable variation in this, and the extent of variety comprises one of the sources of difference among countries. Some are organized as cooperatives or as charities, but most importantly many people work for the state or some other public body. In a capitalist society the state is ultimately owned by private individuals and organizations, and to some extent by other states acting through the market, because modern governments typically have large debts which are in effect repayable, interest-bearing loans held by private interests or foreign governments. Nevertheless, the distinction between private and public ownership has some important implications for the ways in which work is conducted.

Second, not all economic activity is traded on the market. As we saw in Chapter 3, much in the informal and household sectors is undertaken on market principles only in the very broad sense of following rules of barter or understandings of give and take, not the precise, money-based exchanges of the formal economy. Furthermore, in most societies most of the services and many of the goods which the welfare state provides are not allocated according to market principles. For example, the financing of an education system is in large part separate from the allocation of education.

Third, not only do family, community, and household networks not constitute hierarchies, but neither do all capitalist organizations; in very small firms proprietors give their orders to the tiny number of people working with them based directly on their position as the capitalist owner. In fact, some theories of capitalism would not include hierarchy among its basic principles at all. In pure neo-classical economic theory, the labour contract (the relationship between employer and employee) is viewed as any other contract: the employee agrees to carry out certain tasks in exchange for payment; it is an exchange, no power is exercised, and therefore there is no hierarchy. However, realistic managerial theory has long recognized the artificiality of this (Chandler 1977; Coase 1937). Employers and employees (whether individual or collective) could not negotiate over each piece of work to be done, not only without incurring large transaction costs, but also without undermining the whole concept of the right of management to direct and control. This has become embodied in the recognition by transaction costs economics of markets and hierarchies as the twin principles of operation of the capitalist firm (Williamson 1975, 1985). The latter concept indicates the continuity of the relationship and the capacity of management to give orders without constant renegotiation of contracts.

If we now return to the three principles of capitalist work organization set out above, we see that on the first two (private ownership and market allocation) there are areas of exception on both sides of the standard capitalist firm: below in the informal sector, and above in the state. On the third (hierarchy) however the only exceptions are found 'below' in small firms and the informal sector; state and other public employment nearly always takes place within hierarchies.

Within the model of the mid-century compromise society there is tension between the principle of capitalism and those both of the protection of community by sociological liberalism and of mass citizenship (the subjects of Parts III and IV). There is tension with the former, because it guarantees the autonomy of many activities (such as love, family relations, the observance of religious rules, the way in which free time is spent) from subordination to the principles of private ownership, formal market exchange and hierarchy. There is tension with mass citizenship in that rules of ownership, market allocation, and subordination to hierarchy all contradict the citizenship principle of free, unsubordinated, equal actors receiving goods and services as of right.

In their search for profit, capitalist owners and their agents (managers) must be assumed constantly to be seeking the extension of the areas of society accessible to appropriation through the principles of markets and hierarchies, and therefore to be attempting to invade areas of society protected by community and citizenship; these tensions are therefore lively, dynamic, with frequently shifting boundaries, and thus a matter of considerable sociological interest. Either the boundaries that protect other areas from capitalism are maintained by rules guaranteeing institutional autonomy, or they are broken down by the invasion of capitalist requirements. We must examine the form taken by and the limitations of these boundaries in the mid-century model, and subsequent developments over the past half-century.

In traditional societies various coalitions of non-capitalist elites and such guarantors of non-capitalist areas of activity as religious authorities often protected certain institutions from capitalist principles (unless they themselves used their power and resources to become capitalists, which was quite common in European history). In fully modern societies, however, in which most traditional alternatives to rational exchange have been broken down, there are likely to be only three important non-capitalist forces: residual local community and family, organizations of employees (i.e. trade unions), and the state. Both unions and the state tend to grow in significance during modernization, while the other forces decline in scope—though as we have seen in Part I and will examine again in Part III, in the mid-century model the family remained a major source of protection of aspects of life from capitalism through the gender division of labour. The role of the state as a defender of sociological liberalism is ironic and ambiguous; it may itself be one of the major forces limiting such liberalism, and in the history of Europe, Japan, and some other parts of the world it has at times definitely played such a role. Indeed, political as opposed to sociological liberalism is primarily concerned with the protection of society (and, in fact, the market) from the state. Unions of workers represented a distinctly new force in the power structure of modernizing society that had been framed by these earlier confrontations, and have usually had to struggle for their position against all others whose positions are disturbed by their emergence: capitalist forces, obviously; the state, which was often controlled by property-owning interests; and some aspects of traditional society.

In the only other form of industrial society experienced so far—state socialism, now almost disappeared—there were major differences in work organization: there was very little private ownership; markets, including those for labour, existed, but were heavily administered; particularly strong emphasis was therefore placed on the operation of hierarchy through state (or party) structures for the organization of work. In practice, as a number of studies showed (e.g. Phelps Brown 1977) the overall outcome in terms of the detailed occupational structure was not so different from that in capitalist economies. However, the fact that the market was not available to protect society from the state had serious implications for the conduct of daily life and of the economy. Since none of the societies under discussion in this book has undergone a period of state socialism (except Portugal for a brief period in the mid-1970s), we shall not be further concerned with this alternative. Several of our societies have had a period of Fascist or Nazi regimes, but these have been compatible with capitalism and do not raise particular issues for this part of our discussion.

Under the terms of the mid-century compromise, mass citizenship has also been reconciled with capitalism through certain segregations, or divisions of labour, guaranteed by the liberal principle. The welfare state compensated citizens for the inequalities produced by a capitalist organization of work; democratic governments could be used to impose constraints on capitalist power; and trade unions could protect employees' interests within the employment relationship itself. Within those constraints, business firms were left free to pursue their market and profit maximization goals. In practice there was considerable diversity in the extent to which these checks and balances operated, and there is no way of deriving a priori a list of the areas of society which will not be affected by capitalist rules. Differences in the development of the welfare state and the organization of interests will be considered in Part IV, but differences in the operation of capitalism itself will be considered here.

The debate over whether capitalism is compatible with democracy and citizenship has been long, and has been at the centre of political differences and conflicts in all the societies which we are here discussing. It is a fundamental organizing principle of the concept of the mid-century compromise that this should be possible; that is one of the main issues which the compromise is about. Furthermore, since most of the societies under discussion are both capitalist and have presented the world with its most advanced examples of entrenched democratic rights, the answer would seem to be a very simple 'yes'. However, it is worth examining the ways in which this has been achieved and diversity among these societies.

There is then the question of how things have changed since the high period of the compromise. Many authors associated with postmodernist theories would argue that the capitalist character of contemporary society has been diminished by the general diffusion of powers and capabilities associated with postmodern developments, rendering anachronistic the old antagonisms which the compromise expressed even as it tamed (Giddens 1994, 1998). Others, mainly from a Marxist background, see the division around capitalism continuing to be central, if obscured by social complexity. Others again, primarily neo-liberal economists and those associated with them, would see a reinforcement of capitalism in current trends to marketization, but would dissociate this from the implications of inequality, hierarchy, and conflict inherited from Marxian approaches to capitalism.

The argument is partly about whether capitalism as a form of work organization is *within its own terms* (as opposed to the outcome of its encounter with citizenship institutions) capable of being anything other than the expression of markets and hierarchy dependent on relations to ownership of property. This is partly a question of the structure of employment and the distributional implications of the operation of its markets and hierarchies, and partly about the position of capitalist organizations within social structure more generally. The former will be considered in Chapter 5, the latter in Chapter 6.

Chapter 5

CAPITALISM AND INEQUALITY IN WORK

The income that people derive from work profoundly conditions their level and style of living. There has long been evidence on these points from a number of societies. As an illustration we may take some recent research from Sweden, chosen because this is a society that not only has a low level of overall income dispersion (see below) but also, as we shall see in a later chapter, the world's most advanced and redistributive welfare state. Class differences that we observe in Sweden are probably found in more extreme form in other societies. Starrin and Svensson (1992) have shown that liability to various kinds of sickness and early mortality increase as one moves down the skill/authority hierarchy, as do certain indicators of social isolation (such as non-participation in political activity). For these purposes skilled manual workers sometimes have profiles closer to those of routine non-manuals, but at other times closer to unskilled manuals. Research in the UK during the late 1970s showed similar conclusions (Black 1982) concerning health. Starrin and Svensson (1992) also show that risks of poverty and unemployment increase as one moves down the hierarchy, and very similar results are reported for Germany (Ludwig-Mayerhofer 1992). Noll (1997) and Hradil (1997) have reported similar findings across a wide range of Western European countries.

Also, the positions that people occupy in work hierarchies usually affect their positions in other social relations. Finally, not only are educational achievements frequently used to allocate people to jobs, but (as we shall see in Chapter 8) different levels of work income deeply affect the kind of education people are able to give their children. To this we can add the fact that educational background inclines people to particular lifestyles, often reinforcing differences also embedded in income inequalities and differences of hierarchical position. As the research of the French sociologist Pierre Bourdieu (1979; Bourdieu and Passeron 1964) has shown, these lifestyles are passed on within families as a form of cultural capital. This further binds the relationship between work and life in general across generations.

This generalized social importance of occupational position is one of the two fundamental claims of sociological theories of social class. The second is that the multitude of different occupational positions that exist aggregate and cohere into a small number of identifiable classes. Where both these conditions obtain it can be claimed that the society concerned is a class society. The second condition is more problematic than the first and requires some detailed discussion before we proceed with our consideration of European societies.

THE CLASS ANALYSIS OF CAPITALIST SOCIETIES

More has been written at a theoretical level about social class than about any other theme in sociology, and there is a large diversity of approaches. We cannot here appraise this vast field in detail, but we do need to grasp its major outlines. The starting point has always been the distinction between the owners of property and those who work for them—originally Karl Marx's analysis of the economist's distinction between the factors of production, capital and labour, as social groups. This was clearly too simple a model. (In fact, Marx himself did not consider it to be an adequate representation of the complex class structure of the latter nineteenth century; rather, he believed it to be the direction towards which changes in the character of capitalism would eventually lead.) In the first decades of the twentieth century Max Weber (1922 (posth.)) had pointed out that the skills involved in certain kinds of occupation constituted a kind of property right. This made possible the analysis of classes based on something more than the ownership of literal property: position in the labour market.

The normal sociological approach to analysis of the inequalities of capitalist society is therefore to identify, first the distinction between property owners and those who live by their labour, and then a number of different types of occupations among the latter. (There are also, of course, differences among property owners, not only in terms of the size of property holdings; many people own small quantities of capital (such as a house) which do not make them 'capitalists' or relieve them of the need to be part of the labour force, but which might give them some interests in common with major property owners.) However, this is where we encounter the problem that the labour market produces a massive array of minutely distinguished positions, and the task of class theory to reduce this array to a small number of more or less clearly distinguished positions (Giddens 1980: ch. 6). Most current approaches to class analysis use considerations of property, authority, skill, and income to do this, and outline a number of (around eight) different classes. We need to give some attention to the main examples before we begin our empirical discussion.

Wright (1979), who stays closer to a Marxist approach than most contemporary sociologists, initially set up a nine-class model based on a simple criterion of relations to the means of production, giving him six classes: the bourgeoisie, managers and supervisors and workers in a straight capitalist hierarchy; with the *petite bourgeoisie* as a separate group in 'simple commodity production', and small employers and 'semi-autonomous' workers as intermediate between this form of production and the capitalist groups. However, he had difficulties operationalizing this and later (1985, 1997) amended it to the 12-class scheme shown in Table 5.1 which brings him away from a Marxist towards a more orthodox sociological approach. Attempts at using this empirically have not been very successful (G. Marshall *et al.* 1988).

Goldthorpe and Hope (1974) established a model which has been widely used, particularly but not solely in studies of social mobility (Erikson and Goldthorpe 1992; G. Marshall *et al.* 1988; G. Marshall and D. Rose 1990). This originated in estimates of popular perceptions of the relative standing of different occupations, subsequently subjected to sociological analysis in terms of systematic differences of property, authority, and skill. This scheme in its fullest and latest version (Erikson and Goldthorpe 1992) identifies eleven classes:

Table 5.1 *Class scheme of Erik Olin Wright 1985*

Owners	Non-owners				
1. Bourgeoisie	4. Expert managers	7. Semi-accredited managers	10. Unaccredited managers	**Managers**	
2. Small employers	5. Expert supervisors	8. Semi-accredited supervisors	11. Unaccredited supervisors	**Supervisors**	*Management assets*
3. Petit [sic] bourgeoisie	6. Expert non-managers	9. Semi-accredited workers	12. Proletarians	**Non-managers**	
	Experts	**Skilled employees**	**Non-skilled employees**		

Skill or accreditation assets

(I) higher-grade professionals, administrators, managers, and proprietors;
(II) lower-grade professionals, administrators, managers, and proprietors; supervisors of non-manual employees;
(IIIa) routine non-manual employees (administration and commerce);
(IIIb) routine non-manual employees (sales and service);
(IVa) small proprietors and artisans with employees;
(IVb) small proprietors and artisans without employees;
(IVc) farmers and smallholders;
(V) lower-grade technicians; supervisors of manual employees;
(VI) skilled manual workers;
(VIIa) semi- and un-skilled manual workers (not in agriculture);
(VIIb) agricultural and other primary production workers.

Kreckel (1992: 189–211) outlined a nine-class model, based on contemporary German social structure:

(1) senior managerial staff;
(2) the leading professions;
(3) skilled employees with particularly valued skills;
(4) skilled employees with competitive skills;
(5) skilled employees with skills in declining demand;
(6) semi-skilled manual workers and routine non-manual employees;
(7) unskilled workers in 'normal' jobs;
(8) marginalized workers with low skills and various social disadvantages;
(9) workers without rights, such as illegal immigrants or people in the black economy.

This brings together discussion of different levels of security with not only different levels of skill, which is primarily a hierarchy concept, but also the more market-driven idea of the different levels of competitiveness of different economic sectors. This fulfils his aim of a power-resource-based model. Note that the non-manual/manual boundary is only coincidental. Unfortunately, we cannot present data on countries according to this schema, because data are not collected in these terms, but it has many potentialities. For example, it takes separate account of marginalization within the labour market: issues of different degrees of security and segmentation—such as those discussed in Chapter 3—as well as hierarchy. This is valuable for the study of late twentieth-century societies. Relative security within work becomes a dimension separate from relationship to property, authority, or skill. For example, a waitress in a secure job with an established restaurant might be considered to be in a different class position from one with a zero-hours contract in an establishment threatened with bankruptcy, even if they are doing very similar work, on similar wages, and in the same relationship to the firms' hierarchies. There are however problems with taking this too seriously. First, as many workers in apparently well-established employment discovered in the 1980s, security can change very rapidly; and sometimes someone with an insecure contract might even be more secure in a de facto sense than someone whose very job security might make the market position of her employer risky. Also, in some countries—certainly in Kreckel's Germany—collective bargaining often extends to small, non-unionized firms the collective bargains reached in the established firms sector. For example, it has been found that in Germany workers who move into internal labour markets (skilled jobs in large firms) neither experience an initial wage boost nor higher than average wage growth within the firm (Hannan, Schömann, and Blossfeld 1990).

Sadly, despite the theoretical sophistication and value of these schemes, when their proponents come to do empirical work they often have little choice but to imitate popular discussion of class by slipping to crude three- or even two-class models. This is mainly because data are simply not available to realize the ambitions of the analytical schemes. For example, Giddens (1980) moves straight from consideration of the mass of positions possible within a labour market analysis to produce a rough-and-ready three-class scheme of: those in leading or dominant managerial positions; the middle ranks of administrators and non-manual workers; and manual workers.

Erikson and Goldthorpe (1992: ch. 2), in order to compare their findings with the cruder results of other research, often have to move from their full model to a three-class one, though they do so in a systematic way. They first produce a seven-class model by collapsing classes I and II into the very confusingly named 'service' class. (The term has now become almost universally accepted as the name for this top grouping in the population, even though its implications of 'servant' are the very opposite of the place occupied by this class.) Classes IIIa and b are brought together as a routine non-manual worker class; IVa and b as a *petite bourgeoisie*; class IVc remains as a farmers class; V and VI are joined to form a skilled manual class, while VIIa and b remain separate. This is then reduced further to a five-class model, combining I to III as a white-collar class ranging all the way from captains of industry to sales staff in shops; IVa and b remain as a class; IVc and VIIb combine as a farm class; V plus VI and VIIa remain as in the seven-class scheme. Finally they reduce further to give I–IV (non-manual); IVc and VIIb (farm); and the rest as manual.

However, for the rest of their work they use a rather different three-class model, which they describe as a hierarchical scheme (ibid. 45). Although its derivation from their previous analysis is unclear, it is this which is the one mainly associated with their work and which has been almost universally adopted by class analysts outside the Marxist tradition. It is more or less the same as the one Giddens established, but is more precise about the place of some groups (such as the self-employed) within the intermediate class. It runs:

I and II (service class);
III to VI (intermediate class);
VII (working class).

Most of all the work that we have been reviewing here is concerned with developing a model of class structure so that individuals can be given a class label. This is important for that large proportion of sociological research which tests theories whether the social class of individuals is associated with various life chances. For example, do persons from different classes have different possibilities of social mobility? Do they enjoy different levels of health or longevity? However, for other work we want to identify classes as such, not just demonstrate to which class an individual belongs. Aage Sørensen (1991) identified this as the difference between class theories that identify positions independently of the characteristics of the persons occupying them, and those that are concerned to allocate individuals to positions. The work of the Goldthorpe and Erikson tradition is designed for the latter; it is less well adapted for the former.

For example, a very important class for the analysis of social power is the group of wealthy property owners and senior managers who make major decisions and extract high incomes. They are however very small in number; they are part of a larger group of senior managers and professionals in Goldthorpe's class I; when researchers collapse classes I and II to make the general 'service class' which has now become established as the 'top' social class in much sociological research, they are in effect claiming that there are no relevant differences between this group and such people as hospital nurses and schoolteachers (who are members of class II). This is clearly absurd, and the researchers are unlikely to be claiming anything of the kind. What they are saying is that, for the purposes of the kind of research they do, there is no need to take account of such differences (Evans 1992). This is largely a function of the very small size of the category of owners and controllers of large investment property, which means that they are unlikely ever to disturb statistical significance. This is not however helpful if we want to study the actions of the group, which can have an importance quite disproportionate to its size.

Similarly, Goldthorpe (1983), G. Marshall *et al.* (1995), and others have been very concerned to demonstrate statistically that they do not need to take account of the occupational position of working women who have partners in the labour force. The rule of this research approach is to take the occupation of the principal male earner of a household only. The reason why this case has to be argued so strongly is that it becomes very difficult to allocate an individual to a class if more than one household member's job has to be considered in making the allocation. For the research that these sociologists do, the gain in accuracy in the analysis of individuals' economic circumstances that would be afforded by trying to make such estimates is outweighed by the troublesome complexity of the task. However, if our research question concerns not allocating individuals to a class, but the particular position within the society of distinctively female occupations, the standard class analysis cannot help us.

For our current purposes we need both approaches. It is important to be able to learn from the class analysis literature that individuals from different, broadly defined classes have contrasting life chances and lifestyles. This confirms the thesis that class membership is an important variable for understanding contemporary societies. We do however also need to know which classes exist as social forces within those societies, and for this we need a different but related approach.

A fundamental part of Weber's (1922: 678 ff.) contribution to the study of class was to distinguish between three different ways in which societies are ordered: class, defined as objective economic position as already noted; status, defined as the subjective perception of different social positions and their vertical ranking in relation to each other; and party, defined as the capacity of different groups to organize to press their interests. As often with Weber's ideas, he starts with a particular historical observation and moves from there to produce general theoretical categories. He observed how in the Germany of his day capitalists clearly had the advantages of class. However, traditional landowning groups, although declining economically, maintained a superior position within the society because they were perceived by many people to be a superior group (status). At the same time, manual workers, who were economically weak and perceived as inferior, exercised a kind of power by the fact that they organized themselves in parties and trade unions: hence, class, status, and party. The three concepts can then be entirely detached from these particular cases and used in many different circumstances.

The class analysis approach appropriately restricts itself rigorously to the first of the Weberian ideas, class itself (G. Marshall *et al.* 1987). However, if we are studying classes as actors we need to add considerations of status and party as well. For Weber, classes are objective, passive identities, characteristics attributed to a population by the sociological observer, and therefore not necessarily motivating action at all. It is primarily status, which concerns subjective perception, which enables people to perceive themselves as part of a wider group and to consider that group in relation to others. (Party is best left aside until Part IV, where we consider political parties and economic interest organizations. We shall then be able to return to a fuller discussion of class and related issues in Chapter 15.) We therefore need a class/status scheme that we can use in examining the structure of the societies of interest to us.

Sociological theory often sees a sharp distinction between the way in which class structures are organized in industrial-capitalist as opposed to earlier social forms. In feudal or landed aristocratic societies, it is accepted that status structures were defined by social and political elites and frequently incorporated in legal codes. The word Weber used and which is translated into English as status was *Stand*, which more strictly refers to the estates or formal, legally defined social orders of post-feudal Europe. There was always a problem of lack of fit between the formal structure and the social reality; indeed often legal codes were developed precisely because some groups were refusing to keep their place in the social order, and threatened ruling elites therefore used the law to restrain them. (These incongruities were often celebrated in the literature of the periods concerned: for example, the propertyless aristocrat (Don

Quixote) or the *bourgeois gentilhomme* of Molière's play of that name.) This is seen to have changed with the coming of capitalism, which is considered to rely on the labour market to create its social order. Class in the strict economic sense comes into its own, and status becomes a set of solely social perceptions without formal authoritative force.

I believe this to be an error. Throughout Europe capitalism emerged from societies that had been ordered on the *Stand* principle, and the emerging forms were initially interpreted in those terms; for example, the idea of master and servant was often used to define employer and employee. Then basic class divisions which emerged from capitalist structures themselves became embedded in legal orders: these were property-rooted definitions of citizenship entitlements, the right to suffrage most of all. Furthermore, most firms defined their employees into categories: essentially, the basic division between manual and non-manual, though also skill divisions among the former, and later distinctions between managerial and clerical workers. Some of these distinctions also found their way into legal codes. First, the dangerous nature of much manual work, combined with the fact that manual workers in most countries developed a capacity for organization, led to the development of legislation defining workers' rights to safety and various kinds of social protection. Second, partly through the same process, partly through the development of privileges for certain kinds of non-manual and skilled manual workers, pensions and social security systems were developed, giving different rights to people in different occupational categories. Third, educational routes leading to different kinds of certification and qualification, organized or at least regulated by state authorities, further embedded certain occupational categories in law. Finally, the phenomenon of 'party' intervened, and the organization of employees (which often reflected important divisions among occupational types) and of employers were subject to various legal orders—sometimes making them illegal, sometimes legitimating them, sometimes making use of them in and giving them a formal place in the organization of interests of the state.

As in the post-feudal period, certain basic themes of this kind appear right across Western Europe. They were however all implemented by political authorities, usually working alongside employers' concepts of their organizations, at the nation-state level. Partly for deeper historical reasons, partly as a result of new political choices, partly as a result of different constellations of power, differences emerged in the way that basic themes were structured, and these were differences at nation-state level. Furthermore, to revert again to party, all these issues could be and were the objects of political struggle, with varying outcomes. And these struggles would be national political ones. It is this process, combined with the tendency for class positions to be related to levels and types of educational achievement, which reduces the potential mass of different labour market positions to a small number of identifiable classes, varying somewhat country by country (because of the role of political and legal factors in drawing the definitions), but also bearing certain basic similarities throughout the industrial world.

From these complex and protracted processes emerged the patterns of occupational types typical of industrial capitalism. The basic framework was that of the large industrial firm, with some ranks of management and associated professionals, clerical workers, and manual workers ranked by skill levels. This is basically similar to the objective categories produced by the class analysis approach. When G. Marshall (1997: ch. 1) and Evans (1992) demonstrate that their class categories are good predictors of, for example, the degree of employment security enjoyed by different occupational categories, they are often demonstrating a link between class and status.

Status classes are therefore constituted by certain differences in property- and labour-market positions, the educational, cultural, and material-income differences associated with these, and certain authority-driven categorizations (from both legal and employer sources). To the extent that these different sources of differentiation produce similar cleavages, there will be an identifiable class structure. If they run in many different directions, any structure will be far less perceptible and have little social reality. If there are some direct contradictions (between, say, what the labour and property markets are producing and what is produced by private and public authority sources), there is probably some major change in process.

TYPES OF EMPLOYMENT IN CAPITALIST ECONOMIES

We can now consider the main structure that this approach gives us. First, the figure of the entrepreneur is an elusive occupational category in modern capitalism. As we encountered in Chapter 3, the formal category of the self-employed or even of employers does not correspond to this. First, many people who are self-employed in fact lack property and cannot be approximated to the category of employers. Second, many capitalist entrepreneurs have as their employment status the role of employee in the organizations they control. This is because in the modern enterprise entrepreneurship is closely related to position at the head of the managerial hierarchy, and blends imperceptibly with the upper, then middle, then lower ranks of that hierarchy. It is virtually impossible to identify the role of capitalist as an occupational group. This is further intensified by the fact that, in most societies, many if not most of the shares that constitute capitalist ownership are held by persons quite external to the firm as an organization—in fact shareholders are usually other organizations rather than persons. Scott (1997: 278–9) identifies four different types of capitalist in contemporary economies (he calls them types of capitalist 'situations' in recognition of the fact that specific individuals might occupy more than one of these positions). There are the classic owner-entrepreneurs; rentier capitalists who passively own a portfolio of holdings but do not engage actively in their management; senior executives and directors who, whether or not they actually own business assets, have the authority to determine how they are invested; and finance capitalists who hold multiple directorships or executive positions in a number of enterprises.

In all the societies being discussed here capitalism has been institutionalized in this way. As we shall see in Chapter 6, this institutionalization takes diverse forms, but for the present, when we are discussing the occupational structure of capitalism, we find ourselves dealing with managers, not entrepreneurs, as the leading category.

Two fundamental principles are at work in the hierarchy of a modern work organization: that of managerial authority (different levels and types of responsibility); and that of skill (where many different types and levels can be identified). These principles are different but overlap heavily. First, the possession of a skill may endow its owner with a certain kind of authority, or at least a defence against authority being exercised by someone outside the skill group: only he knows how a particular task can be carried out. Second, the exercise of authority, once classified as leadership or management, becomes a kind of skill itself.

Marxist sociologists frequently predict the end of the skill distinctions that divide employees into so many categories (e.g. Braverman 1974). However, most empirical research suggests that only a minority of jobs has been deskilled, the majority moving in the opposite direction, leading to ever more complex skill breakdowns of the workforce (e.g. Kern and Schumann 1987; G. Marshall 1997; Penn 1990; Penn, Rose, and Rubery 1994 (especially Gallie 1994)).

Particularly important among skilled occupations have been those called the professions. These are groups of specialists who have been able to convince authorities and the general public that their bodies of knowledge are so expert that only practitioners of the skills concerned can manage them. (Medical practitioners and lawyers are the most obvious examples.) There has always been tension between the professions and capitalism, as the claims of the former involve protection from both market forces and external managerial authority, and a source of social power and legitimacy that is not based on the ownership of wealth. At the present time that tension is at a high point because in most industrial societies there are strong pressures to extend capitalist systems of organization to a growing range of institutions (Burrage 1990; Collins 1990a; Freedland 1999; di Luzio 1999). Within the state sector, where many members of professions now work, this primarily means privatization, but also the reinforcement of managerial hierarchy and shadow markets, both of which create antagonisms between managers and professions, as has been seen for example in the British health service (Dent 1993). However, for most of the history of industrial society capitalist and managerial groups and members of the professions have had an amicable relationship. Members of professions often establish themselves as capitalist enterprises; many managers regard themselves as members of various professions—especially in France, Germany, and Scandinavia where managerial occupations have a strong element of formal educational preparation.

Bodies of knowledge developing at the present time and under the control of large corporations are less likely to develop the full model of professional autonomy. A good example would be computer specialists, whose skill categories and job divisions are defined by the capitalist corporations which produce either the hard- or software they use or by the organizations within which they work, as a German study shows (Hartmann 1993). This author saw a division in the occupational group between very high-level specialists, most of whom worked in universities, and those doing more managerially controlled, though hardly proletarian work, in firms. There is a kind of 'Fordism' in process in relation to professional work within capitalist corporations, at the very time that the end of Fordism has been proclaimed in much sociological literature.

Beneath the small but important ranks of management and professions the majority of the workforce is ranked according to various criteria of skill and delegated authority. The former usually corresponds to levels of educational achievement reached, and these are more or less ranked with reference to the gradings of the education system. This embodies one particularly difficult point, where the lower-level achievements of the general education system start to overlap with vocational qualifications gained in training processes which have stepped aside from the general hierarchy. Do the former somehow rank higher because they are the lower rungs of a ladder which leads up to the highest levels of educational attainment, or do vocational skills overtake these lower-level general competences? The division overlaps quite closely that between junior non-manual workers and skilled manual ones, one of the most difficult points in the structure for class analysis. Interestingly, the contrasting position in the organizational hierarchy of a firm of the two types of work raises issues similar to their educational differences: the lower non-manual jobs are in a sense part of an office hierarchy that leads to the top levels of management; on the other hand, skilled manual workers are often of more importance to the firm.

In general therefore the main model of classes embodied in both official perceptions and sociological research parallels the internal structure of a large manufacturing firm, with separate offices and factory and overlapping hierarchies within each. It is therefore closely tied to industrial society, and we should expect it to be disturbed by departures from that form of society.

There has recently been some debate, especially in the UK and USA, about the existence of an 'under-class', existing below the levels of the unskilled. The term usually designates people whose general competence level is so low that they cannot organize their lives: they drift between jobs, unemployment, violent crime and, in the case of women, childbearing outside settled partnerships. Much of the writing about this is political rather than sociological (e.g. Murray 1990), with the authors' main aim often being to argue for tough state treatment of these groups to make them accept work discipline. Against this, other authors (e.g. Mann 1992) contend that unstable working careers are produced, not so much by personal characteristics, as by the instability of employment opportunities following the development of flexible and insecure forms of work of the kind discussed in Chapter 3. Below there will be some discussion of this latter possibility, but it is not possible here to evaluate hypotheses concerning the possible psychological characteristics of any part of the workforce.

WORK AND SOCIAL CLASS SINCE THE MID-CENTURY

The mid-century compromise model presented a society in which class divisions were clear and recognizable, but muted in their implications for inequality. It was not a model of classlessness, which would be quite different. The core concept of the compromise was that different, rival elements persist but come to terms with each other. In this sense classes resemble the institutions engaged in the sociological liberalism which will be the focus of Part III: distinct from each other, aware of their difference and potential hostility, but developing means of cooperation. However, in the case of classes the primary mechanisms for achieving the *rapprochement* were the instruments of citizenship which we shall consider in Part IV: political democracy (Chapter 11), which extended formal citizenship beyond the ranks of property owners and therefore contradicted some elements of capitalist domination; the organization of interests (Chapter 12), especially those of labour, which enabled capitalist domination to be moderated within both the workplace and the wider polity; and the welfare state

(Chapter 13), which ameliorated the impact of income inequalities stemming from the labour market and also claimed to break the cycle of inter-generational transmission of occupational positions through extending educational opportunity (Chapter 8). Clearly, we cannot gain a full view of the state of class relations under the compromise until we have examined all these other issues. Our task in this chapter is to consider the starting point: the structures of hierarchy and inequality that stem from the organization of the work process itself.

As in Chapter 4, for the mid-century period itself only a brief analysis can be made because insufficient data are available on a reasonably comparative basis. The International Labour Office (ILO) has regularly produced a very basic breakdown, though it has a major defect in not recognizing different skill categories among manual workers, and it is certainly not free from problems of inconsistencies among countries and over time. However, there is little else available, and the relevant ILO data for both 1960 and the mid-1990s for as many as possible of the countries in which we are interested are shown in Appendix Table A.5.1. Figure 5.1 shows the changes that have taken place in each of the major occupational classes identified. Almost everywhere the ranks of both professional and managerial personnel have risen, the former considerably so; in growing the professions have also recruited a considerably higher proportion of women. The ranks of junior non-manual workers have similarly grown and recruited women. Manual workers remain the single largest category, though they have declined in numbers almost everywhere.

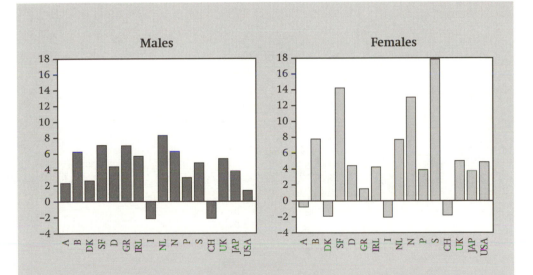

Fig. 5.1a Change in proportion of professional and technical workers, 1960–1995, 16 countries

Notes: For Belgium, the 1995 figure is for 1992; for Germany and Ireland, the 1995 figure is for 1989; for Portugal, the 1995 figure is for 1991; for the UK, the 1995 figure is for 1993.

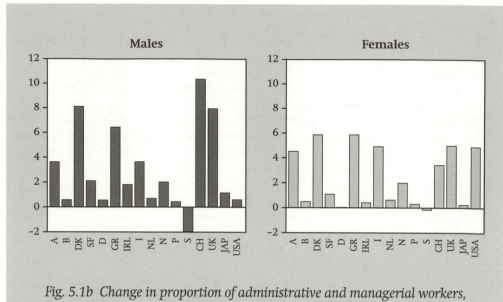

Males   Females

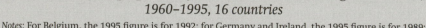

*Fig. 5.1b Change in proportion of administrative and managerial workers,
1960–1995, 16 countries*

Notes: For Belgium, the 1995 figure is for 1992; for Germany and Ireland, the 1995 figure is for 1989;
for Portugal, the 1995 figure is for 1991; for the UK, the 1995 figure is for 1993.

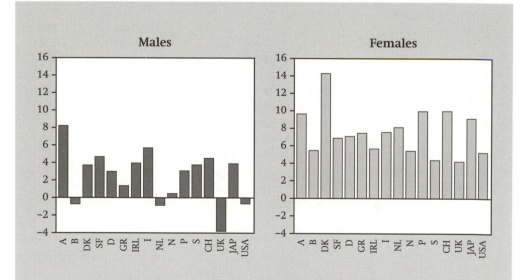

*Fig. 5.1c Change in proportion of junior non-manual workers,
1960–1995, 16 countries*

Notes: For Belgium, the 1995 figure is for 1992; for Germany and Ireland, the 1995 figure is for 1989;
for Portugal, the 1995 figure is for 1991; for the UK, the 1995 figure is for 1993.

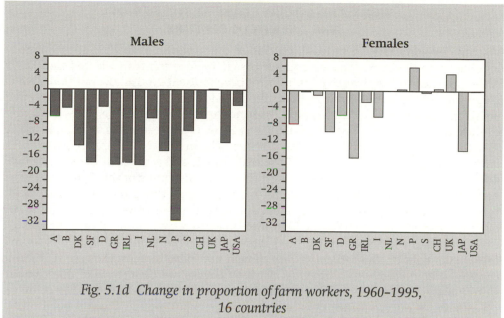

*Fig. 5.1d Change in proportion of farm workers, 1960–1995,
16 countries*

Notes: For Belgium, the 1995 figure is for 1992; for Germany and Ireland, the 1995 figure is for 1989;
for Portugal, the 1995 figure is for 1991; for the UK, the 1995 figure is for 1993.

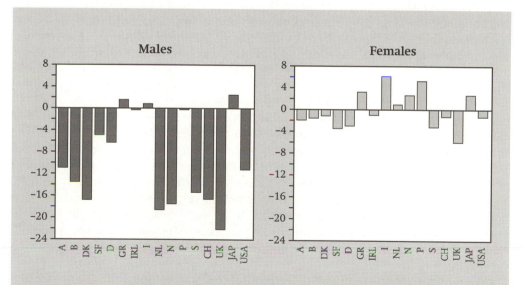

*Fig. 5.1e Change in proportion of manual workers, 1960–1995,
16 countries*

Notes: For Belgium, the 1995 figure is for 1992; for Germany and Ireland, the 1995 figure is for 1989;
for Portugal, the 1995 figure is for 1991; for the UK, the 1995 figure is for 1993.

WORK AND SOCIAL CLASS AT THE END OF
THE TWENTIETH CENTURY

We can develop a more detailed discussion of the situation at the end of the century, looking at individual countries and sectors, if we use figures collected nationally. Although they follow diverse definitions of occupational groups, overall they give us greater insight into the hierarchies of authority and skill. The statistics will be found in detail in Appendix Table A.5.2, and are summarized in Figure 5.2. This shows the overall distribution of 'class' positions for as many of our countries as provide usable data through their national statistical services.[1] The material is all drawn from official national statistics in the censuses of the early 1990s, and as a result the criteria used differ in disappointing ways. At their best they do follow much of the above account of occupational differences: they separate managers and the professions, and divide senior from lower levels of management and from routine non-manual workers; two or three grades of manual skill are identified. In various cases some of these groups are elided, though the boundary between manual and non-manual is usually clear. We often have data on the self-employed, though as I have already warned, this group cannot be identified with a capitalist class. Of course, we cannot make fine comparisons between countries; for example, we have no way of knowing whether someone classified as a middle rather than a senior manager in Denmark would be similarly classified in Belgium.

The manual working population in the early 1990s ranged from 30% to 51%; within Europe from 30% to 43%. Note the different positions of some otherwise similar societies: Denmark's structure was very different from that of Sweden, Belgium from the Netherlands. The class is no longer a majority one in any advanced industrial society with the exception of Japan (where its majority status is very marginal). However, the diversity among the other societies suggests that there is no simple evolutionary trend. Thus, although, as we saw in previous chapters, Germany remained a considerably more industrial economy than the USA, the two had similar proportions of manual workers—with Germany in fact having the smaller share.

Among those countries that report separate figures for different degrees of manual skill, only the three big European states—Germany and to a lesser extent the UK and France—had a majority of skilled workers among their manual workforces. This is a point where we must beware of different definitions of the groups, assessments of levels of manual skill being notoriously difficult to standardize. However, it is unlikely that Germany is counting a wider range of workers as skilled than other countries, that country's system for providing and accrediting skill being particularly rigorous. Furthermore, the UK is the only country to report three different levels of manual skill, and it is therefore unlikely that its definition of skilled workers is more generous than elsewhere.

Different national systems also make it difficult to assess the relative sizes of different grades of non-manual worker. We shall therefore limit our attention to those that identify three levels of managerial employees. This should at least enable us to estim-

---

[1] Greece and Spain, for which class data are available for the non-agricultural economy only, have to be left out of the general comparison; they can however be included in subsequent discussion of individual sectors.

ate in a broadly comparable way the size of senior categories and routine ones (the two extremes of the non-manual range). Some countries, even though they make this separation, amalgamate senior managerial and professional categories. We therefore have to combine these two for all cases. This combined managerial and professional category seems to vary widely in size between 5% and 35% of all employment, between 5% and 27% in Europe; it was notably low in Germany and the UK, notably high in the USA. It is likely that different national methods of counting explain at least part of this difference, especially for those countries (Denmark, France, Germany, Sweden) that count the self-employed as a separate category rather than assimilating them to the hierarchical rankings.

The junior non-manual level amounted to around 20% to 25% (less in Sweden), and was thus relatively similar across countries.

Many of these patterns look different when we take account of gender. If, as was common among studies of social class until a decade or so ago, we look only at males, the proportion of the workforce in manual work rises to above 40% in all countries except Denmark, where it remained slightly lower. It is also notable that among men the proportion of skilled manual workers was higher than of unskilled everywhere except Denmark again (where it was nevertheless only slightly below 50%), Sweden, and the USA. Non-manual workers are disproportionately male at senior and middle levels only. The male workforce therefore still reproduced, in virtually all countries, the mid-century pattern of the capitalist hierarchy: an essentially managerial form of non-manual work and a majority of manual workers, but with the skilled component of the manual working class rarely being smaller than the unskilled as it would be in the traditional model.

The female workforce presents the mirror image of this: the manual working class was below 32% of the female working population in every country except Germany, Sweden, and Japan, and only in Germany was it above 50%. The female manual workers who did exist were overwhelmingly unskilled; only in Germany did the skilled account for more than one-quarter of all manual women. The non-manual majority was heavily weighted towards the junior levels. In every country there was a smaller proportion of female than of male employees in the professional and managerial groups, even though the numbers of the former were often swollen by large numbers of teachers and nurses.

If we see the classical capitalist hierarchy of authority and skill as extending down from non-manual to manual ranks, the gender analysis is highly ambiguous. Women are more likely to be found in non-manual occupations than men, but within both, manual and non-manual, they are in the more junior positions. This echoes ambiguities found in Chapter 4. But there are grounds for questioning the idea of ranking non-manual over skilled manual, as we shall see in due course. For the present we need only note how junior non-manual workers and skilled manual workers are more or less different gender classes.

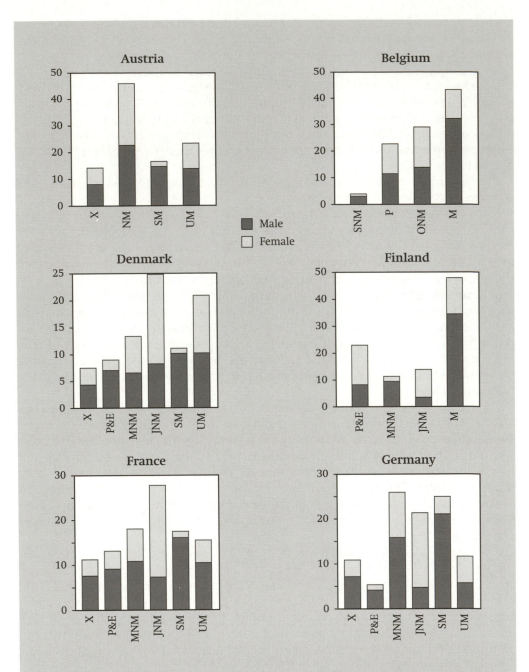

Fig. 5.2 *Occupational classes by gender, national definitions, c.1990, 11 countries*

Key: JNM = junior non-manual; M = manual; MNM = middle-ranking non-manual; NM = non-manual;
ONM = other non-manual; P = professional; P&E = professional and managerial; P&T = professional and
technical; SM = skilled manual; SNM = senior non-manual; SSM = semi-skilled manual;
UM = unskilled manual; X = self-employed and family workers.

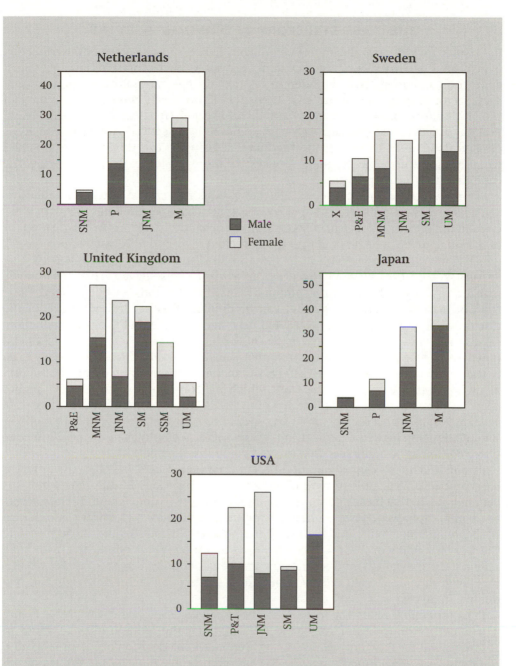

Fig. 5.2 (continued)

Key: JNM = junior non-manual; M = manual; MNM = middle-ranking non-manual; NM = non-manual; ONM = other non-manual; P = professional; P&E = professional and managerial; P&T = professional and technical; SM = skilled manual; SNM = senior non-manual; SSM = semi-skilled manual; UM = unskilled manual; X = self-employed and family workers.

THE CLASS STRUCTURE OF ECONOMIC SECTORS

In Chapter 4 we also saw the importance of considering separately the different sectors of economic activity. We can use the same analysis (carrying forward the same sector definitions and numbers) to consider processes of change in class structures, assuming that Sector II continues some characteristics of the more industrial economy of the mid-century into the current period. As Kreckel (1992) and Esping-Andersen, Assimakopoulou, and Van Kersbergen (1993) have discussed, the prototypical analysis of class structure is heavily tied to the manufacturing sector; the further one moves from this, to for example the public services, the more one leaves the parameters of the capitalist structure of relations.

Esping-Andersen (1993a: 24–6) argues that two distinct class structures are developing within this gender segregation of economic activity, and combines this with a discussion of Fordism. He sees men being employed primarily within the 'Fordist' sector of manufacturing industry (and the closely related distributive Sector III (ibid. 42–5)), while women remain largely within the post-industrial service economy (including Sectors IV and VI as well as V). However, our evidence here suggests that this is partly inaccurate. Sector III is not a predominantly male sector, and it is by no means clear that all manufacturing employment can be dubbed 'Fordist'. Indeed, much of the discussion of post-Fordism has been about new methods of manufacturing production. He also does not consider the extensions of Fordist management within services employment. As we noted in Chapter 3, women who are in paid work are less likely to be in the 'non-Fordist' self-employed category than men; they are often part-time, but usually it is part-time employee status work, which is a 'Fordist' employment type. Further complications are raised by the fact that some Fordist theories include the welfare state as an aspect of such a society, providing specialized, rationalized services to families. The relationship between Fordism and female Sector V employment is therefore complex and cannot be easily seen in terms of two different models.

Esping-Andersen's central idea of different class hierarchies, based on the different organizational structures of typical employment institutions in different sectors, is very helpful, in that these differences are important keys to understanding class in contemporary capitalism. However, he oversimplifies. Managerial, supervisory, and clerical posts are assumed to be limited to the Fordist sectors (II and III) (ibid. 24, 55), despite the fact that many of these will be employed in various service industries; while all scientists, professionals, and technicians are seen as employed in the post-Fordist sectors, even though in reality many (especially scientists and technicians) work in productive industry.

I shall therefore retain the more diversified analysis developed in Chapter 4. Figure 5.3, which is drawn from Appendix Table A.5.2, shows data similar to those in Figure 5.2 but for different sectors. (I have excluded consideration of Sector I, because the definition of workforces in agriculture is often problematic, while the sector has now become very small.)

Productive Industry

Sector II (manufacturing, utilities, and construction) continued to show the familiar class profile of standard sociological theories of capitalism, with well over 50% of the workforce manual. The range of variation in the proportion in manual work was much lower than for the economy as a whole. For the latter, the ratio of the most manual (Greece) to the least (Netherlands) was 2.14. If we exclude Greece as not a typical advanced industrial society, the outlier becomes Japan (ratio of 1.73 to the Netherlands). Within industrialized Europe the biggest range was, surprisingly perhaps, between the Netherlands and Sweden, with a ratio of 1.51. Within Sector II Spain had the highest proportion of manual workers and Denmark the lowest (ratio of 1.51). Spain and Greece both being outliers reinforces the role of a simple development thesis in explaining these differences. If we exclude these two countries as not being 'advanced industrial', the outlier was again Japan, but this time joined by Austria (ratio of only 1.22 to Denmark). These differences are small. Most of the diversity in proportions of manual workers is therefore explained by differences in other sectors rather than by the size of Sector II.

As with the general pattern, men were over-represented in the upper levels of both manual and non-manual hierarchies. Women did not reproduce the classic industrial society class pattern, but were heavily concentrated in routine non-manual work, with some presence in unskilled manual, and very little else. As in the general data, Germany was unusual for its concentration of skilled manual posts, and although as elsewhere women were more likely to be found in unskilled than skilled manual work, the differential is not as high as in other countries. Only the UK approaches German levels of skilled women.

There is evidence from other studies (Prais 1981; Steedman, Mason, and Wagner 1991) that there is a trade-off between managerial staff and the proportion of manual workers who are skilled: if workers are skilled, fewer managers are needed to supervise them. The observation originated in contrasts between British firms, which employ large numbers of managers, and German firms, which have a wider range of skilled workers but fewer managers. Across the six countries which provide both three-category data for professional and managerial staff and for skilled manual workers, there is some support for the hypothesis that, the higher the percentage of skilled workers among manual workers in general, the lower the overall proportion of managerial and professional persons employed—Germany and the USA constituting extreme cases.

The Distributive Sector

Organizations in Sector III have an apparatus of managerial and clerical staff with ancillary professionals similar to that of Sector II, but the workforce that provides the final output is engaged in moving objects around rather than fabricating them. The work of, say, shop assistants is difficult to align with either the routine non-manual or the manual work of a factory. National statistical services mainly allocate shop workers to routine non-manual categories, who indeed usually have this status in firms that use formal definitions of manual and non-manual workers. Other front-line workers in this sector—in transport and communications, with such posts as drivers, postal staff, and telephone operators—are variously allocated. There is considerable arbitrariness here, as is reflected in the fact that there was a wider range than in either Sector II or aggregate national data in the cross-national ratios for proportions of manual workers from 2.15 (Sweden) to 1.00 (Austria).

This all results in a system where the mass workforce comprised a large number of junior non-manual workers rather than manual ones. As in Sector II, in all countries other than Greece there were heavy concentrations of female junior non-manual

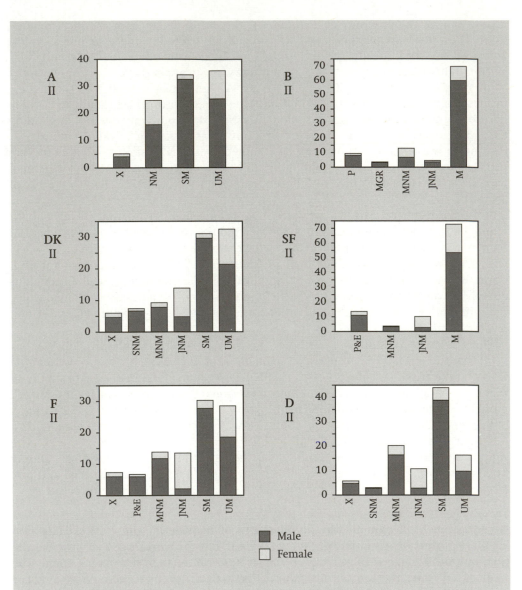

Fig. 5.3a Employment in productive industries (Sector II) by gender and occupational class, c.1990, 13 countries

Key: C = clerical; JNM = junior non-manual; M = manual; MGR = managerial;
MNM = middle-ranking non-manual; NM = non-manual; P = professional;
P&E = professional and managerial; SM = skilled manual; SNM = senior non-manual;
SSM = semi-skilled manual; T&S = trade and sales; UM = unskilled manual;
X = self-employed and family workers.

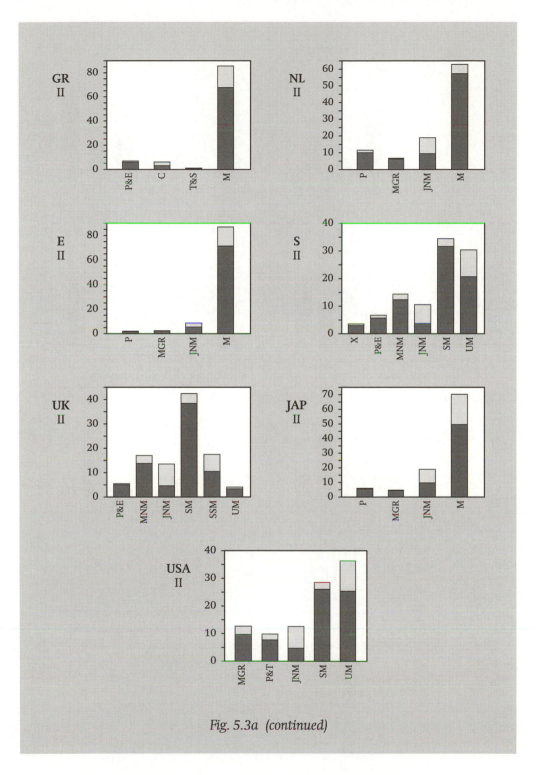

Fig. 5.3a (continued)

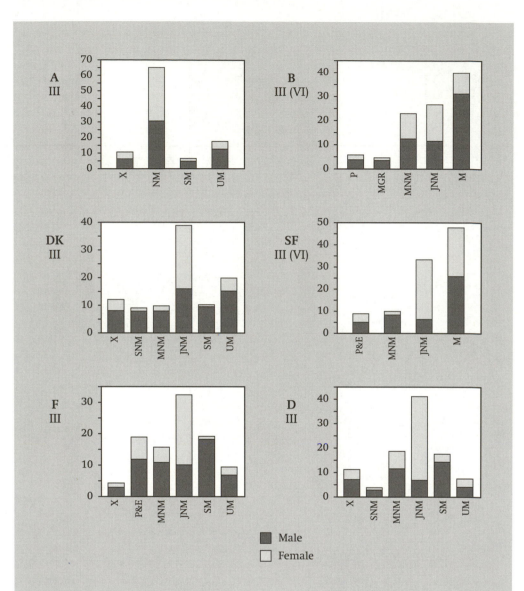

Fig. 5.3b Employment in distribution (Sector III) by gender and occupational class, c.1990, 13 countries

Key: C = clerical; JNM = junior non-manual; M = manual; MGR = managerial;
MNM = middle-ranking non-manual; NM = non-manual; P = professional;
P&E = professional and managerial; SM = skilled manual; SNM = senior non-manual;
SSM = semi-skilled manual; T&S = trade and sales; UM = unskilled manual;
X = self-employed and family workers.

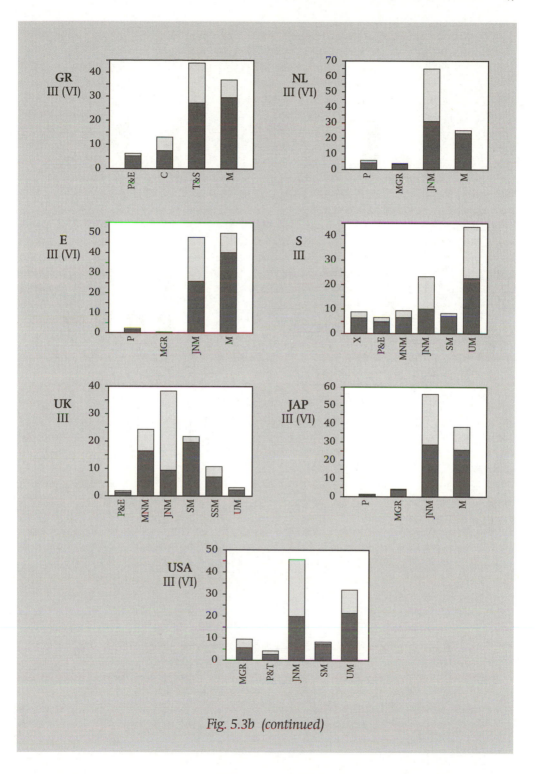

Fig. 5.3b (continued)

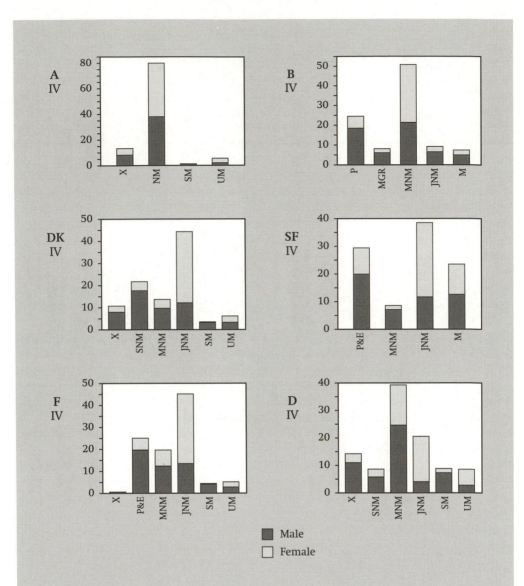

Fig. 5.3c Employment in business services (Sector IV) by gender and
occupational class, c.1990, 13 countries

Key: C = clerical; JNM = junior non-manual; M = manual; MGR = managerial;
MNM = middle-ranking non-manual; NM = non-manual; P = professional;
P&E = professional and managerial; SM = skilled manual; SNM = senior non-manual;
SSM = semi-skilled manual; T&S = trade and sales; UM = unskilled manual;
X = self-employed and family workers.

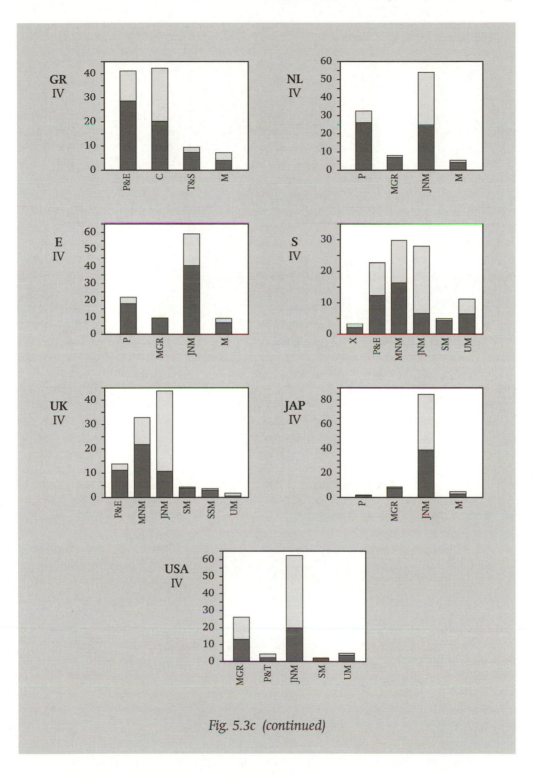

Fig. 5.3c (continued)

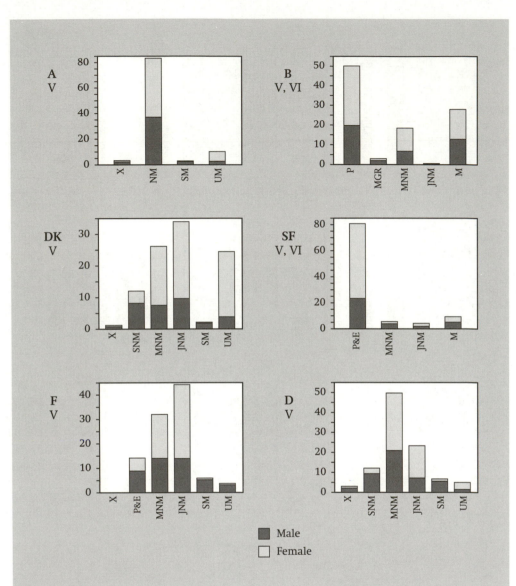

Fig. 5.3d Employment in social and community services (Sector V) by gender
and occupational class, c.1990, 13 countries

Key: C = clerical; JNM = junior non-manual; M = manual; MGR = managerial;
MNM = middle-ranking non-manual; NM = non-manual; P = professional;
P&E = professional and managerial; SM = skilled manual; SNM = senior non-manual;
SSM = semi-skilled manual; T&S = trade and sales; UM = unskilled manual;
X = self-employed and family workers.

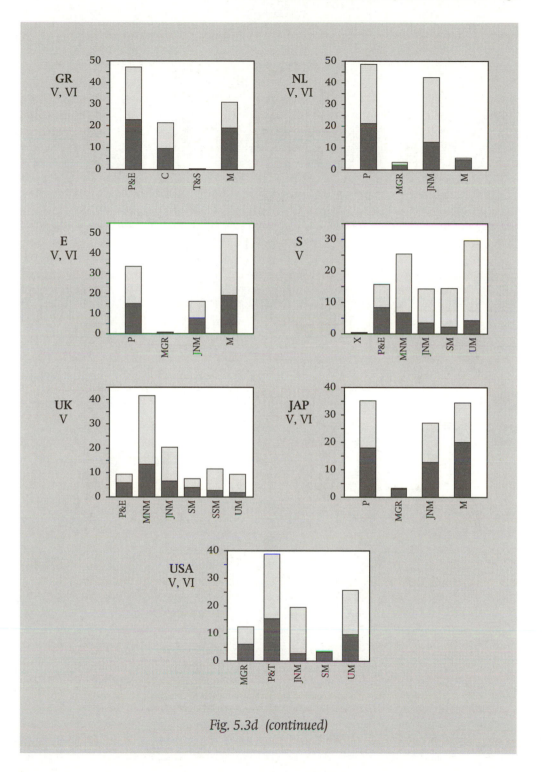

Fig. 5.3d (continued)

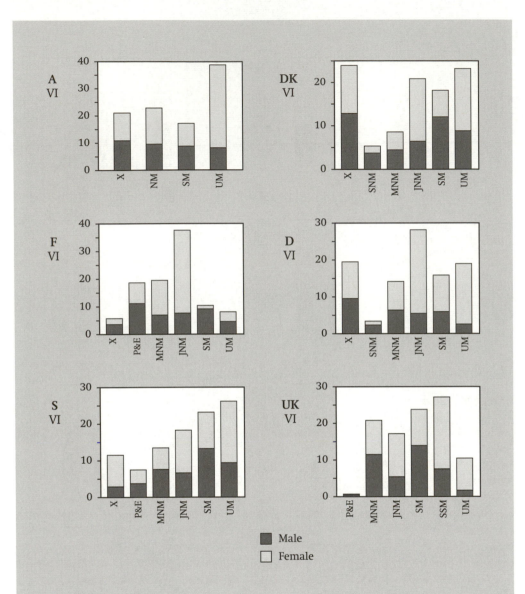

Fig. 5.3e *Employment in personal services (Sector VI) by gender and occupational class, c.1990, 6 countries*

Key: JNM = junior non-manual; MNM = middle-ranking non-manual; NM = non-manual;
P&E = professional and managerial; SM = skilled manual; SNM = senior non-manual;
SSM = semi-skilled manual; UM = unskilled manual; X = self-employed and family workers.

employees. The numbers of managerial professional employees were (except in France and the USA) nearly always small and predominantly male. With the important exception of the relative absence of manual workers, the sector follows the main principles that we have seen to be operating at the general level.

Business Services

Sector IV partly comprises highly specialized services like banking and insurance, though partly tasks that could be handled within a Sector II enterprise but which in practice have been purchased through the market from an independent organization that does not itself engage in production. Sector IV organizations might employ some ancillary or service manual workers (such as cleaners), but by definition not production ones. In every country for which we have data these factors are reflected in the relative proportions of manual and non-manual workers. This is the first sector in which manual workers are a decided minority, and as such this sector—small but growing rapidly—does not correspond at all to the stratification outline of mid-century society. Its class structure largely reflects the non-manual hierarchy from senior management to routine employees. Although everywhere small, the manual proportion of the workforce varied markedly in size, with the extreme ratios of 3.73 (Germany) and 3.48 (Sweden) to 1 (Japan).

It was in nearly all cases a heavily gendered hierarchy with women (present in large numbers) concentrated in the routine jobs. Only in the USA (and, to a considerably lesser extent, Sweden) were women found in large numbers in senior managerial and professional positions. This factor, combined with the very small role of a manual group, intensifies the gendered nature of stratification. This 'post-industrial' sector has a hierarchy that is not at all rooted in the historically and sociologically important break between manual and non-manual work, and its growth is therefore often seen as being part of the development of a non-class or post-class society. It is however hierarchically ordered; it is just that virtually all posts in the structure are non-manual; indeed, this fact makes the hierarchy clear and unambiguous, while its gendered character prevents it from being merely an intra-organizational arrangement of no wider social significance.

Social and Community Services

Most persons within Sector V are providing education, health, social welfare, and public administrative services. They are mainly non-manual workers, though the manual workforce is not as small as in Sector IV. It was particularly large in Sweden, and also Denmark and the UK. It has some complexities that complicate its contribution to national stratification considerably more than Sector IV—which gave us a straightforward gender class schema of non-manual work. This is unfortunately intensified by problems in the collection of data. Several countries do not publish statistics for this sector separately from Sector VI; since Sector V is by far the larger sector and these countries include part of Sector VI (hotels and restaurants) under Sector III, we shall discuss these cases as primarily presenting data on Sector V, but being careful not to draw inferences that might be affected by the inclusion of Sector VI.

Enough is known to enable us to draw certain conclusions. First, in most cases the sector had its core workforce—the equivalent of production workers in manufacturing or shop workers in retailing—among the professions. Numerically therefore the sector was 'top-heavy' in class terms; though if senior management is counted as superior to the professions—a contested issue in many examples of this sector—it should perhaps better be regarded as 'upper-middle' heavy, since the small number of cases that enable us to discriminate between management and professions (Belgium, the Netherlands, Spain, the USA, and Japan) indicate a small top management group as well.

The majority of the large combined managerial and professional group was female in all countries for which we have relevant data except Japan. In those cases where different levels of professional and managerial staff are shown, it is clear that women were found towards the lower end of the professional hierarchy; while the small managerial group that we can sometimes identify was usually heavily male. The USA is an exception on this point, but even there the female managerial majority was not as large as that among the professional and lower non-manual groups. In contrast to Sectors I, II, and III and the overall structure of all societies, the majority of *manual* workers in this sector was both female and low-skilled—important exceptions on both counts being France and Germany.

This large sector of the post-industrial economy therefore embodies a very distinctive and complex class and, in particular, class–gender structure. There is a large professional workforce and a relatively large number of low-skilled manual workers, but few skilled manuals. Women predominate at all except the top levels and among the small stratum of skilled manual workers.

Personal Services

Finally, Sector VI comprises a mix of some professional services (for example in the culture field) with a larger number of primarily manual ones (e.g. domestic cleaners). Most work organizations in this small sector are themselves small, with short managerial hierarchies. Unfortunately we have data that separate this sector from V for only six societies (Austria, Denmark, France, Germany, Sweden, and the UK). Apart from a much larger self-employed sector and (except in France) greater balance between the size of the non-manual and manual workforces, all show a structure rather similar to Sector V: a non-manual hierarchy with male domination at the top levels and large numbers of women at the lower levels; and a manual group dominated by unskilled women (except, again, France, where skilled males are dominant).

EUROPEAN SPECIFICITIES

As with much of the analysis in previous chapters, there are specifically European patterns at only a few points. The USA does not have a particularly distinctive class structure, despite the relatively small size of its manufacturing sector and therefore of its manufacturing working class—a characteristic which has long been a prominent feature of American/German comparisons. Several other European societies have at least as small a manual working class, and any US distinctiveness here is largely the result of the small size of its manufacturing sector: *within* manufacturing the size of its manual workforce is relatively high. More distinctive is the large size of the senior managerial and professional hierarchy in the USA, and its relatively even gender composition. Japan too appears outside the range of internal European variation at only a few points, mainly concerning the large size of the manufacturing working class. Here it resembles southern European countries.

Esping-Andersen, Assimakopoulou, and Van Kersbergen (1993) found a more systematic contrast by looking at the relative capacity of Scandinavian (i.e. Norwegian and Swedish), North American (i.e. US, Canadian, to some extent British) and continental countries (especially Germany) to generate low-skilled work. The first category was able to provide such work predominantly in Sector V through its large welfare states; the second in other services sectors through its unregulated labour markets; but the third did neither. Our own analysis of a slightly different group of countries and more varied sectoral analysis lends some support to this. As can be established from Appendix Table A.5.2, the highest proportions of low-skilled workers in Sector V are to be found in Scandinavia (Denmark and Sweden), the lowest in continental countries (Austria, France, Germany), with the UK and USA in between. Some of these inter-country differences are very large. In Sector III the continental group is again low, but there is no clear difference between the other two blocs, while Denmark is on the same level as Austria. The inter-country differences in Sector IV are too small to invite interest. In Sector VI the Anglo-American group has a larger number of low-skilled workers than the Scandinavians, but the continental group has no fixed pattern. Sectors III and VI are those where unregulated low-skilled work is said to flourish, but there is only partial support for that thesis here. Other contributions to Esping-Andersen's study tend similarly to play down strong contrasts between Fordist and post-Fordist sectors or country groups (Tåhlin 1993; Blossfeld 1993; Gershuny 1993).

THE CLASS STRUCTURE OF SECTORS: A SUMMARY

Clearly, Sector II is no longer emblematic of occupational structure, and to that extent the mid-century pattern of occupational classes no longer exists in its strong form. Nothing has unambiguously replaced it—this lack of clarity of structure being itself as anticipated by postmodern theories. One reason is that Sector II is still a major component, and will remain so for many years to come. Another is that, at least in Western Europe, the core of the biggest single new sector, V, is in public service and therefore stands aside from specifically capitalist structures. A third factor is that gender differences tend to parallel the fault lines of these different hierarchies. If we look solely at male employment (which is after all still the majority form), then not so much has changed since the mid-century pattern. Female employment tells us much more about the future, though women remain located in very specific and relatively junior positions throughout most of the hierarchies in which they are found. This further strengthens the postmodern characteristic of indefiniteness and fragmentation.

As all versions of 'post-' theories would have it, the growth of the service sector economy challenges the class structure of industrial society, which was derived from the manufacturing sector, though the services sectors differ from each other in significant ways and do not fall into the neat classless pattern frequently assumed. Also, they often continue to 'borrow' presentations of their structures from the manufacturing sector, though its appropriateness to that task must by now be in doubt. It is the related processes of the rises of these services sectors and of the employment of women which has produced the large changes in the overall appearance of capitalist class structure.

It is possible that we shall soon need to replace a class model based on the manufacturing sector and levels of skill and types of work with one which reflects different levels of security and type of contract. This would take account of the difference between 'normal' work as defined by the mid-century model of the employee with certain rights in his or her employment and the many deviations from that discussed in Chapter 3.[2] This would not disturb the concept of a managerial hierarchy. Sometimes concepts of this kind, analysed as labour market segmentation, are seen as alternatives or even rivals to class analysis. It seems to me better to view them as *updating* the form taken by class, at least by adding the security concept as in Kreckel's scheme cited above. In favour of such an approach is the fact that the distinction between secure and insecure work is not dependent on the pattern of relations prevalent in any one sector. It can also take good account of gender, and it avoids the growing irrelevance of the manual/non-manual boundary. It also recognizes what I have argued here is a neglected aspect of class structure: the dependence on definitions of status classes by state and management. Law and employers define these categories of security, just as they defined the manual/non-manual difference or the difference between sharecroppers and landless labourers.

Against making such a change of analysis are however some weighty arguments. Insecure positions are sometimes occupied as part of the life course: young or recently retired people are likely to take these posts, the former hoping to move out of them for the main part of their working lives. However, this is not true of all such workers, and it is likely that their numbers will increase. Furthermore, some parts of the existing class structure also embody life-course or career path elements: in particular (for males) the gap between routine non-manual and managerial posts often indicate different stages of careers. A more serious objection is that sometimes insecure workers are doing just the same jobs as secure ones, but simply on different contracts. To the extent that this is true, segmentation will never become the basis of a class structure, as the divisions defined by private and public authority will not correspond to differences in other areas of life. This is a matter for empirical enquiry (Gallie *et al.* 1998).

It is however already possible to see a possible new class structure emerging, as these always do, gradually and obscurely from the mould set by its predecessor. This would be a structure in which a managerial class based on a model of capitalist ownership is clearly identifiable; then a wide variety of more or less secure professional, administrative, clerical, and skilled manual posts; then various insecure categories, with low levels of educational requirements.

INCOME INEQUALITY IN THE CLASS STRUCTURE

Central to the assumptions of class theory is the argument that superiority of position in market and hierarchy will be reflected in superiority of earnings or rewards. It is this ramification of positional (and often educational) inequality by inequality of material outcomes that gives a class structure its strength and social importance. Therefore we

---

[2] In some respects Japanese social class already reflects this. The distinction between manual and non-manual is not important in Japan, but there is considerable difference in the level of rights enjoyed by the core permanent workers of the great enterprises and both the temporary workers in those firms and people working in small enterprises, all of whom lack security.

cannot determine whether the changes we have been discussing, such as the growth of routine non-manual work and the emergence of certain gender classes, have importance for the sociology of contemporary capitalism until we consider their relationship to this issue. In turn, the study of inequality has to be intimately bound up with the study of capitalism. Otherwise it becomes a static study of distribution, ignoring power relations (Kreckel 1992: 31).

It has recently been argued by many scholars as part of the postmodernist thesis that position in the occupational system, or class structure, is no longer adequate for a study of social inequality because other forms of distinction, such as entitlement to social benefits, gender, ethnicity are independent sources (Gorz 1980; Kreckel 1992). Apart from the reference to the welfare state, which has developed strongly only during the second half of this century, there is nothing particularly 'new' about this. Ethnic minorities had distinctive positions in earlier periods: for example, Irish workers in Britain, Portuguese in France, Poles in Germany. Gender was if anything a more important autonomous source of inequality in a period when fewer women participated in the labour force than today when, as we have already seen and will see further below, women can be more easily allocated to distinctive class spaces.

It is not therefore necessary to abandon the study of class as a form of inequality. Rather, we should proceed by giving separate consideration to the impact of class relations, subsequently seeing how these implications are changed, exaggerated, or modified elsewhere in the social structure. In terms of the organization of this book, this means considering in later chapters the impact of mass citizenship (especially the welfare state) and also the extent to which sociological liberalism affects the relationship between the economy and such issues as family membership and ethnicity. Then, at the end of this study we can draw these different threads together.

Unfortunately, it is not possible to make comparisons over time that would enable us to see how recent are the trends that we have identified. The number of countries collecting and publishing data of this kind was very small twenty or thirty years ago; if they did collect them it was usually on a different system from that used now. Our already thin basis for making comparative statements would virtually vanish. It is therefore difficult to answer the question whether inequalities of class have changed in their character—say in the relationship between capitalist and occupational earnings, or between manual and non-manual groups, or between gender classes. Some data give us an indication of change over time, and we shall lean on these heavily for our interpretation of shifts since the mid-century period. In general, however, we must concentrate on considering the present.

INEQUALITIES OF WEALTH

In capitalist societies a crucial component of inequality will be inequality in the distribution of wealth ownership. As noted above in connection with occupational structure, it is not easy to align capitalist ownership with occupational position. In a small number of cases it is possible to do something about this, but in the main it is necessary to consider inequalities of wealth separately. Even at this level we are hindered by a considerable lack of data. Surveys of wealth-holding are very difficult for private researchers to do because wealth-holders are reluctant to divulge information to them, while governments have rarely been interested in discovering this kind of information (exceptions have included official surveys carried out in the 1970s in Norway, Sweden, and the UK). Very little research of any kind has been carried out during the 1980s and 1990s, though these were periods of great change in wealth-holding. It is therefore impossible to provide a reasonably up-to-date summary covering even a few countries. We must restrict ourselves to fragments of out-of-date discussion.

The Scandinavian research (Norway 1982; Spånt 1979) found surprising concentrations of wealth in societies widely believed to be egalitarian. The British Royal Commission on the Distribution of Income and Wealth (UK 1975) also found that nearly all wealth (other than the ownership of residential accommodation) was concentrated in a tiny proportion of the population. If there had been any redistribution it was between the very richest (i.e. the top 1% or 5%) and the rest of the top 10%. There is also evidence that during the 1980s it began to be more concentrated again (Feinstein 1996). Although the distribution of wealth in Germany has probably not changed much since the 1950s (observers think that concentration probably declined in 1969–73, but subsequently rose again (Hornung-Draus 1989; Glatzer et al. 1992: ch. 12.3)), more Germans now have assets of some kind than in the past. For example, the proportion having savings deposits (the most widely distributed form) rose from 60.1% in 1962 to 90.3% in 1983 (Breitschneider et al. 1988). The proportion owning land and buildings rose only from 38.8% in 1969 to 45.5% by 1983, while those owning the form of savings with the highest return (securities) remained relatively small, though rising sharply from 10% (1962) to 29.6% (1983). Kreckel (1992: 109–20) noted that between one-quarter and one-third of all private income in Germany was income from property concentrated in the hands of a small proportion of the population, and not deriving at all from work.

Beyond this we have only fragments of data, usually collected as part of national taxation statistics and therefore liable to many kinds of distortions. It would seem that in France the average self-employed person (whether a farmer or not) has higher earnings than the average employee (France 1993), while in Sweden it is the other way round (Sweden 1997). Data for men (but not women) in Denmark show a pattern similar to France rather than to Sweden (Denmark 1995). This is not surprising if we note that both Denmark and France have a high proportion of small businesses, whereas Sweden has very few. Swiss data permit more nuance, in that they separate different types of employee (Switzerland 1996). Self-employed men rank between non-manual and manual male employees in wealth-holding, while self-employed women rank lower than all groups of employed women. In all cases the sizes of the differences are considerable.

Data on the spread of earnings in Austria (Austria 1994) and Denmark (1995) show a much greater spread among the self-employed than among employees, despite the considerably smaller numbers of the former. The poorest self-employed are among the poorest people in both countries, while some of the richest men (but not women) are also in this formal category. Evidence of the relative poverty of many self-employed corresponds to what we learned in Chapter 3 of the association between self-employment and insecurity; their high earnings at the top correspond to what we expect from knowledge that there is considerable self-employment among certain professional and business groups. Clearly the legal category of self-employed identified by relationship to the means of production does not have an overall sociological meaning. This, like our analysis in Chapter 3, casts doubt on those class analyses which take self-employed status per se as indicating some kind of objective membership of a *petite bourgeoisie* or business-owning class. (This was done, as we have seen above, in the original Goldthorpe–Hope (1974) scale and its recent elaboration by Erikson and Goldthorpe (1992), which put all self-employed persons (including for example window cleaners and gardeners) in an 'intermediate' class along with routine non-manual workers, technicians, and lower-level supervisors. There is some ambiguity whether the authors of this scheme regard the intermediate class as truly intermediate between the professional and managerial grouping and that which they call the working class. Since there is clear hierarchy between the other two, the label intermediate would seem to imply a hierarchical relation, though at some points this is denied (e.g. Erikson and Goldthorpe 1985). As we have also seen above however, in their later (1992) work, Erikson and Goldthorpe move technicians and skilled manual workers into the intermediate class and return to calling their model hierarchical.)

Earnings from self-employment are not a good guide to earnings from capitalist activity, though French data (France 1993) show us that a combination of entrepreneurial income and property ownership is enough to give at least non-agricultural self-employed households the highest average annual incomes in the country. Among the employee groups, both entrepreneurial and in particular property incomes are most heavily concentrated among senior managers (*cadres*). There is then the normal expected gradient as we move down the hierarchy, with little difference between manual workers and routine non-manual. There is a high level of property ownership among the non-working, suggesting the continuing role of persons living entirely off their *patrimoine* (Mendras and Cole 1991).

INEQUALITIES IN INCOMES

Unfortunately, as we shall see below, there are few comparable data covering large numbers of countries which examine the span of earnings by occupational group. However, a fairly recent OECD study (OECD 1995) does provide evidence, based on the Luxembourg Income Study, on overall household earnings dispersion in the 1980s for 12 of the countries with which we are concerned. Table 5.2 presents some of this evidence, showing the levels of earnings from employment (that is, excluding welfare recipients) of both the top and bottom deciles expressed as a ratio of median earnings. The column for the richest decile shows a considerably higher degree of inequality in the USA than in any other country apart from Ireland. Italy and the UK are the next most unequal, while there is a particularly low level of inequality in Scandinavia. The position of the poorest decile also demonstrates the exceptional inequality of US society. (A more recent study of 23 countries, including some in Eastern Europe, showed that only Russia had as high a proportion of people living in extreme poverty (measured relatively) as the USA (Rainwater 1997).)

A further study covering data from the mid-1980s for the European cases discussed in this book (except Austria, Denmark, and Greece) and the USA also shows a strong inter-continental difference (Atkinson 1996). Whereas the bottom decile in the USA earns one-third of the median income, in no European country was the figure below

Table 5.2 *Income of adult equivalents, top and bottom deciles, 1980s*

	Year	Top decile	Rank	Bottom decile	Rank
Belgium	1988	163.20	9	58.50	10
Finland	1987	152.70	11	58.90	11
France	1984	192.80	5	55.40	7
Germany	1984	170.80	8	56.90	9
Ireland	1987	209.20	1	49.50	3
Italy	1986	197.90	3	48.90	2
Netherlands	1987	175.00	7	61.50	12
Norway	1986	162.20	10	55.30	6
Sweden	1987	151.50	12	55.60	8
Switzerland	1982	185.10	6	53.90	5
UK	1986	194.10	4	51.10	4
USA	1986	206.10	2	34.70	1

Note: The adult equivalent statistic is derived by dividing household income by the square root of the size of the household.

Source: OECD 1995.

45% (ibid. 17). These data take account of social income transfers designed to offset market inequalities. US levels of inequality were less isolated where shares of the richest decile were concerned, it being joined at the extreme end by Ireland and southern European countries. Most egalitarian here were the Nordic countries. Using a statistical technique designed to take account of varying inequalities throughout the income range, Atkinson (ibid. 21) found Finland to be the most egalitarian country, followed by Belgium, Luxembourg, Norway, and Sweden. Next came the Netherlands and Germany; then Portugal, followed by the UK, France, and Italy. More unequal still was Spain, and the most unequal were the USA, Switzerland, and Ireland.

Recent comparative research on poverty (Kohl 1992) shows similar results. The author analyses societies in terms of the size of the extremes and the middle of the income distribution, and as a result identifies three groups of societies: the curiously defined Anglo-Saxon (USA, Canada, Australia, UK, but also Israel) in which there is a strong concentration at both extremes, with less than 60% of the population grouped around average standard of living; the Scandinavian (Norway, Sweden), in which over 70% are grouped around the mean; and the Continental European group (here Germany, Switzerland, Netherlands) which comes in-between. Unfortunately, no southern European country was included.

We need an occupational analysis if we are to consider the extent to which membership of distinct class groupings implies barriers and breaks in the overall stream of a distribution of earnings (Kreckel 1992: 105). P. Berger has argued (1989) that material wealth is inherently a stream rather than a series of steps. As we saw above, Kreckel contests this by demonstrating the concentration of wealth in Germany—and in the UK and perhaps some other countries it is even more heavily concentrated. Nevertheless, as Kreckel so well expresses it, it might still be the case that concrete human groups do not easily fit the outlines of the abstract class structure that one can identify (ibid. 148–9). Evidence of an association between an identified class and a typical level of income cannot be taken as evidence for the existence of the class, because the class has been assumed to exist by the way the data were collected. The evidence can simply tell us whether a class that is presumed to exist has some further correlates. Again, we have to rely on data from just a few countries, collected for taxation purposes and not necessarily on a comparable basis for different countries. Only very broad summarizing statements can be risked.

Austrian data (Austria 1994) differentiate only three groups: *Beamte* (civil servants above a certain rank, but including some manual posts—mainly railway engine drivers and postmen); *Angestellte* (*all* white-collar workers irrespective of rank, apart from *Beamte*); and *Arbeiter* (manual workers of all skills levels). The ranking of these groups (further subdivided by gender) conforms to what we might expect from the occupational analysis, which showed women concentrated in routine non-manual and unskilled manual work: manual working men have mean earnings coming between those of male *Beamte* and female *Angestellte*, with manual women coming a poor sixth. The earnings gap between male and female *Angestellte* is very striking. (This is notably not replicated among *Beamte*, where the small number of women who have made this grade actually earn on average very slightly more than their far more numerous male counterparts.)

Spanish data, which simply cover non-manual and manual (*empleos* and *obreros*) show male *empleos* as the *only* group earning above the average, and male *obreros* and female *empleos* at the same level (Spain 1994). In the UK, on the other hand, class (very crudely defined again as manual and non-manual) proves to be, *grosso modo,* more important than gender (UK 1995). Again here, male non-manuals are the *only* group earning above the average.

Greek data are rather defective, giving information for only certain sectors and offering no national mean (Greece 1993). There is considerable sectoral difference, and manufacturing has a superior position over retailing in this economy. Non-manual earnings, *for both men and women*, in manufacturing were considerably ahead of those in retail, and in fact each gender's manual workers in manufacturing earned more than its counterpart among non-manual workers in retailing.

Swiss data give us more useful material on the non-manual hierarchy, and also on the self-employed (Switzerland 1996). Purely male groups monopolize the higher levels, proceeding through senior and other non-manual and then the self-employed, interrupted only by the female senior non-manual group. These are however only slightly ahead of male manual workers. Then come female non-manuals, female manuals, and, last of all, female self-employed.

French material unfortunately does not distinguish between genders, but we know from data above that the most senior of its three non-manual groups (*cadres supérieures*) is heavily male and the most junior (*employés*) is heavily female (France 1993). Like the

UK, France has manual workers (very aggregated) at the foot of the income hierarchy, though whether this would be true if we separated the genders we cannot tell.

Some other countries give us elaborated non-manual hierarchies, skill differences for manual workers and sometimes gender divisions. Sweden (Sweden 1995), like France, has a hierarchy that keeps the means for all types of manual workers below those for non-manuals, even though it distinguishes levels of skill. (The self-employed, as in Switzerland, foot the list.) That the French and Swedish data might look different if account were taken of gender is suggested by the Danish statistics (Denmark 1995). (A study of male and female wages in Sweden has in fact shown that there is a persistent gender wage gap (Le Grand 1991). To the extent that this cannot be explained by the fact that women have on average lower levels of education and work in lower-paying sectors, it seems that the necessity for women to do large amounts of housework holds back their earning capacity. A comparative study of men's and women's earnings in the Netherlands, Germany, and the USA also found that women's split perspectives between domestic and employment responsibilities reduced their relative incomes (Sanders 1993).) These proceed down the non-manual hierarchy only as far as middle-level males; then skilled manual workers come ahead (albeit very slightly) of middle-ranking non-manual women, who are in turn only equal with junior non-manual men and only very slightly ahead of self-employed men. Even unskilled men earn more than junior non-manual women, while unskilled female workers actually earn more than skilled female workers. As in Switzerland, self-employed women are the poorest group of all.

Similar complexities of gender and class are revealed by German data (Germany 1994), which rank a number of grades of both *Angestellte* and *Arbeiter* (comparable data are not available for *Beamte*). Among *Angestellte*, grade II men earn slightly more on average than grade I women—grade I males being particularly highly paid. The highest skilled manual men earn more than the bottom three grades of non-manual women and the bottom two of non-manual men; both the second and third skill grades of manual men more than the bottom two of both non-manual women and non-manual men; and the least skilled manual men earn more than the lowest of non-manual women and men. However, the highest skilled manual women earn no more than the lowest non-manual men; while the lowest non-manual women earn less than even the lowest skilled manual women.

How much overlap is there among these various groups? We should expect overlap, if only because different industries often pay different wages and salaries for similar occupations—and inter-industry differences have demonstrated long-term stability (Molle and van Mourik 1989*a*: 14). Vassille (1989*b*: 144) shows further that inter-industry differences have a cross-national stability, dispersion varying from low in Italy, a little higher in Germany, higher still in France, then the UK, and much higher in the USA and Japan than in any of the European cases. One might expect different levels of productivity to explain differences in pay and overall labour costs. Within manufacturing industry at least there is evidence of what one would expect on common-sense grounds: lowest wages in the clear low-productivity sectors; somewhat higher in the 'Fordist' mass production sectors; and highest in the high-technology sectors (ibid. 146–8). However, beyond the low-productivity industries the correlations are low, with considerable differences among countries. Unfortunately, data that show us ranges for occupational types are readily available for only one or two countries. In general these ranges show us a considerable degree of overlap, though also the general utility of some of these categories.

CHANGES OVER TIME

Researchers who have plotted changes over time in various inter-category pay differentials usually comment on the remarkable stability that these show, despite considerable changes affecting labour markets which would lead one to expect big fluctuations if wages and salaries were determined by market forces alone (Jacobs 1989: 49). We can test the overall trend of aggregate income inequality, though not its link to particular occupational groups, since the OECD study mentioned above includes information on changes in the dispersion of occupational earnings between 1973 and 1991 (OECD 1993). This does not take us back as far as our usual 1960 juncture, but gives us some historical perspective. Nearly all countries of interest to us here are covered in some detail, with the exception of Finland, Greece, Ireland, and Switzerland. The datum on which the report concentrates is the expression of the earnings of the ninth and lowest deciles as proportions of the median. This enables us to see how the richest and poorest members of the occupational earnings distribution have fared in relation to the median level of their society.

Throughout the 1970s—and probably following a similar trend in the 1960s—there was a consistent decline in earnings dispersion in all countries except two: Spain and the USA. A decline did start in Spain at mid-point of the decade—that is, after the end of the forty-year-long dictatorship—so this country is only partially an exception. In the USA, however, earnings became more unequal throughout the period. We can therefore say that throughout the 1970s Western Europe and Japan saw a reduction in income inequalities consistent with theories of the 'taming' of capitalism. The USA was an exception to this trend among *democracies*.

In the 1980s the picture became more complex. Only in Germany did the trend to less inequality continue; in Spain it resumed at mid-decade after a reversal during the first half; in France, the Netherlands, and Sweden the trend lasted until mid-decade before being reversed. In Austria, Belgium, Japan, Portugal, the UK, and USA there were trends to greater inequality throughout the 1980s—also in Australia and Canada beyond the range of our study. However, the inegalitarian trend was small in all these cases except two: the UK and the USA. Here there were sharp deteriorations in the relative positions of the poor while the incomes of the top earners leaped ahead considerably. In the USA (and also Canada) the decline of the poor was not just relative: the poorest 10% were *absolutely* poorer at the end of the 1980s than they had been at the beginning, even though in the USA the previous decade had also seen their relative position worsening.

A Swedish study (drawing on the Luxembourg Income Study) of just five countries (Canada, Germany, Sweden, the UK, and the USA), but giving more detailed analysis of the income distribution (Fritzell 1993) reaches similar conclusions: among the countries in our study: only Germany (also Canada) remained stable; in Sweden, the UK, and the USA inequalities increased sharply, most strikingly of all in the UK.

More recent OECD statistics (see Table 5.3) bring the story up to the mid-1990s for

Table 5.3 Changes in real earnings over five and ten years, full-time workers

	Years	All	Men	Women	Top decile	Bottom decile
Austria	1991–5	5.50	5.80	6.60	12.60	8.40
	1986–95	*1.80*	*2.70*	*3.90*	*7.70*	*0.80*
Belgium	1990–4	9.90	8.00	14.10	13.30	8.10
	1985–94	*16.90*	*15.30*	*25.80*	*20.30*	*15.70*
Denmark	1989–93	0.10	0.00	2.70		
	1984–93	*5.30*				
Finland	1991–5	4.60	4.80	3.40	2.00	8.80
	1986–95	*21.50*	*21.90*	*22.10*	*18.50*	*26.90*
France	1990–4	2.60	2.10	4.40	3.40	3.10
	1985–94	*7.20*	*6.70*	*10.00*	*10.20*	*4.00*
Germany	1990–4	9.90	7.60	15.70	11.70	30.80
	1985–94	*21.00*	*19.70*	*26.10*	*21.50*	*59.60*
Italy	1989–93	0.80	3.10	2.50	0.50	−11.10
	1984–93	*10.40*	*12.40*	*12.60*	*20.00*	*7.40*
Netherlands	1990–4	3.30	2.70	7.70	2.70	3.50
	1985–94	*9.30*	*8.40*	*17.10*	*9.90*	*8.30*
Sweden	1990–4	−2.30	−2.00	−0.20	−1.80	−5.10
	1985–94	*9.30*	*10.80*	*10.00*	*11.80*	*3.40*
Switzerland	1992–6	3.00	3.90	6.20	5.20	3.90
	1987–96					
UK	1992–6	8.50	7.80	11.70	9.10	4.90
	1987–96	*23.20*	*21.90*	*33.40*	*24.90*	*13.80*
Japan	1991–5	4.50	3.30	9.90	5.90	11.40
	1986–95	*17.50*	*15.80*	*24.70*	*19.90*	*24.30*
USA	1990–4	−0.90	−4.80	0.20	−2.10	−7.40
	1985–94	*−3.10*	*−6.30*	*3.70*	*3.10*	*−7.20*

Source: OECD 1997.

most of our countries. This concentrates on the real earnings of full-time workers only. It shows that in the decade ending around 1995 the earnings of the bottom decile increased more rapidly than those of the top decile in only 4 out of 13 countries (Finland, Germany (considerably), the Netherlands (slightly), and Japan). By the last five years of that decade the Netherlands had joined all others in a worsening position of the poorest earners.

CONCLUSION

Disappointing though the chances of carrying out good comparisons have been on the issues covered in this chapter, we can draw some overall conclusions.

First, there are gender classes as well as classes, in that the hourly earnings of full-time men and women on ostensibly similar grades are frequently very different, with women *never* being ahead of men within an individual category. As Kreckel (1992: 233) points out, this exists even though there are, at least in Germany, no longer any significant differences in the qualification levels of male and female employees.

Second, the hierarchical relationship between non-manual and manual work that we see in aggregate data begins to break down once one differentiates within both groups. There are no grounds for regarding the lower levels (however defined) of the non-manual hierarchy as somehow superior, at least in income terms, to the more skilled levels of manual work; indeed, the reverse is the case. To that extent our data refute the significance of a fundamental point of class analysis.

Third, this latter point is partly but not entirely gender-related. As we have seen earlier in this chapter, in virtually all societies junior non-manual workers are mainly female while skilled manual workers are overwhelmingly male. The considerably higher earnings of the latter are therefore in part a component of the gender character of classes. However, there is also considerable overlap among men's earnings across the so-called manual/non-manual divide. It is interesting to speculate whether, as some research has suggested, this is mainly because men in these junior non-manual positions are in effect doing 'women's jobs' (Crompton and Jones 1984). They may be there because they have 'failed' in the race for 'real' male jobs, or because they are in the junior stages of a career which requires them to spend some time in these junior roles before they are moved up the hierarchy, leaving their female colleagues behind.

Finally, we should note that, if skilled manual workers are seen as superior in skill to many routine non-manual ones, the income hierarchy remains a skill hierarchy (Vassille 1989*a* and *b*).

As far as we can tell, there is little difference in the basic pattern in different regions of Europe, except for the relatively egalitarian nature of Scandinavian societies. Evidence from Spain (on the similar mean pay of male manual workers and female non-manuals (Spain 1994)) and from Greece (on the overlapping incomes of gender groups and across the manual/non-manual divide (Greece 1993)) gives at least some grounds for considering that principal generalizations derived from northern experience apply more generally. More detailed evidence would doubtless reveal subtle cross-country differences. However, they are unlikely to disturb this central finding of essential similarity.

We have identified a characteristic which seems to distinguish US capitalism from nearly all European and also from Japanese varieties. In both change over time and current position, the USA has levels of inequality untypical of all other advanced societies, though the UK has come to resemble it in some respects in recent years. That the UK should be changing and beginning to follow the US model is not surprising, given the similarities between the approaches of those countries to capitalist organization (see next chapter). It should be noted that this elongation of the income hierarchy is based on *pre-tax* incomes, and is not therefore directly affected by political forces; as we shall see in a later chapter, changes in taxation in the UK and USA also moved in a regressive direction, intensifying the trend towards inequality. The trend within the labour market was not therefore a compensation to higher paid employees for higher relative taxes but very much the reverse. Evidence from at least the UK also suggests that during a decade (the 1980s) of rapidly rising directors' pay, the relationship between directors' incomes and the performance of their companies actually declined

(Gregg, Machin, and Szymanski 1993). The change is therefore unlikely to be a result of greater market sensitivity.

It is more difficult to determine whether other societies are simply at an earlier stage of a tendency that will affect them all. The trend towards slightly greater inequality in a number of them suggests this possibility, but at present it is too early to tell (see for example some more detailed work on the previously egalitarian Netherlands (CBS 1993)). If the USA, as the largest advanced country in the world, is a trendsetter, post-modern or post-industrial societies will be far more unequal than their mid-century predecessors, and will see a return to levels of inequality of earlier decades and centuries.

Chapter 6

THE INSTITUTIONS OF MODERN CAPITALISM

We now need to look at capitalist organizations—that is, firms—within a wider perspective than employment. While capitalism is a constant in all the countries of this study, its organization can take a diversity of forms. Some of this has been caused by the need of capitalism to come to terms with other elements of the mid-century compromise, and these will be considered in Parts III and IV. But there have also been forms of diversity internal to the structure of capitalism itself, and not necessarily related to external compromises.

It might be thought that a capitalist system is always simply a matter of private ownership of the means of production and services combined with free markets, a straightforward set of institutions essentially the same across the world. This view was especially prominent during the period when Eastern and Central Europe seemed to provide an alternative, state socialist model for the organizing of industrial society, making any differences among capitalist economies seem minor. However, some scholars challenged this model even in the early 1960s, most prominently the British economist Andrew Shonfield (1964). More recently study of the diversity of modern capitalism has developed into a major research field, drawing attention to the social, political, and economic institutions that support and underlie pure market processes, and which can vary among countries or among regions of countries or different economic sectors (see Berggren 1991; Best 1990; Boyer and Hollingsworth 1997; Crouch and Streeck 1997; Dore 1986; Hall 1986; Hollingsworth, Schmitter, and Streeck 1994; Jürgens, Malsch, and Dohse 1989; Kogut 1993; Maurice and Sorge 1989; Sako 1992; Berger and Dore 1996).

FORMS OF CAPITALIST GOVERNANCE

A particularly important feature of this literature has been the delineation of a number of forms of 'governance' of economies. Wherever we find a pattern of social organization that persists in more or less the same form over time, we must assume that some or other mechanism is operating to sustain that persistence, otherwise things would change randomly. The kinds of mechanism can vary enormously. If the social pattern is relatively simple, like a group of friends, there need only be a few informal devices for keeping the group together, defining its boundaries, and punishing behaviour by group members that threatens continuity. If the pattern is vast and complex, like the economy of a modern society, it will need a large apparatus of rules and enforcement mechanisms. The ensemble of these mechanisms in any one institution we can call its pattern of governance. 'Government' is too strong and specific a word, since the processes involved can be more implicit and diffuse than the top-down regulation which that word normally means. Government is a form of governance, but the latter can range more widely.

In fact, the first form of economic governance we need to identify is one that is often seen as the opposite of government: the *market* itself. The existence of markets presupposes a wide range of mechanisms for ensuring that participants in the market behave in ways appropriate to it. For example, they must keep contracts, and accept certain definitions of money.

Large corporations do not depend on the market alone for their activities, but in their relations with both suppliers and their own employees often develop structures of authority based on *organizational hierarchy*. Any large firm is likely to have a structured set of relationships through which orders are transmitted—a system of governance—making companies into social institutions and not just clusters of individual exchanges. Some firms however go considerably further than this and generate entire cultures and communities within themselves. A company culture embodies certain values about specific ways in which work is considered to be conducted in that firm, and becomes the basis for appeals to loyalty. Companies of this kind usually develop internal labour markets and encourage long service among their employees, to the extent of developing a company level of social policy. While these firms can exist within highly competitive product markets, they do suspend the operation of market rules in their labour relations. They can be identified as *institutional companies* to distinguish them from mainstream hierarchical firms.

If we think of governance in the stricter sense of government, we will of course consider the *state* as a further form. States have been deeply and variously involved in the management of capitalist economies, so much so that different state traditions made for quite different rules and outcomes of economic action.

Next, in many societies *formal associations*, such as trade associations and chambers of commerce have organized cooperation between competitors and negotiated collective rules of exchange between groups with opposing interests, thereby both modifying the functioning of markets and firms and adding to the variety among states.

Finally, *informal communities and networks* sometimes control a significant share of certain economies' transactions, and to varying degrees help sustain as well as transform the other mechanisms of governance.

Different forms of governance give us different forms of capitalism. In this chapter I shall analyse these in the following way. First, given the theoretical importance of the idea of capitalism as a market-governed system, I shall take as the paradigm case what capitalism would look like if it followed the form given by the idea of pure free markets. This provides a model of perfectly competitive capitalism with no intervention in the operation of the market from other institutions in society apart from the fundamental need for law to safeguard the ownership of property and the functioning of markets. A purely competitive market is one in which no actors are able, either by acting alone or by combining together, to affect prices. This requires the existence of large numbers of participants, none of which is large enough to have an effect on the market by individual action, and none of which can communicate intentions to others except by signals of prices offered and demanded within the market. This applies to relations among firms, including firms' relations with the suppliers of finance, to relations between firms and their employees, and between firms and ultimate customers.

Furthermore, no external agency (i.e. an agency governed by rules of behaviour other than following the rules of the market) can intervene in the operation of the market, with the necessary exception of a rule-making authority that maintains and enforces the market rules themselves. This means that there is no place in the pure market model for firms so large that they can individually have an effect on the market, or can communicate with each other outside the frame of market signals, or for non-market social or community relationships that condition economic behaviour; or for organizations of firms that might impose an organizational logic of behaviour over and against the market signals; or for economic activity by the state beyond its role as guarantor of the rules of contract and the market.

I shall spell out the implications of this model by designating those characteristics which distinguish pure markets from each of the other main types mentioned above. It is assumed that apart from their points of contrast the other types adhere to the market model in all other respects. This gives us an idea of the range of potential diversity. It is important here to understand the differences between types and cases. Different types of a phenomenon (in this case capitalism) differ from each other in formal ways which should be anticipated by theory. Cases are empirical examples, which might bring together different components of models and types in a variety of ways.

In the second and third parts of the analysis we shall consider which different models of capitalism have in practice been in use among the societies being discussed in both the early 1960s and the 1990s. Fourth, we shall examine whether any particular groupings of countries emerge from this process; and finally we must consider whether there have been any major trends over time.

This approach makes the major and not necessarily correct assumption that there are such things as national patterns, rather than local or sectoral ones, within countries. As noted in the Preface, this assumption is partly given us by the structure of this book, which takes national cases as its main units. To attempt to break down the analysis further would make it too complex, and we must therefore in large part respect this constraint while acknowledging the distortions that it sometimes imposes. Also, knowledge is not evenly advanced on this question, and we would be unable to present a very detailed picture were we to try systematically to provide sub-national and sectoral data for all countries. Nevertheless, where local or sectoral differences seem particularly important, attention will be drawn to them in the construction of the national profiles.

The types which result from this analysis are summarized in Table 6.1. The following discussion introduces the variables from this table and presents the available evidence on each of them for both points in time. After that we shall reorder the material as a series of country profiles, partly in order to try to identify groups of nations. The model starts with the immediate business environment of the firm, and then moves out to: its local community environment; wider, more formal institutional structures; and the nation state. (Entities beyond that have been excluded to simplify the argument.) We are dealing with complex variables which each need to be explained.

Table 6.1 Characteristics of different forms of capitalist economies

Pure market form		Opposites
		Hierarchy
Ai	Small firm size, many in market	Large size, few in market
		Hierarchy (institutional company form)
Aii	External labour markets (rapid turnover, no concern for company culture)	Internal labour markets (slow turnover, development of company culture)
		State involvement
Bi	Low economic role for state (low share of GDP, no state ownership of productive resources)	Extensive economic role for state (high share of GDP, extensive state ownership)
Bii	No state regulation	Extensive state regulation
		Neo-corporatism
Ci	Low membership of formal associations	High membership of formal associations
Cii	Any associations limited to lobbying for observance of market rules	Associations have governance role
		Reciprocity
Di	All relations on a pure contract basis	Interpersonal and community relations supplement pure exchange
Dii	Arm's length, short-term financial arrangements	Close institutional relationship with sources of finance

We shall therefore consider the change between the two time periods on each issue separately.[1]

MARKETS AND HIERARCHIES

First, we deal with factors which determine whether firms are likely to operate in pure markets or to have developed a hierarchical system of governance. It is difficult to gain access to this variable systematically on a multinational basis, since the really appropriate evidence requires many company-level case studies. If we try to reduce the subject to something easily quantifiable we have to move to indirectly relevant variables. I

[1] Where possible statistical data will be used to apply this framework, but very often a qualitative judgement has to be made based on an assessment of the available literature. For both kinds of data we are very dependent on material which happens to have been made available by statistical services or academic research; there is by no means a full coverage for all countries on all issues. Deficiencies are particularly severe in the earlier period, when little serious work was being done on these questions. Even more than in other chapters we shall be relying on patchy data and trying to make extrapolations in order to give a rounded picture.

shall here use two of these. One relates to a central characteristic of firms: their size. If firms are to become organizational hierarchies, they have to develop a critical mass, and, for several purposes, they have to become sufficiently large within their market to be price-makers rather than price-takers. The other refers to their internal structure and their capacity to build company cultures and internal careers; these are at least in part a function of the length of tenure of employees within an individual firm.

Size and Concentration

The requirement that the perfectly competitive market has by definition a large number of actors, none of which is able by its sole activities to be able to affect prices, has a number of implications. Strictly speaking the important criterion for pure markets is not the absolute size of firms but the presence of large numbers of them within a given market, such that none can by itself have an impact on its terms. A thousand firms each employing a thousand workers will be in as pure a market as a thousand firms each employing five workers. Ceteris paribus, however, there will be a tendency for a growth in firm size to indicate a decline in pure market conditions: partly because of the barriers to entry that are likely to exist if large size becomes necessary to participate in a particular market; partly because large firms are likely to develop capacity for various kinds of strategic action, including the development of hierarchical relations with suppliers and of internal corporate cultures. (By strategic action I mean action that shapes the conditions of the market rather than action which responds to market signals.) In a pure market all actors are price-takers and none price-makers. Once an individual firm has become large enough to affect by its sole actions in the market how other market participants will behave, not only have the conditions of the pure market been violated, but the firm will start to develop plans, strategies, for how it can take advantage of this position. This can happen at a level of concentration considerably lower than that which constitutes a formal monopoly.

Unfortunately, it is not possible to find data collected on a comparable basis on the concentration of economies. We therefore have to make a number of approximations. First, the statistical services of the European Community or Union have since the mid-1970s been collecting statistics on the numbers of firms employing more than 500 people, though only for a few countries and only for manufacturing and construction industries. We cannot get any closer to 1960. If we limit ourselves to manufacturing we have at least some data on 10 European countries for the mid-1970s. These are given in Table 6.2.

For the most recent period (around 1991) we can consider data from a wider range of countries recently put together by the OECD (1994*b*). This also includes data on small firms, enabling us to consider whether countries might have concentrations of *both* large and small firms. This is also shown in Table 6.2. Belgium, Germany, Finland, Sweden, and the UK seem to be concentrated economies. Comparison with the USA suggests that European firms are, *on average*, closer to the market model. It is important to bear in mind two facts about the British data. First, that country is alone in including self-employed persons in its figures for small enterprises; second, instead of using the firm as its unit of measurement, Britain takes the smallest possible unit capable of presenting statistical information—which will often simply be a branch or a division, sometimes just a separate building. This is clearly a complete underestimate of the size

Table 6.2 Sizes of firms, 1975–1990

| | Manufacturing, 1975–87 (Firms with more than 500 employees as % of all firms employing 20 or more) | | | | | | | | | Industry and marketable services, c.1990 (% persons employed) | | | |
| | 1975 | | | 1985–7 | | | Change | | | | | | |
	firms	employees	turnover	firms	employees	turnover	firms	employees	turnover	<20	20 to 99	total <100	500+
A[a]										30.54			23.66
B	5.99	55.07	59.98							25.20	20.80	46.00	34.90
DK	9.76	29.56		2.49	25.90		-7.27	-3.67		38.40	18.00	61.40	21.00
SF	4.69	35.65		3.23	28.10		-1.46	-7.55		26.30	21.00	44.30	38.60
F	5.20	56.54	58.12	3.80	50.00	58.90	-1.40	-6.54	0.78	29.10	21.00	50.10	33.70
D	6.66	62.23	65.55	5.80	60.10	61.40	-0.86	-2.13	-4.15	25.90	18.70	44.60	37.20
GR[a,b]	2.91	47.75	50.01	2.00	37.70	43.70	-0.91	-10.05	-6.31	19.40	34.00	53.40	17.30
I[c]	17.25	85.99	90.95	2.90	35.60	41.50	-14.35	-50.39	-49.45	58.20	13.20	71.40	18.70
NL	2.58	25.29		2.33	23.03		-0.26	-2.26					
N[b]										9.30			17.50
P										34.60	25.00	59.60	21.00
E				2.20	29.60	29.50				42.40	23.00	65.40	20.00
S[d]	4.82	44.82		4.60	41.35		-0.23	-3.47		24.40			34.40
CH	7.45	58.90	61.64							32.50	22.00	54.50	25.40
UK[c,e]										33.00	16.10	49.10	33.80
USA										24.60	18.80	43.40	43.10
JAP[f]	0.08	11.73		1.43	18.70		1.35	6.97		36.40	17.70	54.10	27.60

[a] Number of establishments, not enterprises
[b] Firms with less than 10 employees not counted
[c] 1990: enterprises with no employees included
[d] 1990: figure for >500 calculated on different basis
[e] Figures are for neither enterprises nor establishments, but smallest possible unit of calculation
[f] 1990: first two columns are for 1 to 29 and 30 to 99

Sources: OECD 1994b; Austria 1994; Nordic Council 1994; Japan 1994; USA 1994.

of *firms*. Both these singularities mean that British data exaggerate the numbers of small enterprises and fail to show the true size of large ones. Given that even on this count the country ranks as the third most concentrated, it must in reality be a very highly concentrated economy.

France would be allocated to the high group on the grounds of its concentration in firms of 500 or more, but it can also be seen to have a large number of very small firms, which puts it in something of an intermediate position. At the other extreme, Italy and Spain continue to be clearly very decentralized, and are joined there by Denmark, Greece, and Portugal. In intermediate positions between these two groupings comes Switzerland, and we can probably add Austria and Norway. Outside Europe, Japan probably also belongs to this last category, with its combination of a number of truly giant firms with a very large number of extremely small ones.

We can examine differences in countries' concentration levels across a number of industries, to see if we are dealing with consistent patterns or whether countries occupy diverse positions for different industries. This is available for some European countries in Eurostat (1990) data for the mid-1980s. The material is summarized in Table 6.3 and follows the pattern of the general picture. Belgium, France, Germany, and (if account is taken of distortions in the British data) the UK appear fairly consistently concentrated. Italy, Spain, and (where we have data) Ireland and Portugal appear as small-firm-dominated. The only important exceptions are found in the paper, printing, and publishing sector, where German firms are much smaller and Italian ones larger than we would expect. In a recent study of the rise of big business in Europe, Cassis (1997: 63–71) shows how there was a considerable growth of concentration of giant firms in France and Germany in the 1960s and 1970s, but this still left the UK with a more concentrated economy than either. Data collected by Lyons and Sembenelli (1996: 25) on the country of origin of the 200 largest manufacturing firms in the EU area show that France, the UK, the Netherlands, and Switzerland have disproportionately large concentrations of these, and Italy, Spain, and Austria disproportionately small.

In general therefore we can conclude that within Europe, the most concentrated economies are those of Belgium, Finland, Germany, the Netherlands, Sweden, and the UK. France is slightly less concentrated because of the size of its small-firm sector. With it in a mid-position are Austria, Norway, and Switzerland. The least concentrated are Denmark, Italy, Greece, Ireland, and Spain. Europe emerges as very diverse. However, it seems as a whole to contrast with the USA, where concentrations and hierarchies are more extensive, and from Japan, where there is a large small-firm sector as well as several firms which are probably the purest cases of hierarchies in the world.

Table 6.2 suggests that there was some decline in concentration between the 1970s and 1980s, particularly in employment. Therefore, although we know from other data that the *role* of giant firms has increased, in general there has been a growth in the *proportion* of smaller firms, at least in manufacturing. Change over time has little effect on the relative positions of countries.

More detailed research into small business sectors in individual countries throws further light on these developments. Studies of German business (Kotthof and Reindle 1990; Leicht and Stockman 1993) describe the way in which small firms have grown in number and importance. Some of these are developing as client supplier firms to large corporations, others are operating more generally in the market in response to the

Table 6.3 Size of firms in various industries, 1985
(Firms with more than 500 employees as % of all firms employing 20 or more)

	Firms	Employees		Turnover		Firms	Employees		Turnover	
	%	%	rank	%	rank	%	%	rank	%	rank
	Mechanical engineering					*Electrical engineering*				
B	4.20	52.60	2	55.80	2	15.80	77.70	2	73.90	3
DK	2.70					6.90				
F	3.60	33.70	3	39.30	3	6.90	69.90	3	75.20	2
D	7.50	55.30	1	58.50	1	9.90	78.20	1	80.90	1
IRL						3.90	26.80	6	15.90	6
I	2.00	31.00	4	32.80	4	5.20	55.70	4	54.40	4
NL	1.80	20.00	5	30.80	5					
P										
E	0.80	9.90	6	9.40	6	7.00	44.60	5	44.70	5
UK	4.30	37.00		43.30		10.30	60.10		61.30	
	Motor vehicles and parts					*Clothing and footwear*				
B	21.40	91.00	2	96.00	1	0.90	10.00	4	20.50	3
DK	1.90					0.90				
F	12.00	87.30	3	92.50	3	1.90	20.10	2	24.80	2
D	20.20	93.50	1	95.60	2	2.40	24.50	1	27.90	1
IRL										
I	6.00	80.60	4	86.30	5	0.60	9.90	5	9.60	5
NL	6.50	65.20	6	68.00	6	2.30				
P	7.50									
E	10.00	78.40	5	86.80	4	0.50	10.90	3	10.60	4
UK	11.20	76.40		86.00						
	Paper, printing, publishing									
B	5.70	36.70	1	41.00	1					
DK	4.70									
F	2.70	30.10	3	34.60	3					
D	2.20	24.00	4	33.20	4					
IRL										
I	2.40	33.90	2	35.40	2					
NL	2.90	22.30	5	24.00	5					
P										
E	1.80	16.70	6	16.80	6					
UK	3.70	31.60		36.40						

Source: Eurostat 1990.

increased demand for flexibility. They are located in both industry and services, in general tending to carry out traditional craft functions rather than hi-tech operations. As Kotthof and Reindle (1990) suggest, an important advantage of small firms is the informality of personal social relations they provide.

Similarly, Peron (1991) has discussed the survival and modernization of small retail firms in France despite the rise of large out-of-town *hypermarchés*, sustained partly by a regulatory order and partly by social supports. For example, whereas in the past the wives of small shopkeepers might have worked in the shop, today they are more likely to work in an external salaried post and thereby be able to contribute financially from a separate source to sustain the family business (Peron 1991: 188–9). Often these small firms are franchisees who nevertheless acquire some capital in their franchise role and diversify into other businesses, though the author also argues, as we found in Chapter 3, that the old ideal of the 'independence' of the small business is rather broken down by these dependencies on large corporations. It is likely that there are important cross-national variations on this point: C. Lane (1991) summarizes research evidence in a way which suggests that German supplier relations between large and small firms in manufacturing have been placed on a balanced and constitutional basis, while those in France are very conflictual, with also considerable dependence by small firms on a limited number of large-firm customers. British firms came somewhere between the two.[2]

Whether the flourishing of small firms should really be interpreted as an indicator of pure markets is difficult to determine. As Weiss (1988) and Assimakopoulou (1998) have shown, in continental European countries small-firm survival has been rooted in both institutions of local community and legal regulation. The former we shall discuss below, but the latter raises the ironic possibility that the market condition of large numbers of actors can often be sustained only by regulation (which limits freedom within the market). This is true for Greece, Italy, Spain, France, and Germany. Even the definition of special small-firm types, such as *artigiani* (Italy), *artisans* (France), and *Handwerk* (Germany; see Streeck 1987) are anchored in law. These concepts and protections do not exist in the Anglo-American economies. There are therefore doubts about the correspondence between such a ranking and a real measure of the closeness of any individual country to a pure market model.

The Treatment of Labour

Labour markets do not enter much into this analysis, because we have dealt extensively with employment in previous chapters, and shall turn to collective labour relations in Chapter 12. There is however one separate question that needs to be addressed here. In the pure market model of capitalism labour markets share the characteristics of general markets. These include limitation of communications among actors to giving and receiving market signals and limitation of the form of the relationship to pure contract exchange: if a worker is paid to do a certain amount of work she will perform it; no more, no less. In practice, the pure market is combined with hierarchy in anything

---

[2] Sako and Helper (1998) have compared relations between large firms and their suppliers in Japan and the USA. They contrast the supportive, long-term contract nature of these relations in the former case with the more distant, short-term character of US contracts. However, they also show some convergence in recent years, as large firms in both countries try to imitate elements of the other system.

beyond the smallest organizations. Economic models have adapted to this. Managers and employees do not in reality enter into a series of specific small contracts every time the former want some work done; rather, in exchange for an income the employee places himself at the general disposal of the orders and instructions of the manager. The relationship becomes one of authority within one over-arching exchange of the labour contract, not a mass of exchanges.

Further departures from pure labour markets are made wherever there are systems of communication to establish social ties between manager and employees or among groups of employees, going beyond pure cash relations and pure hierarchies (giving and receiving orders). The opposite of a pure market-cum-hierarchy firm is one in which there is considerable communication of this form, aimed at building long-term relations of trust and commitment; this is what I called the institutional company model. Managements sometimes believe that they can extract more, and better quality, effort from their workers if they establish relations of this kind than if they rely purely on the cash nexus supplemented by simple hierarchical authority. In the managerial literature this is usually referred to as the establishment of corporate 'cultures'. Just as in some societies markets have tended to be more flexible than in others, managerial hierarchies have been negotiated with employees in varying degrees.

Since we are not dealing here with industrial relations we shall limit ourselves to the cultivation of company cultures and communities as a managerial tool. It is difficult to collect national-level data on this phenomenon as such, but we can have access to a more easily quantified and available related datum: the average length of employees' tenure with their employers. Under a pure market model this should be shorter than under a company culture one, since in the former case no attempt is made by the employer to offer anything other than the exchange of effort for reward to sustain the contract. Both should shop around and frequently exercise choice. Table 6.4 presents the results for this, based on data collected by the OECD (1993 and 1997), showing average tenures of employees and proportions of employees changing firms after less than one year of employment. Unfortunately, there are no data for the period of the early 1960s, and the earliest we have are for some time in the late 1970s or early 1980s. Even then less than half our countries are covered. The more recent are for the mid-1990s and cover all our countries.[3]

In the earlier period Germany and Spain had long tenures and Finland and Germany low levels of persons leaving jobs within one year; Germany was therefore an unambiguously high-commitment country. The USA was the only country with particularly low levels on both counts, joined by the ambiguous Finland on the tenure count. For the 1990s we have data for all countries, and Italy and Japan then appear as high-commitment countries on both measures (joined by Belgium and Portugal on the first). The USA remains a low-commitment country, but is joined by Denmark, and on different measures by Spain and the UK.

Do studies of company cultures confirm these rankings? On the basis of a comparison of research on management practices and work organization in the USA, France, Japan, Germany, and Sweden, Boyer (1991) concluded that post-Fordist management

3 For both periods countries are considered to have high labour commitment if their labour tenure rate is more than one standard deviation above the 1995 mean and their proportion of workers leaving within one year is more than one standard deviation below the 1995 mean; vice versa for low labour commitment.

Table 6.4 Employment by enterprise tenure, 1979–1995

	c.1979 or 1985					c.1995								Change	
	Year	Average		<1 year		Average		Median		% < 1 year		% < 5 years		Av. years	% < 1 year
		years	rank	%	rank	years	rank	years	rank	%	rank	%	rank		
A						10.00	8			12.60	4				
B						11.20	3			11.60	3				
DK						7.90	16			25.10	16				
SF	1979	7.80	7	5.10	1	10.50	6	5.20	6	17.60	13	49	6	2.70	12.50
F	1986	10.70	3	13.10	5	10.70	5	7.50	2	15.00	9	42	3	0.00	1.90
D	1984	11.10	2	8.50	2	9.70	10	7.50	2	16.10	11	41	2	-1.40	7.60
GR						9.90	9			12.60	4				
IRL						8.70	14			17.80	14				
I						11.60	1			9.50	2				
NL	1985	8.90	4	11.70	4	8.70	14	3.10	9	16.30	12	62	10	-0.20	4.60
Nᵃ						9.40	11	6.50	4	14.90	8	44	4		
P						11.00	4			13.40	6				
E	1987	11.20	1	15.20	6	8.90	13	6.30	5	35.50	18	46	5	-2.30	20.30
S						10.50	6			14.80	7		7		
CH						9.00	12	5.00	7	15.70	10	50			
UK	1986	8.30	6	18.00	7	7.80	17	4.40	8	19.50	15	55	8	-0.50	1.60
JAP	1979	8.90	4	10.60	3	11.30	2	8.20	1	7.60	1	37	1	2.40	-3.00
USA	1978	6.40	8	29.30	8	7.40	18	3.00	10	26.00	17	62	9	1.00	-3.30

ᵃ 1995 figure is for 1991

Source: OECD 1993, 1997.

approaches have developed, all based on the recognition of skills and workers' commitment, decentralization of management and long-run contractual arrangements with suppliers. He saw differences among the countries: Japan has progressed furthest towards incorporating employees' commitment; Sweden and Germany slightly less so, social-democratic versions of the model somewhat limiting direct involvement; least of all in France and the USA, where managements have been more concerned to reinvent Fordist hierarchies. This corresponds to our quantitative findings on tenure in setting Japan and the USA as extremes within which Western Europe, internally diverse as it is, can be set.

We have already seen how, although the German economy is dominated by large firms, small companies have a particular place within it. Research by Kotthof and Reindle (1990) on the separate legal order of the *Handwerk* firm referred to above suggests that often (though by no means always) these institutionally protected firms form strong communities with high-trust relations between managers and employees. The authors express surprise that German managers seemed to be learning about company communities from textbooks on Japan, when in fact their own tradition provided plenty of scope for a local approach to the question (ibid. 363–4).

As to the French case, some studies report strong paternalist relations within *some* large firms, while others suggest very remote relationships. We must therefore regard France as internally diverse. In the early 1980s some noted research by Maurice, Sellier, and Silvestre (1982) established a significant difference between German and French firms, the former being seen as far more likely than the latter to form corporate communities, given the strong sense of distance between different hierarchical groups in France. d'Iribarne (1992) suggests that these differences have long historical roots based on the tendency for German society to be constructed on the basis of occupational organizations, while the French was based on deep hierarchies.

A survey of the introduction of participative forms of organization in Spain (Castillo and Victoria Jiménez 1991) found mixed results: overall not much had been achieved in moving away from managers' and workers' distant relations from each other, and where there was some change it seemed to be accompanied by union involvement. However, the authors stress the unrepresentative nature of their study and the difficulty of making generalizations on the basis of it—though they did cover a good range of industries: motors, banks, construction, electronics, chemicals, and public service. Research evidence suggests that British companies would occupy a similar position to that indicated by Boyer for US ones (Culley *et al.* 1998).

MARKETS AND STATES

We next consider relations between firms and the state; it must again be remembered that we are here not concerned with the latter's welfare or social policy activities, but those that concern the business of capitalism as such. Under pure markets there is no such role beyond the minimum case already mentioned of action to maintain the rules of property and contract. At the other extreme is ownership of the whole economy by the state, as existed for many years in Russia and the rest of Central and Eastern Europe. With complete state ownership there might still be some role for markets: salaries and wages might be used to allocate labour, and prices might partly reflect costs of production and levels of demand. However, these are open to considerable interference and distortion, and by definition there is no market for or private ownership of capital. Full state ownership would therefore be a limiting case in capitalist diversity, representing a situation of no capitalism at all.

Unfortunately, intermediate levels of state ownership do not provide us with an easy measure of state intervention in the economy, as the range of instruments for intervention at the state's disposal are very varied, and they can be used in very diverse ways. For example, it is possible for one government to sustain a number of publicly owned enterprises but to have these operate on more or less commercial lines, while another government removes its state industries from normal market rules of operation. At the same time the first government might sustain a regulatory regime on the private sector of price controls and allocations of raw materials that considerably distorts pure market competition. How do we rank which of these situations constitutes a further departure from the pure market model?

We shall here consider some of these differences and changes in them over time, but shall not use them as the basis of cross-national ranking. Instead we shall use two indicators of the state's economic role. First is a very simple, measurable indicator of the presence of the state within the economy: the percentage of the gross domestic product of which the state is the final consumer.[4] The more a system corresponds to a free-market model, the lower this proportion should be; the more it corresponds to a state-led model, the higher it should be. Second, less easily quantified, we should try to estimate the density of general economic regulation by government of an economy (which should be low in the free-market case, high in the state-led one).

The State's Share of GDP

Table 6.5 presents the basic data. By the standards of the mid-1990s[5] none of these can be considered particularly high; in fact all are low except those of France, Sweden, the UK, and USA. At the very lowest end was Japan, the poorly developed non-democratic countries of southern Europe, and the very rich highly democratic case of Switzerland. Again, the two non-European cases stand at opposite ends of the European range. Clearly a diversity of different forms of state action affects these patterns. In France, the UK, and USA there were large military budgets; such spending is economically important, because both the cost of and the degree of technological invention involved in contemporary weapons systems can have a major economic impact. There were strong welfare states in Scandinavia, the UK, and the USA. The French state was strongly

---

[4] This is not the same as the level of public expenditure, as it excludes all transfer payments. Transfer payments (pensions, unemployment benefit, etc.) involve the state in redistributing private spending power by taxing some people and making cash payments to others; the final expenditure itself is not determined by the state. Transfer payments do constitute an intervention by the state in the market, as the pattern of income distribution is different from that which would have emerged from pure labour-market forces; and the consequent pattern of final spending is probably different as a result. However, there are three good reasons for excluding transfer payments from our assessment of the state's economic involvement. First, the intervention is secondary, in that final spending patterns are those of private consumers, not government itself. Second, transfer payments are overwhelmingly welfare payments, and we are trying to exclude the welfare state from consideration for present purposes (it is considered in Chapter 13). Third, the size of welfare payments varies considerably with the level of unemployment, which distorts the analysis of both change over time and inter-country differences.

[5] Countries are considered to have had a high level of expenditure at either date only if it is more than one standard deviation above the 1996 mean; a low level if more than one standard deviation below that mean.

Table 6.5 Government consumption as % of GDP, 1960 and 1996

	1960			1996			Change 1960–96
	%	rank		%	rank		
Austria	12.97	7	mid	18.10	9	high	5.13
Belgium	12.44	10	mid	14.54	14	mid	2.10
Denmark	13.28	6	mid	25.18	2	high	11.89
Finland	11.92	13	mid	22.94	3	high	11.02
France	14.22	4	mid	19.62	6	high	5.40
Germany[a]	*13.36*	*5*	*mid*	*19.84*	*7*	*high*	*6.48*
Greece	11.70	14	mid	13.82	17	mid	2.12
Ireland	12.45	9	mid	14.13	15	mid	1.68
Italy	12.00	12	mid	16.35	10	high	4.35
Netherlands	12.27	11	mid	14.03	16	mid	1.76
Norway	12.85	8	mid	20.52	5	high	7.67
Portugal	10.54	15	low	18.55	8	high	8.00
Spain	8.40	17	low	16.25	11	high	7.86
Sweden	16.08	3	high	26.24	1	high	10.16
Switzerland	8.84	16	low	14.61	13	mid	5.76
UK	16.40	2	high	21.07	4	high	4.67
USA	16.84	1	high	15.59	12	mid	–1.25
Japan	8.01	18	low	9.67	18	low	1.67

Note: Values <11% rated as low; >16% as high.

[a] The 1996 data are for all Germany. The last year for which separate figures were given for West Germany was 1994, when the proportion was 17.71%, an increase of 4.35% since 1960.

Source: OECD *National Income and Expenditures* (various years).

involved in planning the economy (Shonfield 1964). While in some areas of life, such as police, the southern European dictatorships were very active, overall their involvement in their *economies* through direct spending decisions was very low. The low profile of the Swiss and Japanese states is generally acknowledged, though the Japanese government was at that time actively involved in encouraging various business developments.

During the 1960s and 1970s there were very large increases in the role of the state, as reflected in its expenditure, in all countries. By the end of the 1980s and the early 1990s this had begun to level off and even to decline. To some extent the change represented certain real shifts in state activity, but there was also a knock-on effect from the rise in unemployment experienced by most countries. Rising unemployment leads to a major increase in transfer payments; in order to help pay for these governments may reduce other areas of spending, including areas where it is the final consumer. Nevertheless, if we compare spending in the early 1990s with 1960, the overall trend is of an increase; in no European country had the proportion declined. On the other hand, the range of increases is wide, from over 10% in most Nordic cases to 1% or 2% in Japan, Ireland, and the Low Countries—with an actual decline from the high level of 1960 in the USA. The range of dispersion is considerably greater at this later period, implying divergence rather than convergence. It is important to note that everywhere except the USA the share of the state in national expenditure was higher in the 1990s than in the heyday of the Keynesian economy.

The resulting rank order of countries changes to some extent, with the Nordic countries and the UK clearly heading the range (this includes a major Finnish convergence on the Scandinavian pattern). Japan and Switzerland keep their previous lowest positions. The former dictatorships in southern Europe rise considerably in position (less so in Greece). Only the Nordic countries (though not including Norway) had particularly high levels; only Japan a particularly low one.

State Economic Regulation

It is not possible to quantify levels of overall economic regulation without producing artificial indicators which often have to conceal much of their substantive findings in the initial definitions.[6] The classic European case of state regulation of the economy has been France, where for many years prices and many aspects of trading and industrial relations were governed by legal codes (Boyer 1992; Shonfield 1964). French industrial policy also included the strategy of 'national champions': privileging particular large firms, so that they could be France's representative within a sector, even if that meant harsh treatment for other, competing French firms in the same area of business (Cohen 1995). There were also high levels of regulation in Belgium and in the Fascist economies of Portugal and Spain. A similar regulatory regime existed in principle in Italy, but in a context of considerable evasion (Bianchi 1995).

The Scandinavian states at this time, and especially Sweden, regulated business through detailed Keynesian policies and tax incentives. Beyond that they were more likely to let firms operate in the market. It must also be remembered that these small economies are considerably exposed to international competition, and regulation of the domestic environment is less relevant for the conduct of firms than in a country like France or the USA. There was considerable regulation of Scandinavian labour markets, but mainly through collective bargaining, not the state itself.

Regulation has to be rated low in all other countries. Basic Keynesian demand management was practised in several, especially the UK (and to some extent the USA). The German concept of the social market implied a subtle mix of free markets with regulative support, though it excluded Keynesian demand management (Matzner and Streeck 1991).

Levels of regulation probably increased everywhere during the 1970s, but since that time there has been major change. Following the general rejection of Keynesianism, state ownership, and even state indicative planning of economies, there have been major moves towards economic deregulation. Some of these have been specific to individual nation states, especially the UK. Within the European Union, which now embraces all but two of the European countries discussed here, a general programme of deregulation was initiated as part of the move to a single European market in 1992. Member states dismantled protectionist arrangements and most forms of state subsidy

---

[6] The OECD has recently tried to assess and compare the level of regulation in different national labour markets (OECD 1994a). However, this has been controversial, and in any case is limited to employment issues. To produce an amalgamated index running across the whole range of potential regulation topics would be unrealistic.

to industry, and began the privatization of state-owned industries. More generally, there have been global moves to deregulate, partly in response to the growth of a liberal world trading regime, and partly in response to international investors seeking to 'regime shop' until they find a lightly regulated location for their businesses (Wilthagen 1998). We can probably assume that previously highly regulated cases should now rank as moderate, and that moderate ones become low.

Against all this, it has been observed that deregulation often requires a re-regulation to cope with it (Majone 1993, 1994). In the European cases this means a re-regulation at EU rather than national levels. Whether the content of the new regimes means more or less overall regulation is difficult to determine; there should however be less diversity among EU countries than there had been in the past. On the other hand, the Single Market project has by no means reached all aspects of the economy.

MARKETS AND CORPORATISM

Strictly speaking, formal organizations of businesses should not exist at all within pure market capitalism; firms should discover all the information they need from market signals, and cooperation should be based on contract; anything beyond that is likely to be a conspiracy to form a cartel protecting themselves, against the public interest, from the impact of market disciplines. A state supporting the market order should therefore suppress them. One might see as a limiting case the need to lobby government to maintain the competitive order, so external lobbying of this kind will serve as the form of associational activity closest to the free-market pole. However, we should then have no assurance that lobbies would use their power solely to ensure that the rules of the market are upheld; they might well use them to subvert rules or to have them defined in ways that favour individual firms or industries. In fact, business interests do routinely organize themselves. The issue then becomes whether they will simply perform the lobbying role mentioned—in which case they cannot be regarded as forming a mode of governance, since this necessarily implies some kind of overall responsibility for the functioning of a system, not just the extraction of rents from it. The opposite of lobbying that has developed in the literature is therefore the idea of more or less responsible self-management of a system by organizations of firms within it. The organizations play a double role, both representing and regulating their members. Such systems are known in the literature as corporatist (Cawson 1986; Crouch 1993: chs. 1, 2; Schmitter 1974). This concept is discussed in more detail in Chapter 12, since it has been applied mainly to the study of industrial relations. It can however also be used in other aspects of trading relationships.

We can look at two aspects of this; as with discussion of the state I shall combine an at least in principle quantifiable variable (the membership strength of associations) with one that is less easy to measure, but which is essential if we are to understand the character of systems and differences among them: the mode of operation of such associations.

Associational Membership
Although we might expect to be able to make some simple statistical assessment here, with membership of organizations providing a useful indicator of associational strength, this is in fact not the case. Very few trade associations publish membership

figures, and those that do often provide the useless datum of number of firms. Given how firms can vary in size, we need to know the proportions of the workforce or of turnover represented by an association's membership. This information is very rarely available. We must therefore proceed impressionistically, basing our assessments on the overall thrust of the available literature. Since our primary interest is in capitalists' organizations for commercial or trade purposes rather than industrial relations, our concern is with trade associations rather than employers' associations, though in many countries today the same organizations tackle the two tasks.

During the 1960s no country had a virtually association-free economy of a kind that would correspond fully to the pure market pole, but membership levels were low among French, Greek, and Italian firms. In both France and Italy governments preferred to deal directly with individual firms (Shonfield 1964; Hayward 1995), reducing the incentive for firms to associate, even for lobbying purposes.

Finland, Ireland, Italy, the UK, and the USA all had systems of trade associations considerably more organized than the countries discussed so far, but with only moderately high membership levels. Membership was substantially higher than this and organizations more important in Belgium, the Netherlands, and Switzerland, and even higher and more central to national corporatist coordination in the three Scandinavian countries and Japan. In Austria and Germany compulsory membership organizations, the *Kammern*, give the highest possible membership levels, but membership in voluntary bodies was high too. (For Austria, see Marin 1982; for Germany, see Shonfield 1964; Streeck 1992; for the Netherlands, see Bax 1990: 153–7.) The two then Fascist countries, Portugal and Spain, exhibited high levels.

By the late 1980s a number of studies began to detect a decline in the role of organizations; often this was associated with changes perceived to be affecting the labour market, which we shall discuss in Chapter 12, but in some respects the changes affected trade interests by themselves (Lash and Urry 1987; Offe 1985). It should be noted that this presumed decline followed a rise in importance during the 1970s (Crouch 1993: ch. 8). Changes in the world financial system pressing financial systems towards more short-run calculations by firms (discussed below) often led firms to escape the constraints of membership organizations, especially of a neo-corporatist kind. Competitive pressures within the globalizing economy of the late 1980s and early 1990s often had similar consequences. Individual large firms were now beginning to forge transnational alliances with similar firms from other countries and to cut loose from the constraints of national-level membership associations. Similarly, large firms often wanted to carry out their own lobbying rather than work through associations—a development that started in the USA but which gradually spread also to Europe (Coen 1996). The move to more short-term financing, rapid takeover patterns, and frequent financial mergers also brought a new instability to firms' industrial identities, while associations usually remained defined by participation in a particular industry.

Overall there seems to have been a decline in the level of associational membership in all previously strong or medium-strong cases with the exception of Austria, though France and Italy rise to become moderate cases.

Organizational Modes of Operation
Under pure market conditions firms have low incentives to join organizations because

they can be concerned only with very marginal functions for maintaining the purity of the market or they will be harassed by antitrust law. By definition therefore membership should convey no privileges, and membership levels will be low. The opposite situation is that of neo-corporatism, under which organizations of businesses play a major role, alongside or in place of the state, in regulating their sectors, both representing and disciplining their member firms (Cawson 1986; Marin 1990; Schmitter 1974; Streeck and Schmitter 1985). There may even be an element of compulsion in membership. In any event, membership levels will be typically high. In a midway position should be situations in which organizations exist and play a lobbying, possibly cartelistic, role, but without accepting neo-corporatist responsibilities. Incentives to join here should be strong but lower than in the neo-corporatist cases.

Although neo-corporatist structures constitute a 'worse' form of interference with the pure market than lobbying organizations (as associations have authority over firms and can help shape markets), if they are genuinely governing their sectors they might ensure a more level playing field for market forces than purely self-interested lobbies. This needs to be borne in mind, just as we have needed to take account of the fact that both regulation and reciprocal business networks might sustain the pure market ideal of a large number of small-firm participants better than unrestrained competition would.

As we have noted, in the 1960s in France and Italy governments preferred to deal directly with individual firms, which meant that associations did little, not even lobbying much. Indeed, it seems to be this form of strong statist intervention in individual firms that is associated with the weakest organized business role, not market economies. It is difficult to establish the role of organizations in the Portuguese and Spanish dictatorships. Ostensibly impressive formal, organic corporatist structures existed. However, the evidence suggests that these were virtually shadow organizations that had no real autonomy in relations between the regimes and business interests (Linz 1981). These tended to be carried on through inter-personal contacts between governments, individual firms, and other parts of the social elite, rather as in France.

In the UK and USA associations played an important lobbying role, while rarely accepting corporatist responsibilities (Shonfield 1964; Grant and Marsh 1977; Olson 1982; Hollingsworth and Lindberg 1985). Organizations were more corporatist in Belgium, the Netherlands, and Switzerland, and even more central to national corporatist coordination in the three Scandinavian countries and Japan. In Austria and Germany the compulsory *Kammern* and associations played an important role in self-governance. (For Austria, see Marin 1982; for Germany, see Shonfield 1964; Streeck 1992; for the Netherlands, see Bax 1990: 153–7.) There were important sectoral exceptions to these generalizations (Streeck and Schmitter 1985); the agricultural sector was strongly organized on a corporatist basis virtually everywhere; the defence sector constituted particularly strong lobbies in France, the UK, and USA; and the financial sector took a virtually corporatist form in the UK.

The numerical decline of organizations in the late 1980s was reflected in or reflected shifts in their role, tending to press organizational structures towards the market pole as they tried to hold on to their members rather than regulate them. Corporatist structures began to unravel into lobbies; lobbying increasingly became firm- rather than association-based. On the other hand, lobbying did not diminish in intensity in any way. Tendencies towards deregulation (to be discussed below) placed a stronger premium rather than a weaker one on lobbying governments than did a stable regulatory regime proof against interference; globalizing firms lobbied governments in order to secure privileges and inducements to encourage them to invest in one country rather than another.

These changes did not usually alter the relative ranking of countries, but pressed most of them in the lobbying direction. Thus, lobbying became more lodged in individual firms than in associations in the UK and USA, producing a weakening of associations' role. Swedish associations moved sharply from a neo-corporatist to a (still associational) lobbying role, though largely because of developments in the labour market (Pestoff 1995). Dutch firms, located in a highly international economy with a neo-corporatist structure still rooted in originally religion-based structures, began to move to an individual firm mode (Hemerijck 1992); but by the mid-1990s they had found a revised mode of corporatist relationships, both with each other and with the state (Visser and Hemerijck 1997). Some German firms left their associations to avoid the constraints of imposed decisions. On the other hand, moving in the opposite direction were Finland, gradually acquiring Scandinavian characteristics, and the new democracies in southern Europe, acquiring for the first time autonomous organizational structures. Something similar took place in France and Italy as governments moved away from clientelistic relations with individual firms (Hayward 1995).

MARKETS AND NETWORKS OF RECIPROCITY

Another way in which the pure market model can be distorted is if actors may interact with each other through personal and community networks, or long-standing rather than calculated market links. The exchanges within arrangements of this kind have the character of networks of reciprocity: people do things for each other within the framework of a relationship that they expect to be long term. They therefore do not count the costs and benefits of each transaction, as in pure contract. They expect to receive as well as give, as the term reciprocity implies, but they may be willing to wait a time for reciprocity and they may not make precise calculations of the costs and benefits. This contradicts the market model of precisely calculated losses and gains and short-term relations. We shall look at two different aspects of this: the existence of local community-based, reciprocal economies; and different kinds of relationships between banks and firms embedded in different financial systems.

Reciprocal Economies

The tendency for some local community contexts to generate networks of reciprocation and commitment within which firms may locate themselves was mentioned in Chapter 3. Some arguments about this extend more widely to consider relations between firms and parties, churches, families. It can however also be seen in the character of relations between firms and more immediate components of their local environment: suppliers and competitors.

Informal networks operate through norms of reciprocity and community exchange. A group of small firms located within a community might be able to threaten various sanctions of social exclusion in order to ensure conformity from each other in co-operative tasks in which there are temptations to break rank. More positively, they can pool resources and gain from cooperation in a way that is not possible through pure exchange. This mode of behaviour is not fully consistent with the formal principles of the market, since it includes forms of communication and cooperation not based on pure exchange. In the pure market there are no relations with competitors; and relations with elements of the local community are unimportant.

There is no obvious indicator for the existence of these networks, and we are therefore dependent entirely on ethnographic studies that have considered their existence. A further problem of the data is that this tradition of research is recent. Alfred Marshall (1912) described the phenomenon in some towns of the English Industrial Revolution (e.g. Birmingham and Sheffield), but there seems to be some agreement among observers that it declined with the rise of mass production and the Fordist system. In much literature its re-emergence has therefore been associated with post-Fordism and the move away from mass production in some parts of the economy (Piore and Sabel 1984; Hirst and Zeitlin 1990). However, others point out that the forms of production involved in these local economies is not necessarily 'post-' anything (Voelzkow and Glassmann 1998), and the Italian research which started the current interest is more often dealing with modernized craft production than with something succeeding mass production (Bagnasco 1977; Becattini 1987; Trigilia 1986, 1991). It may therefore be wrong to see these developments as starting in only recent years.

The role of small firms, sometimes very small ones, in some of the most dynamic regions of the Italian economy has been the focus of particular discussion, especially in Emilia-Romagna (Best 1990; Brusco 1992; Bianchi and Gualtieri 1990; Bianchi and Giordani 1993; Leborgne and Lipietz 1988). It was during the 1970s that Bagnasco, Becattini, Trigilia, and others began to note that the familiar division between industrial north and backward agricultural south did not exhaust the diversity of the Italian economy, and that the industrial districts of small firms in sectors such as engineering, advanced ceramics, and textiles in central Italy merited separate consideration. While firms continued to compete, their cooperative relationships facilitated product specialization, with enterprises concentrating on those markets where they had a competitive edge.

One area of Denmark seems also to possess these networks, Jutland (Kristensen 1992); but elsewhere in Scandinavia there seems to be little evidence. There has also been work on Germany, mainly but not solely concentrating on Baden-Württemberg (Tödtling 1994; Herrigel 1989; Maier 1987; Sabel, Herrigel, Deeg, and Kazis 1989) and Nordrhein-Westfalen (Voelzkow 1990). Streeck (1987, 1992) has described such processes more generally among German employers, though these are likely to be associated with formal organizational membership too. Catalonia and Ireland have also been found to possess these districts (Cooke and Morgan 1994, 1998), and the Jura mountains in Switzerland (Glasmeier 1994). Studies of French (Ganne 1992; Le Galès 1993) and American examples seem to be describing exceptions rather than national typicalities, though the latter include some of the most dynamic sectors of US manufacturing, particularly computers and biotechnology (Swann *et al.* 1998).

It is not possible to construct any ranking system for the 1960 period; an incomplete impressionistic scale can be suggested for the early 1990s; Italy clearly possesses strong reciprocal networks, with Denmark, Germany, and possibly Switzerland in a middle position. France, Sweden, the UK, and the USA rank low.

Financial Markets

An important element in the immediate market environment of firms concerns sources of finance. There are no easy indicators for this variable, but the facts are reasonably straightforward and enable us to make some simple rankings. There is a large debate in the literature on the relationship between financial systems and economic activity (Zysman 1983; Mayer and Alexander 1990). From this it emerges that most financial systems can be classified as being either capital- or credit-based, the difference between these two discriminating according to our central criterion of interest: adherence to or departure from the pure market model.

Capital-based systems approximate closely to the pure market concept of arm's length arrangements. Companies' primary means of raising new investment is through the issue of stocks or bonds. These are purchased by numerous individuals and institutions, each free to buy and sell them at will. As a result, relations between owners and their companies tend to be distant, purely market-contractual—or 'arm's length' in Zysman's (1983) phrase; investors will tend to display little loyalty to a given firm, being concerned with short-term perspectives (Soskice 1990). Managers of such firms can ignore this speculative battle for short-term investment if the ownership of shares is separated from control of the corporation, but this can become ineffective if the market places few restrictions on hostile takeovers. In that case, managers who make long-term investments that depress profits face the risk of an outside interest seizing control over the company and raising the share price by cutting investment or selling off the assets of the firm that are undervalued by the market. Even if management is successful in fighting off a takeover bid, it may leave the company in debt to the extent that it cannot afford long-term investments. Even in cases where managers are not directly responsible to shareholders, their investment timescales may be influenced by the dominant financial market in the country and the criteria for evaluating performance which it sets. In general therefore the capital-based model is one closely tied to the pure market concept of capitalism.

Among the countries being considered here Ireland, the UK, and the USA adhere closest to this model. Scott (1997: ch. 4) analyses this form of Anglo-American capitalism, testifies to its longevity and also argues that it is very much a creation of the English-speaking world, and will be found elsewhere among former countries of the British empire (ibid. 92–102). Although this and most other research refers to relatively recent periods, we can also turn to a study based on the early 1960s (Shonfield 1964) which described the UK and USA in similar terms. Since Ireland has if anything moved away from its British past over the years, we can assume that it certainly followed the UK model in the earlier period.

Although these cases approach a free market concept of corporate finance, it is notable that in both the UK and USA firms are involved in what Scott (1997) calls 'controlling constellations', whereby interlocking directorships and cross-dependencies, mainly mediated through banks (ibid. 120–1), enable important groups of capitalists to secure power and stability for their interests in a way that compromises the assumptions of the pure competitive model. It does not however affect the short-term orientation of this form of capitalism, since the interest constellations are able to shift their holdings rapidly from one firm to another. The rise of institutional investment during the 1980s and 1990s has in fact intensified this characteristic (ibid. 122).

Under the alternative form of company financing, credit-based systems, a regulatory framework allows (or even requires) banks or other financial institutions to take long-term ownership positions in industrial companies, creating incentives for institutional shareholders to become more committed to the strategic planning of the enterprise and thereby facilitating communication of a more dialogistic form than is provided by market signals alone. Hostile takeovers are made difficult. Responses to market signals are slower, and judgements may be affected by interpersonal links (the phenomenon known as 'cronyism'). A bank provides management with a stable source of investment and expert advice acquired from its involvement with other major economic actors. In return it secures intimate knowledge of the firm's operations and contributes to its long-term planning, enabling it to safeguard both its equity stake and the loans that it has made to the corporation. Looked at in a different way, within the German system banks can interfere, and rob client companies of autonomy.

This model suits our concept of close institutional relationships with the sources of finance, which is at the opposite pole from the pure market. It has taken a number of different forms. If we look first at the system that existed around 1960, in Germany and Austria banks took long-term stakes in firms through membership of corporate boards (Shonfield 1964).[7] These large universal banks, while very powerful institutions, restricted themselves very much to a national role, which impeded short-term change and flexibility in contrast with the Anglo-American model. Banking in the Scandinavian countries was rather similar. Dutch and Swiss banks had a similar structure but were far more internationally oriented, which locates those systems somewhere between the German and the Anglophone models. Scott (1997: 142–55), who accepts a similar list of countries as belonging to this type, calls this pattern that of 'corporate affiliates', and points to its position as a form of organized capitalism which is being undermined by recent trends to disorganization and the dominance of the Anglo-American model (see also Streeck 1997). Pontusson (1997), in comparing the Swedish system with the German, points to ways in which that country's capitalism too has begun to move away from a classic German model towards an Anglo-American one.

In a comparison between German and British companies, Windolf and Beyer (1996) demonstrated some of the further implications of these structures. The concentration of shareholdings, especially by non-financial institutions, in Germany enabled owners to dominate firms, and interlocking networks of directors tended to link firms in the same industry into what they call 'cooperative capitalism'. The UK followed more closely a pure market model, with ownership of firms highly and anonymously dispersed among shareholders in the financial sector rather than the firms' own industries—what the authors call 'competitive capitalism'. Research into ownership patterns of British firms by Scott (1990) suggests similar results, identifying fragmented constellations of interests as the most important form of ownership of both large industrial and financial firms, as opposed to wholly owned by an individual or family or other forms of control. Over time (between 1976 and 1988) institutional share ownership increased at the expense of other forms, though family ownership had by no means

---

[7] In Japan banks have usually been part of the corporate network of the firm itself, which is further removed from market transactions than the German model. Scott (1997: 192) describes the system as one where relatively decentralized federations of aligned enterprises form the basis of a network of insiders who, within the scope left by their autonomy, develop special relations with each other.

disappeared (ibid. 365). However, he also found considerable stability in patterns of ownership within the constellations: organizations holding shares in major firms changed the size of their holdings only very gradually (ibid. 362–4). A particularly important role seems to have been played in the UK by pension funds investing the pension contributions accrued by employees. Such funds are entirely in the control of the organizations, not the pensioners themselves.

Scott (1986, 1990, 1997) has also found patterns similar to the UK in other English-speaking advanced societies in North America and Australasia. In continental Europe, in contrast, the survival of smaller enterprises had led to the persistence of higher levels of family control (Scott 1990: 369), with firms having more recourse to banks than to other financial intermediaries and with a smaller role for pension funds. Japan emerges from this review as similar to continental Europe (ibid. 370).

In southern Europe (here including Belgium and France as well as Italy, Portugal, and Spain) banks were more specialized and related to specifically defined sectors of the economy and types of firm. Scott (1997: 155–69) sees this pattern as originating mainly in the family-based businesses of these countries, needing to modernize but reluctant to relinquish family control for the anonymity of the German form. He possibly underestimates here the continuing role of family-owned firms in Germany. In these countries, as the state began to seek to engage firms in tasks of national modernization, a gulf developed between large enterprises engaged on tasks of national construction and small family businesses. Financial institutions then developed to bridge this gap and cater for the needs of small firms. In Italy in particular a large number of very local savings banks (*casse di risparmio*) served the needs of local firms in a very close, interpersonal way. This group therefore lies further towards the non-market pole than the German model. There were also elements of public ownership in the banking systems of these countries, which further justifies ranking them further away from the pure market, but in a different way.

The French system went through a brief period of divergence from current trends towards a more market-oriented capitalism during the 1980s, when the main banks were nationalized. However, with the re-privatization of these in the next decade and general other measures for deregulating the French economy, it too has joined the main trend (Boyer 1997).

While there is some stability in the pattern of countries between the early 1960s and the present time, there has been change conforming with a model of 'disorganization' of capitalism (Scott 1997: ch. 8; Lash and Urry 1987: ch. 7). During the 1980s capital markets became increasingly open as a result of a number of developments: legal changes, especially in the UK and the USA, liberalized movements of capital and made it easier for banks and other financial institutions to move resources, to borrow, and to lend; developments in technology opened major new possibilities for speed of movement in dealings in company stock; changes in the organization of stock markets, especially in London, also made the movement of funds more flexible and mobile.

The general changes, described as spreading from the Anglo-American cases to other systems (Tsoukalis 1997: esp. 92–101), push the former further into conformity with their original type, but for others constitute moves against the historical pattern. Changes have therefore been slower to occur. Therefore, although there is a certain convergence on a more market-based system, the immediate implication of this move is to increase the distance between some of the countries because of the different speed of movement. No changes have thoroughly displaced existing systems, though the French one has moved away from the pattern of small, particularistic banks. This was originally achieved through the nationalization of further banks during the early 1980s, but subsequent de-nationalization has left the country with a banking system closer to a market model than before. Similarly, Spain and Portugal have experienced a period of reforms to closely controlled banking systems of the Fascist period, moving closer to a market model. The German and Scandinavian banking systems have become more open to international markets following the liberalization of exchange movements. In several of these countries, as well as Japan, stock exchanges have become far more important than in the past. Ironically, the move to European monetary union might encourage a further move towards the Anglo-American model by the continental economies. Its light level of regulation and lack of deep institutional involvement is more easily generalizable and portable than the various European systems, anchored deeply in the specificities of national business communities, and therefore provides an easier basis on which to build a Europe-wide system (Story 2000).

NATIONAL PROFILES OF CAPITALISM

Two tasks remain to complete our study of the development of modern capitalism. First, we must try to characterize individual countries according to the dimensions we have used, to assess the extent to which they have changed, and to see if they fall into particular groupings. After that we shall be in a position to consider whether it is possible to make any overall generalizations about the development of capitalism in the advanced societies.

Table 6.6 summarizes the results of the above discussion in a way that attempts a characterization of countries in the early 1960s; the work is hampered considerably by an absence of data on several countries and by the fact that some of our data really belong to a slightly later period. It is not possible to cover the theme of reciprocal networks at all. Nevertheless, we can make some tentative assessments.

Some countries have 'pure profiles', meaning having a strong position on all pure market forms or on only one of the forms of deviation from that. Denmark and Norway were corporatist. Finland, the UK, and the USA were concentrated economies. Others combined elements of two alternative forms with pure markets: Austria was neo-corporatist with a reciprocity financial system. Belgium combined concentration and a regulatory state with free markets. France combined a regulatory state and a reciprocal financial system with such markets, and the Netherlands and Sweden combined concentration and corporatism. Portugal and Spain had distinctive patterns of strong government regulation and corporatist membership, but low public spending and low real activity for corporatist structure. Germany fell furthest from the free-market model, scoring strongly on all indicators of deviance from that form except state involvement. Japan depended on a reciprocal financial system.

When we move to the 1990s we can make a more satisfactory analysis as more data are available and they relate to the appropriate period. This is summarized in Table 6.7. We are also able now to take account of reciprocal relations in small-firm networks as

Table 6.6 *Forms of capitalist economies, c.1960*

	Ai	Aii	Bi	Bii	Ci	Cii	Di	Dii
Pure market forms	DK, GR, IRL, I, E	USA	All except F, S, UK, USA	D, NL, USA	F, GR, I	F, GR, I, P E		IRL, UK, USA
Deviations from pure market forms	B, SF, D, NL, S, UK, USA	D		B, F, P, E	A, DK, D, NL, N, P, E, S	A, DK, D, NL, N, S, CH		A, D, F, I, JAP
	Hierarchies		State involvement		Neo-corporatism		Reciprocity	

Note: Intermediate or ambiguous cases, or cases where there is inadequate evidence to form a judgement, are not included.

Table 6.7 *Forms of capitalist economies, c.1995*

	Ai	Aii	Bi	Bii	Ci	Cii	Di	Dii
Pure market forms	DK, GR, IRL, I, E	DK, USA	JAP	DK, IRL, CH, UK, USA	GR		A, B, SF, F, NL, N, P, S, UK, USA	IRL, UK, USA
Deviations from pure market forms	B, SF, D, NL, S, UK, USA	I, JAP	DK, SF, S		A	A	I	
	Hierarchies		State involvement		Neo-corporatism		Reciprocity	

Note: Intermediate or ambiguous cases, or cases where there is inadequate evidence to form a judgement, are not included.

an additional institutional form. Again countries are presented where they contain major divergences from the pure market model.

Austria appears now as primarily corporatist (with otherwise relatively free markets); Belgium, Germany, the Netherlands as concentrated; Denmark as having strong state spending but not regulation; Finland and Sweden as concentrated with strong state spending; Italy is an unusual mix of strong labour commitment and small-firm reciprocity.

A recent comparative study of mechanisms for economic cooperation among 17 OECD countries by Lane Kenworthy (1995) has attempted to provide an index of economic cooperation for these countries. On the basis of available research findings, the author allocates to each country a 1, a 0.5, or a 0 score for the strength of cooperation devices among a number of actors: at macro-level among industries, with unions and relations between governments and unions; at meso-level between purchasers and suppliers, investors and producers, and competing firms; at micro-level between labour and management, among workers and across the production chain. This overlaps to some extent with the above analysis, though its concentration on cooperation is more specific than our contrast between pure markets (which would constitute non-cooperation for Kenworthy) and various opposites. His scale (ibid. 170) resembles the outcome of the above analysis in that those countries with extensive recourse to corporatist and reciprocal networks as well as institutionalized labour and investor relations emerge with the highest scores (Japan, Austria, Germany, and the Nordics), while the Anglophones have least cooperation (in our terms, are closest to the pure market pole). Strength of the state and size of firms are variables not relevant to Kenworthy's concerns, but within the areas of overlap a similar outcome is achieved.

FROM THE 1960S TO THE 1990S: TOWARDS A PURER CAPITALISM?

We now need to draw some conclusions for our central question in this chapter: have economies become more or less capitalist in the period since the peak of the mid-century model? Overall there may have been some return to a purer form of capitalism, not in contrast with the 1960s, but between the early 1980s and the current decade. This mainly takes the form of a loosening of neo-corporatism and the distinct roll-back both of the state and of credit-based finance systems. However, the patterns are complex. Over the longer period such a change is not clear, while a possible rise in the role of small-business networks might indicate a shift, in at least some countries, to a less centralized form of institutionalized capitalism than that predominating in the Fordist period. We can certainly conclude that the economies of the advanced societies are not becoming *post*-capitalist, as has sometimes been claimed by observers of the advanced societies.

We can combine this discussion with evidence from the previous chapter to provide a more definitive summary. The types of change described in the two chapters are similar. In both analyses—of occupations and earning in Chapter 5, of institutions in the current chapter—capitalism can be seen to have changed in a number of respects since the early 1960s, and to have produced a more complex class structure and institutional base, but the changes are reorganizations within an overall capitalist framework, not necessarily implying any reduction in the inequalities associated with the operation of capitalist economies. It is also notable that the two countries which had seen a major increase in labour-market inequalities (the UK and the USA) are also the cases which (apart from the less advanced southern European cases) have the most purely capitalist economies. The historical association between capitalism and inequality seems to continue at the end of the twentieth century.

The question is then obviously raised whether and to what extent institutions of mass democracy, universal citizenship, and the welfare state ameliorate these inequalities, and whether these structures have changed since the early 1960s. In Chapter 12 we shall present these as some of the major defences against capitalist encroachment of non-capitalist areas of society. This will be addressed in the final part of the book. First, however, we must consider some of society's less economically related institutions, since welfare policy is related to developments in these too.

Part III
SOCIOLOGICAL LIBERALISM AND THE INSTITUTIONS OF TRADITIONAL COMMUNITY

As I defined it in Chapter 1, sociological liberalism refers to the capacity of institutions to preserve a mutual autonomy while also engaging in cooperation. It will not be adequate for this to depend solely on tolerant attitudes among a population; we have to identify specific mechanisms that sustain and support it. These mechanisms are liable to change over time and vary across societies, and they may occasionally fail, leading one or another institution to be 'overrun' by the practices and criteria of another. As pointed out in Chapter 1, the best starting point for an understanding of such mechanisms was the organizational form developed in the Netherlands in the late nineteenth century to cope with religious and political divisions. People spent most of their lives interacting solely with members of their own politico-religious groups, but the leaders of these groups co-operated in the management of the society as a whole. The different groups were seen as different pillars (*zuilen*) which together, though separately, sustained the overall edifice of Dutch society in general. There was a subtle mix of mutually respected separation and cooperation. What seems to be a matter of ideas and values is in reality embedded in firm structures of social relations.

In my concept of sociological liberalism the combination of separation and cooperation has to be even more subtle and complex than in *verzuiling*, because I am not carrying over from the Dutch model the concept of separation among the masses and cooperation among elites (Lijphart 1968). Instead, people live their lives in different institutional settings; the separations happen within those lives.

While we shall find instances of this institutional self-protection at a number of different points in the social structure, particular importance attaches to the protection of weaker from stronger institutions. As we have seen in Parts I and II, in capitalist industrial societies there is particular strength and power in economic institutions. For example, the capacity of the economy to reward people with income for participating in it may lead them to choose to spend large amounts of their time working in preference to being with their families or attending religious services. Most institutions will offer rewards of some kind for participating in them (for example, a family will offer love). However, money income differs from all other rewards (except power) in that it is itself a means to other ends. When we pursue money we are able to postpone making a decision about the ends we are actually pursuing, as the money can be held in reserve until such time as we might make a decision. Attending religious services might carry with it a power far greater than this, in that it might affect our eternal souls. However, to pursue religion at the expense of material gain requires a considerable act of faith. In considering sociological liberalism we are therefore particularly though not solely interested in those institutions which might be especially vulnerable to swamping by economic ones. The other powerful institutional structure in modern societies is the state, which has great powers to coerce and enforce obedience. The institutions with which we are concerned here are primarily those which lack the pervasive power of these two great forces, economy and state, and require protection from them if they are to survive.

In particular we are mainly concerned with those institutions inherited from past social forms, when they were more important and economy and state less so, but which have since lost their power. In some though not all cases these are also institutions which lack hard-edged organizational capacities of the kind afforded by the capitalist firm or the state; they depend for their identity on shared assumptions and understandings and have the implicit character of community.

The first to be considered (in Chapter 7) will be the family, resuming the threads of discussion from Part I and returning to the great division of labour between two kinds of work—that in the paid economy and that in the household—which has been one of the major characteristics of modernity. How can we characterize the particular forms of that division embodied in the mid-century compromise form of modernity? What have been the implications for the family of the changes in work in recent decades that we considered in Part I?

The rules of sociological liberalism require that family bonds do not interfere with activities in other institutions, such as employment. (Max Weber included in his concept of the capitalist enterprise the separation of the household budget from that of the enterprise (Weber 1922).) This can be problematic, as families make great claims on the loyalty of their members and seek to use all their resources to assist them. The education system is the point at which this tension is most acute in advanced societies. Educational opportunities are a major element of the citizenship model of these societies, promising that inequalities and disadvantages of social origin can be compensated by people taking advantage of meritocratic educational opportunities. Meanwhile, however, families promise their members that they will do all they can to help them win social advantage, whether by bypassing education or by helping them with the educational process. Since education is concentrated on young people who are still primarily living within their parental families, there is a strong potential clash between the family and the concept of equality of educational opportunity when wealthy or otherwise advantaged families try to carry out this promise for their children.

How have societies of the mid-century compromise tried to cope with this tension? And how has the pattern changed as that form of society also changed? This is the theme of

Chapter 8. Existing research on education, family background, and social mobility is used within this framework to illuminate the changing strength or weakness of the institutional segregation of the family, in the process further illuminating our attempt to define the changing class structure of advanced societies.

Concepts of sociological liberalism began with the protection from each other of religion and state, and of warring religions. Meanwhile, most theories of modernization include secularization—that is the decline of religion—as central to the overall process. A lower level of religious identification should therefore distinguish advanced from earlier societies. How can we reconcile this with the protection of institutions central to the sociologically liberal component of the mid-century compromise? Within such societies we should find that religious institutions are left alone, but by the same token not permitted the non-liberal, totalizing role that they enjoyed in some pre-industrial contexts. If the mid-century model has been eroded by postmodernist forces, we should expect to see certain kinds of religious revival, postmodernism favouring a heterogeneity of cultural expression and a rejection of rationalist domination.

We shall consider these questions in Chapter 9. Religion having been found to be an important force in producing diversity in the work patterns of Western European societies, as well as in family and ethnic experience, is not treated here as a residual institution, but as fundamental to the continuing interaction between work and family during recent changes. The central paradox is that, while religion seems to have become weaker as a force for constructing social identity in nearly all Western European societies, all rivals to it in that role (with the possible exception of national and ethnic identities) have become even weaker. This further helps develop the concept of late modern society being in some ways fragmented.

Overlapping with religion, reinforcing it, rivalling it or even extinguishing it has been loyalty to a human grouping to which people consider they belong by some combination of biological descent, geography, and state organization. For modern societies, including those of the mid-century compromise, these have been national identities. These will be considered in Chapter 10 in the context of the issue of ethnic identities and the place of ethnic minorities and immigrants within European societies.

Mutual protection of national identity and those of other institutions have been fundamental to the dynamics of sociological liberalism, as has the relationship between diverse ethnicities, especially in the expansion of international population movements that has characterized the years since the onset of the mid-century compromise. Liberal individualism would seem to imply a declining significance of nation and ethnicity, especially as the development of mass citizenship implied the absence of ethnic categories of persons. However, the populations formed by this process (which in several countries continues a process of forging national identity began much earlier) were not neutral, acultural entities, but had been formed by states with nation-building projects that embodied distinctive symbolic and practical social specificities. How successful were the nation states in achieving this task? Is nation the most useful level for defining the identity of most European people?

At the same time, the mass population movements encouraged by the successful development of social compromise economies after the Second World War generated considerable mixing of different ethnic groups, a process occurring in very diverse ways in different countries. To what extent did societies make use of segregation devices to resolve these questions? Eventually their resurgence as a source of cultural identity and conflict in many parts of modern Europe—and elsewhere in the world—has become a major social characteristic and one which in its form as multiculturalism is clearly relevant to postmodernist analysis of growing cultural diversity.

Chapter 7

THE FAMILY

As an institution found in virtually all forms of society, the family has often been very broadly defined in order to fit this universal context. Here however we are limited to forms found in industrial and industrializing Europe. We can therefore limit ourselves to a concept of the family as an institution focused on human reproduction: historically, European families have usually been based on marriage, which can be defined as a formal and legally valid relationship between a man and a woman, serving primarily as a means for organizing and legitimating sexual relations between them and also legitimating the children which result from those relations. The couple and such children then comprise what is usually called the 'nuclear' family. Various other recognized connections between this group and others attached to them by similar relationships—uncles, cousins, grandparents, etc.—are part of a wider family network.

Sometimes married couples do not have children or sexual relationships despite an original intention of doing so; sometimes—as will be discussed below—couples live together for prolonged periods and raise families but do not marry; all these are just exceptional types of the predominant form. Rather different are marriages where the couples never intend to have children or even sexual relations, or prolonged sexual relationships between people of the same sex (homosexual partnerships). These are sociologically interesting phenomena, and their incidence is definitely growing. However, to date they affect too few people to justify discussion in a work of the present scope.

We are here in the presence of very different relationships from those which we have considered until now, which were based on calculative exchanges and domination focused on the employment of labour in exchange for money wages. At the heart of the family there is, it is true, a kind of contract, the marriage contract, and certain exchanges of services and indeed money. But in all the societies with which we are concerned there are moral norms which try to limit the application of calculation to family transactions. Concepts of easy exit are not expected to be applied, and relationships can only be rejected and thrown off with difficulty. Family members are expected to develop strong affective and trusting ties to each other, and it is the duties and sentiments resulting from these that are ideally expected to motivate exchanges among family members.

This in no way means that the family is an arena devoid of power relations. The family has virtually always been centred on male power, in particular within modern societies the power of the income-earning husband, often known as the head of the household and sometimes imbued with various kinds of legal authority over his wife and pre-adult children. Most theories of the family in industrial society stress how, with the decline of family-based market activities and the rise of the firm, two extremely important processes took place: women were driven from the labour force into a purely domestic role; and the family became a place of primarily affective and emotional bonds. This is the basis of an application of the idea of sociological liberalism to the family. The family acquired an autonomy as an institution within which different rules were expected to operate from those in the wider society. However, just as the capitalist firm uses hierarchy as well as markets, so the family retained authority as well as love: the patriarchal authority of the husband in particular, but also the intergenerational authority of parents over children.

Sociological liberalism implies the relative autonomy of different institutional areas from each other, but not their complete segregation, since they are interdependent and need to interact. There have to be mechanisms which ensure this combination of integration with autonomy if institutions are to exist alongside each other. The sociology of the place of the family in modernization that developed during the 1950s and 1960s presented a model well suited to our concept of mid-century compromise society (see, in particular, Parsons and Bales 1955). The balance between integration and relative autonomy was to be achieved through gender and age segregation: men and unmarried women would enter the paid workforce in the economic system and behave according to its calculative rules; married women, children, and the elderly would remain outside the formal economy and sustain the family through both domestic work and the maintenance of the family's affective bonds. This separation of roles provided for the separation of modes of action, leading to stereotypical male and female character types, while at many points the worlds of family and economy interacted heavily. The family would nourish and sustain those of its members working in the economy; and as a unit of consumption purchase much of the product of economic activity.

The family's reproductive activities were also relevant. Through reproduction the family would provide new recruits for the workforce and send them to the education system to be prepared for employment. According to modernization theory this system is in turn institutionally separated from the family; educational processes are expected to operate on rational, meritocratic criteria and cannot let the emotional ties and loyalties of the family intervene. We shall submit this idea to some critical scrutiny in the next chapter, while we here assess to what extent the general model of segregation through gender roles might have been true of the industrial societies of the 1960s, and then examine what changes have subsequently taken place.

There has been considerable debate in the sociological literature concerning the timing of certain important events in the development of the prototypical 'modern' family. Early post-war functionalist accounts posited a pre-industrial extended family with widespread functions being gradually knocked back to its limited, nuclear family core during the course of the twentieth century. However, as we saw in the Prologue, socio-historical research has shown that the extended family had not really existed in north-western Europe even during the early modern, pre-industrial period (Mitterauer and Sieder 1982; Seccombe 1992; Sgritta 1989). At marriage couples would normally move away from their parents and siblings to form separate households; elderly parents, especially widows, would possibly live with their married children, but the low life expectancies of the pre-modern period limited the number of people to whom this applied.

There has been similar doubt over the timing of the rise of the patriarchal model of the family. Ideas that the two genders were on a more or less equal footing until capitalist industrialization removed women from the workforce and placed them under male authority cannot be sustained; there is considerable evidence that rural society was very male-dominated (Mitterauer and Sieder 1982). However, the degree of patriarchy and also of gender segregation intensified in the early stages of modernization as women left the workforce and acquired a solely domestic position in economies which were fully dependent on wage labour (Julémont 1993). In one of the few remaining areas of a pre-industrial economy in contemporary Europe, today Greek women in the countryside take a full part in farm work with their husbands; have virtually full responsibility for housework; and may care for both aged relatives and the small children of their own working daughters (Pavelle 1994). Although the division of labour between husband and wife was taken for granted by post-war sociologists, there was often insistence that somehow the post-war family of the democratic world must be a 'democratic' family (Dahlström 1989). But Sogner (1993), in addition to making a similar point to Julémont about the change in the character of housework alongside the decline of the family economy, has suggested that political democracy in the wider society initially *increased* the gap between men and women, because men were first admitted alone into this new sphere that elevated the importance of the non-familial.

Several of these developments are associated with the gradual rise of industrial society in general and not just with the particular, rather recent, form of mid-century compromise society with which we are primarily concerned. Nevertheless, many of them did reach a kind of apogee during the mid-century compromise period. The thesis of relative autonomy leads us to expect a 'strong' family concept; there should be considerable activity around making and sustaining families. This can be translated into several testable propositions:

1. There should be a *high level of female domesticity*: within a 'Fordist' family division of labour, women should be expected to play a central role in domestic tasks and not to participate much in the paid workforce. In many European societies a combination of increased marriage rates, the decline of agriculture and domestic service, as well as the decline of the textile industry in which many women had worked, led to a sharp diminution of full-time female working in the years after the Second World War (Blossfeld and Hakim 1997; Huinink and Mayer 1995: 188).[1]

2. *A low average age of marriage*: second, people should marry young. 'Young' is of course a relative concept; in most human societies, stretching as widely as we can in time and place of which we have knowledge, girls have married shortly after puberty, or the mid-teens.[2]

3. *A high marriage rate*: a strong family concept with a high gender division of labour implies a high marriage rate.[3]

---

[1] To measure this I shall use the concept used in Chapter 2: that proportion of female persons who are not in education, are below the age of 80, and are neither in gainful employment nor registered as seeking work (i.e. unemployed).

[2] Age of marriage is normally measured from the point of view of women; in nearly all societies the average male age of marriage is between 30 and 36 months higher than this. I take data for first marriages only, as clearly subsequent marriages of widows and divorcees tell a different story.

[3] For much of the earlier part of this century the number of marriageable males was heavily affected for some countries by the deaths of the World Wars (especially the first) and certain other major disasters that differentially affected men.

Ideally we want to know the proportion of a population who will be married at some time in their life, but this is difficult to establish for a population which is moving in time. Can we assume that all 45 year-olds who are unmarried at the time we take our survey will never marry? What about 35 year-olds? What assumptions do we make about the potential marriage behaviour of 25 year-olds? The proportion of people in or having

4. *A relatively high rate of fertility*: mid-century compromise society came at the end of the process of demographic transition described in the Prologue, whereby there was an adjustment of low birth rates to low death rates. The population should therefore be expected to reproduce itself, that is on average each woman should produce 2.1 children.[4]

5. *A low rate of divorce*: if families are 'strong' they should remain together. The divorce rate is the most obvious, most easily available, but also a highly misleading indicator of family break-down. It is misleading if we want an indicator of the 'health' of the family, because in contexts where divorce is legally difficult or results in social ostracism, people might be very unhappy within marriages, creating families full of hate and tension, but unable to escape them. Divorce rates, not surprisingly, tend to rise when divorce laws are liberalized. However, provided we accept this and treat the divorce rate as only a measure of the extent to which families hold to-gether, irrespective of the internal *quality* of their relationships, we can make use of these rates.[5]

6. *A low level of illegitimacy*: a final easily available statistic for measuring the strength of marri-age is the proportion of births that are out of wedlock, which should be low where there is a strong model of the married family. This is however again a dubious indicator of the strength of family relations: in societies where the law and social practices impose considerable hardship on unmarried mothers or their children, there are strong incentives not to produce illegitimate children. However, if the law recognizes the rights of illegitimate children (for example to in-heritance) and if there is no social stigma attached to either unmarried mothers or their children, women will be less concerned to ensure that they are married before they give birth. Provided we bear this in mind we can use the datum.

Our concept of the family within mid-century compromise society should therefore give us a pattern of: high female domesticity (low labour-force participation); a low age of marriage (i.e. early 20s); a high marriage rate; a level of fertility of over 2.1 TFR; and low divorce and illegitimacy rates. If the mid-century compromise society thesis is cor-rect, in the early 1960s advanced industrial societies should have been characterized by this pattern, which is summarized in Table 7.1 line (a).

We can make two alternative predictions to what might happen afterwards in post-mid-century compromise society, depending on how we interpret contemporary devel-opments. Is the essential 'modern' project of calculation and rationalization of chosen ends reaching a point where it disrupts and fragments settled institution? Or is there a new postmodern project where people use their opportunities for greatly increased

been in the married state at any one time is the product of several decades of marital behaviour: the marriage rate among 75 year-olds tells us about the popularity of marriage half a century ago; if we are looking for current trends, we need a different datum. It is not possible to make these calculations and we have to make do with something rather different.

We therefore use the number of marriages taking place in a particular year or short run of years as somehow typifying the marriage behaviour of that period. Ideally we should want a figure for this rate for all women between the age when marriage becomes legally possible in a society and around 50 years old, and the rate should be expressed as a proportion of all women potentially available for first marriage, that is the denominator is all women who are not and never have been married. We can come close to this but not precisely: available data do not include an upper age limit, so the (rather small) number of spinsters over 50 enter the denominator, though only a few of them are likely to marry.

[4] We want to know something about the size of families, the number of children that women will have; but at any one time this number includes the fertility rates of past but still surviving generations. Here demo-graphers use a standard figure, the period total fertility rate (TFR), which gives the number of babies the average woman would produce if she experienced current age-specific fertility rates throughout her lifetime; this is a rather artificial figure, but it eliminates the effects of age structure differences when making com-parisons between the fertility levels of different populations (Coleman 1996a: 5).

[5] The same problems apply here as to marriage rates and fertility rates; we want a measure of current reality, and therefore take an annual rate of divorces per 10,000 first marriages.

Table 7.1 Models of family forms

	Female domesticity	Marriage age	Marriage rate	Fertility	Divorce	Illegitimacy
(a) Mid-century compromise	High	Low	High	High	Low	Low
(b) Family decline	Low	High	Low	Low	High	High
(c) New family form	Low	High	High	Medium	Low	Low

choice to produce extensive but viable diversity of ways of life? The alternatives can also be expressed another way. We know from Part I that one characteristic of this society is a major rise in female labour-force participation. According to our thesis this breaches the basis of institutional separation on which the relative autonomy of the family in mid-century compromise society rested. We might predict, either that the family is therefore 'damaged' as an institution, or that it will find new means of protecting its autonomy. The first possibility, which I shall call the *decline of the family* model, should give us, in addition to low female domesticity (high labour-force participation): a high age of marriage, a low marriage rate (both evidence that young people are avoiding entering the state), a low level of fertility (avoidance of family building), and high divorce and illegitimacy rates. This hypothesis is consistent with a pessimistic view of postmodernity as a fragmentation of social relationships, or with a concept of 'exacerbated modernity' according to which the rational calculation and individualism of the modern project itself eventually corrode the strong structures which were a part of the mid-century compromise form. The general model is summarized in Table 7.1 line (b).

The alternative possibility, or *new form of family integration*, would retain from this model the low level of female domesticity and should also be expected to retain a high age of marriage: prolonged female education, a desire to become established in careers and more careful mate selection should be expected. Beyond that however the pattern should more closely resemble that of mid-century compromise society: a high *eventual* marriage rate, a level of fertility above replacement level, and low divorce and illegitimacy rates. This is summarized in Table 7.1 line (c).

Appendix Tables A.7.1 and A.7.2 present the available data on these six items for the early 1960s and the early 1990s respectively for all 16 Western European countries under consideration as well as Japan and the USA. In only a few instances is it impossible to provide figures for a particular country. The tables also give the international means for the various statistics.[6] Data sources for the basic demographic facts about the family,

---

[6] These must be used cautiously: they are the means of each national figure, not for the total population represented by those figures. That is, the three million population of Ireland ranks equally to the 280 million of the USA, so each Irishman or Irish woman contributes 90 times as much to the international average as each

though incomplete and subject to the usual limitations on reliability, are far better than those for the economy with which we have been dealing until now. However, they still give us only the basic contours of family life, and to present a more complete picture we shall be dependent on research evidence which is not available on an even basis for all countries.

In order to determine whether a particular birth, divorce, or other rate was 'high' or 'low' at a particular time we need to relativize these concepts: Were levels on the various indicators for the various countries high or low in 1960 *from the point of view of the 1990s*? Were they high or low in 1990 *from the point of view of the early 1960s*? We shall carry out these exercises for both periods in the following discussion.[7]

THE FAMILY IN MID-CENTURY COMPROMISE SOCIETY

We look first at the early 1960s. We saw in the Prologue how north-western European societies had since the late Middle Ages adopted a pattern of postponed or avoided marriage (Seccombe 1992). The early decades of the twentieth century had seen a continuation of this historic trend, which the economic depressions of the inter-war years and the World Wars themselves further sharpened. In the years following the Second World War there was however a major shift in nearly all advanced societies back towards earlier and more universal marriage. This trend continued until the late 1960s, when the marriage rate began to decline, first in Sweden and Denmark and then in most of the rest of Western Europe, reaching the southern part of the continent in the mid-1970s (Kiernan 1996: 62–3). The mean age of marriage continued to decline during the 1970s; the European average fell from over 24 to 23 between 1960 and 1970. Since then it has begun to rise steadily, again faster in Scandinavia, slower in southern Europe (ibid. 64). Our key year of 1960 was not therefore the high point of the post-war 'popularity of marriage' pattern; however, it was close to it.

Fertility rates in the early part of the twentieth century were also low, in many countries falling some way below replacement level; then came the well-known 'baby boom' after the ending of the Second World War. In most European societies this peaked with remarkable simultaneity within a year of 1964, though in the USA it continued a little

---

American. This is because it is an underlying assumption of the structure of this book that there are such things as national societies, and these 18 units are our object of study.

With the exception of Italy and Spain, there is little internal variation in the demographic behaviour of Western European nation states (Coleman 1996a: 41–7). Jurado Guerrero and Naldini (1996) show that there are considerable inter-regional differences within both these countries. In general, it is the poorer regions that most show the pattern of 'traditional' marriage, with the more modernized ones being closer to a Western European pattern of divorce, illegitimacy, etc. However, the fertility rates of the poorer regions have moved very close to the low levels of the wealthier regions in recent years. De Rose (1992) reports that in 1983 divorce rates were highest in the north of Italy (the most industrial and 'modernized' part), slightly lower in the centre (the very distinctive zone of small-firm modernization), and much lower in the south (which remains economically backward).

7 For each indicator I define a three-point ranking of high, middle, and low. (I regard as middle-ranking all values between the mean and plus and minus half of its standard deviation; levels above that range are high; below are low.) In Appendix Tables A.7.1 and A.7.2 the rankings are shown for the time period itself. In order to relativize the data we derive what would constitute the rankings from the data for 1990 but apply them to the data for 1960, and vice versa. These rankings are not displayed in the appendix tables, but will be represented in tables within the chapter.

longer. Again, while 1960 is not the crucial year in either case, it is located around the high point of the fertility rise.

In the early post-war years there had in a number of countries been extended debate about an alleged collapse of the family following a rise in divorce and separation rates. Such a rise should not have been surprising. In several societies divorce became easier to achieve in liberalizing post-war legal reforms. Also, many people's lives had been massively disrupted by war: vast involuntary movements of populations, active participation in fighting and killing, separation of families. Once we move away from this period into the 1950s we find that levels of divorce and illegitimacy declined, only to rise again in the 1960s and early 1970s—in several societies again a time of new legislation facilitating divorce (F.-X. Kaufmann *et al.* 1997). The years around 1960 serve as a relatively 'still centre' between the two periods of active marital disruption of the mid-1940s and the years following the late 1960s.

From the point of view of 1990, only the Dutch 1960 national family pattern approximated perfectly to the mid-century compromise model (see Table 7.2). The USA comes close, but had a slightly high divorce rate. However, if, given the problems of the marriage rate, we regard as conforming to the mid-century compromise model all those with either high or middle (but not low) marriage rates, we find Belgium now conforming fully and a number of other societies deviating in only minor respects. Several countries—France, Germany, Greece, Italy, Norway, Portugal, and the UK—have middle-ranking rather than low marriage ages. Denmark deviates, not in terms of

Table 7.2 1960s families from the perspective of the 1990s

	Female domesticity	Marriage age	Marriage rate	Fertility	Divorce	Illegitimacy
Austria	M	L	L	H	L	L
Belgium	H	L	M	H	L	L
Denmark	H	L	M	H	M	L
Finland	M	?	M	H	L	L
France	H	L	L	H	L	L
Germany	H	L	M	H	L	L
Greece	H	H	M	H	L	L
Ireland	H	L	L	H	L	L
Italy	H	L	M	H	L	L
Netherlands	H	L	H	H	L	L
Norway	H	L	M	H	L	L
Portugal	H	L	M	H	L	L
Spain	H	M	M	H	L	L
Sweden	H	L	L	H	L	L
Switzerland	H	?	L	H	L	L
UK	H	L	M	H	L	L
Japan	M	?	M	H	L	?
USA	H	L	H	H	M	L

age of marriage, but of a slightly higher divorce rate. Sweden and Switzerland deviate further in having *low* rather than medium marriage rates—particularly surprising given that these were two countries unaffected by the World Wars and therefore without the frequent surplus female population.

This leaves only three countries which deviate enough from the model for us to be unable to say that they experienced our hypothesized mid-century compromise family form. In two (Austria and Japan) the level of female domesticity was moderate rather than high—in each case largely because of rural employment as we saw in Chapter 2. Austria had a low marriage rate and therefore an overall demographic pattern similar to Sweden and Switzerland; Japan had, like several other countries, a moderate marriage rate but unfortunately data on age of marriage are missing. The remaining exception, Ireland, was also predominantly rural, though it had a high female domesticity rate; it differed considerably from the marriage model in having a high age of marriage and low marriage rate.

The exceptions and partial exceptions to the model do not form any particular pattern; it is reassuring to the mid-century thesis that it is among more rural societies that we find most of the departures—though in that case we should have expected Greece, Italy, Portugal, and Spain similarly to diverge.

We can more easily consider sub-patterns within the general pattern if we apply high, middle, and low rankings based on the mean and standard deviation for the 1960 data themselves: from the viewpoint of the patterns of the early 1960s, which patterns corresponded most to the average of the period, which deviated and in which directions? Table 7.3 enables us to consider these questions. We can in particular identify three groups. First, some societies show unusually high divorce and illegitimacy ratings for the period: Austria, Denmark, Sweden (both also having low fertility), and the USA (divorce only); a second group shows unusually low fertility: Germany, Greece, Japan; and a third a late age of marriage: Ireland (also low marriage rate), Italy (also low fertility), Portugal, and Spain.

Overall, we can conclude that the majority of societies corresponded reasonably closely to the model, with two main exceptions: first, certain still-rural societies showed higher ages of marriages and/or lower levels of fertility, indicating the viability of the thesis of the strength of the family 'protected' from the industrial economy; second, the societies which in their different ways seemed at that time generally to embody 'modernism' (Denmark, Sweden, and the USA) evince some signs of strain: high divorce or illegitimacy rates. We may speculate that these societies were showing precocious attributes of post-mid-century compromise family forms.

Across all societies, female domesticity correlated positively with average age of marriage,[8] which suggests that age of marriage had nothing to do with women delaying marriage for education and career. Female domesticity also correlated negatively with the divorce[9] and illegitimacy rates, though in the latter case not statistically significantly. A late age of marriage was very negatively related to divorce;[10] it was also negatively related to illegitimacy, though not significantly. Although late marriage,

---

[8] At the 0.05 significance level, R^2 0.31.
[9] At the 0.05 significance level, R^2 0.29.
[10] Very strongly at the 0.01 significance level, R^2 0.77.

Table 7.3 1960s families in relative perspective

	Female domesticity	Marriage age	Marriage rate	Fertility	Divorce	Illegitimacy
Austria	L	L	L	M	H	H
Belgium	H	M	M	M	M	L
Denmark	M	L	H	M	H	H
Finland	L	?	L	M	M	L
France	M	M	L	M	M	M
Germany	L	M	M	L	M	M
Greece	M	M	M	L	L	L
Ireland	M	H	L	M	L	L
Italy	H	H	M	L	L	L
Netherlands	H	M	H	H	M	L
Norway	H	M	M	M	M	M
Portugal	H	H	M	H	L	H
Spain	H	H	M	M	L	L
Sweden	M	M	L	L	H	H
Switzerland	M	?	L	M	M	M
UK	M	M	M	M	M	M
Japan	L	?	H	L	M	?
USA	M	L	H	H	H	L

high divorce, and high illegitimacy are all attributes of the hypothetical 'family decline' model, they are not associated with each other.

POST-MID-CENTURY COMPROMISE FAMILY PATTERNS

We now look at more recent years to see what kind of changes have taken place. There is a danger that in comparing two years at a thirty-year interval we may be selecting misleading ones; what, for example, if fertility hit a surprising high point in 1960, dropped quickly and then began a gradual rise up to the 1990 level? This is however not the case. Fertility either continued to decline or (as in Ireland, France, Scandinavia, and the UK) bottomed out in the 1980s (Coleman 1996a).

This time we consider available data for the early 1990s *in terms of means and standard deviations for 1960*. This is done in Table 7.4. From this perspective *no* country any longer conforms to the mid-century compromise model. As Coleman (1996a: 31–2) has put it, the post-war generations in Europe saw virtually universal marriage and parenthood; there is now a return of bachelorhood and childlessness. There is also a high and growing divorce rate. This is a so-called 'period effect', that is affecting all marriages in existence at a certain period rather than the cohort that became married during a particular time. Several countries conform fully to the 'family decline' model of Table 7.1(b): Denmark, Finland, France, Norway, and Sweden; if we count moderate as well as low marriage rates as conforming to this model, Austria, the Netherlands, and the UK

Table 7.4 1990s families from the perspective of the 1960s

	Female domesticity	Marriage age	Marriage rate	Fertility	Divorce	Illegitimacy
Austria	L	H	M	L	H	H
Belgium	L	M	H	L	H	H
Denmark	L	H	L	L	H	H
Finland	L	H	L	L	H	H
France	L	H	L	L	H	H
Germany	L	H	M	L	H	H
Greece	L	M	H	L	M	L
Ireland	M	H	L	L	L	H
Italy	L	H	H	L	M	M
Netherlands	L	H	M	L	H	H
Norway	L	H	L	L	H	H
Portugal	L	M	H	L	M	H
Spain	M	H	M	L	M	H
Sweden	L	H	L	L	H	H
Switzerland	L	H	M	L	H	M
UK	L	H	M	L	H	H
Japan	L	?	H	L	M	?
USA	L	M	H	L	H	H

also evince 'family decline'. In Switzerland the illegitimacy rate was only medium, while Belgium diverges further towards a slightly stronger family pattern in having a moderate (rather than a high) age of marriage and a high (rather than low) marriage rate, but otherwise conforms.

No society approximates to the hypothetical 'newly integrated family autonomy model' (Table 7.1(c)), though a number of societies are left with mixed patterns: Greece, Italy, Portugal, and outside Europe the USA and Japan, all show high marriage rates. These countries also deviate in other ways: Greece, Italy, and Portugal share the low fertility of the family decline model but not the high divorce and illegitimacy; the data for Japan are unfortunately defective, but it is possible that it approximates to the Italian or Portuguese pattern. The USA is quite distinctive, and while it is not possible to speak of a single European family system, there is a strong difference between them all and the USA. However, were we to be concentrating on studying the USA we should have to note several very diverse ethnic variants within a national average. Ireland and Spain are alone in having moderate rather than low levels of female domesticity by 1960 standards, and otherwise show quite different patterns from those of other countries; they do not however cling to the mid-century compromise model, as their fertility levels are low and average marriage ages high.

As with the 1960 data, we can better explore anomalies in terms of deviance around the means and standard deviations for the 1990 period itself (Table 7.5).[11] The most

---

[11] Detailed studies of developments during the 1980s for most of the countries studied here will also be found in Kaufmann *et al.* 1997.

Table 7.5 1990s families in relative perspective

	Female domesticity	Marriage age	Marriage rate	Fertility	Divorce	Illegitimacy
Austria	H	H	M	M	M	M
Belgium	H	M	H	M	M	L
Denmark	L	H	L	M	H	H
Finland	L	H	L	M	M	M
France	M	H	L	M	M	M
Germany	M	H	M	L	M	L
Greece	H	M	H	L	L	L
Ireland	H	H	L	H	L	M
Italy	H	H	M	L	L	L
Netherlands	H	H	M	M	M	L
Norway	L	H	L	H	M	H
Portugal	M	M	H	M	L	M
Spain	H	H	M	L	L	L
Sweden	L	H	L	H	H	H
Switzerland	H	H	M	M	M	L
UK	M	H	M	M	H	H
Japan	M	?	M	M	L	?
USA	L	M	H	H	H	M

striking finding here is that, as we should expect, those countries with high levels of female domesticity do tend to retain relative characteristics of the mid-century compromise family form, especially in terms of having lower divorce and (in particular) illegitimacy levels; but they never retain the higher fertility of that period. Belgium, Greece, Italy, the Netherlands, Portugal, Spain, Switzerland all fit this pattern. Austria has high female domesticity but no other mid-century compromise features, while Germany has low illegitimacy but moderate female labour-force participation.

The only other form of deviance from the family decline model within Europe is in the high levels of fertility in Norway and Sweden—with the other Nordic countries having 'high medium' levels. Outside Europe the USA shares this deviance, but deviates further from the model in having a low marriage age and high marriage rate. Given the exceptionally high divorce rate in the USA one might surmise that, while in much of Europe the failure of marriages is associated with declining popularity of the institution, Americans are undeterred by their even greater failure. The other non-European country, Japan, deviates less from European patterns, though our ability to reach conclusions is inhibited by the deficiency of the Japanese data on marriage ages and illegitimacy.

In contrast with the early 1960s, average female age of marriage is inversely related to the level of female domesticity.[12] Even more surprisingly, *the level of fertility varies strongly inversely with female domesticity.*[13] This reflects the recovery of fertility in the

[12] But only at the 0.10 significance level, R^2 0.24.
[13] At the 0.01 significance level, R^2 0.39.

Scandinavian countries and the USA at high levels of female labour-force participation, and low fertility in the southern European countries where this participation is low. The northern continental European countries have low levels of fertility and moderate levels of female labour-force participation, so the relationship is in fact curvilinear.[14] More predictably, both divorce and in particular illegitimacy are negatively related to female domesticity.[15]

Comparison of changes between the early 1960s and early 1990s *means* shows us that there have been: (1) (as we already know) a large fall in female domesticity (from 62.79% to 44.83%); (2) a rise in women's average age at marriage by two years from 23.83 to 25.85 years; (3) a slight *rise* in the female marriage rate from 49.51 per thousand to 52.13; (4) a considerable fall in the fertility rate (TFR) from 2.71 (well above replacement) to 1.62 (some way below it); (5) a considerable rise in divorce from 3.02 to 7.79 per thousand first marriages per annum; and (6) a very considerable rise in the illegitimacy rate from 5.09% to 21.64% of all live births. (If these divorce rates continue, in most countries of Europe outside the south, chances of couples divorcing will be around one in three; in Sweden, Denmark, and the UK, two in five; and in the USA one in two (Kiernan 1996: 72–3).)

The female marriage rate is a strange statistic in that, as we have noted, in the form of data available to us, it includes in the denominator for 1960 the large female surplus population from the early decades of this century who were not realistically 'available for marriage' in the early 1960s. By the 1990s nearly all these women had died, producing an artificial rise in the female marriage rate. If we calculate the changes in the marriage rate between 1960 and 1990 for all countries, we find that the mean change for those countries which did not suffer major domestic slaughter during either of the World Wars (Denmark, Netherlands, Portugal, Sweden, Switzerland, the USA) was a decline, while that for those that experienced such slaughter in at least one of the wars and/or suffered major male slaughter in civil war was a rise.

Two important aspects of contemporary behaviour which are not captured by these statistics but which lie behind some of them and will be discussed further below are the growth of pre-marital cohabitation and the growth of second families following divorce.

Compared with the 1960s very many couples live together for some time before marrying (Kuijsten and Strohmeier 1997). Höpflinger (1997: 105) has shown a considerable rise in virtually all countries for which data are available during just the decade of the 1980s. The only exceptions were Denmark and Sweden, where there was a fall back from the very high levels reached, and Italy, where the proportion remains extremely low. This is part of the explanation of the rising age of marriage and childbirth, and also the rise of illegitimacy, since many of these couples have babies before marrying. It is also possible that many of them will not marry at all, but either separate after a period or remain as unmarried partnerships.

Most divorced persons remarry a new partner at some point and often have children in the new relationship. This produces a complex structure of half-kin, as children share one parent but not the other. Figures for TFR give the impression of a married couple

---

[14] R^2 rises to 0.48 for the second polynomial.
[15]   Both at the 0.01 significance level, at R^2 0.51 and 0.68, respectively.

together bringing up the average woman's 1.62 children, completely concealing the family patterns which result from divorce and remarriage. These complexities have clearly risen with divorce, so changes in family structure since the early 1960s are in fact greater than appears from the numbers alone. It is unfortunately not possible to provide comprehensive data on this. Höpflinger (1997: 121) has statistics on the proportion of children living in one-parent families and step-families for a number of Western European countries, though these often relate to the 1980s and never more recently than 1990. They show a strong growth in both these indicators, though the proportion of single-parent families has nowhere reached 20%, and the percentages of step-families are in single figures.

The conclusions that we can draw from all this are varied. The overall evidence is consistent with the predictions of the initial thesis, that in post-mid-century compromise society the family loses some of the institutional 'protection' that came to it through female domesticity and, as an institution, incurs certain negative consequences. This is seen in both change over time and through a comparison in the 1990s between societies with different levels of female domesticity. However, it is not at all clear that reduced fertility, which might seem to be the most likely consequence of female labour-force participation, is necessarily part of the decline. It may be so where other institutions, such as the welfare state, do not adapt to changes in women's behaviour. For example, in the Netherlands, where female participation in the labour force has increased dramatically and suddenly during the 1990s, women have achieved the change by a major reduction in fertility (Beets, Liefbroer, and de Jong Giervekd 1994).

It is slightly puzzling that illegitimacy should correlate more highly with female labour-force participation than does divorce; indeed the rise in illegitimacy at a period when virtually total control over fertility is possible is surprising in itself. We are not looking at a simple effect whereby female labour-force participation 'weakens' the family, but at some more complicated association between them. The correlation with divorce might seem more straightforward, but as we shall see below, the interesting demographic literature on the question suggests here too some different interpretations.

Other researchers have carried out similar exercises to the above. For example, Jallinoja (1989) established different models of women's roles depending on their participation in the labour force and the extent of their personal care for their young children. She established three patterns: the housewife model (majority of younger married women are not in the paid labour force); the moderate sex role pattern (women either interrupt employment or take part-time work when their children are small); and the employed woman pattern (women continue to work through their children's younger years). She found that in 1960 the Netherlands, Norway, Italy, Sweden, France, the UK, and Germany followed the first model; within Western Europe only Finland followed the second; and none the third. By 1980 (the last year considered) only the Netherlands and Italy remained with the housewife model; only Finland was in the employed woman model; all others were in the second category. With the partial exception of the Dutch case, this separation of Scandinavia, western Central Europe, and southern Europe corresponds somewhat to our findings above—though adding some Eastern European countries as Jallinoja does gives less weight to some of the contrasts we found within Western Europe. In particular it leaves Finland (interestingly, Jallinoja's own country) as the only Nordic case separable from western Central Europe. (Finland is 'western' in the geopolitical sense, meaning that it was not, or at least was only marginally, part of the Soviet bloc; if these compass terms are given a solely geographical rather than geopolitical meaning, Finland is unambiguously eastern.)

The more educated women are, the older they begin childbearing (see F.-X. Kaufmann *et al.* 1997 for Western Europe in general; Klein and Lauterbach 1994 for Germany). Diekmann (1990) argued that the human capital effect could be seen at work in Germany, with educational expansion leading to a reduction in marriage rates. However, Blossfeld and Jänichen (1990: 469–71) found that in Germany the low relationship between education and both marriage and having children was solely due to the difficulties placed in the way of marriage and family building by being a student rather than any long-term effect of perspectives, constituting a source of postponement rather than avoidance. Highly educated women were no less likely to marry and become mothers in the longer run (ibid. 472).

In a similar exercise to that carried out here, Boh (1989) put together indicators of female working, marriage, and reproductive patterns and identified high, medium, and low models across 14 countries for the period around 1980. This allocated Germany, Italy, and the Netherlands as unambiguously in the category of low female employment, low marriage rates, low fertility; Sweden, the UK, Belgium, France, and Norway as having a mix of low and medium values; Finland and certain Eastern European countries as a mix of medium and high positions; and only some Eastern European cases (including East Germany) as fairly unambiguous highs. These are again similar results to those of Jallinoja and our own discussion, though it is notable that Germany joins Italy and the Netherlands. More recent research by L. B. Knudsen (1997) argues that in Denmark the full-time housewife has virtually disappeared; only among older generations does one find women who are not in paid employment.

On the basis of her 1980 data, Boh pointed out that there is no unambivalent support for modernization theses here, and that a variety of viable family patterns is emerging. The most recent data available to both Jallinoja and Boh were those for 1980; our own data extend to 1990, and it is partly this that detaches Germany and the Netherlands from southern Europe, following the more recent rise in their female labour-force participation. It is however useful to remember that in 1980 both these countries resembled what we are now able to regard less ambivalently as a 'southern' model.

BEYOND DEMOGRAPHY: THE SOCIOLOGY AND ANTHROPOLOGY OF THE FAMILY

The essentially demographic approach we have been following so far tells us a good deal about contemporary family structure, but we can better understand some of the dynamics of the processes by examining the findings of the more sociological or anthropological literature on the quality and character of family relationships. In particular they can help us throw further light on our choice between an 'exacerbated modern' model of decline of the family and a postmodern one.

An obvious candidate in explaining differences in family patterns is religion, given that European religions in general and Roman Catholicism in particular place considerable stress on the strength of family and marriage and have distinct views on sexual relations. Also, in Chapter 2 we found the political role of religion to be a relevant variable in explaining female labour-force participation, which is in turn very relevant to family patterns. The Belgian demographer Ron Lesthaeghe (1995: 42–5) found the strength of Protestantism (as opposed to Catholicism, that is) and the economic variable of GNP per capita to be the crucial factors in determining the pace of what he has called the second demographic transition (declining concern for the formal institution of marriage). Even in the most recent period, his analysis shows a 'straight line of positive influence that runs from Protestantism via individual autonomy and female emancipation to the demographic dependent variables' (ibid. 51).

Religion might affect behaviour at the level of peoples' autonomous responses, or by shaping the legal and welfare policy framework that gives incentives to behave in certain ways (Lewis 1993). For example, if the children of unmarried parents encounter severe difficulties in inheriting property, potential parents have a stronger incentive to marry than those in countries where the law does not discriminate in this way. To take a more specific and different kind of example, during the 1970s German family policy changed from one supporting large families of conventional form to one aimed at incorporating families of various sizes and types according to their means within a general framework of welfare-state provision (Lüscher and Schultheis 1988). Castles and Flood (1993a) have combined all these factors in a model of five 'families' of national legal regimes: the Anglophone common-law system; Scandinavia; the German-speaking countries; countries where the Code Napoléon was in force (France, Belgium, Netherlands), and countries where for much of the earlier period canon (church) law governed (Italy and Ireland—Portugal and Spain were not included in their study). They then related changes in divorce rates in the period since 1960 to these legal regimes, more directly to religious belief and to various indicators of modernization.

Their findings were as follows. During the period 1960–76 different approaches to divorce embodied in the different regimes explain most of the cross-national difference in divorce rates. After that, however, matters changed. Those countries which had previously strict divorce laws (and which usually had low levels of social and economic modernization) began to liberalize very rapidly, except where the Catholic Church remained strong. (In Ireland divorce did not become a legal possibility until after a referendum majority in favour in 1995 (Kennedy and McCormack 1997: 198–9).) As a result, divorce started to rise much more rapidly in ostensibly less 'modernized' countries. The main exception to these trends was the USA, whose exceptionally high and rising divorce rates cannot be explained by the model, but for Western Europe it held up well. This suggests that religion may affect family-related behaviour both indirectly through legal regime, but also directly through social behaviour even if the legal regime changes.

In related research on a different aspect of family life, Therborn (1993) used the same 'legal families of nations' approach to consider the development of law affecting children. He saw these rights developing in an historical progression from: (1) recognition of the child-centred family as opposed to patriarchy; through (2) recognition of the rights of children born outside marriage; to (3) recognition of children's rights to personal autonomy (e.g. prohibition of corporal punishment). By the 1990s only the Nordic countries and possibly Austria had reached this last; the Common Law group tended to come second in developing children's rights; third the Germanic; and last the Latin group (with Greece). This last combines two of Castle and Flood's groups: the in principle very secular Code Napoléon and the Catholic canon law groups.

Religion is clearly important in these categories, with a tendency for Lutheran countries to liberate individuals from families the earliest, and Catholic ones (and Greek Orthodox) the latest. However, Therborn puts an interesting gloss on the working of these differences. Catholic countries tended to undergo upheavals in their legal system at some point between 1789 and the end of the nineteenth century—a time when concepts of adult male dominance (patriarchy) were still entrenched. Therefore patriarchy became embodied in otherwise modernized systems. In the Nordic and Anglophone groups there were not similar upheavals; patriarchy remained embodied in continuing traditional systems, which were not disturbed by revolutionary change and therefore remained unmodernized until reform waves of the mid-twentieth century, when patriarchy was becoming outmoded.

He also points out, in a comment which we shall find of considerable importance in Chapters 9 and 11 (on religion and political parties, respectively), that Protestant and Catholic teaching do not really differ on family issues; what differs is the far weaker capacity of Lutheranism (and Anglicanism) to mobilize people around their social causes, leaving them incapable of realizing Christian family forms within the societies where they are dominant. (Calvinism is a different case, as we shall see in Chapter 9.) For example, in Denmark (L. B. Knudsen 1997) and Sweden (Meisaari-Polsa 1997) illegitimate children have virtually the same rights as those born to married couples, and cohabiting couples have virtually the same legal status as married partners. The situation is similar in France (Muller-Escoda and Vogt 1997); while this is a Catholic country, the exclusion of the Church from formal public life for most of the period since the 1789 revolution has given it a position not dissimilar from that of Lutheran Europe— again an issue to which we shall return in Chapter 9.

Often churches' political influence is a result of powers exercised at earlier historical moments but continuing to be embedded in law and practice. It is also notable that, as Swiss experience makes clear (Fux 1997: 359–61), Christian parties are particularly concerned to have influence in this policy field. The diversity of historical experience of these questions within Western Europe has helped produce considerable variety in contemporary behaviour. We must similarly note that, although Germany was dominated by Lutheran values during the fundamentally important period of nineteenth-century modernization, during the first four decades of the western Federal Republic, Catholic social values were dominant. This was reflected in a family policy which gives strong incentives to married couples with children and breadwinner husbands (Daly 1996; Federkeil 1997). Another exception is the very favourable treatment accorded to single mothers by social policy in Catholic Italy (Menniti, Palomba, and Sabbadini 1997). In the Netherlands a long period during which social policy strongly encouraged the male breadwinner family was followed by a sudden change in the 1980s to encourage mothers' labour-force participation (Kuijsten and Schulze 1997: 261). This change, which followed the rapid secularization of the country (see Chapter 9) was followed by a strong rise in women's participation in paid employment.

FEMALE EMPLOYMENT AND FAMILIES

At the centre of our discussion has been the impact of married women's employment, which earlier chapters have already shown to be one of the most significant social processes of the present period. For example, Huinink and Mayer (1995: 191–5) argue that it remains difficult to combine work and motherhood in West Germany, and that this explains delayed fertility. Women either do not work, and therefore have reduced incomes and independence, or work in contexts where little is done to help them—by husbands or employers—combine the roles. Federkeil (1997) sees a polarization of German family forms resulting from this: women either pursue careers but remain in non-family households, or form families but withdraw from the labour force. Germany is the country where declining fertility has had most impact, leading to actual population reduction, but similar processes can be seen elsewhere. (German men and women are less likely to 'approve' of mothers being in paid employment, especially full-time, than British or American (Alwin, Bruan, and Scott 1992).) On the basis of data from a number of countries in Europe, the USA, and elsewhere, Chafetz (1995: 71) shows that women in paid employment want to postpone childbearing (more than marriage), and that the rise in their employment is positively associated with the rise in divorce. On the other hand, Swedish women are more likely to combine motherhood and paid employment if they have a high level of education (B. Hoem 1993), and it is women with higher education who are most likely to have large families.

Married women have proved to be very flexible employees, either being willing to work part time, or even if full time often willing to accept that their work was somehow secondary to that of their husbands. Research evidence suggests that, in most families where the mother is in paid employment, it is she who makes most of the adaptation to combining the two worlds with little impact on the husband's role (Kuijsten and Strohmeier 1997). This is possibly exacerbated by the fact that much female employment comprises childcare related activities within the welfare state—'turning mothers' tasks into female tasks' as it has become known in Scandinavia where this development is seen at its fullest (Jensen 1995: 226–7). At the same time this has reduced the relative involvement of men in these childcare related occupations. Jensen argues that ironically the gender gap in relationships with children within the family has if anything widened with the growth of married women's employment. Concomitantly, Nave-Herz (1989) summarizes a number of researches from several different European countries which indicate that, while men participate more in household tasks when their wives are in full-time—though not part-time—paid employment, they tend to do only typically 'male' tasks (see also Kiernan 1992 (a number of countries); and Horrell 1994: 102 (UK only)).

Chafetz similarly concludes that 'research in numerous industrialized nations has revealed that husbands of full-time employed wives do little more domestic and childcare work, on average, than do husbands of full-time homemakers' (Chafetz 1995: 68). Research suggests that women do twice as much of the total burden of informal work in the Netherlands (housework, shopping, childcare, charity, etc.) (de Hoog 1994: 60). It is only in the small amount of time devoted to home maintenance and charity that male effort exceeds female. In the central housework and childcare areas, women do more than three times as much as men, but only twice as much shopping. Research in both Finland and France shows that men increase their role in the home by only a few minutes a day when children are born, whereas women increase theirs by a number of hours (Michel 1989).

Studies of family divisions of labour rarely report men doing more than one-third of women's share (Kuijsten and Strohmeier 1997). Data for Sweden (Björnberg 1992b), where women's labour-force participation is well entrenched, report this figure, as do those for the Netherlands (Arts and Hermkens 1994; Kuijsten and Schulze 1997), where that participation has only recently started to grow. The Dutch research reports very considerable differences in male and female contributions to housework, though both men and women claimed to find the divisions 'fair'. The crucial variable, according to the authors, is that the spouse who has the higher earnings and the higher level of education participates less in housework; this is usually the man. Other research on the Netherlands (van der Lippe, van Doorne-Huiskes, and Siegers 1993) reached compatible conclusions: men are more likely to share housework to the extent that their wives earn money. Comparative work on Sweden, Norway, the USA, and Canada (Kalleberg and Rosenfeld 1990) suggests that men make little adjustment of their own working lives to take on housework tasks, while women often do; in Scandinavia women seemed to adjust their working hours to ensure they carried out their household tasks; in the USA, where little is available in the form of part-time work or childcare, housework took the strain. Muller-Escoda and Vogt (1997: 69–70) report that French fathers take little share of childcare; Bertaux and Delcroix (1992) support the argument with a different datum: the observation that, after divorce, only 20% of French men seek custody of their children and only 9% are granted it. Similar results have been summarized for most Western European countries by F.-X. Kaufmann et al. (1997).

According to Nave-Herz (1988a), in Germany the concept of shared household tasks between husband and wife is more an ideal than actual practice. As a result, mothers still retain the main burden of household tasks (see also Federkeil 1997). A further aspect of this asymmetry is that, while women strain anxiously to combine roles as mothers and as workers, men are not clear what the role of father means; the old authority role has gone, but few fathers are in practice prepared to share mothers' nurturing roles. This is reported for at least Sweden (Björnberg 1992b), Finland (Nurminen and Roos 1992), Italy (Bimbi 1992), and France (Bertaux and Delcroix 1992). In Switzerland (in contrast with the Dutch and US findings), men help *less* with housework if their wives have children (Charles and Höpflinger 1992). The husband's participation in housework was unrelated to wives' labour-market participation. It seems that in this society families with children are more likely to believe in traditional role models, and therefore in a strict gender division of labour.

In Portugal, where women have entered the normal paid workforce in large numbers in the past twenty-five years, the evidence is that they continue to bear the greatest share of family housekeeping too (Portugal 1988). The society's symbolic evaluations have not changed alongside the changing reality: especially in rural Portugal, it is considered effeminate for men to share these tasks. Research carried out in 1988 suggested that while 50% of Portuguese husbands shared in shopping expeditions, little more than one-third assisted in the preparation of meals, and cleaning tasks were shared by fewer still (washing dishes and house cleaning around 20%; washing and ironing clothes, less than 5%); over one-quarter of husbands took no part in housework at all (ibid.). Also, daughters were far more likely than sons to participate in these tasks. Later research in 1994 suggests continuing imbalances (Portugal 1994; Lopes 1994).

On the other hand, there is some contrary evidence, or at least of change over time. It must first be remembered that, except among very poor people, as a result of the automation of the kitchen through the inventions of vacuum cleaners, washing and dish-washing machines, and various electrical food-processing equipment, housework requires less time than in past generations. For example, already by 1977 the average non-working German women spent 41.7 hours per week on housework and childcare —a decline of 16.4 hours since 1952–4 (Lakemann 1984). Gershuny, Godwin, and Jones (1994) also found that, although British men seemed to change their habits very little in response to their wives' involvement in paid work, there had been a definite increase in their acceptance of domestic tasks between the early 1970s and the late 1980s—a lagged effect which they were able to find also in data from France, Netherlands, Norway, Finland, as well as the USA and some other countries outside Western Europe. The early socialization of men and women seems to explain this: husbands and wives whose own parents had experienced joint working were more willing to adapt to changed roles by both partners. There is also evidence that German men have begun to take a share in some chores (Müller-Wichmann 1987). Generational changes have also been noted in Spain, where mothers born since the mid-1950s have been more likely to combine paid employment with motherhood than earlier generations (Delgado 1993).

Eurobarometer research suggests a gradual rise in couples *wanting* a diminution in sex-role divisions; by 1987 only 25% of respondents offered the mid-century compromise model of male breadwinner family as their ideal. There was little difference between male and female responses on this, though with the expected differences between northern Europe (Scandinavia and the UK), the central continental countries, and the south (Kiernan 1996: 81–3). However, research on the actual division of labour between couples rather than on stated attitudes suggests a far less even picture, with the expected variations between Scandinavia and southern Europe (ibid.).

Despite what we saw above concerning the different behaviour of husbands of part-time as opposed to full-time working women, in a study of couples with different kinds of working arrangements in Britain, Horrell, Rubery, and Burchell (1994: 102) did find fathers becoming involved in childcare after school if they returned home before their wives. It is a distinctive UK practice that British part-time working wives often work in the evenings, at night, or in the early hours of the morning—times when their husbands are at home and can look after children. This point helps us to understand what might otherwise have been surprising: these researchers also found that part-time working wives were more isolated from other members of their households than either full-time working or non-working wives. The finding that married women's part-time work is more likely to take place at unsocial hours than full-time work of either men or women is an interesting insight into the contribution to economic flexibility being made by these women as they try to reconcile these two different worlds. The authors point out a potential clash between the ostensibly mutually convenient developments of women's working lives and employers' demand for 'flexibility': joint-job families need considerable predictability in their working habits in order to plan their family patterns.

Part-timers demonstrate contemporary women's double commitment—to paid work and to family work—very clearly indeed. They are a very distinctive part of the labour force and cannot simply be seen as workers who are spending a little less time in paid work than others (Blossfeld and Hakim 1997). In Britain there is evidence at least from manual-working families that women fully accept that their return to work after childbirth will be part-time, with a possible return to full-time work in the longer term (McCrone 1994). This makes it difficult for them to think in terms of a 'career' for themselves; or, to put the matter differently, they have chosen a certain combination of paid work and family work rather than opted for a stronger career emphasis on paid work only.

Although the double commitment can impose considerable strain, these women have in a sense not put all their eggs into one basket and can therefore be relatively more relaxed about job change, job reduction, or even job loss than husbands who still see themselves, and are seen by their wives, as family 'breadwinners'. This has been an attribute of married women that employers have found very attractive at a time when they have been seeking more flexibility and less insistence on employment rights. Ironically, therefore, the very characteristics that mean that married women are less likely to be 'fully' members of the world of calculative economic exchange makes them more likely than men to behave as a labour 'commodity' when they *are* in that world, since men have to accompany their participation in market exchanges by their felt need to provide for their families.

As was discussed in Chapter 3, Pfau-Effinger (1993) has related differences in Finnish and German female labour-force participation to pre-industrial differences in family divisions of labour. Similar links between pre-mid-century and very recent changes have been made by Déchaux (1994: 40), considering initially the French case, but doubt- less with wider implications. She distinguishes between those kinds of familial help that *protect* the recipient from society (caring, affording access to informally produced goods) and those which facilitate (re-)insertion within the wider society (looking after children, helping in the search for work). An ironic consequence of this occurring at a time of growing participation in the labour force by married women is that the ex- tended family is being revived. Thus, France is now witnessing a rise in the role of grandmothers in caring for children while mothers work. This makes an interesting contrast with the argument of R. Knudsen (1991), discussed in Chapter 2, that in the Scandinavian countries female employment was curiously assisted in a society with existing records of female independence by the *absence* of family support: welfare-state institutions grew to assist working mothers, 'replacing' the absent extended family and in turn providing more female work opportunities. This reminds us of the *importance* of the family in Scandinavian perspectives, policy-makers regarding it as important to support and complement family activities (see the studies in F.-X. Kaufmann *et al.* 1997). This begins to demonstrate the possibility of alternative 'flexible' forms of the develop- ment of female employment: one compatible with the mid-century social compromise and taking the form of the welfare state; the other departing from that compromise and comprising the informal economy.

MARRIAGE CHANGES AND COHABITATION

Clearly, adapting to the paid employment of wives and mothers is an issue that has to be and is being faced by millions of families in contemporary Europe. Our analysis above demonstrated a statistical relationship between female working and divorce and other indicators of strain on marriage. We must be careful how we draw conclusions from this. It might be argued that there is an ecological fallacy in the linkage of national family indicators with those for female domesticity: how do we know that it is the working women who are divorcing? In fact, women in paid employment *are* more likely to become divorced than those who are not (e.g. for Italy, see de Rose 1992; for Germany, Italy, and Sweden see Blossfeld *et al.* 1995). (When considering the high Swedish divorce rate, it is necessary to remember that the procedures for divorce and legal separation are virtually the same (J. Hoem 1991).) To some extent the point being made *is* an ecological one: it is something about the societies that brings these phenomena in association, not necessarily the individuals. This might work in the following way: if women see a high risk of divorce around them, they may be more likely to sustain their workforce position as an 'insurance' against a possible future need to be financially independent (Ermisch 1996). (Ermisch suggests similar interactions between fertility rates and divorce: a high rate of divorce might deter couples from having children, while an absence of children might reduce the bonds that link the couple, making them more vulnerable to divorce.) Alternatively, as Lutz, Wils, and Nieminen (1991) argue with reference to the Finnish case, divorce rates among young women are high, not because a young age of marriage is associated with divorce, but because they have entered marriage during an epoch when the risk of divorce is high.

Behind this lie further issues. Increased divorce is by no means associated only with married women working; there also seem to be some quite separate factors imparting a fragility and hesitancy to contemporary marriage. This was partly seen above in the low marriage rates taking place in many countries. In Denmark, 46% of males and 67% of females between the ages of 20 and 30 were married in the mid-1960s, but by the 1980s the proportion was down to 15% and 27%, respectively (Matthiesen 1993). It is difficult to tell from demographic statistics whether a new generation of young people is postponing marriage or deciding never to marry. There is certainly widespread evidence of postponement today, but in some countries it now seems increasingly that a growing minority, including a growing minority of couples, is choosing not to marry at all (for the UK in particular, see Clarke and Henwood 1997: 159; more generally, see Kuijsten and Strohmeier 1997). As we shall see below, some authors have seen in this an anxiety and a reluctance about entering the commitments of marriage, which they then relate to wider questions of values and culture in contemporary society.

There might however be further reasons associated with the economic insecurities of recent years. Young people need to be confident that they have equipped themselves for future employment, which means a prolonged period of education, and for acquiring a home, before they risk marriage. For example, Kennedy and McCormack (1997) find such anxieties to be the main explanation of the postponement of marriage in Ireland, while Huinink and Mayer (1995: 178) argue that a particular cause of delayed marriage in Germany could be the need for men—and increasingly for women—to guarantee future economic security through prolonged education and training. There is also a growing tendency for mates to have similar educational levels—and even a rise in the proportion of females with superior levels (ibid. 179–81). However, among cohorts born during the 1950s working women married sooner than non-working ones.

These authors disagree with the economists' thesis that educated women try to avoid marriage and family building; rather they postpone it until they have established themselves in careers. However, this may make it more difficult to find a partner, and leaves childbearing until late.

As already noted, alongside the postponement of marriage there has also been a considerable rise in the amount of cohabitation outside formal marriage in several countries of Western Europe (Kiernan 1996: 64–5). Is this to be interpreted as an aspect of family decline, or as a reaction to that decline and an attempt at restabilizing the institution? The growth of cohabitation started in Denmark (L. B. Knudsen 1997) and Sweden (Meisaari-Polsa 1997). (High levels of unmarried cohabitations in Sweden seem to date back to the pre-Christian (i.e. twelfth century) era (ibid. 302–3).) It has now spread to become a normal pre-marital stage in at least France (Muller-Escoda and Vogt 1997), Germany (Federkeil 1997), the UK (Clarke and Henwood 1997: 160). It is also gradually extending to countries with previously more conservative patterns: Ireland (Kennedy and McCormack 1997: 198), Switzerland (Fux 1997: 373–5). It is sometimes argued that in Scandinavia cohabitation is often an *alternative* to marriage, whereas elsewhere it is usually a brief *prelude* to it. In fact, although many Swedish and Danish couples often have one or even two children in cohabiting unions—this helps explain the high illegitimacy rates—they still frequently marry at a later stage in life (Kiernan 1996: 66–7). In Sweden women's mean age at first marriage is higher than their mean age at birth of their first child (Meisaari-Polsa 1997: 304). In Germany (Federkeil 1997), the Netherlands (Kuijsten and Schulze 1997: 273), and Switzerland (Fux 1997: 469) however, cohabiting women are unlikely to have children. These patterns have not yet developed in southern Europe. A survey by Eurobarometer (1991) of cohabitation among men and women aged 15–24 suggested a far lower level for Italy and Spain than in other countries. Extremely low southern cohabitation rates are also reported in other studies: for Italy by de Rose (1992) and Menniti, Palomba, and Sabbadini (1997), and for Spain by Delgado (1993).

More generally, a rise in divorce has been found to be associated with a number of factors. Blossfeld *et al.* (1995) claim that female education will be initially associated with a rise in divorce as the 'liberating' effect on women disrupts marriages, but that as divorce becomes more widespread and different living arrangements become established, more women become engaged in the liberation, divorce spreads, but becomes less confined among the educated. They demonstrate this in a comparison between Sweden, Italy, and West Germany. We can therefore see a by now familiar grouping: Scandinavia and France (Muller-Escoda and Vogt 1997); the rest of central Western Europe; southern Europe.

Young people who cohabit before marriage are often doing so in order to test whether their union is likely to last. Cohabitational relationships break down faster than do marriages. This is the case in Sweden, the country where cohabitation has progressed furthest (B. Hoem and J. Hoem 1987; Jensen 1995: 226–7). Sweet and Bumpass (1990) suggest the same for the USA; and Toulemon (1994) for France. On the other hand, consensual unions are often seriously intended: in the late 1980s about 80% of Danish consensual unions had lasted for more than two years and 40% for over five years (Matthiesen 1993), and only 16% of Danish cohabitants under 25 did not consider the possibility of marriage (ibid.). In a comparison of British and French cohabitation behaviour, Lelièvre (1994) noted that in both countries premarital cohabitation began to rise sharply from around 1970. Young British women were found to marry earlier, divorce more frequently, but cohabit less frequently than their French sisters.

Klijzing (1992) found that on a first view Dutch and Swedish evidence alike suggested that prior cohabitation was associated with *increased* risks of divorce. However, in the Netherlands (though not Sweden) this could be explained by certain social characteristics of the group concerned (in particular, social origin, composition of parental household, composition of the new household). When these effects were taken into account, cohabitation seemed to be negatively associated with risks of divorce.

In a study of the relative happiness and well-being associated with different forms of living among young adults in Belgium, France, Germany, and the Netherlands, Lesthaeghe and Moors (1996) distinguished among cohabitation, marriage, living alone, and living with parents. They found most dissatisfaction with and anxiety about life among cohabitees, least among the married (especially married women). The finding is consistent with the general argument the authors develop that cohabitees are constantly appraising whether or not they are content with their living arrangements. This is a plausible explanation of the puzzling finding that divorce rates were higher among couples who had cohabited before marriage: these people are more demanding on relationships, because of their high need for self-fulfilment (Lesthaeghe 1995: 24–5). A similar paradox has been noted by Chafetz (1995: 72): couples who are both in paid employment have more in common and have greater intimacy than traditional couples; but ironically they also have more conflicts and find these difficult to resolve, hence their higher divorce. Such couples do not have a clear division of function between the partners.

Lesthaeghe is aware of the danger that Ermisch (1996), Becker (1981), and others who take an economistic approach neglect exogenous values originating in other parts of the society that can affect family behaviour (Lesthaeghe and Moors 1996). He therefore tries to link contemporary changes in family behaviour to arguments about changing values associated with post-materialism and post-industrialism. He argues that young people now have very high expectations of individual fulfilment from relationships and wish to be able to revise decisions and commitments that do not succeed; a low value is placed on commitment. Unfortunately, he and Moors do not say much about national differences, but across all four societies that they studied they report that all home-leavers and, especially, cohabitants are less likely than those living with parents or married to hold traditional Christian beliefs or support Christian Democratic political parties, and more likely to support radical social movements and post-material values. Those living alone and cohabitants are less likely than home-stayers and married couples to rate fidelity as a value, but more likely to stress tolerance and understanding, and also symmetrical relations (see also Lesthaeghe 1995: 23). They place the adult couple at the centre of their concept of a partnership and place less emphasis on children. When it comes to the education of children they stress the instilling of values of independence and imagination rather than of obedience and hard work.

Again, these conclusions suggest the continuing role of historically embedded forces producing different outcomes in different national contexts rather than any changes resulting from recent overall transformations of the form of society. Nevertheless, much of the above account is consistent with the thesis of a growing use of calculation in human relationships, having (for better or worse) a destructive effect on certain kinds of social institution.

FERTILITY

Other light is shed on a potential 'crisis' of the family by evidence on fertility: both its general decline and the rise in extramarital childbearing. According to an original argument of the French demographer Ariès (1980), the fertility decline of the 1960s and 1970s marked the end of the era of the child as couples became more adult-centred. On the other hand, the smaller the number of children in a family the greater the amount of resources (money, love, time, attention) can be devoted to each one.

One explanation of the former has been that proposed by economists writing about the rationality of family decisions, especially Gary Becker (1981). According to this theory, as the importance of education rises, so does the human capital investment cost per child, providing a strong incentive to have smaller families (Becker 1981; Ermisch 1996). This will be especially true when there is reliance on wives' earnings to sustain the families' level of living, since even with paid maternity leave childbearing is likely to mean the temporary removal of the mother from the paid workforce, and probably a move to lower-paid part-time status and a diminution of career opportunities. On the basis of British data, Ermisch (1988) is able to show that women's relative wages are negatively related to the likelihood of having a further child. The link can be broken when higher-earning women purchase childcare (as in the USA, possibly the UK), or when there is widespread state-subsidized care (as in Sweden). It is notable that these are all countries which are bucking the low fertility trend despite having high levels of female labour-force participation.

As Pinnelli (1995: 84) has concluded: the recent rise in fertility in northern Europe suggests the hypothesis that 'the factor that seems most important for levels of fertility is the extent to which institutional conditions make it possible for women to reconcile productive and reproductive roles'. This development is the only major factor which suggests that one option within post-mid-century compromise society is a new form of family integration model. It is certainly a testimony to the desire of couples who have virtually total control over their fertility to continue to raise families—especially if childcare is available as in northern Europe—despite both having paid employment and despite high levels of divorce (Bernhardt 1993). Whether it will become the basis of a new institutional autonomy for the family is more doubtful; apart from a recent decline in Sweden, divorce rates in these countries continue to rise.

Rises in *extramarital* fertility (indicated by the rise in illegitimate births shown in Table A.7.2) are surprising in that since the 1960s a variety of highly effective contraceptive methods have been developed and are known to be extremely widely used. There seem to be two forms of births out of wedlock. One refers to the prominence of cohabitation, even after the birth of one or two children, as a normal, planned manner of family building, found particularly in Scandinavia and France (Strohmeier and Kuijsten 1997: 6). Research from Denmark, France, Norway, and Sweden shows that only a small minority of unmarried births are to one-parent families; the great majority are to cohabiting couples (L. B. Knudsen 1997: 17; Muller-Escoda and Vogt 1997: 60–1). Although by 1990 the proportion of extramarital births in France had increased to 30%

(from 6% in 1965), only 4% of all births were born to women neither married nor co-habiting; meanwhile, among women under 30 pregnancies outside marriage are more common than those within (Toulemon 1994). In several countries it is however characteristic of this extramarital pattern that there are very few such births to unmarried teenagers, and that the age of unmarried mothers is rising (L. B. Knudsen 1997: 17).

The other form of extramarital birth is a sign of an incapacity to plan life, found particularly among young girls with no settled partners. Anderson, Bechhofer, and Kendrick (1994) showed that for a sample of British families, people who were less able to plan their lives in general—e.g. the unemployed or those in economic insecurity—also felt less able to plan their reproductive behaviour and were more likely to have unplanned children than the better established families who were, ironically, better equipped to cater for additional children. The authors also note however a reluctance by all types of parent to admit to planning in this sphere of life; many respondents who clearly had planned the arrival of their children nevertheless thought that they ought to sustain a myth of spontaneity and avoidance of calculation.

Illegitimate births of this second kind, demonstrating lack of control, have become peculiarly concentrated in the Anglophone world: the UK, Australia, and the USA (Clarke and Henwood 1997; Höpflinger 1997: 104). In the USA 75% of unmarried births are within single-parent families (Jensen 1995: 229), while Britain (or at least England and Wales) is unusual within Europe in continuing to experience high fertility among adolescents, the great majority of whom are unmarried girls not in cohabitation relationships (Coleman 1996a: 23). In France nearly all children born out of wedlock had been recognized by both parents before their first birthday (Lelièvre 1994). Clarke (1992) describes the considerable rise in the number of British children living in lone-parent (mother) families, and the considerable likelihood that they will be living in poverty. Both divorce and an absence of initial marriage have contributed to this rise. On the other hand, there is evidence of a growing proportion of British unmarried births at least being registered jointly by mothers and fathers, even if they are not always cohabiting (Clarke and Henwood 1997: 162). While this is most likely to be the case among older unmarried mothers, it is growing among the young ones too.

Lone-parent families (in 80–90 per cent of cases lone-*mother* families) have however been increasing generally because of the rise in divorce, particularly in the UK, Scandinavia, and the USA, but not in southern Europe (Jensen 1995: 232-3; for Italy in particular, see Menniti, Palomba, and Sabbadini 1997). In France too there was a considerable rise in single-parent families during the 1980s. These were mainly a result of divorce, but the statistics also include cohabiting couples wrongly regarded as single-parent units by statistics counting only married partners as forming couples (Lefranc and Thave 1994).

In a study covering most Western European and some other societies, Rainwater and Smeeding (1994) found that children were more likely to live in poverty than adults, even among two-parent families. The effect was most extreme in the USA, but only in the Netherlands were children less likely to be poor than adults. Recent evidence in the UK also shows a shift towards increased child poverty (Clarke and Henwood 1997: 178). However, in Denmark, as a result of state social policy, the real income of families with children (including single-parent families) has improved faster than that of childless families (L. B. Knudsen 1997: 41). This poverty was always concentrated among lone-parent families. In the USA the combination of an extreme in the general adult/child difference with an exceptionally high rate of single parentage means that one in eight US children live in poverty against one in 100 in Belgium, the Netherlands, Sweden, Finland, or Italy. In most European countries the situation was stable, but in the UK and USA the number of poor children was increasing rapidly; this is consistent with our findings in Chapter 5 concerning the trend in incomes in those countries. On the other hand, the rise in part-time working among both men and women in the Netherlands seems to have been associated with a considerable rise in child poverty in families with only a single earner (Kuijsten and Schulze 1997).

The argument of Lesthaeghe (1995) cited earlier that marriages are increasingly centred on the couple rather than children suggests either an imminent change as contemporary young people become parents, or yet another misfit between values and practice. Much other research suggests a *growing* importance of children within marriages. Schütze (1988) found a major change in the approach of parents to children in Germany between the 1950s and the 1980s. In the earlier period children were seen in terms of their capacity eventually to advance or sustain the position of the family. By the 1980s parents were more concerned to develop the autonomy and free will of their children, while at the same time making them and love for them the central object of the family's life; this latter reached the extent where the parents' relations with their children became more important than their relationship with each other. It is also important to note that the low birth rate in Germany is not the result of a trend to single-child families. Instead there is a polarization, with some young women choosing to have careers and no children at all, while others continue a traditional role as non-working wives and mothers with two or more children (Federkeil 1997: 94). In Italy in contrast, where cohabitation rates are low, the impression given by the summary statistics of single-child families corresponds to the reality (Menniti, Palomba, and Sabbadini 1997: 228).

A similar argument has been made about a wider range of countries by Björnberg (1992a). Studying a period similar to that covered in this book (from the early 1960s to the 1980s), Nave-Herz (1988a) argued that, again in Germany, marriage and family have changed in a number of ways. Marriage is now likely to be entered only at the point when a couple want to have children, and caring for children has become a principal purpose of marriage. Furthermore, German children are expected to share housework tasks less than in earlier decades. Similar conclusions have also been reached more recently by Peuckert (1996: 268). In Sweden too marriage is frequently embarked on only once a couple has children, and divorce rates are considerably higher among couples without children, as though marriage had become primarily an arrangement for children (J. Hoem 1991).

These facts, while supporting the thesis of increased calculation in human relationships, suggests a distinction between calculation and *individual* happiness maximization. Furthermore, in a study of 19 countries (including most of those in our study), Mastekaasa (1994) found a positive association between being married and happiness; least happy of all were the divorced, who were unhappier than the widowed, and the single were less happy than the married. The effect was the same for both genders, though especially for men. There was little variation by country, though Germans (both genders) and Japanese women seemed least dependent on marriage for their happiness.

One recalls here the finding of Lesthaeghe and Moors (1996) of most dissatisfaction with and anxiety about life among cohabitees, least among the married (especially married women). On the other hand, the married (and especially women) were least likely to report feelings of pride in an accomplishment, demonstrating the costs to the individual of a strong family. Flaquer (1994) also relates the strength of the family in Spain to the relatively weak development of an individualistic approach to social values of private life.

The churches' loss of control—a control which had lasted for many centuries until the post-war period—is also part of the explanation of the second demographic transition. This transition essentially takes the form of an assertion of individual autonomy which involves a rejection of all expressions of external institutional authority—something that extends far wider than demography (Lesthaeghe 1995: 20–1). Lesthaeghe (ibid. 26 ff.) claims that from the 1960s individual autonomy (which is not the same as individualism) rose alongside community involvement as values of personal responsibility, embodying rejection of external authority. *However*, he notes that from the 1980s both Dutch and US research suggest a decline in the community component. This would suggest that the family has begun to lose its collective, trust-based—and also of course patriarchal and hierarchical—character and has been affected by the calculative, individually maximizing forms of behaviour associated with the economy.

Von Trotha (1990) also sees the family as becoming, like the pre-modern family, less autonomous and more open to public control. She is thinking here, not of the subordination to the economy that we have identified as a counter to the increased openness of post-compromise society, but a subordination to two other forces: children's peer groups; and the state through its school and counselling services and childcare or family-related services of the welfare state. These, as we have seen, began to grow as part of mid-century compromise society and in many ways embodied the logic of specialization of that form of society. What we witness here however is what she calls the breaking down of the high walls (*die hohen Mauern*) of the modern family, and its replacement by an open family (*offene Familie*).

However, we must also remember that, in this chapter, in addition to discovering the vulnerability of the family we have discovered the determination of people to sustain it. This takes various forms. In the USA people continue to form marriages and families despite increasing difficulty in sustaining them. In northern Europe people are using the welfare state to assert their determination to have children even if the family structure within which those children will live is in a state of uncertainty. In continental, in particular southern, Europe people seem to resolve the paradox by keeping families small but continuing to recognize an extensive set of obligations within the circle. Jurado Guerrero and Naldini (1996), using World Values Survey findings, show that southern families are more likely than other Europeans to recognize mutual duties of both parents and children—'duties' not being a word that matches the individualistic set of values described by Lesthaeghe. They point out that, according to the surveys, Italians and Spanish (and French, here part of the south) place more weight on the desirability of having a child than do northern Europeans (in this case Danes, British, and Germans), and yet Danes and British have larger families than Italians and Spaniards. Values and practice do not necessarily correspond. They ascribe the differences to the poor development of the welfare states in southern Europe, and in particular to the poor development of the capacity of those states to recognize the position of working mothers. Where strong family obligations continue to be recognized *despite the pressures of modern individualism*, and the welfare state offers little support in this task, people resolve their dilemma by restricting their assumption of such obligations. They can however do this only laterally (by postponing marriage) and downwards (by not having many children); they cannot evade obligations to parents, or perhaps to siblings and cousins.

THE WIDER FAMILY

It is not possible in a book of this scope to discuss in detail the many other aspects of family life: the changing character of parent–child relationships from authority to friendship; the relative role of kin and friends in people's lives. Nevertheless, some discussion of these issues is necessary to complete our picture.

Early in the chapter we noted the mythical nature of much of the idea of the extended family in pre-modern Western Europe. There was however considerable experience of elderly widows living with their married children, and of unmarried children staying in the families of the ageing parents until the latter died. The decline of this is very recent. For example, in the early 1960s 42% of elderly people in Britain lived with one of their children. By the mid-1980s this had dropped to 14% (Grundy 1996: 285–6). Data are not available for many societies on this, but Grundy (ibid. 287) reports considerable diversity in the 1980s: Netherlands 11%, UK 16%, Italy 35%, Ireland 43%.

This decline should however not be taken to mean that people are today likely to cut off contacts with elderly parents. Living separately is something that has been made possible for many elderly people through improved health and combinations of improved social facilities and domestic technology. Improved travel and communication arrangements then make it possible for them and their adult children to retain considerable contact. Caring becomes 'caring about', arranging for either private services or the welfare state to care for an elderly or otherwise dependent relative (Waerness 1989: 221). The pattern of people living alone in Europe is as might be expected: most in the Scandinavian countries; then Germany, France, the Netherlands; then southern Europe (J.-C. Kaufmann 1994a). There is however a strong difference between the two main groups living alone: the elderly and the young. Women dominate in both cases: among the former because of their greater longevity; among the latter because young men are less skilled in housework and are more likely to stay in their parents' home.

Daughters and daughters-in-law continue to be important sources of direct care for the elderly, even when the latter remain in their own homes (Waerness 1989: 228). Elderly people themselves, and especially grandmothers, are often involved in *caring for* other members of their families: their own divorced adult children, or their grandchildren while their own daughters go out to work (Grundy 1996: 290). This is important in sustaining the high level of mothers' labour-force participation despite low levels of public childcare in the UK (Clarke and Henwood 1997: 180). The role is also important in Italy (Menniti, Palomba, and Sabbadini 1997: 247). Déchaux (1994) described these developments in France. These are family bonds that are likely to have been tightened rather than loosened by certain recent family changes—changes which are otherwise indicators of family weakening. According to Déchaux, familial aid can take three very different forms: domestic work to maintain the household (normally performed by women); maintenance of a network of contacts that can be used to facilitate access to the wider society, performed by the extended family in general; and financial support, usually taking the form of inheritance and *patrimoine* passed down the family line (ibid. 43). Societies vary considerably in their capacity to generate resources of this kind. France may be unusual here in the strength of the importance of *patrimoine*—as either reality for the reasonably well to do or as aspiration for everyone else—resulting from the property-owning peasantry of post-revolutionary France (Mendras 1988). Two-thirds of the French population report having received some kind of financial assistance from their family network (Déchaux 1994).

Von Trotha (1990) claims that many family changes, which bring to an end the 'modern' family, produce a kind of return to the variety of family forms of the pre-industrial period. Where high mortality rates produced large numbers of step-parents and caring grandparents, so the postmodern family does the same through divorce. We might also note that high mortality produced complex relationships of stepbrothers and stepsisters similar to those being produced by divorce and remarriage today. (Anxieties produced by these complexities might explain the prominence of difficult step-parent relationships in traditional folklore and fairy stories.) The mid-century period, coming after the reduction of mortality rates but before the rise in divorce, may well have been a point of historically unusual stability and simplicity in family structures. Von Trotha (ibid.) also notes that the prevalence of single-mother families in some societies also produces a new matrilineal pattern, though with these mothers being part-time mothers as in the past fathers were only part-time. She therefore sees the mother–child dyad as at the centre of the family, which contradicts the research of Lesthaeghe and others, who see the adult couple as the focus.

Renewed unemployment and economic uncertainty lead to growing recourse to family ties. Morris (1994) reports on the widespread dependence on kin of unemployed families in a north-eastern British manufacturing town, with both relatives and friends providing not just material support but also vital news about job vacancies; wives tended to be the co-ordinators of such activity. Research among manual workers in Sweden suggests a very strong concern to keep problems within the family rather than turning to professional helpers (Waerness 1989: 233–42), men being more dependent than women on their marriage partner in particular.

Families remain an important source of routes to occupations for young people (an issue that will be explored more generally in the next chapter). Déchaux (1994) reports however that, at least in France, the kinds of employment found by family members are less likely to require formal qualifications than those obtained through more public means (school, official advertisements). This probably follows from the fact that such mechanisms by definition work within narrower circles—except for those at the top of society, for whom family networks are contiguous with those of national elites. Against this 'deficiency' of the familial model stands the fact that there are affective and normative gains from such exchanges that are largely missing from the formal market and bureaucratic world.

A pattern of prolonged living with parents among young adults found in southern Europe, especially Italy (Menniti, Palomba, and Sabbadini 1997: 227) and Spain (Jurado Guerrero 1999), is a further form of a continued importance for the family which should not necessarily be seen as a residual practice that will decline with further modernization. Jurado Guerrero and Naldini (1996) point out that this pattern exists alongside the very 'modern' phenomenon of low fertility, and among causes of it are the recent phenomena of high employment and economic insecurity. Höpflinger (1997: 99) has argued that such developments demonstrate the limited usefulness of modernization theory to studies of the family, as reassertion of the traditionalism of this institution can become a source of respite from modernization pressures—from our current perspective, an example of the mid-century compromise at work.

Bouverne-de-Bie (1994) has argued that today young people are subject to contradictory pressures: socio-culturally they are pressed to become independent ever earlier, while as a result of education and youth unemployment their period of economic dependency on parents is longer than in the past. In this context it is particularly interesting to note that, although the numbers of young adults living with parents in France is considerably lower than in Italy and Spain, and declined during the 1960s and 1970s, during the 1980s it began to rise again (Lefranc and Thave 1994; Jurado Guerrero 1999). By 1990 37% of 24-year-old men and 21% of women were living with their parents, an increase from 28% and 17% respectively in 1975 (ibid. 1314–15). This trend is particularly strong among the unemployed. There has however also been a rise in young French people aged 16–24 living alone; what has declined is the number in unions (marriage or cohabitation) (ibid. 1315–18). Many young French adults, of both sexes, report being pressed to leave by their parents (Bozon 1991). The median age of leaving home was around 20, with between two and four years then elapsing before first marriage or cohabitation (Bozon 1991: 1545, 1550). The phenomenon of increased stay in the parental home has also been observed in the Netherlands (De Jong, Liefbroer, and Beekink 1991; Kuijsten and Schulze 1997), where it again seems to be associated with unemployment. Parents who are themselves poor are also particularly unable to help their children leave home. On the other hand, children who had experienced caring childhoods were less likely to seek to leave home in order to find independence. The main reason for leaving the parental home remained marriage. Research in the Netherlands (and in some other countries) suggests that young people in the 1980s and 1990s had friendly, egalitarian relations with their parents, probably contrasting with a more antagonistic situation when parental authority roles were being challenged in the 1960s (van Well 1994). In the UK, on the other hand, there has been the opposite trend of young people increasingly leaving the family home early to establish single-person households (Clarke and Henwood 1997: 167).

As we might by now expect, families remain generally important in southern Europe: in Italy members of extended families live closer to each other and visit each other more often than in northern Europe, and people recognize extensive kinship obligations beyond the nuclear family (ISSP 1986). Waerness (1989: 228–9) points out this concentration of multi-generation families within southern (or 'Mediterranean') rather than other parts of Europe and argues that it corresponds to a far older, pre-industrial pattern when southern Europe (but not northern Italy) lagged behind the north-west in developing the European marriage pattern (Wall, Robin, and Laslett 1983). However, she also concludes (Waerness 1989: 226) from her surveys that close relatives are still very important in the case of children in modern urban European families, the most important figures being grandmothers. There is also evidence that German and

Austrian families are more likely to sustain family contact than American ones, and that these Europeans are more likely than Americans to depend on kin in preference to friends (Haller 1989). There seems in general little evidence that family links are becoming less important to people in contemporary Europe (Höpflinger 1997: 125).

Recourse to family rather than friends implies a relatively ascriptive, less individually chosen approach to life. In a Spanish study, Requena Santos (1994) found that people with larger friendship networks were happier than those with small numbers of friends, but that happiness declined with the intimacy of friendships. On the other hand, intimacy of *family* relationships improved happiness. Also, the lower a person's social class the more they depended on family rather than friends. In a study of elderly Germans, Schütze and Lang (1993) found that social status was not relevant in determining numbers of friends. Men were more successful in finding friends than women, unless women had had earlier experience of participating in the public sphere. Elderly women were however more dependent than men on friends, because most of them were widows.

In research on family life in two German cities (Bremen and Cologne) Lüschen (1988) found little evidence of the 'isolated' nuclear family anticipated in the theoretical literature. Wide circles of kin (aunts, cousins, nephews, etc.) were recognized as important by most persons studied, though more for friendly relationships than for practical tasks like borrowing money. In what seems to have been a contrast with the findings of London research carried out in the 1970s (Young and Wilmott 1973), kinship ties were as important as friends for *Bremener* and *Kölner*, and in particular they tended to mix friends and relations in their social networks.

In general, as has been indicated a number of times in the above discussion, it is women in nearly all societies who sustain family networks. The relationship between adult daughter and her mother is often the core, and even men are more likely to have recourse to a female relative rather than a male one at times of need (Haller 1989). In addition, research reveals an extraordinary dependence of men on their wives for help and advice on personal matters; women have recourse to a wider range of kin and friends (ibid.). This returns us to an issue considered at the very start of the chapter. If men are somehow the gender which is more rooted in the economic world of calculative exchange, and women more in the family world of trust and affective ties, then it is unsurprising that it should be women who manage personal and emotional questions for men and women alike. Whether this would change with a more thorough breakdown of the mid-century compromise model of separation of economy and family it is as yet too early to say.

CONCLUSIONS

Pinnelli (1995: 88) offers a summary of recent family developments that well serves as a conclusion of the above discussion:

[in Western Europe] marital instability, cohabitation, and extramarital births are taking place where the conditions of development have gone beyond economic well-being, where there is a high value on non-material aspects of the quality of life, and where women enjoy economic independence and relatively great political power. . . . Divorce, cohabitation and extramarital fertility are most widespread where women enjoy economic independence and are in a position to face the possibility of being a single mother without becoming, for this reason, a social subject at risk.

Nuptiality does not correlate so well, she argues, because it is found both where there is a high level of cohabitation and where there are structural obstacles (e.g. unemployment) in its path in poorer countries. Fertility does not follow the trend because of the way in which some of the richer countries ease the strain of being a working mother (ibid. 90).

It remains interesting that couples who cohabit before they marry are more rather than less likely to divorce. Meanwhile it must be remembered that the great majority of young people continue to form couples and produce children. Becker's (1981) economic paradigm argues that the decline of the family results largely from a reduction in the gains from marriage for women and in the opportunity costs of parenthood. This is challenged by those who point out that marriage and family building are often postponed rather than avoided, suggesting that it is a matter of increased quality standards rather than opportunity cost (Oppenheimer 1988). This turns our attention to the idea of a *search for quality* in family relationships, not just decisions about whether to marry or whether to have children (Lesthaeghe 1995). The economic approach assumes certain more or less fixed criteria of choice and preferences that are always seen from the perspective of a maximizing individual. It does not recognize the possibility that people's expectations and calculations can be strongly shaped by the general cultural ambience in which they live, and pressures imposed by those around them. We therefore need to relate these family changes to points of reference in the culture or prevailing values, and to search for changes in these that might explain family change.

Our evidence has in fact been rather ambiguous on the role of children within contemporary families. On the one hand, they may be pushed out of prominence as the adult couple concentrate on maximizing the quality of their own (often problematic) relationship. On the other hand, it was the need for particularly large investment in children—and therefore intensified concern for the individual child—that made necessary a reduction in fertility—not a desire to avoid children altogether.

Dahlström (1989) discusses four contradictions of the modern family: that between parenthood and gainful employment; that between bureaucratic culture and primary-group culture; that between insistence on individual freedom by marriage partners and children's need for stability; that between a male-dominated public sphere and a familial and private one with gender equality. This also covers similar themes to the above discussion, except again that if we have neglected any it is that of children's lives. We shall now consider them in more detail, but in connection with the bridge between the two institutions which specifically dominate the lives of children: the family and education.

Chapter 8

FAMILIES, EDUCATION, AND SOCIAL MOBILITY

Children within a family are preparing for adulthood, which gives their lives a character distinct from those of adult members who are already engaged in either paid or domestic work. Their parents (or substitutes for these) are heavily involved in this preparation, but in all modern societies a major role is also played by formal agencies of socialization and education: schools, colleges, and universities of various kinds. The process is partly about work roles, but not entirely so as education and, in particular, family socialization, are concerned with preparation for adult life in a more general sense. Until recent years of female labour-force participation this can be seen in the case of the education of girls. It is true that until the second half of this century in many countries most education was aimed at boys only, with both parents and educational institutions taking the view that girls' education was less important, mainly because they would not be entering the labour force. However, at least some education was provided for them, primarily at lower levels. Initially the education they received aimed at providing them with skills for housekeeping and for being appropriate companions for their husbands.

The thesis of sociological liberalism implies that educational institutions do their work of preparing the young without major interference from other relevant institutions. For education these would be the state, religion, the economy, and the family. The relative roles of state and religion were fought out as a central social issue in nearly all countries in the late nineteenth century and the first half of this. Especially in Roman Catholic countries, the Church had seen its control of the educational systems that existed as fundamental to its ideological power. The determination of states to establish their own education systems—sometimes in direct ideological rivalry with the Church, sometimes for more technical purposes of looking to the skill needs of an industrial economy—produced considerable social conflict in late nineteenth-century Europe. We shall encounter other dimensions of this struggle when we examine religious and political structures. For the present we need to note that it took place. Its eventual settlement saw a dominance of state education with a certain space given to church schools and sometimes (as, for example, in Italy and the UK, but certainly not in France) a guaranteed space for religious worship within the state's own schools. These settlements had usually been reached by the end of the Second World War, even if aspects of the conflict rumbled on for a longer period. (For example, French and Spanish politics in the 1980s were punctuated on a number of occasions by disputes over the respective roles of church and state; and in the 1990s a controversial decision by the German constitutional court ruled the display of crucifixes in Bavarian schools as contrary to the constitution.)

A different issue has been the control that the state itself might exercise over the education process. The cruder elements of political interference in education in the western part of Europe largely ended with the defeat of the Fascist powers in the Second World War, though they lasted until the mid-1970s in Greece, Portugal, and Spain. More subtle conflicts between governments and the education profession over definition of the curriculum and appropriate methods of study can however occur at any time, and can involve such politically controversial issues as the way in which history is taught or the relationship between schools' assessment procedures and wider principles of social selection. A number of examples can be found in the records of British educational debate in the 1980s and 1990s. However, at the simplest levels and in comparison with many other kinds of society we may assert that, during the post-war years, education did achieve at least some crucial aspects of autonomy in most of the countries under discussion as they entered the mid-century compromise.

Whether or not the education system has autonomy from the economy is a different and also very difficult issue. Since much of its work is a preparation for adult life, a major component of which is the world of paid work, its scope for autonomy is clearly limited. There are important questions here over whether providing what is seen as necessary by current employers actually fulfils economic needs; whether education better serves the economy by operating under its own guidelines but hoping to approximate to economic requirements; or whether it should resolutely avoid any link. Again, the history of our various countries provides a number of examples of these struggles. Windolf (1992) attempted to measure the extent to which higher educational expansion over the period 1870–1990 in France, Germany, Italy, Japan, and the USA was a response to economic growth. He found little correlation in the European countries, where if anything educational expansion was counter-cyclical, but, significantly, a considerable correspondence in the USA. There has been some tendency in some European countries to use extensions of education as a means of keeping young people out of a labour market perceived as overcrowded, rather than as preparation for it.

We shall however concentrate here on the relative autonomy of education from the family, and shall approach its relationship to economic institutions by way of this other link. The thesis of the sociological liberalism of modern society should predict that a child's experience in the education system should be more or less independent of his or her family background; that there is a kind of barrier between the socialization process of the family and that provided within schools. Most optimistic theories of industrialization and modernization emerging from US sociology during the 1950s and 1960s did predict something of precisely this kind (the most influential and frequently cited examples being the theoretical contribution of Parsons (1970) and the research of D. J. Treiman (1970)). The mechanism perceived by these and similar writers works through a hypothesized double disconnection of the occupational system from the family, with education being involved at both disconnections.

First, the thesis of the rational efficiency of modernization predicts that the process of allocation to jobs will be on meritocratic grounds: people will acquire posts because they have had an educational preparation and achievement suited to performing them, and not because their families have managed to acquire posts for them. Pre-modern society is commonly perceived to have been based on various forms of the latter principle: this is demonstrated in the hereditary principle of transmission of property and authority, as well as in the common practice of children being inducted into the same occupation as their parents, whether in agriculture or in apprenticeship to urban crafts. When principles of this kind are in operation, one may well have a clear moral duty to use whatever means are available to secure positions for members of one's family; indeed, people are often not perceived as individuals with destinies separate from the lives of other family members. This can be seen, for example, in the belief within the Roman Catholic Church that it is possible for the prayers and devotions of family members to reduce the time spent in Purgatory by a deceased person: an individual's ultimate fate can be determined by the actions of their families as well as of themselves. A rejection of this view in favour of the concept of the individual standing alone with God was an essential part of the Protestant critique of Catholicism during the Reformation, and this fundamental conflict was itself associated with the rationalization and modernization of society.

In essentially 'modern' societies attempts to help family members other than by assisting them to improve their own performance becomes stigmatized as 'nepotism', a moral offence. Societies undergoing rapid modernization often experience difficulties as people are called upon to adapt to this radical change in ethical requirements: what is a moral duty under one regime is a moral defect under the other, and vice versa. The matter is made even more difficult by the fact that in no societies is nepotism likely to be seen as completely illegitimate: 'modern' monarchies are still based on the hereditary principle; inheritance of large quantities of property, sometimes bringing with it rights of power and control over extensive economic resources, is universally permitted and accepted, even applauded and regarded as appropriate behaviour by those at the very peak of society.

Second, educational opportunities themselves are predicted to be made available on as open a basis as possible, with no privileges being reserved to children from particular family backgrounds. This follows partly from the rational efficiency principle again —a modern society based on achievement must make maximum use of all the talent available to it and not accept artificial restrictions according to family backgrounds; and partly from the claims of democracy that all children in a society should have opportunities to achieve within national educational institutions. In the years after the Second World War political elites in virtually all European societies made the promise to their electorates that US leaders had made for many previous years: although the society would not have an equality of outcomes, there would be equality of opportunity; and the main path to opportunity in an increasingly scientific and technical world would be through education.

An education system corresponding to these ideals would itself therefore manage to select on merit and separate itself from family influence; and would in turn replace family influence as the channel for recruitment to occupations. Theories that predict this outcome either ignore the response that privileged families are likely to make to this situation, or assume that they will be defeated. From the point of view of the family however the situation looks very different. Families are responsible for the early stages of socialization of their children; and they have a series of motives for wanting to achieve 'the best' that they can for them. They should be expected to deploy whatever resources they have to help their children secure a good place in adult life, whether by helping them to direct access to employment, through making advantageous

marriages, or by using family resources to enable children to acquire levels of education that will assist them in the subsequent competition for occupational advantage
(de Graaf and Ganzeboom 1990). The resources at the disposal of families for this task
are both diverse and very unequally allocated. Wealth, contacts, and influence can be
used either directly to secure the desired advantages for children, or indirectly to help
the children acquire education if this becomes the principal means through which
such goals as a good job can be accessed. Given that there is a fairly unbroken continuum between the socialization that takes place in the home and the education that
takes place in formal institutions of schools and colleges, a family can also use its
cultural resources to assist its children educationally.

The role of marriage as a means of social mobility is limited by the strong tendency
for people to choose marriage partners from social classes close to themselves—this
being especially true for propertied groups (for France, see Bozon 1991). The pattern is
somewhat confused by the broad character of routine non-manual employment
among women, which might give the impression that many male manual workers are
'marrying up' when they marry an office worker, when this is not really the case. There
is also (at least in France) evidence of an educational dowry (*la dot scolaire*) whereby
women from artisanal or commercial families who acquire a good education are able
to marry into higher social groups. However, in general Erikson and Goldthorpe (1992:
261) concluded from a study of marital mobility in nine European countries: 'If we
know how men of a given class origin have themselves become distributed within
the class structure in the course of their employment, we can predict, with no great in-
accuracy, how their "sisters" will have been distributed through marriage.'

That these diverse familial resources are possessed unequally is clear. We saw in
Chapter 5 that material resources of wealth and income are unequally distributed,
these inequalities being strongly based on the rewards available from the occupational
system. Similarly, ability to use influence and take advantage of contacts to help children in that system will depend on the family members' own positions within it. Finally, families' ability to help their children will depend, partly on material resources,
but even more strongly on adult family members' own past educational achievements.
To the extent that educational level was important in securing the adults' own occupational positions, we have a series of tight linkages between the educational and
occupational positions of successive generations. The different material and cultural
resources available to different members of generation A enables them to acquire
different levels of education; these give them access to different kinds of occupation;
these in turn give them different material resources, kinds of contacts and influences
which, combining with the continuing legacy of the cultural capital established by
their own education, enables them to help their children in generation B to acquire
different levels of education. And so it continues.

According to these cultural reproduction theories families should be expected to
pursue a different logic from that of the 'requirements' of modernization. The logic of
modernization insists that only certain routes should be used to secure occupational
places, and that the educational channels that form important components of those
routes should be open to children from many different backgrounds. The logic of the
family says that children must be helped by whatever means are available; these means
might involve bypassing educational routes; or ensuring that children will be success-

ful within such routes; or, in the case of families lacking material and cultural advantages, merely hoping that the promises of open and fair access to meritocratic channels are trustworthy. We should not therefore expect sociological liberalism in the sense of the autonomy of education to be unchallenged. It must also be remembered that the elites who enunciated and took responsibility for the promise of meritocracy and equality of opportunity have been endogenous. That is, they are themselves members of societies, usually with families and children of their own; being, by definition as members of elites, people with material, influential, and cultural resources, their own commitment to egalitarian meritocracy must be in some doubt.

A number of sociological theories have argued along these lines, producing predictions very different from the 'optimistic modernization' school. The French sociologist Pierre Bourdieu developed from this idea the concept of cultural capital: just as families have financial capital which they can use to benefit their children, so they have reserves of culture which can be passed on (Bourdieu and Passeron 1964; Bourdieu 1979). Cultural capital has a great advantage over financial capital in that it can be 'used' without being 'used up': a child drawing on his or her reserve of family socialization in order to take advantage of educational opportunities in no way diminishes the family's stock of culture, but may indeed further enrich it. Other authors have gone so far as to argue that educational credentials are used primarily to legitimate inequalities of family access to subsequent occupational differences (Collins 1979; Bowles and Gintis 1976). According to this argument, it is necessary in a democratic society to justify cross-generational transmission of privilege. The children of privileged groups are therefore required to demonstrate superior educational success before they can inherit their parents' high positions. Therefore both they and the children of the underprivileged are required to enter the educational process, where the cultural advantages of the privileged enable them to demonstrate their superiority and therefore the appropriateness of the cross-generational transmission of advantage. In this way the drive of modernization towards extended, widely available education and the desire of privileged groups to sustain their families' positions are reconciled.

However, while there is probably an overall association between modernization and a shift towards reliance on formal educational qualifications, many factors will interfere with this simple generalization. As Erikson and Goldthorpe (1992: 304) point out, national systems exhibit different degrees of closeness between education and employment. In an apprenticeship system like the German one, formal educational channels are almost obligatory for any employment choice; in England, France, and Italy the links are far less strictly developed, and families' cultural and financial resources will be deployed in other ways. Occupational types also differ: the professions always require specific educational preparation; entrepreneurial careers will be considerably assisted by the existence of family wealth or family businesses; while many administrative and managerial careers need neither of these. Further still, once more potential candidates for particular forms of employment have acquired the appropriate formal educational qualifications than there are vacancies, employers may fall back on such 'pre-modern' criteria as family and ethnic contacts, local and cultural loyalties, to select the successful ones. It is therefore possible that an increase in educational opportunities might actually lead to a reduction in reliance on education as a recruitment criterion.

A number of detailed studies of parents and children have demonstrated the mechanisms through which these processes operate. Some recent Dutch research (Janssen and Ultee 1994) established a model similar to that assumed here: parents' own education and financial resources should influence children's performance. The study distinguished between fathers and mothers, sons and daughters, and also compared two age cohorts: those born between 1917 and 1946, and those between 1947 and 1961. Both parental education and financial circumstances explained a good deal of variance among both cohorts, but whereas the latter was more important among the older group, parents' education was more important in predicting the educational success of the younger cohort.

This is consistent with the expectation that educational and cultural rather than purely financial background has become more important as a predictor of educational success over time. Fathers' education had considerably more influence than mothers' on their children's performance—especially in the case of daughters. In a pure socialization model of cultural transmission, one would expect mothers' cultural background to be more important, as they have much greater responsibility for children's upbringing. Fathers' dominance might imply that it is the general cultural environment of the home produced by a traditional 'head of household and breadwinner' father rather than specific socialization that transmits the family influence. Consistent with this interpretation of the evidence is the fact that in the younger cohort this gender difference had virtually disappeared—during a time period when the concept of male 'head of household' was also declining.

Pioneering work on inter-generational cultural transmission was carried out in the 1960s and 1970s by a British sociologist, Basil Bernstein (1970). He drew particular attention to language and identified two different speech codes: a 'restricted' one consisting of short sentences, limited vocabulary and syntax, and a 'elaborated' code of long and complex formal language. Everyone was able to use the restricted code, but people of low educational level had access to it alone. This disadvantaged their children at school, where they suddenly encountered elaborate speech patterns. Bernstein's work was criticized for oversimplifying into two codes what in reality was likely to be a wider diversity. However, his insights into one of the basic forms taken by the processes that Bourdieu describes continue to have value. Although his ideas developed originally on the basis of research in London, they have been found useful in very diverse contexts. Most recently, research on Portuguese children (Morais 1993) has demonstrated the continuing viability of the Bernstein approach. In particular, it reveals a considerable gap between children's capacity to acquire knowledge and their capacity to use it. While children from families with restricted codes might well be able to acquire knowledge, their capacity to use it was restricted by their lack of access to the elaborated code.

In a carefully observed study of families' socialization and education practice in Geneva, a French-speaking Swiss city, Kellerhals and Montandon (1991) demonstrate some of the diverse ways in which parental background affects children's educational performance. They conclude that, even in what they regard as the *situation postmoderne* of the contemporary city of Geneva, social class was a major determinant of parents' approaches to their children's education. They developed two variables in parental approaches. In internal family relations there was a contrast between families which kept children tied tightly to family norms (*fusion interne*) and those which encouraged their autonomy. Externally families might be either open to or closed against external influence. Manual working and routine non-manual families were likely to be externally closed, but internally of either type. Professional and managerial families were more likely to offer internal autonomy with either closure or openness. Professional families therefore placed far more emphasis on expression and participation among their children and the values of self-regulation. It is interesting to note that on many indicators skilled manual families more closely resembled professional and managerial than did the lower non-manual levels.

Research on Ireland (a country only recently acquiring many of the characteristics of 'modernization') also suggests that there is a shift from direct transmission of family position to doing so through education (Breen and Whelan 1993). These authors also found evidence for the ironic twist suggested above that, as education becomes more widely available, the advantages in possessing it decline, and individuals may again start to have recourse to 'traditional' mechanisms of social networks to secure employment advantages. Similarly, Duru-Bellat, Jarousse, and Mingat (1993) argue that in France social advantages of family background are increasingly translated into an educational advantage which is then *legitimated* by formal qualifications. These parents also show a persistence in allowing their children to remain out of the labour market while repeating qualifications in order eventually to enter from a high educational level. Families from poorer backgrounds are less likely to see the advantages of doing that or to be unable to afford to permit it.

Whether or not the educational qualifications so received constitute credentialism, in the sense that they are not really needed, is difficult to prove. It is however possible to submit to some test the idea that modernization will involve a simultaneous broadening of educational opportunities but continuing inequality of educational outcomes. Other research on Ireland enabled Raftery and Hout (1989) to go further and hypothesize the following. Under the pressure of modernization, educational opportunities will expand. However, existing privileged families, using their cultural and financial advantages, will take up the bulk of these opportunities until their demand for a particular level of education has been 'saturated'; from that point underprivileged groups will begin to share in the gains from education. They call this the 'maximally maintained inequality' (MMI) thesis.

Against the predictions of the modernization theorists we must therefore set those of various kinds of class or inequality theorists. These will predict that sociological liberalism will be heavily compromised by continuing differential success of the children of existing advantaged groups. This will be reflected in both recruitment to desirable occupations and in educational success. In this chapter we shall first consider the latter and then the former.

Ideally we should want to examine to what extent this was happening in the heyday of mid-century compromise society in the early 1960s; and what, if anything has subsequently changed. However, the necessary data cannot be accessed easily from widely available statistics; we require sociological research to have been undertaken which relates children's educational achievements to those of their parents. This is not available for all countries in which we are interested. There is another problem affecting all research on interaction between generations, which we have to some extent encountered in the previous chapter: the difference between cohorts and periods. At any one point in time the educational backgrounds of the population reflect the educational policies, structures, and approaches of a variety of different past decades—but not those of the present decade. When we enquire into the educational backgrounds of the adult population of the early 1960s, we are looking at the effects of education systems of the 1940s, 1930s, and earlier; it is only when we turn to the 1990s that we see the outcome of 1960s education. We cannot therefore carry out a cross-sectional comparison between the two periods, but instead generally consider changes that have taken place over time. It is too early yet for research evidence to be available on experience during the 1990s, but some studies enable us to consider the situation in the 1980s, at least for certain countries (Shavit and Blossfeld 1993; Müller *et al.* 1989).

SOCIAL ORIGINS AND EDUCATION

Most theories of post-industrialism argue that the stratification systems of industrial society are broken down by the new fluidity of occupational systems. Also, in a context of frequent change and of a general upgrading of skill levels, we should predict a further decline in the power of family to influence educational outcomes since mid-century compromise society. This is in line with the general hypothesis being tested in this part of this book, that the tendency towards fragmentation and individualization embodied in theories of postmodern and post-industrial should ramify and take further the existing pressures towards sociological liberalism of mid-century compromise society. On the other hand, we have seen in Chapter 5 that many of the predictions of declining class inequality have been oversimplifications; the clarity of class identities may be declining, but levels of inequality associated with them might be increasing.

In examining the research findings we are therefore seeking to discover answers to two questions: to what extent did family origin continue to influence inequalities in educational achievement during the development of post-war compromise society? (In other words, is an MMI or an equalization of opportunity thesis better supported by the evidence?) And can we detect any subsequent developments of either a loss of family influence through the fragmentation of classes or of its perpetuation despite fragmentation?

Blossfeld and Shavit (1993) studied the association between social origins and educational attainment across much of the twentieth century in 13 countries, including the following among those of interest to our present study: Italy, the Netherlands, Sweden, Switzerland, part of the UK (England and Wales), Japan, and the USA. They used a theoretical approach which enabled them to appraise some of the theories of modernization cited above, though they did not address any specific changes or intensifications of change that might be expected to occur in post-compromise society. They concentrate on certain key educational transitions: the proportions of a particular age cohort remaining in school after the primary stage (around age 11); entering post-compulsory (usually post-16) secondary education; and entering higher education (universities and equivalent). Modernization theories making assumptions of sociological liberalism will predict both that these proportions will rise with the needs of the modernization process for a more educated population and that the chances of children from different family backgrounds achieving success will gradually become more equal. Cultural reproduction theories will predict that even with expansion inequalities in the chances of children with different family backgrounds will remain strong, children from culturally disadvantaged families being able to advance in educational performance at a particular level only when privileged groups have saturated their demand for that level, after which they will go on to predominate at a new, higher level.

Blossfeld and Shavit certainly found evidence of an enormous expansion of education, with compulsory secondary education becoming virtually universal everywhere in the years following the Second World War. Inequalities in opportunity at this first transition point virtually disappeared. However, at the later transition points, into advanced secondary education and into higher education, a lack of expansion of supply concomitant with the new large numbers coming through from universal secondary education led to new bottlenecks. Almost everywhere this produced a reassertion of social selection based on parental advantage. The thesis of maximally maintained inequality (MMI) seems to have been confirmed: in most countries children from 'lower' social backgrounds did not experience an increase in their educational opportunities until 'higher' groups had fully satisfied, or saturated, their demand for it.

If parental background is fundamental in explaining children's educational success, we would expect this background to have a declining effect on chances as children move away from sole reliance on it, that is as they become older and move from the initial to the later transitions. This is certainly confirmed for all the cases studied, except Switzerland where family influence did not seem to decline in importance (ibid. 15–18). In other studies Jonsson and Mills (1993*b*), comparing England and Sweden, and Müller and Haun (1994), studying Germany, also found that social (that is primarily family) background had most effect on children's chances at earlier stages of the education process. Jonsson and Mills (1993*b*) thus found the impact of compulsory secondary education particularly important, as before its introduction family background had been of fundamental importance in determining children's tendency to remain at school at these relatively young ages. They report considerable gross equalization of chances among classes between cohorts born before and after the Second World War, the period when compulsory secondary education was being extended in Sweden and the UK. On the other hand, the authors point out, privileged classes were also making large gains in their access to more advanced levels of education.

Similarly, Müller and Haun (1994) traced the educational careers of German men and women born in successive decades from 1910–19 to 1960–9, and showed that for both genders the gaps between children from professional and managerial families and various other social groups had become progressively smaller, though it remained high, especially among women. The authors argue that the progress made in reducing the impact of cultural inequalities tells against Bourdieu's argument that these differences would become more significant as socio-economic ones became less important.

Van der Ploeg (1992) showed similarly that expansion of the basic education system was the most important factor producing an increase in participation in higher education in the Netherlands: the more that young people acquired during their basic education, the more likely they were to proceed to higher levels. However, Koppen (1991) has described considerable inequality in educational opportunity in the Netherlands, showing that here as in many other countries expansion of higher education mainly favoured social groups already taking advantage of such levels. He identified the brief period 1969–75 as the only one in which there was a real democratization of educational opportunities.

The Netherlands was in fact one of only two countries—the other was Sweden—in the Shavit and Blossfeld (1993) study in which lower social groups had been able to secure an educational advance before privileged classes had reached saturation point; at the other extreme, in the USA, even saturation of educational demand by privileged groups failed to have an effect, the position of lower social groups actually *worsening* despite the apparent saturation effect (Hout, Raftery, and Bell 1993). Only expansion of the system improved the educational chances of young Americans from underprivileged families, but any gains they made were prevented from becoming relative gains by the constancy or intensification of social selection at later stages. The authors, two of whom had developed the MMI thesis during their earlier Irish research, comment that although their US evidence confirms their thesis, they did not anticipate such an emergence of an educational under-class of school drop-outs with declining performance as is now taking place in that country (ibid. 43). They point out that this cannot be explained by popular theories about broken homes and single-parent families, since their research method, concentrating on both mothers and fathers, required them to study only persons who had remained in full two-parent families throughout their childhood (ibid. 46). It is notable that in the USA there is considerable emphasis on the pursuit of equality of opportunity through education but not at all on the redistribution of material resources, which, as we saw in our consideration of incomes in Chapter 5, are more unequal, and are becoming even more unequal, than in virtually any other advanced society.

The MMI thesis has also been sustained by evidence from Germany (Blossfeld 1993: 62–70); Italy (Cobalti and Schizzerotto 1993); and Switzerland (Buchmann, Charles, and Sacchi 1993). It was also the case in the UK, where—in a society almost rivalling the USA for its recent increases in income inequalities—between those born in the 1940s and those born in the 1950s there was actually an increase in inequalities of educational opportunity among different social groups (Kerckhoff and Trott 1993: 141–3).[1] In a separate study Müller and his colleagues (Müller *et al.* 1989; Müller and Karle 1993) compared 9 European countries in terms of the relationship between social origin and educational attainment, finding only slight variation among nations and very strong inequalities, hindering the opportunities of manual workers' and rural families' children.

It seems that we can safely conclude from this research that, up to and past the heyday of mid-century compromise society, educational systems did not acquire an autonomy from family as would be anticipated by the thesis of sociological liberalism, but tended to continue and reinforce differences among families. The theories of class analysts (such as Erikson and Goldthorpe 1992) and the cultural capital school such as Bourdieu would seem to come closer to describing reality than those of Treiman and other advocates of the modernization hypothesis. A somewhat different conclusion would appear were we to compare these countries with some in the Third World,

---

[1] In Japan too the ostensibly widespread reforms of the national system imposed by the US occupation authorities after the Second World War seem to have had no impact whatsoever on the consistent patterns of inequality of Japanese education (Treiman and Yamaguchi 1993: 248). The surprise expressed at this by Treiman and Yamaguchi is perhaps misplaced, since US educational outcomes are not particularly different.

where inequalities are far steeper.[2] A more reasonable conclusion would therefore be that there is a tendency for advanced industrial society to be associated with a growing autonomy of education from family background, but that this tendency is checked and limited, the checks and limitations stemming primarily from the efforts of families to use their highly unequally distributed resources to assist the next generation.

RECENT CHANGES

Some of the national studies brought together by Shavit and Blossfeld contain some evidence for the 1980s, which might give us an early insight into any possible changes associated with post-compromise society. Blossfeld (1993: 71) reports how the decline in vocational training places associated with more difficult economic circumstances in Germany has led to a growing association between relatively advantaged social backgrounds and apprenticeship success. J. O. Jonsson (1993) suggests that the gradual trend to decreasing inequality in Sweden seems recently to have been declining. Kerckhoff and Trott (1993: 141–3) saw a reassertion of inequalities in their most recent English cohort, but this was research carried out in 1972. In a different analysis of the effect of the Education Act 1944 in England, Blackburn and Marsh (1991) show the progress and effects of the social struggle that takes place over education. They show that during the 1920s and 1930s inequalities of access to education had been worsening. The 1944 Act, by making secondary education universal and compulsory, massively expanded access to it and thereby reversed that trend. However, as the effect of the post-war increase in fertility began to increase competition for the selective form of secondary education, parents in professional and managerial occupations deployed their material and cultural capital to ensure that their children would do best in that competition. Inequalities increased again to become greater than they had been before the 1994 Act. As already noted, Hout, Raftery, and Bell (1993) also report a recent worsening in the performance of the 'lowest' social groups in the USA and an increase in high-school drop-outs.

This is a small number of countries on which to base conclusions, though it does include the largest European society (Germany) and the world's largest advanced society (USA). Tentatively, it seems that the intensified labour-market competition of the post-Keynesian economy has led, as one would expect, to advantaged social groups deploying their resources to ensure that their children succeed in the educational competition which precedes that for employment. For this process to take place it is not necessary for class identities to be strong; merely that there should be clearly recognized differences between advantageous and disadvantageous occupations, and an accurate idea among at least the successful of the role of education in achieving the former.

GENDER DIFFERENCES

In previous chapters we have frequently noted that one of the main changes between compromise and post-compromise society is the altered position of women. We find

[2] See, for example, the data collected by Treiman and Yip (1989) on 21 countries, which set such countries as Brazil, India, and Taiwan against many of those covered in the present study.

similar evidence in the educational data. Among the older cohorts, that is people born in the earlier parts of the twentieth century, Blossfeld and Shavit (1993) report considerable difference in girls' and boys' achievements in every country where evidence was gathered on girls' performance, with girls lagging considerably. These girls had been educated at a time when it was expected that they would spend very little time in the paid labour force. This is consistent with a strong vocational motive in parents' pursuit of educational qualifications for their children, and with the concept of the family 'protecting itself' from the occupational system by keeping one gender less involved in the latter. Among later cohorts, people born from mid-century onwards, there has been a very considerable advance in the position of girls against boys, in all countries. This is consistent with what we have learned about the new occupational ambitions of women, though it seems that these ambitions might have been initially encouraged by parents who did not themselves envisage such an outcome.

Until the most recent years, research in many societies has shown a tendency for girls to outstrip boys in educational performance until the end of compulsory schooling, when they were overtaken. (See the evidence for earlier birth cohorts in Shavit and Blossfeld 1993.) Their earlier superiority can probably be explained in terms of the behaviour patterns of compliance with adults and obedience that are more strongly expected of girls in most cultures, a higher level of 'naughty' and unruly behaviour being tolerated among boys. During the years of compulsory schooling 'good behaviour' includes trying to succeed at school work. However, at the end of the compulsory period girls have often been told that it is time they now directed their concerns to marriage and domesticity, while boys have been encouraged to prepare for occupational success, often by means of prolonged and successful education. At this point, to be a 'good girl' ceased to mean striving to excel educationally.

In recent years however girls have begun clearly to overtake boys throughout the school range. Furthermore, Müller, Steinmann, and Schneider (1997: 213–18) show that, whereas among the generation aged 55–64 in the early 1990s men were about three times as likely as women to have degrees, this gap reduced decade by decade. Among those aged 25–34 women were slightly more likely than men to have a degree in Denmark, Austria, Portugal, and Spain; there was gender equality in Norway, Sweden, Ireland, France, the Netherlands, and Italy; and in Finland, Germany, the UK, and Belgium male superiority had become very small. Only in Switzerland were young men twice as likely to have a degree than their female counterparts. In the USA too there now seems to be female superiority in educational performance, with young men from underprivileged backgrounds dropping out particularly early from education (Hout, Raftery, and Bell 1993: 39). There is clearly a relationship between these developments and women's changed approach to the labour market, as we discussed in Part I.

Apart from their intrinsic interest, these findings on female improvement assist our general appraisal of the effect of family background and other social factors on educational performance. It is remarkable how rapidly girls' educational performance has improved, equalling and then overtaking boys after decades of inferiority; meanwhile class inequalities seem almost impermeable and indeed recently have seemed to widen. Arguments about unequal material and cultural resources do not apply to the gender difference. Once families decide that they will apply their stock of cultural capital to help their daughters as much as their sons, there is nothing in social theory to suggest that they will not be able to succeed. Between-family class differences, however, are the results of far more persistent variables (Müller, Steinmann, and Schneider 1997).

CULTURAL AND MATERIAL LEGACIES

The role of family in determining who has access to certain kinds of education has clearly remained important in both post-war compromise and subsequent social forms, with exceptions in only a very small number of countries. We can also expect sociological research to tell us something about the mechanisms through which this process takes place. In particular, and following on from the last point made in the discussion of gender differences, we can ask what is more important about parental background: the parents' purely cultural legacy, or the material and other standards of the family while the child was growing up? And what kinds of education transmit family advantages?

The first question can be tested by considering what is more important: parents' own earlier education or their current occupational positions? There is then a subsidiary question whether it is fathers' or mothers' position that matters more. Comparing parents' and children's educational levels is relatively straightforward, but consideration of occupations raises the issue of how these are to be ranked. Within modern sociology there are broadly two approaches to this question: a concept of occupational prestige and one of social class. The former derives mainly from US sociology and ranks occupations hierarchically according to an ordering of their prestige as adjudged by sample surveys of popular opinion. The gradings are then sorted into categories, and the ordering is always seen as vertical, based on a summation of subjective views. The class approach, which is more European in background, identifies a number of objectively defined socio-economic positions based on criteria of the kind discussed in Chapter 5.[3] This approach is 'objective' in that it results from an analysis of social positions, not of subjective perceptions; also, it does not necessarily produce a clear hierarchy. This is consistent with what we saw in Chapter 5, with for example considerable ambiguity surrounding the question of whether routine non-manual work can be ranked 'above' skilled manual.

These two approaches are radically different in their conceptions of how to analyse social differences. We shall examine these in more detail below, when we discuss occupational rather than educational mobility, and in the final chapter, when we examine the overall class structure of society. For the present we simply need to note these differences, but also the fact that they can be less profound in their practical implications than in their theoretical derivation: in the US prestige approach professional, managerial, and entrepreneurial occupations tend to be ranked at the top and unskilled positions at the bottom; these groups also form separate classes in European class theory.

The national studies collected by Shavit and Blossfeld (1993) make use of both approaches, depending on the theoretical model preferred by the researchers. It is difficult to say whether this affected the outcomes in any important way, but we shall here have to treat them as more or less equivalent; some of the national studies in fact used

---

[3] For an exposition of the prestige ranking approach, see Treiman (1970); for one of class analysis, see Erikson and Goldthorpe (1992: ch. 2).

both and found they give very similar results. Nearly all studies consider fathers' rather than joint parental backgrounds. It is interesting that in most countries fathers' educational backgrounds were more important than their current occupations: Germany (Blossfeld 1993: 61); Italy for men but not for women (Cobalti and Schizzerotto 1993: 164); the Netherlands (de Graaf and Ganzeboom 1993: 88–96); German-speaking Switzerland (Buchmann, Charles, and Sacchi 1993: 180–2); Japan (males only studied) (Treiman and Yamaguchi 1993: 248). In the USA however it was the other way round (Hout, Raftery, and Bell 1993: 46). In Sweden both factors had declined considerably in importance, but parental education background had declined more steeply except among the children of unskilled manual workers and farmers (J. O. Jonsson 1993: 124–6). The English research did not consider fathers' educational backgrounds (Kerckhoff and Trott 1993).

It may be significant that the USA differs from the other countries. In Europe and Japan education has long been associated with the cultural styles of historical social elites, generating an educational culture that possibly inhibits groups from different backgrounds, even if their fathers have reached relatively senior occupational positions. In the USA, on the other hand, education has been a more functional phenomenon, perhaps creating fewer purely cultural barriers. At the same time sheer wealth might be more important to children's educational success in the USA, where the costs of education are more likely to have to be borne by families and individuals, favouring those with fathers in prestigious (and therefore well paid) occupations.

The studies that considered a class rather than a prestige approach were able to reach some further interesting conclusions. In particular, in the Italian study Cobalti and Schizzerotto (1993), who tried both prestige and class approaches, were able to show some interesting differences between urban and rural classes: the urban working classes and urban *petite bourgeoisie* made gains at the expense of the rural working class (ibid. 165–7). Furthermore, separating bourgeois from professional and managerial sections of the 'middle classes' revealed that the former had a relatively poor educational experience, the large number of owners of small and medium-sized enterprises in Italy (see Chapter 6) often not having had any significant educational background.

The Cultural Diversity of Educational Paths

An important issue in studies of educational careers concerns the distinction between general (often called academic) education and vocational education. It is usually assumed in research that the former ranks as superior to the latter, partly because it is the main gateway to the very highest levels of the education system itself, and partly because educational preparation for professional and managerial careers usually lies through that path, even if it becomes itself 'vocational' in the latter stages. If we adopt a vertical prestige model of occupations we also have to accept this unambiguous ranking of educational routes. However, if we follow a class approach to occupations, first identifying different groups and only secondarily deciding whether they can be ranked vertically, we can do the same to the different kinds of educational route. This draws our attention to national differences in the ways that general and vocational education are related to each other. There are in general four main forms of this relationship:

1. The education system itself can provide just general education, with those who seek ad-

vanced qualifications remaining in the system for as long as possible while others seek employment, any vocational training they are likely to find being provided by the employer.[4]

2. After a certain point (usually the end of lower secondary education) the choices offered to young people within a single formal education system can include both academic (or general) and vocational branches. This is very widespread, being found both in countries following the French model of a single centralized state education model and most Nordic countries: Belgium, Finland, France, Italy, the Netherlands, Norway, Portugal, Spain, and Sweden (Crouch, Finegold, and Sako 1999: ch. 4).

3. There can be a formal separation of academic and vocational courses at the end of lower secondary education, with the latter being carried out as apprenticeship, students in these branches spending part of their time in school but part with a potential employer. This is found in countries following the German model of educational organization: Austria, Denmark, Germany, and Switzerland (ibid., ch. 5).

4. Finally, there can be a mix of all of these patterns, as in Ireland and the UK (ibid., chs. 4, 5, 6).

It is interesting to note that the two cases where research suggests a real decline in inequalities of educational opportunity (the Netherlands and Sweden) are both instances where students following vocational tracks after compulsory school-leaving age were counted *by the researchers* as having made an educational transition just as much as if they had remained in the academic stream. In the German and Swiss research however, young people opting for the vocational route after the ending of compulsory schooling were seen as having left the educational system. While it is true that Dutch and Swedish students can in theory switch to an academic stream partway through their course, while Germans and Swiss are almost certainly committed to their choice for life at the age of 14 (Blossfeld 1993: 53), in practice this difference is unimportant. This difference of treatment of routes could well explain much of the strong contrast shown between the Netherlands and Sweden, on the one hand, and Germany and Switzerland, on the other.

If they persist with their vocational courses German, Swiss, and probably also Austrian and Danish, apprentices will achieve formal recognition as the practitioners of a publicly recognized skill; usually though by no means necessarily a manual one. In doing so they are likely to be sustaining a family pattern, since, as we know, the earlier in life that decisions are made the more dependent they will be on family background. They therefore certainly lack choice. Do they suffer a disadvantage? If we follow the prestige-score approach we must almost certainly answer 'yes' in all cases where prestige rankings indicate a low status for practitioners of manual skills. However, in a class model of occupations the matter may be different. The young people continue a family tradition that leads to the award of a certificate confirming their membership of a certain kind of occupational group, and probably therefore of a social class defined positively in terms of skill according to the more or less formal ideas of class considered in Chapter 5. They are likely therefore to have a strong class identity; how this ranks them within an *invidious* scale depends on how relations between these classes work within the wider society. As Blossfeld and Shavit (1993: 14) express it, both kinds

---

4 This model is pursued in both Japan and the USA, though with the strong difference that the transition from school to employer and subsequent training is systematically organized in the former country but not at all in the latter (Crouch, Finegold, and Sako 1999: ch. 6; Dore and Sako 1998). This emphasis on generalism is valid in the USA only for those who leave education before university level; US higher education has many branches that resemble forms (2) and (3) below.

of vocational-track system, the Dutch/Swedish and the German/Swiss, involve a compromise in the stark choice between elite and mass systems of education.

It then needs to be asked why the Italian system does not seem to confer the same vocational education chances as the Dutch and Swedish ones. Is this a particular weakness of Italian institutions? Or is a system based on a strong *welfare* state (as in the Netherlands and Sweden) more likely to achieve egalitarian outcomes than one based simply on a strong state? Italy is not a good case on which to base a judgement here, as although its policies are based on the model of the strong French state, it has never been able to achieve the capacity of its exemplar. To examine the subject further we would need evidence from France itself, which unfortunately was not included in the Blossfeld and Shavit study.

The most extreme comparison is between forms (1) (the US variant) and (3) (apprenticeship). Under the former one's social status is never finally confirmed and options for exit from lower social groups potentially remain open, though we know from the research evidence that in practice they are most unlikely to occur. In the latter case options are closed but a clear route is maintained to achieving a publicly recognized diploma. Also, as Kappelhoff and Techenberg (1987: 10) pointed out in a comparison of German and US mobility patterns, in recent years there has been increasing evidence of social selection in US high schools resulting from a rise in the relative numbers of working-class youths, exclusionary practices by schools, and the impact of residential segregation on school choice. Here both forms (2) and (3) contrast with form (1) (in both its Japanese and US versions), in that the first two confer a public attribution of educational qualification, while in form (1) this remains dependent on decisions of employers.

The British system is difficult to analyse, since that country has historically had and continues to have a bewildering variety of educational routes. (There are in fact major differences between the educational systems of Scotland and the rest of the UK, Scotland coming closer to systems of form (2). However, for the present arguments these are less important than the location of Scotland within the overall British labour market.) Particularly interesting in that country is the relatively high number of people who, having been unsuccessful in their initial education, return in later years to follow various less orthodox routes to qualifications of various kinds (Kerckhoff and Trott 1993: 146). Indeed, this occurred to such an extent that in some cohorts more men had benefited from tertiary education than had from advanced secondary. However, while it might be thought that these alternative routes might be used particularly by people from educationally disadvantaged families having a second chance after some adult experience, in fact the opposite proved to be the case: uptake of alternative opportunities was even more skewed towards those from relatively privileged backgrounds (ibid. 146).

These issues of the relationship between family background, educational paths and opportunities, and types of occupational definition and identity are fundamental to the analysis of social class in modern societies, and they bring together themes from all parts of this book. We shall therefore resume discussion of them in our final chapter. We may also note here how theoretical traditions relate to particular social structures. For example, the low position accorded to all manual labour in the prestige ranking approach of US sociologists can be seen as a reflection of the position of skilled manual work in that society, where, with the exception of very few traditional craft occupations, manual skills are not externally certificated occupations, conveying some autonomous social status and in the organization of which trade unions might have some role, but the property of employers. The Erikson and Goldthorpe (1992) model, which, as discussed in Chapter 5, places manual skills in the middle ranks of the social structure, more closely fits the social reality of most Western European cases, consonant also with Weber's concepts of established occupational skills conferring a kind of property right. These very real differences in the meanings accorded to different occupational forms in different societies need to be borne in mind when cross-national comparisons of class structure are made, particularly in the area of social mobility, the topic to which we now turn.

SOCIAL MOBILITY

So far we have considered the role of family, culture, and other factors in affecting access to education, but the end of a project of transferring capacities across generations ends, not with the education of the second generation but with its occupational destinations. We assume that families will seek to 'do their best' for their children's adult future, but this can take two different forms. It might mean *sustaining* the family's present way of life across generations; or it might mean *improving* on the past—temporarily begging the question of what constitutes 'improvement'. For many families these goals mean quite different things. For example, for a family with strong roots in a peasant or industrial manual-working culture a desire to maintain traditions across generations means to forgo major chances of improvement. On the other hand, for a wealthy propertied family or a family in one of the well-established professions to maintain tradition can also be compatible with the ideal of improvement. Clearly, the bigger the gap between the culture and tradition of the family of origin and that of what are considered to be more desirable positions, the more difficult it will be for a change to be made.

We have seen some of the ways in which these processes operate in the major educational transitions. As we have however also noted, education is not the only means of protecting or advancing a family's social position. We therefore need to consider both the link between education systems and occupational outcomes and the overall link between social origins and occupational outcomes in a way that takes into account non-educational forms of allocation of people to careers.

As with the educational transition, we are dependent for our knowledge of comparative social mobility on a small number of major research projects, which will not necessarily have covered all the countries of interest to us. The most recent large-scale study is that by Erikson and Goldthorpe (1992), though this covers only 9 of our countries: France, Germany, Ireland, Italy, Netherlands, Sweden, the UK (as three separate studies: England and Wales, Northern Ireland, Scotland), Japan, and the USA. More seriously, despite the recent publication date of the study, most of the empirical material on which it is based was gathered between 1970 and 1978 and can therefore tell us only about the period of the post-war compromise, nothing about any possible subsequent shifts. Consistently with this, the research is mainly (though not solely) concerned with male employment and with contrasts between agricultural and industrial, not services, sectors.

Fundamental to the Erikson and Goldthorpe study is a distinction between absolute and relative social mobility. The former concerns shifts that take place through changes in the size of occupational groups and in the family sizes of people in these groups in the parent generation. The latter concerns any changes that take place in mobility chances once the former have been taken into account. For example, let us imagine a society with no immigration from abroad and with just two relevant occupational groups: managers and workers. If over time the demand for managers grows relative to that for workers but existing managerial families do not produce enough children to fill the new managerial posts in the next generation, then some workers' children must experience mobility into the managerial class even if nothing happens to improve equality of opportunity and managerial children continue to have privileged opportunities to succeed their parents. The mobility that then takes place will of course be highly significant to the individuals concerned and may involve certain interesting social changes through the arrival of 'newcomers' to the managerial class. However, it would be wrong to interpret such a change as marking any increase in the openness of the society or in its equality of opportunities. This latter occurs only if relative mobility takes place, that is if people from workers' families are moving into the managerial class in greater numbers than required by changes in the size of the families of the two groups in the parental generation and of the occupational groups in the second generation.

Erikson and Goldthorpe therefore consider these two forms of mobility separately. They relate their work to bodies of theory in a similar way to that carried out at the outset of this chapter. They too make use of what they call liberal theories of industrialism, using similar US sociologists from the 1960s and 1970s as used here and in earlier chapters to establish the orthodoxy of mid-century compromise society. As in our earlier accounts and in that of Blossfeld and Shavit (1993) they identify these authors with optimistic predictions of increased options, equality of opportunity, and freedom from family inheritance associated with modernization. Against these writers they set Marxist predictions of a deskilling of the population of the kind noted in Part I of this book. Finally, they consider a number of theories similar to others discussed earlier in this chapter which anticipate a limitation to relative mobility as existing families from advantaged backgrounds struggle to sustain their children's positions (see especially Featherman, Jones, and Hauser 1975).

They find the Marxists quite wrong in their predictions, but also find the liberal theorists to be very mistaken. Erikson and Goldthorpe find no trend to increased openness or decline in the cross-generational inheritance of occupational positions. Overall, looking at birth cohorts of the first half of the twentieth century, they find quite wide fluctuations over time in absolute rates as waves of expansion and contraction succeeded one another, but no trends at all in relative mobility. This is consistent with the 'trendless fluctuations' approach of Featherman, Jones, and Hauser—hence the title of Erikson and Goldthorpe's volume, *The Constant Flux*.

They decompose their model of this stability into four components which will account for patterns of mobility between classes: hierarchy, inheritance, sector, and affinity. Hierarchy refers the different authority levels which distinguish some occupations from each other. (Erikson and Goldthorpe adopt a class rather than a prestige-ranking model of social stratification; therefore hierarchy is not built into their class scheme by definition; nevertheless, they recognize certain hierarchical tendencies separating some classes from others.) Inheritance refers to the tendency of families to transmit class positions across generations. Sector refers primarily to the difference between rural and industrial social experience, and affinity to the social links that relate some classes closer together.

They develop a core model of mobility experience based on aggregate data from all their countries (Erikson and Goldthorpe 1992: esp. ch. 4). Broadly, this suggests that the most important factor determining mobility chances is sector (that is, the boundary between the agricultural and all other sectors), while the most important set of factors is a cluster of different aspects of inter-generational inheritance. Hierarchy and affinity were considerably less important, though they did have some effect. This is in itself a powerful argument in favour of the authors' contention that stratification in advanced societies cannot be seen in terms of an ordered prestige hierarchy.

Although they are able to generalize extensively across nations with these findings, some interesting cross-national conclusions also emerge. England (and to a lesser extent Northern Ireland and Scotland) and France appear as similar countries in which inherited social position most closely follows their core model (ibid. 147–8). Sweden also follows the core model but, as we might expect from earlier discussions of that country, with far flatter contours indicating greater mobility chances (ibid. 164–6). Germany diverges from the model in two respects, again as anticipated earlier in this chapter. First, the vocational education system imposes particularly strong barriers between manual and non-manual employment, though not necessarily of a hierarchical form (ibid. 148–51). Second, as we saw in the Prologue, distinctions between non-manual and manual (or *Angestellte* and *Arbeiter*) were established in law during the crucial stage of industrialization in the late nineteenth century. In a further study, König (1987: 70) argues that it is the rigidity of the German vocational training system that leads to there being less within-career mobility for both men and women in that country than in France. On the other hand, the work of skilled German manual workers includes some functions that, in the USA and some other countries, would be classed as managerial and performed by managers having authority over the manual workers rather than by the latter themselves (Kappelhoff and Techenberg 1987: 45). More puzzling is the Dutch case, which showed an unusually high amount of mobility between routine non-manual workers and the professional and managerial group, and a low level of mobility between the former and non-skilled industrial and agricultural workers (Erikson and Goldthorpe 1992: 171–2).

Ireland and Italy diverged from the model for reasons primarily related to the low mobility chances of their agricultural populations, which strengthens rather than weakens the role of the model in accounting for mobility patterns in primarily *industrial* societies. Ireland otherwise differed in only minor ways from the core model (ibid. 154–6), which we might expect given the historical relationship of that society to Britain. The Italian case also suggested considerable differences between the more modern north and the 'backward' south, as is consistent with much other sociology of that country (ibid. 170–1); removing the Mezzogiorno from the account of Italy led to that country resembling England and France as one closely following the core model.

As with the educational mobility research, Erikson and Goldthorpe also found that, despite the widespread view of the USA as a country of high mobility chances, in practice the mobility pattern found there was quite similar to that of the European countries, though admittedly towards the upper end of their range.[5] Japan (ibid., ch. 10) failed to show any particularly distinctive characteristics.

In general therefore this research suggests some rather common features to social mobility patterns among industrial nations, industrialization being the main variable causing cross-national variation. Two fundamental features of class relations—relative similarities and differences between classes and varying degrees of hierarchy among them—accounted for the main structures of relative mobility chances, testifying to the continuing validity of occupationally based classes as structural features of modern societies. And in each case the strength of inheritance demonstrates the continuing role of families in sustaining class patterns across generations. As already noted, Erikson and Goldthorpe are primarily concerned with the development of advanced industrial society, and cannot tell us much about the hypothesized shift to post-industrialism, which in most countries developed strongly only after the years in which their data were gathered. The prime sectoral transition with which they are concerned is that from agriculture rather than the transition between manufacturing and the various services sectors in which we have been primarily interested in this volume; male manual workers in manufacturing industry stand at the centre of much of their analysis, and there is very little on the emerging new class of routine non-manual women in various services.

Their approach to class makes it difficult for them to deal with women, as their chapter devoted to them (ibid., ch. 7) shows. Class is seen by Erikson and Goldthorpe as an attribute of individuals but derived from their total household circumstances. This is determined by the character of their study, which is to examine the mobility trajectories of individuals. Such an approach is less easily able to consider classes themselves as collectivities with certain shared attributes and behaviours, unless it can be assumed that the individuals who comprise a class have overall household characteristics which derive primarily from the characteristics of the class. This assumption is fulfilled in the case of people who are the predominant earners in their households, of which they are the 'heads'. In such cases the income and other conditions associated with the occupations that comprise the class will be similar across all households of class members. The classic mid-century compromise society of a male breadwinning workforce would be an example of such a society. Where most working women are concerned the assumption is not satisfied: the occupational classes they form are often comprised of people coming from diverse household backgrounds, and the earnings of these households are usually not predominately derived from the women's own labour-market position. Indeed, to the extent that women contribute to household income, the central assumption ceases to be true for men as well as women.

This development has important implications for classes as social collectivities. It is interesting that Erikson and Goldthorpe say with respect to their solely male class of routine non-manual employees and sales personnel that it is problematic whether it can be considered to have a demographic or social identity at all (ibid. 226). In fact, as we have seen in previous chapters, the majority of members of this category are female,

---

[5] They drew a similar conclusion for Australian data too, though in fact that country corresponds more closely to the American dream of egalitarian mobility chances than does the USA itself (ibid., ch. 9).

with even more diverse household backgrounds; and this class is one that has been growing considerably in size. It is likely to be a class that fails to meet many of the criteria required for a class to be a demographic entity with widely shared characteristics among its members. We shall return to some of the implications of this for the class structure of post-industrial society in the final chapter.

While the difficulties of Erikson and Goldthorpe's approach in dealing with female employment are particularly important and have attracted most critical attention, it should also be noted that the approach would experience similar difficulties in dealing with men who are not the dominant earners in the families—such as men living in their parental homes. From the evidence we encountered in Chapter 7 we know that this imparts a northern European bias to assumptions about household structure.

THE TRANSITION FROM EDUCATION TO OCCUPATION

Using the same data set as Erikson and Goldthorpe, and therefore telling us about post-war compromise society rather than any recent changes, Müller *et al.* (1989) have compared the transition from social origins to education with that from education to occupational destination. They found more differences among nations in this latter than in the first transition. This seems to result from considerable diversity in the formal rules which relate educational qualifications to occupational placement. Where legal or bureaucratic norms prescribe a particular educational preparation for a certain career, there is little opportunity for someone with low educational achievement to enter that occupation. Where rules are left much looser they might have more chance.

Müller (1994) has also distinguished three basic means by which this is achieved, based on the historical cases of England, France, and Germany. The findings run parallel to those we considered in Chapter 5 in connection with the development of the professions. In England rulers made little use of formal qualifications for the selection of a state bureaucracy and relied on informal contacts and the concept of the committed amateur. There was little interest in developing formal vocational education. In France, in contrast, the state—even before the Revolution of 1789, but particularly in the subsequent attempt to construct a new, modern French state—sought to construct a highly trained elite for state service and for those professions of particular interest to a modernizing state (e.g. certain branches of engineering). Outside that, however, the state was not interested in what took place and did not therefore develop advanced systems of education. The young German state of the latter nineteenth century developed itself in some ways similarly to the French, but also had a particular niche as a state based on industrial and technical pre-eminence. It made use of its own medieval legacies of craft skills to develop a concept of virtually all occupations having some of the qualities of the professions.

These origins have left their mark. In England education continued until the early 1990s to be relatively unimportant, with rather small numbers going on to higher levels, but in consequence with a relatively low social gradient of opportunities. In France there is far more concern to gain access to higher educational opportunities, which therefore tend to be monopolized by children from privileged backgrounds. Educational opportunities are therefore far more highly skewed towards privileged families than in England. In Germany access to those professions requiring academic training is similar to what is found in France; but there is a considerably wider range of educational opportunities of other kinds, which tend to be taken up by families from manual working backgrounds. Young Germans therefore face a very hierarchical set of educational opportunities, which tend to confirm them in their class of origin in a rather fixed way; but it is possible to pursue an educational course conveying considerable status honour within the manual or technical tracks.

A similar account of the Franco-German difference has been given by Maurice, Sellier, and Silvestre (1982), and by Garnier, Hage, and Fuller (1989), who see the French state differentiating strongly between elite and mass education, not only because it was mainly concerned to create only its own elite, but also because it was responsive to the pressure from existing privileged families to restrict competition for elite places.

Although the Swedish system differs considerably from the German one in a number of respects, J. Jonsson and Mills (1993b) distinguish between the English and Swedish systems in similar terms: in the UK an emphasis on academic streams of education has historically meant that pupils who remained a long time in education but did not achieve academic success were likely to be defined as failures, whereas in Sweden a wide number of vocational courses were available to them. This has a similarly ambiguous consequence in Sweden, as several authors have also noted for Germany (Müller and Shavit 1998), that children from manual working families are less likely than in the UK (or the USA) to attempt academic education, but more likely to find success in other forms of education. Müller and Haun (1994) also comment that German children from manual working-class families are often motivated to remain within the education system because they understand the role of formal education and training for skilled *manual* work in their country. Alternatively, as Kappelhoff and Techenberg (1987: 11–46) express a similar point, in comparison with US workers, German skilled manual workers enjoy a level of security and relative income advantage that affords them a kind of collective as opposed to individual social mobility.

Allmendinger and Hinz (1997) compared social and occupational mobility in Germany, Sweden, and the UK, and reached conclusions both very compatible with the above characterizations of those and linking with some themes that we shall consider further in Chapter 13. In the UK a primarily market model of society with a residual welfare state meant that people entered the labour market young and remained there until they were old. Their working lives being long and links between qualifications and jobs being rather weak, British workers experienced frequent occupational mobility; however, it tended to be mobility within a range of similar jobs and therefore was not often class mobility. In Sweden, where the universal welfare state meant that considerable emphasis was placed on renewed educational opportunities throughout the life course, there was also considerable occupational change, which was also likely to incorporate class change or social mobility. There was least mobility in Germany, which was primarily characterized by stability, but the overall level of qualifications was high, so far fewer people than in Sweden or the UK found themselves in unskilled jobs.

The most direct study of the education to occupation transition is that recently completed by Müller and Shavit and their colleagues (1998). Being based on research carried out in the 1990s, this is also telling us about society after the decline of the mid-century compromise, though of course most of the people sampled will have completed their education and major occupational transitions during the earlier period. In fact their findings show considerable continuity with the earlier studies: with a wider range of nations they demonstrate the interesting irony implied in Müller's three-country comparison: where educational qualifications are closely tied to occupational destinations, a smaller proportion of young people will pursue academic education, but a larger proportion will pursue *some* form of education leading to a recognized qualification granting them an occupational identity.

They distinguish degrees of vocational specificity, the extent of standardization, and the extent of stratification of systems. They conclude that the association between qualifications and occupations is stronger where the education systems are stratified, where there is a high level of vocational specificity and where the overall proportion attending tertiary education is low. Education was particularly important in determining entry to professional and managerial occupations in Germany, Italy, and Switzerland (also Taiwan, outside our study). It was lowest in Sweden, the UK, Japan, and the USA. On the other hand, people with lower-level vocational qualifications were less likely to enter unskilled occupations in the former group of countries. They also found that the extent to which vocational secondary education enhances employment in skilled rather than unskilled employment is strongly determined by the specificity of vocational training in the country. In some countries (France, Germany, and the UK in our group) a vocationally specific secondary education can be a better protection against unemployment among men than can a general education even if at a higher level. In Ireland and the USA, where employers have far lower expectations of specific skills, this is not the case. Among women the situation is slightly different, with general education being more helpful than vocational except in Italy and (in comparison with men) the USA.

In Germany and Switzerland qualifications have far more effect on occupational outcomes than in the UK, Japan, or the USA (ibid.). In Germany, Italy, and Switzerland university graduates are 2,000 times as likely as the least qualified to enter professional or managerial employment; in the USA the comparable difference is less than 90; in the UK less than 30. In Germany and Switzerland vocational education means that the odds of becoming skilled rather than unskilled workers are 10 to 30 times as great, while in Ireland, Sweden, or the UK the ratio is only 2 to 4 times. The authors conclude that the more specific a vocational training, the earlier the differentiation into tracks, and therefore the stronger the role of parental influence and barriers to inter-track mobility.

CONCLUSIONS

This has some important implications for the formation and identity of social classes, which will be pursued in the final chapter. For the present we are interested in the implications of this difference for the institutional relationship between family, education, and economy. In the general systems families have little choice other than to place all their emphasis on their children maximizing opportunities of any kind; and the education system has no particular need to adapt itself to signals coming from the occupational system about types of qualifications. On the other hand, as we have noted, there is a much clearer hierarchy running down from managerial positions, with manual work of all kinds being lowly ranked. In the more vocationally segregated education systems this hierarchy is interrupted by the strong sense of status honour possible for skilled manual positions, and a lesser strong subordination of them to managers within the employing organization. This shows up most clearly in American/German comparisons.

There is little sign that much has changed in the role of family in determining education and mobility chances between the decades of the post-war compromise and more recent years. We might however note the following points:

First, since the number of manual positions has been declining, the significance of this group and its internal divisions as forming the large base of the class mobility pyramid has also declined. Erikson and Goldthorpe's (1992) study similarly shows the importance of the rural peasant class as a mobility base in many European countries for at least the first half of the twentieth century.

Second, our finding in Chapter 5 that material inequalities have risen in recent years in the UK and the USA (general education model) while declining in Germany (vocationally segregated model) suggests that there is no necessary positive association between the openness of educational systems and more egalitarian outcomes.

Third, the implications of one very major change have yet to be felt. In previous chapters we have noted the concentration of female workers in relatively junior economic positions, and with lower educational profiles than men, to the extent that some class positions have virtually become in post-compromise society gender classes. This is consistent with the story told in this chapter of *past* inferior educational achievement by girls. However, as the recent evidence shows, this has now begun to change dramatically in most societies, showing a capacity to change never evinced by class inequalities. This attrition of gender inequality just at the moment when gender has been becoming a major constituent of class inequality will have major implications in coming years. This constitutes further evidence that the kind of society currently being formed 'post-compromise' is very much a transitional stage, with some characteristics which are unlikely to be sustained for long. It is unlikely that we have reached an 'end to history' in education and social mobility.

Chapter 9

THE PARADOX OF RELIGION

Nearly all chapters of this book deal with some or other aspect of tangible, material relations among human beings. However, in addition to having such relations humans also imbue their lives with 'meaning'. They very frequently express the need for there to be a 'point' to what they do, especially when what they are doing is stressful or seems to involve sacrifice. One of the main means that people have found in human history for solving the problem of meaning is to identify their lives and those of their immediate group within a wider community which is in turn located within something of far more encompassing importance and moral purpose, preferably something going beyond the contours of all knowable material experience and constituting something external, mighty, the embodiment of meaning and often the idea of goodness itself. Great chains of ideas, beliefs, and social institutions have been constructed around this singular human project. They are known as religions, and the trans-human embodiment of meaning is usually known as God or a number of gods. The sociology of this set of institutions is therefore important to the study of any society or group of societies.

There are other ways of defining religion, but for our purposes we need an approach which is sociologically rather than theologically useful. My emphasis on its role in identifying the individual with a wider human community which is then invested with transcendent implications belongs to the classic tradition of the sociology of religion associated with Emile Durkheim. This differs in emphasis from recent literature, more typical of which is the following, which puts the emphasis on beliefs rather than on identity and meaning:

Religion for us consists of actions, beliefs, and institutions predicated upon the assumption of the existence of either supernatural entities with powers of agency, or impersonal powers or processes possessed of moral purpose, which have the capacity to set the conditions of, or to intervene in, human affairs. (Bruce 1992: 10–11)

Relevant here is the contention of several recent sociologists of religion that there is an important distinction between 'believing' and 'belonging'; in particular, people in the UK are today said to 'believe without belonging' (Davie 1994). In a review of religious belief and practice in Germany, however, Kecskes and Wolf (1993) were not able to find evidence of a difference between belief (*Glauben*) and experience (*Erfahrung*); rather, people exhibited to different degrees a 'general religiosity' (*allgemeine Religiosität*). Only level of religious *knowledge* seemed to identify a distinctive group. They found similar evidence from studies in the USA. There is possibly evidence here therefore of a British (or English) specificity.

This thesis has been developed to deal with the evidence from a number of surveys of religious belief and practice that many people seem to have a sense of belief without wishing to belong to any particular religion—unless it is a kind of rudimentary adherence to their country's major national church from whose nominal membership it takes effort to escape. They 'believe' in God, or sin, or prayer, or possibly hell; but they are far less likely to attend church or even to be members of one.

The distinction is useful, but it misses something out. To suggest a shift from belonging to believing implies a shift from the social act of membership of a group to the intellectual one of adopting various theological positions. This exaggerates the meaning to be given to 'believing'. Belief is obviously of great importance to religions. They are inherently concerned with phenomena beyond the range of material experience and therefore beyond that of the 'knowable', whether in the everyday or more scientific sense of that word. Religious beliefs therefore have to be developed and sustained without much chance of evidence as normally understood. There is therefore a constant risk of both a failure to believe (loss of faith) and the invention of alternative beliefs (heresies) which are no more amenable to proofs than the initial ones. But these beliefs are developed at very diverse levels of sophistication and detail. Nearly all religions are accompanied by specialists in the interpretation and development of beliefs, but only a small part of their work filters down to the non-specialist community of ordinary adherents to the particular faith.

Moments like the Reformation, when individuals and informal groups start questioning profoundly the particular structure of beliefs they have inherited, are unusual. Most of the time most people's religious beliefs are difficult to establish. Social surveys have to latch on to a few central concepts, and can perhaps probe a little what lies behind them; they will rarely be able to demonstrate that, say, Catholics 'believe' in the concept of the transubstantiation[1] in the same sense that people 'believe' that if they go out in the rain they will get wet. This is probably not a singularly modern phenomenon. In far earlier centuries, those usually regarded as the peak of the Christian era, ordinary people were very rarely asked about their beliefs: *cuius regio huius religio*, as we saw in the Prologue. And coercion was often employed to prevent them voicing unorthodox ones. It is quite likely that magical and pagan beliefs long outlived the ostensible 'conversion' of a population—which usually meant the conversion of its ruler. In a world very remote from the Middle Ages, in the inner London suburb of Islington in the late 1960s, Abercrombie *et al.* (1970) found considerable evidence of superstition as the main form taken by 'religious' beliefs.

If the concept of belief is unsatisfactory, so is that of belonging (or not belonging). Clearly belonging in the sense of actively retaining membership of a church indicates a fairly strong statement of religious identification, especially if this is accompanied by regular attendance at services and participation in specifically church-based activities. However, there is also the question of belonging in the wider, perhaps vaguer but possibly more profound, sense of having a religion as a component of one's identity, including being located within a social framework in which religious symbols and institutions are very salient. We can here look back at the strong form of belonging represented by *verzuiling* and split it into two components: participation in religious acts as such; and having one's secular life embedded in wider aspects of the faith. A distinction between these seems important. This also helps us to come to terms with a difficulty of the idea of 'membership'. As Gill points out (1992: 91), membership is

---

[1] This is the belief that, at the moment that a Christian eats the wafer and sips the wine offered at the Mass these items are literally changed into the body and blood of Christ.

essentially a concept of dissident Protestant churches, not of either the 'universal' Catholic Church or the Protestant or Orthodox national churches.

I therefore prefer to use the concept of religious identification. Very simply, do people identify themselves with a religion, and what does this mean to them? This gives us no preconceptions about what 'real' religion might be. If we learn that many people are concerned to undertake certain acts that associate them to a religion but do not share any specific theological beliefs with their church, we take that as a social statement in its own right indicating a certain meaning of religious adherence. We might compare and contrast it with other approaches to religion, but we are not necessarily concerned with whether it is an adequate statement of 'real' or 'true' religion.

RELIGION AND SECULARIZATION

But whether viewed as behaviour, identification, or beliefs, does religion warrant a major position in a study of social change in contemporary Western Europe? Virtually all major theories of modernization of both the nineteenth and twentieth centuries predicted a decline of religion as an accompaniment of modernization, in a process usually known as secularization. As defined most clearly and perhaps over simply by Bryan Wilson (1966: xiv), secularization is 'the process whereby religious thinking, practice and institutions lose social significance'. To some extent this concept incorporates the idea of sociological liberalism as applied to religion. The process whereby various social institutions secured their autonomy from ecclesiastical control necessarily implied a decline in the wider social significance of religion.

However, the two ideas are not the same: as we shall see below, not all social significance of religion is concerned with control or even influence over other institutions; and secularization can involve questions other than this. Karel Dobbelaere (1981) distinguished three dimensions or levels of secularization. The first corresponds most strictly to Wilson's idea: at the level of the society there is a process of laicization, a structural differentiation whereby other institutions develop autonomy. Second, at the sub-system level, he speaks of a change within religious institutions themselves. Finally, at the level of the individual is another process with which Wilson was concerned: a decline in religious involvement, in the degree of normative integration with religious bodies. Since our concerns in this book are with religion as an aspect of society in general, we can devote little space to the second of these. The first is our primary concern, but we cannot leave the situation there; we cannot note a separation of religion from other institutions without having an idea of what religion is as a social institution per se, and not just in relation to others. This involves examining the relationship between individuals and religion.

Wallis and Bruce (1992) follow Wilson's idea of secularization as a declining social significance of religion, and they see this occurring in the main overarching processes associated with modernization: social differentiation, societalization (by which they mean the replacement of community by society), and rationalization. However, Brown (1992) has shown that religious participation increased in England, Scotland, and certain American cities during the process of nineteenth-century industrialization and urbanization, in particular as new forms of Protestant dissent developed to represent the concerns of the new population.[2] McLeod (1992) shows similarly a high level of religious participation in London and New York in the late nineteenth and early twentieth centuries—but not in Berlin, a third city which he studied. In an argument that reinforces David Martin's thesis (1978—to be discussed below) concerning the role of state churches in creating barriers of hostility against excluded social groups, he argues that the identification of German Lutheranism with the deeply conservative Prussian state alienated both liberal middle-class and working-class groups. The greater diversity of social forms of religion available in London and New York both reduced this element and also brought the greater choice available in diversity.

We shall return to this last question in due course, but in general we can at this point see certain aspects of secularization as religion's 'share' of the general modernizing process of sociological liberalism. In much discussion however religion is seen as having a particular problem with modernity in that religious beliefs are seen as challenged by science and rationality. Especially in the nineteenth century, Marxists stood alongside liberal writers in seeing these beliefs as part of a world of magic that was incompatible with modern systems of thought. At the level of ideas modern sociology has seen the question more subtly. Daniel Bell (1976), one of the most prominent theorists of post-industrialism, places religion in the more general context of the fate of culture and values. Using concepts similar to those of sociological liberalism, he argues that advanced societies have less need than past ones for coordination and ordering by values. As a result values themselves become less important; authorities in general as well as ordinary people care less about what happens within the cultural sphere, and that sphere becomes isolated. For example, in a more traditional society (say a Western European society of the late nineteenth century) religious innovations could be matters of major controversy if they confronted values that were considered important by political and other social authorities. In that sense religion was at the centre of life. This can still happen today: there is widespread uneasiness over sects which recruit young people and encourage them to live in religious communities apart from their families (for example, the Moonies in the UK, or Scientologists in Germany). There is also continuing difficulty in the encounter between many societies and radical Islam. In general, though, purely religious innovations attract far less attention and are widely seen as being solely the business of those concerned—the hallmark of sociological liberalism. There is a trade-off here; alongside the autonomy comes a social marginalization and reduction of importance.

For Bell not just religion but the whole area of culture and values is involved in this marginalization as a paradoxical consequence of liberalization. Many other writers however have concentrated on the specific loss of engagement with other social institutions suffered by religion. Wilson (1966) shares my account above of religion as a form of identification, linking the individual, the community, and a realm of ultimate meaning, but sees the impossibility of this being a process of any strength in societies where the bonds tying the individual to the community have themselves become so weak. Declines in attendance at religious services then seem consequent on that community decline and serve further to push religion to the margins of life.

---

[2] Finke (1992) shows that urbanization and industrialization are still associated with higher levels of religious participation in the USA.

Some writers have contested the secularization thesis. In the 1960s, David Martin (1965) argued that declines in, say, church-going were really only changes in social patterns, and that plotting the course of the role of religion should not become tied to particular forms of action that might be specific to particular historical periods. Attendance at many other mass-participative events was also declining since people stayed at home and watched them—including religious services—on television. However, he later amended this position to one more specifically concerned with Europe, which came to seem the continent where the process of religious decline was concentrated.

Indeed, the choice of indicators of religious decline has theological implications. For Catholics religious faith can only be expressed through the Church; for most Protestant groups the emphasis is placed on the individual's relationship with God, and although the community of joint believers represented by a church is important, it is not as indispensable as with Catholicism. Therefore, to use participation in church activity as a measure of religious adherence is to some extent a 'Catholic' interpretation of religion. An alternative would be directly to assess religious beliefs. However, the 'Catholic' model is also more sociological, treating religion as a social institution, not as a set of inner feelings of individuals. An important objection to this is that religious participation might be constrained rather than freely chosen. Church attendance among inhabitants of a village where the local lord exacted a fine on anyone not seen regularly in church tells us less about people's values and inner beliefs than similar attendance by a modern urban population. However, if we are interested in the power of religious institutions and their relations of autonomy with other institutions, the coercive actions of a local lord may tell us a good deal.

Ironically, that dependence of churches on local secular authorities may have been a counter to sociological liberalism that eventually induced only a heavier dose of rejection of religion. As already noted, Martin has argued (1978, 1994) that the central problem for many European churches was their past association with the state—an association to which they had clung for protection and an assurance of survival. During the process of modernization many states—and alongside them state churches—became heavily associated with particular classes, geographical regions, or ways of life which excluded large proportions of the population and limited the extent to which they could use the Church as part of their own identity construction. (As in several other chapters, problems of space require me to talk mainly in terms of national patterns, whereas in many of the countries being discussed here there are highly distinctive regional patterns to religious observance (McLeod 1997: 133).) Furthermore, in the struggle for democracy this exclusion was challenged, and state churches often found themselves defending the old order against the challenge—with the result that the previously excluded groups never forgave them, and either became non-religious or joined dissenting sects. Therefore, Martin argues, it was not religion itself that was rejected, but its particular social integument—and he is able to cite the more flourishing condition of religion in the USA, where there has never been any official church, in evidence.

Confirmation of this thesis also comes from the high level of religious adherence in contemporary Ireland, a country where for centuries the state was under the control of the British—an external force with a different, often opposed, religion. A similar account can be given of Greece, which was ruled from the sixteenth to the early nineteenth centuries by the Islamic (though tolerant) Ottoman Empire; even after 'liberation'

Greeks had a Catholic Bavarian king imposed on them by the then European powers, who proceeded to appoint *Protestant* German officials to rule; Greek Christianity became the national symbol par excellence (Kokosalakis 1994: 131–40). Similar again is the case of Poland, a country outside this study but one where religious observance has remained high—alongside Ireland the highest in the whole of Europe—and where for over a century the state was ruled by external (Austrian, Prussian, and Russian) forces, the latter and more important two of which were not Catholic. This was followed in the latter half of the twentieth century by an atheistic Communist regime imposed by Russians.

The high level of religious adherence in post-war Germany has also been attributed to the fact that the two German dictatorships of this century (the Nazis and, in the East, the Communists) were atheist (François 1994: 82). Protestant urban Germany had been a highly secular society, the state Lutheran Church having identified itself totally with the conservative Prussian state (McLeod 1992). By the late 1940s the situation looked very different; there was a distinct return to religion in Germany. It is also interesting to note how in Spain, where the upper reaches of the church hierarchy became associated with a dictatorship which suppressed local autonomy and lasted into the 1970s, Spanish popular Catholicism developed during the twentieth century as a series of very locally based Marian cults (Albert-Lorca 1994). In a tacit, subtle way, Albert-Lorca suggests, people were indicating that the Virgin Mary, not Generalissimo Franco, ruled their lives, and she did so through their small community, not the Spanish state. At the national level, where the Church hierarchy (which cooperated with the Franco regime) operates, the Church has had difficulty establishing a strong position in democratic Spain.

These arguments help explain the apparent religious weakness of Europe, as a continent exhausted by past struggles over the association of religion with politics. But is this a rejection of religion or of the politicization of religion? Wallis and Bruce argue that to try to get beyond this is to try to search for some meaning of 'true religion', which is beyond the sociologist's task. However, in seeing no space between religion as 'true' (a theological concept) and the involvement of religion in other social spheres, they exclude the possibility of regarding religion *in itself* as social as well as theological. If people identify themselves, or locate themselves in some framework of meaning through the use of religious ideas, affiliations, rites of passage, then that is surely religion being its own social self, rather than intruding into other sociological selves or retreating entirely from the social into the doctrinal. It is important not to exclude this third possibility, as most debates over secularization seem to do. This returns me to my insistence on treating identification as a fundamental element of the sociological role of religion, combined with a willingness to see this identification change its form in different social contexts.

As to the argument that scientific rationality should somehow have disposed of religion, some anthropologists have pointed out that, just because our societies contain within them institutions of advanced scientific reasoning, it does not follow that all human action follows the canons of science. We do not conduct our daily lives as a series of experiments, otherwise life would become impossible; we have to take many things on trust, not only other human beings but also material objects, many of which we use without understanding them. Similarly, just because someone might be a qualified scientist in some area of knowledge does not prevent him from acting out of unreasoning prejudice when outside his specialist field. A conflict between science and religion is a potential encounter for modern mankind, but it is not a permanently potent one (Hervieu-Léger 1994).

At the same time the importance of scientifically 'erroneous' beliefs to the integrity of various churches needs to be placed into perspective. Much of the inaccurate science carried as baggage by the Church during the first 1,500 years or so of its existence had been imported into it when it took over ancient Greek science and decided to make this part of God's revealed truth. This was incidental to other aspects of the Church's role, though for centuries it deployed its authority in its support. Had the Greeks correctly observed the movement of the earth around the sun, for example, cosmology would not have led the Church into its dispute with early astronomers. In terms of the daily life of the religion, of religious identification, these intellectual matters do not have much importance. Identification is not an intellectual exercise or a rational calculation but a matter of something becoming so taken-for-granted as a part of the life around one that it becomes part of the self. Identifications of that kind might become unimportant; but only in extreme situations does one actually reject them.

RELIGION AND SOCIOLOGICAL LIBERALISM

Religion therefore deserves to be taken seriously by contemporary sociology, and particularly for a study such as this which is including an examination of the survival of traditional institutions within the framework of social compromise. One of the earliest meanings of the idea of liberalism in Europe was the assertion of a right to autonomy of political and private life from the claims of organized religion as embodied in their overwhelmingly dominant form as the Christian churches. In turn the term later came to refer also to the autonomy of economic and other spheres of life—including very prominently religion itself—from the state. This reminds us of the sociological, as well as political and cultural, centrality of religion in pre-modern Europe. Religious authorities exercised or tried to exercise authority over many areas of daily life: sexual practices and relations between the genders and within families in general; forms of artistic and cultural expression; the character of scientific knowledge; relations between social classes. In such a context the issue of sociological liberalism as defined in this book was highly problematic.

On the other hand, the Church's claim was never total. As we saw in the Prologue, from the days of its rapprochement with the Roman Empire in the fourth century after Christ it had accepted a certain autonomy of, or at least a division of labour with, the secular state. The authority of the Roman Empire at that time (that of its rather fictitious re-establishment by Charlemagne in the year 800), and thereafter the authority of a variety of Christian kings and other European rulers, was seen as deriving from God as much as did that of the Church itself.

The history of the subsequent growth of sociological liberalism can be written as the gradual relinquishing by the Church of its claims on other institutions. It was in this way that the Middle Ages were defined as giving way to the modern period: art and science began to achieve autonomy from rules prescribed by religious authority; the Reformation produced, in the Protestant churches, forms of religion that did not make as extensive a claim on other social institutions as did Catholicism.

As we also noted in the Prologue, a further major contribution of religion to the development of sociological liberalism after the Reformation was embodied in the pattern of relatively peaceful co-existence but strict segregation between groups of different religions, primarily embodied in Dutch social organization. The Netherlands were unusual in the relative importance enjoyed by this kind of institution within their social order, and for the historical earliness of its development. However, as we shall see, significant traces of it can be found elsewhere. For example, the long record of mutual antagonism between Catholic and Protestant parts of Germany only began to lose its venom and become a kind of co-existence when identities had been clearly established, and the constant provocations of mixed marriages reduced in extent, making it possible for two confidently separate communities to establish mutual relations (François 1994: 77). A similar process took place in Switzerland, especially on the part of Catholics after they were defeated in the civil war of 1847 (Campiche 1994: 93). Far less explicitly, British Catholics also constructed a rather separate minority social world for themselves (Hornsby-Smith 1992).

In the late nineteenth and early twentieth centuries, secular movements in societies with very strong religious cultures often felt the need to go further than simply setting up specific, instrumental organizations, and began to establish rival worlds of non- or even anti-religious social and cultural life (McLeod 1997: 37–53). These usually worked most successfully when allied to mass political parties of the communist or socialist kind. Such structures became particularly important where the dominant religious culture was Catholic (Austria, France, parts of Germany, Italy, Spain). These were mainly rooted in mutual antagonism rather than the combination of separation and cooperation that marked the tolerant Dutch model (ibid. 134), and were involved in much of the turbulence and social disorder which affected those countries in the middle years of the century.

As noted in the Introduction to this Part, Dutch *verzuiling* or pillarization stands as a kind of type for the entire concept of sociological liberalism on which this part of the book is based. The essential points are the subtle mix of separation and cooperation; and the fact that what seems to be a matter of ideas and values is embedded in firm structures of social relations.

We can now examine the situation of religion in Europe at the two time points of central interest to this study.[3]

---

[3] As in previous chapters, we shall proceed initially by analysing available general quantitative material, going on to consider more detailed and qualitative studies. The basic statistical evidence available on the state of religious identity around 1960 is presented in Appendix Table A.9.1; that for more recent years in A.9.2. Data on this topic are not as easily available as those for many of the preceding chapters, especially for the earlier period. A diversity of sources has had to be used; comparability cannot be guaranteed; and for some countries there is no information at all. As in previous chapters I include figures on Japan and the USA where possible to provide a framework for considering Western Europe. Figures in the text of the chapter illustrate the salient points from these tables.

RELIGION AT MID-CENTURY

The religious inheritance of post-war Western Europe was the result of successive historical overlays described in the Prologue: a continuing small Jewish presence (made far, far smaller following the slaughter of millions of Jews by the Third Reich in Germany not long before our period begins); a small part of the eastern Orthodox form of Christianity, almost entirely in Greece; a very extensive Catholicism rooted in nearly two millennia of European presence; large, state forms of Protestantism now nearly half a millennium old; smaller, nineteenth-century forms of Protestantism; secularist movements, also from the nineteenth century though earlier in France. After the waves of both new Protestant dissent and *laïque* movements petered out in the early twentieth century, Europe was to produce little further religious innovation. From time to time new cults and minor variants of Christianity have formed, but the main novelties have been brought from outside, as immigrants from other parts of the world have moved into Europe. Around 1960 these movements were still just a trickle; when we come to deal with the 1990s we shall give them more consideration.

A certain religious map has resulted from the distillation of these processes, which still mainly bears the imprint of the most important change of all, the Reformation. Over subsequent years various wars, massacres, and expulsions clarified the immediate post-Reformation patchwork a little, but essentially three kinds of territory have persisted within the Western Church:

(1) those lands where Catholicism remained virtually the sole form of Christian religion: Austria; Belgium; France; several, mainly southern, German principalities; Ireland, once that country was freed from English domination; Italy; Portugal; Spain;

(2) those from which Catholicism had been more or less expelled at the Reformation: by the 1960s this applied solely to the Nordic countries; the mainly northern German areas and large areas of England and Wales to which such a description could once be applied had become more like category (3);

(3) and those where Catholic and Protestant churches had gradually, and sometimes only through recurrent bloody conflict, come to accept that they shared the territory and also some form of access to secular rulers: the Netherlands; Switzerland; the German Federal Republic; the United Kingdom (throughout, but especially in Scotland and, less successfully, in Northern Ireland).

(It is notable how Germany appears in all three alternative forms; historically several German principalities had had to manage intricate internal balances of Catholic and Protestant groups and to cooperate with neighbours of different religious contours (François 1994: 69). A similar pattern occurred in Switzerland, where to some extent religion was a matter of different but neighbouring cantons falling on different sides of the divide, but where some cantons had remained mixed in themselves (Campiche 1994: 90).)

The central prediction of the theory of post-war compromise society should be that, under the impact of sociological liberalism, religion both concedes autonomy to other institutions and receives autonomy from them. If we compare religious observance with much earlier periods, when churches could dominate societies in a manner incompatible with liberalism, we might expect to find evidence of secularization. However, within the terms of the compromise secularization should not reach a point where religion has become a small minority activity. Religion should therefore hold an important but not dominant place within society.

PATTERNS OF BELONGING

We start with the most basic datum: declared religious adherence by national populations. In some countries these data are collected as part of the national census; in others they are discovered through social surveys from time to time. What meaning we adduce to these declarations we shall explore later, but they at least give us an initial indicator to use for comparisons over time and across countries. Figure 9.1 presents this information for as many countries as it has been possible to locate the statistics.

In 1960, in those countries where long ago the Reformation Protestant challenge had been successfully resisted or crushed, overwhelming majorities of the population still affirmed at least a basic identity with the Roman Catholic Church: Austria, Belgium, France, Ireland, Italy, Portugal, Spain.[4] It is notable that in France the numbers declaring to have no religion at all was low, despite a secularization process dating back to 1789, and with Liberal, Socialist, and Communist political parties having been rallying points for *laïcisme* since the mid-nineteenth century.

The Orthodox Church had also been highly successful in maintaining its hold on the identity of Greeks.

The post-Reformation grouping of entrenched Lutheran churches continued to be evident in Scandinavia. Again, it is remarkable to note the stability of these state churches as points of basic identity for their populations; and the weakness of all other religions.

The four countries which emerged from the Reformation with an unresolved religious identity had continued in the same way: Germany, the Netherlands, Switzerland, and, rather differently, the UK. The first three continued to be mixed roughly 50% Catholic and 50% Protestant among believers (mainly Lutheran in the German case, largely Calvinist in the other two).

The British pattern was somewhat more complex. Initially the triumph of the national Church (the Church of England) had been as solid as that of the Scandinavian churches, with the exception of recusant Catholics in Ireland. Scotland was at that time a separate kingdom, with a religious settlement similar to that of the Netherlands and Switzerland: a dominant Calvinist majority and a Catholic minority. The union of England and Scotland in the early eighteenth century saw the Reformed (Calvinist) Church, the Church of Scotland, continue to be the national church north of the border. Then came a wave of other Protestant dissent in the nineteenth century, an influx of Catholicism in Scotland and England from Ireland, but then a simplification of matters with Irish independence in 1921. Therefore the mid-century patchwork was not really the same as the one left by the Reformation, as is the case with the other countries; if the Church of Scotland is included as a state church alongside that of England, the proportion declaring allegiance to one or other state churches was 67% in 1960.

There is a further problem with the British case in that it is possible to regard oneself as a member of the Church of England without formally being a member, rather in the

---

4 No precise statistics are available on this for Portugal. However, it will become evident from subsequent tables on church attendance etc., that this statement must be valid.

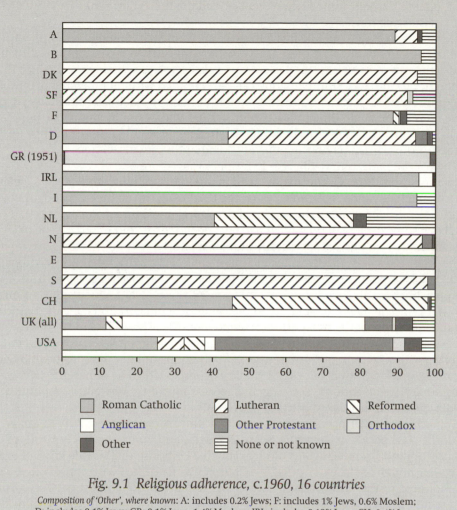

Fig. 9.1 Religious adherence, c.1960, 16 countries

Composition of 'Other', where known: A: includes 0.2% Jews; F: includes 1% Jews, 0.6% Moslem;
D: includes 0.1% Jews; GR: 0.1% Jews, 1.4% Moslem; IRL: includes 0.12% Jews; CH: 0.4% Jews;
UK: includes 0.93% Jews, 0.93% Moslems, 0.69% Hindu; USA: includes 3.24% Jews.

same way that one can regard oneself as a supporter of a French trade union without actually paying membership dues to it. If we count only actual members, then not only is the Catholic Church slightly larger than the state church, but the UK becomes by far the most secular society in the industrial world. However, we cannot estimate how many British people would have formally joined the Church of England in 1960 had they been told that only by doing so could they regard themselves as adherents to its form of Christianity.

The US case is rather different from the European ones. The fact that no church or even small number of churches has a privileged place here immediately sets it aside. It was a mixed Catholic/Protestant country, like Germany, the Netherlands, and Switzer-land, but the Catholic minority was smaller, and the Protestant ranks far more divided, than in those countries.

Japan clearly stands outside this Europe-based frame of reference, never having been part of the Christian world; there is a Christian minority in Japan, but it is difficult to find estimates of its size at this period. Japan also displays a distinctive dualism in that adherence to the state Shinto religion can be combined with membership of one of the Buddhist cults.[5] As a result of the overlap it is difficult to establish how many Japanese have no religion at all, though it has been argued that as few as 25% of the population really regarded themselves as believers. Japan does resemble most of Europe (but not France or the USA) in having an officially dominant national religion.

The overall pattern that emerges in Europe is therefore one of continuity with a Re-formation past. Indeed, the major movements of Protestant dissent or secularism which affected France, Scandinavia, and the UK during the eighteenth and nineteenth centuries subsided, leaving the earlier edifice more or less intact. Furthermore, if there had been some decline in religion, it had not been to the favour of secularism or *laïcisme* as such. Little remained of specifically humanist or other explicitly secularist organiza-tions other than very small groups in Scandinavia and the UK (McLeod 1997: 145), and various *laïque* political parties. Political parties will be discussed as such in a later chapter, but we can here bring forward some of the relevant conclusions. As already noted, in Austria, Belgium, and the Netherlands, the pillarization concept historically extended to include the non-Catholic component of working-class movements, that is the Socialist movement of parties and unions, and in Belgium and the Netherlands the liberal parties, as pillars. That means that these groupings were seen as having a meaning similar to that of religions, and encompassed their adherents in a web of community organizations, sporting and leisure interest clubs and communications media similar to that constructed by churches.

Something similar occurred in France and Italy, more clandestinely in Spain, and until the Nazi period in Germany. Socialist parties and unions built a network of com-munity organizations. This was often as much a response to a hostile state as against religion, though to the extent that the Church was identified with conservative forces it amounted to the same thing. However, in general, if the contest between religion and secularization is a matter of which 'side' had the strongest formal organizations and articulated systems of belief, then religion ruled undisturbed by the early 1960s.

Overall, at this rather minimal level of religious observance, the thesis of soci-ological liberalism is sustained rather than that of secularization. Only in France, the Netherlands, and the UK did numbers of non-adherents exceed extremely small numbers, and this includes all cases where adherence was simply not known to those carrying out the surveys.

RELIGIOUS PARTICIPATION

So far we have discussed only formal adherence, a mere indication that requires virtu-ally no effort—except in Germany, where to declare adherence to a religion is to make

---

[5] Aggregate religious adherence in Japan therefore comes to considerably more than 100% of the popula-tion. The country has therefore been excluded from Figure 9.1.

Table 9.1 Baptisms, c.1960 and c.1990, as proportions of total infant population

	1960			1990			Change, 1960–90		
	RC	L	A	RC	L	A	RC	L	A
B	93.60			82.00			−11.60		
DK		67.00			73.40			6.40	
SF		89.00			82.00			−7.00	
F	82.00			64.00			−18.00		
D					35.00	35.00			
I				98.00					
P				93.00					
E				95.00					
S					72.00				
UK			50.00			33.30			−16.70

RC = Roman Catholic
 A = Anglican
 L = Lutheran

Sources: Various national censuses, and chapters in Davie and Hervieu-Léger 1994 and Mol 1972.

a tax contribution to it (François 1994: 82–3). We should also investigate levels of participation in the main rites of life's passage, equivalents of which are exhibited by very many of the world's religions. What I have taken as the defining task of religion, imbuing human life with fundamental meaning, is here developed in one of its most significant ways. At birth, puberty, marriage, and death the life of the individual is made significant before the community and God. Unfortunately, there are few data for the early 1960s, but where we do have them they help us construct a narrative that resembles that of the previous discussion of basic adherence.

First, Table 9.1 looks at baptism. Although we have information for only 5 countries, they give us 2 Catholic cases (Belgium and France), 2 Nordic Lutheran countries, and the mixed case of the UK. They show that the parents of between two-thirds and almost the whole infant population of these diverse countries were putting their babies through this important symbol of religious initiation. In the UK case one must remember that no account is taken in the figures available of baptism into Catholic and other Protestant faiths.

Unfortunately, we have data on very few countries for confirmations of church membership at puberty (though a figure as high as 90% has been given for France), or on religious funerals (though a figure of 84.3% is stated for Belgium). We have more information on weddings (Table 9.2), and for a wider range of countries than in Table 9.1, though unfortunately these do not all give comprehensive information for all the main religions within a territory. In particular, Dutch data are available for Catholics but not Calvinists; the Swiss data are vice versa. (The figures for the *total* numbers of church weddings in these countries should therefore be roughly doubled.) Nevertheless,

Table 9.2 Religious marriages as proportions of total weddings, c.1960 and c.1990

	1960					1990							Change				
	RC	L	R	A	O	RC	L	R	A	O	OC	I	RC	L	R	A	O
A	75.00					55.00							-20.00				
B	86.10					57.00							-29.10				
DK							57.00										
SF							80.00										
F	78.00					50.00						10.00	-28.00				
D	40.00	38.00				28.00	25.00						-12.00	-13.00			
GR					100.00					91.50							-8.50
I	98.00					83.00							-15.00				
NL	40.00					20.00		3.00					-20.00				
N		82.00					69.00							-13.00			
P						82.00											
E						81.50											
S		94.00					72.00							-22.00			
CH	55.00		45.00			38.00		31.00					-17.00		-14.00		
UK[a]	12.30			47.40		8.00			45.00				-4.30			-2.40	
USA[b]						15.00					34.00						

RC = Roman Catholic   L = Lutheran   R = Reformed   A = Anglican   O = Orthodox   OC = Other Christian   I = Islamic

[a] Figures are for England and Wales. In Scotland, 18% of weddings were Catholic in 1960, declining to 12% by 1990. The Anglican figures for England and Wales are in fact for all Protestants (mainly Anglican). In Scotland 65% of all weddings in 1960 were Protestant (mainly Reformed), declining to 47% by 1990.
[b] Figure for all Protestants

Sources: Various national censuses, and chapters in Davie and Hervieu-Léger 1994 and Mol 1972.

there is enough here to demonstrate that the great majority of couples marrying in many European countries in the early 1960s sought a religious blessing on their union.

These figures all indicate high levels of affirmations of religious identity. They do not however tell us anything about religious behaviour. Here the key indicator would be regular participation in church services. Unfortunately, we have here data only for nine countries (Table 9.3). These indicate far more minority participation than in the rites of passage, but as regular monthly or often weekly commitments they must rank among the largest scale of collective activities in existence in these countries at the time. Roman Catholics showed considerably higher levels of adherence than Protestants in European countries, but not in the USA.

It is, overall, reasonable to regard at least many parts of Western Europe in the 1960s as being fundamentally Christian. Religion seemed to have secured its place according to the terms of the mid-century compromise and survived the attacks of a century or more of secularism.

RELIGION AT THE *FIN DE SIÈCLE*

The most important religious innovation in Western Europe in the intervening thirty years has been that brought by the waves of immigrants from other regions of the world, and subsequently by their descendants. Most important have been Moslems, European Christendom's historic and antagonistic neighbours, but there have also been Buddhists and Hindus, other religions from the Indian subcontinent, and new varieties of Christianity. In the cases of Belgium, France, the Netherlands, the UK, and to a limited extent Portugal and Spain, these people have come from former colonies. In Germany, Scandinavia, and Switzerland they have come from a variety of countries, usually seeking work. We shall consider the general phenomenon of these population movements in more detail in the next chapter, but here we note their importance in Europe's religious diversity.

PATTERNS OF BELONGING

Figure 9.2 displays the basic patterns of religious adherence in the early 1990s. Again, we have information for all the countries of interest to us except Portugal, though we know from other data that it remains strongly Catholic in many respects. As in the early 1960s, between two-thirds and virtually all the adult populations have some declared religious adherence. The basic patterns are also repeated:

(1) the Catholic predominance group continues, with the only major new challenge from other faiths being the growing number of Moslems in France and of various ethnic minorities in Austria;

(2) the Nordic countries retain a very heavy Lutheran dominance;

(3) the mixed Protestant/Catholic group of Germany, the Netherlands, Switzerland, and the UK also retains its basic pattern, with a rise in non-Christian groups following immigration waves, especially in the UK.

Table 9.3 *Attendance at religious services as proportions of adherents of faith, c.1960 and c.1990*

		1960					1990								Change		
		RC	L	R	O	OC	RC	L	R	O	OC	J	I	Other	RC	L	OC
A	weekly	34.50					22.92										
B	weekly	34.00					47.69								-11.08		
B	monthly																
DK	monthly		5.30					11.00								5.70	
SF	weekly		10.00														
SF	monthly		5.00														
F	weekly	20.00					14.93		5.00				10.00		-5.07		
F	monthly						25.37					22.00					
D	weekly						55.29	11.66									
D	monthly						40.87	13.99									
IRL	monthly						87.00										
I	weekly						35.00										
I	monthly						53.00			1.00							
NL	weekly	64.40		20.00			37.50										
NL	monthly								59.09					37.04			
N	monthly							9.44									
P	weekly	15.00					36.90										
P	monthly																
E	weekly						29.70										
E	monthly						38.70										
S	monthly							11.56									
CH	weekly					15.00	33.00	33.00									
UK	weekly	40.00					51.19										
UK	monthly										21.24[a]						
USA	monthly	47.00				44.00	49.36				69.70[a]				2.36		22.70

RC = Roman Catholic   L = Lutheran   R = Reformed   O = Orthodox   OC = Other Christian   I = Islamic   J = Jewish

[a] All Protestants

Sources: Chapters in Davie and Hervieu-Léger 1994, European Values Group 1992, and Mol 1972.

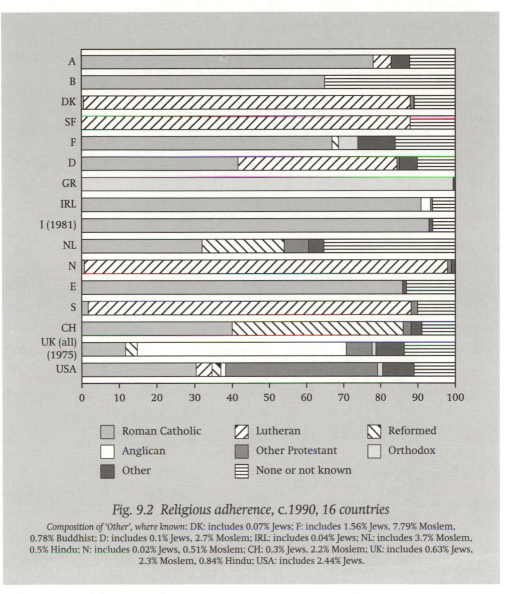

Fig. 9.2 Religious adherence, c.1990, 16 countries

Composition of 'Other', where known: DK: includes 0.07% Jews; F: includes 1.56% Jews, 7.79% Moslem, 0.78% Buddhist; D: includes 0.1% Jews, 2.7% Moslem; IRL: includes 0.04% Jews; NL: includes 3.7% Moslem, 0.5% Hindu; N: includes 0.02% Jews, 0.51% Moslem; CH: includes 0.3% Jews, 2.2% Moslem; UK: includes 0.63% Jews, 2.3% Moslem, 0.84% Hindu; USA: includes 2.44% Jews.

The USA has had a similar experience to the third group; there is little change in Japan.

However, as Table 9.4 (which shows change between 1960 and the 1990s) enables us to see, in almost every country for which we have data for both periods, there is a clear increase in the proportion of Western Europeans (and of Americans) not associated with any religion at all. The only slight exception is Norway, while the Greek Orthodox Church has suffered hardly any reverse at all. Elsewhere the religious decline ranges from around 5% to the extreme case of the Netherlands, at 16.8%. The combined total of those with no religion or those whose faith was not known to the researchers has

Table 9.4 *Change in religious adherence by type of faith, c.1960–1990*

	RC	L	R	A	OP	O	J	I	H	B	S	Other	None or not known
Austria	-10.99	-1.01										3.71	4.82
Belgium	-31.00												
Denmark		-7.60											8.30
Finland		-4.40											8.30
France	-23.00		0.10			4.89	0.56	7.19		0.78			5.98
Germany	-2.50	-7.60			-2.50		0.00	2.70				0.70	9.70
Greece						1.52	-0.07					-1.42	0.00
Ireland	-3.29			-3.02	-0.39							-0.19	5.86
Netherlands	-8.40		-15.60									7.20	16.80
Norway	0.54	-0.89			-1.71							0.39	-0.15
Spain	-13.90												12.90
Sweden		-11.78			-0.25								
Switzerland	-5.40		-6.60		1.60		-0.10	2.20					7.90
UK (members)	-1.55		-1.20	-1.54	-0.30	0.12	-0.30	1.38	0.14				
UK (total community)	-0.28		-1.26	-10.74	-0.50	0.12	-0.30	1.38	0.14				6.66
Japan					0.45					-2.58	11.67		
USA	4.69	-2.81	-3.27	-1.53	-7.52	-0.83	-0.80					4.71	7.39

RC = Roman Catholic   R = Reformed   OP = Other Protestant   J = Jewish   H = Hindu   S = Shinto
L = Lutheran   A = Anglican   O = Orthodox   I = Islamic   B = Buddhist

reached levels of over one-third in the Low Countries (Belgium and the Netherlands). The very largest declines are registered among French Catholics and Dutch Calvinists,[6] though big drops were also experienced by Austrian and Dutch Catholics, Anglicans, and US Protestants of various kinds.

However, from a certain perspective these declines are small. Given that secularization has been in progress since the late nineteenth century, and a century earlier in France, that Liberal and Socialist or Communist political parties in these countries have been rallying points for *laïcisme*, the persistence of Christianity is remarkable. Michelat (1990), tracing a decline in French religious practice, notes the close relationship between practice and a family background of observance. Perhaps unsurprisingly, the higher the devotion to church attendance the more orthodox and firm a person's faith. There is here clearly a religious subculture which, although declining, remains an important component of French society. In general, and with the possible exception of the Netherlands (where ironically we have identified the origins of sociological liberalism), the mid-century model emerges from this examination slightly battered by recent developments, but basically intact.

The secularist organizations and counter-religious Communist and Socialist party cultural structures which we noted in the early 1960s as a form of *laïcisme* have declined very sharply indeed. In particular, political parties have become vote-gathering machines and have lost much of their role as cultural or counter-cultural organizations (see Chapter 11). This decline has been far more severe than anything suffered by the churches. If the contest between religion and secularization is one between organizations and articulated systems of belief, then religion rules undisturbed. Its 'enemy' is not an aggressive *laïcisme* but indifference, as Lambert comments with specific reference to France (1989: 49), an enemy which it shares with its erstwhile secularist opponents.

RELIGIOUS PARTICIPATION

Tables 9.1 and 9.2, which we have already examined for data on the early 1960s, also show us the situation for more recent years, and (for those countries where we have material for both time periods) enable us to compare changes in the main religious rites of passage between the two periods. We now have information on baptisms from 10 European countries, with a good range of Catholic, Protestant, and mixed cases. This rite remains a majority experience for the infants of all countries for which we have details except the UK. (We should note that we have no information on the Netherlands here, which may well resemble the UK.) The very high levels recorded in Italy and Portugal give us confidence that it is correct to regard these countries as still strongly Catholic, despite the absence of up-to-date statistics on religious adherence. However, with the exception of Denmark, there has been a fairly strong decline in all countries for which we have evidence at both time points.

With again the strong exception of the Netherlands (and Dutch Protestants in particular), religious weddings remain a majority experience for European populations. There is considerable diversity here. In some countries the figure remains at over 80%, in some cases well over: Finland, Greece, Italy, Portugal, Spain. It is notable that these are all countries which, although coming from three different religious families, share

---

[6] It should be noted that no data are available for the small Belgian and French Calvinist communities.

the experience of having industrialized during the post-war period. It should also be noted that in Italy church baptism and marriage extend far beyond the proportion of the population which in the past voted for the Christian Democratic Party and must include many who voted for explicitly secularist parties. Within the global Italian figure there was considerable regional differentiation, with most of the south (except the city of Naples) having higher levels of religious marriage than the north (Dittgen 1994). In Spain too there were far lower proportions of such marriages in the more industrialized parts of the country. It must be remembered that Greeks have had the right to civil marriage only since 1982 (Kokosalakis 1994: 144). In most other countries the figure is around half or a little more: Austria, Belgium, Denmark, France, Germany, the UK, and the USA. In between come Norway, Sweden, and Switzerland, with levels around 70%; these cases fit less easily into the 'timing of industrialism' thesis.

As with baptisms, these mainly high levels are nevertheless considerably lower than 30 years before: in every case where we have comparable data, we can see an important decline, in Belgium and France very strongly so. We still have little information on confirmations and funerals. The French confirmation figure has dropped from 90% to 43% over the period, a very steep decline. However, 80% of Swedes still confirm their faith in their mid-teens.

A useful indicator of the extent to which adherents of different religions see themselves as members of different communities is the extent to which they are willing to marry members of different religions or no religion. Those Western European countries with large numbers of both Catholics and Protestants (Germany, Netherlands, Switzerland) enable us to see this particularly clearly. In a comparison of Germany and the Netherlands, Hendrickx, Schreuder, and Ultee (1994) traced these patterns since the beginning of the century. They show that people in these countries are more likely to marry someone from their own religious group than to marry outside, but that this preference has declined for most of the century and is now very small. A major decline in religious homogamy took place in Germany immediately after the Second World War; in the Netherlands it did not occur until the major cultural changes of the late 1960s, once again confirming the significance of that period for religion in the Netherlands in particular. (Indeed, according to Bax (1990: 115) there was a growing *aversion* to mixed marriage during the 1947 to 1960 period.) Early in the century Catholics tended to be more homogamous than Calvinists (except for the Orthodox Reformed Calvinists in the Netherlands), but today there is little difference. Swiss evidence too (Switzerland 1995) shows a tendency for Protestants and Catholics to marry co-religionists, but to a declining extent.

Jews however remain considerably more homogamous than Christians or non-believers (Hendrickx, Schreuder, and Ultee 1994). Not surprisingly, there was a particularly abrupt rise in Jewish homogamy from immediately after the start of the Nazi period in Germany, and following the German invasion in the Netherlands.

There were inadequate data available to consider fully a crucial test of religious adherence—regular attendance at religious services—in 1960. We can however say more about the early 1990s (see Table 9.3). Within Western Europe there is still a clear and consistent difference in the approaches of Catholics and various kinds of Protestants to church attendance. Outside France, at least one-third of Catholics attend church monthly, and over a quarter do so weekly. Among Italians, the Irish, and the largely Irish Catholic population within the UK, the monthly level exceeds 50%. With the exception of Dutch and Swiss Calvinists, little more than 10% of Protestants are regular church attenders. We see here a contrast between types of Christianity which was not evident with the earlier indicators: within Europe the official state churches of Anglicanism and Lutheranism in England and the Nordic countries attract far lower attendances than Catholics and Calvinists. France has a level of religious observance considerably below other Catholic countries and more closely resembling a Protestant case. In many respects that exclusion of the French Church from public life that took place for large parts of the nineteenth and twentieth centuries has made French Catholicism more like a form of Protestantism in its lack of public demonstrativeness; it is notable that in Chapter 7 we found that in several aspects of family behaviour France resembled the Scandinavian countries more closely than it did Catholic southern Europe or even Germany.

There is a very striking contrast between European and US Protestants, with the various categories of the latter being the most reliable church attenders in the advanced world apart from Irish Catholics.

Recent research on *strength* of adherence to one's church gives us further insight into national variations (Table 9.5). In general, predominantly Catholic countries score highest, Lutheran ones the lowest, with the mixed Catholic/Protestant nations coming in between. Germany however is more religious than one would expect on that basis, and the rather special case of Northern Ireland considerably more so. France is for once closer to the Catholic norm, though it is the weakest of the Catholic countries.

The higher level of religious participation in the USA than Europe can be placed in context here. Its Catholics are not so different from their European co-religionists, though certainly attending more frequently, but it is among US Protestants that

Table 9.5 Orientations to church membership, c.1990

	B	DK	F	D	IRL	I	NL	N	P	E	S	GB	NI
Core[a]	9	3	5	12	14	8	23	8	9	5	4	13	23
Modal[b]	21		11	22	73	44	6		32	38		9	44
Marginal[c]	38		45	56	9	33	21		32	44		35	23
All practising	68		61	90	96	85	50		73	87		57	90
Lapsed[d]	18		25	9	3	8	28		8	8		21	7
Never[e]	14	8	13	2	0	7	21	10	21	5	19	21	3

[a] At least monthly attendance, plus participation in church organizations
[b] At least monthly attendance
[c] Attendance less than monthly
[d] Formerly a church member, but no longer
[e] Never a member of a church

Source: European Values Group 1992.

participation is particularly high. This is in line with Martin's (1978) arguments that the weakness of religion in much of Europe results from past associations between established churches and the state. While the main European Anglican, Calvinist, and Lutheran churches largely succeeded in regaining hegemony within Protestantism in their various countries once the waves of nineteenth-century dissent had died down, they remained 'quiet' churches. There have been virtually no waves of new, non-established Protestant 'enthusiasm' in these countries of the kind which fuels religious activity in the USA.[7]

PATTERNS OF BELIEF

The theology of Western Christianity always stresses beliefs, the creed or *credo* of the faith. Some other of the world's great religions—Judaism, for example—do not share this emphasis on a catalogue of more or less intellectual belief statements. A general sociology of religion is also not particularly interested in fine details which are usually barely understood by most adherents, but we are interested to learn if adherence to a religion has any major implications for beliefs and values taken *grosso modo*, if only because that can tell us something about the relationship of adherence to a religion and values and behaviour exercised in other realms of life.

We cannot obtain detailed comparative material on this question for our 1960s starting point, though we can probably accept McLeod's (1997) conclusion from what research does exist on the period 1945–60 for most of Western Europe:

The overall picture in this period seems to be one of a very widespread acceptance of some form of Christian doctrine, ethics and identity, combined with a good deal of uncertainty about specific items of Christian teaching and low levels of institutional commitment. . . .

In the years 1945–60 religious change had been fairly slow and there remained large areas of continuity with the pre-war years.   (ibid. 135)

For the 1990s, after the great waves of religious change which then intervened, we have some more detailed, though still by no means comprehensive, information. Some recent findings by the International Social Attitudes Survey for a small number of countries are summarized in Table 9.6.

The most basic item—belief in God—is too widespread and diverse in potential meaning to be of much use for comparative research, but the more severe test of Christian orthodoxy used by the Survey included belief in the devil, heaven, hell, miracles, and the Bible. If one sets aside Northern Ireland as a special case, the higher level of orthodox belief in the USA compared with Europe is very striking. Among European

7 Another aspect of US religion which seems to differentiate it from most of Europe is the high level of activity on the political far right of the small US Protestant sects. These are large in number, attract a high level of active participation, and take up fundamentalist religious as well as far-right political positions (Finke 1992). Were the USA to be at the centre of this book, we should need to spend time considering the paradox of a growth of fundamentalist religion in what is ostensibly the world's most 'modern' society. The US branches of the major global forms of Christianity (largely Catholicism and Episcopalian Protestantism), which have tried to come to terms with 'modernism' broadly conceived, are in decline as they are in Europe (ibid. 151–4). It is religions which insist on literal interpretations of the Bible, reject ecumenicism, and advocate traditional models of social behaviour far more ardently than do the major churches which are thriving. (For example, while the Catholic Church in the USA and elsewhere is unequivocal in its opposition to abortion, it has never associated itself in any way with the campaign by some American Protestants of murdering medical practitioners who carry out abortions.) Here however we simply need to note the contrast with European societies.

Table 9.6 Indicators of orthodoxy of religious beliefs, 1990
(10 = highest possible orthodoxy level)

	D	IRL	I	NL	N	UK		USA
						GB	NI	
Regular Catholic	6.60	7.10	7.00	5.00	—	7.50	8.00	7.70
Irregular Catholic	4.60	5.20	4.80	4.00	—	5.80	7.00	6.80
Regular Protestant	6.60	—	—	7.00	8.70	6.50	8.00	8.60
Irregular Protestant	4.30	—	—	4.90	4.00	4.50	6.60	7.20
Other	7.10	—	—	6.80	7.50	6.50	—	4.50
None	2.90	—	2.10	2.80	2.80	3.30	5.60	4.40
All	4.80	6.60	5.90	4.00	4.40	4.70	7.60	7.40

GB = Great Britain; NI = Northern Ireland

Note: Regularity refers to frequency of church attendance.

Source: Jowell et al. 1993.

countries the two Catholic ones have higher levels of belief than the others, and the only solely Lutheran example (Norway) is slightly lower than two of the three mixed countries (Britain and Germany), though the third, the Netherlands, ranks lowest of all. Without a wider range of countries it is not worth trying to interpret this datum. It is also difficult to interpret the differences between Catholics and Protestants in the different countries.

Possibly more important evidence of the extent to which churches are able to teach their adherents a series of attitudes and beliefs can be seen in the fate of the Catholic Church's teachings on sexual behaviour. (The Protestant churches in most European countries have not attempted to steer behaviour on these matters for many years; the Church of England however finally dropped its objections to divorce only in the 1990s.) Referenda in favour of divorce (1974) and abortion (1981) both secured majorities of the Italian population despite the strong Catholic identity reported in the above tables, though it is true that areas of the country where the Church was strongest were less likely to vote for these reforms (Cipriani 1989: 28). Perhaps less surprisingly the French Church suffered similar reversals in parliamentary votes on similar issues (sale of contraceptives (1967); abortion (1974 and 1979) (Willaime 1994: 165)). Ireland remained the only country to maintain a strong Catholic position on these questions until the mid-1990s. The evidence reviewed in Chapter 7 that birth rates in the Catholic south have now become the lowest in Europe also suggests that church teaching on birth control has little force, though it is true that within those countries birth rates remain higher in the more strongly Catholic areas.

On the basis of the evidence from the European Values Study, Davie concludes (1994: 58) that religion has declined as institutional practice but not as a set of beliefs—'believing without belonging'. The evidence above however leads one to suspect it might be the opposite: there is a clear sense of belonging to one church or another (usually the dominant national one) but little corollary in beliefs and wider values. Eva Hamberg (1990: 33–57) has indeed explicitly used the phrase 'belonging without believing' to describe the state of religion in contemporary Sweden. For the Scandinavian countries this might well be appropriate, but more generally applied it would be too glib. On the basic item of belief in God, there is still much evidence. For example, in 1985 32.1% of Italian Catholics believed and practised; 36.1% believed but rarely practised; and 17.3% believed but did not practise (Cipriani 1989: 43). Both belonging and belief may be questioned; both may be alternatively defined as, in their different ways, strong. In line with my argument near the start of the chapter, I prefer to avoid these difficulties by talking instead about changes in the pattern of religious identification.

Many of these changes are very recent. Without much knowledge of earlier periods we must be careful about speaking of major new historical departures rather than fluctuations, but it does seem that the present period, the end of the twentieth century, is one of change of some kind in the structure of values, including those affecting religion. The main theme is one that we encountered in Chapter 7: individualization. This emerges from a number of studies carried out on value change.

Nesti (1985) speaks in relation to Italian Catholicism of 'implicit religion', where beliefs are generally unspecific with just a core of central ideas. The great majority of people in all but two European nation states and the majority in the remaining two (the Netherlands and the UK) clearly affirm some kind of religious identity as part of their sense of who they are in relation to the mass of general humanity. Even the Danes, who are the least religious people according to all surveys of religious belief, identify in large numbers with their national church, the great majority of them having their children baptized; for 47% of Danes rites of passage are the main things they want from their church and 39% of the adult population attends the Christmas Eve service which is for them more important than Easter Sunday (Riis 1994: 119–21).

Campiche (1994: 109), using the terminology of Pierre Bourdieu, makes a similar point when he remarks that young Swiss people still want *un habitus religieux*; but they will not accept *une tradition confessionnelle*. Young French people have also indicated their desire for an individually defined religion in replies to opinion polls (Willaime 1994: 169). At its weakest this amounts to religion as an element of lifestyle, alongside one's taste in music or perhaps only as a fashion statement; Willaime talks of *religion à la carte* (ibid. 170). Voyé (1994: 205) makes the point with reference to contemporary Belgium—though he could have referred to almost anywhere in contemporary Europe —that while people are willing to adhere to the great rites of the Church, they are no longer willing to *obey* it. Similarly in Italy, home of the Vatican, the Catholic Church survives (and in many respects thrives) by accepting considerable diversity in beliefs and religious practice (Pace 1994: 219; Cipriani 1989: 39–41).

Churches have been becoming more tolerant of their members discovering their own form of worship and faith within the framework of previously dogmatic forms. This is seen perhaps most strongly in both Catholic and Protestant churches in the Netherlands and Switzerland (Campiche 1994: 97). It is perhaps understandable that, in these religiously plural societies, once Catholic and Protestant hierarchies had begun to take an ecumenical approach towards each other, it was difficult to sustain a rigid insistence on doctrine within any one church; less than one-third of Swiss Christians believe that there is any important doctrinal difference between the two principal forms of Western Christianity (ibid. 104). At the same time, Campiche reports that about half of Swiss still move largely within circles of co-religionists, marry within their faith and tend always to be aware of the religion of people they meet (ibid. 106).

Some European churches have long embodied this kind of internal diversity: Danish Lutheranism; the complex web of Protestant churches in northern Ireland; the diversified localism of Spanish Catholicism (Albert-Lorca 1994); Greek Orthodoxy (Kokosalakis 1994: 147). But the recent changes embrace a far wider range. There is also some small growth of small Protestant groups of an American kind, and of some fringe non-Christian religions within Europe. These groups have attracted an extraordinary amount of research interest, but overall they affect proportions of the population too small to be considered in a survey of the present kind. In general the major European churches are today less challenged by either internal fragmentation or organized secularism than in the nineteenth century. Indeed, organized anti-religion has suffered far greater reversals than organized religion, with the collapse of humanist, Marxist, and other organizations (McLeod 1997: 145). Instead however they do have to come to terms with the consequences of individualization in the sense of a declining organizational competence.

BEYOND LIBERALISM?

This brings us to make a final assessment of the adequacy of sociological liberalism as the concept through which late twentieth-century European religion can most usefully be viewed. The Second Vatican Council 'deregulated' the system of belief, says Pace (1994: 231), using the terminology of economic policy debate of the 1990s but thereby perhaps achieving an accurate linkage with behaviour in the USA, the home of economic deregulation. It is here that the pluralistic jumble of religions that make up the USA come into their own, as faiths capable of suiting individuals' needs like products. On the other hand, there are considerable paradoxes about the American religious market. Bruce (1992: 173) points out that while there is enormous diversity across the country overall, within particular regions there is often only one or a very limited number of dominant faiths. He also points out that the historical importance of religion to immigrants in the USA was to enable them to continue to live in their habitual religious world, not to enable them to make a free-market choice of faith (ibid. 191). We must also note that the two European countries which seem to provide most diversity, the Netherlands and the UK, are those with the lowest levels of adherence.

This returns us to Martin's (1978, 1994) arguments that it is perhaps to differences between the European and American pasts and the linkage of established religion to exclusionary state forms in the former that we should look in order to explain religious decline on the *vecchio continente*. Here the more complete sociological liberalism of the nineteenth-century US state appears as an advantage to Christianity, not its weakness as maintained by most theories of secularization.

This however only leads us to a further paradox. The biggest departures in the advanced world from sociological liberalism occur today in the USA. While some of these changes, a great growth of multicultural religious diversity, are fully consistent with the expectations of postmodernist theories, other components of the change mark moves in an *opposite* direction, not anticipated by any of our theories. Fundamental to the formation of the American state was an avoidance of any formal association between that state and a particular religion or small number of religions, much of the founding US population being themselves refugees from Europe's state churches. At the same time Christianity, and later a more widely conceived Judaeo-Christianity, has long been seen as one of the fundamental building blocks of the national unity of this vast diverse society. The emphasis on the institutional separation of religion therefore falls entirely on the evasion of a specific church–state link, it does not inhibit a diversity of sects from using all means of political campaigning and lobbying to assert their social policy agenda. Some contemporary US Christianity is extremely politicized, almost entirely on the extreme right of politics, and masks demands for engagements between religion and the state which are not compatible with sociological liberalism in general or its historical US manifestations in particular. This extends from demands to have biblical rather than scientific theories of the origins of the human species taught in schools, to demands for limitations on the right of women to have abortions. These developments mark a break from recent trends in European Christianity since the Second Vatican Council, though they are more consistent with the very long past of Christian political action (Robertson 1989).

Diverse though Western European religion is, there does seem here to be a striking contrast between all forms of it and the situation in the USA; and England, so often seen as closer to the USA than to the rest of Europe, here stands as a secular extreme contrast with the American case.

The quiet, slowly declining persistence of the various European churches needs to be understood in its own terms. Wallis and Bruce (1992: 17–21) argue that religion declines alongside modernization unless it 'finds or retains work to do other than relating individuals to the supernatural' (ibid. 17). They see two forms of this 'work', both of which imply the survival of strong separate communities. First is that of cultural defence, where a threatened ethnic or status-group culture uses its particular religious identity to affirm its specificity in the presence of other, usually hostile groups. Wallis and Bruce, who both studied religion in Northern Ireland, have that region, the last site of bloody, low-level Reformation warfare in Western Europe, particularly in mind.

Second is what they call 'cultural transition', the strong religious commitment usually associated with immigrant groups. This latter might be thought to result from the fact that immigrants to today's advanced societies typically come from traditional and therefore less secularized cultures; however, a similar high level of religious adherence was noted among European colonial elites in Africa, India, and elsewhere. Also, research on religious observance among European immigrants to the USA in the late nineteenth and early twentieth centuries suggests higher levels than among the population in the country of origin (McLeod 1992).

The idea of a search for identity and meaning can embrace these various minority forms and also account for the stubbornly persistent even if undemonstrative place of religion among 'normal' European populations. The important point is to note that this search might take very different forms in different circumstances. A resident of a medieval village, embedded in a constraining and unavoidable network of relations with family, neighbours, and virtually no one else, his or her life surrounded by potentially fatal risks of harvest failure, injury, and disease will make a different and more fervent and community-bound kind of demand for reassurance of identity and meaning than an urban resident of a late twentieth-century Scandinavian welfare state. Both these figures however inhabit worlds where most people around them are similar to them in important cultural respects; different again will be the approach of someone constantly reminded of difference and cultural cleavage by living in a historically mixed region or by being an immigrant from a different culture, or indeed living among immigrants from such cultures. Contemporary Americans and contemporary Europeans are similarly likely to express their search differently, given the 'bad history' of the European case.

It is possible that, in the case of national churches where there are few corollaries in religious behaviour to accompany the basic indications of religious adherence (the Nordic countries, the Netherlands, and the UK, though in rather different ways), religious identity is mainly a component of national identity; in the Nordic lands and Greece (different though the last might normally seem from these far northern countries) the Church is virtually a branch of the civil service, with ministers of religion as government employees and a minister (in the Nordic cases within the Ministry of Education) responsible to Parliament for Church affairs. Here religion still operates in the public domain, or at least it negotiates between individuals' private lives and their public ones, because adherence to an organized religion and participation in its rites of passage indicate some desire to locate oneself in relation to something beyond individual private life. Hervieu-Léger has argued (1994: 13) that in the division between public and private life that is fundamental to modern society, religion belongs to the private sphere. This is very much a French perspective; from a Scandinavian, German, or southern European one different conclusions might be reached.

While Catholicism is always a supranational rather than a national religion, it too has taken decidedly national forms. This is perhaps seen especially strongly in Italy, the 'world headquarters' of the faith, where the historical and continuing public presence of the Church provides what Cipriani (1989) calls 'diffused religion', so extensive that even oppositions to it take their form and style from its own distinctive patterns. Since these patterns are frequently public, they assist the general Italian tradition of public *manifestazioni*, whether as celebrations or as protests, opportunities '*scendere in piazza*'.

We need not only see religion as an identity in the challenged and therefore activist contexts allowed by Wallis and Bruce. The quiet absorption by a Dane of her sense of the national church as an aspect of Danishness, or the inseparability of Catholicism from Italian-ness for even an atheist Italian, are just as much part of an identity, even if passive. Identity is a different concept from belonging; it implies that the person concerned takes the identifying institution or symbol as an aspect of his own persona, whereas belonging implies more of an engagement with an institution and its practices. Identification may therefore be particularly suitable to the form of association with large collectivities that can be reconciled with the conditions of an individualized society. Wilson (1966) argues correctly that the kind of identification with community that gave strength to religion in past times sprang from the tight and embracing world of the local community. Clearly neither this way of life nor acceptance of that kind of control is likely to thrive in today's circumstances. On the other hand, many people might find in religion some residual form of identification—with some general idea of community, with their nation, or with some ultimate framework of meaning—which does not cease to be sociologically relevant just because it has become quiet and undemonstrative.

We are still likely to see secularization in the sense of a decline in the wider social significance of religion, but this may be more accurately seen as a change in the form taken by religion as part of the long-developing implications of sociological liberalism rather than a process of decline that ends with its eventual disappearance.

Chapter 10

NATIONS, CULTURES, AND ETHNICITIES

In the previous chapter identity with nation appeared alongside that with religion; sometimes, as outstandingly in the French case, as a rival; more frequently, as in Scandinavia and the United Kingdom, as an ally or even as an aspect of the same phenomenon. Nation and certain related ideas such as ethnicity and local culture therefore require separate consideration.

The core concept for this discussion is ethnicity, by which I mean shared cultural characteristics which enable an extensive and more or less homogamous group to distinguish itself from others it encounters, and which are seen as having endured since a remote past. Nothing is said here about the size of the group so perceived or its geographical spread; it could be a few hundred thousand; it could be tens of millions. Homogamy (marriage within the group) is fundamental, because if large numbers marry outside the culture becomes diluted as the generation formed by the mixed marriages produces a new joint culture. However, provided a substantial majority remains homogamous there is scope for some external marriage without a threat to the group's survival. If members of two or more such groups intermarry extensively over a period they will produce a distinctively new ethnicity. Most extant ethnicities have resulted from this kind of process; they are subject to constant, slow change.

It is homogamy which gives ethnicity its ostensible 'racial' and 'biological' characteristics. Attempts at scientifically defining races in biological science identify a far smaller number of human types than the number of ethnicities that can be identified by sociologists and anthropologists. (See Chapman 1993 for an extensive discussion of the relationship between biological and sociological or anthropological approaches to ethnicity.) This is because the kinds of biological differences that are produced by these patterns of intermarriage are rather superficial in terms of human evolution. Repeated homogamy within even a large human group will, given enough time, reproduce certain characteristics (such as skin colour, nasal shape, typical height), but these will not affect more fundamental issues of biological differentiation. Also, the occasional heterogamy that always takes place prevents any really strong demarcations between populations in close mutual contact.

For our present purposes the central question is how nationality and ethnicity relate to models of modernity, and in particular to that of the mid-century social compromise. As traditional institutions not deriving directly from industrial capitalism, they appear here among the institutions requiring the protection of sociological liberalism if they are to survive. This is unambiguous where ethnicity is concerned, but the relationship of nationality to modernity is far more complex. The process of nation building has long been associated with modernization and even ndustrialization (see particularly the works of Reinhard Bendix 1977 and Ernest Gellner 1965, 1982, 1983, 1994). As such, construction of the modern nation state is commonly regarded as part of the construction of rational institutions. It is widely believed that such things as 'nations' can be perceived as social realities, and that it is more sensible and orderly if the geographical boundaries of these become the boundaries of states. One sees this most clearly in Africa where, following independence from European colonial powers, leaders tried to construct institutions and loyalties based on the state boundaries that they inherited from the colonial period. Loyalties based on the tribal structures that had preceded the European invasions are generally seen as disastrously irrational res- idues from 'primitive' times. International agencies and Western governments have encouraged this process. Only a few nations (as opposed to tribes) in fact existed in Africa before these states were established. These are states trying to construct nations, not nations realizing themselves as states. Nevertheless, this is believed to be import- ant to modernization, even if the development of national identity involves emotions and symbols just as 'irrational' as those associated with tribes.

Something similar occurred in the Western world. Several nation states developed their symbols and loyalties in struggles with not tribal, but relatively local, sub-state identities. As we saw in the Prologue, this process derives its reputation for rationality from the historical circumstances of the first two 'modern' states: France and the United States of America. We also saw how similar concepts were used elsewhere: Germany, Italy, the nations that comprised the Austro-Hungarian Empire. More recently the eventually ill-fated republic of Yugoslavia presented itself as building a non-national Yugoslav identity. 'Nations' in this multicultural state were seen by the Yugoslav elite to be such traditional entities as Serbia, Croatia, Bosnia-Herzegovina. When civil war struck in the early 1990s the outcome was the destruction of Yugoslavia in favour of these smaller nations. However, during the period of its construction Yugoslavia was to be a modern, supranational force, though in constructing it the elites used the same symbols and emotional appeals as those in France, the USA, and more obviously 'na- tional' nations.

It is not clear that the nation-state building process deserves to be regarded as par- ticularly rational, the principles underlying it being so diverse. As Benedict Anderson has expressed it (1983), nations are 'imagined communities'. They are too large to be actual communities, but it is possible to conceive of fellow members of a national group as being sufficiently similar to oneself that they could potentially be members of the same community—more readily than someone from another nation. However, the conceptions that we have of who constitutes our fellow nationals are mainly the past residues of what successful or once-successful political leaders have managed to con- struct and to project. Dahrendorf (1988: 30) is historically correct in arguing that the nation state came to be essential in guaranteeing the rule of law, but whether there is something intrinsic to its form that gave it this benign role is very difficult to establish. Had the city-state form managed militarily to resist the onslaught from nation states, would it have been less capable of ushering in a world governed by the rule of law in due time? The fact that Dahrendorf, like most others, goes on to build a concept of national citizenship that in fact finds its most powerful origins in urban citizenship makes the question reasonable, if ultimately unanswerable.

Nor is it clear that the association with modernization and industrialization is accurate. It seems to be so in the Third World, where nation states are among the accoutrements of modernity bequeathed by the West to new nations. Within Western Europe, the birthplace of the concept, the process was more closely associated with warfare. The region was unusual in having for several centuries a variety of political forces, none of which could fully conquer the others. States that were successful in acquiring territory and power did so by acquiring empires outside the Western European cockpit itself: either towards the east (Austria) or overseas (in particular Britain, but also Belgium, France, the Netherlands, Portugal, Spain). Within Western Europe they had to remain on guard against each other and to strengthen their potential military power. Eventually this process exploded into the two great world wars of this century, both principally European wars, but *en route* the various states did everything they could to maximize their strength. Building the populations of their territories into loyal, patriotic subjects was of fundamental importance to the process. Those European nations who ruled over colonies in other parts of the world had a particularly useful instrument for this purpose; all classes of the imperial nation could feel part of a common community defined against the colonialized peoples. The task was not therefore primarily rational, only incidentally modernizing, and not immediately designed to ensure the tolerance and cooperation required for sociological liberalism.

Industrial society, unlike the social forms that preceded it, has always been organized on the basis of nation states. These states are not passive collections of individuals who happen to be grouped territorially; the leaders of nations expect the loyalty of their populations, even to the point of demanding the sacrifice of the individual's life under the cruel and terrifying conditions of warfare. Warfare in turn has to be seen as an integral part of industrial societies. Contrary to the expectations of optimistic nineteenth-century thinkers, who believed that capitalist industrial society would be less military than its agricultural aristocratic and monarchical predecessors (e.g. Spencer 1864; Comte 1844), the military technology made available by industrialism has unleashed wars of unprecedented destructive intensity. Industrial states sustain a permanent capacity for waging war that earlier state forms did not possess.

The deeply ambiguous relationship between nationalism and modernizing rationalism received some limited resolution in the post-war period which can be attributed to the role of sociological liberalism. European nationalisms had twice brought war to virtually the whole world within three decades, and the Nazi period had brought to Germany and its allies probably the biggest example of genocide and racist persecution in human history. Inter-ethnic and inter-national relations were therefore high on the agenda of social concern. Within Western Europe itself a process of cross-national integration began with the Treaty of Rome and construction of the European Economic Community and European Coal and Steel Community. Now the expanded process being continued by the European Union as the enlarged successor to these Communities has become the most extensive example of sociological liberalism affecting national identities among a group of still sovereign states to be introduced in the world. During the same period those European states which had maintained colonial rule over people of various non-European ethnicities throughout the world began to accept the need for withdrawal from these territories and the establishment of independent countries with their own governments. This process began with the British acceptance of the independence of India and Pakistan in 1948, and ended with Portuguese with-drawal from its colonies in Africa and elsewhere in the mid-1970s. In between the rest of the British empire and lands ruled over by France, Belgium, and the Netherlands underwent a similar experience.

Some authors have claimed that most advanced societies in the contemporary world have now developed something called 'liberal nationalism', a form of national identity and pride that does not depend on hostility towards and rivalry with other national-ities—a concept very similar in its implications to sociological liberalism in this field. Other scholars, particularly Germans for obvious reasons (e.g. Habermas 1998), have tried to develop a concept of constitutional patriotism, whereby a visceral pride in ethnic origins is replaced by a rationalistic pride in the achievements of one's country's constitution. It is doubtful whether this has much resonance outside intellectual groups, but it is significant as an element in the continuing struggle to accommodate nationality to both rationalism and social compromise. It is also true that, if a European identity is ever to develop at the level of the EU, it will have to take a Habermasian form, since the EU eschews all militaristic and nationalistic or ethnicist appeals in its attempts to build a social Europe.

Sociological liberalism in the sense of relations of mutual tolerance between nation and other institutions proceeded less dramatically. For example, while the privileged appointment of family members to economic positions is, in modern societies, regarded as 'nepotism' and an offence against rational meritocracy, most governments maintain rules privileging the employment of persons holding the nationality of the country by requiring special permission for the appointment of foreigners. Governments have usually also maintained controls on cross-border movements of persons and trade and have planned communication routes to emphasize borders (Deutsch 1966).

From the 1960s to the 1990s the Western European states have been involved in successive waves of international negotiations which have liberalized trade. However, while interacting intensively in economic and some other areas, individual states jealously guard their sovereignty and distinctiveness in other fields, in particular in the maintenance of national education systems, in which the cultural expression of nation states takes its most powerful form. Furthermore, at the very time that these various forms of globalization have been taking place, controls on the movement of persons across countries have intensified, and xenophobic movements have strengthened in many countries. Among the factors involved are the globalizing forces themselves, which lead some people to feel that stabilities of their identity are being threatened. The compatibility of nations with sociological liberalism depends on a certain pattern of restrained identity: without a sense of national identity nation states would find it difficult to continue as the core organizing structures whereby social life is related to systems of order spread across geographical space; but if that sense becomes very strong it produces intolerance of other identities.

This brings us to the biggest challenge from sociological liberalism affecting con-temporary states: relations between the dominant ethnicity or culture within the nation state and minorities within its borders. For Western European societies this challenge takes two forms: surviving quasi-national or submerged identities below the level of the established nation state (Scots, Basques, etc.); and immigrant populations or populations descended from immigrants. The two groups can be distinguished from each other as follows: the former have been settled in a specific territory since long before the foundation of the present nation state, that territory usually having had an autonomous political existence at some point in the past; the latter, immigrant populations or their forebears, entered the nation state at some point and have never had a settled territory within it, being likely to live in scattered clusters. In general these latter are relatively recent arrivals: immigrants from past centuries are likely to have been absorbed by the host society by now. Jews form the principal exception to this.

It is also possible for migrations within a nation state by people from distinctive cultures to raise some of the same issues as those by immigrants from more remote locations. Given the artificial construction of most nations, this should not surprise us. Before the Republic of Ireland became an autonomous nation state the movement of Irish people to England and Scotland was strictly speaking internal migration, though it raised major questions of linguistic, cultural, and religious differences. After 1922 these movements in theory became international migration, though since over the years the differences between Britain and Ireland have diminished, the cultural implications of these moves have become much smaller. In the 1960s the large numbers of migrants who left southern Italy to find work in Turin and other growing industrial cities in the north found that they were often treated as people coming from a remote culture, their 'peasant' rural practices contrasting sharply with the urban way of life.

SOCIOLOGICAL LIBERALISM AND DIFFERENT FORMS OF ETHNIC RELATIONS

The ethnic awareness of minorities and the cultural nationalism of majority populations are essentially similar: identities that enable a person to answer the question 'who am I?', not in a manner having transcendental implications as with religion, but still in a fundamental way in that the identity is with a large entity encompassing many aspects of life and a large, wide reference group. On occasions these secular cultural identities can overlap fairly completely with religious ones, and consequently become more powerful. It is important to perceive the matter in this way, as it is easy to slip into the habit of regarding ethnicity as something possessed by minorities alone, with majority populations somehow being in a rational world above cultural particularities (for a good discussion of this, see Smith 1986: 27).

Let us assume a situation in which two or more groups which see themselves as of different ethnicities find themselves in a relationship of host majority and immigrant minority, and where the majority is both wealthier and possesses greater access to centres of political and other forms of power within the society. (A very similar analysis could be carried out for the majority and minority religions discussed in the previous chapter.) The host ethnicity clearly comprises a dominant group, even if it is itself divided by class and other relationships. This is the case when societies receive immigrants from countries that are in general poorer, as with most immigration to Western Europe in recent decades. It is therefore the model with which we are mainly concerned. There is however also the possibility that the dominant group is small and immigrant but rich and powerful. This was the case with the European colonial settlements in other continents which took place from the fifteenth to the twentieth centuries. We would normally describe these as invasions rather than immigrations.

Encounters between groups that perceive themselves as different are potentially difficult, for three principal reasons. First, any or all the groups involved may regard their culture as an asset that they wish to preserve. They may therefore want to protect it from mixture with the other culture(s), whether by members of the group adopting the practices of the other or, most important of all, by intermarriage leading to the possible disappearance of the group. Majorities as well as both immigrant and territorial minorities may have this concern. It is more realistic in the case of minorities, since the chances of their culture being 'swamped' by the one which they have entered are very high. The challenge to the majority culture is far less likely, but it may be strongly felt, partly because the majority feels that this is 'their' country and that other cultures have no legitimate place in it; and partly because the impact of the minority may be concentrated in specific classes and geographical areas. What is overall a small minority presence might in some locations be far larger.

Second, the trust that people extend to each other in everyday life often requires some knowledge of the general social characteristics of the others. If I recognize people to be in some ways 'similar' to me, I may well be more likely to trust them or at least to feel I can predict their behaviour than if they seem very different. The assumption may be entirely false—this error permits confidence tricksters to thrive—but it is extremely common and makes people wary of entering into detailed relations with others who seem 'different'.

Third, members of majority host cultures may perceive members of minorities, especially immigrants, as unnecessary sources of competition. This is likely to be most apparent at times of important scarcities; unemployment is probably the most significant case in contemporary societies. Members of the host group may believe that if only the 'outsiders' would go away, things would be easier.

Three broadly distinguishable institutional responses are possible to these difficulties: segregation, assimilation, and integration.

SEGREGATION

The first, which I shall call *segregation*, occurs when the life of the minority is almost entirely separate from that of the host society. This is the ghetto model which for many centuries governed the lives of Jews in many European societies. This segregation may be chosen by the minority (or at least by dominant members of it), may be imposed on it by the majority, or may be wanted by both sides. Under segregation the minority sustains its original culture and social practices with virtually no reference to the majority. Social interaction, especially anything which might lead to marriage, is strictly avoided. Since many individuals in both cultures might be expected to want to deviate from the segregation rules, a segregation system is likely to persist only if there are formal or informal 'gatekeepers' on one or both sides of the line. These might be religious authorities who refuse to permit intermarriage, or senior figures in a community who discourage contact. In the case of the gatekeepers of the majority culture there can also be imposition of laws restricting the movements and dealings of the minority.

It is important to note that only one side needs to desire segregation for it to be effective; it is alone among the three models in this. If a minority wishes to enter more fully into a society, but the majority will not let it, then the minority must remain segregated; if a minority insists on remaining separate then it will do so, even if the majority welcomes its assimilation or integration. This assumes unity of practice and preference within both groups. In practice it is likely that some individuals from the minority will become associated with at least parts of the majority society.

For the minority segregation preserves the inherited culture of the group and minimizes the risk of its dilution and eventual disappearance, but at a certain price. Opportunities within a small immigrant society are likely to be restricted. Higher education and career advance are likely to be possible only within the host society. Therefore a segregated minority is virtually doomed to low social mobility. Also, although possible friction with members of the host community is reduced to a minimum by restricting contact with it, when contact does take place it is particularly likely to be difficult because the groups are so separate. For the majority culture segregation keeps minorities at a distance, but at the price of maintaining groups *within* the host society but not really *of* it.

ASSIMILATION

At the other extreme from segregation stands *assimilation*. Here members of the minority gradually lose all distinguishing characteristics, drop their original cultural practices at all points where they differ from those of the host society, and freely intermarry. After a while all that remains is possibly a foreign-sounding surname or a remembered origin. This clearly requires no gatekeepers, but indeed either their absence or gatekeepers committed to the assimilation project. A minority can only venture on this strategy if enough people in the host society are willing to accept it. The advantage for the minority is that before long all problems of being a minority disappear. However, this takes place at the cost of losing the original culture, and the intermediate steps as individuals break from it and link with the new one may well be painful. Just as majority societies have sometimes insisted on segregation, so they have also insisted on assimilation, for example by refusing to accept minority languages and insisting on putting minority children in schools that do not recognize their culture in the teaching of culturally relevant subjects. Host societies can be divided about their approach to assimilation. They can change their minds, with devastating consequences if members of a former minority are suddenly told that, after all, their cultural membership is remembered and their affiliation to the host society rejected. This was the experience of many assimilated and secularized Jews in Germany in the 1930s.

INTEGRATION

Between these two extremes lies the process that we can call *integration*. Here the minority retains key aspects of its distinctive culture and a sense of its identity, but in all other respects mixes freely with the host society and takes advantage of the opportunities it provides. Usually the divided life that this implies relates to a conception of private and public spheres. Private life, mainly domestic activity (family life, cuisine) and here including religion, will be kept within the culture, while public life (work, participation in formal associations) will take place within the host society.

In some respects this is a 'best of both worlds' model. The minority retains precious elements of its culture while losing none of the opportunities of the larger society; the larger society gains the commitment and loyalty to its institutions of a new population, and in addition gains from the presence of an additional set of cultural practices. However, it is also a model fraught with problems along the private/public line. Intermarriage is likely to become frequent following interaction with members of the majority society in the public sphere, and intermarriage of course threatens the minority culture within the private sphere. What happens in practice is that some members of the group intermarry while many do not; but behind this outcome lie many difficult dilemmas and choices for individuals and their families.

A CONTINUUM OF RELATIONS

These three concepts—segregation, assimilation, and integration—mark the formal extremes and mid-point of a continuum, but between segregation and integration and between assimilation and integration there are several other possibilities. For example, an assimilated group might retain some symbolic indicators of origins—celebration of certain holidays, wearing of certain emblems—which do not in any way hinder assimilation, but sustain some sense of continuity of a culture at least as folk memory. There is similarly scope for considerable variety in the number and type of areas of life 'reserved' for cultural separation in an integration model. In some cases interaction might be limited to economic transactions, apart from which an almost complete segregation is maintained.

So far we have assumed a simple case in which majority and minority cultures are somehow static. In practice this is unlikely. Both are likely to be changing: to some extent as a result of the interaction itself, but also for exogenous reasons. As we saw in Parts I and II, at the present time a number of important globalizing factors are at work. Global products are changing cultures in such important areas as eating habits, dress styles, and artistic and leisure practices. Transnational corporations either bring the employee and customer relations of one country to others, or develop a non-national corporate culture of their own. This means that the cultures with which majorities and minorities alike identify are constantly challenged by novelty and change. Responses to this can be very diverse. According to postmodernist theories, the change and heterogeneity induced combine with the heterogeneity of immigration to produce rapidly changing cosmopolitan cultures in which senses of specific belonging and of historical rootedness disappear, enabling individuals to *choose* their cultural identity from the available ensemble rather than having one imposed as an ascribed inheritance (Fishman: 1985; Soysal 1994). On the other hand, members of both majority and minority cultures might find globalization disturbing. This can lead members of majorities to blame immigrants for changes which really have nothing to do with them; and can lead minorities to develop extreme conservative defences of the traditional culture against all challenges from modernity. Certain forms of Islam and fundamentalist Christian groups currently provide the main examples of this.

Interaction between majorities and minorities also produces change itself. Alund and Schierup (1991) have shown how the cultures of immigrant groups in Sweden have not remained as static 'traditional' cultures, but have developed to become something new and different in response to the encounter with Swedish society. These changes, which can also affect a majority culture, can have diverse consequences. Under one model, host cultures become influenced by the minorities in them, with the consequence that the society to which the minority assimilates or within which it integrates now includes some elements of its own culture, which in turn has started to change itself in response to the encounter with the host culture. This process can reduce the strain of assimilation and integration processes. Such a concept lay behind the US model of the 'melting pot'. While all immigrant groups were 'melted down' in the sense of losing their specific characteristics, the substance from which they had been made then formed part of the pot within which others would be melted. As successive waves of immigrants entered, so they contributed parts of their culture to the mix that eventually becomes American culture. The USA is a special case here, being a society of immigrants; it is difficult for minorities in European host societies to have quite the same effect, though elements of it can be seen. Also, the capacity of a group to make a noticeable contribution will be varied, depending on its size, its influence and the strength of its culture.

At the same time, groups within majority and minority alike might resent the evidence that they see of practices from the other culture entering and thus 'diluting' their own, and may respond with hostility and extreme redefinitions of their cultures designed to change them so that they differ more from the other.

Both extremes of the range from assimilation to segregation are incompatible with sociological liberalism, as neither embodies the concept of a respect for mutual contributions within a shared frame. All intermediate positions that include some component of integration are however compatible. Dutch *verzuiling* would come somewhat towards the segregation end of an integration model, since in its classical form people of different denominations kept larger areas of their life separate than required strictly for religious purposes—but they did interact within a single Dutch society, so it is an integration model rather than a segregation one. In such a system, if the balance among groups shifts so that one or more become clearly less powerful than others, then *verzuiling* could slide into a ghetto model. One must remember that Dutch social thought underlay the former South African concept of *apartheid*—essentially a Dutch word.

It is also important for our purposes to relate to this analysis the contemporary idea of multiculturalism, as this seems to exemplify a postmodernist fragmentation of identities *away from* sociological liberalism, changing and in some respects destroying or transcending it (Glazer 1996; Gitlin 1995; Hollinger 1995; Waters 1990). According to its strongest definitions, mainly emerging from the USA, multiculturalism is a form of segregation. In the US context this means that, rather than groups being expected to conform to the melting pot, they should be enabled to remain separate for the foreseeable future. In particular there should be no pressure to learn the language of the new country or join the organizations of its formal political and associational life; rather, the host society should facilitate teaching of the language, history, and culture of the group, and should deal with its separate institutions. On the other hand, this can be seen as simply an adjustment of sociological liberalism, shifting the balance more to defending identities but still within a framework of integration with the main society. Although this discussion originates with the issue of ethnic minorities, it can be linked also to pressures for sub-state autonomies and to a general postmodernist deconstruction of national societies under pressures from globalization (Lapeyronnie 1993; Touraine 1992).[1]

TERRITORIAL MINORITY CULTURES

Our main test of the role of sociological liberalism within the mid-century compromise in the field of ethnicity and nationality will concern relations between dominant native cultures, on the one hand, and immigrant minorities and their descendants on the other. Significantly however, with the partial exception of the UK, these had not begun to arrive in large numbers in Western Europe until the 1960s, and hence after the formative years of the mid-century compromise. Attention also needs to be given to the question of the place of existing territorial minorities. Initially however it is necessary to establish some theoretical base for relating the model of sociological liberalism to study of inter-ethnic relations.

Determining whether a settled minority exists with sufficient distinctiveness to form a culture or even a nation is difficult. There need to be at least some firm signals and symbols that the group has consciousness of itself, though this can be problematic if there is widespread disagreement within the group over the use of these. Sometimes small minorities of cultural separatists within the wider minority try to articulate a separate identity but find that this is not widely shared. Since even the most successful examples of nation-state consciousness have their origins in deliberately constructed attempts of this kind, it is not so easy to dismiss such activities as 'artificial'. There will also be gradations from a general vague awareness of being interestingly distinct from some identified 'core' culture of the nation state, to outright demands for separate national status and secession. Within any group there are likely to be grades of opinion along this continuum. Ideally we would have at hand detailed studies on the strength of these sentiments across a wide range of groups. Unfortunately, however, the available literature is patchy in its coverage.

We might also want evidence of something more than sentiment to establish the reality of a group. One way of assessing this is to study easily measured aspects of actual behaviour. A path-breaking study of this kind is that of the American demographer, Susan Cotts Watkins (1991). She examined the fate of identities at levels below the European nation state through the lens of demographic change. In the discussion of family change in Chapter 7 we took for granted that we could work in terms of national units: the French birth rate, the Greek marriage rate, etc. But is there really such a thing as a French birth rate, rather than a Breton one, a Burgundian one, etc.? And are

---

[1] It is easy to exaggerate the unity of the US melting-pot concept. In practice American approaches to this have varied over time and according to ethnic groups. In the mid-nineteenth century there was considerable tolerance of multilingualism. This changed in the late nineteenth century as groups from outside Protestant northern Europe began to predominate in the waves of immigration, and there was far more pressure to inculcate a model of Anglophone Americanization in schools and elsewhere. Later, in the inter-war years various ethnic groups—still mainly European ones—began to organize themselves and became the most important base of popular political organization in the USA. When the black population began to stress ethnicity and the need for special rights in the 1960s it was not therefore initiating something totally new. There is scope for considerable oscillation between more segregationist and more assimilationist emphases within the integration model.

these more similar to each other than they are to, say, the Bavarian birth rate or the Hamburg one? The answer that Cotts Watkins gives is that by 1960 one could (for most nation states) make such national generalizations, but that 90 years before the internal diversity of today's nation states was far wider.

This might seem to be an odd way to examine national and other identities. Should we not look at expressed opinions, or the use of regional as opposed to national flags, the foundation of separatist movements? One problem here is that expressed opinions have been measured on such issues only for the past thirty or forty years, whereas the most important changes took place long before that. A second problem is that political movements are often attempts to construct or develop identities; they do not tell us whether there really are differences among the people whom, it is claimed, should be part of different nation states. The attraction of Cotts Watkins's use of birth rates and marriage behaviour is that it gets beneath symbolic questions that can be wielded politically while having no real sociological meaning, and takes us to elements of behaviour that are not easily manipulated. As she persuasively argues, views about the appropriateness of marriage and ideas about when to have children are likely to be discussed and developed among women, the area of consensus over a particular answer being broadly coterminous with their interlocking social circles. If there is a barrier to detailed communication, it is likely to form a boundary around certain practices of this kind. Therefore, if we find that women in one province have very different ages of marriage from those in a neighbouring one, that suggests that there is little interaction across the province boundary. Identities and loyalties of various kinds are likely to stop at that boundary too. If a state successfully breaks down that boundary, we should see a homogenization of marriage ages across the provincial divide.

Today both the European Union and various international trade agreements have considerably changed many of the means which Cotts Watkins analysed as nineteenth-century ways of securing national identities. There are still cross-national differences in the way people in different European countries dress and eat; but they are diminishing. Overall, however, during the nineteenth and twentieth centuries states built national rather than provincial societies. Discriminations in favour of persons from one's own region for purposes of making job appointments, forming marriages, choosing friends died out, but very gradually.

Was the eventual triumph of nation states a growth of sociological liberalism at the level of the nation, in the sense that place of origin within the national territory ceased to matter, ceased to affect chances in other aspects of life? We must recall that sociological liberalism implies a mutual tolerance; one institution does not interfere with another, but is permitted its own space. If therefore a sub-state identity is permitted to express itself and its culture while not intervening in other areas of society, a condition of sociological liberalism at the level of the nation state can be said to exist. If however the state has reduced the wider social influence of local identities only by suppressing them, then we cannot speak of liberalism. For example, when the English banned Scots from wearing the tartan and playing the bagpipes and encouraged them to regard themselves as 'North Britons', there was hardly sociological liberalism. Once they dropped these prohibitions, incorporated these symbols into the British Army itself and established a regime whereby different Scots and English legal and financial institutions could co-exist with considerable ease of exchange, one may describe such a condition.

Have the powerful emotional and political concentrations of power in nation states been deployed in a manner compatible with sociological liberalism in relation to other institutions within the boundaries of the nation state, and with respect to other nation states and their people? Do different socio-cultural groups organize elements of social life? On the basis of approaches of this kind it is possible to build up some kind of continuum of territorial subcultures for different countries. An attempt is made to do this in Table 10.1. It is offered as an impressionistic summary only, based on a wide range of different literature but not on a systematic study of evidence.

The starting assumption is that in most societies there will exist a 'core' subculture, one identifying itself before others with the core symbols of the nation state; if this core has some further subcultural identities these are not defined in ways that distance the group from another subculture which is in turn seen as being closer to the core. (Class and other identities within the group may stand in the way, but here we are concerned solely with alternative territorially based identities.) It is then assumed that there may be parts of the society where people see themselves as less close to the

Table 10.1 Regional subcultures in Western Europe and elsewhere

	Core groups	Soft subcultures	Hard subcultures	Separatist subcultures
A	Inhabitants of the capital, Vienna, would regard themselves as a core, but this would be rejected by various other subcultures who would regard Vienna as too cosmopolitan.			
	Vienna	Alpine communities Burgenland		
B	Neither of the two dominant subcultures can now regard itself as core, Belgium being seen as constituted by the two as distinct entities.			
			Flanders Wallonia (German-speakers)	Some Flemish and Walloon
DK	Danes	The various islands and Jutland		
SF	Finns		Swedes Lapps	
F	Paris and the Ile de France	Brittany Burgundy Provence Languedoc Normandy	Rousillon	Corsica
D	While there are certain distinct regional cultures, none of these successfully establishes itself as 'core'			
		Certain cities and regions	Bavaria	

Table 10.1 (continued)

	Core groups	Soft subcultures	Hard subcultures	Separatist subcultures
GR	Greeks		Small ethnic minorities	
IRL	Irish		English Protestant groups	
I	While there are certain distinct regional cultures, none of these successfully establishes itself as 'core'. However some are certainly marginal to any core while others can be separatist.			
		Mezzogiorno Sardinia Sicily	Alto Adige Some parts of Alpine French- and German- speaking groups	Lombardia and Veneto
NL	Dutch		Fresians	
N	Oslo would regard itself as the core, but rural groups would regard it as cosmopolitan (in a Scandinavian context) and therefore inadequately Norwegian.			
			Oslo (speakers of Riksmål) Rural periphery (speakers of Nynorsk) Lapps	
P	Portuguese			
E	Castille		Andalucia Navarra	Catalonia Basque country Galicia
S	Swedes		Lapps	
CH	German Swiss	French Swiss	Italian Swiss	
UK	Home Counties (South-east of England)	North and West of England	Wales	Scotland Northern Irish Protestants and Catholics
JAP	Japanese	Some rural groups seen as coming from different tribal roots		
USA	While there are certain distinct regional cultures, none of these successfully establishes itself as 'core'			
	White non- immigrants	The various regions	Native Americans	Blacks

nation-state core than others, and where certain symbols of difference are deployed, though with virtually no claims to a separate institutional identity. These are set out in Table 10.1 alongside the identified core group. Groups which have gone further than this and established various kinds of institutional or behavioural separations are indicated in a further column. Real survival of a regional language or dialect, for example, counts as evidence of an institutional separatism. The table does not distinguish between groups that actually demand political separation and those that simply maintain their separateness within an accepted nation state, as this is primarily a political rather than a social and cultural variable. Similarly it does not necessarily concern itself with territories of regional government, as these regions need not correspond to cultural identities.

As can be seen, there is considerable diversity here within modern Europe. In France, Spain, and the UK—three long-established, large, former colonial states—there is a clear sense of a core part of the nation state in the territories surrounding the national capital, with distinctive alternative identities developing as one moves to more remote regions. The strongest of these are in areas that had at some time in the past been autonomous states (e.g. Burgundy, Scotland, Catalonia), but there is now considerable difference in their relative importance. Two hundred years of a centralist state that had no place for culturally defined regions in its administrative map have finally weakened most of the sense of separateness in French regions that once either had a totally distinct language (as in Brittany) or had been autonomous kingdoms (Burgundy), though Cotts Watkins (1991) found evidence of the continuing demographic vitality of some of these below the surface. The population of the island of Corsica also produces powerful resistance movements to French authority. The Spanish state, on the other hand, has never been able to suppress the very strong cultural and linguistic nationalisms of Catalonia, the Basque country, Galicia, and Valencia, and now gives these more formal recognition than in the past. The British case lies somewhere between these two. As Cotts Watkins showed, for a long time more socially homogeneous though less determinedly centralist than the French state, the British one now finds strong residues of former autonomous nationhood in Scotland, linguistic survival in Wales, and a regionalism superimposed upon a religious and nationalist struggle sometimes leading to open violence in Northern Ireland.

During the early 1960s, the period hypothesized here to be a strong moment for sociological liberalism, there was in fact a low level of that quality in these three cases. Spain, as a Fascist country, clearly lay outside the terms of the compromise. But also in France and the UK there was little political tolerance of strong expressions of cultural diversity in any area that might have political implications; minority languages, for example, were not encouraged. The 1990s therefore appear as more strongly sociologically liberal than the so-called peak period. The most dramatic reversal has been in Spain, where politically, linguistically, and culturally a considerable level of diversity is now fully accepted. The UK has seen a growth, first in the acceptance of minority languages (mainly Welsh) and eventually by the mid-1990s political self-expression for Scotland and Wales. There has been far less change in France.

The two other large Western European states, Germany and Italy, lacked the strong centralizing historical forces of these three countries. One consequence is the absence of a 'core region' and in particular a core city able to establish a cultural hegemony.

Rome, once by far the Western world's most important city, might have achieved hegemony within modern Italy had it not been located in the poorer south of the country and had it not also included the Vatican, the headquarters of the Roman Catholic Church, which opposed an Italian nation state until the very last years of the nineteenth century. Even then, regional and city loyalties had become deeply embedded in Italian culture during centuries of city-state government, an absence of a central authority, and difficulties of communication caused by the country's mountainous terrain. The populations around such cities as Milan, Venice, Bologna, Florence do not see their culture as somehow subordinate to that of Rome. There are also distinct antagonisms between parts of the country, in particular one between north and south that follows fault lines of economic development. Northern and central Italy contain some of the richest regions of the modern world, while parts of the south and the islands are among the poorest in Europe—and the poverty takes the form of a failure of modernization, not a decline of former industry as in the UK. Nevertheless these tensions do not reach the level of separate *national* identities as are found in Catalonia or Scotland. (The recent advance of a separate northern creation to be called Padania by certain separatist groups in northern Italy has a contemporary political and economic, but no historical or sociological, meaning.)

Germany equally lacks a central core. The country's religious divisions and the fact that eventually it was unified under the leadership of a remote, backward, eastern region (Prussia, in particular Brandenburg and the area around Berlin) prevented that from occurring. The more advanced western parts never conceded that national leadership implied cultural hegemony. This historical characteristic was reinforced by the Second World War which divided the country for four decades and left Berlin, the former capital, split in half and within the East German state. However, post-war Germany has not developed the regional tensions in evidence in Italy. Even Bavaria—a former state with as good a claim to nationhood as Scotland or the dissident Spanish regions—while keeping certain emblems of isolation, developed its culture as a part of German culture, not as a separate Bavarian one. German post-war development strategy prevented the development of more than minor economic differences among regions. German cultural unity now faces new challenges following unification with the eastern *Länder*, but they are beyond the scope of this book.

The post-war German republic has been thoroughly sociologically liberal on these questions throughout the period. Similarly, Italian diversity has always had to be accepted de facto, and linguistic diversity as well as special political status for the border regions and islands were built into the post-war constitution. These two countries therefore score highly on this factor at both periods.

The smaller nations of Europe fall into two groups: the homogeneous and the diverse. The first includes Denmark, Greece, Ireland, Netherlands, Portugal, Sweden, with Austria and Norway being slightly exceptional. The second comprises Belgium, Finland, and Switzerland.

Denmark and Portugal are possibly the only countries to have no territorial minority cultures at all. There is a small Protestant community of English descent in Ireland; inhabitants of the Dutch region of Frisia sustain a language part-way between Dutch and English; there is a small Lapp community in northern Sweden; and minorities from various other Balkan states in various parts of Greece. Norway experienced considerable cultural conflict during the late nineteenth and early twentieth centuries as the country freed itself from a long legacy of Danish and Swedish rule. Nationalists tried to discover a rural Norwegian culture and in particular a language that had not been 'corrupted' by these influences. They constructed what was regarded as an original Norwegian language (though they called it *Nynorsk*, new Norwegian), which is still sustained by some rural inhabitants of Norway's long, isolated and sparsely populated terrain as a cultural opposition to Oslo and the urban speakers of *Riksmål*, 'official' Norwegian.

Austrians have historically experienced major problems over their cultural identity. Vienna was the capital of the German or Holy Roman Empire, but, failing to sustain a political and military hegemony over the various German states despite the widespread recognition of a shared German culture, the empire developed its power and strength in the Slav lands to the East. Over the years many people from these lands came to Vienna and other Austrian cities. The core population was therefore German with various subordinate Slav communities, as well as a large Jewish population. A sense of Austrian as opposed to German nationhood has really developed only since the establishment of the Second Republic after the Second World War.

In none of these countries has sociological liberalism been put to the test particularly strongly in terms of territorial minorities during the period under review. The situation has been very different and more complex in Belgium and Switzerland, which are both divided into distinctive language-based subcultures. The region of Belgium known as Wallonia has long been French-speaking, and historically this population formed the dominant group: the royal family and aristocracy, the main families of capitalist wealth and the main artistic life were all French-speaking. The capital city of Brussels has formed part of this world, though it is located in the Dutch-speaking part of the country, Flanders, and is therefore itself bilingual. There is also a small German-speaking minority. Since the Second World War Flanders has risen economically and demographically while Wallonia has declined, over 60% of the population now being Flemish-speaking. However, the cultural hegemony of the French speakers remains. There is therefore a complex interplay between different forms of dominance, and linguistic differences do not exactly parallel regional ones, largely because of the location of Brussels. It is no longer possible to describe either French or Dutch culture as the 'core' one; this has been reflected in the country's constitutional arrangements, whereby nearly all domestic political affairs have been decentralized to regional and linguistic bodies.

The Swiss have long known this kind of complexity. The religious pattern discussed in the previous chapter follows different fault lines from the linguistic differences, creating a large number of subcultures. (For example, there are French- and German-speaking Catholics, and French- and German-speaking Protestants.) Although the German language is clearly dominant it is not a true core culture, as French-speaking Switzerland includes some major parts of the country. The Italian cantons are clearly more minoritarian and marginal, as is the residual group speaking the old Swiss language, Romansh. Again, political arrangements reflect and re-create this heterogeneity.

Switzerland has therefore long had sociological liberalism built into its structure on these issues; Belgium has increasingly acquired it in recent years.

Disputes over an imposed nation-state identity continue to produce violent incidents in the Spanish Basque country, Corsica, and Northern Ireland, and separatist political parties are important in Flanders, Scotland, Wales, Lombardy, the Veneto, and several parts of Spain. However, with these important exceptions historical ethnic intolerance and difficulties have declined in importance in most Western European states in recent decades. In some countries there has been a stable situation of sociological liberalism throughout the period; in some others—Belgium, Spain, the UK—it has notably increased in recent years. To that extent the 1990s represent more of a 'peak' than our so-called peak of the early 1960s.

IMMIGRANT MINORITIES

We can now consider the situation of recent immigrant minorities and their descendants. Apart from the UK, few countries had experienced much inward migration of this kind by the 1960s, and it is not possible to give a good statistical account, as few countries had useful means of identifying such populations at the earlier time. We shall therefore consider (in Table 10.2) a comparison between 1965 and 1990 for just one country, Germany, which has become one of the largest immigrant countries, and one which had clearly not been an instance of sociological liberalism on this issue in the pre-war period. The growth is too large to require comment. For most Western European countries sociological liberalism had not been 'put to the test' on this question in the 1960s, the high point of the mid-century compromise. In an important respect therefore immigrant communities were not parties to that compromise in Western Europe. They come afterwards, and contribute to a period when postmodern concepts are perhaps producing a different form of social compromise, one based more on ideas of multiculturalism.

Immigration into at least some Western European countries has been of three kinds: as in the late nineteenth century, from areas of Western Europe not benefiting from

Table 10.2 Foreign population resident in Germany, 1965 and 1990

Origins	1965	1990	% change
All Europe	525,200	2,101,700	300.17
Western Europe	407,200	1,439,000	253.39
Greek	42,000	320,200	662.38
Italian	197,000	552,400	180.41
Spanish	44,000	135,500	207.95
Eastern Europe	118,000	904,700	666.69
Polish		242,000	
Yugoslav	16,000	662,700	4,041.88
Turkey	7,000	1,694,600	24,108.57

Source: Germany: *Statistisches Jahrbuch* (various years).

progress (e.g. from Italy and Spain to Germany; from Portugal to France); from colonies and former colonies to the old imperial country (e.g. from the Indian subcontinent and the Caribbean to the UK; from North Africa and Indochina to France; from south-east Asia and the Caribbean to the Netherlands (S. Castles and M. J. Miller 1993: 71–3)); and from developing countries, usually when special labour migration agreements were signed with Western European governments (e.g. from Turkey to Germany). By the 1960s the Nordic countries began to recruit foreign workers, initially from southern Europe and then from further afield. It is remarkable that these migrations, some of them involving large geographical and cultural journeys, pre-date the move of women from domestic life to the economy. To express it graphically, the journey from a valley in India to the factories of a northern English town often proved easier to make than that from a kitchen in the same town.

During the full-employment years of the 1960s these migrations were welcomed and encouraged by governments and employers in the host countries as a means of allevi- ating labour shortages. They were however organized in various different ways and, as S. Castles and M. J. Miller (1993: 39) show, had different implications for the citizenship rights and other aspects of the subsequent position of immigrants in their new coun- try. As Withol de Wenden (1988) has argued, there is an extraordinary diversity of approaches to the rights of foreigners among Western European countries. It is not simply a question of citizenship rights, as citizenship can be detached from the status of resident, which in turn can acquire varied social and economic rights. In several cases the treatment of migrant workers was organized explicitly in treaties between governments of the receiving and sending countries. Often, and particularly in the Ger- man case, they were seen as labour-only migrations: migrants would come as workers, normally young men without families; and after a time they would return with their savings to their country of origin. There would be no dependent children, no sick people, no elderly; if they became unemployed or incapacitated they would return, or be sent, home. They therefore imposed no burdens on the local welfare state, and re- ceived no rights in the new country.

By the early 1970s these migration models had changed, and in contrary directions. The years of labour shortage were ending and high unemployment was returning to Western Europe; also the presence of people from remote cultures, small in number though they were, was creating antagonistic responses from some parts of the native societies. Governments began to close down immigration schemes or to ban new arrivals. On the other hand, the model of the temporary male labour migrant who would eventually return home was becoming unrealistic. Although it is estimated that over half the 20 million guest workers recruited into Western European countries between the end of the war and the general end to recruitment around 1973 did return home, the same economic downturn that produced the recruitment block now also made return home to countries with even worse economic difficulties unattractive (Münz 1996). The workers stayed and were joined by other members of their family; young women joined the young men; they married and had children. They began to make the same demands on the welfare state as natives, and since their population consisted primarily of young adults their birth rate was usually higher than that of the existing population.

When immigration was supporting vigorous growth it created fewer social tensions than when there were employment crises (Limousin 1988). During the decades of eco-nomic growth following the Second World War employers and officials tolerated and even encouraged clandestine immigration in order to strengthen the workforce (Marie 1988). This tolerance could change as economic conditions worsened. Hochet (1988) points out that there were as many foreigners in France in 1930 as in the late 1980s, and Etienne (1988: 115) argues that in Marseille the foreign population of 1936 was *double* what it had become fifty years later. However, it was during the latter period that a primarily Arab minority was defined as highly problematic in French political debate.

Ancient Roman concepts of citizenship continued to determine the ways in which modernizing European nation states perceived the issue. Some, particularly the British, still conscious of having been an imperial power, maintained the Roman imperial model: if one was born anywhere in the territories of the Roman (British) Empire, one could call oneself its citizen. The Roman *civis romanus sum* became *civis brittanicus sum*. In other countries (for example France) where citizenship was based on the Roman con-cept of *jus solis* (literally, the law of soil, or the acquisition of citizenship according to the territory in which a person was born), the descendants of immigrants could gain citizenship relatively easily.

In Germany matters were different. Germans, having been a people longer than they had been members of a shared nation state, had developed a concept of themselves as joined by common descent, or *jus sanguinis* (law of blood relations). This had enabled not only the inhabitants of the different little states that constituted historical Ger-many to see themselves as part of the same group, but also those whose ancestors had migrated to the Slav lands of the east. It is thought that from 1950 to 1994 around 3.2 million of these ethnic Germans left Poland, Romania, Russia, and Central Asia for the Federal Republic (Münz 1996); in addition more than 5 million citizens of the Soviet-bloc state of East Germany moved across the border to West Germany during the years of the existence of the former state (1949–90); for much of the period these movements were not counted as cross-border at all by the Federal authorities, who did not recognize the existence of the border that divided their country (Leggewie 1996: 4). Accordingly, granting formal citizenship rights and the less formal sense of 'being German' to the son or daughter of a Turkish guest worker presented difficulties to German law-makers.

However, contrasts between Germany and other countries should not be exagger-ated. By the early 1970s France had decided that the powers of assimilation of the French republic did not easily extend to non-Europeans, and that therefore north African immigrants should be encouraged to return 'home' (Schain 1985). British governments gradually reduced the rights of inhabitants of Commonwealth countries to emigrate to the UK unless they had at least one grandparent who was born in that country—a clear case of *jus sanguinis* rather than an imperial citizenship right. Furthermore, less legal but sometimes more substantive elements of what (as we shall see in Chapter 13) con-stitute the rights of citizenship, such as access to the welfare state, were gradually accorded to guest workers in Germany, their families, and their descendants. Indeed, it has been argued that, given that the German welfare state is so much more generous than the US one, a non-citizen immigrant to Germany probably has more substantive rights than a citizen immigrant in the USA (Soysal 1994).

In a further paradox, West Germany, while being the state that had most difficulty with immigration, became the European country which had the largest number of immigrants. This happened for a number of reasons. First, as the most prosperous large country in Europe Germany was attractive to immigrants. Second, partly consequent on Germany's appalling record of treatment of ethnic minorities during the Nazi period, the Federal Republic, while not wanting to be a country of immigration, was willing to offer shelter to refugees and asylum seekers on generous terms. Third, located where it is, a highly wealthy country on the frontier of west and east, it was a highly attractive location, first for escapees from eastern-bloc countries during the Soviet period, and more recently as a migration target for people from those territories seeking a more prosperous life.

Therefore, against the expectations of the early post-war decades, the countries of Western Europe, instead of becoming territories of easy but temporary access for guest workers, have become territories of difficult access for permanently settled ethnic minorities, with a gradual extension of citizenship rights to these non-citizens (Guiraudon 1998).

THE DEMOGRAPHY OF IMMIGRANT COMMUNITIES AND THEIR DESCENDANTS

Figure 10.1 (based on Appendix Table A.10.1) gives for recent years an indication of the proportion of the populations of Western European countries who can be regarded as immigrants (or at least as resident foreigners), or (in some cases) as the recent descendants of immigrants. As usual, there are major problems in the accuracy and comparability of these data.[2] We can however see the relative importance of particular world zones for European immigration. The different patterns of origins of minorities in the different countries is striking. As S. Castles and M. J. Miller (1993: 19–24) argue, immigration is not an economic process whereby individuals seek to maximize their opportunities in global labour markets, but a socio-political one. Governments (both

---

[2] First, widespread immigration into virtually all these countries has become illegal and yet takes place; illegal immigrants are unlikely to declare their existence to official census authorities and are therefore almost certainly under-reported. Second, there is a difference between resident foreigners and persons born abroad, though the categories overlap. Persons born abroad will not be regarded as foreign if they have citizenship of the country to which they are emigrating; this may mean that they are a member of the 'native' group of the host country whose family has been living abroad, or they may be members of a former colony and have citizenship according to its imperial concept. Whether second- and subsequent generation populations are defined as members of foreign groups will depend on a country's citizenship law. In the German *jus sanguinis* case all such persons (except the small number who have been able to acquire formal German citizenship) will be listed. Third, Germans returning to Germany from Central and Eastern Europe are not recorded in these statistics at all: for the German statistical office they are simply Germans coming home (Leggewie 1996: 4). Finally, the British do not calculate their data on the basis of precise national origins (apart from residents from other European Union states), but use a very broad racial criterion which gives no indication of the heterogeneous character of white immigration.

In setting out this analysis I have used a different geographical pattern from that adopted by most national authorities, in order to place greater emphasis on relative proximity to Europe and to give a very rough indication of cultural zones. This means three things in particular: distinguishing between Central and Eastern Europe, on the one hand, and Western, on the other—a division of major economic, political, and often cultural significance for the entire post-war period; distinguishing between Mediterranean Africa (the so-called Near East, geographically and historically a zone very close to Western Europe), and sub-Saharan Africa; and generally breaking down the culturally and geographically useless concept of 'Asia' into its various constituent parts. Unfortunately, the aggregation process of many national statistical services does not enable this to be fully achieved.

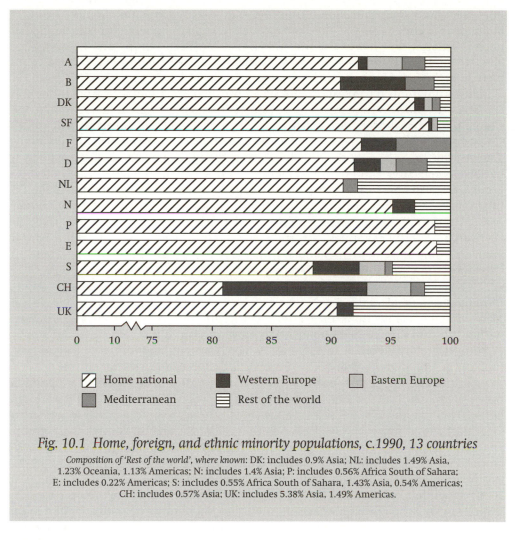

Fig. 10.1 Home, foreign, and ethnic minority populations, c.1990, 13 countries

Composition of 'Rest of the world', where known: DK: includes 0.9% Asia; NL: includes 1.49% Asia,
1.23% Oceania, 1.13% Americas; N: includes 1.4% Asia; P: includes 0.56% Africa South of Sahara;
E: includes 0.22% Americas; S: includes 0.55% Africa South of Sahara, 1.43% Asia, 0.54% Americas;
CH: includes 0.57% Asia; UK: includes 5.38% Asia, 1.49% Americas.

sending and receiving ones) have shaped policies to encourage some movements and
discourage others; migrants themselves have established communities.

Appendix Table A.10.2 enables us to compare the totally different situation in the
USA. In that territory (as in Canada and Australia) the original population had been
subject to a genocide during the nineteenth century by European immigrants, who
then constituted the core population of the modern society. In addition to noting the
origins of recent immigrants, the US census authorities enable 'existing' Americans to
indicate their general lines of ancestry if they wish. Since people can nominate more
than one such ancestry the total figure amounts to more than 100%. This is of course a
heterogeneity not experienced by any European country.

Bearing in mind all the defects of the data, we can at least draw a number of
broad conclusions. There has been an extraordinary growth in migration to Western

European lands since 1960. Some countries—in general those most remote from the main areas of emigration (i.e. the Nordic countries) and those which at that period had not yet entered the club of the prosperous (i.e. southern Europe and Ireland)—had virtually no immigrants in 1960. In the former case this situation has changed completely; in the latter it has begun to change.

Many immigrants into Western Europe are Moslems, or Hindus, or from other non-Christian religions. Even when they are Christian, as with the great majority of people from the Caribbean, they are usually members of distinctive churches. They often speak non-European languages or, as in the case of West Indians in Britain, distinctive dialects; this can create more difficulties than a foreign language, as they are likely to be seen as speaking 'bad English' rather than a distinctive language. Nearly all these groups are also easily distinguished by skin colour. These various points make immigrants a target for hostility among certain groups within the majority culture. Assimilationist strategies are therefore problematic. Integration may be tried and there are significant examples of its success, but it is difficult, especially if it is hard to secure housing and employment outside the networks of the minority itself. There are therefore strong pressures towards segregation.

Intra-European Immigrants

Many 'foreign' populations in Western European countries come from elsewhere within Western Europe, with a particular emphasis on those from close and similar cultures (Dutch and French to Belgium; French, German, and Italian to Switzerland; Irish to the UK). In the earlier period Europeans dominated the scene entirely.

As in the late nineteenth century, these groups will probably pursue an assimilationist path, especially where, as with southern European immigrants in France, the cultural and linguistic boundaries are low and Catholic origins ensure few barriers to intermarriage. Within capital cities and other major immigrant centres these groups in turn continue the process they began in the last century of amending the native cultural pattern a little after the manner of the melting pot. However, the ease of this assimilation must not be exaggerated. Recent French historians have found it useful to remind their fellow citizens of the melting pot (le creuset) character of their own society (Noiriel 1988). Schnapper's contention (1991) that immigrants in France, unlike in the USA, found their place as individuals not as groups in ghettos is refuted by Noiriel's work on the location of Italian, Belgian, and other immigrants in different parts of late nineteenth-century France and the difficulties they experienced, long before consternation at the formation of north African ghettos in Paris, Marseille, and elsewhere in the past few decades (Schain 1996). Milza (1988) points out that although Italians and their descendants integrated fully into French society, this took a lengthy period and occurred during periods of economic growth and reduced social competition.

Ex-Colonial Immigrants

By the 1990s we see a particularly strong presence of immigrants from former colonies (in France, from the Near East and Indochina; in the Netherlands from the Far East and Caribbean; in the UK from the Caribbean and the Indian subcontinent). The former French colonies in the North African Near East, Western Europe's close neighbour, are particularly important, but (with some exceptions that will be considered below) the same is not true of sub-Saharan Africa, whose populations have been so poor and so disconnected from the world of population movements that few of them have moved to their former colonial countries (mainly Belgium, France, the UK).

These groups have often encountered severe difficulties in establishing their relationship to their new country, with the exception of descendants of previous settlers from the original country (e.g. white Australians coming to the UK) who assimilate virtually immediately. Most of these people come from Third World societies, which not only means that they have cultures quite different from those which they find in Europe, but also that they are often poor and therefore congregate in areas of poor-quality housing and in low-skilled jobs. Even if they possess high skills in their own countries, immigrants are likely to find it difficult to find corresponding employment, partly because it may be difficult to secure recognition for these skills, and partly because they lack the personal contacts that often have to accompany formal skills in the pursuit of good employment.

Meanwhile, younger generations of immigrants want to move beyond the position of their parents as rather marginal manual workers doing jobs that natives did not want to undertake. This can increase the sense of competition between them and natives (Leveau and Withol de Wenden 1988).

Labour Recruitment Schemes

We also see evidence of the special recruitment schemes, such as the Turks in Germany. In these cases, where both the host society and the immigrants initially saw the engagement as a temporary labour-only migration, the idea of assimilation or integration in the new society is particularly difficult, and a reinforcement of the segregation implied by temporary labour status becomes particularly likely.

As we discussed in Chapter 8 in connection with education, there are often alternative mechanisms, where Germany and the USA serve as particularly strong contrasts. Faist (1993) demonstrates this in a comparative study of young German Turks and US Mexicans who fail to gain access to higher education. Both groups suffer from social exclusion, but in different ways. In Germany young Turks find it difficult to gain access to the vocational training system that provides the best forms of employment for those who do not have university education. On the other hand, works councils have worked hard to assist the employment of Turks in mass-production industry, and many young Turks are found training for the artisanal or craft sector. In the USA, in contrast, there is not the same formal corporatist organization of education and training opportunities and therefore fewer formal obstacles to participation. On the other hand, US pluralism is organized on lines of ethnic loyalties and solidarities; young Mexicans do not receive help from trade unions, and they are particularly *under*-represented in the craft sector.

Alba, Handl, and Müller (1994) demonstrate the educational disadvantages experienced by ethnic minorities in Germany. However, they also show that much of this can be explained by cultural disadvantages (in particular parental competence with the German language), which should be expected to decline with time. Also, among the four ethnic groups they studied (Greeks, Italians, Turks, and Yugoslavs), it was Italians and Turks who suffered most disadvantages and Greeks the least. This suggests that the problems are not specifically 'Turkish' or 'Islamic'.

Eastern and Central European Immigrants

For Austria, Germany, and Scandinavia the main current sources of immigrants are the countries of Central and Eastern Europe. During the period of the Soviet bloc people from this region entered the West with great difficulty, often at the risk of being shot by border guards; on arrival in the West they were given a special welcome. Now that they can come easily they find that Western nations have replaced the so-called Iron Curtain with their own border guards, immigration controls, and a tendency to refuse admission. However, many have succeeded in gaining entry, mainly to Germany and Austria. Four million Central and Eastern Europeans left their home countries between the fall of the Berlin wall in 1989 and 1993 (Fassmann and Münz 1994), while as many as 5 million more left former Yugoslavia because of the civil wars of the early 1990s. The data presented here having been collected during that time, former inhabitants of that territory loom particularly large; at a slightly later date many Albanians began to enter Italy following upheavals in their own country.

The Immigrations of African Poverty

Finally, there are now some migrations from such east African countries as Somalia and Ethiopia, where major economic problems are driving people northwards. These often arrive in Italy and Spain, and more recently also Greece and Portugal, countries accustomed to being centres of emigration rather than the opposite and completely unprepared both administratively and in terms of everyday interaction for the new situation (S. Castles and M. J. Miller 1993: 81–2). These immigrants are usually among the world's poorest people, and in Europe they eke out a totally marginal existence, being more or less homeless and working as beach or street traders, their presence usually being illegal and giving them no rights whatsoever to services.

SOCIOLOGICAL LIBERALISM, MULTICULTURALISM, OR WHAT?

It would be difficult to argue that the pattern of settlement of most non-European immigrations to Western Europe exhibits the sociological liberalism of modern societies in action (Schierup 1998). Tendencies towards ghettos will be found wherever people of contrasted cultures live. Immigrants and their descendants tend to establish residential communities. Access to places of worship, preferred cultural and recreational activities, shops selling familiar foods, dress styles partly shape this. So do a series of informal and formal processes whereby both host society and immigrants seek the company of those familiar to them and avoid that of 'strangers'. Landlords, house purchase finance agencies, employers, and local governments tend to steer immigrants towards some areas and away from others. Immigrants themselves will often want the company of people of familiar appearance, language and remembered past way of life. Ghettos clearly inhibit assimilation and tend towards segregation rather than integration.

Two examples of opposite policy leading to the same outcome demonstrate the difficulty of ethnic relations. The German authorities, not wanting Turks to try to become German, provided special teaching in Turkish language and culture and in the Moslem religion for guest workers and their children. The aim was to encourage them to seek their future back in Turkey, though ironically the strategy amounted to the same as would result from a separatist multicultural demand; it certainly involved no forced assimilation into German culture. Since return to Turkey was not seen as desirable by most of these families, they have remained in Germany but with the segregationist mode of behaviour that had been pressed on them by German 'gatekeepers'. As a result there are often complaints from Germans that Turks are incapable of integrating or assimilating.

The French republic has, as would be expected, been more severely assimilationist. It has for example banned Islamic religious symbols (such as the wearing of veils by girls and women) from French schools. This has caused considerable conflict. French people have resented the demands; the north Africans have seen the ban as a threat to their religious practice and many of them have responded by adopting a segregationist mode, the strains of integration being difficult to bear when the host society makes such assimilationist demands. The issue has to be seen in the French context. It was through such strategies that French national society was built among the disparate provinces that constituted the population of French territory; banning the symbols of the Catholic Church (such as wearing a crucifix around the neck) from the schools of the republic had been important in establishing that republic as secular. This had involved severe conflict with the Church for many years.

The French republic would defend itself against the charge of authoritarianism on this matter by pointing to the distinction it has long drawn between public and private life. In private, one could display a crucifix as much as one wanted, but not while in the public institutions of the republic, of which school is an example. Having asserted this stance against the Christian religion of the majority of the French population for two centuries, it is not easy for France to treat differently the Islamic religion of a fairly small minority. However, the Islamic religion does not share the Christian concept of a separation of the heavenly and earthly kingdom, which was a fundamental historical building block in the construction of European sociological liberalism. For certain— though not all—denominations of Islam a woman must always wear the veil outside the home; for a state to rule otherwise is a blasphemy and an interference with the will of God. Such actions by the French government have been interpreted by many Moslems as a mark of the impossibility of coming to terms with French society and has strengthened the voices of segregationist strategies, therefore having the opposite result to that intended by the French state. Increasingly north African immigrants organize themselves through primarily Islamic associations separate from French ones (Barou 1994).

This all challenges deeply what might be called the 'pre-sociological' rational universalism of republican French nation building: the French republic treats people as individuals, not as members of groups; it is therefore blind to ethnicity in a liberal way (for an example of this approach to ethnic integration, see Schnapper 1991). However, if the lives of individuals are deeply affected by their ethnicity and the ethnicity of those around them, this liberalism is achieved by viewing the individual in only some of his or her attributes. As with the individuals of economic theory, individuals are not 'people' but analytical units. In the French case this is reconciled with reality because one's life as a citizen of the republic relates to only certain parts of one's personality— the messy ethnicity-ridden, province-ridden, gender-ridden parts being left to the private sphere. This can simply mean that public life ignores problems that eventually force their way to its attention.

Conflicts between hosts, on the one hand, and immigrants and their descendants, on the other, are not always as incorrigible as this one. Uniformed British public services have permitted Sikhs from India to wear the distinctive turbans that are for them an important religious symbol rather than the peaked cap of the uniform; however, a peaked cap does not have the same resonance for the unity of the British state as does the absence of religious symbols for the French republic. Swedish society, ethnically one of the most homogeneous in the world, has accommodated a wide range of multi-cultural arrangements designed to make a totally new space within Swedish society for diversity. It will take a number of years to discover whether this multiculturalism becomes an occasion for irredentist separatism, a postmodern fragmentation of cultures that have little to do with each other, or helps ease an integration of a textbook kind that would become a clear instance of sociological liberalism. (For a discussion of how multiculturalist assumptions might be more consistent with sociological liberalism in a German context than in a US one, see Leggewie 1994 and 1996; for France, see Schnapper 1991.) Meanwhile the small size of immigrant groups in Europe, together with the strength of the nation-state model of citizenship, have considerably limited any major impact on these societies (Joppke 1998a, 1999).

The recent waves of immigration from the East and across the Mediterranean have coincided with a time of rising long-term unemployment and pressure on social services in Western Europe. The combination has been difficult, and makes it difficult to analyse the emerging situation as one of cheerful postmodernist heterogeneity. Governments have tightened their controls over immigration, and private acts of intolerance and sometimes violence against minorities have increased considerably (Wiegand 1992). Several violent incidents have occurred in Germany; perhaps no more than in other countries, but arousing particular memories of the last period of mass unemployment in the 1930s. Eurobarometer surveys have from time to time measured feelings towards immigrants from outside Western Europe within EU countries. They report a considerable jump in hostility since the late 1980s (Hofrichter and Klein 1994). In both France and the UK, the combination of acquisition of a 'European' identity and rejection of a past nationalistic and imperial role has had the paradoxical effect of creating new barriers against immigrants from Third World communities which had developed strong cultural and linguistic links with the former imperial power (Krulic 1988).

At the same time, attempts at integration or assimilation continue. Evidence of them can be seen in the rising levels of educational success among ethnic minorities and, perhaps most significantly, intermarriage between members of minority and majority populations (Leggewie 1996: 2; Tribalat 1995). Growing minorities of young Germans and Turks, French people and North Africans, English people and Indians are building lives together.

Immigrant minorities were outside the terms of the mid-century compromise in Western Europe, if only because they had not yet arrived in the subcontinent in more than small numbers. Here the compromise was far more in evidence in the USA. Since that time one can identify a few developments in the majority of countries which change that situation, but in general it still could not be claimed that sociological liberalism was seen at its strongest in this aspect of social relations. For Europeans, taming the mutually antagonistic ethnicities of their nation states was the first and biggest challenge after they had brought the world to two savage wars in the first half of the century. Coping with existing internal heterogeneity was a second, smaller task. Relations with new immigrant groups is an issue still being encountered.

Part IV

CITIZENSHIP

Some of the institutions discussed in the previous Part, particularly the family and religion, are those which pre-dated the onset of capitalist, industrialist society and required some kind of 'protection' if they were to survive their encounter with these two disruptive and creative forces. There are other elements of society which were produced by capitalist industrialism but which could similarly be overwhelmed by it. The main examples were the subordinate social classes which were the product of industrialization, but whose social position was not secured by capitalism itself since they owned little property. Somewhat differently, industrial and capitalist activity has a number of general needs for social infrastructure and various forms of support—including the purchasing capacity of the mass population—which cannot easily be provided by the market process itself.

According to the pure theory of capitalist markets, the underprivileged have no particular need for concern. The operation of competition and the laws of supply and demand should prevent accumulations of property and extreme concentrations of income and wealth. As for infrastructural needs, the incentive of capitalists to meet the wants of customers should ensure that demand for goods and services not currently met by the market will eventually be so if in genuine demand. It is beyond our task in this book to investigate the validity of these contentions of the self-rectifying characteristics of market processes. However, it has historically been the case that working classes in particular have not been prepared to trust these assurances but have sought other, non-market means of securing economic security, basic provision of health services, education, and welfare, and some constraint on the degree of economic inequality generated by the labour market. The main outcome has been a politics of redistribution and a political concern for ensuring that basic goods and services are provided by some criteria of right or desert that are not directly expressed through the market.

These concerns have overlapped with the other question of the provision of social infrastructure. Examples are a network of public roads, or an educated workforce (the latter overlapping heavily with popular demand for educational opportunities). There has also been suspicion that the market cannot itself deal with some forms of damage produced by the dynamic energy of industrialism but which is not part of the arena of market transactions—what economists call 'externalities', environmental pollution being the main example. As with issues of redistribution and the expected shares of different social classes, there are solutions proposed to these problems from within the market framework, but again there has historically been widespread lack of confidence in the efficacy of these. Or, even if market processes can be devised for, say, reducing pollution, it is frequently argued that markets will only do this job if they and their incentives are in some way managed and varied by political action.

It is not our task to pronounce on the relative merits of these arguments, merely to note that in many countries there has been a search for institutions other than the market to address these issues. This has usually taken the form of demands for 'public' action, public here being contrasted with market processes which are seen as essentially private. Various voluntary and organizational forms can be part of this public, but the most important in modern societies has been the state. It is the body which is seen as having a general responsibility for externalities. In societies where there is mass participation in politics, or political democracy, there is the further question that groups who feel let down by the operation of the market can seek remedies in state actions.

This leads us to the issue of citizenship. In a highly influential essay in 1950, the British sociologist T. H. Marshall (1963) suggested that entitlement to certain levels of social welfare and levels of living should become an aspect of the rights of citizens, just as they were entitled to the rights to judicial process and to vote. To the extent that he was describing a development that was taking place at that time, particularly in Britain and in Scandinavia, as much as advocating something as desirable in principle, he was dealing with a major component of the mid-century compromise. Citizenship implies a capacity both to seek action for what one defines as the public good, and to have the right to benefit from any such action.

Our consideration of this area starts (in Chapter 11) with the political process itself. In what ways have the various social interests we have identified in earlier chapters— classes, genders, ethnic groups—managed to have themselves represented politically? This requires a discussion of systems of representation, which is for our purposes mainly a matter of political parties and their electoral support bases. If mid-century society saw political representation of the major interests around which it was organized, what is happening now in this field to parallel the changes that have taken place in that model?

Alongside political parties within the state itself, various social interests have founded formal organizations to work for them outside the direct possibilities afforded by market and state, or often to enhance their activity within these two arenas. These are the themes of Chapter 12. Such rationally and instrumentally focused organizations can be seen as a quintessentially modernist replacement of the diffuse, unreflective mechanisms of community in traditional societies. Formal organizations of this type have often developed in a dialectical relationship with community subcultures, both building on them while transcending them. Class has often served as the mediating mechanism for this process. Meanwhile, post-Fordist, postmodernist, and some post-industrial theories predict a fragmentation of these organizational structures within the context of their anticipated decline of mass populations (whether perceived occupationally as in post-Fordism and post-industrialism, or culturally as in postmodernism. Does such a collapse occur? To the extent that it does, is it replaced by fragmented localism ('back to community') or by an absence of organization? If the latter, does this mean societies with neither traditional community nor rationalist organization as bases of social cooperation?

A major hypothesis of developmental sociology is that welfare states 'replace' affective ties and ascriptive communities during the course of modernization. In those countries which industrialized during the nineteenth century, however, this development tended to take place after the initial stages of industrialization when working-class organizations had become able to express demands for their admission into citizenship. It is this later stage that we have identified as the antecedent of mid-century compromise society. The welfare state became the major mechanism through which groups unwilling to trust pure market processes have tried to secure what they believed to be the basic needs of human welfare and also to limit material inequalities. These are discussed in Chapter 13.

There are some problematic issues here. If the welfare state replaces institutions like family and church, how is the tension between mass citizenship and community managed? And what are the implications of any post-industrial, post-Fordist, or postmodernist movements away from the mid-century model? As with some other institutions that we have considered, there are contradictory indicators. On the one hand, we have already seen in Part I that employment in the welfare sector has been a major motor of the move to post-industrialism. On the other hand, some elements of post-Fordist and postmodernist theory would predict a decline in the welfare state; it can be seen as part of the rationalization embodied in social modernization, in that it replaces the diffuse, affective efforts at human welfare of family and community by specialized expert institutions.

The relationship between citizenship and community is therefore not straightforward, and while we cannot here examine the philosophy of this difference in detail, some preliminary discussion is required. Central to the strong concept of citizenship is the idea that certain aggregates of human beings can be said to form communities, in the sense that within a sphere where a certain kind of common identity is acknowledged among members, there is acceptance of mutual obligations and rights. In the essay cited above, Marshall (1963) saw citizenship rights deriving from membership of a shared community of felt joint experience, not from an abstract rationalistic entity. In practice the nation state has been the most effective level for establishing mutual recognition of this kind, and that is certainly the entity that Marshall had in mind. However, this is not without its difficulties. Although community is frequently used in ordinary speech to denote groups which constitute little more than 'an aggregate of persons', within strict sociological theory it should refer only to such aggregates within which there are dense, frequent, and important interpersonal interactions and relations of reciprocity. Society is here used to describe all secondary, impersonal, and non-affective relationships. (The *locus classicus* for this analysis is the important distinction between society and community (*Gesellschaft* and *Gemeinschaft*) established by Tönnies (1887) and central to much late nineteenth-century sociology.)

Under citizenship, participation and entitlements are acquired through membership of a formally constituted political entity. In contrast, allocations within community institutions are based on affect and custom, the major examples being families, households, and informal groups. Both active and passive participation in community are defined by a complex web of rules, but there are no formal processes for claiming one's rights as exist for citizens. Within a community claims have to be based on moral and emotional appeals to fairness, past practice, or the mere fact that one is a member of the community.

Advocacy of citizenship rights often co-opts the attributes of community or altruistic moral commitment. (For example, see Richard Titmuss's (1970) analysis of the UK's voluntary blood transfusion service as the embodiment of the principles of the welfare state; in practice the model of a voluntary service based on altruism is not paradigmatic for British or any other welfare state service delivery.) However, the formal, legal, and bureaucratic institutions of citizenship differ in crucial respects from this and have often been its enemy; the arbitrariness, family character, and lack of universality of community are often a major impediment to the egalitarian and universalist aspirations of citizenship. This was true for liberal republican post-1789 French concepts, in which intermediate loyalties of locality, guild, and above all church were seen as standing in the way of the citizen's relationship with the state. It has also been true of twentieth-century social democratic welfare-state versions, where the inequalities of these same intermediate entities, but in particular perhaps the family, were seen as major enemies of the spread of citizenship.

Marshall and many other citizenship writers try to resolve these problems by relying on the tradition which depicts the nation state as a kind of community which somehow retains the senses of belonging and identity while also attaining a kind of universalism. In fact of course the so-called 'universe' defined by a nation state, even a large one, is very restrictive. As we saw in Chapter 10, states define themselves in arbitrary, affective terms similar to those of community. As we also saw, the community attributes of nation states are in reality invented or, at best, 'imagined' (Anderson 1983). Neither true communities nor genuinely universal, states claim to have and even to embody both these mutually inconsistent attributes. To put the claim in Scandinavian terms, if national social policy can retain a proper sense of 'caring', it can remain a community or a *folkshemma* (people's home). Meanwhile, acquiring the size of a nation state (even a small one of Scandinavian size), enables it to outgrow the arbitrariness of really small communities and to approach universalism. These arguments have a distinct Hegelian sense to them, with the nation state somehow embodying a rationality that is denied to other forms of organization. It is also the French concept of the modern state that we have noted in earlier chapters, seen as separate from and in a clear sense superior to and more rational than the arbitrary mass of loyalties that make up the communities of everyday life. This may indeed be how that entity seems to a resident native from the nation's core ethnic group; whether the ethnic and cultural minorities we encountered in Chapter 10 take the same view is another matter.

Chapter 11

DEMOCRACY AND MASS PARTICIPATION

A fully comprehensive survey of social structures would include a thorough discussion of political institutions. Politics, or the processes of maintaining order and attending to the collective tasks of a society, is a fundamental aspect of large-scale social relationships. More than that, the main justification for treating nation states as being automatically 'societies' is the strong role that states and other political actors have played in shaping social behaviour, or at least (as we saw in the previous chapter with reference to the work of Cotts-Watkins (1991)) shaping the spaces within which distinctive forms of social behaviour are created. One could therefore write an account of social structures which sees these as in part the product of political action. The study of political institutions and government action has indeed developed as a fully autonomous area of research, the achievements of which in the comparative study of European societies far exceed the current state of purely sociological knowledge of most other institutions. My central concern is to remedy this latter deficiency, and focus on social structures and the impact they have on various institutions, including the polity. In other words, my concern with politics is focused on how it is shaped by society rather than the opposite (what Bartolini (forthcoming) calls the sociology of politics rather than a political sociology). I do not adopt this position out of any belief that it has priority or is more valid, but merely because of the impossibility of tackling all angles in one book. Even while we concentrate on the sociology of politics, it is important to remember that the relationship between society and politics is in fact reciprocal and interactive.

I am therefore leaving aside the study of politics in the sense of government and the process of making legislation and regulating society, with the exception of two questions which directly concern the translation of social forces into political ones. These are the social bases of political parties and of organized interests. To some extent we shall examine the reciprocal process, the way in which political action affects society, in Chapter 13 on the welfare state.

Our concept of the mid-century model has included the idea of segregation into clearly established social identities, through the Fordist organization of work, the elaboration of a class structure, and through the mutual institutional defences of traditional identities afforded by sociological liberalism. A concept of citizenship consistent with such a model would include the existence of strong organizations rooted in social identities, which would define, express, and safeguard interests. This is by no means the only possible form of citizenship guarantee; it can and normally is also embodied in individual rights secured through legal redress. However, the particular challenge for the mid-century compromise was to protect people and a diversity of social institutions from being overwhelmed by the forces of capitalist industrialism, and this required more substantial defences. The dissolution of social identities implied by the theory of post-industrialism and/or postmodernism should lead us to predict a crisis of organization, fragmentation, and a loss of democratic capacity by those groups most dependent on collective identities for expression of their political interests. Meanwhile, we should expect certain new interests to be enabled to take the political stage through these same processes of change.

CLEAVAGES OF PARTISAN ALLEGIANCE

All the countries covered by this book today have systems of government generally called democratic, in the sense that virtually all persons regarded as adult have an opportunity to vote for political representatives at national and various local levels, with the government being either drawn from or further selected by those elected. However, as Table 11.1 shows, the arrival of democracy is a recent development in European history. Few countries have enjoyed it throughout the twentieth century; women usually acquired democratic rights some time after men—in Switzerland spectacularly so. And in three of our countries (Greece, Portugal, and Spain) a sustained period of democracy did not begin until well into the brief time period covered by this book. Nevertheless, political allegiances, partisan attachments to one set of political biases rather than another, have become embedded in all these countries. It was particularly remarkable to note how, when people in Portugal and Spain regained the vote after forty or fifty years of fascist dictatorship and a very thin prior democratic history, they rapidly began voting in a manner that was recognizable from the perspective of other European cases and to do so consistently over a number of elections.[1]

As Table 11.2 shows, large majorities of people take advantage of their rights to vote (at least in national elections; the picture at a local level is often very different). These turnout levels fluctuate from election to election and overall there is no general trend for them to rise or fall. It is however notable that a fairly large fall was registered in virtually all countries during the most recent period reviewed (the 1990s). Whether this is a start of a major and enduring trend to reduced participation in democracy it is too early to determine. Certainly to date no public in Western Europe apart from Switzerland evinces a level of interest in the democratic process as low as that in the USA. Political participation is only sporadic; for the great majority of people the only political action is voting, and this takes a very short time and is exercised only at intervals. Nevertheless, the high level of participation and the tendency for most people to sustain a political preference for a number of years suggests that this is behaviour that people find meaningful.

The question therefore arises of how electoral choices are made and structured. According to the simple model of liberal political choice, individuals deliberate about which of the various candidates available to them will be most likely to advance their interests, or alternatively will have the general qualities likely to make them good representatives. The language of election campaigns assumes that this is the process at work. Candidates and groups of candidates propose policies and invite voters to view

---

[1] Eastern Europe has been very different. The Portuguese and Spanish dictatorships had been capitalist ones, so important elements of underlying social structure were no different from those of other capitalist societies. State socialism changed more social variables.

Table 11.1a The timing of universal suffrage: adult males

	1848–1900	1900–13	1914–18	1919–38	1939–45	1946–64	1965–
A		24 (1907)	suspended during WW I	20 (1919)	dictatorship and invasion	20 (1945)	19 (1968)
B				21 (1919)	invasion	21 (1946)	21
DK			29 (1918)	25 (1920)	25	23 (1952) 21 (1961)	20 (1971)
SF	state founded 1907	24 (1907)	24	24	suspended during WW II	21 (1945)	20 (1969)
F		25	suspended during WW I	25	dictatorship and invasion	21 (1945)	18 (1975)
D	25 (1871)	25	suspended during WW I	20 (until 1933) (dictatorship)	dictatorship	21 (1949)	18 (1970)
GR							dictatorship 1967–73; 18
IRL	separate state not founded until 1921			21 (1921)	21	21	18 (1972)
I		30 (1913)	suspended during WW I	21 (until 1924) (dictatorship)	dictatorship	21 (1946)	21
NL			25 (1918)	25	invasion	23 (1945)	21 (1965) 18 (1972)
N		25	25	23 (1921)	invasion	23; 21 (1946)	21
P				dictatorship	dictatorship	dictatorship	18 (1976)
E	21 (1869–76)			21 (1932–38)	dictatorship	dictatorship	18 (1977)
S	24 (1909)	24	24	23 (1921)	23	21 (1945)	19 (1969)
CH	20 (1848)	20	20	20	20	20	20
UK			21 (1918)	21	suspended during WW II	21	18 (1969)
JAP						20 (1947)	20
USA	21 (1868)	21	21	21	21	21	21 (1971)

Table 11.1b The timing of universal suffrage: adult females

	1848–1900	1900–13	1914–18	1919–38	1939–45	1946–64	1965–
A				as men	dictatorship and invasion	as men	as men
B						21 (1948)	as men
DK			as men	as men	as men	21 (1961)	as men
SF	state founded 1907	as men	as men	as men	suspended during WW II	as men	as men
F						as men	as men
D				as men	dictatorship	as men	as men
GR						as men	dictatorship 1967–73; as men
IRL	separate state not founded until 1921			30 (1921) 21 (1923)	as men	as men	as men
I						as men	as men
NL				as men		as men	as men
N			as men (1915)	as men	invasion	as men	as men
P				dictatorship (1926)	dictatorship	dictatorship	as men
E				as men	dictatorship	dictatorship	as men
S				as men	as men	as men	as men
CH							as men (1971)
UK			30 (1918)	as men (1928)	suspended during WW II	as men	as men
JAP						as men	as men
USA				as men (1920)	as men	as men	as men

these as superior to those of other candidates, either because they suit some general interest or because they will advance the specific interests of particular groups. Individual candidates also stress their personal capabilities.

In reality however this a very artificial model of the electoral process in mass situations and dealing with complex issues. It is not possible to approach voting as a set of rational calculations. Most claims made by political parties presenting themselves to voters take the form: if we take approach A instead of B, we shall reach goal X. But only very rarely is it possible to establish that such a causal connection really operates. In the case of a widely shared goal, if the causal sequence is known, all parties will adopt the appropriate approach, ruling out that issue from party differentiation. The formulation really only operates effectively if some parts of the population want goal X and others goal –X, in other words a goal which contradicts X. In many (though not all) cases candidates have a motive to conceal such differences in goals and interests. To argue 'I am associated with goal X' is to lose the support of the defenders of –X; better therefore to find goal Z, which everybody wants, and to claim to be associated with that—which reverts us to our original problem.

A further complication is caused by the fact that there will normally be a very large number of such goals, and in the rational choice model of voting electors have to know their own preference ordering of these, and reach conclusions of the following kind: 'I know that candidate X supports goals G, H, and I, which I support, but she also supports goal S, which I dislike more than I support the other three combined. Although candidate Y does not support H and I and is neutral on S, at least he supports G, T, and V, which in combination is more important. Therefore I shall vote for Y.' This is a very artificial representation of the voting process. At times of rapid change in either an individual's identity or in that of the issues being pursued by politics, something of the kind may happen, but we must expect voters to want to avoid doing it as much as possible.

Politics is about collective, public business. One reasonable solution for voters is therefore to argue: 'Which party or parties seem to be most closely allied to the concerns of people like me?' Or more simply: 'How do people like me usually vote?' There remain two problems. First, the voter has to work out who are 'people like me'. In other words, she must have one or more social identities that are significant to her. Second, there is a strong possibility that political parties will associate themselves with particular identities merely through the use of symbols and without doing anything substantive for the interests of the people denoted by the identity. These are the hazards of the political process.

In previous chapters we have encountered the major issues which have shaped social identity and prepared the great segregated blocs of the mid-century social compromise: the gender division; the cleavages of the occupational structure, which besides being important in their own right also have ramifications in standards and styles of living, educational and culture style and level, and place in general structures of social authority; family; religion; ethnicity. This leads us to expect that the political divisions of societies engaged in that compromise will reflect similar themes, and indeed the literature on political identities and allegiances draws on this same stream of issues.

The seminal work in this field is an essay by the American sociologist Seymour

Table 11.2 Turnout in general elections, 18 countries, 1960–1997

		1960–4	1965–9	1970–4	1975–9	1980–4	1985–9	1990–4	1995–7
A	level	93.80	93.80	92.10	92.50	92.60	90.40	84.10	82.70
	change		0.00	−1.70	0.40	0.10	−2.20	−6.30	−1.40
B	level	92.30	90.80	90.50	94.90	94.60	93.40	92.70	91.10
	change		−1.50	−0.30	4.40	−0.30	−1.20	−0.70	−1.60
DK	level	85.60	88.90	87.90	87.20	85.80	86.30	83.60	
	change		3.30	−1.00	−0.70	−1.40	0.50	−2.70	
SF	level	85.10	84.90	81.80	74.50	75.70	72.10	72.10	68.50
	change		−0.20	−3.10	−7.30	1.20	−3.60	0.00	−3.60
F	level	68.70	80.50	81.30	83.30	70.90	72.30	68.90	68.00
	change		11.80	0.80	2.00	−12.40	1.40	−3.40	−0.90
D	level	87.70	86.70	91.10	90.80	88.50	84.30	78.40	
	change		−1.00	4.40	−0.30	−2.30	−4.20	−5.90	
GR	level	82.10	—	79.50	81.10	78.60	82.40	82.50	78.70
	change			1.60	−2.50	3.80	0.10	−3.80	
IRL	level	70.60	76.00	76.60	76.30	74.20	70.90	68.50	65.90
	change		5.40	0.60	−0.30	−2.10	−3.30	−2.40	−2.60
I	level	92.90	92.80	93.20	92.20	89.00	90.50	86.70	82.90
	change		−0.10	0.40	−1.00	−3.20	1.50	−3.80	−3.80
NL	level	95.10	94.90	81.30	88.00	84.00	82.90	78.30	
	change		−0.20	−13.60	6.70	−4.00	−1.10	−4.60	
N	level	79.10	84.60	80.20	82.90	82.00	83.30	75.80	78.00
	change		5.50	−4.40	2.70	−0.90	1.30	−7.50	2.20
P	level	—	—	—	86.60	81.10	72.40	68.20	66.70
	change					−5.50	−8.70	−4.20	−1.50
E	level	—	—	—	68.10	79.80	70.20	77.30	78.10
	change					11.70	−9.60	7.10	0.80
S	level	84.90	89.30	89.50	91.20	91.40	87.90	86.70	
	change		4.40	0.20	1.70	0.20	−3.50	−1.20	
CH	level	64.50	63.80	56.40	50.20	48.90	46.80	46.00	42.30
	change		−0.70	−7.40	−6.20	−1.30	−2.10	−0.80	−3.70
UK	level	77.20	76.00	74.60	76.30	72.80	75.40	77.80	71.30
	change		−1.20	−1.40	1.70	−3.50	2.60	2.40	−6.50
JAP	level	71.60	70.40	71.10	70.00	70.20	69.90	69.80	
	change		−1.20	0.70	−1.10	0.20	−0.30	−0.10	
USA	level	64.40	62.30	57.10	55.80	55.10	52.80	55.30	
	change		−2.10	−5.20	−1.30	−0.70	−2.30	2.50	

Source: Lane and Ersson 1999: 141.

Martin Lipset and the Norwegian political scientist Stein Rokkan (1967), which established the main shaping factors in the political cleavages in Western European development as having been: religion, social class, geographical region, and the somewhat
circular concept of political tradition. The fact that their analysis has been used re-
peatedly by subsequent scholars testifies to its utility and viability. Its main terms
embrace or can be extended to include nearly all the main themes that emerge from
our past discussions, with just two distinctions. First, their concept of geographical
area needs to differentiate between geographical distance as a marker between centre
and periphery and the tendency of geography to be associated with ethnic and other
cultural differences. Second, it is necessary to relate family to their account. Families
are too small to be forms of political identity in themselves in modern mass societies.
(In those which existed almost everywhere until at least the late eighteenth or the
nineteenth centuries, the very small number of wealthy families that dominated politics were indeed the principal units of political organization—monarchical dynasties
being the most outstanding examples.) However, they continue to be important transmission routes for socio-political identities and as such are important actors in the
mobilization of political tradition identified by Lipset and Rokkan. This can be seen in
the record of many studies of political allegiance, which show how people who move
into a different class or geographical region from their parents nevertheless often retain their parents' political preferences.

Lipset and Rokkan were describing political change during the industrialization
process. By the time of the starting point of our study, that of the high tide of 1960s
industrialism, the balance of these factors had changed. According to the theory of the
mid-century compromise, issues of industrialism should have taken predominance
over others in shaping the way in which citizens related to the representative political
systems of their societies, though with 'reserved areas' for religious, historical intra-
European ethnic, and regional identities. Parties defined by class should therefore be
the largest, with those defined by the other structural cleavages next in line. Parties
not rooted in such structured identities should be very small. Postmodern theories
would then anticipate a subsequent decline in the strength of class and an increase in
more voluntaristic, cultural forms of political attachment. I shall investigate these propositions using the approach of most other chapters, examining the situation in the
early 1960s and the mid-1990s.

I shall try as far as possible to characterize parties solely in terms of their social
composition and associations, ignoring their ideologies or policy programmes. In other
words, the fact that a party calls itself a 'labour' party and presents policies claiming to
represent workers' interests in particular does not make it a manual workers' party; it
will be defined as such if it attracts high proportions of manual workers to vote for
it and if its electorate primarily comprises manual workers. (This is very different from
the approach taken in the main current political-science text on this subject, by two
Scandinavian political scientists (Lane and Ersson 1987; 4th edition 1999). These authors (1999: ch. 3) analyse parties in terms of their names, statements, and affiliations,
and then proceed to attribute social structural attributes to many of them on that basis
rather than on direct knowledge of their actual support.)

I shall similarly examine political action by citizens in terms of their observed
behaviour rather than expressions of belief. This means that as far as possible data will

be drawn from voting in elections. One problem in studying either political actions or opinions is that they fluctuate; parties' fortunes can vary quite widely from one election to the next. Indeed, one aspect of political change, consistent with postmodern arguments, is that in most countries political opinion and voting behaviour fluctuate far more widely today than forty years ago. There will therefore be occasions when my 'snapshot' approach catches individual parties at particularly strong or weak moments and distorts the picture. I shall draw attention to such instances.[2]

POLITICAL CLEAVAGES AND SOCIAL IDENTITIES IN THE EARLY 1960s

The following party types existed in the early 1960s in the countries of concern to us:

1. *Manual working-class parties*: These drew their strength more from manual workers and their families[3] than from any other category. They can be subdivided into two sub-groups. Sub-group a *major parties* received the support of at least 40% of the category; since manual workers have formed such a large minority of the electorate, this was enough to make a party a major party within the state. Sub-group b *minor parties* attracted only small minorities of manual workers' votes; since by definition these parties relied primarily on this class, they were necessarily minor parties within the state.

2. *Christian parties*: These drew their strength primarily from regular church attenders, and can again be divided into two sub-groups. Sub-group a *major parties* attracted the support of at least 40% of regular churchgoers of a particular faith, that faith itself being sufficiently large within the society for such a level of support to make the party a major one within the state. These cases

---

[2] In order not to spend time on parties which, however internally interesting, represent only small proportions of the electorate, I shall look only at those receiving 5% or more of the vote in the election being considered (rounding up votes to the nearest full percentage point for this purpose). To examine social class I consider (where the data are available) manual workers, lower non-manual workers, and agricultural workers. This excludes full consideration of managers, the professions, senior non-manual staff, and the self-employed. However, these are small groups often problematically defined; the main point here is to present illustrative examples. I also consider religious affiliation (usually defined in terms of church attendance), gender, and geographical differences represented by either distinctive regions of the country or different types of settlement (mainly, villages or similar small communities against large cities).

The information produced by such an analysis is presented in full in Appendix tables. There are two ways of considering party support. First, there is the distribution of political support across main political parties of certain segments of the population. This looks at the situation from the point of view of which parties were supported by particular sections of the population. This is presented in Appendix Table A.11.1 for the early 1960s and Appendix Table A.11.3 for the 1990s. Second, we can also examine the social composition of the parties by examining the social character of the support of a particular party. This sometimes gives us different answers. For example, we may find that a particular small party is supported by only 5% of women; but it could be that 75% of the party's support was female. These data are presented in Appendix Table A.11.2 for the early 1960s and Appendix Table A.11.4 for the 1990s.

Lane and Ersson (1987) assembled data of a similar kind on a more extensive basis, covering the period from the mid-1960s to the mid-1970s. They considered a slightly different variable: not the social characteristics of supporters of particular parties, but the social characteristics of the regions of a country in which parties are strong. This ecological approach does not tell us which characteristics a party's supporters *possess*; it might even tell us to which characteristics they are objecting—for example, when racist parties among the majority ethnic group are strong in areas where many people from ethnic minorities are living. The main findings of this work are summarized in Table 11.3. Unfortunately, they dropped this form of analysis in their most recent (4th, 1999) edition, so it is not possible to bring it up to date.

[3] In the social survey practices of the period people were normally classified occupationally according to the job of the so-called 'head of household', usually the oldest male in paid employment.

were mainly concentrated in primarily Roman Catholic countries. Sub-group b *minor parties* either attracted the support of only small minorities of the regular churchgoers on whom they were dependent, or found strong support among minority religions.

3. *Agrarian parties*: These drew their strength from farmers, usually farm owners, tenants, and sharecroppers rather than from agricultural employees.

4. *Cultural or ethnic parties*: These drew their strength overwhelmingly from people distinguished primarily by their cultural or ethnic characteristics rather than by other social features. These can be subdivided into: a *dominant majority nationalist parties*, which sought to represent the interests of the majority ethnicity of the nation state against either internal minority ethnicities or other nation states; and b *cultural minority parties* representing ethnic or national minority groups, usually being resident in culturally distinct regions of a country.

5. *Primarily secular, higher-class parties*: These drew their strength from proprietorial, professional and upper non-manual categories, or from those who did not work at all, and were not distinguished by particularly significant levels of church-going. They can be further subdivided into: a *major parties*, attracting the support of majorities of non-working-class categories and large minorities of the total electorate; b *minor parties*, attracting the support of only minorities of these categories.

6. *Other parties*: A final residual category for parties whose support base does not seem to be dominated by any one interest. Such parties might have represented no structural interest at all, or they might have had a mix of bases which is obscured by the statistics. This can only be determined by discussion of the individual cases.

According to our central hypothesis, parties of types 1 and 5 should dominate the political landscape, with some role for types 2, 3, and 4. There should be no important parties that cannot be accounted for by these five types, unless there are type 6 parties which combine two or more of the others.

Table 11.4 summarizes the overall distribution of parties in those societies enjoying near-universal adult suffrage in the early 1960s. It is based on Appendix Tables A.11.1 and A.11.2, as well as on the general literature on political parties of the period. The mid-century compromise model is confirmed for all Western European societies for which we have data, to the extent that the five main types account for virtually all party support, and in that the class parties have a major role. However, cross-class Christian parties often have a greater prominence than we would expect were class issues to have moved into a truly dominant position. We can learn more about the situation by examining the position of the party types in different countries in more detail.

MANUAL WORKING-CLASS PARTIES

In most Western European countries there was at least one party which relied on manual workers and their families to provide at least 40% of its support and relied on this class more than it did on any other class. The same was not true for Japan or the USA, so this is a true 'European' characteristic.[4] However, in four countries no party achieved the status of being a category 1a party. In France, Ireland, Italy, and the Netherlands strong Christian parties attracted too large a share of manual workers' votes for the main working-class party to achieve dominance within that class. However, in only one case, Ireland, was the party attracting the plurality of the class's

---

[4] The Japanese Socialist Party and the US Democratic Party attracted particularly strong shares of the working-class vote, but were not highly dependent on the class.

Table 11.3 Coefficients of social composition of party support, 1960s–1970s

	Party	Av. share of vote	Ind. empl.	Agric. big units	Income/wealth	Religion		Language or local culture	
Austria	SPÖ	48.10	0.52	-0.29	0.18	-0.66		-0.14	German
	ÖVP	43.80	-0.51	-0.31	-0.28	0.63	Cath.	0.11	German
	FPÖ	6.00	-0.04	0.21	0.32	0.03	Luth.	0.03	German
Belgium	CVP/PSC	31.40	0.27	-0.44	-0.39	0.89	Cath.	0.72	Dutch
	PSB/BSP	27.30	0.04	0.39	0.08	-0.71		0.60	French
	PLB/BFP	19.40	-0.47	-0.08	0.03	0.01	Cath.	-0.32	non-Dutch
	VU	10.40	0.31	-0.29	-0.26	0.48	Cath.	0.95	Dutch
	RW/FDF	7.40	-0.33	0.46	0.55	-0.61		-0.80	non-Dutch
Denmark	SD	30.90	0.41	-0.17	0.00	-0.29		—	
	VE	17.10	0.71	-0.20	-0.48	0.59	Luth.		
	FRP	14.70	-0.11	0.19	0.02	0.31	Luth.		
	RV	10.90	0.18	-0.15	-0.12	0.08	Luth.		
	KF	10.50	-0.38	0.13	0.39	-0.31			
	SF	6.70	0.33	0.15	0.64	-0.73			
	CD	5.00	0.06	0.15	0.34	-0.22			
Finland	SDP	25.50	0.63	0.06	0.53	-0.38		0.06	Finnish
	SKDL	18.30	0.21	-0.25	0.10	-0.40		0.29	Finnish
	KESK	18.20	-0.57	0.35	-0.60	0.27	Luth.	0.55	Finnish
	KOK	16.50	0.30	-0.08	0.46	-0.20		0.44	Finnish
	SMP	6.90	-0.35	-0.13	-0.32	0.12	Luth.	0.06	Finnish
	LKP	5.90	0.27	-0.37	0.54	-0.37		0.55	Finnish
	RKP	5.70	-0.05	0.15	0.05	0.25	Luth.	0.98	Swedish
France	UDR	38.60	0.02	0.32	-0.16	0.45	Cath.		
	PCF	21.30	0.11	-0.21	0.31	-0.64			
	PS	18.60	-0.13	0.19	-0.25	-0.23			
	REF	11.80	-0.01	-0.04	0.06	0.25	Cath.		

Germany	CDU/CSU	46.30	-0.13	0.37	-0.53	0.74	Cath.	-0.27	refugees
	SPD	39.40	0.25	-0.30	0.48	0.55	Luth.	0.21	refugees
	FDP	9.40	-0.10	-0.25		0.38	Luth.	0.11	refugees
Greece	ND	44.00	0.03	-0.11	-0.17				
	PASOK	29.00	0.02	0.00	0.06				
	EDHIK	11.30	-0.07	0.17	-0.01				
	KKE	11.20	0.10	0.26	0.27				
Ireland	FF	45.90	-0.37			0.48	Cath.	0.70	Irish
	FG	34.60	-0.67			-0.31		0.06	Irish
	Lab	15.30	0.77			0.16	Cath.	-0.35	Irish
Italy	DC	38.80	-0.04	-0.39	-0.20	0.61	Cath.		
	PCI	29.50	0.12	-0.55	0.17	-0.35			
	PSI	11.00	0.29	0.06	0.21	-0.04			
	MSI	6.40	-0.48	-0.44	-0.59	0.18	Cath.		
	PSDI	4.90	0.29	-0.22	0.32	-0.24			
Netherlands	PvdA	25.20	-0.04	0.25	0.00	0.80	Cath/Calv		
	KVP	22.00	0.27	-0.32	-0.20	0.95	Cath.		
	VVD	11.80	0.41	0.14	0.61	-0.32			
	ARP	9.10	-0.42	0.28	-0.16	0.95	Cal. (Geref)		
	CHU	6.40	-0.43	0.09	-0.19	0.74	Cal. (Her)		
	D'66	4.80	0.43	0.11	0.55	-0.30			
Norway	DNA	41.40	0.21	0.33	0.01	-0.53	anti-ab.	-0.50	Nynorsk
	HOE	20.60	0.20	-0.36	0.45	-0.15	anti-ab.	-0.25	Nynorsk
	KRF	11.00	-0.12	-0.30	-0.20	0.64	anti-ab.	0.54	Nynorsk
	SP	10.00	-0.68	0.42	-0.30	0.33	anti-ab.	0.36	Nynorsk
	SV	6.30	0.21	0.13	0.08	-0.38	anti-ab.	-0.31	Nynorsk
	VE	5.40	0.00	-0.22	-0.01	0.17	anti-ab.	0.27	Nynorsk
Portugal	AD	42.60		-0.58	0.36	0.75	Cath.		
	PSP	35.40			-0.21	-0.32			
	PCP	15.40		0.58	-0.29	-0.74			

(continued over)

Table 11.3 (continued)

	Party	Av. share of vote	Ind. empl.	Agric. big units	Income/ wealth	Religion		Language or local culture	
Spain	PSOE	35.60	-0.07	0.31	-0.18	-0.12		0.18	Spanish
	UCD	25.70	-0.36	-0.22	-0.30	0.14	Cath.	0.25	Spanish
	AP	13.40	-0.21	-0.22	-0.17	0.07	Cath.	0.14	Spanish
	PCE	8.00	0.10	0.45	0.10	-0.07		-0.06	Spanish
	Ethnic	5.00	0.57	-0.15	0.52	0.37	Cath.	-0.51	Spanish
Sweden	SAP	43.80	0.38	-0.13	0.05	-0.48			
	M	19.80	-0.30	0.29	0.41	-0.01			
	CP	19.20	-0.67	0.20	-0.56	0.67	Luth/ non-conf.		
	FP	9.20	-0.18	0.12	0.21	-0.03			
	VPK	5.30	-0.15	-0.19	0.31	-0.40			
Switzerland	SPS	23.80	0.49	0.13		0.66	Prot.	0.14	French
	FDP	22.40	0.19	-0.17		-0.04		-0.04	German
	CDV	21.20	-0.71	-0.24		-0.72	Prot.	0.19	German
	SVP	10.60	-0.11	0.03		0.46	Prot.	0.00	German
UK	Lab	42.80	0.76		-0.66	-0.41	CofE	-0.01	English
	Cons	42.10	-0.61		0.49	0.21	CofE	0.40	English
	Lib	11.80	-0.41		0.42	0.34	CofE	-0.10	English
	SNP	1.20							
	PC	0.40							

For abbreviations see Appendix Table A.11.1.

Source: Based on Lane and Ersson 1987.

support different from the party which depended most on the class. This latter party (the Irish Labour Party) is therefore an example of a type 1b party. Outside Europe the Japanese Socialist Party was also of type 1b. In Finland and Norway there were type 1b parties in addition to a strong type 1a example. In addition to the type 1b parties featured in the list, very small parties failing to pass the 5% hurdle for inclusion in the analysis also existed in several countries.

Type 1 parties were the most widespread party type of the period, constituting the main evidence of the role of occupational class in shaping political identity in these societies. All, whether minor or major, enjoyed considerably less support in attracting other classes, though some were able to attract agricultural as well as industrial manual workers. All except the Danish Social Democrats (SD) were more attractive to men than to women; the Japanese Socialist Party had no gender bias in its support. It will be remembered that in the early 1960s married women tended not to be present in the paid labour force; research in a number of countries demonstrates that those women were more likely to vote for working-class parties than were housewives. It therefore seems that it was the actual experience of the workplace and work community that generated support for working-class parties, and although much of it was transmitted to wives through family mechanisms, there was less than full success in this.

Nearly all these parties were weak in attracting the support of practising Christians, especially Catholics; it should here be remembered that women are always more active churchgoers than men. The only exceptions were the British Labour Party and US Democrats who had particular success in attracting the Catholic minorities in their countries.[5] The parties were also associated with other correlates of the growth of the industrial working class: residence in large rather than small towns; either a low level of agricultural support or support among workers in large-scale rather than peasant agriculture (i.e. that most resembling factory conditions).

Venturing beyond a purely sociological approach to party analysis, we can confirm that all the parties listed here shared some central ideological and political concerns, and most were members of two major recognizable political families. In every case except three (France and Italy, and for very different reasons the USA) the main working-class parties were members of the Socialist International: a group of parties dedicated to the non-revolutionary transformation of the capitalist economy in order to redistribute power and wealth towards the interests of workers, using such devices as government intervention in the economy, development of the welfare state, and advancement of the rights of organized labour. Each of these parties maintained strong formal or informal links with trade union organizations.

In France and Italy the most important working-class parties (both called communist parties) were members of a different political family, often opposed to those from the Socialist International. This distinction followed paths initiated in the 1920s, when the leaders of the communist revolution in Russia had called on all other parties regarding

5 It is however notable that Labour is the sole example in Europe of a type 1a party attracting Catholic voters in such large proportions. The anomaly results from the past history of relations between Britain and Ireland. The great majority of British Catholics are immigrants from Ireland and their descendants. The British Conservative Party's orientation towards both anti-Catholicism and maintenance of Ireland as a British colony until the early twentieth century, and its association with the Protestant population in Northern Ireland (continuing at least until the 1970s) led Irish Catholic immigrants in Britain and their descendants to support the Labour Party.

Table 11.4 *Party types, 15 countries, 1960s*

	Working-class		Christian		Rural	Cultural and ethnic		Secular, higher class		Other
	major 1a	minor 1b	major 2a	minor 2b	3	majority 4a	minority 4b	major 5a	minor 5b	6
A	SPÖ		ÖVP			FPÖ			FPÖ	
B	BSP/PSB		CVP/PSC						PLB	
DK	SD				V				KF, RV	SF
SF	SSP	SKDL			KESK		RKP		KK	LKP
F		PCF		(Majorité)				(Majorité)	PS, Centre	
D	SPD		[CDU/CSU]						FDP	
IRL	Labour		[FF]	[FG]					FG	FF
I		[PCI]	[DC]			MSI			[PLI, PRI]	[PSI, PSDI]
NL		[PvdA]	[KVP (Cath)]	[ARP, CHU (Prot)]					[VVD]	
N	DNA			[KrF]	SP				Høyre, [V]	
S	SAP	VPK			CP				Höjere, FP	
CH	SPS		CDV (Cath) SVP (Prot)		SVP			Freisinnig		
UK	Labour		(Con.)	(Lib.)				Con.		Lib.
JAP		JSP	—	—	(LDP)					LDP
USA			Rep (Prot)							Dem.

Notes: Parties may appear in more than one category. Cases in square brackets, [ ], indicate allocations made partly on the basis of the general literature, statistical data in the Appendix Tables being deficient. Cases in parentheses, ( ), indicate doubtful allocations. For key to abbreviations of party names, see Appendix Table A.11.1.

Sources: Appendix Tables A.11.1 and A.11.2.

themselves as workers' parties[6] to join them in revolutionary struggle and to abandon participation in and loyalty to the political structures of their individual nation states. The response of the parties in Western Europe had been mixed, and in nearly every case produced a division. In general, those who had seen little chance of political progress within their national political system had supported the Russian call and formed parties which, while organizing and contesting elections within the system, did not believe that much could be achieved without a full revolution and an alliance with the Soviet Union. These forces had tended to predominate in polities very resistant to pressure from the industrial working class, primarily France and Southern Europe, though to a considerable extent also in Germany. Those who regarded their political systems as potentially permeable had abjured the revolutionary call.

In the former group of countries parties allied to the Soviet appeal and usually called communist parties became the major form of working-class party, alongside small reformist socialist or similarly titled parties. In the second group majority reformist socialist, social democratic, or labour parties formed the majority wing, though usually small communist parties also emerged. In inter-war Germany the movement remained divided between large social democratic and communist parties, as well as other revolutionary groups who did not ally with the Soviet appeal.

In subsequent years relations between the two wings of the labour movement everywhere became very bitter indeed, changing temporarily during the Second World War when the Soviet Union was an ally in the war against fascism. After the war relations reverted to hostility of an even more intense kind, as the communist parties were now associated with the potential enemy power in the global confrontation that started in 1947 and continued until the collapse of the Soviet system in 1989. In Germany many communists were killed by the Nazi regime, and survivors moved to the communist state of East Germany after the war. The Communist Party was in fact made illegal during the formative years of the post-war Federal Republic.

By the 1960s, communist parties, while still existing, had sunk below the 5% threshold in most Western European countries and Japan. They remained however the dominant working-class parties in France and Italy, important in Finland, and above the threshold in Sweden. Communist parties were more likely than reformist ones to be male-dominant and decidedly less likely to attract active Christians. Although usually urban, they were in some cases associated with isolated rural regions. It is important to note the complex significance of the decision to rally to the Russian call. It was and remained primarily a symbol of extreme alienation from the national political system.

The minor working-class parties were primarily variants of the two dominant forms, communist and reformist. The Irish Labour Party and the Italian Socialist Party belonged to the Socialist International. In the Irish case it had been unable to combat the hegemony of two parties which took their identity from the country's civil war in the early 1920s; the Italian Socialist Party had been dwarfed by the Communist Party. A new type of party was formed in some countries during the 1950s by activists in working-class politics who were dissatisfied with the compromises made with the capitalist

---

[6] The Communist Party of the Soviet Union, as it became called, saw itself as a labour party and regarded its revolution as a workers' revolution, despite the fact that the country had hardly started the process of industrialization at the time and few industrial workers were involved in the party or the revolution.

economies by Socialist International parties, but who disliked the dictatorial political regime in the Soviet Union with which the communist parties were willing to be associated. The Danish Left Socialists (SF) were the only case to pass the 5% threshold, but it is interesting to note that its support base did not make the criteria for a type 1b party, being inadequately representative of manual workers. It therefore counts here as a category 6 party.

CHRISTIAN PARTIES

If the occupational structure cleavage seems to follow a similar pattern in all countries, that of religion is more diverse, following lines familiar from Chapter 9 of the central division between Catholicism and Protestantism and a subsidiary one between forms of the latter. In all countries where the Catholic Church was the dominant religion it managed to become associated with political parties which then had considerable success, winning a large minority of votes of manual workers, as well as majorities among rural populations, more privileged socio-economic groups, and women in general. We can identify a number of parties which depended very heavily indeed on regular churchgoers: in Austria (ÖVP), Belgium (CVP/PSC), Norway (KF), Switzerland (CDV and SVP), and outside Europe the US Republicans among Protestants. It is known from less statistical sources that Germany (CDU/CSU), Ireland (two parties, Fianna Fáil and Fine Gael), Italy (DC), and the Netherlands (three parties, KVP, ARP, CHU) also had parties of this type (Lane and Ersson 1987, 1999; and Mommsen-Reindl 1980; Merkl 1980a; Schäfers 1990: 299–301; Zariski 1980). More complex are France and the UK. Various elements within the French *majorité* were predominantly Catholic, in particular the Mouvement Républicain Populaire, while other components were decidedly *laïque*. We have already noted how the British Labour Party was something of a Catholic Party. The Conservative Party in that country was disproportionately representative of adherents to the English state church; it was not chosen by them as decidedly as Labour was by Catholics, but Anglicans were more numerous within the country as a whole and therefore provided a higher proportion of Conservatives' support base than Catholics did of Labour. Meanwhile, the Liberal Party was disproportionately representative of the small and declining non-conformist Protestant denominations.

Some of these parties attracted sufficient support from large Christian groups to be dominant parties in the state and therefore type 2a parties: the Austrian ÖVP, the Belgian CVP/PSC, the German CDU/CSU, Irish Fianna Faìl, Italian DC, Dutch KVP, Swiss CDV and SVP; the UK Conservatives if they are counted as a Christian party and, outside Europe, the US Republicans. With the exception of CDU/CSU (which was both Catholic and Protestant), SVP, Conservatives and Republicans, all these parties were Catholic. Among the exceptions, while CDU/CSU was in principle a combined Catholic and Lutheran party, it drew its support predominantly from Catholics; SVP was as much a rural as a Christian party; and the Conservatives were less clearly a religious party than most of the others. Within Europe therefore it is only the Catholic Church which has been able to mobilize major political parties.

This leaves as type 2b parties the Catholic elements of the French majority, Fine Gael, the ARP and CHU, KrF, and the Liberals. With the exception of the French and Irish, these were all Protestant parties.

The French case requires some comment. With the ironic exception of the Communist Party, French parties did not take the form familiar elsewhere in Western Europe of fairly firm organizational blocs. Rather, small groups of politicians (*notables*) would organize themselves separately from each other but with more or less recognizable relationships to the series of divisions that had deeply marked French politics from the time of the 1789 Revolution onward: for or against the Church; for or against the Republic; for or against central authority; for or against the political role of the working class. During the Fifth Republic these gradually came together to form larger, slightly more cohesive blocs in a basic confrontation between defence of a capitalist, centralized but democratic republic (*la majorité*) and support for or at least reduced antipathy towards communism (*la minorité*). Unlike in the countries listed in the previous paragraph, no party based primarily on the Church could form the main basis of the anticommunist or anti-socialist position, French Catholicism having experienced the fate described in Chapter 9. There was a Christian party (the MRP), but it was small and became just a part of the *majorité*.

The *majorité* comprised two separate broad groupings: the Rassemblement pour la République (RPR), which centred on the author of the Fifth Republic, General Charles de Gaulle, and the Parti Républicain (PR), which supported him in preference to the PCF but which had grave reservations about his authoritarianism. It is notable however that these differences make only a minor appearance in the support base of the two parties. As one might expect, the PR was more urban and secular than the RPR, but only in small measure. Both appear as not quite Christian democratic; they attracted the support of the majority of Catholic voters, but these voters were not so important to their support base as in the more straightforward Christian democratic cases.

While not found as universally as parties of type 1a, parties of type 2a were in general the most successful type of all in the years between the end of the Second World War and the early 1960s, dominating governments in Western Europe apart from the north (the UK—unless one counts the Conservatives as a 2a party—and the Nordic lands). Like type 1a parties, these parties of type 2a form a mutually recognized political family, known generically as Christian democracy. (British Conservatives were not of this group.) Since all these appeared as the main rivals of the working-class parties, they often came to play the role of being major representatives of interests hostile to organized labour; as can be seen from Appendix Tables A.11.1 and A.11.2, supporters of 1a and 1b parties were the most remote from the Church. This dominant role was a novelty for these Catholic or Christian democratic parties, since in the first decades of their existence, from the 1890s to the Second World War, they had often been marginalized by privileged groups, even those with strong church attachments, who at that period had often preferred anti-democratic solutions to the political challenge of labour. These attempts had culminated in the fascist and nazi movements of the 1920s and 1930s which, with the exception of Portugal, Spain and to some extent Greece and Italy, had completely disappeared in 1945.

AGRARIAN PARTIES

Distinctive though rural and agricultural life has been, it has been only in the Nordic countries and Switzerland that parties drawing their support almost wholly from the farming community have passed the 5% barrier and played an important role in political life (Danish V, Finnish KESK, Norwegian SP, Swedish CP, and Swiss SVP). (With the exception of the Danish party, whose name means 'Left', and the Swiss, which is called a people's party, all these are named 'Centre' parties.) Outside Europe, the Japanese LDP shared several of the attributes of an agrarian party at this time. Elsewhere the traditionalism of rural society has produced an association with the Church, and sometimes with landed aristocracy, to submerge the distinctive political identity of rural voters within the larger bloc of Christian Democratic or, in the British case, Conservative support. The Nordic parties largely attracted the support of farming proprietors, and did so very successfully; employed farm labourers were more likely to vote with their urban counterparts for type 1 parties. This again contrasts with the Catholic countries and the UK, where working-class parties were rarely successful in the countryside —though in certain regions of France and especially Italy there was a certain association between self-employed agricultural smallholders and communist voting.

CULTURAL AND REGIONAL PARTIES

Lipset and Rokkan (1967) fully recognized the role of regional parties representing historical local cultures, or established ethnic cultures in the sense of Chapter 10. By the time the great oppositions of church versus secularism and the working class against capitalism had claimed the centre ground of politics in most countries, little was left to the autonomous political expression of such identities, though they might contribute to wider ones based on class and/or religion if a region was heavily characterized by particular classes or minority religions. For example, the population of Brittany tended to vote strongly for Catholic parties because the Church (itself excluded for so long from national participation) adapted itself locally to express the marginalized culture of Bretons. We have also already noticed the local cultural associations of communist voting in some countries, especially France and Italy. In fully industrialized societies the agricultural parties discussed immediately above also take on some of the character of regional cultural parties.

Ethnicity and regional cultures therefore have had a larger importance than is evident from a look at the main indicators. This can be seen in the part of Lane and Ersson's scheme (Table 11.3) which relates politics to linguistic groups. Although by the 1960s only a small proportion of the Irish and Norwegian populations in specific regions spoke Gaelic and Nynorsk respectively, Fianna Fáil in Ireland and the Norwegian farmers' SP were particularly strongly represented in those regions. Similarly, although only a proportion of the Welsh population, and a very small proportion of the overall British population, spoke Welsh, the weakness of the Conservative Party in Wales was enough to give it a significantly negative association with minority languages and mark it as partly an English national party. Given that the party had defined itself in the late nineteenth century as Unionist (that is, opposing self-government for Scotland, Wales, and Ireland), the continuing implication of minority language does tell us something about the social identity base of this party even in the 1960s. A similar point is conveyed by the strength of its association with the Church of England and its weakness among Roman Catholics (mainly Irish) and nonconformist Protestants (concentrated in Scotland and Wales, as well as in parts of England remote from the Conservatives' base in the South).[7]

Beyond these ethnic or regional components of the support base of some more extensive parties, ethnic or at least regional culture broke the bounds of the primarily class and religious divides of 1960s politics and produced a small number of parties of type 4 that succeeded in passing the 5% barrier. In Finland the RKP had long represented the interests of the Swedish-speaking minority there, being incorporated into the political and governmental system without ethnic tension. More controversially, both the Flemish and the Francophone linguistic communities that together comprised the great majority of the Belgian population produced small parties representing the interests of one community *against* the other (the CVU in Flanders, the RW in Wallonia and its associate the FDF representing French speakers in Brussels). In the early 1960s these parties did not reach the 5% threshold; by the end of the decade they were to do so, and the tensions associated with them were to have more profound implications for the Belgian political scene, as we shall see below.

Other cases existed but either failed to pass the threshold—for example regional parties within the UK (in Scotland, Wales, and Northern Ireland; which in this last took the opposed forms of a Catholic subculture that often sought withdrawal from the UK and adherence to the Republic of Ireland, and a Protestant subculture that stressed the union with Britain, but which also enjoyed domination of a provincial parliament which enabled it to express its particular set of social identities). Such movements in Spain were unable to express themselves through parties at that time, because the country was ruled by a dictatorship, but they appeared immediately in the young Spanish democracy of the 1970s, as can be seen from Lane and Ersson's data in Table 11.3 which extends to the 1970s.

In terms of ideology and political strategy most of these parties sought to advance the interests of a clearly delimited community. They did not seek further support bases in order to represent wider numbers of people; hence they remained small parties— type 4b rather than 4a. Overall they tended to derive more support from routine non-manual than from manual workers and from men rather than women.

The Italian MSI is a rather different case. According to our sociological approach it counts as a regional party because its support was very heavily concentrated in the south of the country. However, unlike the Belgian parties it did not explicitly define itself in these terms, but rather the opposite, standing as an all-Italian nationalist party. It was therefore a party of type 4a. It was in fact the historical successor to the Fascist party that ruled over Italy in the dictatorship of Benito Mussolini from the 1920s until the latter days of the Second World War.

The Austrian FPÖ is difficult to allocate. Superficially a liberal party, it was in fact a party representing a specifically German orientation for Austria. This dated back to the late nineteenth century when the country was facing dilemmas between its imperial legacy as an Eastern European military power dominating primarily Slav lands, and a future as an industrializing western country. The latter logically seemed to imply a closer relationship with a Germany which was rapidly modernizing and which had

---

[7] There were important but complex elements of regional and ethnic support in the two great US parties, largely emerging from the Civil War, which was only just a century away in the early 1960s.

recently unified all German-speaking lands in Western Europe except for Austria and German-speaking Switzerland. The antecedents of the FPÖ lay in the latter orientation, which allies it to certain strands of modernizing liberal politics. However, by the 1930s and 1940s identification with Germany came to mean alliance with Nazism, which is how this party interpreted its role. In post-war Austria it was therefore caught ambiguously and highly incongruously between a continuation of that strand (which was anathema throughout the world after the collapse of the Hitler regime) and an aspiration towards a liberal position between the two main blocs of labourism and Catholicism—on the lines of the German FDP. It attempted to do the latter and clearly had a social profile appropriate to a liberal party, though it continued to draw on ethnic support to the extent that it stressed the German character of the Austrian destiny—as opposed to the Slav and Jewish components that had been important in the imperial past.

PRIMARILY SECULAR, HIGHER-CLASS PARTIES

Most of the remaining parties of Western Europe can be defined as largely drawing their support from primarily urban middle- and upper-class groups. These classes being small, these parties could rarely attain a large size and are therefore mainly of type 5b. The only exceptions were the Swiss Freisinnige party, components of the French majority coalition, and the very large British Conservative Party—though, as we have seen, this party drew relatively heavily on a certain kind of Christian support and therefore belonged partly to type 2a and partly to type 5a.

Before labour-movement parties attracted the identities of the male manual workers —and eventually a smaller proportion of their wives—who moved into the electorate in such large numbers during the twentieth century, the Rokkanian nineteenth-century battles between modernity and tradition, religion and secularism, town and country, industry and agriculture were played out within the upper- and middle-classes of society through a different confrontation. This was not yet fully the politics of the mass, which required the manipulation of major symbols of social identity and raised grave challenges to the mobilizing capacity of parties rooted in the earlier order. In much of continental Europe conservative interests tackled the problem of mass appeal by supporting the fascist route of wielding major mass symbols of national and racial identity but without democracy.

The essentially modernizing bourgeois interests of nineteenth-century reform— usually known as liberal parties of some kind—were less able to find a voice in mass politics. Attempts at alliances with the growing young labour movement, although initially successful, eventually fell behind Catholic attempts to do the same, partly because liberals so clearly represented the political interests of employers' within the new industrial economy. Such parties survived in almost every country into the mid-century, but usually attracting only low levels of popular support; typically the third force in a system dominated by one or more labour parties and one or more church-based parties. The majority of the parties of type 5 are members of this historical group: the Belgian PLB, Danish RV, the German FDP, the Italian PRI and PLI (too small to pass the 5% threshold), the Dutch VVD, the Norwegian V, Swedish FP (also both too small to pass the 5% threshold), the Swiss Freisinnige. All continued to be far weaker than Christian parties in attracting working-class and agricultural support. They remained as they mainly began, parties of the urban bourgeoisie. However, by the 1960s their original *laïque* character within Catholic countries had weakened considerably; while less religious than the explicitly Christian parties, they were more likely to attract churchgoers and have a higher proportion of churchgoers among their supporters than working-class parties.

Two major countries, France and Britain, present unusual liberal patterns. The British Liberal Party was never *laïque* but non-conformist Protestant; by the end of the nineteenth century it had also become strongly associated with causes of Catholic emancipation and independence for Ireland. It therefore removed itself from the metropolitan elites which in other countries continued to support Liberals and became, like its Scandinavian partners, a party representing groups who identified neither with the industrial working class nor with the symbols of conservative nationalism. This led it into rural areas that felt culturally remote from Conservatism, whether through non-conformist religion or other elements of traditional regional cultures.

French liberalism had been cross-pressured by the many divisions of nineteenth-century France, becoming eventually a rallying point for all those who were unable to identify with either the communist-dominated labour movement or a conservative wing of politics that stood for either Catholic forces or an authoritarian form of French republicanism. By the 1960s, when these latter forces were grouped in a series of quasi-party fragments around General de Gaulle, remaining liberals began to assemble under certain symbols of liberal republicanism, but were tied into the Gaullist-led anti-communist majority in a manner that made it difficult for them to develop an independent profile; though less Catholic than the Gaullists, they were considerably more so than the parties of the left.

A final doubtful case of liberalism concerns Fine Gael in Ireland. Irish political divisions, like those in the USA, have primarily been formed by those of a civil war and have then survived following loss of the original rationale. As things stand, Fianna Fáil in Ireland emerges as rather similar to a Christian democratic party, mobilizing across classes and attracting disproportionate support from churchgoers. Fine Gael, as a less churchgoing, non-labour party seems to fit the mould of liberalism. However, it would have to be a liberal party of the British type: it was not *laïque* (there was no space for such a politics in the most loyally Catholic country of Western Europe), and its support was more rural than urban. Also, like the Austrian FPÖ, earlier in the century it had been removed from the liberal camp by the association of its predecessor (Poblachta na Gael) with fascism. Strangely, it was eventually Fine Gael and not Fianna Fáil that allied itself to the Christian democratic group in the European parliament during the 1970s.

RESIDUAL PARTIES

This leaves a few parties which cannot be fitted into our essentially structuralist analysis. Danish SF has already been discussed: a new-left socialist party which however failed to attract a support base of the kind it desired; Finnish LKP and the UK Liberals, essentially liberal parties with less higher-class bases than most parties of that kind in type 5; the small Italian PSI and PSDI, small social-democratic parties with less working-class bases than most parties of type 1. It might be considered that the parties of the Gaullist majority in France should be included in this residual, unstructured category. However, the heterogeneity of this grouping resulted from the fact that it comprised a group of parties coming together to form a majority; individual units of that majority embodied clear social-structural characteristics.

The only large parties that cannot be fitted into categories 1 to 5 are the US Democrats and Japanese LDP, which makes the social structural characteristics of the great majority of parties in the other countries a true Western European distinctiveness—though in fact the Democrats rather resembled the French *majorité*, comprising a number of different segments, each itself strongly structured by class, geographical or, above all, religious and ethnic characteristics.

PARTIES IN THE EARLY 1960S: CONCLUSIONS

This detailed analysis of the parties shows that it is not so easy to separate clearly class and other 'identity' parties from each other and from any not primarily rooted in social identity, as these currents all cross each other within the organizational structures of certain parties. This is part of the ambiguity of class identity already hinted at in Chapter 5: class as an objective economic criterion based on labour-market position can only acquire social meaning and become a basis for identity when it is shaped by organizational forces and creative action. This is often most easily done if the class position can feasibly be allied to other, more immediately meaningful identities: religion or anti-religion, region, or ethnicity. This helps explain why the mid-century compromise thesis only partially accounts for the pattern of political support in this period; in particular why religion plays a larger role than we should expect on the basis of that thesis.

The Catholic Church (and, where they existed, the Calvinist churches) in particular being highly successful at the mobilization of identity, the strength of class as such was weaker in shaping political identities the stronger the role of those faiths within a society. Therefore, the countries which conformed most clearly to a strong class form of the compromise model were the Nordic countries and Britain; those which conformed least those of the Catholic heartland: Belgium, Ireland, Italy, and to a lesser extent France and Germany. However, overall the broader expectations of the compromise model, that voting behaviour will be predominantly explained by strong social identities, is overwhelmingly confirmed.

PATTERNS OF ALLEGIANCE IN THE 1990S

Postmodernist theories expect political allegiance in the advanced societies to float free from social structural constraints and be increasingly determined by individual preference and fluctuating cultural patterns. There has been much interest in these possibilities in recent years following the researches of Richard Inglehart (1977, 1984, 1990), who has argued that voters in the advanced societies have moved on from the materialist concerns of an earlier generation to various post-materialist values (such as the natural environment, or the realization of cultural styles). One corollary of this would clearly be the break-up of the class blocs which defined material interests and the opening of a fragmented range of cultural and other sources of voting behaviour. The concept of a relatively fixed political identity should itself become less useful, as social identities become more flexible and temporary. These theories therefore lead us to expect a collapse and fragmentation of the mid-century model in contemporary societies. This is a straightforward matter for testing, by comparing the demographic profiles of partisan support for the most recent years available with those that we assembled for the early 1960s. Appendix Tables A.11.3 and A.11.4 respectively present the main evidence available for appraising this, in the same manner as Appendix Tables A.11.1 and A.11.2 did for the 1960s.

Several of the observed changes are consistent with the fragmentation hypothesis (Lane and Ersson 1999). First, participation in elections itself has somewhat declined, implying less rootedness of political behaviour in identities. Second, there has been a decline in the proportion of the vote secured by most of the working-class and Christian parties which formed the core of the post-war system. Third, there is some evidence of growing electoral volatility, and voters who are increasingly likely to change their vote between elections cannot have strong political identities. Fourth has been the rise of a number of new parties within category 6, that is established on no clear social bases. Finally, in several societies there has been considerable change in the identity of parties, especially in Belgium and Italy where there were major changes in the entire spectrum. These changes indicate instability, though, as Mair (1997) has pointed out, the overall contours of a party *system* might remain the same even if the precise party organizations within it come and go.

The overall picture is somewhat more nuanced, as we shall see in the following discussion. For example, Van Deth and Janssen (1994) used Eurobarometer data to identify the proportions of voters in Western European electorates whose voting behaviour showed no basic identity to a single party over the 1973–88 period—a period covering much of the interval between our two moments of observation. Contrary to the expectations of postmodern theory, this suggested that in all the countries considered (the 12 members of the European Community until the enlargement of 1995) the majority of voters did sustain a partisan loyalty. Among some societies in which this tendency was particularly strong are some cases where major changes might have led to considerable volatility: Spain, where the party system had not emerged from dictatorship until 1975; Ireland and again Spain, which underwent particularly rapid transformations of an agricultural economy; the UK, which experienced a particularly severe de-industrialization; and Belgium, which saw a transformation of its party base. (In fact, this last involved a strengthening rather than a weakening of social base.) In most of the 12 countries between three-quarters and nine-tenths of the electorate sustained their political allegiances.

Those party types which we identified as having the most clearly defined social bases continued to enjoy the most stability throughout the period, volatility being highest among a form of party (ethnic) that was not very important in the 1960s and one (green) which had been non-existent. We can examine this further by returning to the six party types of our earlier discussion. The overall position is summarized in Table 11.5.

Table 11.5 Party types, 18 countries, 1990s

	Working-class		Christian		Rural	Cultural and ethnic		Secular, higher class		Other
	major 1a	minor 1b	major 2a	minor 2b	3	majority 4a	minority 4b	major 5a	minor 5b	6
A	SPÖ		ÖVP			FPÖ			FPÖ, LIF	Grünen
B	BSP, PSB		CVP, PSC				All, plus VB, VU		PRL, PVV	AGALEV, ECOLO
DK	SD				V			V	KF, RV	FRP, SF
SF	SSP	SKDL			KESK		SVP		KOK	LKP, VIHR
F		PCF				FN		RPR, UDF		PS, Verts
D	SPD		[CDU/CSU]						FDP	Grünen
GR	PASOK	KKE	ND							Pol Spring
IRL		Labour	[FF]	[FG]					FG	FF
I	PDS			PPI, CDU		AN	PD			FI, Verdi
NL		[PvdA]	CDA	SGP				[VVD]		D66
N	DNA			[KrF]	SP			Høyre	SV	FRP
P	PS			CDS				PSD		
E	PSOE	PCE	PP/AP			FN	CDS, PNV, CIU, HB	PP/AP		Verdes
S	SAP	V			CP			M	FP	MP
CH	SPS		CVP (Cath), SVP (Prot)		SVP			FDP		GPS
UK	Labour			(Lib.)				Con.		Lib.
JAP		JSP	—	—	(LDP)					LDP
USA			Rep (Prot)							Dem.

Notes: Parties may appear in more than one category. Cases in square brackets, [ ], indicate allocations made partly on the basis of the general literature, statistical data in the Appendix Tables being deficient. Cases in parentheses, ( ), indicate doubtful allocations. For key to abbreviations of party names, see Appendix Table A.11.3.

Sources: Appendix Tables A.11.3 and A.11.4.

WORKING-CLASS PARTIES

There have been some changes in the identities of the parties in this group. The Belgian PS has been affected by the split of all national Belgian parties. Each of the three main families (working-class, Catholic, and liberal) split into linguistic/regional components. Where before there was a single party of type 1a there are now two of type 1b. The Francophone party, the PSB, is in fact the dominant party in Wallonia but the BSP is a relatively weak party in the larger region of Flanders.

In all three countries emerging from dictatorship in the 1970s a reformist working-class party appeared as an important one claiming the plurality of the working-class vote and becoming either the governing or the second party in the state. In all three countries previously clandestine communist parties became important examples of type 1b parties. The labour politics of these countries therefore rapidly acquired a very normal European form.

Both communist parties (French and Italian) have changed; given the collapse in 1989 of the Soviet Union, in relation to which these parties took their primary definition, this is not surprising. The PCF has declined so much in support that it now a very small case of type 1b. The Italian PCI took a totally different path. It gradually distanced itself from the relationship with Moscow during the 1970s and 1980s, culminating in a symbolic name change, first to Partito Democratico del Sinistro (PDS) and then to Democratici del Sinistro (DS), dropping the reference to party altogether. It is now a reformist party of type 1a. Members opposed to the change split away and formed a continuing communist party (Rifondazione), which in 1998 split further; both became examples of type 1b parties.

Elsewhere existing type 1a parties remained, as they had been in the 1960s, major forces in their states. In comparison with the earlier period some of them had declined in overall share of the vote. Those that show no apparent decline (such as the Austrian ÖSP) had in fact experienced considerable growth during the intervening years, followed by decline in the 1980s. In every case the decline is partly explained by the decline in the size of the working class that had taken place. However, most of these parties have also become less popular among remaining members of that class. Overall therefore all these parties have become far less clearly manual working-class parties than in the past. In several cases this decline was compensated by an increase in the proportion of routine non-manual workers supporting them. More detailed studies of some countries (e.g. Austria, Germany, Scandinavia) suggest that this is largely the result of public-service employees voting for working-class parties. It will be recalled from Chapter 4 that the majority of such employees have been women. This shift in voting patterns is therefore also associated with a decline in the former strong masculine bias of these parties; in some cases they are now more strongly supported by women than by men (e.g. Austria, Sweden).

Apart from the PCF the working-class party in heaviest decline during the period was British Labour until 1997, which, like the PCF, notably failed to pick up non-manual voters and also retained a marked male emphasis; in 1997 it changed trend completely on all these points. It is interesting to note that in both countries these parties had particularly low levels of non-manual support in the early 1960s. These were parties that relied heavily on their manual base and were very slow to learn how to move out from it. There the resemblance between them ends. The PCF, as a communist party, was isolated from the mainstream of French political life and voting for it was an act of alienation from the national polity. Labour was a major party constantly in contention for dominating the government of the British state, and doing so for several spells during the period under review. During the early 1980s the party did however go through a major crisis leading to a split and the temporary formation of a new Social Democratic Party among a minority which rejected much of the socialism of the majority. By 1997 the Labour Party had relaunched itself (informally changing its name to New Labour) as a non-socialist party.

Alongside the PCF, other parties of type 1b did not fare well. Small communist parties dwindled even further as the Soviet Union moved towards collapse, all sinking below the threshold. Small breakaway socialist parties in Scandinavia similarly declined or at least failed to advance beyond their earlier toe-hold. Rather different was the experience of the Italian PSI. After a lengthy period when it had seemed to be heading towards major party status and playing a major role in the state, it finally entered total oblivion following its involvement in a number of severe corruption scandals which generally engulfed the Italian political scene in the early 1990s. (Similar scandals affected Socialist parties in Belgium, France, Greece, and Spain during this period, as well as parties from some other political families, particularly in Italy.)

The overall appraisal of the fate of working-class parties is complex. On the one hand, there has clearly been decline, both absolutely and in the working-class character of the parties. On the other hand several of them have acquired a new social base among public-service employees which gives the parties an *entrée* into a growing type of employment, a more extensive class base, and better prospects with female voters. This is likely to be a valid extension of social base rather than a temporary accretion of volatile votes, because these parties have logically appeared as the main defenders of the welfare state within which public-service workers have their employment. Also, while the Scandinavian parties have lost their former dominance of their national systems, working-class parties in southern Europe have enjoyed an historically unprecedented period of importance including spells of government. This has resulted partly from their strength in the new democracies of Greece, Portugal, and Spain, which quickly developed the European pattern of having a strong working-class-based party as one of the most important in the state. It also resulted from the change in Italy from PCI to (P)DS, and from a prolonged period of socialist government in France. The French PS was not considered a group 1 party in 1960. Today its position as a party of public-service employees, especially teachers, seems more in line with general trends within type 1a, and it is now a major party in the French state.

CHRISTIAN PARTIES

There have been similar changes in the other great historical bloc, Christian democracy. These parties have gradually become smaller with the decline of Catholic observance, though, unlike the working-class parties, they have not lost ground within their core electorates. Specifically Christian voters have become less important to them because often they retain their initial post-war position as the main rallying point for members of the electorate who do not identify with the manual working class. They have therefore attracted large numbers of the strongly growing non-manual group, even when these are not particularly interested in religion.

Some parties have done particularly poorly. By the early 1990s the Austrian ÖVP had lost much of its support, largely to the FPÖ—the implications of which will be discussed below. Belgian Christians underwent the same split into Wallonian and Flemish organizations as did the socialists. In this case the Flemish part was stronger (Flanders being a more devout region), and since it is considerably more populous, the CVP has become the biggest single party in the state. Italian Christian Democracy, like the PSI, was broken on the rack of severe corruption scandals and then split into three small parties. One then allied itself with PDS, the other two with parties of the centre-right and right, though one subsequently joined the centre-left. Each of these became parties of type 2b, leaving the core country of the Catholic world without a major Christian democratic party.

Dutch Catholics and Protestants, faced with declining support given the rapid depolarization of their society, followed the 1949 example of their German colleagues and united to form one Christian democratic party, the CDA. Like the CDU this became a primarily Catholic party. The small strict Calvinist ARP, renamed as the SGP, continues autonomously as a type 2b party.

British Conservatives, always only marginally a member of the Christian category, became less characterized by an association with regular church-going. Small Protestant Christian parties in Scandinavia made some electoral advance, but only in Norway enough to bring them above the threshold and into political prominence.

Greek Orthodoxy never had the same political possibilities as Catholicism or Calvinism, so it is not surprising that there are no specifically Christian parties in Greece. It is however notable that in neither Portugal nor Spain have explicit Christian democratic parties appeared as the central rivals to a working-class party. One must remember here that European Christian Democrats had originally been those Catholics who supported the struggle for democracy in the late nineteenth and early twentieth centuries when other conservative forces opposed it. Very few Iberian church groups opposed the dictatorships which lasted until the mid-1970s. Parties associated with these churches were therefore in no position to assume a Christian democratic mantle. Nevertheless, there is a Christian party in Portugal, and the main national party of the democratic Spanish right tends to have far stronger support among Christians than does the PSOE: it is unambiguously a de facto Christian party, which is the main point for our analysis.

Like the working-class parties, Christian parties have had an ambiguous recent history. In several respects their social base has declined, and some of their number have been major casualties of change. However, in most countries of Europe a party of this type remains one of the two biggest in the state. The only real decline has taken place in Italy, though the three successor parties to DC occupy strategic positions across the spectrum.

AGRARIAN PARTIES

Purely agrarian parties have declined with industrialization as we would expect. Several have however managed to reshape themselves to appeal to new electorates, particularly in Denmark where Venstre has become the most important focus of opposition to social democracy.

CULTURAL AND REGIONAL PARTIES

Ethnic and regional parties have grown considerably. We shall first consider those of type 4b, which are easier to define. Here bilingual Belgium is the extreme case, with every established party splitting into linguistic wings alongside the existing specifically regionalist parties which have in turn strengthened their position since the early 1960s. Following the general collapse of existing parties that accompanied the corruption crisis of Christian democratic, socialist, and some other small parties in Italy, one of the major new forces to emerge was the Lega Nord, seeking separation from Italy for the prosperous northern part of the country. In the UK regional parties became strong in Scotland and Wales, while the parties of Northern Ireland broke completely with those of the mainland and organized themselves almost solely around a Protestant/Catholic antagonism and orientation to either the UK or to Ireland. However, these British parties, though very important within their regions and significant in national politics, do not pass the size threshold for the UK as a whole.

Assisted by some strong regional languages, distinctive regional economies, and a legacy of clandestine organization under the dictatorship, soon after democratization the Spanish regions began to produce parties which stressed their identity against the central state: in the Basque country, Catalonia, Galicia, and Valencia. These are often separatist, but they are split between groups prepared to work for autonomy from Spain within the existing political framework and those wanting to use armed struggle. Like those in Belgium and Wales, these parties use historic national languages as symbols of autonomy.

In the 1960s the only sociologically identifiable cases of a party of type 4a—a party of existing nation-state nationalism—were the Italian Fascist party the MSI and possibly the Austrian FPÖ. This is because a majority nationalist party can be identified demographically only if its support is either concentrated in what is regarded as the potentially hegemonic regions of a country, or if minorities are significantly excluded from its support. If the minorities in question are aliens who do not have the vote this will be difficult to determine.

By the 1990s the MSI had changed its name to Aleanza Nazionale, but retained its strong southern association. It is also notable that its share of the electorate has increased very significantly. Alongside this went a move of the party out from the isolation to which fascist parties were condemned after 1945, it having become part of an alliance with a major new primarily secular, higher-class party (Forza Italia, see below) and having had a brief spell in government in 1994–5. A sociologically similar party is the French Front National. Its support is concentrated in the southern part of France, though it articulates not southern regional separatism but French national integralism. The sociological significance of the French *Midi* is different from that of the Italian *Mezzogiorno*. The towns and cities of the former have been (alongside Paris) the major areas of settlement for immigrants from North Africa, while having also been in the 1950s the major areas of return to France for French North African colonialists driven from Algeria and elsewhere by movements for national autonomy. The Italian south is also a major focus for African immigration, but there is not the same background there of returned natives from colonies. In fact, AN tries to avoid being seen as a racist party and has rejected offers of collaboration from FN.

During the 1980s the FPÖ resolved its earlier dilemma between being a liberal and a quasi-fascist, anti-foreigner party in unambiguous favour of the latter. Since then the party has grown considerably and could before long overtake the ÖVP as the second party in the state. Liberal members of the party formed the new LIF in response, with some moderate success.

Other new parties with a population base in core populations and an anti-foreigner stance existed elsewhere (e.g. the Republikaner in Germany), but without crossing the 5% threshold. Apart from their regional or cultural base these parties tend to share a social profile with working-class parties, receiving disproportionate support from manual workers and being more male than female.

PRIMARILY SECULAR, HIGHER-CLASS PARTIES

Secular, non-working-class parties have expanded considerably. It is necessary to separate out those which have a clear identity as primarily parties of higher classes rather than those which simply lack a class identity, since only the former really belong in category 5. Others must be reckoned within category 6. One factor behind the growth of such parties has been the growth in the social categories represented by them. In some cases this has enabled them to become major parties within the state and thus of type 5a: Danish Venstre has been able to shift its support base from being an essentially agrarian party to being of type 5a; Dutch VVD, Norwegian Høyre, and Swedish Moderaten (the former Höjere party renamed) are all in this category. The three new democracies all produced parties of this type too: Greek New Democracy, Portuguese PSD, and Spanish PP/AP. It is interesting that these are all countries where, for different reasons, classical Christian democracy has been weak or divided. Where Christian democracy has been strong, it has held voters from these classes within more socially diverse parties.

Other parties of this basic sociological type remain within 5b: the Belgian liberals, the anomalous Danish far-left party, German FDP, Norwegian SV, and Swedish FP. The Belgian party has split into Flemish and Walloon wings, but together these occupy a similar vote share as in the past, as do Italian and German liberals. Support has been lost by Norwegian and Swedish liberals, whose former voters seem to have clustered round more conservative parties better able to counter the dominant working-class party.

UNSTRUCTURED PARTIES

Parties of category 6, sociologically undefined parties, have grown considerably in conformity with the postmodern hypothesis. Even more in keeping with this, the growth has mainly taken the form of new organizations. One of these has already become among the largest in the state: Italian Forza Italia. This is in some senses the world's first truly postmodern political party; ideologically it belongs with the new anti-tax, anti-state parties to be discussed below, but it has been considerably more successful than them in extending its social base. It is rooted, not in an existing political group or social movement, but on a business enterprise, or chain of related enterprises, called Fininvest and located within the growth centres of the post-industrial economy: financial services, national television stations and newspapers, a leading football team, a supermarket chain, and condominium apartment blocks. As a political organization it does not require a membership base or local structures; its money comes from the firms it owns; to the extent that it needs people on the ground it can deploy employees of these; instead of fighting to win the attention of the media it simply uses its own television stations and papers. With these assets the party was able to become one of the leading two or three in the state—and temporarily to dominate a government—within weeks of being founded. It is however also notable that it has formed a close electoral partnership and potential coalition with a party with more traditional nationalist loyalties, the neo-fascist AN.

Other parties in category 6 can be divided into two main groupings: Green parties—most of which align themselves to the political left—and anti-tax and racist parties—which align with the right. Greens developed strongly during the 1980s. In terms of formal ideology they are likely to be most clearly marked by strong opposition to the capitalist economy, which is seen as the source of most ecological damage. They therefore tend to be close to socialists on several issues, though have problems with the interests of *industrial* workers; they are likely to incline to anarchism, or better what Kitschelt (1990) has called 'left-libertarianism'; they have often been linked with wider movements for peace and various minority rights. They are more or less neutral on religious questions, though they often have an important Christian wing. In some respects the British Liberals now belong in this group.

While ideologically Green parties can be distinguished from most other secular, non-working class parties, sociological analysis fails to show them as any different from these, except for a tendency for Green parties to be more female than pro-capitalist new parties. To some extent this is consistent with a postmodern account of politics, with individuals reaching political positions without much sociological determination. However, there have been two critical responses to this. Klaus Eder (1993) suggests that unrest about environmental and related issues becomes itself a new class fault line within society. This is of course a very different meaning of class from the conventional occupation-related approach, and will be discussed again in Chapter 15. The central point however is that environmentalist politics are by this approach seen to be rooted in social structural attributes and positions, and not as free-floating individualistic choices. The second argument, which is consistent with Eder's but does not require such a break from conventional class analysis, locates environmentalism with particular social-structural segments, such as public service professionals and those employed in the media and creative worlds (Kriesi 1989; Vester 1989). Differences among these new forms of non-working-class party may well therefore be far more structurally determined than at first appears. It is also notable that their social structure somewhat resembles that towards which category 1 parties have been moving.

The second group, the anti-tax populist parties, mainly exist in Scandinavia, though in some respects Forza Italia belongs here, and the earliest case was D66 in the Netherlands. Founded in 1966 as its name implies, originally D66 was more concerned just with taking a stand against the entrenched interests of the rest of the Dutch party scene, but over time it has followed the pattern set initially by the Danish FRP and then imitated by parties in the other Nordic lands. The ideological programme of these parties is therefore close to some of the parties in category 5 (such as the British Conservatives), though unlike these they are 'rebel' parties and not part of the national elite. For example, they tend to oppose military as well as welfare spending, which conservative parties rarely do. Just as FI has joined with the anti-immigrant party AN, so several of these parties have started to combine hostility to immigrants and other foreigners in their programmes. Were we to be able to analyse their support base sufficiently closely, we might find that they are beginning to acquire the attributes of type 4a parties—in which case they would no longer constitute unstructured parties.

CONCLUSIONS: TOWARDS POSTMODERN POLITICAL ALLEGIANCES?

Peter Mair (1997: ch. 4) has analysed the change in shares of the vote of 'old' parties in 14 Western European countries, conveniently covering the same period as that followed in this book: from the early 1960s until the 1990s. The share of the vote of these parties has declined in all cases, but in only three cases did it decline by more than 15%: Belgium (where the regional split produced divisions in each major party), Switzerland (where women were enfranchised during the period), and Sweden (where the old parties had achieved 99.9% of the vote in 1960 and had to expect some decline). Considering the change in political issues, the occupational profile of the electorate, and also the sheer growth in numbers of voters, reductions in voting age and change in individual identities through the processes of death and maturation, Mair is more impressed by the stability than the change of this situation.

The main consensus of studies seems to be that those changes which have taken place have resulted from changes in the demographic profile of societies rather than in the political orientations of specific social groups. For example, the volatility of British voters clearly increased between the late 1960s and the 1990s, but this was because the proportion of Britons having a clearly defined historical class identity declined. Those who had such identities (e.g. less skilled manual workers, or property owners) continued to express their traditional political preferences (Heath 1992). However, if those forces in the population which had particularly strong political profiles are declining in size, the question arises whether newly emerging groups are developing them. If they are, then the social structure of political cleavage will change, and we need to understand its potential shape. If they are not developing clear profiles, then we may be entering a period in which political allegiance is less socially determined, where the ability of sociology to explain that allegiance declines, and where postmodern expectations may be validated.

In many ways the findings of this chapter on political allegiances are similar to those of Chapter 9 on religion—and the two phenomena are of course related. The old structure of the mid-century compromise model of social cleavages has clearly weakened considerably, but it remains in place and is still a majority system. It is difficult to perceive an alternative structured system emerging to replace it. This might mean that we are moving towards a period where there are no structures, as anticipated by postmodern theories. Alternatively it might mean that we cannot discern the overall outline of a new structure, and confuse this with structurelessness. We have however also seen, as we did in Chapter 10, that structured cleavages around ethnicity might be growing in importance. This is a cleavage that stood outside those negotiated by the mid-century compromise, but it is certainly a cleavage and can be a very powerful one.

Chapter 12

THE ORGANIZATION OF
SOCIAL INTERESTS

Apart from party allegiance, social interests may also find political expression through organizations which seek to represent them within the public sphere, either by lobbying governments or by sharing directly in the administration of public business. A wide range of interests can be involved in such activities. Here there is space to consider only one, that which is most important for the mid-century social compromise model: associations of workers and their employers. This has become a form of economic citizenship in many industrial societies. For associations of employers or manufacturers this has long been established in such forms as urban guilds, and in fact constitutes one of the earliest forms of European citizenship since the medieval period. For workers it has been an achievement of the twentieth century, often of the second half of that century.

As discussed in the Introduction to this Part, all achievements of citizenship have been set in a context of class relations: at one level universal citizenship constitutes an abatement of the power of class, a legal affirmation of the existence of rights that exist irrespective of class resources of wealth and power. On the other hand, these class resources can be deployed within the frame of formally equal citizenship rights in order to gain substantive advantages. For example: all citizens have equal rights of access to the legal procedures and the law courts; but a rich person can buy a better lawyer to represent him in the courts. Organizational rights have followed the same pattern. It usually took workers' organizations far longer to win them than their capitalist counterparts. Then followed a strange asymmetry. Workers were more dependent on them than capitalists or employers, since the latter already had the organizational structure of the firm to protect their vulnerability as human individuals; but because they possessed both that capacity and greater wealth in any case, it was easier for employers to form organizations than it was for workers (Offe and Wiesenthal 1980; Streeck 1992). In turn this became a major element in the political shaping of class identities. Particularly relevant then becomes the question of which parts of the workforce are organized within the same structures.

The model of mid-century compromise society legitimated the organization and expression of various interests, provided they did so in a form that could be integrated within the capitalist economic order. The organization of employees clearly posed the most problematic challenge here, since potentially this was the interest that was most difficult to reconcile with capitalism. During the nineteenth and early twentieth centuries it often proved irreconcilable in all countries covered by our study, and was occasionally involved in some of the most extreme conflicts, extending to violence, fascist takeovers and civil wars. By the time mid-century compromises were installed in most of the countries under review, there were two main modes whereby these interests could be organized consistent with citizenship: bargained corporatism and pluralism. This left two possibilities outside that framework: contestation and authoritarian corporatism.

FORMS OF INTEREST ORGANIZATION

All four of these forms are needed for an analysis of the early 1960s. They will therefore be defined before we consider the state of organized interests at that time and then again in the 1990s (see Crouch 1993 for a fuller analysis of these forms).

CONTESTATION

Contestation is the most simple. It refers to a situation where either employers or workers or both refuse to accept the right of the other side to organize. It does not however necessarily follow that overt conflict in the form of strikes and other disruptions will be endemic or even frequent. Were they to become such the system would enter major crisis. This would be quelled either by the breaking of workers' organizations altogether or by a move to either pluralism or corporatism. Contestation represents an absence of citizenship, because there is no agreed structure through which interests can express their concerns through autonomous organizations.

PLURALISM

Pluralism, or pluralist collective bargaining, stems from Anglo-American industrial relations traditions. In countries which traditionally had extensive civil liberties and where the state had no use for the role of organized interests but by and large did not interfere in their growth, organizations of interests developed in a rather chaotic, competitive manner, coming to resemble an organizational market of free choice (Clegg 1975; Dahl 1961; Dunlop 1958). The processes involved were not really markets: there were no constraints to match supply and demand and not even a pricing mechanism. Therefore the analogy never really held, and at any time there could be a growth of unregulated demands that could cause crises in the system. For many years this did not matter, as only relatively skilled workers were able to organize and in the slack labour markets of much of the first half of the century employers had the power to break labour's organizations if they became difficult. In other words, an element of contestation was perhaps a condition of the balance of the system.

The model is clearly one of citizenship, in that rights to participate are mutually accepted, but the fact that it can only operate smoothly if not too many workers start exercising their rights within it creates certain problems of universality. Typically two very different types of employee have been left out of these systems: non-manual workers, especially at the higher levels; and low-skilled workers including those in flexible labour markets of the kind discussed in Chapter 3. When the former are excluded, the industrial relations system becomes one of the ways in which the manual working class achieved certain citizenship rights not available to groups often regarded as being 'above' them in the class scheme. The exclusion of the latter also creates a limitation to the idea of universal citizenship, but of a less surprising kind.

BARGAINED CORPORATISM

Bargained corporatism describes a form of organizational behaviour in which associations, while representing the particular interests of their members, also discipline them in the interests of some wider collectivity. It can be applied to a number of organizational situations. The *verzuiling* arrangements of Dutch religious structure described in Chapter 9 have distinct affinities (Daalder 1974). It can also refer to the work of trade associations, in relations with governments or with each other (Streeck and Schmitter 1985). Applied to systems of industrial relations it usually refers to long-term arrangements for keeping collectively negotiated wage development in line with price competitiveness (Dell'Aringa 1990; Crouch 1993). It has therefore been particularly associated with voluntary incomes policies.

The significance of corporatism is that it might enable firms, unions of employees, and other participants in a market economy to achieve a high level of cooperation and shared pursuit of collective goods that also serve a wider public interest, despite the fact that they are also in competition and conflict with each other. For these reasons it is an appropriate form of interest organization for citizenship within the mid-century social compromise framework: it grants participation, at least to representatives, and it is oriented towards the public sphere.

However, from the perspective of economic theory, when interests organize themselves they are likely to conspire against the public interest; it is argued that they will pursue their shared collective interest by rent-seeking and by dumping or externalizing the costs of what they do on to those outside their circle, that is the general public. For example, they might exercise political pressure to receive special treatment for their activities, or they might fix artificially high prices for their products. From this perspective corporatism, as defined here, is impossible to achieve. There are however three kinds of situation in which they might not act in this way:

1. When the organized group is so large that (a) its actions have a clear, perceptible effect and cannot just disappear into the general 'noise' of everybody's special pleading; and (b) its membership overlaps with at least a large minority of the general public. In such instances the distinction between insiders who gain at the expense of outsiders who lose breaks down, as the two groups become partly coterminous. This is the case that Olson (1982) described as 'encompassing organizations'. Examples would be large, centralized national trade union organizations bargaining on behalf of, say, 30% of the employees in a country. Whereas the leaders of a small union might argue that any inflationary consequences of their actions will be (a) infinitesimally small and (b) in any case borne in general by outsiders, the leaders of a centralized national federation know that the outcomes of their bargaining will (a) have a macro-economic effect that will be (b) directly borne by their members as part of the general public.

2. Where the group is sufficiently large and responsive to its leaders for the latter to have a strategic capacity enabling them to identify and respond to negative consequences that would eventually be felt by the group were it to maximize its immediate interests. Examples would be centralized employers' associations and unions bargaining: (a) in a context where they know that any inflationary outcome of their bargaining will lead to deflationary action by a central bank likely to create unemployment in the sector (Lange and Garrett 1985; Crouch 1994; Streeck 1994); or (b) in an industry heavily dependent on price-sensitive export trade (Crouch 1990).

3. Where the group is small, decentralized, and operating in a context of many rival groups analogous to a pure market: that is, no one group can affect the overall outcome or have more than an infinitesimally small impact.

Cases 1 and 2 are both examples of where the organizations are likely to behave in a corporatist way, as they have strong incentives to restrain their pursuit of self-interest, if necessary disciplining their members in order to do so. Case 3 is an example of organizations compatible with the public interest achieved under pluralism, *not* corporatism. The optimal conditions of corporatism and pluralism are therefore the opposite of each other, and pluralism serves as a useful antithesis to corporatism in the study of different systems of organized interests. Corporatism will be more stable the more oligopolistic, the more centralized and capable of strategic action are the organizations; pluralism will be more stable the more there is a highly competitive free market in organizational capacities.

Corporatism is a citizenship model in the double sense that it extends rights to participation, and that it embodies duties and responsibilities—an essential element of the citizenship concept. In principle corporatism does not have the problems of pluralism of operating best when many interests are not represented, since in theory it operates best when organizations have to take responsibility for a whole. In practice however life may be made easier for bargaining organizations if there exist some parts of the economy which can bear the strain of any bargains made while not interfering with them. This becomes a kind of corruption of corporatism and will cause resentment among the excluded groups.

From this it follows that both corporatist and pluralist systems begin to acquire the rent-seeking attributes associated in economic theory with interest organizations as they start to converge, that is if they slip towards the middle ground between them. This middle position would exist if there were a number of competing interest organizations, each too small to have strategic capacity but too large and too uneven and partial in their coverage to produce a true market. It is an interesting case of a middle-ground position being less stable than the two extremes on either side of it, a bipolar or U-curve model of stability. Research evidence has supported this theory of interest group behaviour and the public interest (Calmfors and Driffill 1988; Crouch 1993).

AUTHORITARIAN CORPORATISM

Corporatist industrial relations appear to us today as a system of cooperation among highly and autonomously organized workers and employers, associated in particular with strong social democratic trade union movements. However, it is a form of industrial relations accepted initially by labour movements only with great reluctance. The origins of corporatism as a set of economic ideas rested in various social Christian ideas emerging in the late nineteenth century as a reaction against the individualism of capitalism and the class conflict associated with socialism. Then in the years after the First World War it was taken up by a new and surprising source: the Fascist movements emerging in southern Europe were also staking a claim to being alternatives to capitalism and socialism, and included a good deal of romanticism in their rhetoric. A corporatist model of industrial relations fitted this perfectly and was developed in Fascist ideology (Williamson 1985). In reality none of the Fascist regimes really developed corporatism in the way that had been envisaged by the nineteenth-century writers. Since existing labour leaders were all executed, imprisoned, or exiled, and no open debate was permitted, the organizations established became little more than dummies for the Fascist parties, empty shells with few real functions. This was not therefore a form of citizenship.

One way in which authors have tried to make clear the distinction between bargained corporatism, on the one hand, and both authoritarian corporatism and that of nineteenth-century Catholic social theory, on the other, is to call bargained corporatism 'neo-corporatism'. This is less cumbersome than repeated use of the adjective 'bargained'. From now on in this chapter, 'neo-' will be added to the words 'corporatism' and 'corporatist' whenever contemporary bargained corporatism is intended, and simple 'corporatism' used only if reference is being made to the full range of corporatist phenomena.

FORMS OF ORGANIZATION AND DEGREES OF POWER

Neo-corporatism is potentially unstable because it involves central actors working at a level of the strategic interests of the overall system, while local, decentralized actors are also invited to participate. It can therefore only be established in stable form when the organizations possess a high degree of *articulation*, that is when there is a strong two-way communication flow such that central actors (leaders) can both commit their local units to a course of action and have been initially informed by those units so that they do not reach agreements that are unacceptable to them. I prefer this term to the more obvious ideas of centralization or coordination, since these focus only on the one-way flow of authority and competence from the top to the base. This does this not capture the complexity of what has to occur in voluntary organizations where members are free to rebel or even to leave the organization, and this possibility is important if corporatist organizations are to be aspects of citizenship.

Pluralist collective bargaining does not make the same stringent demands and therefore does not face the same organizational complexities if it is to correspond to a citizenship model. On the other hand, pluralism becomes unstable when the density, competitive character, and activism of the organizations involved in the system press conflicting demands that exceed what is available to be gained (to take a very relevant example for industrial relations, when everyone demands a wage increase greater than everybody else).

Stability can return to a neo-corporatist system through either a reassertion of articulation or a breaking of the organizational capacity of at least one partner, that is a move to contestation, or perhaps authoritarian corporatism. Stability can return to a pluralist system only by a reduction in pressure being exerted. This might take the form of a regrouping of interests into a neo-corporatist form or by a weakening of the power of some of them (contestation). A move to authoritarian corporatism is unlikely given that this is a rather remote form of organization for a pluralist case. There is therefore a certain asymmetry between the two citizenship-compatible models: neo-corporatism either reforms itself, becomes authoritarian or is broken; pluralism either becomes neo-corporatism or is broken, perhaps in order to re-form at a weaker level of action.

In practice there is a further asymmetry. Within a capitalist economy it is far easier for labour's organizations and citizenship to be broken than those of capital. We can therefore reformulate the previous paragraph as follows: Stability can return to a neo-corporatist system by either a reassertion of articulation or a breaking of labour's organizational capacity through either contestation or perhaps authoritarian corporatism. It can return to a pluralist system only by a reduction in pressure being exerted. This might take the form of a regrouping of interests into a neo-corporatist form, or by a weakening of the power of organized labour (contestation).

THE ORGANIZATION OF INTERESTS IN THE EARLY 1960S

According to the citizenship hypothesis of the mid-century model, we should find that by the early 1960s all societies in our group were converging on either a neo-corporatist or a pluralist model. That was broadly the case, though there were important exceptions. In Finland, France, Greece, and Italy far more contestative forms dominated; and Portugal and Spain exhibited authoritarian corporatism. Very major elements of contestation were also present in Japan and the USA.[1] Communism in the labour movement (or opposition to it) was at that time the main cause of contestation being the predominant form of industrial relations; communist components were of major importance to the movements in Finland, France, Greece, and Italy.

CITIZENSHIP MODELS OF INDUSTRIAL RELATIONS (1960S)

Neo-Corporatism with Strong Labour
In Austria, Sweden, Norway, and Denmark, unions and employers' organizations had become deeply engaged in a range of national-level institutions that enabled or required them to participate in economy-wide decision-making on wage movements and in the administration of various labour-related services, moving especially in the Swedish case into aspects of labour-market policy.[2] These were the most clearly neo-corporatist cases of the period. These were all systems in which unions represented the great majority of the workforce, either directly through high memberships (in the Scandinavian cases) or through the extension of bargains to all parts of the workforce in Austria.

Neo-Corporatism with State Support
Similar institutions existed in Belgium and the Netherlands, though limited to a somewhat narrower range of issues and needing continuing government support to enable them to operate—the latter increasingly also becoming a feature of Danish incomes policy.[3] In Belgium this took the form of *programmation sociale*, a series of national tripartite agreements on incomes development and a broad range of social policies.

---

[1] In Japan installation of the distinctive form of cooperative corporatism was preceded by a violent purge of communist trade unionism; and in the USA both anti-communism and the occasionally violent rejection of unions by employers also left wide areas of contestation.

[2] For a general overview, see Crouch 1993: 205–32. For more detailed information on individual countries, see: *Austria*: Kotthof 1985: 85; Lang 1978: ch. 5; Talos 1981: ch. 7; Traxler 1982: 191–253, 1986; *Denmark*: Hansen and Henriksen 1980: 150–64; Rasmussen 1985: 393–404; *Norway*: Kvavik 1976: ch. 3; Olsen 1983; *Sweden*: Hadenius 1976; Kjellberg 1990; Korpi 1978; Micheletti 1984; Olsson 1991: 25–9; Rothstein 1985.

[3] For a general overview, see Crouch 1993: 205–32. For more detailed information on individual countries, see: *Belgium*: Brande 1973; Gevers 1983, 1987; van de Kerckhove 1979; Spitaels 1967: 30–78; *Netherlands*: Hemerijck 1992; Scholten 1987; Windmuller 1969.

These would sometimes be incorporated into legislation. Given the deadlocked nature of Belgian party politics over the language issue at this time, legislation was often implemented by the democratically dubious device of royal decree, prior agreement to a policy in *programmation sociale* enabling the government to bridge this democratic deficit while simultaneously enhancing the acceptance of national responsibility by organizations of employers and employees.

In the Netherlands institutions for the formal involvement of business and union organizations in exercising public responsibilities alongside the state had been developed since the war, using ideas initiated in the 1930s and based on the *verzuiling* concept. These mechanisms were fully in place through a Stichting van de Arbeid and a Sociaal-Economisch Raad by the 1960s. They never gave unions the degree of general economic policy influence that had been originally envisaged, but involved them in widespread consultation and included a binding tripartite incomes policy.

Both these cases achieved a high level of extension throughout the workforce, if only through statutory imposition.

Neo-Corporatism with Decentralization
Arrangements in Germany and Switzerland also took a neo-corporatist form, except that there remained in these countries a split between national level participation by confederal and union leaders and more localized collective bargaining.[4]

The Japanese organized interest system bore a complex relationship to corporatism (Aoki and Dore 1994; Dore 1972). At the level of business organizations there was a tight, straightforward system of relations between government departments and organizations representing firms. Much of the growing innovation of the Japanese economy during that period was organized in that way. However, labour's organizations were not involved at that level. Instead, in the large corporations of the Japanese economy, trade unions were organized at company level and there operated in a very corporatist manner. In no European country or the USA were unions organized as company unions in this way, and there were often suspicions among external observers that this pattern more closely resembled authoritarian than bargained corporatism. However, other observers insist that real bargaining took place in these forums, and there was also a certain amount of strike activity.[5]

Pluralist Collective Bargaining
Ireland and the UK, and outside Europe the USA, were pre-eminent cases of strong collective bargaining, the countries having converged from rather different positions in the post-war years.[6] Irish industrialization had increased the importance of unionized

---

[4] For a general overview, see Crouch 1993: 205–32. For more detailed information on individual countries, see: *Germany*: Armingeon 1987, 1988: 65–81; Bergmann 1985; Hirsch 1966: 155–88; Leminsky 1965: ch. 3; Simon 1976: ch. 6. *Switzerland*: Höpflinger 1976; Kriesi 1986; Parri 1987.

[5] From a European and North American point of view there are some doubts about describing as citizenship an institution limited to the level of the firm. There is considerable debate about this in the relevant literature. From the point of view of some authors Japanese citizenship is weak and defective for this reason (Morishima 1982); others however argue that Japanese firms are more like communities or villages than are Western firms (Dore 1972, Aoki and Dore 1994). Quite apart from the cultural differences in the concept of the firm that this raises, it also suggests the interesting question of the relationship between citizenship and community.

[6] For a general overview of Ireland and the UK, see Crouch 1993: 205–32. For more detailed information on individual countries, see: *Ireland*: Lee 1989: 401–4; McCarthy 1977; *UK*: Clegg 1972: chs. 2, 4, 6; 1979: chs. 3, 5; Crouch 1977: chs. 4, 11; Currie 1979: ch. 5; Fox 1985: ch. 8; Middlemas 1979: Pt II, 1990.

labour, giving governments some interest in encouraging shared understandings going towards a neo-corporatist model, though the system remained largely one of straight pluralist bargaining. Meanwhile the British, who had seemed to be embarking on a 'Scandinavian' neo-corporatist path in the early post-war years, had reverted to a purer collective bargaining model as Conservative governments lost interest in economic coordination, while unions and employers lost a temporary capacity for articulation that they had acquired under the pressure of wartime emergency. Collective bargaining was shifting to the unofficial shop-floor level, in a manner quite disarticulated from branch-level negotiations—though this was to change during the course of the 1960s when there was an increasingly frantic search to re-establish institutions of the kind that had deteriorated during the 1950s. British bargaining was quite extensive, the unions representing a high proportion of manual workers, and certain mechanisms being in place at that time to extend the results of bargaining throughout a sector.

The USA had not passed through a strong neo-corporatist episode in the 1930s or 1940s. It had come close to it with New Deal policies, but the main consequence of partnership between government and unions was to establish a legal framework whereby unions could gain recognition from employers. Left to themselves many US employers pursued a contestation policy, refusing to let labour have autonomous representation. Bargaining tended to be at company level only, with few capabilities for extension and with non-manual workers usually excluded.

There was therefore by the 1960s a kind of Anglophone zone of pluralist bargaining, though, as noted, in large parts of the US economy conditions more closely resembling either contestation or no worker organization at all predominated, and the system lacked extensiveness compared with the British and Irish cases.

MODELS OF INDUSTRIAL RELATIONS DENYING CITIZENSHIP (1960S)

Contestation

Finland, France, and Italy are relatively clear cases of contestation.[7] In Finland, government control of income development had been instituted after the War. This had been relaxed in 1956, but instead of a transition to a centralized Scandinavian model, the system shifted to one of intensive and conflictual bargaining. Political conflict divided the labour movement between a social democratic majority and a communist minority, the latter being guaranteed a certain status in the country by virtue of Finland's special relationship with the Soviet Union. This did not make for central coordination of industrial relations, though governments persevered with efforts to encourage co-operative behaviour through intensive consultation of interest groups.

In France and Italy the beginnings of a citizenship model of industrial relations had been established at the end of the War, with the erection of various national institutions, and legislation for bargaining and workplace representation rights. However, these remained rather frozen in their tracks as the bulk of the labour movement became

---

7 For a general overview, see Crouch 1993: 205–32. For more detailed information on individual countries, see: *Finland*: Elvander 1974*b*: 431–4; Knoellinger 1960: 168–78, ch. 7; Mansner 1989; Nousiainen 1971; *France*: Brizay 1975: 101–8; Hayward 1966: ch. 3; Keeler 1987: ch. 1; Lefranc 1976: 159 ff., 191 ff.; Reynaud 1975: chs. 4, 5; *Italy*: Bull 1988: 78–82; Contini 1985; de Carlini 1972: 62–74; Collidà 1972: 93–104; LaPolambara 1964: chs. 8, 9, 11; Martinelli 1980: 71–7; Martinelli and Treu 1984; Turone 1981.

associated with communist parties and as employers refused to recognize unions within the firms. In both countries there was some growth in collective bargaining, led by the state industries, in the early 1960s. This was undertaken for political at least as much as for industrial-relations reasons: governments were seeking to reinforce national unity in the face of the continuing level of class conflict. Unions were in general weak: membership was low and finances poor. However, to compensate for this, unions would demonstrate their mobilizing power by frequent strike calls which secured widespread support.

Even less institutionalized were industrial relations in Greece. A low level of industrialization and a split between socialist and communist wings of the labour movement meant that worker organization was weak and divided. The few important manufacturing firms tried to avoid union recognition.

In all four countries the level of industrialization and therefore the size of the organized working class was relatively low, so bouts of contestation only fitfully threatened real system instability. By the late 1960s this was to change, culminating in the major incidences of social conflict of that time. The level of industrialization and union capacity for militancy rose. In Finland and Italy this was a gradual and persistent process; in France it was more sporadic but occasionally dramatic (as in 1968 above all); in Greece a military coup in 1966, in response partly to labour unrest, temporarily removed Greece from the ranks of democratic societies. In the first three countries governments and employers responded to the instability with varieties of pluralism and neo-corporatism; in Greece the response was one of authoritarian corporatism.

AUTHORITARIAN CORPORATISM

Greece then joined Portugal and Spain, where Fascist dictatorships had continued since the 1920s and 1930s, respectively, with a form and rhetoric of authoritarian corporatism, behind which very few real industrial-relations exchanges occurred (Amsden 1972: chs. 5–7; Ariza 1976). However, in Spain government had responded to unrest by establishing a form of elected shop-floor committees for dealing with local grievances. Although these were permitted no overt links with clandestine autonomous unions or parties, in practice it was activists from these, especially communists, who took advantage of the new institutions and secured election to places on them.

SUMMARY, EARLY 1960S

Overall therefore most but by no means all countries had systems of organized interest representation matching one or other of the two forms compatible with the citizenship of the mid-century compromise. Those which had taken the neo-corporatist route were largely those with a prior history of involvement of trade associations in public business extending back to before the rise of liberalism in the nineteenth century (Austria, Denmark, Germany, the Netherlands, Norway). In Sweden that interruption had been only brief. Switzerland was an unusual case in that its very early, medieval, liberalism had always operated *through* organizations of interests. Belgium is slightly odd, having resembled France in much of its prior social organization. In these cases the main pre-condition for a neo-corporatist system was the admission of labour to the circle of legitimate interest. This was achieved either (as in Scandinavia; more weakly in the Netherlands and Switzerland) during the 1930s when the growing strength of the labour movement made necessary a social compromise over capitalism of the mid-century social compromise kind, or following internal turmoil and violence as capitalist forces rejected compromise until the fascists they supported were defeated in war (Austria, Germany).

Where liberalism had de-legitimated close relations between states and organized interests (France, Ireland (when an English colony), the UK, and the USA) associations could not achieve the level of integration with public power as in the corporatist cases, and therefore tended not to develop internal articulated structures themselves, the incentive to develop a central competence being that much lower. By the same token the issue of whether labour was to be included or not raised less intense questions: admission to the club of legitimate interests in a liberal system brings fewer returns. As labour movements in the Anglophone countries managed to achieve some strength they gained that admission.

In France liberalism had been more resistant to organized interests becoming involved in the state. Also, in that country as in Finland, Greece, and Italy delayed industrialism and the existence of a strong communist component to the union movement rendered labour that much weaker in making its claim for admission. These countries and the two Fascist survivors—Portugal and Spain—therefore stand outside the mid-century social compromise model.

There is therefore a distinct geography to the diversity of interest organization around 1960, and to some extent it follows a pattern we have encountered in earlier chapters: a distinct Scandinavia; a distinct southern Europe outside the mid-century social compromise citizenship frame, though here divided between a contestative Greece and Italy and an authoritarian corporatist Portugal and Spain (soon to be joined by Greece); an Anglophone belt that is more coherent than we have found in other chapters; and a complex European continental core. Here, and in contrast with discussions of demography and religion, France belongs more with the southern group, while the German-speaking countries (especially Austria) and the Low Countries belong more with Scandinavia. Japan stands somewhat alone. If anything it is assimilable to the German/Swiss model of decentralized neo-corporatism, though the absence of strong citizenship raised by its company-centred rights raises questions of whether there are not elements of authoritarian corporatism here.

The mid-century compromise model was valid in one or other of its forms for many of our countries, but not for Finland, France, or southern Europe. Given the diversity within Europe and the similarities between the UK, Ireland, and the USA, there was no distinctive European form of industrial interest organization. Japan is rather different, though in ways which can be related to the general analysis.

THE ORGANIZATION OF INTERESTS IN THE 1990S

Postmodernist and post-industrial theories should anticipate a collapse of the tighter forms of interest organization associated with neo-corporatism and a convergence on the pluralist model, with its more fragmented structures and its great compatibility with the limited levels of union organization to be expected following the decline of the manual working class. The pluralist model also permits more variety and implies fewer constraints on forms of action or choice of organizational form. Postmodernist theorizing in this field therefore stresses the concept of *disorganization* (Lash and Urry 1987; Lash and Bagguley 1988; Offe 1985), as we also saw in Chapter 6. If these theories are correct, we should find a collapse of previously viable corporatist arrangements and also a weakening of the role of labour organization.

With the exception of Austria and Switzerland all our cases had seen a resurgence of industrial conflict and institutional instability sometime between 1968 and 1970; after 1973 the first 'oil shock' had produced a wave of inflation and decline in purchasing power throughout Western countries that wreaked havoc with expectations and institutions (Crouch 1993: ch. 7). Virtually everywhere—except perhaps Japan where recovery was rapid—the initial response of governments to this crisis had been to appeal to central organizations of capital and labour to help restore stability. This implied at least an element of neo-corporatism, whether as a reinforcement of existing forms or as a shift away from pluralism or contestation.

However, a further new phenomenon which has to be taken into account was a shift in the locus of workers' collective action: disaggregated, localized shop-floor strength of a tenacious kind, differing considerably from either the conservative defensiveness of traditional skilled craftworkers or the transient eruptions of anger and unsettled grievances that every system had known from the early days of industrial relations. The new form of action was a product of unprecedented full employment, and it began appropriately enough in the UK, a society that had experienced both sustained full employment and a labour movement already less centralized than most. All this made neo-corporatism more difficult to achieve since it threatened the articulated character of union (and to some extent employer) organization fundamental to the model. Disarticulation made for good examples of pluralism, but under conditions of growing union power that rendered the model unstable.

This period therefore saw a kind of convergence on neo-corporatist arrangements *which became increasingly difficult to manage*. In general those that had already established systems of this kind tended to control their crises reasonably successfully, though with their patterns of central coordination and articulation fraying badly at the edges. Those with other kinds of system sometimes managed to set up the formal apparatus of neo-corporatist coordination and organized interest participation in managing public business, but frequently with continued conflict as this was resisted by newly powerful and non-articulated decentralized levels. Meanwhile, the changes in the structure of the labour force which we have discussed in previous chapters also made management of the labour market more difficult. Either the more heterogeneous workforce was represented in the unions, in which case the bargaining system had to try to manage much more diversity of market positions, or unions remained representative of traditional manual workers, in which case they were being overtaken by social change and in danger of marginalization.

In general the inflation of the 1970s ended in recession, and in many countries the political response was a sharp shift to the right. Domestic politics apart, international monetary agencies and powerful international investors looked to deflationary policies to remove the heat from the labour market. In many instances Keynesian demand management was abandoned. Even where forces favourable to the labour movement retained political power, they and their policies were affected by these developments; where parties of the right governed, they amplified them. Labour had shown its potency in the decade or so following 1968, leading many conservatives to question the wisdom of their post-war compromise assumptions of seeking to pacify unions by incorporating them. The recurrent recessions of the 1980s and 1990s now led them to question whether such propitiatory policies were even necessary. The restructuring crises which have affected all economies both reduced the size of the workforces in export-oriented manufacturing industries which had borne the burden of wage restraint, and shifted the locus of problem-solving to the company, away from the sectoral or national level where neo-corporatist arrangements had been most prominent. Within general economic policy there was a return to popularity of free-market solutions, which tend to exclude any constructive role for organized interests. Finally, for the great transnational corporations the globalization of the world economy has reduced the importance of individual national associational networks. All these changes undermined the importance and effectiveness of neo-corporatism in particular, but also pluralist collective bargaining in those cases where employers used their new power to return to a position of refusing to recognize labour's right to participate through autonomous organization.

The major overall tendency in countries previously exhibiting strong levels of neo-corporatism has been for a shift in the centre of gravity towards industrial relations at the level of the individual firm. Advocates of the disorganized capitalism thesis (e.g. Lash and Bagguley 1988) see important confirmation of their arguments here. In some cases (especially in Scandinavia) this has been a development of considerable novelty. However, there was a major difference between those countries where decentralization to the firm level took the form of a collapse of wider organized structures (e.g. the UK) and those where the decentralization was managed by employers' associations and trade unions who wished to keep some capacity for general strategy and organized action but who also wanted both to reap the benefits of sensitivity to the individual company and to retain a capacity to act more generally if need arose.

This latter model has been termed 'co-ordinated decentralization' by the Austrian sociologist, Franz Traxler (1995). This concept is a useful way of describing the types of system now developing in some of those countries which used to conform most closely to the neo-corporatist form of compromise. While the organized interests in these cases retain some capacity for action, within bargaining it is increasingly of a residual, steering kind, oriented to a few macro-economic concerns of wage restraint, while accepting that most detailed bargaining is conducted at the level of the individual firm, or possibly a small sector. However, the residual level can become important at certain moments, and the organized actors continue to be active in renegotiating the terms of employment citizenship in terms of government legislation affecting labour and often, welfare questions.

CITIZENSHIP MODELS OF INDUSTRIAL RELATIONS (1990S)

Neo-Corporatism with Decentralization
Austria continues to exhibit many of the features of its previous almost pure form of neo-corporatism (Traxler 1998). The system has become slightly displaced: privatization

of the state industries that had been important to the manageability of the model has removed an important lever of control from the central actors; unemployment and demands for deregulation have made it more difficult to achieve consensus outcomes. However, the Austrian system has long incorporated an absence of political influence over key economic variables, since the economy and the currency have been so dependent on Germany and the Deutsche Mark. The kind of loss of control in a context of globalization that is causing disequilibrium for several neo-corporatist cases is therefore already anticipated in the Austrian model. Similarly, decentralization to works councils of several aspects of industrial relations had already, as in Germany and Switzerland, included aspects of articulation and decentralization. Because the system had long included both manual and non-manual workers without trying to erode the salary differentials of the latter, changes in the structure of employment have not had a heavy impact on extensiveness. The growth of a flexible sector outside the scope of the system, particularly among immigrant workers, is however causing some problems of representativeness, and the unions' membership has been stagnant for a long time. The Austrian case therefore remains relatively stable.

Denmark, where paradoxically neo-corporatism had been collapsing for a number of years, had by the 1990s become the clearest case of a negotiated and thorough 'centralized decentralization' (Due *et al.* 1994). Something similar has also taken place in Norway (Dølvik and Stokke 1998). One aspect of these developments is the extension of the loose remaining central framework more fully to include non-manual workers, services sectors, and public employment; earlier Scandinavian models had been heavily based on manual workers in manufacturing—a declining group, as we have seen in Part I. Therefore, although the new coordination arrangements are 'loose', they are in some respects more comprehensive than the former centralized model had become by its latter years.

Finland had been gradually moving from its earlier contestative system to a set of neo-corporatist arrangements similar to those of its Nordic neighbours throughout the 1970s and 1980s. It anticipated Denmark and Norway in firmly incorporating areas outside manual work in manufacturing. Paradoxically, Finns were then given an added incentive to achieve cooperative and coordinated industrial relations by the extraordinary shocks delivered to their economy by the collapse of the Soviet Union—a crucial trading partner—at the end of the 1980s (Lilja 1998).

In Belgium, as in the Netherlands and to some extent in Scandinavian countries, there have been important instances of government intervention in wage determination through statutory incomes policies (Arcq 1997; Vilrokx and Leemput 1998). These are to be interpreted as failures of neo-corporatism rather than of its presence, since they denote a mistrust by government of the capacity of the bargaining parties. It is a form of mistrust that nevertheless envisages or at least aspires to a re-establishment of neo-corporatist arrangements. Belgian social partner organizations, rather like the other cases discussed so far, retain a framework of coordination in order to search for consensus and new compromises in order to manage the decentralization and the breaking of the boundaries of the former compromise that are certainly taking place.

Ireland, which had previously been part of a pluralist 'Anglophone' world of organized interests, had been developing neo-corporatist arrangements since the 1970s. As in Denmark, the Netherlands, and Norway, this had been temporarily interrupted in the early 1980s, but by 1987 flexible but extensive, coordinated agreements of the new 'Danish' kind had become fairly well established (Hardiman 1992). In the context of a small country it was relatively easy to establish understandings between different levels of the system to ensure a reasonable level of cooperation. Ireland now seems to have left the Anglophone belt for one of the more European models, and in particular a northern European one.

Neo-Corporatism with Decentralization (Weak Labour)

The Netherlands had also experienced a crisis of the former model in the early 1980s and reconstructed it with a much lower level of cohesion. In many respects the Dutch model now seemed to be a rather exhausted attempt to sustain decentralization within a neo-corporatist shell merely because that had for so long been the Dutch way (Hemerijck 1992). However, by the mid-1990s this set of institutions had been used to negotiate very wide-ranging reforms of the Dutch labour market, introducing elements of neo-liberal deregulation but through consensus and with important security guarantees to workers. The 'old' system is now generally regarded as having rediscovered its purpose and to be operating effectively as a case of coordinated decentralization (Visser and Hemerijck 1997). The country still counts as one of weak labour, because union membership had declined during the 1970s and 1980s to one of the lowest in Western Europe (Visser 1990). It is however notable that it began to rise again slightly during the 1990s following establishment of the revived neo-corporatist model (Visser and Hemerijck 1997). It is not yet clear how successfully it can start to extend to the very large proportion of workers now in the flexible labour market.

There has long been an important company-level component to some neo-corporatist arrangements, in particular in Switzerland (Fluder and Hotz-Hart 1998). This, combined with the continuing absence of economic crisis in that country, has left its arrangements very stable, though it is notable that very little has been done in recent years to modernize or adapt the system to change.

In Japan, as we have noted, it is only at the company level that labour has been important, and some of the European changes have resulted from firms trying to imitate the Japanese model of company cultures. This can develop a new form of neo-corporatism, but it is one that strains the concept of organized interests as an aspect of citizenship, since citizenship refers to rights and practices at a general public level, not to exercises in corporate personnel management. Japan has therefore remained stable in its position; the character of its company citizenship has however come under some strain as that country adjusts to new uncertainties.

Neo-Corporatism in Crisis

All the above cases except Switzerland have undergone moments of crisis, leading in most cases to major reform of the system. In Sweden however the crisis has been engaged but there is to date no clear sign of the character of the system that will eventually emerge from it (Kjellberg 1998; Ryner 1998). In the late 1980s the main organization of employers (SAF) made it clear not that they wished to dismantle their associations (as the British seemed to do), but to change their role from neo-corporatist cooperation to a more aggressive, US-style lobbying (Pestoff 1991). This difference may partly reflect the different economic structures of Denmark and Sweden. As we saw in Chapter 6, the former economy comprises many very small companies which both need to pool and share resources and which build on informal, or sometimes even formal, cooperative networks with other firms and local deals with local governments and trade unions. The large and often multinational firms which dominate the Swedish economy do not have the same dependence, either on each other or on the Swedish national economy.

Given the strength and representativeness of the unions in Sweden, it would be difficult for SAF to achieve its goal of an Anglo-American system. Dismantling of neo-corporatist institutions would lead to pluralism with both sides powerfully organized, and therefore probably considerable conflict. The changes currently taking place in that country are therefore consistent with the expectations of postmodernist theory, with a possible fragmentation of organizations. On the other hand, the employers' bloc is not united over such proposals, several industry associations preferring a decentralized neo-corporatism, and it is therefore possible that after a few years this country will join the first group discussed above. Although the model is in clear crisis, the neo-corporatist citizenship model has not been overturned.

Partly because of the difficulties of that country following unification with the east, the German economy has experienced considerable problems of competitiveness (Jacobi, Keller, and Müller-Jentsch 1998). Many employers have responded to this by a crisis of confidence in their industrial relations system and, as in Sweden, by seeking to imitate American and British systems. In particular, in what has become known as the *Flucht aus den Verbänden* (flight from the associations) they have begun to resign from membership of their own membership associations. Nevertheless, the German system continues to reproduce several neo-corporatist forms of behaviour, and to some extent the absence of reform can be said to reflect the existing degree of decentralization built into the model. Another change in the German model since the early 1960s has been a strengthening of the unions, so that the country no longer counts as a case of neo-corporatism with weak labour, though they continue to have problems representing non-manual workers in the private sector.

Social Pact Neo-Corporatism

All the above have been cases of existing forms of neo-corporatism in decline or being reshaped. Meanwhile some countries which in the past embodied pluralist, contestative, or authoritarian corporatist forms of industrial relations have been adopting certain neo-corporatist characteristics in continuing attempts to establish social consensus. To some extent Ireland belongs in this group, though the institutional mechanisms there seem sufficiently institutionally embedded not to require the frequent overtly political support of appeals to social pacts that are fundamental to this model.

While the search for new compromises in this next group of countries no longer centres on dealing with powerful labour militancy as in the 1970s, there is in them all anxiety, especially among governments, that if workers and their representatives are not involved in discussions about economic adjustment they will become alienated or angry. If the content of social citizenship (in both an orderly form of industrial relations and welfare policy of the kind to be discussed in Chapter 13) are to be diminished, at least this should take place in a manner that recognizes citizenship rights to participate in the discourse.

Italy stands apart from the rest of this group in that developments there have been so complex, and in many respects a fully effective bargained corporatism has been achieved (Regini and Regalia 1996). In the north and centre of the country there has been a remarkable growth of branch- and regional-level tripartite administrative agencies as well as bargaining, often in association with some regional tiers of government. While this is rarely linked to balancing structures at plant level, it otherwise forms an embryonic 'German' system, but in part of the country and therefore not characteristic of a national system. Meanwhile, at national level government engages with union leaders in a mutual and often effective search for agreement on the main lines of economy policy in order to encourage wage moderation, on a classic 1970s model of seeking to establish neo-corporatist understandings. Unions are also formally involved with discussions on the reformulation of social policy, particularly since they have a legal role in the co-determination of pensions systems. They are also acquiring a role in regional development policies, especially where the distribution of European Union funds is concerned (Grote 1998; Regalia 1997). At the same time, highly autonomous local organizations of workers continue to dissent from union tendencies to reach agreements in these fora, while in some parts of the south labour continues to have virtually no representation and, because it is often in the black economy, to lack any occupational citizenship rights at all. The entire variety of possible European forms of industrial relations is contained within this one country.

In the early 1960s Spain had been under authoritarian corporatism. Soon after the country democratized governments embarked on a strategy of encouraging tripartite social pacts and accords, attempting explicitly to replicate a version of northern European neo-corporatism, though on the basis of a very small but frequently militant union movement. Strong agreements are made difficult by the division of the union movement between socialist and communist wings, which rivalry prevents either from risking too much of a role in neo-corporatist discipline. There is however genuine collective bargaining and employers are well organized in a powerful central association. Despite several failures, there continues to be a commitment to returning to new national agreements of a social pact form. Spain is now clearly a case of citizenship in the politics of industrial relations. Its union movement is however very weak in membership terms (Martínez Lucio 1998; Richards and García de Polavieja 1997).

Moves to erect neo-corporatist central arrangements have also been attempted in Portugal, where there is an orderly if divided union movement with participation rights in national fora (de Lucena and Gaspar 1991; A. V. de Lima 1991; Barreto 1998). Here, as in Spain and also in France and Greece, one now sees systems oscillating between contestation and a weak neo-corporatism (in the Spanish case, one with weak unions). It is primarily a matter of judgement and an assessment of the past durability of pacts that leads one to place the Iberian pair here and the other countries in a later category of 'problematic cases'.

One aspect of the Italian complexity is widely shared: an attempt by government, unions, and to some extent employers' organizations to erect a national forum for achieving consensus, but on the basis of a disparate and decentralized bargaining system that in some parts of the economy moves into a contestative mode. This case and the others in this group can be interpreted by advocates of the disorganization thesis as proof of the failure of neo-corporatist systems to develop during the 1980s and 1990s if they had lacked prior roots. In other words, the conditions of this particular period have been hostile to coordinated organizations of interests, as the postmodernists argue, and it is only where these arrangements can extend their life on the basis of a past institutional inheritance that they can survive (as in the Danish or Dutch cases). On the other hand, it can be argued that the frequent recourse to the attempt of social pacts, and the recurrent if not fully consistent commitment of the social partners and governments to such attempts argues against any strong claims of the disorganization thesis. As often in social science, it is a case of whether one prefers to describe a glass as being half full or half empty. At least we can conclude from this that the glass is neither completely full nor empty.

A particularly important stimulus for very recent attempts at social pacts has been the introduction of the European Monetary Union. This is for two reasons. First, the need to meet the criteria of the Treaty of Maastricht for preparing countries to enter the new single currency imposed considerable strains on several economies, involving increases in unemployment, public spending reductions, and difficult reforms of the welfare state. These moves have placed a premium on social consensus, with the unions being important components of that consensus. Philippe Pochet (Pochet 1998; Pochet and Van Lerde 1998), who has done most to plot this development, lists Finland, Ireland, Italy, Portugal, Spain, and less successfully Belgium, as countries where social pacts of this kind have developed.

Second, within a single currency it will be impossible for individual countries to use devaluation as a means of resolving problems in the labour market. (If high wage increases in the export sector make a country's goods uncompetitive, export prices can be reduced by a devaluation of the currency without a need to reduce workers' nominal wages. However, increases in the price of imports reduce the purchasing power of wages, while if a country has frequent recourse to devaluations the currency experiences crises in the foreign-exchange markets.) This has led some governments, unions and even employers' organizations to return to ideas of minimal overall wage coordination. Some authors see this as a beginning of a possible EU-wide level of bargaining (Pochet 1998), while others regard maintenance of different national systems as fundamental to tackling problems of economic adjustment given wide differences in the various European national economies (Crouch 2000a).

As in several of the themes discussed in this book, European integration sets something of a puzzle. As Due *et al.* (1991) point out, on the one hand, twenty to thirty years of existence of the European Community seem so far to have hardly any effect on convergence or harmonization of its industrial relations systems. On the other hand, the most recent developments in that process, particularly the achievement of the single market and now the single currency, might be the beginnings of really serious integration processes that could change that. There is possibly already some convergence in the combination of a new decentralization of previously heavily centralized systems and the improved coordination of some previously very disaggregated and contestative ones (especially Italy).

PROBLEMATIC CITIZENSHIP

The remaining countries are more difficult to analyse, partly because they are internally mixed, and partly because they are changing in ways that are difficult to interpret. They are all cases of institutional weakness that come considerably closer to confirming the disorganization hypothesis than that of coordinated decentralization.

The French union movement has been far weaker and more divided than that in Italy, and the French state has had a long record of rejecting cooperation with organized interests of the kind under review (Goetschy 1998). However, a prolonged response to the disorders of 1968 has meant that not only successive governments but also organized employers have changed their approach to unions and begun to involve them in tripartite actions. There has also been a sustained programme of legal change designed to give a more orderly place to negotiated relations, trying to replace the classic French combination of state regulation alongside contestation by a degree of pluralist bargaining and certain elements of neo-corporatism. Both forms of these arrangements usually leave out the communist CGT union which normally refuses to sign agreements. (It may also be argued that most of the agreements reached comprise employers taking advantage of union weakness in order to secure commitments from the union representatives that they would not give at times of tighter labour markets. However, that is not our immediate concern.)

It has become very difficult to rank the UK (Edwards *et al.* 1998). Historically it has probably been the world's foremost example of a pluralist bargaining system, with some dramatic but extremely weak attempts at neo-corporatism. However, following the major failures of these last and the major political shift to the right in the country during the 1980s, many of the institutions that supported that structure have been dismantled. Employer associations have collapsed as effective participants in collective bargaining, governments have marginalized trade unions from national debates, and changes in occupational structure combined with a period of very high unemployment have weakened the unions. In that context many employers have found it possible to reject union recognition. The system now therefore appears as a mix of company-level pluralist bargaining (mainly in large firms in the manufacturing sector, certain financial institutions, and the public service) and contestation elsewhere.

The USA represents an even more extreme example of this case (Kochan, Katz, and McKersie 1986). Also in the past a certain exemplar of pluralist bargaining, the rather weak US labour movement has been unable to withstand a wave of aggressive de-unionization drives by US employers. The system is now primarily contestative with certain surviving islands of pluralism, and a system that increasingly represents only small parts of the manual workforce and some public employees. Japan continues to practise its very distinctive, company-based kind of citizenship, though this is possibly threatened by the country's economic problems of recent years.

Japan and the USA are very different from each other, and the European countries differ from each other too. Nevertheless, in their different ways both Japan and the USA seem further removed from all the European cases than any of these from each other—though the UK may be starting to approach the US model. Virtually all the European cases now seem to have some approximation to a citizenship model of industrial relations. Meanwhile in the USA, whose pluralist system was once among the most advanced citizenship cases, this is disappearing. Japan's system continues to exhibit *company* citizenship, which is difficult to interpret in European terms.

CONCLUSIONS

Between the 1960s and the present decade there has been a distinct advance in the organizational citizenship of industrial relations systems, as Finland, France, Greece, Italy, Portugal, and Spain, all moved from contestative or authoritarian corporatist structures to at least attempts at pluralism or neo-corporatism. However, to some extent these new guests at the citizenship party arrived just as others were leaving. Only the USA and to some extent the UK could be said to be leaving citizenship behind for contestation, but the terms of both citizenship forms of industrial relations were clearly under strain everywhere; and the strains related to the decay of the mid-century compromise model of society.

As a result of these various moves the strong geography of neo-corporatism, pluralism, and contestation that we saw in the 1960s is if anything stronger today, but with an end of 'southern European' authoritarian corporatism: Finland has more obviously joined the Nordic group of coordinated decentralization, though there are currently serious question marks over the place of Sweden here. Setting that country and the UK aside, the rest of Norden, Ireland, and the Netherlands comprise a north-western zone of very coherently and deliberately reformed systems. A kind of 'central belt' comprising Austria, Belgium, Germany, and Switzerland remains similar, but with far less coherence in the reform and, at least in the latter two, some institutional fragility. France and all the 'southern' countries comprise a category of 'weak but aspirant' organizers and coordinators, though moving at very diverse speeds. The UK stands apart as, with the USA, the only case fully conforming to the disorganization thesis. The Anglophone group therefore continues, though without Ireland. However, whereas in 1960 the pluralism of the UK and USA constituted a very advanced form of organizational citizenship, those two countries are currently experiencing a decline in that quality. The closest to them elsewhere in the democratic world is now France, where a citizenship industrial relations system remains very fragile (Pochet and Van Lerne 1998).

Interesting developments have been taking place within the company and within the geographical region (Grote 1998; Regalia 1997). This parallels an important pair of divergent trends in contemporary post-mid-century compromise economies towards both the local and the global, away from the nation. The global shift leaves neo-corporatism very much at a disadvantage. Neo-corporatist structures exist only where there are strong disciplined organizations which become involved in a dense web of interactions. This cannot take place at the world level. It happens to some extent at the level of the European Union, where interest organizations play a growing part in the formulation of policy. There is even evidence of admittedly very limited forms of collective bargaining among sectoral employers' associations and unions at the European level (Dubbins 1999). However, European associations of business and labour have a very low capacity for self-discipline over national affiliates, and are rarely part of substantial neo-corporatist relationships. Euro-corporatism remains an extremely weak, diluted phenomenon.

The European Commission tends to attract interest organizations into a relationship with it as it extends its own influence. Here a type of exchange resembling neo-corporatism in form but concerning primarily symbolic business takes place. The

Commission and the associations exchange legitimacy: the Commission can grant an association a voice at an important level of decision-making, which is particularly important to trade unions at the present time; the associations can help the Commission acquire some of the attributes of a national state. It is a form of neo-corporatism with weak labour, paralleling national developments where governments fear threats to social order: Spain, sometimes France, Italy, occasionally the new united Germany— though neither German nor Italian unions need social promotion to realize their strength. Weak associations are grateful to be taken into the circle of those consulted by the state; states want to demonstrate their centrality and stability to groups who might challenge them. However, the European level is not yet one at which citizenship can be said to have been established, while transnational capitalism operates at an even higher level where the concept of citizenship cannot even be considered.

The rise of the individual firm, although ostensibly the opposite of globalization, amounts to the same thing where giant corporations are concerned. This raises the 'Japanese question': can arrangements at the level of the firm, where formal rights are vested in owners alone, be regarded as a relevant level for citizenship? The question becomes a very practical one as this level becomes more important in industrial relations systems in most countries. The answer that has long been given by the German and Austrian systems to that is: yes, if the company-level system is tied to a pattern of formally established rights and with some scope for coordination at levels above the firm. The key question for the future therefore may be to what extent these conditions continue to obtain in the post-mid-century compromise economy.

Advocates of the disorganization thesis (e.g. Lash and Bagguley 1988) emphasize the emergence of divisions within the modern (or postmodern) labour force, distinguishing in particular between 'a "core" of white male skilled workers in private firms in the international sector against a "periphery" of often female, part-time, and/or temporary workers in the public sector' (ibid. 323). As we know from Part I of this book, this is an oversimplification of tendencies. These authors do however go on to demonstrate empirically a move to decentralization in each of the countries they study: France, Germany, Sweden, the UK, and the USA, though with only the UK evincing a radical change of system.

However, some other accounts—all considerably more recent than Lash and Bagguley —see less in the evidence to support the disorganization thesis. Schmitter and Grote (1997) place the question into a broader historical perspective by speaking of the neo-corporatist Sisyphus, in a reference to the character in Greek mythology who was condemned to spend eternity pushing a heavy rock up a steep slope; as soon as he nears the top, the rock crashes down to the bottom, whereupon he starts all over again. For Schmitter and Grote, the task of erecting neo-corporatist institutions has a similar quality of collapsing just as they near completion. They are however also concerned to point out the way in which the task is then recommenced. In opposition to those, like the disorganization theorists, who argue that organized capitalism and neo-corporatism have reached an 'end of history', they point to the rich diversity of attempts at neo-corporatist construction that have taken place during the 1990s, especially in Finland, Ireland, Italy, the Netherlands, Spain, Portugal, and also in most of the post-communist countries of Central and Eastern Europe which lie beyond our present scope.

Traxler (1996), in an analysis which admittedly stops at 1990, takes a statistical rather than, like Schmitter and Grote, a narrative approach, and concludes that a *polarization* of cases is taking place, rather than a convergence on neo-corporatism, pluralism, or disorganization. This occurs, he argues, because industrial systems tend to be embedded in past practices and develop in ways consistent with past trajectories. In a typology related to but different from that adopted here, he distinguishes between inclusive and exclusive patterns of collective bargaining. The former are characterized by multi-employer bargaining with arrangements for extending the scope of bargains to all firms in either a sector or a whole country; this is clearly a heavily organized and coordinated form. The latter are characterized by single-employer bargaining with no arrangements for extension; this is a disorganized form. Distinguishing statistically between these forms he is able to allocate countries as follows. In the former category he puts Austria, Australia, Belgium, Denmark, Finland, France, Germany, the Netherlands, New Zealand, Norway, Portugal, Spain, Sweden, Switzerland. In the latter fall Canada, Great Britain (*sic*), Japan, and the USA. With the exception of Japan, this does not allocate into the category of disorganization any country rated above as having continuing coordination. Traxler's method gives him more confidence than the above account of designating France as coordinated.

He did not include Greece, Ireland, or Italy because of difficulties with data. In more recent work (Traxler 1997) he adds Ireland and Italy and considers the simpler question of whether or not multi-employer collective bargaining predominates within a country, the existence of such non-localized bargaining being a refutation of postmodernist, or what Traxler refers to as post-Fordist, theories of disorganization. Countries divide as in the bargaining extension analysis, with Italy being added to the multi-employer group with Ireland having neither form predominant.

In a similar analysis of the early 1990s Visser (1996) concludes that, within Western Europe, only in the UK has there been a collapse of collective bargaining and union rights. Elsewhere 'national sectoral agreement, multi-employer bargaining, nation-wide union recognition and legal or public policy supports of various kinds' (ibid. 38)—the hallmarks of either pluralist bargaining or neo-corporatism, the two forms of industrial relations compatible with citizenship—have survived. He does however indicate tendencies towards decentralization or even fragmentation in most cases, with employers usually trying to distance themselves from strongly integrated arrangements in favour of the company level. This is fully compatible with the pluralist model, but is a challenge to the corporatist one. If any overall trend emerges from Visser's study it is mainly of the kind of 'coordinated decentralization' already noted: a tendency to shift to less aggregated levels than in the past with some retention—or even a *renewal*—of capacity for coordinated intervention at important moments. As we saw above, a recently important reinforcement for the tendency to renew long-stop coordination has been the introduction of the European Monetary Union. A similar argument has been made by Pestoff (1994), with respect both to the trend towards a kind of coordinated or centralized decentralization and to the restraint placed on the *Flucht aus den Verbänden* by the growing dependence of firms on the European level and their need for representative associations to advise them about that level. This point may however be strongest for small and medium-sized firms; the very largest are increasingly establishing a company presence in Brussels (Coen 1996).

The overall evaluation of the disorganization form of the postmodernist thesis must be that it has greatly exaggerated the tendency for organizational forms to collapse, and that in several countries which had previously exhibited weak forms of interest organization, changes have taken place in the opposite direction to that proposed. On the other hand, the loosening of institutions which is observable in a number of previously 'strong' cases does conform to the expectations of the thesis. It is also important to note that in all countries it is employers' organizations which are straining at the constraints of organizations and pressing for the priority of the individual firm. This follows what I indicated at the outset concerning the differential relationship of employers and workers to organizations: employers find it easier to form them, but workers are more dependent on them. Traxler (1995) finds this old logic of organizational capacity confirmed for recent years. If there is disorganization in progress, it is not the fragmentation of all forms of social coherence as maintained by many postmodern theorists, but one very much consistent with the reaffirmation of the coherence of capitalism. It is firms, finding their class strength in the capitalist market, which are seeking to reduce the role of organizational citizenship.

Chapter 13

MASS CITIZENSHIP AND WELFARE STATES

During the course of the twentieth century, mass citizenship came to include various forms of social policy whereby people were either protected from misfortunes that can in the absence of collective risk-bearing only be managed through extensive personal wealth, or enabled to take advantage of what became defined as 'essential' services. These again could otherwise only be available to people with wealth. Social policy was therefore one of the ways in which people in industrial societies became protected from the full implications of the risks of the capitalist industrial economy and the inequalities of its distribution of income and wealth on which their societies otherwise depended.

The attempt to meet certain perceived basic needs other than through market processes pre-dates modern social policy. Historically the most important organizations involved have been religious; the word 'charity', deriving from the Latin *caritas*, had originally a very specific meaning in the early and medieval Church, referring to the kind of love for fellow human beings that Christians were enjoined to express. From there developed the secular concept of charitable activities. Families and local communities were overall the major sources of what we today call welfare or caring, though they obviously lacked the professional expertise that we associate with modern educational, health, and social support services. The caring and welfare provided in advanced societies, whether privately or publicly, offer considerable professionalism but possibly sacrifices for that the warmth and emotional support of family and community. Often there are attempts to recover this in ideas of moral purpose in welfare policy and in appeals to support the welfare state (largely by paying taxes to finance it) as an aspect of sustaining the nation as an extended community and basis for solidarity or compassion. Such an idea is embedded in the Scandinavian concept of the welfare state as *folkshemmet* (the people's home).

This returns us to the discussion in Chapter 10 and the strange role of the nation state in claiming to bridge the gulf between emotional community and 'modern' purposive rationality. The concepts of membership of a shared national community on which appeals to the solidarity of citizenship, especially social policy citizenship, are based, make particular use of the emotional and affective loyalties of the national community. It is made rational, partly through the professionalism of the services involved, and partly through the citizenship concept.

Charity and community, however kindly they might operate, do not confer rights; neither do some forms of state intervention in the welfare field. Here there is a difference between the appeal to compassion and the appeal to solidarity. The former does not necessarily confer rights on its recipients: they are identified as mobilizing moral concern to do something for them, but that does not give them a right to demand help, and it tends to treat them as objects of concern rather than as fellow citizens. Appeals to solidarity stress the shared identity of the society in providing for needs, and is therefore far more likely to embody the concept of mutually enforceable rights available by virtue of a claim to *membership* of the society. This contrasts *both* with being an object of pity (and thus in a sense excluded from the group of insiders capable of bestowing pity) and with buying welfare products in the market (which does not require any membership). It is only when such membership rights to various kinds of social benefits exist that one can speak of welfare *citizenship*.

As Lewis (1993: 4) has pointed out, this issue is also deeply affected by issues of gender: whether 'community' means family or modern voluntary-sector services, it usually means the provision of services by women *without remuneration*. We also know from Chapter 4 that welfare delivery by the state mainly means the provision of services by women as remunerated career work.

Welfare citizenship needs therefore to be understood in relation to themes from the rest of the book: the markets and occupations that constitute the heartland of the capitalist economy, and the communities that formed much of the analysis in Part III. A series of reciprocities and antagonisms among citizenship, capitalist markets, and community institutions provides the basis for a sociology of citizenship, especially when extended to embrace the welfare state. Blame for many of the problems experienced by community institutions is often lain at the door of citizenship, or the *combined* impact of citizenship and markets. A 'crisis' of the family might be attributed to the welfare state both invading traditional family functions and providing paid employment outside the family for mothers, rather than—or in addition to—being attributed to provision of female employment at unsocial hours by contemporary capitalism. A 'destruction' of local community might be perceived to result from major road- and office-building projects by the combined non-local forces of government planning agencies and big business. A rise in the threat of criminality to a neighbourhood might be perceived as related to the presence of ethnic minorities, introduced into an area by both the capitalist labour market and the insistence of public authorities that such people should enjoy certain rights.

On the other hand, a frequent aim of social policy has been to enable families to sustain their joint life. This can mean protecting them from the poverty and insecurity that can undermine them as in early plans for the British and Swedish welfare states (Beveridge 1942; Myrdal 1944). In the mid-century model this was likely to mean sustaining the male breadwinner family form as in much continental European welfare policy as well as in Beveridge's original UK formulation (Lewis 1993). But it might mean facilitating the joint family tasks of couples where both partners are in the paid workforce as in Scandinavia (ibid.). Finally, as suggested by some recent Portuguese research on the introduction of social security into traditional rural communities, the welfare state might actually improve the quality of family relationships by reducing rigid hierarchies of financial dependence on the old by the young (Samouco 1995).

WELFARE CITIZENSHIP AND THE MID-CENTURY MODEL

Welfare citizenship therefore has a prominent place in the mid-century model of so-ciety. It is one of the institutions softening the impact of the capitalist market and mediating between industrial society and traditional institutions. Also, inequalities stemming from the market can be limited by the taxation needed to fund the welfare state, attenuating social cleavages. In nearly every society under review here public spending expanded during the years of construction of the mid-century model. The only exceptions were Greece, Portugal, and Spain, which we have consistently seen to be then excluded from the model. Certain perceived basic needs—primarily health, education, and security—were increasingly provided through non-market means. As we have seen in Chapter 8, this has been very important in education, where without non-market guarantees of rights to participate there could be no equality of oppor-tunity. However, as we also saw in Chapter 8, few welfare states have been powerful enough radically to change the distribution of education that would emerge from either the market or elements of family privilege that must be seen as one form taken by the operation of community. The main exceptions that we encountered there, Scandinavia and the Netherlands, are, we shall discover below, among the strongest welfare states in general.

Not all expenditure by the modern state is welfare spending: defence, police, general bureaucracy, maintenance of the general legal system, subsidies to various economic activities, and the ceremonial activities of the state have minor or no welfare compon-ent. In recent years it has become possible to analyse different components of spending on a comparative basis across countries, but in the earlier part of the period in which we are interested this was not available. We therefore have to make do with a cruder level of data. It is usually possible to differentiate defence spending, which is both a large non-welfare item and also one that varies considerably across countries. Ap-pendix Table A.13.1 presents data for all public expenditure except defence for as many countries covered by our study as possible, at five-yearly intervals from 1960 to 1995.

Table 13.1, based on this table, shows that this expenditure grew for all countries for most of the period, consistent with the hypothesis that the citizenship component of the mid-century model continued to expand for a considerable time after 1960. In some cases however there is a check to that growth in later years, consistent with the hypo-thesis that the citizenship model has now peaked and might be in some decline. Beyond that point experience is more differentiated. In six countries (Denmark, Finland, Spain, Sweden, Switzerland, and Japan) no decline is evident at all. In a further four cases (Austria, Belgium, France, Portugal) a decline sets in by 1990, but spending expands again by 1995. In a further four (Germany, Ireland, possibly the Netherlands though the data are defective, the UK) the decline starts slightly earlier, but again growth is re-sumed in the most recent period. In the USA decline started even earlier, by 1980, but a very gradual rise was then resumed. In Greece and Norway decline starts only in the mid-1990s. Finally, Italian public spending has fluctuated more than that of other coun-tries, but with an overall upward trend. The six countries which have seen no reversal of growth are a very mixed group: two which have consistently had some of the highest levels of spending (Denmark and Sweden), two with consistently low levels (Japan and Switzerland), and two which have risen from low levels in the early years (Finland and

Table 13.1 *Total public spending on welfare, 18 countries, 1960–1995*

		1960	1965	1970	1975	1980	1985	1990	1995
A[a]	level		22.83	25.14	28.43	35.85	38.05	36.66	40.12
	change			2.31	3.29	7.42	2.20	−1.39	3.46
B	level	20.78	22.56	25.25	32.89	38.76	39.60	34.66	
	change		1.78	2.69	7.64	5.87	0.84	−4.94	
DK	level					40.74	39.46	41.56	44.96
	change						−1.28	2.10	3.40
SF	level	16.98	19.92	21.77	25.85	25.44	29.63	36.59	43.96
	change		2.94	1.85	4.08	−0.41	4.19	6.96	7.37
F	level			27.48	31.88	34.29	38.24	36.27	39.63
	change				4.40	2.41	3.95	−1.97	3.36
D[a]	level	22.40	23.64	25.20	34.00	34.11	33.38	31.42	32.21
	change		1.24	1.56	8.80	0.11	−0.73	−1.96	0.79
GR	level	12.85	15.17	15.96	15.85	19.84	28.97	30.61	38.24
	change		2.32	0.79	−0.11	3.99	9.13	1.64	7.63
IRL[a]	level			24.06	32.15	32.48	35.05	29.81	30.06
	change				8.09	0.33	2.57	−5.24	0.25
I	level	23.47	27.33	25.77	31.91	27.16	31.53	33.66	
	change		3.86	−1.56	6.14	−4.75	4.37	2.13	
NL	level	18.11	23.23	27.56	34.19			31.08	31.00
	change		5.12	4.33	6.63				−0.08
N	level			25.66	32.08		31.63	38.89	33.37
	change				6.42			7.26	−5.52
P[b]	level	9.71	9.51	10.16	19.53	26.04	36.26	23.52	30.35
	change		−0.20	0.65	9.37	6.51	10.22	−12.74	6.83
E	level				8.91	17.44		28.72	29.93	33.95
	change				8.53			1.21	4.02
S[a]	level		22.78	29.16	37.01	43.68	43.18	44.57	49.98
	change			6.38	7.85	6.67	−0.50	1.39	5.41
CH	level	12.70	15.56	16.74	22.75	25.40	27.09	26.99	34.48
	change		2.86	1.18	6.01	2.65	1.69	−0.10	7.49
UK	level	17.18	18.57	21.61	27.65	32.69	29.62	28.19	32.03
	change		1.39	3.04	6.04	5.04	−3.07	−1.43	3.84
JAP	level		12.36	11.12	16.77	19.25	19.66	19.88	22.40
	change			−1.24	5.65	2.48	0.41	0.22	2.52
USA	level	13.82	15.11	19.45	24.76	22.42	22.98	23.11	23.10
	change		1.29	4.34	5.31	−2.34	0.56	0.13	−0.01

[a] 1995 data are for 1994
[b] 1995 data are for 1993

Source: OECD *National Income and Expenditures* (various).

Spain). Overall we can conclude that while the onward march of public expenditure no longer seems as ineluctable as it did during the 1970s, there is no clear new downward trend.

In the early 1960s, expenditure defined in the above way fell into the narrow band between 21% and 24% of GDP in 6 of the 15 countries for which we have data (Austria, Belgium, Germany, Ireland, Italy, and Sweden) and was almost certainly in that range in Denmark, France, and Norway too. All other countries had lower levels, and these fall into distinct groups. Five countries (Finland, Greece, Japan, Portugal, and Spain) were at distinctly lower levels of industrialization at that time, and the Iberian countries were not democracies. Two (the Netherlands and Switzerland) were cases where religious organizations assumed a particularly important role in charitable services. The other two are the Anglo-American pair of the UK and the USA.

By the late 1990s the modal range had risen considerably to 30%–35% of GDP. Ten European countries were concentrated there: Germany, Greece, Ireland, Italy, the Netherlands, Norway, Portugal, Spain, Switzerland, and the UK. All previous low European outliers, including the 'retarded development' cases, had now reached at least this modal level, marking a considerable convergence of European welfare states embracing even the previous dictatorships of Portugal, Spain, and (for part of the earlier period) Greece. In four of the remaining six European cases (Austria, Denmark, Finland, and France) spending was higher still, within the range 40%–45%, with Sweden as a further upper outlier at 50%. (No details are available for Belgium.) Norway had been at similar levels until the mid-1990s, making this a primarily Nordic block; Finland had moved from low outlier in the early 1960s to reach this very high level. To add to this emerging geographical pattern of public spending in the mid-1990s, Japan and the USA fell considerably below all European levels with public spending below 25% of GDP.

To an extent that was not the case in the early 1960s, the welfare state had by the mid-1990s become a distinctive Western European social characteristic. It is however premature for us to start trying to group countries into sociologically or politically relevant blocs. The causes of particular levels of welfare spending are very diverse and it cannot be concluded that they all reflect political decisions or the outcome of social conflict. For example, the ageing of the population, a major factor in many European countries, produces a rise in spending on retirement pensions, health services, and various welfare facilities. A rise in unemployment, as experienced by all countries during the 1980s and continuing for most during the 1990s, also leads to an increase in spending on unemployment benefits of various kinds. It is of course possible, if the prevailing political climate is hostile to welfare spending, for governments to respond to these developments by restraining payment levels or qualifying criteria, or by cutting other services, so the overall outcome will be the result of a complex interaction between the social and the political. It is entirely possible that a rise in the proportion of elderly people in a population and of unemployment will lead both to an increase in spending and to a tightening of eligibility criteria in an attempt to restrain that rise. The tightening of criteria might well be used in a way which undermines the citizenship entitlement characteristic of the welfare system in question. Therefore, if we simply take overall spending levels as an index of citizenship development, we might be drawing conclusions *opposite* to those which are really appropriate.

However, we can make some further progress by considering different components of spending, as different forms of expenditure respond to different pressures. For example, if a rise in the elderly population occurs at the same time as a decline in the birth rate over a prolonged period, increasing pressure on health services will be offset by reduced demand for education. A look across the range of spending issues therefore helps us to gain a more detailed picture of what is going on in particular countries.

Given the absence of detailed breakdowns by category in the earlier period, and its patchy presentation even now, we have to start with a crude approach and consider expenditure which took the form of final government consumption rather than transfers. The meaning of this distinction is as follows. Some public spending is devoted to the direct provision of substantive services: schools, hospitals, and various forms of care are the main examples. Other expenditure takes the form of transfers of money, the government acting as the agent which takes resources from taxpayers and then redistributes them as such payments as pensions, social security benefits, subsidies. In government final consumption, the government decides the objects of spending; in transfers, it simply decides who should spend it. For our purposes, concentrating temporarily on the former enables us to disregard both some of the main items which are not really part of the welfare state (subsidies) and the big transfer payments that are determined more by demographic and economic development rather than by policy decision (pensions and unemployment compensation). However, still included in government final consumption will be police and administrative costs that are not part of the welfare state, while much spending on hospitals and education is strongly determined by demographic change and unemployment.

As can be seen from Table 13.2, government final consumption rose more slowly than public spending overall, reflecting the exclusion of the more volatile transfer payments. In many cases (Belgium, Denmark, Finland, Ireland, Italy, Sweden, Japan, the USA) the end of expansion appears earlier than that for public spending overall. Often these expenditures were taking the strain as governments had political difficulty raising taxes, but were unable to restrict the demand for increasing transfer payments consequent on population ageing and rising unemployment.

Since 1970 it has been possible to examine the breakdown of government final consumption figures for specific services for most of our countries. This enables us both to lose non-welfare components of expenditure and to examine individual types of spending. This is possible for education, health, social welfare, and housing. It is also possible to separate those transfer payments which were devoted to social insurance and social assistance, as opposed to such items as industrial subsidies; if these sums are added to welfare final consumption we can achieve a reasonably good estimate of overall welfare spending. Appendix Table A.13.1 presents these data for the four services. They have to be interpreted with care, as governments do not necessarily follow the same definitions of categories and may effect changes of definition over time. For example, some Swedish health services were redefined as welfare services during the 1980s, leading to part of the decline in Swedish health-service spending during those years.

Education spending has risen in most but not all countries. The biggest rises have been in Germany, Greece, Portugal, and Spain. The presence of Germany in this group, which otherwise comprises 'retarded development' cases, may seem surprising. However, it should be noted that in Germany (and Austria) an important part of the cost

Table 13.2 *Government final consumption spending on welfare, 18 countries, 1960–1995*

		1960	1965	1970	1975	1980	1985	1990	1995
A[a]	level		12.17	13.61	16.13	16.82	17.67	16.80	18.10
	change			1.44	2.52	0.69	0.85	-0.87	1.30
B	level	9.43	10.15	11.18	14.07	15.07	14.35	11.75	
	change		0.72	1.03	2.89	1.00	-0.72	-2.60	
DK	level					24.11	23.14	23.20	23.42
	change						-0.97	0.06	0.22
SF	level	11.17	12.90	14.37	17.06	16.70	18.82	21.15	20.28
	change		1.73	1.47	2.69	-0.36	2.12	2.33	-0.87
F	level			10.44	11.42	15.13	16.17	14.96	16.41
	change				0.98	3.71	1.04	-1.21	1.45
D[a]	level	10.34	11.33	13.00	17.71	17.50	17.24	16.20	16.02
	change		0.99	1.67	4.71	-0.21	-0.26	-1.04	-0.18
GR	level	7.26	8.15	8.00	8.42	10.63	14.12	15.78	14.71
	change		0.89	-0.15	0.42	2.21	3.49	1.66	-1.07
IRL[a]	level			14.79	19.00	19.87	18.55	15.73	15.48
	change				4.21	0.87	-1.32	-2.82	-0.25
I	level	10.17	12.50	10.66	11.70	13.05	14.37	15.51	14.58
	change		2.33	-1.84	1.04	1.35	1.32	1.14	-0.93
NL	level	9.51	11.68	12.94	15.13			11.46	11.32
	change		2.17	1.26	2.19				-0.14
N	level			11.82	13.71		16.88	19.36	17.58
	change				1.89			2.48	-1.78
P[b]	level	6.76	5.54	7.05	10.96	19.40	28.04		15.18
	change		-1.22	1.51	3.91	8.44	8.64		
E	level			8.91	9.94		12.76	14.06	16.61
	change				1.03			1.30	2.55
S[a]	level		13.60	17.92	21.20	26.07	24.96	24.58	25.21
	change			4.32	3.28	4.87	-1.11	-0.38	0.63
CH	level	8.84	10.49	10.48	12.62	12.73	13.35	13.44	15.03
	change		1.65	-0.01	2.14	0.11	0.62	0.09	1.59
UK	level	10.26	11.00	12.90	17.40	19.03	15.72	15.99	17.36
	change		0.74	1.90	4.50	1.63	-3.31	0.27	1.37
JAP	level		7.57	6.51	9.06	9.18	8.76	8.38	9.02
	change			-1.06	2.55	0.12	-0.42	-0.38	0.64
USA	level	8.57	9.69	11.53	13.22	11.59	12.12	11.85	10.02
	change		1.12	1.84	1.69	-1.63	0.53	-0.27	-1.83

[a] 1995 data are for 1994
[b] 1995 data are for 1993

Source: as Table 13.1.

of education takes the form of compulsory provision of apprenticeship training by employers, which does not count as public spending. Over the years there has been a relatively strong growth of those aspects of the education system falling outside the apprenticeship model, in particular the universities, giving an exaggerated view of the rise in overall spending.

In only some countries has education spending risen as a proportion of GDP without interruption since 1970, and each of these were countries that had been particularly poor in the earlier period: Finland, Greece, Portugal, Spain. Elsewhere a complex pattern of fluctuations prevails. In the earlier period the range among countries was between 1.2% (Spain) and 5.3% (Sweden). By the mid-1990s there had been considerable convergence, all countries for which we have data falling in the range of 4% and 6% of GDP except Germany, Japan (both low), and Greece (now a surprising upper outlier). The reasons for the German exception have already been explained. In Japan much education is in the hands of employers, though not through a publicly organized apprenticeship as in Germany. (The German system of an obligation on firms to provide apprenticeships is compatible with a citizenship model of a right for young people to receive free education. The Japanese model corresponds to a different concept whereby private firms acknowledge a public obligation, but there are no publicly enforced guarantees for young people.)

Health expenditures too have fluctuated, though here a number of countries in addition to all the 'retarded development' cases have seen uninterrupted increases. A previous European range of from 0.7% (again Spain) to nearly 5% (again Sweden) has now been reduced to one from 2.5% (Greece) to 5.6% (Germany). However, if we include the extra-European countries, Japan would occupy the lowest point at both dates, hardly moving from 0.3% to 0.4%. Unfortunately, data from the USA are considerably out of date, but it seems that public spending on health in that country is also very low, being today at similar levels to those found in the southern European dictatorships in the early 1970s.

Welfare expenditure has seen far more dramatic increases; this is where the apparently relentless rise of welfare state spending has been concentrated, both in overall quantitative terms and as unambiguous increase. It must be remembered that retirement and unemployment transfer payments are included here. Some countries show recent interruptions to the upward trend (Austria, Germany, UK), or generally fluctuating levels (Italy), but the overall upward surge is clear. In 1970 within Europe these expenditures accounted for between 7% (Portugal and Spain) and 16% (Italy), though in Japan they were at only 4.9%. By 1995 the European range was between 15% (Portugal) and 30.7% (Sweden), with both Japan and the USA falling below Portugal.

Direct provision of housing has been a far smaller component of public spending, and in most cases has followed a historical downward path. In some cases revenue from either the rent or the sale of public housing has today produced negative levels of expenditure under this heading. The only exceptions to this generalization are France (where spending is over 1% of GDP and on something of a rising trend), Portugal, Spain, and Japan (rising).

Overall, this once more suggests the existence of a general Western European level of welfare citizenship which is not shared by Japan and the USA. The latter country does however seem to share a European citizenship approach to education.

For a small number of countries it has been possible in recent years to obtain accounts of total spending, not just government final consumption, under the headings of education, health, welfare, and housing. Those available are displayed in Appendix Table A.13.1. Unfortunately, they are too sparse to permit detailed conclusions. They do however confirm the picture of a check to growth across all categories in more recent years, except in Portugal (the only case of a previously 'retarded development' country). There has been no general rise in education spending during the 1980s and 1990s, slightly more evidence of a rising health trend, and largely decline in housing. It is welfare payments alone which account for any overall rise in public spending over these years. These detailed statistics therefore lend a little more support to the view that the growth of welfare citizenship has peaked. Alternatively, it could be argued that the demographically and economically driven growth of demands for pensions and unemployment pay has forced a shift in the orientation of the citizenship model towards these transfer payments.

To conclude this part of our discussion: the early 1960s did not constitute the peak of the welfare state; much growth took place during the 1960s and 1970s. If one disregards the impact of unemployment compensation, this began to falter in the 1980s and to be distinctly reversed in the 1990s. The rise in unemployment presents a major analytical problem. If one simply counts unemployment payments within an indicator of the welfare state, one has the impression of an enormous welfare state development, which would be misleading. On the other hand, if one leaves it out one is unable to take account of the fact that many governments reduced their other forms of spending only because unemployment compensation was taking so much of their resources.

THE REDISTRIBUTIVE IMPACT OF WELFARE STATES

The next step in our analysis is to examine to what extent welfare states have served to redistribute resources in a manner different from that embedded in market processes. If the theory of the mid-century compromise maintains that citizenship institutions have been some kind of counter to industrial capitalism, we should find different principles of distribution at work in them. Has this been the case? How has it varied among countries? And what changes have there been since the 1960s? We can begin our account by examining the effect of welfare-state action on the distribution of income, but as usual we face considerable deficiencies in the data available. Only a small number of studies cover more than a few of the countries in which we are interested, and none go back as far as the 1960s. Several recent studies have looked at change since the early 1980s, so we can look at more recent trajectories of change and at least reach some narrative conclusions about what happens as at least some societies move from industrialism to post-industrialism.

The earliest comparative study is that by Sawyer (1976), who gave estimates for the redistributive effect of taxation and welfare benefits in 1970 for 12 countries. This established France, Italy, Germany, and the USA as having the most unequal post-tax and benefit distributions; Spain, Canada, and the Netherlands were middle-ranking; and the UK, Japan, Australia, Norway, and Sweden were the most redistributive. The relatively redistributive position of then-Fascist Spain is notable. Looking at the actual impact of transfers on the distribution of income among a smaller group of countries, Sawyer (ibid.) saw the biggest reduction in the share of the top quintile through taxation and social benefits occurring in Sweden, then Spain, Germany, France, the UK, and Norway. The ordering for increases in the shares of the bottom quintile ran (from the most redistributive down): Sweden, Spain, Germany and the UK, Norway, France. Again the position of Spain is remarkable, as also is the contrast between Norway and Sweden. However, many criticisms were made of Sawyer's rankings. These were based primarily on concerns over the comparability of national data, which seemed in particular to exaggerate the level of German inequality (Atkinson, Rainwater, and Smeeding 1995).

Atkinson, Rainwater, and Smeeding (1995) attempted to assess the situation in the early 1980s using comparable data made available through the Luxembourg Income Study (see also Smeeding and Coder 1993). One interesting feature of their work is that it tries to estimate the distribution of inequality among *individuals* by looking at *household* income. To do this it has to assume that all adult members of a household have equal access to its income regardless of whether they were the actual earners or not. As the authors acknowledge, this is a contestable assumption, and in particular probably exaggerates the access of women to income. However, without far more detailed studies of how households share their resources it is difficult for a macro- and cross-country study to make appropriate adjustments. Using material from national surveys of households' budgets they consider all sources of money income regularly received: post-tax remuneration, profits and rents, cash transfers from the welfare state.

Table 13.3 shows their principal findings. There is no simple answer to the question: which country has least post-tax income inequality: it is possible for the very rich to be way out in front but the poorest not to be too far behind the median (as in Ireland), or for the opposite (as in the UK). However, some basic conclusions do emerge, which are perhaps best summarized by the overall Gini[1] scores. The Scandinavian countries are the most egalitarian. After that there is not much pattern within continental Europe.

We would need more data from Spain, Portugal, and Greece to know whether the high level of inequality in Italy represents a 'southern' generality, though the limited data available for Portugal and Spain suggest that it does. Even then, it is notable that quite remarkable relative reductions in inequality and increases in welfare-state expenditure took place in Spain, Portugal, and Greece between 1970, when still under dictatorial rule, and 1990 (Maravall 1997: 98–101). In the mid-1970s spending on social policy in Spain had been 9.9% of GDP in Spain, compared with 22.6% in Italy and 22.9% in France (ibid. 142); by 1991 it had reached 21.4%, with similar levels in Greece and Portugal.

With the exception of Switzerland there seems to be a broad positive relationship between overall national wealth and equality within Europe, though outside Europe the richest country of all (with the exception of small Luxembourg), the USA, is to the extreme of the entire European pattern in the extent of its inequality, more resembling the European south. Change during the 1980s largely took the form of: a big rise in the position of the very rich in the UK and the USA; a small *general* shift towards increased

[1] The Gini co-efficient measures the share that a decile of the income distribution secures in income compared with the share that it would have if income were distributed equally.

Table 13.3 Income distribution, 1980s, 16 countries

	Percentage share of total income of:			Gini coefficient
	Poorest 10%	Poorest 50%	Richest 10%	
SF (1987)	4.50	35.60	17.80	20.70
S (1987)	3.30	34.60	18.10	22.00
N (1986)	3.90	33.90	19.40	23.40
B (1988)	4.20	33.80	19.70	23.50
Lux (1985)	4.30	33.50	19.60	23.80
D (1984)	4.00	32.90	20.60	25.00
NL (1987)	4.10	33.00	20.60	26.80
F (1984)	3.00	29.90	23.70	29.60
UK (1986)	2.50	28.70	22.90	30.40
I (1986)	3.10	28.70	23.80	31.00
CH (1982)	2.80	29.00	27.50	32.30
IRL (1987)	2.50	27.10	24.90	33.00
E (1980s)		28.20	24.50	n/a
P (1980s)	3.10	28.70	24.20	n/a
USA (1986)	1.90	26.20	23.70	34.10

Source: Atkinson, Rainwater, and Smeeding 1995.

inequality in the Scandinavian countries, the Netherlands, the UK, and to a smaller extent Belgium; no change in France, and a decline in inequality in Portugal.

These findings echo those of our examination of pre-tax and pre-benefit incomes in Chapter 5. These new figures reflect the effects of both the initial distribution of inequalities and any subsequent redistribution through the tax and benefit system. For the purposes of this chapter we need to isolate the latter. Unfortunately, this has not yet been done with a large number of countries. We can however look at some more restricted studies.

In research on the impact of taxation and welfare policy changes during the 1980s in five countries (Canada, Netherlands, Sweden, UK, and USA) Jäntti (1993) found that in all cases except the already relatively egalitarian Netherlands the changes had helped to reduce inequalities emerging from the market. Dutch national research (CBS 1993) also suggests that in that country there was a sharp shift of disposable income away from the poorest and towards the very rich from the late 1980s, resulting mainly from regressive changes in taxation. In a study of changes in the impact of direct taxation alone between 1980 and 1985 on the distribution of incomes in a slightly different group of countries (the Netherlands was dropped but Germany and Australia added), Bishop, Chow, and Formby (1993) found that taxation was: moving in a direction of greater equality in Canada, Germany, and Sweden; moving in the *opposite* direction in the UK; static in the USA; and unclear in Australia.

Ayala *et al.* (1994; cited in Maravall 1997: 188) compared the evolution of post-tax income inequalities in France, Spain, the UK, and the USA from 1979 to 1985, giving us some insight into a southern European former dictatorship. While the share of the bottom decile had remained static in France, fallen by 10.7% in the UK, and 8.7% in the USA, it had *risen* by 17.9% in Spain to stand at a level (3.2%) comparable with France (3.2%) and the UK (3.5%), and considerably higher than in the USA (1.9%).[2] The top decile in Spain saw its share drop by 5.4% of national income, while that in France fell only 1.6% and those in the UK and the USA rose (by 9.5% and 6.4%, respectively). The total share of the top decile was rather similar in all four countries (around 24%).

In a comparison of pre- and post-tax incomes among full-time working males between 25 and 54 years old in 6 countries during the mid-1980s, Bradbury (1993) found the same rankings before and after tax, with Sweden the most egalitarian, then Australia, Germany, Canada, the UK, and the USA. The most redistributive tax system[3] was the Canadian, followed by the German and Swedish cases (very similar to each other), then the Australian, the US and the least the British. With the exception of the redistributive Canadian tax system, this broadly suggests that countries with the most egalitarian pre-tax income ranges also have the most egalitarian taxation.

In a study of social policy expenditure over a number of years in 17 countries, including all those considered in this book except Greece, Portugal, and Spain, Huber, Ragin, and Stephens (1993) also found support for the power resource theory using a completely different approach. They found that the degree of redistribution achieved by welfare policy correlated strongly and positively with the length of government by labour-movement parties. At the same time, these authors also found continued support in recent years for the 'logic of industrialism thesis' that welfare-state expenditure will be highest among wealthy countries, originally demonstrated for an earlier period by Wilensky (1975, 1976).[4] In other words, where the wealthy have particularly strong positions in initial income distribution, they also seem to be able to resist redistributive taxation, and vice versa. This is consistent with the arguments of those welfare state theorists who see policy as the outcome of the differing capacities of different groups to mobilize power resources, rather than as the expression of a consensus that inequalities should be alleviated, or as a general improvement in societies' capacities to tackle social problems as they become more industrialized and/or wealthier.

A further way of gaining access to the politics of redistribution is to examine the criteria used by different governments to assess poverty; since definition of someone as in poverty creates a certain imperative to take action, one would hypothesize that the higher the level of income at which a government sets its definition of a poverty line, the more prepared in principle is that welfare state to intervene to improve citizens' living standards. Especially if the levels are set in relation to general income levels within the society, the idea of a poverty line embodies assumptions about how much inequality a political system wishes to tolerate. In a sample of 10 countries Gustafsson and Lindblom (1993) found that the highest poverty lines (defined in terms of percentage

[2] In fact, even in 1980 the Spanish bottom decile had a greater share of national income than did their US counterparts.

[3] The redistributive character of the tax system was measured by expressing the difference between the Gini coefficients of a country's pre- and post-tax distributions as a proportion of the pre-tax Gini coefficient.

[4] We must however note that their measure of 'industrialism', per capita GDP, does not really enable them to contribute to a debate about post-industrialism; GDP measures wealth from all sectors, not just the secondary.

of mean incomes) were set in Germany, the Netherlands, Norway, Sweden, and the UK; lower down were Australia, Canada, France, and Switzerland; on its own with the lowest poverty line was the USA. With the exception of the generous approach of UK welfare policy, this confirms the general picture of these countries that emerged from our discussion of welfare state forms, and in particular suggests the outrider position of the USA against north-western European countries.

It will be recalled from Chapter 5 that the UK and USA were the two countries in which pre-tax income inequalities had grown most in recent years; and from Chapter 12 that their industrial relations citizenship is also declining. In these two countries therefore an increase in market-driven inequalities has been exacerbated by a decline in the impact of institutions designed to offset the impact of such inequalities. One study has estimated that in any five-year period about 50% of the US population will experience poverty (based on estimates of what is needed to buy goods affording reasonable minimal survival) for at least a year (Rainwater 1992).

A wider range of countries and some change over time was studied by Van den Bosch (1996), who considered trends in poverty, though over the relatively brief periods of the 1980s. The relief of poverty is only one aspect of the welfare state, but it brings together some of its most important elements, and since he is considering disposable income he also takes account of the impact of income-related taxation. Poverty is here defined relatively, as the proportion of persons whose total income from all sources is less than half the average income. The impact of the social security transfers of the welfare state can be estimated by looking first at the proportion who would be in poverty if social transfers and taxation were not counted when estimating their income, and then considering the proportion again after the transfers are included. We can then also estimate the extent to which a reduction in poverty was produced by the social transfers. By considering two points in time—around 1980 and around 1990—we can examine trends of change.

Van den Bosch found that in all cases the proportion who would have been in poverty around both time points had it not been for social transfers is high. Much of this is due to the presence of the elderly, most of whom have retired from work. The rich among the elderly will have private income; the moderately well off will often have some form of occupational pension plan; but many will be dependent on state retirement pensions. However, even figures for adults under 65 years old show between one-fifth and one-quarter in poverty without state transfers. In all countries surveyed, except the Netherlands, pre-transfer income inequality increased during the 1980s, though this was partly due to the rise in the proportion of elderly persons. If we consider only adults below 65 we find inequality increasing only in the Nordic countries (though only a restricted number of years, starting in the late 1980s, is covered for Denmark and Finland), France (but no data later than 1984), and the UK. These data will be heavily affected by the rise in unemployment that took place in many countries during the decade, but they also confirm the impression we have from other evidence that the only European country to experience a sharp rise in initial income inequality was the UK.

The effect of social transfers is extensive in all countries, relative poverty being reduced to between 5% and 13% of the population whether one takes account of the elderly or not. Room (1990: chs. 5, 6) found poverty levels among both the elderly and large families to have declined considerably in most EU countries, while in Germany

Hausner and Neumann (1992) found the elderly constituting a lower proportion of the poor and people of working age a higher one. Over time, looking first at all persons, the welfare state more than offset the growing inequality of pre-benefit incomes in all countries except the Nordics (apart from Denmark) and the UK. The pattern was the same among adults below 65, though here there was no reduction in the welfare state's impact in Norway. These outcomes were the joint result of the changes in pre-benefit incomes and in the impact of the benefits themselves. Both for all persons and among adults below 65 only, this rose in all countries except Finland and the UK. The effectiveness of the Finnish welfare state diminished slightly; that of the British very considerably.

Using these data we can rank several of our countries by the redistributive power of their welfare states at both the beginning and the end of the 1980s. Starting with the most egalitarian, in 1980 the ranking in terms of post-transfer incomes for all persons was: Sweden, Norway, Germany, Netherlands, UK, France; but among adults under 65: Norway, Sweden, Germany and UK, Netherlands, France, indicating the effect of different proportions of elderly people. By 1990 the order for all persons for a slightly different group of countries was: Norway, Belgium and Denmark, Sweden, Finland, Netherlands, UK; for adults under 65: Norway, Belgium, Denmark, Finland, Netherlands, Sweden, UK. We begin to see some disintegration of the Nordic egalitarian bloc, but the only clear outlier is the UK, with a far higher level of poverty than any other northern European country. Unfortunately, we do not have recent data for France, in the early 1980s another high-poverty country, nor do we have anything from southern Europe.

We cannot be completely certain that, had there been no welfare state, the proportion of those in poverty would really be as high as implied by a simple removal from the sum of their income of social transfers. In the absence of welfare payments a number of these people would have found some kind of work that would have raised their incomes and that enjoyed by their children from above these levels. However, if that effect were to be important we should find that, the larger the role of social transfers in reducing the poverty gap, the higher should be the initial pre-transfer inequality among adults of working age. In fact, there is no discernible relationship of this kind. We must therefore presume that any overall impact of this factor is small.

A similar study by Fritzell (1993) of the redistributive effects of taxes and transfers in Germany, Sweden, the UK, USA, and Canada found that during the 1980s only Germany and Canada saw increased equalization. In the other three both pre- and post-tax incomes became more unequal, though most increase in inequality took place before the effect of redistributive measures. Figures for the UK in particular saw a decline in the number of middle incomes and a growth of both the rich and the poor.

OVERALL REDISTRIBUTION OF TAXES AND TRANSFERS: CONCLUSIONS

Nowhere does the impact of the welfare state radically change the distribution of resources flowing from the market. However, it does have significant effects, and there is considerable cross-national variation. There is a particularly strong—though declining—vertical redistribution effect in the Nordic countries; strongly rising inequality in the UK; a mixed pattern elsewhere, with inadequate evidence from southern Europe preventing us from fully establishing whether less redistribution takes place there than in other continental countries. There is however some evidence from Spain to suggest a considerable redistributive move in recent years (Maravall 1997: chs. 3 and 4).

A major change in the orientation of welfare states has been produced by the growth of unemployment and the emergence of new poverty levels among the employed. To some extent these are often seen as alternatives: there is either unemployment or low income. But the two also accompany each other, either as unemployment reduces the labour-market power of those in work, or as incomes are forced down to prevent unemployment from rising (Room 1990: ch. 6). In most European countries the employed have been constituting a growing share of those requiring social assistance—whether in an advanced welfare state like Germany, one being dismantled as in the UK, or those newly emerging in southern Europe (ibid.). In France (and probably Spain) in particular the rise of low-wage temporary employment of the kind discussed in Chapter 3 has left many wage earners in poverty. When welfare rights are based on employment records, there can then be a paradoxical *reinforcement* of the inequalities and dualisms of the labour market by those of the protective system itself (Kreckel 1992: 185–200; Room 1990: chs. 9, 10).

The absence of comparable data from the 1960s or even the 1970s prevents us from drawing any strong conclusions about whether the redistributive character of the welfare state reached a peak with the height of industrialization. However, the crude measure of the rising share of social spending in national income suggests that growth continued after the early 1960s and indeed, consistently with Bell's thesis (1974), accelerated at the time when post-industrialism was gathering pace. To some considerable extent this is true by definition; as we saw in Chapter 4, employment in community and social services has been part of the form taken by post-industrialism, and much of the expenditure on the welfare state (apart from personal transfers) is devoted to staff costs. However, in more recent years there is evidence that the rise in spending has peaked, and the subsequent reduction has combined with a sharp regressive turn in the redistributive impact of the welfare state in the UK and USA—two countries that have been in the forefront of post-industrialism. There has been some start to the same process elsewhere, especially in some particularly redistributive countries: the Netherlands and Sweden. This tendency, if confirmed for a longer period and a longer time, would validate forms of postmodernist theory that see a fragmentation of the countervailing power of social groups in weak positions in the capitalist market. There might however also be divergence among countries which, power-mobilization theorists would argue, would reflect changes in capacity to organize politically.

DIFFERENT FORMS OF WELFARE STATE

These basic data cannot tell us about the forms taken by welfare states. Major contributions to this analysis have been Gøsta Esping-Andersen's (1990) classification of the so-called 'three worlds of welfare', and a different grouping of three European models by Pekka Kosonen (1994). For our present purposes we are interested in these only insofar as they help us to examine the relationship of the citizenship content of these different types to the rest of the mid-century model, and changes within these.

Esping-Andersen's starting point is the same as that adopted here: the welfare state is a means by which labour escapes some of the implications of capitalism. He calls this 'decommodification', reducing the extent to which labour is treated as an economic commodity like fixed capital or goods. Decommodification is said to take place to the extent that workers are able to maintain their standard of living when not able to work. There have been pressures to do this in all capitalist societies because, unlike the other factors of production, labour is embodied in human persons who seek treatment different from that of the commodity form, such as citizenship or community membership. Once again we find the triad of economy (market), polity (citizenship), and society (family, community, religion). Esping-Andersen's account of the decommodification of labour can therefore be related to different outcomes of major power confrontations around these.[5]

MARKET-ORIENTED WELFARE

Where modern, liberalizing capitalist elites achieved hegemony during modernization there were two alternative possible subsequent developments. First, where the challenge against capitalists was weak and bourgeois capitalist groups preferring market liberalism retained hegemony, the challenge to the commodification of labour was restricted. However, certain problems of the commodity form of labour and the social marginalization and pauperization of large sections of the labour force could not be ignored—both in terms of the social cost of underperformance and in terms of political demands raised by labour itself. What modern economics recognizes as problems of public goods and externalities, requiring minimal collective action, also became evident (Esping-Andersen 1990: 42–4). There was therefore a development of welfare provision, but of a very basic, needs-related social assistance kind, designed specifically to interfere as little as possible with workers' performance in and subordination to the laws of the labour market. Claims for welfare therefore had to be made on the basis of abject need.

The citizenship capabilities of this model are minimal. State social security benefits

[5] He compares different national social policy regimes across a number of dimensions relevant to the decommodification theme (ibid. 47): (1) rules of entitlement to benefit (there is more decommodification if access to benefits is easy, affords rights to an adequate standard of living irrespective of previous economic performance, means tests, or past financial contributions based on prior employment); (2) income replacement standards (there is more decommodification if benefit levels come close to employment income); (3) range of entitlements (there is more decommodification if a wide range of conditions make one eligible to receive benefit, the end point being a citizen's income where benefit is completely detached from prior work experience).

In practice he operationalizes these dimensions by allocating each country's regime a score for: (1) the severity of rules for the prohibition of eligibility, (2) the strength of built-in disincentives to make claims, and (3) the replacement level of earnings provided. The resulting summed score is then weighted by the percentage of the population eligible for benefit to give a combined decommodification index of the national welfare state (ibid. 49). We must note the limited concept of welfare state being used here: this is a study of income replacement only and does not cover health-service delivery systems, housing policy, education, or other elements of welfare. Huber, Ragin, and Stephens (1993) have shown in an analysis of 17 countries that one gets very different results whether one estimates welfare-state strength in terms of transfer payments, or general government revenue, as an estimate of total welfare state effort. Even within the field of income replacement, one can analyse different aspects of policies. Gough *et al.* (1997) analysed social assistance schemes across all OECD countries according to a number of dimensions, such as the extent of coverage, the generosity of payments, whether they give general help or according to distinct categories of need, the extent of means-testing they embody. This resulted in a seven-category scheme, against the three categories of Esping-Andersen's analysis. Were we to expand our range of comparators beyond Japan and the USA, we would see that Canada and Australia, despite their respective geographical locations, resembled the Western European cases, while Eastern and Central Europe resembled Japan and the USA.

themselves do not constitute a citizenship right in the sense of offering a full participation in which all citizens expect to share, but a small residual to which most people expect to be able to find superior alternatives. Rather than a right to be enjoyed, the benefits are more likely to be a stigma to be endured; in order to protect work incentives, there have to be deterrents to relying on welfare. The only citizenship component comes in the acceptance that there are levels of income and security below which citizens should not fall, irrespective of their market capacities.

With the growth of political democracy and a growing working class, these systems made major adjustments towards universalism and citizenship in the context of the mid-century compromise, though they continued to develop their welfare states primarily on their existing basis, and by the 1980s when the threat of an organized working class had started to recede, they began to move back to a needs-based, now *re*commodified form of labour policy. Esping-Andersen calls this model liberal and associates it primarily with the so-called 'Anglo-Saxon' countries—mainly the USA, Canada, Australia, and New Zealand.

The UK itself and Ireland do not fully conform to this group. The UK did produce a powerful labour movement. As a result for a long period (roughly 1945 to 1979) the British model was a mixture of the liberal form and the social democratic or Scandinavian one to be discussed below. However, as the home of bourgeois liberalism and the country in the world which has had, alongside the Netherlands, Switzerland, and the USA, the most coherent capitalist class, a basic liberalism remained far more important than in other societies where labour became powerful. The main abiding characteristics of these cases have been the development of residual welfare states, with benefits allocated in ways least likely to interfere with work incentives: strict tests for eligibility, minimal provision through the state system, and a general expectation that most people will find their own security provision for old age, sickness, etc. through the market in private insurance policies. The post-war British welfare state, receiving a new infusion of energy during the 1960s, embodied a stronger form of state provision. Although there was always an important private insurance market, especially for pensions, the basic state pension was seen as a citizenship right for all rather than something for those unable to cope by themselves; and attempts were made to provide benefits rivalling most occupational schemes. However, during the 1980s the system began to change more in the direction of the minimalist US one (Kosonen 1994).

The reasons why societies which have been dominated by pursuit of the market economy should have a residual concept of social citizenship are clear. British exceptionalism, far from being a problem for this category in the analysis, strengthens it: twentieth-century British political history has been dominated by an unusually unresolved struggle between economic liberalism and social democracy, with the former gaining ground during the 1980s and 1990s. This is compatible with the findings discussed above of the sharp inegalitarian decline in the UK in recent years, and its slow convergence towards an essentially US American model.

THE FULL CITIZENSHIP MODEL

Where liberal capitalist elites did not have the protection of ex-colonial status they were vulnerable to demands from rising working classes. This was particularly true when they were located in hegemonically Protestant countries and therefore lacked the advantage of a religiously and culturally divided working class that protected traditional elites in most of continental Europe (and liberal ones in religiously divided Netherlands, Switzerland, and the UK). This left Scandinavia as a highly distinctive part of the world where unified labour movements achieved political hegemony. Finland is a somewhat separate case, as we have seen in previous chapters.

As forces hostile to the reduction of labour to pure commodity form, these labour movements tried to achieve high levels of social citizenship and therefore, in Esping-Andersen's terms, the decommodification of labour. Welfare claims became based on straightforward citizenship rights 'against' markets. As already noted, the UK shares something of this model and something of the liberal one, having moved from the latter to the former under the pressure of the mid-century compromise, and back again to the latter in more recent, post-industrial times.

These welfare states have been universalist, high-citizenship systems, offering more or less equality of high standard services within the state sector. According to the logics of these systems, in their pursuit of basic security needs, individuals should be liberated from the constraints of both market and family. They should use the state's services because they are entitled to do so as citizens, and the services should be worthy of them. Paradoxically, this latter meant the extension of the welfare state beyond the immediate manual working-class constituency of the social democratic movement itself. Particularly during the 1950s and 1960s a number of crucial decisions extended coverage to groups who had previously been excluded as outside the original class that championed the model: the self-employed, farmers, middle-income non-manual groups. This then is a full concept of mass citizenship, though moving towards something more articulated and diverse as it moved beyond its original core constituency.

Admission of middle-income non-manual groups was the most important and most controversial. In order to retain the loyalty to state welfare of the growing middle-classes who were being wooed by more generous pensions from the private sector, Scandinavian (and British) social democratic governments accepted that benefits should be paid partly on an income-related basis; those who had retired from work on a high salary were able to expect in retirement a higher pension than those who had been on lower incomes. The principle of equality had to compromise with that of universal citizenship if public support were to be retained. (In fact, Esping-Andersen points out that social democratic welfare states are in practice always part of class *coalition* strategies.)

Social democrats pursued strong demand-management policies; for many years they were able to sustain very high levels of employment. Furthermore, (especially in Sweden), they initiated active labour market policies designed to ease the transition of workers from declining industries to new ones with maximum efficiency and minimum disruption. Perhaps most important, the form taken by their welfare states drew large numbers of women into employment, as we saw in Chapter 4. There was a double effect here. Because social democracy was committed to the extension of citizenship as freedom from both market and family, it was not inhibited (as was Christian democracy) from providing social services that relieved mothers of the burden of childcare, facilitating female employment. In turn, the employment that large numbers of women found was in the welfare state itself, to some extent 'replacing'—though as we noted above also professionalizing—family caring. In that sense therefore the welfare state might be said to have *commodified* female and family work (Stephens 1996).

It is therefore possible to argue that the Scandinavian welfare states were able to develop their citizenship model so fully because the political forces driving them were inhibited by few concerns for either markets or community and traditionalism. These were not Catholic countries, and as we saw in Chapter 9 the Lutheran faith has not been a strong defender of community; but in any case social democrats were rarely strongly attached to religious values. As a new social force in the industrializing late nineteenth century they represented a distinctive commitment to modernity and had few ties to small-town community life. On the other hand, just as their commitment to citizenship embodied its own accommodation to the market by encouraging maximum work participation, so they embodied elements of community in the welfare state. It was regarded as sustaining and helping families, not making them redundant. And the use of the concept of *folkshemmet*, though it might become rhetorical, had resonance in small countries where populations took for granted cooperation with neighbours in either harsh climates (Finland, northern Norway, and Sweden) or islands (much of Denmark).

These cases therefore represent the fullest expression of the mid-century compromise model, and validate a power-resource rather than a functionalist account of that model. On the other hand, as anticipated earlier in the discussion, accelerated development of the welfare citizenship component accompanies weakening of the industrial component. We saw above that very recent years have seen some decline in the redistributive power of the systems. In contrast with the UK, the tendency of policy in Scandinavia has been to make quantitative reductions but to leave the basic framework of a universalist citizenship model intact (Kosonen 1994: 87–90; Clayton and Pontusson 1998), though at a certain point quantitative reductions provide an incentive to seek private services and therefore the beginning of the residualization of the citizenship base of public provision.

WELFARE AND COMMUNITY

Where traditional social elites dominated the European modernization process, their main concern was to sustain the relation of the mass of the people to traditional communities and feudal deference (families, neighbourhoods, churches, occupational groups in the form of local guilds) (Esping-Andersen 1990: 38–40). The elites themselves might inhabit the world of national state power, but this was not how they situated the mass of the people, who were not expected to become citizens. On the other hand, these elites were often worried about the effect on these masses of the free markets of liberalism, which would uproot them, both releasing them from the bonds of social deference and throwing their lives into disarray. They therefore developed welfare policy to protect labour from the capitalist form through essentially corporatist devices. (It will be noted that this usage of 'corporatism' differs from that which I adopted in the previous chapter. The two overlap in seeing citizenship defined in terms of occupational position. However, the sense of corporatism embodying strategic capacity which was important to the concept in Chapter 12 is explicitly absent from the idea of a corporatist welfare state.) According to Esping-Andersen, these mainly took the form of the occupation-based social insurance schemes initially associated with the conservative reforms of Bismarck in Germany and von Taafe in Austria. From the elites' point of view these had the advantages of a link with the past (occupationally organized guilds), of preventing general thrusts for citizenship, and of retaining a capacity for considerable inequality by social status. Claims were based on work performance and therefore largely restricted to male breadwinners.

Even by the period when democratic mass citizenship had arrived (securely after 1945) these countries continued to develop their welfare states on this basis. Their main abiding characteristics have been a concern to limit the disturbance caused by extensions of citizenship to the institutions of traditional society—to community in the terminology adopted here. In particular this has meant three principles. First, they have retained status-based, guild-like structures rather than built up universal national social security schemes. This does not only imply respect for a certain form, but also inequalities in benefits. Second, they respect the family and therefore, and in strong contrast with social democratic welfare states, they are so structured to discourage female labour-force participation. Van Kersbergen (1996: 145–7) finds that Christian democracy explains low female labour-force participation better in 1980 than in 1960. This is not surprising, since as we have seen in previous chapters it is participation in non-agricultural work that seems to be negatively associated with social democracy. In 1960, especially in Catholic countries, there was still much agriculture.

Looked at differently, societies following this pattern have done least to disturb the family, and therefore it remains able to take responsibility for many caring functions. This is, for example, still very important in Portugal where the strength of family and local community compensates for a low level of welfare state development (De Sousa Santos 1994). Third, especially in Catholic lands, since the Church had been the main provider of most caring services before the development of the welfare state, care was taken to ensure that state services did not compromise their operation. Christian democratic thought has been distinctly communitarian in the welfare field (Dierickx 1994). Application of the concepts of both mass and citizenship are therefore qualified.

These welfare states have fewer qualms than liberal ones about interfering with the market. Typically therefore they provide benefits more generous than these, though not as generous as in social democracy. They are more importantly distinguished from the latter by their lack of vertical redistribution (following the protection of occupational categories) and by their failure (or refusal) to replace the family and thus encourage female labour-force participation. Similar findings emerge about the relative lack of redistribution associated with Christian democratic welfare states from the study of 17 countries by Huber, Ragin, and Stephens (1993). They also noted that these welfare states were mainly concerned with sustaining income during periods when people could not work, a kind of substitution for temporary loss of commodity power by the worker.

However, as our review of expenditure patterns above showed, there is considerable heterogeneity within this group of countries, and in particular there are difficulties in allying France, Germany, and Italy closely with each other. In Portugal and Spain the very residual welfare provision of the Fascist period excluded any concept of citizenship rights and was in fact far closer to the US liberal case than to the corporatist systems of democratic Catholic Europe (De Sousa Santos 1994: 52).

Esping-Andersen's analysis brings together as 'traditional': the Protestant corporate state of Bismarck's Germany that had only recently ceased its *Kulturkampf* against Roman Catholics; the anti-corporatist, fiercely secular, liberal French republic; strongly Catholic, corporatist Austria; and the consociational, incipiently corporatist Netherlands. Welfare policy had not begun in Italy or Spain. If we shift to the development of modern welfare states since the Second World War, the pattern of complexity changes, in some ways favouring the Esping-Andersen thesis but in others not. The Catholic Church's influence certainly grew in Germany, where post-war partition of the country gave the Western Bonn Republic a Catholic majority in place of the previous Lutheran one. In social policy it then accommodated itself without difficulty to the corporatist structures of the Bismarckian legacy.

The Church was also influential in some aspects of French policy, though that country remained resolutely anti-corporatist except for a brief period immediately after the war, as we saw in Chapter 12. France was never fully part of Christian democratic Europe, the *laïque* component of the country's politics being too strong. There was however a coincidental consensus over one area of policy which produced a de facto policy convergence. Catholics wanted a strong family policy; and this coincided with republican concern at the long-term stagnation of population growth. The consequent natalist policies suited the interests of both, but with scope for divergence: republicans were not concerned with limiting female employment as were Catholics, with the result that the encouragement of childbearing did not prevent policies enabling a high proportion of French mothers from taking paid employment. France continues to be notable as a rare European country outside Scandinavia willing to give special forms of assistance to single mothers (Room 1990: 69) and generally departing from the Catholic social policy model on gender-related issues.

In Austria social democracy displaced much of the earlier influence of a particularly conservative form of Catholicism. Not dissimilarly, a consensus among Calvinist, Catholic, and social democratic forces developed policy in the Netherlands, but initially post-war Catholic social policy developed its corporatism as the very opposite of the Bismarckian model. Its aim was to obstruct the attachment of workers to the Protestant state and instead to run a generous social policy through religious organizations (van Kersbergen 1996: 128). This was also quite different from France. As time passed church social services received state financial support and became integrated with state services, with the net effect that the main distinction of welfare systems of the Dutch kind is simply that there is heterogeneity of providing organizations.

Esping-Andersen acknowledges the Netherlands as a mixed case, coming between the social democrats and the corporatists. This would be completely straightforward, except that in some respects it is an *extreme* 'traditionalist' one in his terms. Not only was Christian teaching particularly influential, but the organization of service delivery is the most thoroughly corporatist of all, being structured through pillars of the kind discussed in Chapter 9. Also, and as we saw in Chapter 2, until very recently it has been a country of particularly low female labour-force participation. On the other hand, it is the closest to the social democratic model of advanced welfare state development in terms of spending of all countries outside Scandinavia. An attempt by Gran (n.d.) to apply the Esping-Andersen model to old-age policy is only able to make it work by counting the Netherlands as *unambiguously* 'social democratic'. Even then the hypotheses based on the model underestimate the French position. Given that the research covered only 6 countries (the others were Sweden, Germany, Australia, and the USA), these are worrying weaknesses.

On the other hand, Kohl (1992) in a study of poverty levels in a number of countries was also able to make use of the Esping-Andersen analysis but by including the Netherlands as an *unambiguously* 'continental' (i.e. corporatist) country. His analysis otherwise supports Esping-Andersen's identification of a so-called Anglo-Saxon group, that term here being oddly extended to include Israel (in addition to Australia, Canada, the UK, and the USA); the Scandinavians (Norway and Sweden); and the 'continentals', which are here however limited to the highly specific group of Germany, Netherlands, and Switzerland.

When Italy developed a welfare state it strengthened the impression of a Catholic welfare bloc. But Paci (1997) and Ferrera (1996) have suggested that both here and elsewhere in southern Europe the welfare state took on a particular dualist form. At one level it has resembled France in having a very centrally determined bureaucratic system, but beneath that structure welfare is, especially in southern regions, in practice administered more locally and through forms of particularistic clientelism; benefits are not allocated according to the formal criteria but according to whom one knows and how one votes (see also van Kersbergen 1996: 153–67). This is a true traditional *community* model of welfare delivery, and it has very little in common with what occurs in France, Germany, or the Netherlands.

The Spanish Fascist welfare system for many years most closely resembled the liberal one, with low coverage for needs-restricted cases. It was during the more prosperous years after the late 1950s that it began to acquire more obviously corporatist characteristics and ended resembling a mean version of a corporatist scheme—a cross between a liberal and a corporatist one (Guillén 1992). In addition to raising an interesting question concerning the relationship between liberalism and Fascism, this throws considerable doubt on the concept of traditionalism: it was when Spanish Fascism became less traditional that its welfare state acquired less liberal and more corporatist characteristics.

We can resolve these problems of the analysis fairly easily by splitting the concept of community into its component parts: primarily family; guild structures (corporatism); church; non-democratic authority. These different elements are found in very different combinations in different continental European welfare states, and they are not interchangeable. Esping-Andersen tends however to conflate them. For example, speaking of the occupational base of German welfare in particular, he remarks that '[t]he collective solidarity of guild, fraternity or mutuality was clearly closer to the family unit, and hence more capable of serving its needs, than was the more remote central state' (1990: 61). This excludes the possibility that the Prussian and Austrian states cultivated guilds for purposes of state development—partly because of their encouragement of occupational identification and partly because they were building their forms of modernity on the basis of corporatist structures.

The family was most strongly protected where the Catholic and Calvinist Churches were strongest: thus, as we can gauge from Chapter 9, stronger in Italy than in Germany; stronger in Germany than in France. As we have seen in Chapter 12, corporatism was stronger in Austria, Germany, and the Netherlands than in France or Italy.

Non-democratic authority was protected in many of these cases until the mid-twentieth century, and in Portugal and Spain for considerably longer.

SEVERAL WORLDS OF WELFARE

Esping-Andersen's analysis presents us with a view of Europe that is widely shared by popular perceptions, especially by people outside Catholic Europe: Scandinavia rather homogenous and separate; the UK rather more like the USA; and continental Europe all rather similar. Closer investigation suggests however that this residuum can be broken up further, though in an unsatisfactory way. There is something distinctive about southern Europe; but the countries of central Western Europe do not comprise a convincing category, divided as they are by the specificities of the French and German states. As we saw in earlier chapters in connection with family practices and religion, France has a unique history of *laïcisme* and cultural modernism that in some respects places it closer to Scandinavia than to the rest of southern Europe on some questions, particularly those relating to mothers (Lewis 1993: 5). Meanwhile, Germany, while divided religiously, remains more dominated in its politics by Christian and even by specifically Catholic ideas than France—and hence sometimes closer to southern Europe. As we saw in Chapter 12, France also differs from most other countries in the autonomy of its state from interest associations, while the German state frequently co-operates with such associations. Among the other countries of western-central Europe, Austria, the Netherlands, and Switzerland share certain features with Germany; Belgium some with France but some with Germany.

For our purposes the liberal model can legitimately be seen as that form of welfare provision which compromises most with the market and therefore develops citizenship the least; while the social democratic form represents the furthest end-point in the welfare state as citizenship: universal, equal, available as of right and extensive. While criticizing those who overgeneralize on the basis of the Swedish model, Esping-Andersen also takes this view and sees the social democratic or universalistic model as the most complete form of welfare state; he is concerned to pick out the conservative-corporatist model as a distinct type and not simply as a point on a continuum between minimal and universalist forms. Van Kersbergen's (1996) attempt to pay more attention to the distinct autonomy of the Christian democratic form (a major constituent part of the corporatist model) similarly does not disturb a view of the social democratic welfare state as in some way the most developed.

The different patterns all seem strongly rooted in their societies, but in appraising whether the mid-century model is changing we have to question this rootedness. It is always difficult to know whether currently perceptible changes mark major new historical departures or only oscillations around existing trajectories which we should not notice from the perspective of a few years' time. However, already in 1990 J. Berger (1990), in an analysis of the place of the post-war welfare state within the overall social structure which closely resembles that offered here, saw a major historical disjuncture approaching. He expected to see a decline in welfare state provision, alongside a move to flexibility and individualization. In an ironic comment, he saw the capital-labour agreements of the kind discussed in Chapter 12 (which had ushered in the post-war welfare state model) as also demobilizing working-classes so that they acquiesced in welfare decline.

It should certainly be noted that in every country changes during the 1990s, or in some cases since the 1980s, have been at least slightly towards the liberal model of residual welfare and a decline in the citizenship component of social policy. In the UK, and even more the USA, it has been possible for major steps to be taken in this direction because of the initial predisposition to the liberal approach. Elsewhere the evidence is more of a general decline in scope than of a change of system type. However, even in Scandinavia Esping-Andersen (1996*a*: 10–15) does report a return of eligibility criteria in entitlement to benefit, though with an attempt to keep very extensive, co-ordinated coverage and a stress on social investment; for example, welfare and family support policies are used to encourage female employment. As Stephens (1996) has pointed out, the fact that these welfare states have always encouraged high levels of labour-force participation may continue to make it possible for them to adjust the work incentives aspects of their current welfare packages without fundamentally breaking the mould.

CONCLUSIONS

Chapter 14

IS THERE A WESTERN EUROPEAN FORM OF SOCIETY?

In the course of this book we have been seeking answers to two different sets of questions. First, we have been exploring the diversity or similarities among the societies of Western Europe: Is there a form of Western European society which can be distinguished from that of the USA, Japan, and other industrialized parts of the world? Within Western Europe, can we identify groups of societies—e.g. north versus south, Catholic against Protestant? Or are there just individual, unique countries? Is there a sociological as well as an economic, administrative and legal European integration process at the level of the European Union? Second comes a series of questions concerned with how these societies have been changing over time. In these two concluding chapters I shall try to establish the answers that emerge from the preceding discussions to these two sets of questions, starting in this one with the search for a possible Western European form of society.

A major initial difficulty in distinguishing something specific about Western European societies is their relationship to the other main example of an advanced society, the United States of America. The USA originally grew out of a diversity of European cultures, and at least since the Second World War it has in turn been a powerful influence on nearly all European countries. Since the USA constitutes the single biggest comparator for European societies, this complicates the question of defining 'Europeanness'. Often the characteristics that render Western European countries similar to each other and different from most others, including in some respects those in Central and Eastern Europe, are also those which they share with the USA: a Judaeo-Christian base; a shared cultural inheritance; 'modernism'; a lengthy history of industrial capitalism and an associated system of social stratification; stable democracy, advanced civil rights, and citizenship in the second half of the twentieth century. As the Catalan sociologist Salvador Giner (1994) has put it, the earlier colonial Europeanization of much of the world now 'echoes back' to Europe, largely from the USA, with a consequent loss of distinctiveness of the idea of 'European'.

The fuzziness of Europe's boundaries makes the problem even more difficult. If we are considering social and cultural patterns, the various political definitions of a European identity are of little help. The formal boundaries of the European Union imply that Swedes and Danes have some characteristics in common with the Irish that they do not share with Norwegians; Austrians more with the Portuguese than with the Swiss. In the very early years there was a more or less Christian Democratic European Economic Community of the original six. After that the entry of countries as diverse from that model and from each other as Denmark, Greece, and the UK removed any real identity. If one regards the continuing anomalies of Norway and Switzerland as of minor importance, it is only since the entry of Austria, Finland, and Sweden in January 1995 that there has been any social and cultural significance to the boundary of the European (Economic) Community or Union; if the institutions of the EU are expected to construct a European society embracing the whole of Western Europe, that is a task in its very earliest infancy. It is also one which is fated to change direction again when the new entrant countries, largely from Central Europe, join the Union. Although (with the small exception of Cyprus) these countries all belong to the Catholic and Protestant cultures already entrenched within the EU, they mark an extension to Slav culture and also to countries which have experienced an extensive period of communist government.

The histories of France, Germany, and the UK show that it is possible to construct fully integrated nation states out of a pre-existing diversity of smaller societies. However, in each of these cases the task took many years and was accompanied by violence and threats of violence to force recalcitrant subcultures into conformity, as well as hostility and often open war towards most neighbouring states. Any suggestion of the use of force either internally or externally is completely ruled out by the EU institution-building process.

The last time that violence was used at a transnational European level was by the Nazi powers in the late 1930s and 1940s. That rapidly led to military defeat, with the dominant military power in the western part of the continent being the USA. The US victory at the end of the Second World War cannot be called a military conquest of Europe, since it took the form of a liberation of nation states against German Nazi domination. The Americans were however left in a position of institutional dominance similar to that which often results from military conquest, and acquired various forms of hegemony that have never since been dislodged. Not only were such institutions as presses, broadcasting media, and intellectual disciplines, which had been crushed by Fascist rule, reconstructed under strong American influence, but, as Therborn (1995) notes, European science never recovered from the flow of many of its best brains to the USA. Only an institutional vacuum equivalent to that left behind by the Nazis could enable such a massive reconstruction according to one hegemonic perspective. That is not going to occur within contemporary Western Europe, so there is no way in which any Europeanizing force would be able to exercise an equivalent power to dislodge the results of post-war US hegemony. This reality has to be added to the more usually noted fact of the continuing power of nation states to attract the loyalty and identity of their citizens.

Most sociologists who have examined the prospects of a European *society* (as opposed to a polity) have reached similar conclusions (e.g. Delanty 1998; Giner 1994; Haller 1994) about the weakness of any such phenomenon and about the unacceptable prerequisites of anything more substantial. These include not only military conquest but the more realistic prospect of the development of a strong sense of where Europe's social boundaries lie, which primarily means making sharp distinctions between 'Christian' Western Europeans, on the one hand, and Moslem Arabs to the south and Orthodox Christian Slavs to the east. At that point their discussions become very exhortatory, and declare that Europeans must not do anything of such a kind, but must create a different kind of society, which must somehow combine a strong sense of European institutions without any culturally exclusive sense of identity (Delanty 1998; Haller 1994). The net result is the advocacy of something resembling Habermas's (1985) idea of constitutional patriotism. Whether this is at all realistic is not our concern here, as our discussion is analytical and not normative.

Cotts Watkins's (1991) study of the gradual 'nationalization' of family formation patterns which we discussed briefly in Chapter 10 showed that the construction of national societies in the nineteenth century was assisted by a simultaneous expansion of previously very local forms of communications media to a national level: railways, roads, newspapers, magazines, and goods distribution systems. Today's equivalent advances in communications—mass air travel, international television and motion pictures, the Internet, the globalization of economic exchange—completely transcend specifically European boundaries and pre-date the conscious construction of a European social space. Whereas in the nineteenth century the building of railways and establishment of magazines addressing national readerships constituted unambiguous extensions of previously localized systems, any attempt today to build specifically European networks for these phenomena would constitute an impossible restriction of an already achieved internationalism. The fact that most of today's communications media are dominated by US corporations and US cultural perspectives reduces the extent to which this is a genuine 'internationalism', but only further emphasizes the central problem of social Europeanization.

In only three areas can there today be said to be a Western European culture, in the sense of a mass of interactions that involve large numbers of people in social rather than political relationships at levels transcending individual nation-state boundaries but with a more or less perceptible, vaguely defined European boundary. These are classical art, classical music, and association football. The first two relate essentially to the past, to the period from the Middle Ages to the end of the nineteenth century when there was—at least at an elite level—both a good deal of what today would be regarded as cross-border interaction within Western, Central, and much of Eastern Europe, and an absence of any shared and complicating extra-European point of reference. Today football is about the only activity that performs such a role—and of course it extends far beyond any elite. The organization of competitions, the labour market, mass media coverage, and wider participation at the level of amateur and young people's clubs all have a distinctly cross-national, European dimension. Significantly, it is one of very few widespread cultural or social activities where the USA has a very weak presence (Markovits 1988).

To search for a European society being shaped by the formal process of European integration is therefore either a too easy negative task or a premature one. It is too easy to point to all the ways in which the construction of an economic union has not yet produced much social integration; given how slow and deeply rooted social processes are, no one should expect anything to have happened yet. This is not to say that in the long run it will not do so. Despite the absence of force, the Union does have a gradually developing legal code and the European Court of Justice to administer it. This is slowly influencing a wide range of areas of life at the ordinary social rather than purely political level (for example gender relations). Also, monetary union and further economic integration might be expected to have some homogenizing effects. To discuss this however would be to speculate. All we can do on the basis of our knowledge of how they are today is to consider whether Western European societies already share enough characteristics to comprise a distinctive [Western] European social form. As through-out the book, we have to take it for granted that nation states rather than certain sub-national entities do constitute the basic building blocs for a discussion of 'societies' —certainly an oversimplification in the cases of Italy, Spain, and the UK.

A TYPICALLY EUROPEAN SOCIAL FORM?

Such a search has some positive results, but it is necessary to make use of a variously expanding and shrinking concept of Europe, a 'variable geometry' Europe. It is very important to be clear when this is being done, or one asserts a European unity that does not really exist. This is for example often done by Kaelble (1987, 1997), one of the few to attempt a systematic and empirical, rather than speculative and normative, examina-tion of sociological Europeanization. Unfortunately, he is sometimes willing to speak of 'Europe' when he has evidence limited to Germany, France, and/or Britain.

RELIGIOUS, ETHNIC, AND PARTY BLOCS

The most extensive generalization possible—in that it includes a considerable portion of Central and Eastern Europe as well as Western (excluding only the Islamic lands of Turkey, Albania, and some of the nation states formed in recent years in the south of the former USSR)—emerges if we put together some of the findings of Chapters 9, 10, and 11. Virtually all European societies have historically had a restricted range of reli-gious and (often associated) ethnic diversity, with a clear and sometimes official concept of one or just possibly two dominant, established Christian churches (Martin 1978). Any wider diversity has been limited to small, marginal groups. Although the identity of the dominant forms of Christianity varies considerably from country to country (being variously Catholic, Orthodox, Lutheran, Anglican, Calvinist), all Europeans have one or another model of this kind as part of their cultural heritage.

American experience has been different. White Anglo-Saxon Protestant hegemony over a Catholic minority in some ways once resembled the structure of England, Holland, Switzerland, and various historical forms of the German state; but there was never a dominant church within American Protestantism, and certainly not an estab-lished state church as in the European examples (except Switzerland). Similarly with ethnicity, although White Anglo-Saxon Protestants (WASPs) still maintain a distinct hegemony, no one is in a position to define which groups are the 'core' Americans and who the outsiders. There have been two very major exceptions to this generalization in US history. First, the various aboriginal inhabitants of the territory were eventually subjected to a virtual genocide by the British and other European settlers. Small sur-viving groups of them largely remain unintegrated into US society. Second, the black population originated in slaves forcibly brought to America from Africa, and slavery counts as the most extreme form of social segregation known to mankind. Although slavery was eventually abolished—though only 140 years ago—Afro-Americans have continued to experience particular difficulties in achieving integration, and find them-selves being overtaken by successive waves of immigrants.

Setting these important exceptions aside, this central difference of European and US American approaches to dominance and diversity, originally rooted in religious and ethnic matters but eventually extending further, is of abiding importance and affects some surprising areas of life. If and when religious and ethnic minorities in European countries were tolerated, this eventually took the form of the sociological liberalism we discussed in Part III, a process of mutual recognition of cooperation in separateness which took its purest form in the Dutch concept of *verzuiling* (Bax 1990; Daalder 1974).

In more recent decades one can report a further similarity that applies to nearly all European countries, very recently reaching the previous exceptions of Ireland, Poland, and Belgium: the declining authority of religion over people's lives—though not necessarily of basic religious identification—that we identified in Chapter 9. This contrasts starkly with US experience of growing church membership and participation, and an increasingly prominent role in politics for various religions. In a global context it is Western Europe's secularization which seems exceptional rather than American religiosity (Martin 1994).[1] On the other hand, the concept of *authority* in US religion is complex, and taking full account of this might reduce the contrast (Beckford and Luckmann 1989; Brown 1992; Finke 1992). Nevertheless, this is certainly one area where any current change in the European situation does not take the form of an Americanization.

Religion has also been a principal source of intra-European divisions. The separation between Orthodoxy and Catholicism/Protestantism is fundamental to those between East and West,[2] and within Western Europe those between Catholicism and Protestantism are central to the south–north divide. However, while this latter helps us at many points to separate Catholic southern Europe (Italy, Spain, Portugal) from Lutheran (or ex-Lutheran) Norden, the two fundamentally important countries of France and Germany disturb the stereotypes in complex ways. While France resembles southern Europe on some variables, the fact that its Catholic Church was expelled from public life for much of the past two centuries gave it a certain quietist, private 'Protestant' *Innigkeit*. On the other hand, Germany, while predominantly Protestant for the first six decades of its history as a nation state and being partly shaped by that experience, was a Catholic-majority country for the first four decades of the history of the western republic after the Second World War. This is why we found Germany sharing certain 'southern' characteristics more than does France on some questions.

The clarity of north–south religious stereotypes is further disturbed by: the odd position of the various British churches; the position of Belgium and Ireland as northern Catholic countries; the distinctively divided religious structures of the Netherlands and Switzerland; certain features of Austrian society that separate it on several variables from the Catholic south; and the position of Greece as Orthodox rather than Catholic.

Related to the central characteristics of longer-term religious background is the fact that in all Western European countries political allegiance is rooted in certain major

---

[1] Japan shares Europe's characteristics here, though of course on the basis of a non-Christian heritage.

[2] The post-1945 politico-military division of Europe temporarily obscured this, as several Catholic and some Lutheran lands were included in the newly defined 'eastern half' of Europe. It is notable how post-Cold-War Europe is gradually overriding this divide and reverting to the older one: the Central European countries now formally confirmed as being in the queue for admission into the EU are all Catholic or Lutheran, none Orthodox. The earlier inclusion of Greece in the EU constitutes something of an exception. However, *ancient* Greek culture has been formally embodied as part of the Catholic Church's *acquis culturel* since the earliest Christian centuries.

class and/or religious cleavages, even though the parties thereby generated then reach out to wider sections of the population (Lipset and Rokkan 1967). This produces a pattern similar to the religious and ethnic one: two or three parties defined by class and religion dominate the polity, leaving space for a varying number of small parties. Diverse though European party systems are, they all adhere to this basic form. The US cleavage pattern is far more complex, subtle and incoherent than this, with the paradoxical result that at federal level a total two-party monopoly reproduces itself over the years with only rare and temporary lapses.

The coherence of all Western European models has been compromised in recent years, as the declining salience of class and religion has weakened the hold of the dominant parties, leading to a growth of new ones, particularly those representing ethnic or regional interests and ecological concerns. However, the old class and religious bases still provide the biggest parties, and the recent changes remove European party patterns even further from the US duopoly form.

SHARPLY DEFINED CLASSES WITH BLUNTED INEQUALITY

Closely related to the role of class in political allegiance is the fact that in all Western European countries much culture has historically been class-specific; in the USA there has been a more complex pattern of cultural (mainly ethnic) differentiation. The fundamental paradox of the post-war European/American contrast here is captured by Kaelble (1987), who speaks of most of Europe having comparatively restricted social mobility and sharper class divisions than the USA, but lower social inequality (see also Haller 1989). As we saw in Chapter 8, research has thrown considerable doubt on the oft-repeated claims of particularly high social mobility in the USA, but the rest of Kaelble's point is well documented. He also captures well the associated tendency of European social life to be segregated into different occupationally based *milieux*, establishing boundaries of social intercourse and delineating cultural styles (Kaelble 1997: 33–6). In particular he identifies the *bourgeois*, *petit bourgeois*, proletarian, and peasant *milieux*. As a result of all these factors European class distinctions have been far more perceptible. For example, empirical studies by Max Haller and his colleagues (Haller and Holm 1987; Haller 1989) have found that Germans and Austrians are more likely to see their societies as unequal than Americans do theirs, when in fact the opposite is the case. Western European lower classes have therefore found it easier to mobilize themselves politically and autonomously in order to pursue their distinctive interests than have their American counterparts. This has probably been an important force in the reduction of inequalities in northern Europe as compared with the USA which we observed in Chapters 5 and 13.

To understand this contrast further we need to distinguish between class differences which are invidious and those which are not. For example, the German educational system makes a fairly clear and early distinction between children—usually those from manual working-class families—who will become manual workers and those who will follow non-manual careers, distinguishing further among the educational levels of these latter. We saw in Chapter 8 that Germany has a low rate of social mobility, but that those who pursue the manual path receive a strong vocational education which equips them with an occupational identity that can be a source of pride. Also, within

German firms there is often more involvement by manual workers in functions usually reserved for managerial staffs in many other countries (Geißler 1994a). To be manual working class does not mean to have an identity which one should try to shed at the first possible moment or be regarded as a social failure, as is probably the case in the USA as well as in several other European countries.

One form taken by the class struggle made possible by the European mode of organized class politics has been political pressure for strong welfare states. This is not however a generalization fully embracing the whole of Western Europe, as it does not fully extend to the south (i.e. Italy, Spain, Portugal, Greece)—though as Maravall (1997) describes, important attempts were made by southern governments in the 1980s to strengthen their welfare states. There are also the important differences that we observed in Chapter 13 between the universalist models of Nordic and to some (though diminishing) extent British welfare states, the more insurance-based systems of France and Germany, and the more paternalistic pattern found in southern Europe. On the other hand, some of this development is relatively recent: at mid-century one would have regarded the democratic welfare state as a Scandinavian, British, Dutch, and American (New Deal) phenomenon, with a rather different non-democratic Bismarckian model in the German legacy.

It has recently been fashionable to draw a distinction between a European 'preference' for welfare at the cost of high unemployment (resulting from high indirect labour costs needed to pay for welfare and labour-market regulation as well as possibly reduced work incentives) and a US preference for high employment levels at the expense of low welfare provision and extensive poverty among the working population. However, within Western Europe this trade-off does not seem to operate, the highest unemployment and poverty levels being in southern countries with the lowest levels of welfare spending and with the least protected labour markets, not in the heartland of the northern welfare states (Crouch 1998). Meanwhile, the UK increasingly follows an American path. Any contrast between an unemployed 'Europe' and a fully employed USA is in any case a very recent development, reversing the pattern of earlier decades when US unemployment was regularly higher than that in at least northern Europe. Even now it may well relate to certain conjunctural developments associated with the differential timing of emergence from recession. In particular, the economic problems of several European countries have been associated with difficulties in sustaining a balance among European exchange rates in the wake of German reunification. It is doubtful whether this variable has become a fundamental structural feature.

At the same time, there is strong evidence that levels of social inequality—in both the pattern of incomes deriving from the labour market and in levels of inequality after account is taken of the effect of taxation and the distribution of welfare benefits—have been rising steeply in the USA for at least 25 years, followed since the early 1980s by the UK. Initially this seemed to mark a further divergence between the USA (and UK) and much of continental Europe, in much of which an egalitarian trend persisted. This was seized on by both advocates of a distinctive model of 'social Europe' and by its opponents. (The latter saw here evidence of a 'sclerotic' Western Europe (and Japan) continuing to provide security and high minimum standards while more dynamic societies were rewarding their innovators and entrepreneurs with higher initial incomes and lower taxation.) However, in more recent years the egalitarian trend seems to have fallen off in much of Western Europe too. Significantly, these changes have been rather strong in Scandinavia, which had previously been particularly egalitarian. There is therefore some sign of both convergence among countries (with an adjustment of the previous egalitarian outliers) and a shift to more inequality, as well as a rise in poverty. The degree of convergence is limited by the fact that inequalities in the UK and USA have increased particularly extensively. The inegalitarian trend is stronger than the convergent one, but if there is convergence it is more on a US model.

At the same time, the post-industrial economy produces a more diffuse class structure than did industrialism, lacking in particular the large, potentially alienated and often politically well organized manual working class that organized itself in most Western European countries, especially in the northern part of the subcontinent. European class structures are becoming blunted while the level of inequality becomes sharper—an 'Americanizing' trend.

EUROPEAN FAMILIES

Kaelble (1987, 1997) relates European welfare state development to the long-term historical specificity of the European family pattern. He here indicates an important connection, but (as he acknowledges in a later work (1997)) the generalization must be limited to northern Europe only. He argues that 'Europeans' (sic) were historically less able to rely on extended family support in old age and times of difficulty than people in other societies, and may therefore have had a greater need to develop welfare states. One recalls here the Scandinavian term for welfare state as *folkshemma* (people's home). More detailed research is needed to relate the timing of, and differences in the relationship between, family and welfare state change in different societies. However, it is notable that the northern European zone of a distinctive family form does roughly parallel the region of early welfare state development. Southern Europe has followed a different path, but one consistent with the overall thesis of a negative relationship between welfare state and family strength. Here, weak and late developing welfare states have been associated with strong communities and extensive family obligations towards kin.

The role of the Catholic Church was fundamental in the establishment and maintenance of the southern pattern, in that it sustained a strong natalist policy, insisted that caring roles belonged with the family (or Church organizations) and not the state, and both directly and through its influence on state social policy encouraged married women to base their lives on the family and discouraged their labour-force participation. Recently however this pattern has run into difficulties. Increasing numbers of southern European women have aspired to a life not bound by family obligations, but, in contrast with their Scandinavian sisters, find little help with these obligations from the welfare state. They seem to have responded by reducing their childbearing rate as the only means available to reduce caring responsibilities. As a result the Catholic countries of Italy and Spain now have the lowest birth rates in Western Europe, while the highest are found in Sweden.

This is one of those variables where France has certain 'northern Protestant' characteristics while Germany could be part of 'southern' Europe. In the former country, natalism became one of the points of reconciliation between the Catholic Church and a Republicanism concerned over long-term French population decline. Natalist policies then developed mainly under the impulse of the latter, and did not include the Church's concerns to sustain traditional maternal roles alongside a high birth rate; childcare policies could therefore be developed. Meanwhile, post-war German family policy has been strongly affected by Christian democratic dominance of politics. These differences are now reflected in patterns of female working and fertility, where France allies itself to a British/Nordic pattern of relatively high female employment and fertility, while Germany has more in common with Italy and Spain—relatively few in the paid workforce and a low birth rate.

North/south or rather Protestant/Catholic divisions produce further intra-European diversity on the issue of marital stability, with high rates of divorce in the Nordic countries and the UK and far lower ones in Italy and Spain, with France, Germany, and the Netherlands falling in between. There is a related contrast on the question of births outside marriage, with these running at a far lower level in southern than in northern countries. There is however a sharp difference within the latter group. In Nordic countries children born outside marriage are usually born to mothers in settled partnerships and aged over 30. In the UK, in contrast, there is a highly distinctive pattern of large numbers of births to women under 20 and with no settled relationship.

On these family issues the USA resembles the newly developing northern European pattern rather than southern ones: reduced concepts of family obligations, high levels of married women's labour-force participation, relatively high rates of both births in general and those out of wedlock, and extremely high divorce rates. There are however some distinctive aspects. Unlike in the Nordic lands, the high rate of labour-force participation has been achieved despite a low level of public childcare provision. The relatively high fertility level is partly explained by continuing high immigration levels; and the pattern of extramarital births follows the British rather than a Nordic pattern.

A CONCERN FOR SOCIAL CONSENSUS?

The issues of reduced inequality within class divisions and of the welfare state suggest another possible and much discussed European/American contrast: a putative European concern for overall social consensus, especially based on the labour market. But there has been extraordinary diversity in European experience. In the immediate post-war years there was a widespread drive for social and industrial consensus throughout both Western Europe and the USA (with the exception of still Fascist countries in the south of Europe). The USA of the New Deal age as well as Scandinavia and, slightly later, the UK provided a model for Europeans of how class struggle could be turned into collective bargaining and welfare policy. Soon afterwards countries went their very different ways. In particular, where communist wings of trade unions were strong, as in France and Italy, the pursuit of consensus was quickly abandoned. Overlapping with this the legacy of suspicion between states and organized interests in countries where the latter had been associated with Catholic opposition to republican states contrasted with the different approach emerging from Lutheran experience, leading to different post-war patterns of industrial relations organization (Crouch 1993: ch. 9). This, in contrast with the record on family and social policy, is a point where France appears as part of southern Europe and Federal Germany as more closely allied to Scandinavia.

In recent years rather than as a long historical tendency, and with the exception of the UK, political and business elites throughout Western Europe have worked to develop various models of social cooperation (see Chapter 12). In particular, those in France and Italy have begun to look to German models. Governments in southern— and also in Central and Eastern—Europe have encouraged social pacts among themselves, organized employers, and unions. Meanwhile the USA has taken a very different turn, with policy following the same withdrawal from New Deal arrangements as in the welfare state area. The reasons for this difference relate to the point discussed previously concerning social class. If the predominant form of social stratification and division in most of Western Europe has been class, that in the USA has been ethnicity. Classes are bound together in the division of labour. If they need to resolve conflicts they have to do it by constructing cooperation from bases rooted in difference. Ethnic groups can instead seek separation from each other and the right to their separate worlds. In Europe the upheavals of the late 1960s that broke the overall social peace of the initial post-war decades primarily took the form of industrial relations or class issues. This posed the need for a pursuit of consensus, which by then the decline of communism was making possible even in France and Italy. The conflicts of the same period in the USA came to focus on race, as well as the crisis of national coherence signified by the Vietnam war. This implied very different policy responses.

THE EUROPEAN CITY

The phenomenon of corporatist organizations of interests and the idea of organized public institutions that were neither fully private nor truly part of a central state appear today mainly in such fields as industrial relations; but much of the long history of that very distinctive concept of intermediation between private and public lies in the emergence of the autonomous urban systems of the great European commercial city belts (Black 1984). This is a theme which we have not had a chance to discuss in detail in this book, but which needs some discussion if the story is to be complete.

Throughout much of Western Europe the typical city has had a centre (not a 'downtown') that expresses historical and civic identity and continuity, remaining relatively immune to major subsequent human interference (apart from war damage). The typical American city lacks these features and is the product of recurrent changes in market forces. Many European urban authorities, like European states, have a capacity to define some issues and some physical spaces as 'special', almost sacred. The realm of collective goods is able to benefit from past associations of public authority, especially monarchy, with religion. There is still a Durkheimian sense of there being something distinctive and valuable about the public arena. With the probable exception of the armed forces, it is difficult to make such a statement about public authority in the USA.

This generalization is subject to many exceptions. This 'European' urban form is concentrated in the belt of cities that for several centuries escaped concentrated rule by wider territorial states: the Low Countries, Germany, Burgundy, Switzerland, and northern and central Italy. It is not so prominent elsewhere. Today, throughout Europe the newer parts of most cities and the entirety of nearly all new cities follow the US pattern; while in contrast some major US city centres have a 'European' character. To the extent that it is valid, however, the generalization can be related to two major forces which differentiate the USA from much of Europe: obviously, the absence of a medieval urban legacy in the USA; and, in the twentieth century, the stronger persistence of administered planning and regulation of urban development by public authorities in most European cities.

This latter point is well developed by Kaelble (1987, 1997), and by Therborn (1995), who stresses the European city as a form in which there is a good deal of planning and public space, but which affords opportunities for considerable human freedom. One implication of this centrality of European urbanism for Therborn is his analysis of the European Union as being essentially a union of city belts. The dominance of France and agricultural policy in the first few decades of the European Economic Community was unlikely to have led to such a statement, but today one sees its value. An emphasis on the European city might now seem dated, contradicted by the Americanization of European cities, by neglect of public services and space, by extensive motorization and intensified criminality. However the point has important historical resonance and connects with the issue of the welfare state, as it brings out the stronger concept in much of Europe of the role of public authorities in creating and safeguarding a set of common concerns.

ECONOMIC STRUCTURES AND INSTITUTIONS

If we remove the UK and Ireland from our concept of Western Europe, we can make the important economic generalization that most countries in that region have financial markets and approaches to company ownership that privilege long-term institutional stability over rapid flexibility (see Chapter 6). Within most of Western Europe, stock exchanges tend to be weakly developed; hostile takeovers are rare; and company development is therefore governed primarily by technical and engineering, rather than by financial, criteria. The shared Anglo-American financial system, with its concentration on short-term asset flows and the treatment of companies as bundles of tradable property rights rather than as institutions, is the direct reverse of this.

Kaelble (1987) does not include this theme in his analysis, but he alludes to two other economic questions which are related to it: the industrial employment structure and company size. By the latter he means that Europe has tended not to develop giant corporations on the US scale. This is partly related to the role of financial markets. Where, as in Germany, France, or Italy, hostile takeovers and asset acquisition are difficult, companies have to grow by expansion of their productive capacity and by their conquest of markets rather than by acquisition of other enterprises. It is significant that within Europe the British, who have a financial system similar to the American, depart from the European generalization about company size. So however do Germany, Sweden, and Belgium.

By the industrial employment structure Kaelble means the fact that at some point in the twentieth century European societies saw proportions of their populations employed in the manufacturing sector greater than those known elsewhere, including the USA. What strikes him about the contrast with the USA is that the latter began much earlier to develop a large tertiary sector of employment. This apparent Euro-American contrast also has weaknesses, as Kaelble (1997: 31) acknowledges. Until recent de-industrialization, there has been considerable geographical diversity within US employment structures, some of the most heavily industrialized city regions of the world being in parts of the north-east and far west, with strong agriculture in the mid-west and elsewhere. Similarly, on the basis of our analysis of sectors of employment in Chapter 4 we can show that, within Western Europe, Belgium, Germany, Switzerland, and the UK were heavily industrialized, while France, Italy, and Spain remained for a long period more agricultural. Kaelble's point here is rather a description of certain features shared between the USA and much of *southern* Europe, though the American economy has in no way been labour-intensive in the southern European manner. Similar tendencies of tertiarization now affect all economies, though the fact that they embarked on this process from different points of the earlier move from agriculture to manufacturing, and develop different patterns of service because of differences in their welfare states, imparts some elements of continuing diversity.

More recently, as in the case of social inequalities, there are signs of a convergence on something closer to a US style of economic organization (Albert 1991; Crouch and Streeck 1997). Capitalism is now far less strongly associated with industrialism than in the recent past. The most dynamic elements of capital since the period of deregulation and globalization are financial institutions which do not have the extensive sunk costs of industrial enterprises. The contemporary economy is characterized by both new and rapidly changing opportunities for investment (as the unregulated global economy expands) and considerable risks of adverse change (as we leave behind the Keynesian years of muted trade cycles and relatively stable demand). In such a context many firms want to have their hands free to move resources as quickly and as flexibly as possible. This is far easier to achieve in the stock-exchange-dominated financial systems of the Anglo-American type than in the characteristic northern European (and Japanese) economies of long-run commitments.

CONCLUSIONS

The above survey permits two overall conclusions.

First, Western Europe is diverse, and most of the generalizations that one can make about it usually relate to rather specific parts of the subcontinental whole—these parts themselves varying from issue to issue.

Second, however, and generalizing rather broadly, there is something that runs through several of the above numbered discussions which imparts a certain unity, a kind of *Wahlverwandschaft*, to different elements in the character of 'European-ness'. One can define it as ordered, limited, and structured diversity, and contrast it with American unstructured and pluralistic diversity bounded by a framework of overall national or market homogeneity. This distinction is a kind of meta-diversity, as it concerns the way in which diversity itself is handled rather than substantive social characteristics. A somewhat similar categorization of European societies as highly organized and rather formal is presented by Hradil and Immerfall (1997*a*), though their analysis of the USA as more inter-subjective and informal is addressing different variables from those considered here.

With respect to the first conclusion, it is notable that it is the 'northern' Europe of the welfare state, muted social inequalities, and rather regulated capitalism that most contrasts with contemporary North America. However, these are the very parts of Europe that in other respects most resemble the USA: for example, a high level of general education, technological sophistication, increasingly egalitarian gender relations. The southern Europe that contrasts with the USA on these points is more similar to the latter country on questions of social inequality, weak welfare state development, and relatively small manufacturing sectors.

However, we have also found it necessary to use the often discussed north–south division with care. Its extreme form, the Baltic contrasted with the Mediterranean, does work for a number of variables. Reference to these two seas is not solely figurative. Baltic Western Europe could include northern Germany as well as the Nordic countries, and those parts of Germany are indeed those secularized, Lutheran *Länder* that least equivocally resemble Scandinavia. Meanwhile, Mediterranean Europe includes southern France, which again belongs to the European south more clearly than does northern and central France. But the central core of Western Europe can neither be allocated to north or south nor be turned into a region of its own. This analytical difficulty is caused by the complex politico-religious histories of France and Germany, the distinctive patterns of the smaller countries of the region, and the unusual position of the UK. While the last is sometimes seen as being part-way between a European and an American identity, the former component is further attenuated by the fact that the part of Europe which Britain most usually resembles is the 'non-core' Scandinavian region.

The second conclusion, concerning a possible European preference for ordered, limited, and structured diversity, merits some more discussion. It is most strongly seen in religion, politics, and class structure, and contrasts strongly with American society. Interestingly, the national structure of the two subcontinents embodies the difference in itself: one comprises separate, sovereign, internally relatively homogeneous, historical nation states; the other one large, internally highly heterogeneous federal state. The difference is then seen most clearly in the contrasting characters of European and American religious organization: limited and structured diversity against pluralism within the overall unity of 'the American way'. Very much the same can be said about ethnicity—once one takes account of the major exceptions, particularly Afro-Americans, noted in the US case.

The pattern then finds a strong echo in the organization of political cleavages: clear divisions with a more or less known content against a heterogeneity that is pressed into just two parties with uncertain identities. It is then further reflected in the associated contrast between relatively clearly defined class identities but restricted class inequalities, on the one hand, and restrained class identities but very extensive and growing inequalities, on the other. Related to this is the further contrast between the inclusive welfare states, ordered industrial relations institutions and regulated, structured city environments of much of Western Europe and the American pattern of residual welfare and industrial relations systems, and cities with no structured centres. (By 'ordered' industrial relations I do not necessarily mean state-regulated, because the ordering is often carried out by organized interests of the social partners. The relative roles of *l'état* and *Verbände* will depend on the extent to which the country in question draws on French or German institutional traditions.)

From these points one might move to consider the distinctiveness from US patterns of the preference of firms in many Western European countries for strong corporate identities with secure assets and stable ownership.

For those European societies which follow the stereotypes an encounter with a new form of internal diversity is usually difficult, because there will have to be either a rejection of it or a kind of public, formal recognition. Religions and classes have had this struggle over centuries; one now sees it happening again as Europe's new (and some old) ethnic minorities begin to seek citizenship and recognition of their cultures. In the USA, and with the exception of Afro-Americans, it is more difficult to determine whether a group has been 'recognized' or not, or what social recognition might mean; if inclusion is unclear, so is exclusion.

Two images capture the contrast: the old Dutch concept of *verzuiling* against the American melting pot. Both are means of producing an integrated society from various forms of diversity and division. In the former, groups constituting separate subcultural pillars retain separate identities but use certain organizations stemming from these to construct social compromises and together constitute the society. If there is just separation without an agreed process of organization and compromise, such a model produces ghettos rather than pillars, and for many centuries did so, whether among ethnic, cultural, or class blocs.[3] In the US melting pot concept all ethnicities and subcultures, usually seen as immigrant newcomers, were expected to enter the pot and have their distinctive characteristics melted down until they were turned into Americans; however, these characteristics then remained in the pot to form part of the constantly changing definition of what being American actually constituted. The outcome was a highly variegated, complex, heterogeneous communality.

It remains important when developing this theme to remember intra-European diversity: the contrast between *verzuiling* and the melting pot works best as a contrast between north-western Europe and the USA. It does not really embrace France, where social integration is much more routed through the state; or Greece, Portugal, and Spain, which are still in early decades of post-dictatorship. Italy presents a more complex pattern; ethnic homogeneity has accompanied considerable inter-regional differences, while the country has also contained both the global headquarters of the Catholic Church and for many years the largest communist party outside the Soviet bloc. This has produced important mechanisms for conflict *avoidance*, which is not the same as institutionalized *reconciliation* of differences on the Dutch model. Nevertheless, as Italy emerged from its great religious and political confrontation, it is remarkable to see how closely its structures began to assume a basic consociational form. Immigration has been a very recent experience for the southern countries, which lack institutions for coping with ethnic and cultural pluralism. The major intra-regional diversities in Italy and Spain call forth primarily formal political rather than sociological responses. The paradoxical result in these countries has been higher levels of class and other inequalities, leading them more closely to resemble the USA in this respect, as we have seen.

Meanwhile, both Western European societies and the USA seem vulnerable to a cultural fragmentation which disturbs their various inherited forms. US new religious

---

[3] As noted in Chapter 10, transferred to the largely Dutch-settled country of South Africa, it produced *apartheid*.

pluralism and European secularization are equally cases of this; and a declining authority of the family is indicated by both high British, Scandinavian, and US divorce rates and low Italian and Spanish fertility. The only major new source of social identities to have become salient during recent years of globalization and Europeanization has been ethnicity: both among those identifying with the 'imagined communities' (Anderson 1983, 1991) of existing nation states or certain parts of them, and among new minorities. (New political movements based on ecological concern have been important, but do not express the politics of social identity, except among very small communities of ecological activists.) Although labour is far less mobile than capital, the globalization of the economy, the ease of modern communications and the facts that geographical regions of the world experience very diverse fates leads to considerable population movement. This has produced the groups of new but now settled ethnic minorities in most Western European countries, as well as in the USA where it reinforces an existing well-established pattern. Mobility of both capital and labour, but the latter far more saliently, then produced a defensive reaction among some native European and US populations. These seek reassurance and security at a time when flexibility is making work prospects insecure, but this often takes the form of resentment against minorities from whom they perceive a cultural challenge to their life in the community.

The resulting heterogeneity of ethnicity, when viewed in conjunction with the rise in divorce and other changes in conventional family forms, and the decline of strong class identities among the mass of the population, challenges both *verzuiling* and melting pot principles for handling diversity. The European model seems to be disintegrating under the pressure of secularization, the decline of class, the collapse of social hierarchies—in short the collapse of all institutions which made possible the obedience and deference which were important characteristics, both of traditional European social orders and of the class-structured and strongly organized character of oppositions to them. The Netherlands, originator of the *verzuiling* concept, is one of those changing most rapidly (Bax 1990). Meanwhile the US melting pot model is also under considerable pressure from multiculturalism (Hollinger 1995), which also represents a form of resistance to order and obedience, the order that required conformity to the model of 'becoming American', the mass homogeneity or cultural and social Fordism that has prevented the diversity and pluralism of American society from becoming unmanageable. Some authors go so far as to see multiculturalism as the most likely model for the development of advanced societies (Leggewie 1994, 1996; Soysal 1994).

Overall it is perhaps the more rigid European form of combining diversity with overall order which has most difficulty with contemporary trends towards fragmentation and individualization. On the other hand, it is necessary to place this fragmentation in perspective as occurring around a core of institutional stability that survives in reduced form. Most marriages do not end in divorce; most Europeans retain a basic religious identity; ethnic minorities remain small proportions of European populations. The mid-century pattern of Christian, labour, and liberal parties remains the dominant form of Western European politics even if its hegemony has diminished. Furthermore, multiculturalism is possibly easier to accommodate within segmented European structures than within a melting pot.

PROSPECTS FOR CONVERGENCE

While the main emphasis in the above discussion has been on the very limited character of Western European similarities and on intra-continental differences, concealed
beneath many of the arguments have been certain prospects for a greater convergence
in the future. We should certainly expect some convergence, not so much because of
any processes specific to Europe, but because European societies are caught up in
certain general trends that seem common to all advanced societies. These include the
changes stemming from economic globalization, the associated growth of the power of
international financial capitalism, and the partly associated, well attested spread of
certain forms of the ethic of individualism that we considered in Chapters 7 and 9, as
well as the struggle of women for an end to their subordination in domesticity. We
must however also take some account of the explicit Europeanization project of the
European Union, which contains some ironies and paradoxes.

Those who advocate a distinctive 'social Europe' can point to the arguments concerning 'sharply defined classes with blunted inequality' as evidence that something of
this kind is rooted in recent European history, has been slowly extending to southern
Europe too, and could therefore form a convincing way in which the future European
integration process might run with the grain of the post-war European past. In the
words of the Swedish sociologist, Gøran Therborn (1997), Western Europe might become to the world what Scandinavia has been to Europe: a northern corner of strong
social citizenship and relative equality. However, and as Therborn fully recognizes, this
process clashes completely with another one: the 'Americanizing' trend towards greater
inequalities and a more finance-driven capitalism. This latter is no mere cultural borrowing, but rooted in the circumstances of the post-Keynesian and globalizing economy. Capital being in general more mobile than labour, it benefits disproportionately
from the opening of alternative courses of action produced by globalization and deregulation, strengthening its position in relations with any national pool of labour. This
has implications for the superior rewards that capital can enjoy in the market, and for
the demands it can make on governments in terms of taxation and welfare state policy.

Furthermore, important elements of the European integration process itself conflict
with the 'social Europe' elements and foster this 'Americanization' of Europe. First, as
is well known, European integration proceeds fastest when what is being sought is
'negative' integration, the breaking down of impediments to trade; 'positive' integration, the establishment of particular new institutions, requires a more difficult consensus (Scharpf 1994). European integration measures therefore primarily take the form
of breaking down highly specific organizational forms in favour of those that most
closely resemble pure markets. This frequently means adoption of a US model. Second,
the rigid criteria for economies to enter the European Single Currency, together with
the long-term rules for managing the new currency, are making it difficult for many
European governments to operate generous welfare states, Keynesian solutions to demand management, or even their historical forms of banking and financial systems
(Story 1999).

This implies a distinctive kind of European convergence: 'Europeanization' takes
the form of the spread of certain American characteristics to most if not all European
societies. Meanwhile, none of the existing tendencies to Americanization discussed at

the outset are weakened by the chang[...] first instance, global economic deregulation increases the power and scope of the largest corporations and the most homogeneous products. Although there are many European multinationals, the greatest number are American, particularly in the field of culture which is particularly important for deeper social influences.

Hradil and Immerfall (1997a) similarly identify an Americanization process affecting Europe, though they see this in more normative and evolutionary terms. For them the USA represents, almost by definition, the next stage in any modernization process. They also see greater flexibility in its institutions. What might be criticized is their conflation of what they see as the informal and interpersonal nature of US American society with the individualization of the market. As we have seen at various points, the abstract individualization of the market can be very different from concern for the human person. At some points they conflict quite strongly—particularly in terms of employment and welfare rights, as we saw in Chapters 12 and 13. These aspects of a decline in citizenship in the USA need to be taken into account when any superiority of the American social form is being assessed.

However, it is always dangerous to base predictions on the continuation of existing trends without taking account of the capacity of institutions to respond to an external challenge and thereby turn a potentially convergent force into a new kind of diversity. We have already seen how the *common* development of a demand by women for more autonomy led to a paradoxical *divergence* in birth rates between Scandinavia and southern Europe with opposite effects from those anticipated, as this common demand encountered different institutional constraints. Similar processes must be expected in the economic field. Since this moves us into the realm of speculation, I will conclude with hints at one possible example.

European monetary union appears to be a strongly homogenizing force—though it must be remembered that most economists predict that the single currency will lead to increasing economic specialization of different regions, and therefore increased economic diversity. Nevertheless, as it impacts on the labour markets of different countries, it will encounter institutional arrangements with very different capacities of response. Among countries which have retained or, more likely, reformulated fundamentally neo-corporatist industrial relations systems, there are likely to be attempts to use labour market institutions to adapt to the behaviour of the European Central Bank, in the same way that pre-unification West German labour market institutions used to soften the potential impact of the Bundesbank by pre-emptively adapting to its demands (Crouch 1999; Hall and Franzese 1998). As we saw in Chapter 12, during the past few years there has been a considerable revival and reform of neo-corporatist industrial relations capabilities in a number of countries: in particular Denmark, Ireland, the Netherlands, but also to some extent Austria, Belgium, Italy, and Norway. To the extent that these responses are successful, the neo-corporatist structures will be confirmed in their effectiveness, and a distinctive, very non-American characteristic of certain Western European political economies will be enhanced. At the same time, by no means all Western European states have such capacities, so the internal diversity of Western Europe will also grow.

SOCIETY
HABITING?

Now that we have some provisional measure of the range of diversity and the degree of European specificity in current changes within the advanced world, we can conclude our study with an attempt to characterize the kind of society which seems to be emerging, and the implications of changes to the model of mid-century compromise society. In previous chapters we have considered the value of mainly three potentially explanatory theories: post-industrial ones, and optimistic and pessimistic forms of postmodern theories. All suggest a fragmentation of the strongly defined structures of the mid-century model.

POST-INDUSTRIALISM AND POSTMODERNITY

POST-INDUSTRIAL THEORIES

For post-industrial theorists the key to understanding contemporary society is the decline of industrial employment and the rise of the services sectors, the occupational structures of which depart from the essentially factory-based model of the compromise structure. This makes sense of many of the wider changes: it anticipates the rise of the social and community services sector of employment, and therefore both the extra-ordinarily important shifts in the gender basis of employment and the rise of the welfare state. The former then leads the concept of post-industrialism on to explore changes in the family consequent on the changes in the gender division of labour. The latter leads it to examine the rise of citizenship.

The explanatory power of post-industrialism can be taken further if the transition from industrialism to post-industrialism is linked to that from materialism to post-materialism. This brings us to the popular thesis for explaining contemporary value change as 'post-materialist' associated with Robert Inglehart (1977, 1990, 1997). This is used to explain the decline of class-based political identities and the rise of such themes as ecology. The combined post-industrial and post-material thesis can there-fore embrace large parts of the changes that we have identified.

There are however weaknesses. The thesis tends to be very optimistic. It correctly predicts the rise in the educational level of much of the workforce, but is blind to those developments in the services sectors (especially personal services) discussed in Chapter 4 which see a return of low-skilled jobs of an almost pre-industrial kind. It is also un-likely to account for the rise of atypical work of the kind we considered in Chapter 3. The post-materialist component of the thesis also presents problems. We saw in Chapter 11 that the decline of class voting was also accompanied by a decline in voting for Christian parties; it is difficult to envisage a definition of the contrast between materialism and post-materialism that defines religion as part of the former. But perhaps most important of all, while the post-industrial thesis is useful for interpreting the rise of citizenship that we have described, it has much less to say about the return of purer forms of capitalism that we have identified in some chapters. Most post-industrial theorists tend to identify capitalism with industry and the public and charitable sectors with post-industrial services. They are therefore well equipped to account for the rise in social citizenship of the 1970s, but are taken by surprise by the more recent resurgence of capitalism.

POSTMODERN THEORIES

Postmodern theories concentrate on different themes. Postmodernism developed initially as a cultural concept, and it was only as a secondary development that some sociologists tried to apply it more generally (see discussions in Lash 1991). The original formulations remain the stronger: it is in the less economic areas of society that we find most evidence supporting a postmodern account of contemporary social change. As we concluded in Chapter 14, nearly all countries seem vulnerable to the cultural fragmentation anticipated by these theories.

Optimistic postmodernity theorists see a fragmentation of the reality of the class structure as its component parts move apart: the bases of social position become more diverse, organizations become more flexible, past inheritances of wealth and culture become less relevant to the contemporary world. More pessimistic (sometimes Marxist) versions of these theories see a persistence of the prevailing structures of a capitalist society behind processes of fragmentation that are superficial and illusory.

Much of our discussion of the family in Chapter 7 can be analysed in postmodern terms. A useful summary of these developments has been offered by Meyer (1993). He sees three different forms of what he calls private life which are replacing the 'normal' (in our terms the mid-century compromise) family: the child-centred, concerned with upbringing and education of children (*erzieherische Handlungsthematik*); couples (married or not) without children, who are concerned with developing their partnership (*partnerschaftliche Handlungsthematik*); and those living alone or in communal households rather than families who have an individual project (*individualistische Handlungsthematik*). Chapter 7 was mainly concerned with the first two, though the third is also a major component of a postmodern form. It is the second, the partnership dyad, also regarded by Meyer as postmodern, that we mainly saw emerging into prominence. Associated with this we can also note that in many countries, especially in Germany and southern Europe, there is no convenient fit between the expectations placed on family behaviour by social policy and the demands of the economy (Kaufmann 1990; Federkeil 1997: 79). This is consistent with a fragmentation model and contrasts with the 'Fordist' family of the mid-century period. On the other hand, Meyer (1993) also reminds us of the continuing importance of the family centred on child-rearing, which he sees as an essentially modern (rather than postmodern) form.

The evidence from the discussion of individualism in religion points in the same direction of a decline of organizational structures and of external constraint on individuals' choices rather than any decline of faith as such. Observers of both France and Germany comment on the declining capacity of churches to have their authority accepted on matters of sexuality and other areas of private life (Chadwick *et al.* 1994). In Spain Torcal Loriente (1992) found that it was not so much a conflict between materialist and post-materialist values that separated older from younger generations—this had been the conflict between the old and those now in middle years. For the young the important issue was personal liberty and autonomy. In France the 1960s seem to have been a turning point in secularization (Lambert 1993), a marked and rapid decline in religious belief and practice taking place from then onwards, particularly among young generations. However, as he comments, this runs alongside rising belief among the young in astrology and other '*croyances parallèles*'. It would again seem that it is not so much the idea of supernatural belief that is rejected here, but *organized* forms of religious practice.

This enables us to understand a major shift in the basis of the mid-century compromise, relating especially to the specifically European characteristic identified in Chapter 14 of strong formal organizations wielding some kind of authority over their members. Once that characteristic declines, in the way that postmodern theories predict, the model starts to unravel. Studies of the paradigm case, the Netherlands, have demonstrated how pillarization declined over a lengthy period (from the 1950s to the 1980s), affecting different institutions in turn in a kind of domino effect (Bax 1990: ch. 5; Van Praag 1991).

As Hervieu-Léger has remarked (1994: 20–1), the biggest component of the current decline of religious institutions is the individualization and subjectivization of many aspects of life. Halman (1994) and Halman and Pettersson (1994) stress the need to distinguish the growing general individualism in values which they observe from selfishness, and to see it more in terms of a drive for autonomy and an avoidance of collective or authoritative constraint. This leads us to further issues concerning the impact of a possible postmodernity on structures typical of the mid-century compromise, and to alternative interpretations of the post-materialist phenomenon.

Changes towards multiculturalism and ethnic diversity similarly support postmodern accounts of the fragmentation of solid structures and increased diversity. The general concept of a fragmentation of strongly organized structures also makes better sense than does post-materialism of the political changes we observed in Chapter 11: the decline (albeit gradual) of such structures in party identity.

However, there are problems with the postmodern approach. First, it misunderstands the relationship of the phenomena it describes to classical modernity. And second, its optimistic versions fail to see a certain selectivity in the institutions being affected by fragmentation.

To the extent that the changes observed—for example those in the family and religion—embody increasing individualism and refusal to accept the constraints of existing institutions, they can be said to represent an *intensification* of the rationalistic search for maximizing gain which is at the heart of modernization, not its transcendence. In other words, they may be the very reverse of what optimistic postmodernists perceive. This is very much as anticipated by the argument of Giddens (1990: 36 ff.) discussed in Chapter 1, that this is better interpreted as reflexive modernism rather than as postmodernism (see also Beck, Giddens, and Lash 1994). For example, the family is being refashioned to fit a different economic framework, where both the capitalist economy and the welfare state need high participation in the paid economy by men and women alike, not the 'breadwinner' family. Alternatively, in the words of Ulrich Beck (1986), whose concept of *Risikogesellschaft* has been felt by many to capture particularly well the 'essence' of contemporary society, these changes are far more *'ein Weg in eine andere Moderne'* ('a way to another modernity') than a transcendence of modernity as such. Risk calculation is an extreme form of the rationalistic, calculative temperament (see also Genov 1997). This is fully consistent with the growth of individualism that has been observed in so many studies.

As to the claims of a new structurelessness, it is important to note some skewedness in the way in which this occurs—something which the more Marxist versions of postmodern theory can comprehend, but not the more optimistic ones.

First, any fragmentation in structures of authority that might be undermining families, churches, or political parties is not affecting authority embedded in the labour contract or in management. True, as we saw in Chapter 3, firms are being deconstructed in the sense that many workers are being placed in various atypical employment positions. Processes of de-layering and contracting-out, as well as frequent mergers and takeovers and the rapidly shifting patterns of ownership that are facilitated by today's financial markets make the firm a far less solid structure than it seemed during the Fordist period. However, this does not compromise managerial authority; rather the reverse. Persons in atypical work are usually more subordinate to management than are established employees, because their countervailing rights against authority are so much weaker. The contemporary capitalist firm embodies clear principles of authority and order and precisely rationalistic criteria of decision-making and resource allocation. If it becomes more flexible in organizational form (as in the labour market), this is only in order to improve its capacity to pursue its core profit-maximizing rationale— Giddens's reflexive modernity or Beck's *andere Moderne* again.

This is a dialectic in the relationship between goals and the organizational means used to pursue them which can be traced back to the debate over Weber's model of bureaucracy and to which we referred in Chapter 1. Eventually bureaucratic rule-following undermines the *Zweckrationalität* (goal-oriented rationality) of which it is intended to be the instrument. The response of those in control of institutions is then to try to fashion more flexible means of achieving their goals. This might give the appearance of a de-structuration, a postmodern collapse of bureaucratic hierarchy—and there might indeed be subsequent problems of control as the dialectic between aim and form enters a new phase. However, this is in no way a de-structuration that implies a loss of capitalist control.

At the same time, new information technology has enabled the principles of operation of essentially hierarchical, Fordist firms to be newly extended to many services sectors (for example, banks and insurance companies). Furthermore, many public services and public bureaucracies are being reorganized along broadly Fordist lines according to the concepts of new public service management. Both in the original industrial heartland and in their new private and public service applications, 'Fordism revived' incorporates far more labour flexibility than the original model. However, the aim of these flexibilities is to have employees (or ostensibly self-employed subcontractors) perform tasks more efficiently and more clearly under managerial control than was possible under former systems. They therefore represent an enhancement of the capitalist search for rationalized efficiency, not a departure from it.

A RE-ANALYSIS OF THE MID-CENTURY COMPROMISE

What implications do these arguments have for the interpretation of current social change? Previous chapters have established a basic viability of the concept of mid-century compromise society as the main form existing in Western Europe, Japan, and the USA around the early 1960s. There were some important departures from the model in Finland, Ireland, and in southern Europe (Greece, Spain, Portugal, southern Italy), but these can be seen as 'late developers' in the classic sense of modernization theory. More challenging and interesting is the fact that the compromise model does not imply the *maximization* of each element of the model. The capitalist character of society in the early 1960s was less pronounced than it had been in the 1930s; welfare citizenship did not peak until later; indeed, the development of the welfare state was part of the move away from industrial society. The 1960s was a peak for the overall model, but not for its individual elements.

This is not a problem for the model but an aspect of its expression. As set out in Chapter 1, the whole point of the mid-century compromise concept is that it is a balance among four potentially antagonistic elements; development of any one of them beyond a certain level can come only at the expense of one or more of the others. We can see this in a rapid and rather stylized review of a much longer-term development of their relationship. The institutions of traditional community were deeply threatened by the growth of modernism in general and capitalism in particular, with its gradual application of calculation to all actions and relationships and its disturbance of traditional authorities and ways of life. Polanyi (1957) demonstrated how much of the history of the rise of markets was the history of a struggle against tradition and community. At the same time however capitalist institutions often made use of community networks to establish zones of trust within which risky transactions could be executed. The international financial systems established in the late Middle Ages by Italian and Jewish banking families are important cases in point: family and community played an important part in sustaining trust networks that were vital to capitalist development. Fred Hirsch (1977) reminded us that Adam Smith himself saw capitalism as requiring an inherited moral legacy of behaviour (essentially a legacy of community mechanisms) which it could not itself create.

In more recent centuries, market forces also became allies of community in a joint struggle against the extension of citizenship, especially in its twentieth-century socialist and social democratic forms. In the name of the superior right of the democratic state, citizenship institutions challenged many areas of autonomy of both market and community. As a result the latter often came to share the former's demand for clear restrictions on the state role. The economist's laissez-faire and the priest's *subsidiarité* could amount to very much the same thing—especially when the Church relied on rights of private property to defend its autonomy. From the French Revolution onwards the Church's network of charitable activities has faced various choices of being destroyed by the state, fighting it, or (increasingly today) finding an accommodation alongside it. During the formative years of the early twentieth century, and despite the anxiety of defenders of community institutions concerning certain aspects of capitalism, confrontation with the citizenship state proved on balance more important. From this emerged the alliance between Christian democracy and the capitalist economy which, as we saw in Chapter 11, became the most important political force in continental Europe for the second half of the twentieth century.

Community had historically also been used, but even more challenged, by the rise of industry. Many early industries were based on local communities and drew support from local human resources; but in the long run the construction of both large workplaces and large industrial towns and cities threatened the viability of family, church, and neighbourhood.

Meanwhile, markets and citizenship, despite their oppositions, have occasionally united in universalism and modernism or at least anti-traditionalism. The non-discriminatory laws of citizenship were crucial in providing the 'level playing field' that markets require for their operation. The rights needed to act in the market—to make contracts and have them enforced, to own property and have it protected by public authority, to enforce payment for goods and services sold—can all be citizenship rights.

The relationship between capitalism and industrialism was more symbiotic, though by the early twentieth century the latter had begun to be problematic for capitalism. Questions of planning and of needs for social infrastructure were raised, as well as problems of pollution and of damage to persons not party to capitalism's market exchanges. Industrialism also produced—ironically often through the *communities* that industrial workplaces and towns generated—the manual working class that became the first (and to date only) class to pose a sustained and partially effective challenge to the dominance of capitalist rule.

These last struggles took the form of the advance of citizenship. This was partly at the expense of community, such institutions as church and family being functionally challenged by the rise of state welfare. However, the family at least often gained from the stability afforded to its members by the welfare state. Local communities also benefited from the tendency of welfare states to try to support employment and other economic structures in regions that might have suffered severe loss as a result of unmediated market forces. Furthermore, community and citizenship could sometimes find a *rapprochement* in rejecting the negation of non-calculative human bonds that is implied by the market form.

In this longer historical perspective, mid-century compromise society can be seen as a particular moment in the constantly shifting balance of these different social forces. The central problems which this particular model was required to tackle were: (1) to prevent the strong forces embodied by capitalist industrialism from gradually invading all community institutions which did not correspond to their rationalistic, goal-seeking logic; and (2) to reconcile those forces with the aspirations of the working class which they had created but placed in a highly subordinate position.

The former was approached in the following way. In the wake of the defeat of Fascism and the rejection in the West of communism, most of the nation states with which we have been concerned acquired (or retained) a sociologically liberal institutional structure, ring-fencing community institutions against both the invasion of capitalist industrialism and their own internal hostilities. In addition to state and other forms of regulation which maintained these boundaries, a particularly important barrier between capitalist industrialism and the world of family and local community was the male breadwinner model of paid employment. With some exceptions, men spent much of their lives working in the formal economy while married women worked for family and neighbourhood (Dahlström 1989). The incorporation of the industrial working class was achieved by acceptance that nearly every adult possessed certain rights of membership, of citizenship. These took the form of universal male suffrage, political participation by voluntary organizations representing working-class as well as other interests, and the social citizenship of the welfare state.

Expressed in this way alone however, the model seems to embody certain functionalist assumptions. It is important to recognize therefore that responses to these 'needs' for the defence of community or citizenship depended very much on the forces represented by them being able to mobilize some form of power to express such needs. If they were weak or could be easily suppressed, there was little need for capitalist industrialism to make compromises. Therefore, traditional institutions retained most power where Christian democracy was a powerful political force, the Catholic Church emerging as the main defender of the traditional family and, of course, Christianity (van Kersbergen 1996). Where trade unions and social democratic parties were strongest, citizenship could develop most extensively (Korpi 1983). Societies therefore developed differing responses to these questions, ensuring continuing diversity within the overall uniformity. For example, its industrial component was found in its strongest form in Austria, Germany, and the UK; its capitalist character was most exemplified in the USA; the Netherlands was the most outstanding instance of sociological liberalism; citizenship was most advanced in Scandinavia.

The point can be illustrated further by looking in some more detail at the particular case of the rise of the welfare state, since within the academic literature there are both functionalist and power resource accounts of this. The former see the growth of welfare as a functional process, part of the logic of industrialism or of modernization, implying a kind of automaticity whereby once societies reach a certain stage they 'need' to develop welfare states. These theories do not consider the possibility that, for 'need' to be recognized, its expression may require the mobilization of some power (Esping-Andersen 1990: ch. 1; van Kersbergen 1996).

On the other hand, the functionalist approach embodies some important arguments. It argues that, since the advance of markets and urbanization destroys community institutions, the functions that these performed have to be replaced by professional and bureaucratic services made available on a rational basis of entitlements. This suits very well the contrast between community and citizenship mentioned above, and we certainly find some evidence of this 'functional replacement'.

There is also a Marxist version of functionalist accounts, a 'logic of capitalism' approach which argues that the welfare state develops, either as a means by which capitalism defends itself from attack by trying to smooth over its internal contradictions, or as a means whereby capital reproduces the kind of skilled, healthy workforce and advanced social infrastructure that it requires for the more advanced forms of capitalism (Gough 1979). To some extent the analysis of Fordism of the *régulationiste* school shares this kind of functionalist perspective: when masses of people are either poor or their standard of living threatened by insecurity, they are unable or unwilling to spend money freely, and hence they slow down market processes. It was important to the functioning of the economy that the combination of the welfare state and Keynesian demand management smoothed the insecurities endemic to a pure market form of capitalism so that the joint risks of becoming marginalized and of failing to be able to sustain consumption standards were reduced.

Some authors then developed a new concept of the crisis of capitalism by arguing that eventually the capitalist economy becomes unable to pay the cost of social policy while continuing to need its products (O'Connor 1977). This kind of argument, like that of the logic of industrialism, embodies important insights but spoils the case by implying too much automaticity and by exaggerating its explanatory power. For example, while one might explain the development of basic public health measures as being in the interests of capitalist development, it is difficult to account for the widespread availability of sophisticated medical care, needed by small numbers of people but made available through public health services.

The 'power resource mobilization' school argues very differently from all forms of functionalism. The main work here is Korpi's (1983) study of the rise of the Swedish welfare state. Social policy developed, Korpi argued, only when groups who 'needed' a particular policy were able to organize themselves and mobilize power to put pressure on the policy-making system in order to achieve it. Therefore, the particular strength of the Swedish working class (in both its political and industrial wings, as we saw in Part IV) explains the subsequent strength of the Swedish welfare state. This approach is an important corrective to functionalism, though as Esping-Andersen (1990: 16–18) and van Kersbergen (1996) have pointed out, it generalizes too much on Swedish experience and omits to note that groups other than the working class have had an interest in developing welfare policy, or (and here the point applies to Sweden too) that the working class often needed allies in other classes to press home its goals, having to compromise with these others in the eventual design of the social state *en route*.

Our findings in Chapter 13 on the distribution of income through the welfare state enabled us to make some appraisal of the relative value of power as opposed to functionalist or compensatory models of the taxation and benefit system. The latter would hold that social policy acts to redress inequalities emerging from the market, perhaps in the interests of some social balance; this is clearly its general direction, at least at the level of transfer incomes and income-related taxation. However, this theory would also expect the largest compensations to take place where initial inequalities were largest, whereas our evidence showed the opposite. According to the power mobilization thesis, if the degree of income inequality resulting from the labour market can be taken as an indicator of the relative power of different groups within that market, then the countries with the most egalitarian pre-tax, pre-transfer distributions are those in which lower-income groups have most countervailing power. We would expect them to use this to ensure redistributive welfare and taxation systems, and therefore there should be more redistribution in countries where the pre-tax and pre-transfer distribution was already relatively low. This is broadly what we found.

MOMENTS OF CHANGE (1): THE REINFORCEMENT OF CITIZENSHIP

Our model of the mid-century compromise therefore embodies the likelihood of a constantly adjusting equilibrium produced by alterations in the balance of power among the social forces contributing to it. In fact, if the model describes an equilibrium at all, it resembles that of a person riding a bicycle: balance is achieved by constant movement and adjustment, not by a static state of rest, and an exaggerated movement in any direction can cause major disturbance. Two major change episodes in particular can be identified during the model's short history, the cumulative effect of which has been to change its character considerably.

During the post-war years labour, especially that of manual workers, acquired an important position in most Western economies. The Fordist system of mass production spread from the USA to Western Europe. This used mass production methods to produce cheap goods which were bought by the workers whose earnings came from mass production, giving capitalists in general an optimism that working-class consumption could expand and be a new motor of economic growth. In several parts of Europe this combined with Keynesian economic management which similarly used the need of this class for social services to make possible a high level of public spending, which in turn created full employment and further strengthened working-class consumption and political power. This phenomenon was reflected in the role of mass welfare citizenship in the initial formulations of the compromise, but as workers' social position stabilized under the new conditions of mass prosperity, their demands were further incorporated into the social design. Following increases in strikes and other forms of industrial militancy in many countries in the late 1960s and early 1970s (Crouch and Pizzorno 1978) there was extensive growth in the welfare state in most Western European societies—and also for a time in the USA (see Chapter 13). This meant a rapid increase in public expenditure as a proportion of gross domestic product: the only time that such an increase had taken place in peacetime. The growth took place earliest and in the most pronounced way where the welfare state was already strongest and traditional community institutions weakest, that is in the relatively secularized societies of northern Europe.

This disturbed the equilibrium of the compromise in the following ways. First, as we saw in Chapter 4, the consequent expansion of employment in the education, health, and welfare sectors was an element in the de-industrialization of employment, or the move to a post-industrial society. Since the new employment involved large numbers of women, the family segregation model of mid-century society was also disturbed (Chapter 7). In part welfare state growth took the form of removing women from unpaid family work and employing some of them instead as paid carers. In this way the place in the compromise of community as well as that of industrialism was changed.

Industrialism was a 'loser' from this process in the sense that labour shifted increasingly to welfare production rather than goods production. It is important to stress that industrialism 'lost' solely in terms of the balance of the mid-century model. Industrial production continued to rise, but because productivity in the manufacturing sector tends to grow more or less constantly, ever less labour is required for a given unit of output. Growing numbers of jobs in the welfare state did not therefore 'rob' industry of workers which it needed, but maintained overall employment levels when manufacturing's labour needs were declining. Productive efficiency often also gained from the social infrastructure provided by welfare policies, particularly the advance of education. Similarly, although community 'lost' through the growth of the welfare state, childcare and early education provided through welfare policy often became the main means by which female employment and family stability could be reconciled.

The shift of employment and activity to the public sector (or, particularly in the USA, the charitable sector) and the de-commodification of certain goods and, in particular, services through the welfare state also weakened the capitalist component of the model. Not only were an increasing number of economic activities carried on outside the nexus of capitalist ownership and market exchange, but the taxation used to finance the welfare spending also reduced—albeit slightly—the structure of inequality resulting from market forces and property ownership. However, it can also be argued that capitalism gained from the stability accorded to people's lives by certain welfare guarantees enabling them to spend more of their disposable income on the products of capitalist firms, including in particular residential property which considerably increased the proportion of the population having a stake in capitalist property ownership.

Alongside the growth of the welfare state, there was also a growing role for another limb of citizenship: the role of organized interests, especially in the labour market. One consequence of the full employment which became characteristic of the period was a tendency towards inflation. Not wishing to abandon the policies which produced full employment, governments came increasingly to rely on the system of collective bargaining, which was the usual result of freely developed labour market interest organization, for wage restraint which would contain inflation. As we saw in Chapter 12, systems based on neo-corporatist arrangements were usually able to respond to this challenge, but with growing internal strain as inflationary tendencies grew; those based on pure pluralist collective bargaining experienced considerable difficulty and were under pressure to move in a neo-corporatist direction. This growth of the role of the system of organized interests in determining the functioning of the labour market placed further strain on the capitalist free market model of the economy.

In terms of class structure these changes were ambiguous. On the one hand, capitalist classes were being challenged by the pressures for a frequent extension of citizenship rights, but so was the manual working class because it was declining in size. The main classes that were gaining in both size and social advantage were various groups—professional and routine non-manual, and to some extent manual service workers—within the social state. These changes were partially concealed by the fact that the new employment in these areas was predominantly female—male employment remaining more clearly embedded in industrialism, and sociologists tending at that time to confine their attentions to male occupations and classes.

As we saw in many of the preceding chapters, changes in gender relations have been fundamental to this unwinding of the original form of the mid-century compromise. They link changes in occupational structure to those in the family, to religion, and to the welfare state—this last in its dual role as employer of women and either facilitator or handicap to women's employment. Esping-Andersen (1996a) has demonstrated how the effect of the Church on state policy in several countries of Western Europe explains low levels of female employment. In a more detailed analysis of policies, Daly

(1996; see also Pfaff 1992) has shown how the German and British welfare states make diverse assumptions about family structure, the former (since the Second World War being deeply influenced by Christian democratic thought) assuming far more of a 'male breadwinner' than the more liberal British scheme. Vielle (1997) similarly examined the indirect costs of family responsibilities in 7 European countries. She showed how national social policy regimes differed considerably in their recognition of these costs, with considerable implications for women's capacity to join the paid labour force. Countries therefore varied on this dimension of change.

MOMENTS OF CHANGE (2): THE RESURGENCE OF CAPITALISM

More recently there has been a further change of direction. As a result of the inflationary crises of the 1970s, governments adopted deflationary and non-accommodating fiscal and monetary policies; combating inflation became a far higher priority than securing full employment. At the same time the manual working class was declining in size, losing its political importance. The classes that were replacing it lacked manual workers' party-political and trade-union profile. By the 1980s aspects of economic globalization—primarily the liberation of international capital markets and increasing scope for global production systems—were releasing capital from its dependence on individual national pools of labour and hence from dependence on particular national regimes for protecting labour's interests (Michie and Grieve Smith 1995).

The balance of class forces that had propelled the development of citizenship institutions was now being challenged by a resurgence of capitalism and a decline in industrial employment. This decline had initially been stimulated by the growth of welfare state citizenship itself, but now served to diminish the political support base of that very citizenship by reducing the size of the social class that had been its principal supporter.

The strains of economic management imposed on systems of organized interests in the labour market began to mount, even in some previously stable neo-corporatism systems. On the one hand, many workers came to resent the restraining role being played by trade unions which they expected to press their interests, not restrain them. On the other, capitalist and managerial interests resented the shift in economic power from themselves to their own associations and, worse still, workers' organizations, that neo-corporatism entailed. Meanwhile, systems that had retained characteristics of pure collective bargaining continued to be viewed as problematic because of their inability to perform such a role of economic responsibility. In the USA, whose model of pluralistic industrial relations citizenship had been such an example of democratization to continental European countries in the immediate post-war years, there was a virtual disappearance of collective bargaining.

Just as the growth of the citizenship model had challenged the place of capitalism within the original mid-century compromise by excluding the provision of certain major services from private ownership and market distribution, so the capitalist resurgence implied the opposite: what Therborn (1996) has called the rise of 'post-democratic liberalism'. This has included a growing commercialization of social life, including the marketization and/or privatization of the welfare state. Also, if less obviously, the place of traditional community institutions is challenged: the challenge to regulations protecting the Christian Sunday from extensive trading activities is an example. Similarly, in many occupations the concept of a normal working day has been changed by extensions of round-the-clock working, sometimes to take maximum advantage of expensive, capital-intensive production processes, sometimes in response to the increase in demand for leisure activities amongst the working population. This can be seen as an invasion by markets of periods of time previously reserved for engaging in non-traded activities, in particular for remaining within the family. Ironically, some of the invasions of time are made necessary by the need of families to reconstruct the time available to them. For example, if increasing numbers of fathers and mothers are in paid employment during the 'normal' working day, other people (often other fathers and mothers) have to work at abnormal times to enable the former group to shop, travel, and engage in other activities when they are not working. As the 'protection' of family space that was achieved through the domestic division of labour in mid-century compromise society breaks down, so market forces have filled the space.

To some extent the citizenship forces of the welfare state anticipated capitalism by partially commodifying domestic (normally female) labour; it brought many caring and support activities into the labour market, even though the services themselves were neither distributed by market means nor available for private ownership. The next step, beginning only now, is to marketize distribution, and even to privatize ownership, of these services. This occurs both to the form of offer of public services to the ultimate consumer (medicines, certain kinds of educational and health services) and to transactions among units of public service provision. For example, relations between different branches of a service are frequently placed on a basis of purchaser/provider, contracting or market testing. A final step takes place if and when services are finally privatized, that is removed from public ownership and sold to the general class of owners of capital. Very frequently the prior processes of marketization have been a prelude to full privatization.

If the thesis of capitalist resurgence is correct, we should expect to see a rise in inequality among industrial societies and a reversal of the earlier rise of citizenship. And if these changes are common to all societies and are at least in part mobilized by general, transnational changes, there should be some convergence in inequality patterns. As we saw in Chapter 13, there is evidence of this kind, in growing inequalities in both the pattern of incomes deriving from the labour market (Chapter 5) and in those after account is taken of the effect of taxation and the distribution of welfare benefits (Chapter 13)—particularly in the UK and USA, the two countries where the capitalist resurgence has been seen most strongly. On the other hand, we must also remember the evidence in Chapter 13 that, in Europe though not the USA, the level of welfare state spending remains at considerably higher levels during the 1990s than during the heyday of the compromise in the 1960s.

The evidence of developments in industrial relations systems was similarly ambiguous: trade unions had declined in most countries, and all systems were needing to pay more attention to market forces. On the other hand, with the exception of the UK and the USA, reconstructions of social partnership systems were taking place in all countries—even if some of these seemed to stand little chance of real success in organizing their labour markets.

A further component of the capitalist resurgence has been a growth of individualism, which has been measured as a value change by the European Values Survey (Halman

1994; Halman and Pettersson 1994). When a particular aspect of life is within the purview of a non-market institution (e.g. church, family, political party), it is normally governed by some form of collective or hierarchical decision-making; it is through that means that the institution in question keeps an area reserved. For example, if children live entirely within their family they can enjoy goods and services only if the governing institutions of the family (usually the parents) so decide. Similarly, if a national church is able to determine which days shall be work days and which various forms of holy days, its authority structures are able to decide on which days individual members of the society will be able to use certain marketed services (banks, public transport, certain kinds of shops, etc.). Marketization of the area concerned means that individuals can make choices for themselves free from these institutions. Once children start earning some money they can begin to consume in ways that their parents dislike; when religious trading restrictions are lifted, individuals can choose to shop on Sundays if they want. There is a liberation of the individual from the family, but the individual's dependence on capitalist institutions, as employee and/or as customer, is simultaneously strengthened.

It would however be wrong to interpret the rise of individualism solely as a response to the recent recrudescence of capitalism. First, it seems to have pre-dated it, starting with the youth revolts of the late 1960s. Second, there are some ostensibly autonomous forms of it. As we saw in Chapters 7 and 9, recent changes in fertility, divorce, and other aspects of family behaviour are difficult to explain without recourse to the idea of some search for individual happiness maximization; while changes in religious practice show a desire for less authoritative, more individually selected forms of expression. The growth of individualism seems to be an autonomous value-change and not a mere by-product of economic developments. If anything, the resurgence of capitalism can be seen as a *counter* to individualism, offering an institutionally limited and channelled form for its potentially anarchic expression. Capitalism is not a system which gives total freedom to individuals to choose, but one which permits them to make those choices which are made available by markets—a potential clash between the requirements of a capitalist economy and those for postmodernist expression.

Capitalism is now far less strongly associated with industrialism than during the peak period of the mid-century compromise. The most dynamic elements of capital since the period of deregulation and globalization are financial institutions which do not have the extensive sunk costs of industrial enterprises. It is financial capital which epitomizes the concept of 'footloose' capitalism, and this is the form which has been becoming more important as technological advance extends its information and mobility capacities, and as the Anglo-American mode of financial organization and regulation forces out various other models (see Chapter 6). Globally mobile finance capitalism is considerably less committed to the concept of a social compromise than was the industrial form. It is not tied to or embedded in individual nation states and their internal social arrangements, and lacks industry's requirement for elements of social and physical infrastructure, which are often delivered through citizenship institutions. At the same time, the post-industrial economy produces a more diffuse class structure than did industrialism, lacking in particular the large, potentially alienated and often politically well organized manual working class. These characteristics all further disturb the equilibrium of the mid-century compromise and make it less necessary for capitalist interests to make any compromises at all with other social forces.

THE RESURGENCE OF CAPITALISM AND THE QUESTION OF CLASS

Both the changes discussed have been particularly driven by class forces: the rise of citizenship can be seen as the means by which underprivileged classes secured an attenuation of class inequalities of both power and material resources; the subsequent resurgence of capitalism is reversing aspects of those changes. We therefore need to take a closer look at the development of class structures and relations.

Class structures always comprise bundles of social attributes stretching across the three zones of economy, polity, and community (respectively a fundamental economic location, the political expression of that location in relation to other groups, and the set of subjective identities that make the system operate). In the case of the mid-century compromise the bundle took the following form. As we saw in Chapter 5, categorizations of different types of employment had been designed by earlier generations of capitalist employers and governments, indicating both relationship to the capitalist processes of ownership and work authority and occupational and skill categories of industrial work. These designations, since they defined work groups and income categories, and both drew on and created different levels and types of educational and cultural preparation, imparted comparable fates to members of the various categories and led them to form communities. These occupational and class communities competed and coalesced with other community identities based on religion, gender, and ethnicity to form the characteristic identities of capitalist industrial society. These in turn became the building blocks of political identity within mass societies moving towards democracy, in turn again forming the battleground over different encounters between the capitalist market and the process of citizenship.

Labour and social security law placed people in variously defined categories attracting different kinds of rights depending on the kind of work they did (manual versus non-manual, dependently employed versus self-employed, remunerated versus domestic). This resulted from opposing forces: on the one hand, attempts by employers and governments to order the working population into controllable groups; but, on the other, the political mobilization and organization of subordinate classes as they fought to overcome some of their disadvantages within such a system. Although this opposition produced many violent and difficult struggles, eventually the mutual interest of both sides in an orderly structure based on these emerging definitions of class categories helped forge the mid-century compromise, and the link between economy and polity that helped produce the organization of classes that eventually fuelled the political system of capitalist democracy.

Another aspect of the same process was the mutual interest of manual workers and employers in ramifying the resulting structure in the organization of industrial relations between employers' associations and trade unions. It was therefore the originally pejorative definition of them as inferior class categories that enabled manual workers to organize themselves for citizenship—the strength of autonomous political and organizational power of labour often correlating closely with the extent of their exclusion as a class from political citizenship and other rights.

From this process emerged the characteristic class relations of the compromise, which in an ambiguous way froze the contours of the class structure while abating the inequalities implied by them—the relatively clearly defined class identities but restricted class inequalities identified in the previous chapter as a core element of Western European rather than of US American forms.

However, this could not remain static. A combination of a capitalist labour market and modern technology continue to produce a constantly shifting mass of different job titles with minutely varying associated levels of income and combinations of skill and authority. The faster that technology and methods of work organization change, and the more effective the market processes become, then the less can the occupational and associated class structure be squeezed into static forms. Although occupational change was producing new, ambiguously located occupational groups from the late nineteenth century onwards, the manual working class in manufacturing continued to grow in absolute and often relative size until the decade of the 1960s—and in some cases later. A crucial change was therefore registered when this process reached its peak, and the class and sector which by their size and growth had provided the paradigm for the entire class order of industrial capitalist society began to decline.

It becomes increasingly difficult for either analysts or social actors to discern class-like groupings within the population. It is important to note that this *more* purely, not less, reproduces a capitalist labour market. As Kreckel (1992: 140) has pointed out, one of the central historical tendencies of the development of market forces is the destruction of intermediary non-market forms of solidarity and group formation: class *as a set of social identities* is vulnerable to that process precisely as the fundamental power relations of capitalist class relations grow. This leads, as Kreckel expresses it, to *Klassenverhältnis ohne Klassen*—class relationship without classes. The class character of society intensifies and declines simultaneously (ibid. 149). This is a central example of the general paradox of the changes described as postmodern: behind an apparent fragmentation of society and a multiplication of social goals, the underlying logic of capitalist rationalization is in fact intensifying. Indeed, that logic partly takes the form of the fragmentation.

It is unlikely that we shall ever reach a pure labour market, in which virtually nothing groups occupations into clusters. Certain basic similarities among jobs will lead employing organizations, if only for administrative purposes, so to group them. Perhaps even more important, educational performance will continue to influence occupational opportunities for many and probably most working people; if anything the influence of education on job placement is likely to continue to increase. Since education places people in large, differentiated and identifiable bands and streams which inculcate cultural levels as well as intellectual and other achievements, it will continue to bracket together large groups of occupational destinations as broadly similar to each other. Today these divisions increasingly concern gender and also different levels of security rights in employment. Broad class groupings determined by cultural level and consumption patterns associated with certain types of occupation within a hierarchy will therefore continue. It is however unlikely that they will have the same clarity of differentiation of vast, settled masses of the population that developed out of the encounter between post-feudal and industrial society, especially since those whose occupational positions are defined by insecurity are unlikely to develop a capacity for strategy on behalf of an occupationally defined interest. Gender might prove to be an exception, but gender, though a clear and powerful source of social identity, does not easily become a basis for defining interests. To be defined as an interest in a conflictual context, an identity must normally be rooted in shared life experiences, and so long as heterosexual partnerships remain a principal form of human relationship the mobilizing power of gender will be weakened.

As we have seen, the same forces of disintegration do not apply to the class of capital. Recent developments in capital markets impart to the owners of capital a capacity for strategic action and an autonomy from other interests within societies (Scott 1997). This is especially true when the class of capital overlaps heavily with an international managerial class. Management is an occupational category already defined by its separation in authority structures. Today it is also increasingly a class whose interests are structured and catered for by a sophisticated and expensive range of consultant services, specialized journals and other aids of a kind which are not available to other groups in society except perhaps the professions. It is true that neither capitalists nor managers are a thoroughly distinct group; both capital ownership and the exercise of managerial authority are ranged along continua that extend very deeply down into the workforce or indeed, in the case of capital ownership, the general population. However, at the level where active, strategic decision-making occurs it is possible to identify a small class of more clearly defined actors. Capital with its associated management therefore becomes the class which retains the clearest definition in what at first sight seems to be a classless society (Crouch 1996).

This finding is of course consistent with the conclusions of both our critique of postmodern theories and our account of the second moment of change in the mid-century compromise. At the same time, we must also remember the prior record of the first moment of change, the growth of welfare citizenship, and the fact that much of the legacy of that change remains.

How then are we finally to characterize the societies in which we are living? In the case of the European countries which are our principal concern, I do not think we can go beyond the idea of a fractured compromise. A point made by Mair (1997) concerning political allegiance can be made more generally: the institutions of a previous period—the high period of the compromise—still structure much of how society operates. Even if they have been fractured and have lost dynamic energy, the structures they established were powerful and little has emerged that directly challenges them. The most energetic point of social power emerging in late twentieth-century society was clearly that of a globalizing capitalism, but this is checked in the amount of social change it can achieve by two factors: first, the sheer facticity of the institutions of the compromise just noted; second, the major advance of citizenship institutions of the 1960s and 1970s, which largely remain. Is the assembly of non-capitalist interests represented in much of this simply a dead weight carried over from the past, or does it contain a potentiality for new action? If it is the former, we should expect capitalism to make further advances; if the latter, we should expect the emergence of more productive forms of compromise, either in individual countries or just possibly at the level of the European Union.

The situation in the USA, and perhaps the UK, is different. Here the new strength of capitalism is that much greater, and the power of initiative among non-capitalist institutions considerably weaker. One can therefore be more confident in predicting that these societies will increasingly take a less compromised capitalist form. One of the conclusions of the previous chapter was that Americanization is a potent influence among European societies. If that is so, we may more confidently expect that the European societies too will increasingly lose those features which do not conform to the dominance of capitalist markets.

STATISTICAL APPENDIX

Appendix Table A.2.1 Work activities of total populations, 18 countries, c.1960

Category	Austria[a]			Belgium			Denmark[b]			Finland[c]		
	Male	Female	Total	Male	Female	Total	Male	Female	Total	Male	Female	Total
Percentages of total population												
Age 80+	6.25	8.46	7.43	1.44	2.21	1.83	1.49	1.74	1.61	0.61	1.22	0.93
Age 15 and less	23.94	20.10	21.89	24.61	22.65	23.61	25.39	23.94	24.66	31.70	28.41	29.99
Domestic	4.41	29.25	17.67	13.38	53.30	33.77	2.27	41.88	22.24	7.69	33.70	21.16
Education (F/T)	4.41	2.54	3.41	2.33	1.96	2.14	7.13	4.28	5.69	2.45	1.86	2.14
Unemployed	1.23	0.61	0.90	1.47	0.49	0.97	0.91	0.46	0.68	0.88	0.52	0.70
P/T employees	0.91	6.48	3.89	0.57	3.20	1.91	3.31	12.94	8.17	1.84	3.68	2.80
Family workers	3.21	8.33	5.95	1.68	1.54	1.61	0.00	1.05	0.53	4.15	8.17	6.23
Unclassified	0.00	0.00	0.00	1.14	0.01	0.56	0.00	0.00	0.00	0.00	0.00	0.00
Own account	11.43	3.67	7.29	10.80	3.07	6.86	15.66	1.05	8.29	14.63	2.77	8.48
F/T employees	44.21	20.55	31.58	42.58	11.57	26.74	43.84	12.66	28.12	36.05	19.67	27.56
TOTAL	100.00	100.00	100.00	100.00	100.00	100.00	100.00	100.00	100.00	100.00	100.00	100.00
Percentages of non-dependent population (i.e. excluding 80 and over, 15 and under, those in full-time education)												
Domestic	6.74	42.45	26.27	18.68	72.84	46.63	3.43	59.79	32.69	11.78	49.18	31.62
Unemployed	1.87	0.89	1.33	2.05	0.67	1.34	1.38	0.66	1.01	1.36	0.76	1.04
P/T employees	1.40	9.40	5.78	0.79	4.37	2.64	5.02	18.47	12.00	2.82	5.38	4.18
Family workers	4.91	12.10	8.84	2.35	2.11	2.23	0.00	1.50	0.78	6.36	11.92	9.31
Unclassified	0.00	0.00	0.00	1.59	0.01	0.77	0.00	0.00	0.00	0.00	0.00	0.00
Own account	17.47	5.33	10.83	15.09	4.20	9.47	23.73	1.50	12.19	22.42	4.05	12.67
F/T employees	67.61	29.83	46.94	59.45	15.80	36.93	66.44	18.08	41.33	55.26	28.71	41.18
TOTAL	100.00	100.00	100.00	100.00	100.00	100.00	100.00	100.00	100.00	100.00	100.00	100.00
All in employment	91.39	56.66	72.39	79.27	26.49	52.03	95.19	39.54	66.30	86.86	50.05	67.34
M less F employment			34.73			52.78			55.65			36.81

Category	France[b]			Germany			Greece[c]			Ireland[b]		
	Male	Female	Total	Male	Female	Total	Male	Female	Total	Male	Female	Total
Percentages of total population												
Age 80+	1.42	2.86	2.16	1.28	1.62	1.46	1.36	1.84	1.61	1.58	1.88	1.73
Age 15 and less	25.99	23.72	24.82	23.04	19.48	21.15	26.30	24.07	25.16	31.19	30.22	30.71
Domestic	13.05	44.57	29.25	7.20	42.17	25.73	10.07	44.90	27.91	6.92	43.54	25.13
Education (F/T)	1.40	1.27	1.33	4.53	3.30	3.88	2.52	1.41	1.95	1.10	1.23	1.17
Unemployed	0.50	0.40	0.45	0.46	0.20	0.32	1.11	1.14	1.12	2.20	1.10	1.65
P/T employees	1.38	4.59	3.03	0.96	9.21	5.33	0.00	0.00	0.00	1.22	2.68	1.94
Family workers	1.95	4.29	3.16	1.76	5.32	3.64	8.89	15.78	12.42	7.14	1.13	4.15
Unclassified	0.00	0.00	0.00	0.00	0.00	0.00	0.13	0.04	0.08	3.32	0.61	1.97
Own account	12.42	2.82	7.48	9.36	1.77	5.34	27.29	3.70	15.21	16.86	3.36	10.15
F/T employees	41.89	15.47	28.31	51.42	16.92	33.14	22.34	7.12	14.54	28.47	14.25	21.40
TOTAL	100.00	100.00	100.00	100.00	100.00	100.00	100.00	100.00	100.00	100.00	100.00	100.00
Percentages of non-dependent population (i.e. excluding 80 and over, 15 and under, those in full-time education)												
Domestic	18.33	61.77	40.81	10.12	55.78	35.00	14.43	61.77	39.15	10.45	65.32	37.85
Unemployed	0.70	0.56	0.62	0.64	0.27	0.44	1.58	1.57	1.58	3.33	1.65	2.49
P/T employees	1.94	6.37	4.23	1.35	12.18	7.25	0.00	0.00	0.00	1.84	4.02	2.93
Family workers	2.74	5.95	4.40	2.47	7.04	4.96	12.74	21.71	17.42	10.80	1.69	6.25
Unclassified	0.00	0.00	0.00	0.00	0.00	0.00	0.18	0.06	0.12	5.02	0.92	2.97
Own account	17.44	3.90	10.44	13.16	2.34	7.26	39.08	5.09	21.33	25.50	5.04	15.28
F/T employees	58.85	21.45	39.50	72.26	22.39	45.09	31.99	9.80	20.40	43.05	21.37	32.23
TOTAL	100.00	100.00	100.00	100.00	100.00	100.00	100.00	100.00	100.00	100.00	100.00	100.00
All in employment	80.97	37.67	58.57	89.24	43.95	64.56	83.99	36.66	59.27	86.21	33.03	59.66
M less F employment			43.31			45.29			47.33			53.18

Appendix Table A.2.1 (continued)

Category	Italy			Netherlands			Norway[b]			Portugal[d]		
	Male	Female	Total	Male	Female	Total	Male	Female	Total	Male	Female	Total
Percentages of total population												
Age 80+	1.09	1.45	1.27	1.30	1.56	1.43	1.68	2.18	1.93	0.85	1.37	1.12
Age 15 and less	24.49	22.91	23.68	31.28	29.55	30.42	26.60	25.09	25.84	27.56	26.69	27.11
Domestic	12.05	52.87	32.90	7.48	50.38	29.02	8.77	53.25	31.08	4.37	58.31	32.49
Education (F/T)	1.97	1.10	1.52	3.12	2.31	2.71	2.27	1.51	1.89	1.00	0.55	0.77
Unemployed	2.39	0.46	1.40	0.55	0.17	0.36	0.70	0.25	0.48	1.30	0.04	0.64
P/T employees	1.75	1.91	1.83	3.12	7.10	5.12	4.43	9.08	6.76	1.62	2.15	1.90
Family workers	3.63	3.19	3.41	1.72	0.91	1.31	1.70	0.09	0.89	4.39	0.31	2.26
Unclassified	0.00	0.00	0.00	0.00	0.00	0.00	0.00	0.00	0.00	1.28	0.17	0.70
Own account	15.76	2.25	8.87	9.83	0.49	5.14	12.81	0.70	6.74	13.09	1.06	6.82
F/T employees	36.87	13.86	25.12	41.59	7.53	24.49	41.04	7.85	24.38	44.54	9.35	26.19
TOTAL	100.00	100.00	100.00	100.00	100.00	100.00	100.00	100.00	100.00	100.00	100.00	100.00
Percentages of non-dependent population (i.e. excluding 80 and over, 15 and under, those in full-time education)												
Domestic	16.63	70.93	44.74	11.64	75.67	44.35	12.62	74.77	44.19	6.19	81.68	45.76
Unemployed	3.29	0.61	1.91	0.86	0.25	0.55	1.01	0.36	0.68	1.84	0.06	0.90
P/T employees	2.42	2.56	2.49	4.86	10.66	7.82	6.37	12.75	9.61	2.30	3.01	2.67
Family workers	5.01	4.28	4.64	2.68	1.37	2.01	2.45	0.12	1.27	6.22	0.43	3.19
Unclassified	0.00	0.00	0.00	0.00	0.00	0.00	0.00	0.00	0.00	1.81	0.24	0.99
Own account	21.76	3.02	12.06	15.28	0.74	7.85	18.44	0.99	9.58	18.54	1.49	9.60
F/T employees	50.89	18.59	34.17	64.68	11.31	37.42	59.10	11.02	34.67	63.10	13.09	36.88
TOTAL	100.00	100.00	100.00	100.00	100.00	100.00	100.00	100.00	100.00	100.00	100.00	100.00
All in employment	80.07	28.46	53.35	87.50	24.08	55.10	86.37	24.88	55.13	91.97	18.27	53.34
M less F employment			51.61			63.42			61.49			73.71

Category	Spain[d]			Sweden[e]			Switzerland[e]			United Kingdom[b]		
	Male	Female	Total	Male	Female	Total	Male	Female	Total	Male	Female	Total
Percentages of total population												
Age 80+	2.14	3.24	2.71	1.71	2.17	1.94	1.23	1.95	1.60	1.31	2.48	1.91
Age 15 and less	27.96	25.60	26.75	22.55	21.32	21.94	24.42	22.53	23.46	24.81	22.09	23.40
Domestic	4.59	57.24	31.69	10.07	46.87	28.51	7.51	47.63	27.95	6.84	45.13	26.62
Education (F/T)	1.06	0.43	0.74	4.72	3.85	4.29	0.91	0.53	0.72	1.71	1.03	1.36
Unemployed	0.63	0.13	0.37	0.34	0.16	0.25	0.09	0.07	0.08	2.06	0.76	1.39
P/T employees	0.00	0.00	0.00	3.29	11.83	7.57				1.20	11.12	6.32
Family workers	6.71	2.65	4.62	1.42	0.51	0.97	2.84	1.51	2.16	0.32	0.23	0.27
Unclassified	0.00	0.00	0.00	0.00	0.00	0.00	0.00	0.00	0.00	0.00	0.00	0.00
Own account	15.50	1.83	8.46	10.22	0.67	5.43	11.63	2.02	6.73	5.74	0.76	3.17
F/T employees	41.40	8.87	24.65	45.68	12.61	29.11	51.38	23.76	37.31	56.01	16.40	35.55
TOTAL	100.00	100.00	100.00	100.00	100.00	100.00	100.00	100.00	100.00	100.00	100.00	100.00
Percentages of non-dependent population (i.e. excluding 80 and over, 15 and under, those in full-time education)												
Domestic	6.67	80.93	45.40	14.18	64.50	39.69	10.23	63.53	37.66	9.47	60.66	36.31
Unemployed	0.91	0.19	0.54	0.48	0.23	0.35	0.12	0.09	0.10	2.86	1.02	1.89
P/T employees	0.00	0.00	0.00	4.63	16.28	10.54	0.00	0.00	0.00	1.67	14.94	8.63
Family workers	9.75	3.75	6.62	2.00	0.71	1.34	3.86	2.01	2.91	0.44	0.30	0.37
Unclassified	0.00	0.00	0.00	0.00	0.00	0.00	0.00	0.00	0.00	0.00	0.00	0.00
Own account	22.51	2.59	12.12	14.39	0.92	7.56	15.83	2.69	9.07	7.95	1.03	4.32
F/T employees	60.15	12.54	35.32	64.32	17.36	40.52	69.96	31.69	50.26	77.61	22.04	48.48
TOTAL	100.00	100.00	100.00	100.00	100.00	100.00	100.00	100.00	100.00	100.00	100.00	100.00
All in employment	92.41	18.88	54.06	85.34	35.27	59.96	89.65	36.39	62.24	87.67	38.32	61.80
M less F employment			73.53			50.08			53.27			49.35

Appendix Table A.2.1 (continued)

Category	Japan			United States[e]		
	Male	Female	Total	Male	Female	Total
Percentages of total population						
Age 80+	0.49	0.96	0.73	1.16	1.63	1.40
Age 15 and less	31.25	27.62	29.40	31.88	30.06	30.96
Domestic	5.97	32.11	19.28	7.84	40.27	24.29
Education (F/T)	3.83	3.12	3.47	2.59	2.06	2.32
Unemployed	0.50	0.23	0.36	2.88	1.44	2.15
P/T employees	4.35	10.00	7.22	4.83	6.55	5.70
Family workers	5.72	11.60	8.71	0.21	0.38	0.30
Unclassified	0.00	0.00	0.00	2.29	0.91	1.59
Own account	14.79	3.49	9.04	7.04	0.86	3.90
F/T employees	33.10	10.87	21.79	39.28	15.84	27.39
TOTAL	100.00	100.00	100.00	100.00	100.00	100.00
Percentages of non-dependent population (i.e. excluding 80 and over, 15 and under, those in full-time education)						
Domestic	9.27	47.01	29.03	12.17	60.78	37.19
Unemployed	0.77	0.34	0.54	4.47	2.17	3.29
P/T employees	6.75	14.64	10.88	7.50	9.89	8.73
Family workers	8.88	16.98	13.12	0.33	0.57	0.45
Unclassified	0.01	0.00	0.01	3.55	1.38	2.43
Own account	22.95	5.11	13.61	10.94	1.30	5.98
F/T employees	51.37	15.91	32.81	61.03	23.91	41.93
TOTAL	100.00	100.00	100.00	100.00	100.00	100.00
All in employment	89.96	52.65	70.43	83.36	37.04	59.52
M less F employment			37.31			46.31

F/T = full-time; P/T = part-time; M = male; F = female

[a] aged 70+, not 80+
[b] education data 1965
[c] education includes part-time
[d] aged 75+, not 80+
[e] assumed gender share of education

Sources: ILO Yearbooks; OECD Employment Outlooks (retrospective data); OECD Education at a Glance.

Appendix Table A.2.2 Percentages of working or non-dependent populations in various work activities, c.1960

	A	B	C	D	E	F	G	H	I	J	K	L	M
Austria	22.80	12.08	28.60	18.30	67.61	91.39	46.94	72.39	42.45	34.73	5.78	8.84	10.83
Belgium	7.20	0.69	34.70	21.40	59.45	79.27	36.93	52.03	72.84	52.78	2.64	2.23	9.47
Denmark	17.50	1.48	28.50	22.10	66.44	95.19	41.33	66.30	59.79	55.65	12.00	0.78	12.19
Finland	35.50	12.52	21.60	14.80	55.26	86.86	41.18	67.34	49.18	36.81	4.18	9.31	12.67
France	19.80	6.46	26.90	20.10	58.85	80.97	39.50	58.57	61.77	43.31	4.23	4.40	10.44
Germany	13.40	7.31	36.40	18.90	72.26	89.24	45.09	64.56	55.78	45.29	7.25	4.96	7.26
Greece	53.90	21.49	13.40	12.10	31.99	83.99	20.40	59.27	61.77	47.33	0.00	17.42	21.33
Ireland	35.20	2.11	17.00	18.80	43.05	86.21	32.23	59.66	65.32	53.18	2.93	6.25	15.28
Italy	28.20	7.50	28.20	14.20	50.89	80.07	34.17	53.35	70.93	51.61	2.49	4.64	12.06
Netherlands	10.70	0.60	29.90	23.50	64.68	87.50	37.42	55.10	75.67	63.42	7.82	2.01	7.85
Norway	19.50	0.90	25.50	18.40	59.10	86.37	34.67	55.13	74.77	61.49	9.61	1.27	9.58
Portugal	42.30	3.11	20.30	14.60	63.10	91.97	36.88	53.34	81.68	73.71	2.67	3.19	9.60
Spain	41.30	6.71	21.90	13.90	60.15	92.41	35.32	54.06	80.93	73.53	0.00	6.62	12.12
Sweden	13.80	0.82	34.20	19.80	64.32	85.34	40.52	59.96	64.50	50.08	10.54	1.34	7.56
Switzerland	11.20	0.91	39.70	19.00	69.96	89.65	50.26	62.24	63.53	53.27	0.00	2.91	9.07
UK	3.80	0.13	34.80	24.40	77.61	87.67	48.48	61.80	60.66	49.35	8.63	0.37	4.32
Japan	32.30	16.75	21.70	14.80	51.37	89.96	32.81	70.43	47.01	37.31	10.88	13.12	13.61
USA	6.50	0.64	26.50	24.80	61.03	83.36	41.93	59.52	60.78	46.31	8.73	0.45	5.98

A = agricultural work as per cent of all employment
B = female agricultural work as per cent of all female employment
C = manufacturing work as per cent of all employment
D = 'services' work as per cent of all employment
E = per cent of all non-dependent males in full-time employee status
F = per cent of all non-dependent males in employment
G = per cent of all non-dependent persons in full-time employee status
H = per cent of all non-dependent persons in full-time employee status
I = per cent of all non-dependent women in domestic status
J = per cent non-dependent males in employment less per cent non-dependent females in employment
K = per cent of all non-dependent persons in part-time employee status
L = per cent of all non-dependent persons in family worker status
M = per cent of all non-dependent persons in self-employment

Source: As Appendix Table A.2.1.

Appendix Table A.2.3 Work activities of total populations, 18 countries, c.1995

Category	Austria (1994)			Belgium (1990)			Denmark (1996)			Finland (1995)		
	Male	Female	Total	Male	Female	Total	Male	Female	Total	Male	Female	Total
Percentages of total population												
Age 80+	2.16	5.07	3.66	0.81	3.58	2.23	2.64	2.71	2.67	1.83	4.59	3.25
Age 15 and less	18.64	16.63	17.60	23.45	21.65	22.53	18.05	16.53	17.27	19.95	18.16	19.03
Education (F/T)	8.22	4.42	6.26	2.62	2.32	2.47	9.51	9.32	9.41	9.80	10.78	10.30
Domestic	13.94	33.74	24.14	23.13	37.20	30.32	9.78	23.67	16.86	14.72	21.22	18.05
Unemployed	1.87	1.59	1.72	2.92	2.39	2.65	3.35	4.13	3.75	9.29	7.55	8.40
P/T employees	1.43	8.71	5.18	0.80	7.92	4.44	5.76	10.52	8.19	2.44	4.22	3.36
Family workers	0.79	1.94	1.38	0.43	1.78	1.12	0.00	0.00	0.00	0.40	0.19	0.29
Unclassified	0.00	0.00	0.00	0.60	2.96	1.81	0.00	0.00	0.00	1.61	1.72	1.66
Own account	6.06	3.04	4.50	7.84	2.11	4.91	6.88	2.72	4.76	8.65	3.93	6.23
F/T employees	46.89	24.87	35.54	37.42	18.08	27.53	44.04	30.40	37.08	31.31	27.64	29.42
TOTAL	100.00	100.00	100.00	100.00	100.00	100.00	100.00	100.00	100.00	100.00	100.00	100.00
Percentages of non-dependent population (i.e. excluding 80 and over, 15 and under, those in full-time education)												
Domestic	19.64	45.67	33.32	31.63	51.35	41.67	14.01	33.13	23.87	21.51	31.93	26.78
Unemployed	2.63	2.15	2.38	3.99	3.30	3.64	4.80	5.78	5.31	13.58	11.36	12.46
P/T employees	2.02	11.79	7.15	1.09	10.93	6.10	8.26	14.73	11.59	3.57	6.35	4.98
Family workers	1.11	2.62	1.90	0.58	2.46	1.54	0.00	0.00	0.00	0.59	0.29	0.44
Unclassified	0.00	0.00	0.00	0.81	4.09	2.48	0.00	0.00	0.00	2.35	2.58	2.47
Own account	8.53	4.11	6.21	10.72	2.91	6.75	9.85	3.81	6.74	12.64	5.91	9.24
F/T employees	66.06	33.66	49.04	51.17	24.96	37.83	63.08	42.55	52.49	45.76	41.58	43.64
TOTAL	100.00	100.00	100.00	100.00	100.00	100.00	100.00	100.00	100.00	100.00	100.00	100.00
All in employment	77.73	52.19	64.31	64.38	45.35	54.69	81.19	61.09	70.82	64.91	56.71	60.76
M less F employment	25.54			19.04			20.10			8.20		

Category	France (1994)[a]			Germany (1994)			Greece (1994)			Ireland (1995)		
	Male	Female	Total	Male	Female	Total	Male	Female	Total	Male	Female	Total
Percentages of total population												
Age 80+	3.08	6.11	4.63	2.50	5.87	4.23	2.97	3.27	3.13	2.08	3.52	2.81
Age 15 and less	20.53	18.54	19.51	16.46	14.70	15.55	18.27	15.95	17.07	25.47	23.17	24.31
Education (F/T)	9.48	10.53	10.02	4.18	3.84	4.01	7.54	6.71	7.11	3.45	10.99	7.25
Domestic	19.10	26.07	22.68	17.97	36.11	27.29	18.13	44.24	31.60	18.45	32.14	25.35
Unemployed	5.83	5.55	5.69	4.32	3.19	3.74	3.45	4.43	3.96	6.14	3.67	4.89
P/T employees	2.12	7.34	4.79	1.86	10.56	6.33	2.33	3.48	2.92	2.53	6.68	4.62
Family workers	0.81	0.00	0.40	0.24	1.14	0.70	2.61	6.54	4.64	0.45	0.49	0.47
Unclassified	0.00	0.00	0.00	0.00	0.00	0.00	0.00	0.00	0.00	0.00	0.00	0.00
Own account	6.96	2.63	4.74	6.02	2.03	3.97	20.93	4.86	12.64	12.63	2.07	7.31
F/T employees	32.10	23.23	27.55	46.46	22.56	34.18	23.76	10.51	16.93	28.80	17.26	22.98
TOTAL	100.00	100.00	100.00	100.00	100.00	100.00	100.00	100.00	100.00	100.00	100.00	100.00
Percentages of non-dependent population (i.e. excluding 80 and over, 15 and under, those in full-time education)												
Domestic	28.55	40.22	34.44	23.38	47.77	35.81	25.46	59.72	43.47	26.74	51.58	38.63
Unemployed	8.72	8.56	8.64	5.62	4.22	4.91	4.84	5.98	5.44	8.90	5.88	7.46
P/T employees	3.16	11.32	7.28	2.41	13.97	8.30	3.28	4.70	4.02	3.67	10.72	7.04
Family workers	1.21	0.00	0.60	0.32	1.50	0.92	3.67	8.83	6.38	0.65	0.79	0.72
Unclassified	0.00	0.00	0.00	0.00	0.00	0.00	0.00	0.00	0.00	0.00	0.00	0.00
Own account	10.39	4.05	7.20	7.83	2.69	5.21	29.39	6.56	17.39	18.31	3.32	11.14
F/T employees	47.96	35.84	41.85	60.45	29.85	44.85	33.36	14.20	23.28	41.73	27.70	35.02
TOTAL	100.00	100.00	100.00	100.00	100.00	100.00	100.00	100.00	100.00	100.00	100.00	100.00
All in employment	62.73	51.21	56.92	71.00	48.01	59.28	69.69	34.29	51.08	64.36	42.53	53.91
M less F employment			11.52			22.99			35.40			21.83

STATISTICAL APPENDIX

Appendix Table A.2.3 (*continued*)

Category	Italy (1994)[b]			Netherlands (1995)			Norway (1995)			Portugal (1994)[c]		
	Male	Female	Total	Male	Female	Total	Male	Female	Total	Male	Female	Total
Percentages of total population												
Age 80+	4.59	7.19	5.93	1.85	4.18	3.03	2.71	5.32	4.03	2.05	3.07	2.58
Age 15 and less	21.60	20.11	20.84	19.01	17.76	18.38	20.36	18.91	19.63	8.66	15.43	12.18
Education (F/T)	1.80	1.02	1.40	7.28	6.71	6.99	10.52	10.31	10.41	4.93	3.86	4.37
Domestic	20.51	43.12	32.12	15.02	31.92	23.57	10.67	19.49	15.13	28.00	35.73	32.02
Unemployed	4.81	4.58	4.69	3.37	3.46	3.41	2.86	2.12	2.49	2.54	2.69	2.62
P/T employees	2.19	5.01	3.64	6.04	19.93	13.07	6.50	20.30	13.47	2.42	5.92	4.24
Family workers	1.29	1.85	1.58	0.20	0.92	0.56	0.38	0.55	0.46	0.76	0.97	0.87
Unclassified	4.81	4.57	4.69	0.00	0.00	0.00	3.43	2.21	2.81	0.39	0.51	0.45
Own account	13.32	3.95	8.50	6.70	2.85	4.75	6.06	2.16	4.09	13.57	8.73	11.05
F/T employees	25.08	8.60	16.62	40.52	12.28	26.23	36.51	18.62	27.47	36.68	23.10	29.61
TOTAL	100.00	100.00	100.00	100.00	100.00	100.00	100.00	100.00	100.00	100.00	100.00	100.00
Percentages of non-dependent population (i.e. excluding 80 and over, 15 and under, those in full-time education)												
Domestic	28.48	60.16	44.72	20.91	44.74	32.92	16.07	29.78	22.95	33.19	46.02	39.60
Unemployed	6.67	6.39	6.53	4.69	4.85	4.77	4.31	3.23	3.77	3.01	3.46	3.24
P/T employees	3.05	6.99	5.07	8.41	27.93	18.25	9.79	31.01	20.43	2.87	7.63	5.25
Family workers	1.79	2.58	2.20	0.28	1.28	0.78	0.57	0.84	0.70	0.90	1.25	1.07
Unclassified	6.68	6.37	6.52	0.00	0.00	0.00	5.16	3.37	4.27	0.47	0.65	0.56
Own account	18.49	5.51	11.84	9.32	4.00	6.64	9.12	3.30	6.20	16.08	11.24	13.66
F/T employees	34.83	12.00	23.13	56.40	17.20	36.64	54.97	28.45	41.67	43.48	29.75	36.62
TOTAL	100.00	100.00	100.00	100.00	100.00	100.00	100.00	100.00	100.00	100.00	100.00	100.00
All in employment	64.85	33.45	48.76	74.40	50.41	62.31	79.62	66.98	73.28	63.79	50.52	57.16
M less F employment			31.40			23.99			12.63			13.28

Category	Spain (1995)[c]			Sweden (1994)			Switzerland (1994)[d]			United Kingdom (1993)		
	Male	Female	Total	Male	Female	Total	Male	Female	Total	Male	Female	Total
Percentages of total population												
Age 80+	2.31	5.03	3.70	3.31	6.04	4.69	2.17	5.24	3.73	2.35	4.14	3.26
Age 15 and less	19.24	16.98	18.08	19.85	18.40	19.12	17.48	16.27	16.87	20.78	18.40	19.56
Education (F/T)	11.16	11.72	11.45	7.56	7.62	7.59	2.27	1.25	1.76	5.13	4.89	5.00
Domestic	16.62	40.46	28.80	17.66	21.38	19.54	15.00	30.83	23.04	14.95	30.27	22.77
Unemployed	9.12	9.20	9.16	4.70	3.14	3.91	2.46	1.89	2.17	7.03	3.16	5.05
P/T employees	1.21	3.38	2.32	3.14	10.21	6.72	5.21	20.61	13.03	2.59	15.07	8.97
Family workers	0.98	1.38	1.18	0.21	0.25	0.23	0.83	2.28	1.57	0.00	0.00	0.00
Unclassified	0.09	0.07	0.08	0.00	0.00	0.00	0.00	0.00	0.00	0.00	0.00	0.00
Own account	9.56	3.40	6.41	7.17	2.50	4.81	9.66	4.37	6.97	8.13	1.43	4.71
F/T employees	29.72	8.37	18.81	36.39	30.47	33.40	44.91	17.25	30.86	39.06	22.64	30.67
TOTAL	100.00	100.00	100.00	100.00	100.00	100.00	100.00	100.00	100.00	100.00	100.00	100.00
Percentages of non-dependent population (i.e. excluding 80 and over, 15 and under, those in full-time education)												
Domestic	24.69	61.06	43.14	25.49	31.47	28.49	19.21	39.92	29.68	20.83	41.71	31.56
Unemployed	13.56	13.88	13.72	6.79	4.62	5.70	3.15	2.45	2.79	9.79	4.35	7.00
P/T employees	1.79	5.10	3.47	4.54	15.02	9.79	6.68	26.68	16.78	3.61	20.77	12.42
Family workers	1.45	2.09	1.77	0.30	0.37	0.34	1.07	2.96	2.02	0.00	0.00	0.00
Unclassified	0.14	0.11	0.12	0.00	0.00	0.00	0.00	0.00	0.00	0.00	0.00	0.00
Own account	14.21	5.14	9.61	10.35	3.68	7.01	12.37	5.66	8.98	11.33	1.98	6.53
F/T employees	44.17	12.63	28.17	52.54	44.85	48.68	57.53	22.33	39.74	54.43	31.20	42.50
TOTAL	100.00	100.00	100.00	100.00	100.00	100.00	100.00	100.00	100.00	100.00	100.00	100.00
All in employment	61.75	25.06	43.14	67.72	63.92	65.81	77.64	57.63	67.53	69.38	53.94	61.44
M less F employment			36.69			3.81			20.01			15.44

Appendix Table A.2.3 (continued)

Category	Japan (1993)[e]			United States (1994)[f]		
	Male	Female	Total	Male	Female	Total
Percentages of total population						
Age 80+	1.36	4.42	2.88	1.64	3.97	2.83
Age 15 and less	17.11	16.55	16.83	23.77	21.39	22.55
Education (F/T)	6.84	6.03	6.43	8.57	8.09	8.32
Domestic	10.00	28.66	19.30	9.07	20.81	15.11
Unemployed	1.56	1.17	1.37	3.51	2.76	3.12
P/T employees	8.21	16.28	12.23	4.12	8.21	6.22
Family workers	0.00	0.00	0.00	0.05	0.09	0.07
Unclassified	0.00	0.00	0.00	0.22	0.25	0.24
Own account	0.00	0.00	0.00	5.59	3.03	4.27
F/T employees	54.92	26.90	40.96	43.46	31.41	37.26
TOTAL	100.00	100.00	100.00	100.00	100.00	100.00
Percentages of non-dependent population (i.e. excluding 80 and over, 15 and under, those in full-time education)						
Domestic	13.39	39.26	26.13	13.74	31.27	22.79
Unemployed	2.09	1.61	1.85	5.32	4.14	4.71
P/T employees	10.99	22.29	16.56	6.23	12.34	9.38
Family workers	0.00	0.00	0.00	0.08	0.14	0.11
Unclassified	0.00	0.00	0.00	0.34	0.37	0.36
Own account	0.00	0.00	0.00	8.47	4.55	6.45
F/T employees	73.54	36.84	55.46	65.82	47.19	56.20
TOTAL	100.00	100.00	100.00	100.00	100.00	100.00
All in employment	84.52	59.13	72.02	80.94	64.59	72.50
M less F employment			25.39			16.35

F/T = full-time; P/T = part-time; M = male; F = female

[a] family worker and own account data 1990
[b] 75+, not 80+; some calculations provided
[c] 75+, not 80+
[d] several data 1990, not 1994
[e] provisional data
[f] 85+, not 80+

Sources: ILO *Yearbooks* (various years); OECD *Employment Outlooks* (various years); OECD *Education at a Glance* (various years).

Appendix Table A.2.4 Percentages of working or non-dependent populations in various work activities, c.1995

	A	B	C	D	E	F	G	H	I	J	K	L	M	N
Austria	7.20	3.40	26.80	29.40	66.06	77.73	49.04	64.31	45.67	25.54	7.15	1.90	6.21	18,469
Belgium	2.40	0.60	18.70	41.00	51.17	64.38	37.83	54.69	51.35	19.04	6.10	1.54	6.75	18,618
Denmark	5.50	1.40	20.10	43.80	63.08	81.19	52.49	70.82	33.13	20.10	11.59	0.00	6.74	20,066
Finland	8.00	2.60	19.90	28.30	45.76	64.91	43.64	60.76	31.93	8.20	4.98	0.44	9.24	18,744
France	5.10	2.70	19.30	39.80	47.96	62.73	41.85	56.92	40.22	11.52	7.28	0.60	7.20	19,727
Germany	3.30	1.60	18.50	37.50	60.45	71.00	44.85	59.28	47.77	22.99	8.30	0.92	5.21	20,520
Greece	22.30	1.40	29.10	33.30	33.36	69.69	23.28	51.08	59.72	35.40	4.02	6.38	17.39	8,827
Ireland	12.80	9.90	18.70	22.70	41.73	64.36	35.02	53.91	51.58	21.83	7.04	0.72	11.14	11,802
Italy	7.50	1.00	16.80	28.70	34.83	64.85	23.13	48.76	60.16	31.40	5.07	2.20	11.84	18,129
Netherlands	4.20	2.70	19.50	29.00	56.40	74.40	36.64	62.31	44.74	23.99	18.25	0.78	6.64	18,067
Norway	6.10	1.20	16.70	42.70	54.97	79.62	41.67	73.28	29.78	12.63	20.43	0.70	6.20	18,762
Portugal	11.20	1.70	15.80	42.50	43.48	63.79	36.62	57.06	46.02	13.28	5.25	1.07	13.66	10,950
Spain	9.50	5.50	17.00	30.70	44.17	61.75	28.17	43.14	61.06	36.69	3.47	1.77	9.61	13,462
Sweden	3.70	1.60	22.00	33.00	52.54	67.72	48.68	65.81	31.47	3.81	9.79	0.34	7.01	19,615
Switzerland	5.40	1.00	20.20	45.70	57.53	77.64	39.74	67.53	39.92	20.01	16.78	2.02	8.98	23,563
UK	2.00	0.40	18.90	36.90	54.43	69.38	42.50	61.44	41.71	15.44	12.42	0.00	6.53	18,044
Japan	6.90	3.10	23.00	29.30	73.54	84.52	55.46	72.02	39.26	25.39	16.56	0.00	0.00	20,612
USA	2.80	0.60	16.80	45.40	65.82	80.94	56.20	72.50	31.27	16.35	9.38	0.11	6.45	23,748

A = agricultural work as per cent of all employment
B = female agricultural work as per cent of all female employment
C = manufacturing work as per cent of all employment
D = 'services' work as per cent of all employment
E = per cent of all non-dependent males in full-time employee status
F = per cent of all non-dependent males in employment
G = per cent of all non-dependent persons in full-time employee status
H = per cent of all non-dependent persons in employment
I = per cent of all non-dependent women in domestic status
J = per cent non-dependent males in employment less per cent non-dependent females in employment
K = per cent of all non-dependent persons in part-time employee status
L = per cent of all non-dependent persons in family worker status
M = per cent of all non-dependent persons in self-employment
N = per capita gross domestic product in US dollars at purchasing power parities, 1990

Source: As Appendix Table A.2.3.

Appendix Table A.3.1 Changes in occupational forms, 1960–c.1995, 18 countries (percentages of non-dependent population)

	Austria			Belgium			Denmark			Finland		
	Male	Female	Total	Male	Female	Total	Male	Female	Total	Male	Female	Total
Domestic 1995	19.64	45.67	33.32	31.63	51.35	41.67	14.01	33.13	23.87	21.51	31.93	26.78
Domestic 1960	6.74	42.45	26.27	18.68	72.84	46.63	3.43	59.79	32.69	11.78	49.18	31.62
Change	12.90	3.22	7.05	12.95	-21.49	-4.96	10.58	-26.66	-8.82	9.73	-17.25	-4.84
Unemployed 1995	2.63	2.15	2.38	3.99	3.30	3.64	4.80	5.78	5.31	13.58	11.36	12.46
Unemployed 1960	1.87	0.89	1.33	2.05	0.67	1.34	1.38	0.66	1.01	1.40	0.76	1.04
Change	0.76	1.26	1.05	1.94	2.63	2.30	3.42	5.12	4.30	12.18	10.60	11.42
P/T employees 1995	2.02	11.79	7.15	1.09	10.93	6.10	8.26	14.73	11.59	3.57	6.35	4.98
P/T employees 1960	1.40	9.40	5.78	0.79	4.37	2.64	5.02	18.47	12.00	2.82	5.38	4.18
Change	0.62	2.39	1.37	0.30	6.56	3.46	3.24	-3.74	-0.41	0.75	0.97	0.80
Family workers 1995	1.11	2.62	1.90	0.58	2.46	1.54	0.00	0.00	0.00	0.59	0.29	0.44
Family workers 1960	4.91	12.10	8.84	2.35	2.11	2.23	0.00	1.50	0.78	6.36	11.92	9.31
Change	-3.80	-9.48	-6.94	-1.77	0.35	-0.69	0.00	-1.50	-0.78	-5.77	-11.63	-8.87
Own account 1995	8.53	4.11	6.21	10.72	2.91	6.75	9.85	3.81	6.74	12.64	5.91	9.24
Own account 1960	17.47	5.33	10.83	15.09	4.20	9.47	23.73	1.50	12.19	22.42	4.05	12.67
Change	-8.94	-1.22	-4.62	-4.37	-1.29	-2.72	-13.88	2.31	-5.45	-9.78	1.86	-3.43
F/T employees 1995	66.06	33.66	49.04	51.17	24.96	37.83	63.08	42.55	52.49	45.76	41.58	43.64
F/T employees 1960	67.61	29.83	46.94	59.45	15.80	36.93	66.44	18.08	41.33	55.26	28.71	41.18
Change	-1.55	3.83	2.10	-8.28	9.16	0.90	-3.36	24.47	11.16	-9.50	12.87	2.46
All in employment 1995	77.73	52.19	64.31	64.38	45.35	54.69	81.19	61.09	70.82	64.91	56.71	60.76
All in employment 1960	91.39	56.66	72.39	79.27	26.49	52.03	95.19	39.54	66.30	86.86	50.05	67.34
Change	-13.66	-4.47	-8.08	-14.89	18.86	2.66	-14.00	21.55	4.52	-21.95	6.66	-6.58

	France			Germany			Greece			Ireland		
	Male	Female	Total	Male	Female	Total	Male	Female	Total	Male	Female	Total
Domestic 1995	28.55	40.22	34.44	23.38	47.77	35.81	25.46	59.72	43.47	26.74	51.58	38.63
Domestic 1960	18.33	61.77	40.81	10.12	55.78	35.00	14.43	61.77	39.15	10.46	65.32	37.85
Change	10.22	-21.55	-6.37	13.26	-8.01	0.81	11.03	-2.05	4.32	16.28	-13.74	0.78
Unemployed 1995	8.72	8.56	8.64	5.62	4.22	4.91	4.84	5.98	5.44	8.90	5.88	7.46
Unemployed 1960	0.70	0.56	0.62	0.64	0.27	0.44	1.58	1.57	1.58	3.33	1.65	2.49
Change	8.02	8.00	8.02	4.98	3.95	4.47	3.26	4.41	3.86	5.57	4.23	4.97
P/T employees 1995	3.16	11.32	7.28	2.41	13.97	8.30	3.28	4.70	4.02	3.67	10.72	7.04
P/T employees 1960	1.94	6.37	4.23	1.35	12.18	7.25	0.00	0.00	0.00	1.84	4.02	2.93
Change	1.22	4.95	3.05	1.06	1.79	1.05	3.28	4.70	4.02	1.83	6.70	4.11
Family workers 1995	1.21	0.00	0.60	0.32	1.50	0.92	3.67	8.83	6.38	0.65	0.79	0.72
Family workers 1960	2.74	5.95	4.40	2.47	7.04	4.96	12.74	21.71	17.42	10.80	1.69	6.25
Change	-1.53	-5.95	-3.80	-2.15	-5.54	-4.04	-9.07	-12.88	-11.04	-10.15	-0.90	-5.53
Own account 1995	10.39	4.05	7.20	7.83	2.69	5.21	29.39	6.56	17.39	18.31	3.32	11.14
Own account 1960	17.44	3.90	10.44	13.16	2.34	7.26	39.08	5.09	21.33	25.50	5.04	15.28
Change	-7.05	0.15	-3.24	-5.33	0.35	-2.05	-9.69	1.47	-3.94	-7.19	-1.72	-4.14
F/T employees 1995	47.96	35.84	41.85	60.45	29.85	44.85	33.36	14.20	23.28	41.73	27.70	35.02
F/T employees 1960	58.85	21.45	39.50	72.26	22.39	45.09	31.99	9.80	20.40	43.05	21.37	32.23
Change	-10.89	14.39	2.35	-11.81	7.46	-0.24	1.37	4.40	2.88	-1.32	6.33	2.79
All in employment 1995	62.73	51.21	56.92	71.00	48.01	59.28	69.69	34.29	51.08	64.36	42.53	53.91
All in employment 1960	80.97	37.67	58.57	89.24	43.95	64.56	83.99	36.66	59.27	86.21	33.03	59.66
Change	-18.24	13.54	-1.65	-18.24	4.06	-5.28	-14.30	-2.37	-8.19	-21.85	9.50	-5.75

Appendix Table A.3.1 (continued)

	Italy			Netherlands			Norway			Portugal		
	Male	Female	Total	Male	Female	Total	Male	Female	Total	Male	Female	Total
Domestic 1995	28.48	60.16	44.72	20.91	44.74	32.92	16.07	29.78	22.95	33.19	46.02	39.60
Domestic 1960	16.63	70.93	44.74	11.64	75.67	44.35	12.62	74.77	44.19	6.19	81.68	45.76
Change	11.85	-10.77	-0.02	9.27	-30.93	-11.43	3.45	-44.99	-21.24	27.00	-35.66	-6.16
Unemployed 1995	6.67	6.39	6.53	4.69	4.85	4.77	4.31	3.23	3.77	3.01	3.46	3.24
Unemployed 1960	3.29	0.61	1.91	0.86	0.25	0.55	1.01	0.36	0.68	1.84	0.06	0.90
Change	3.38	5.78	4.62	3.83	4.60	4.22	3.30	2.87	3.09	1.17	3.40	2.34
P/T employees 1995	3.05	6.99	5.07	8.41	27.93	18.25	9.79	31.01	20.43	2.87	7.63	5.25
P/T employees 1960	2.42	2.56	2.49	4.86	10.66	7.82	6.37	12.75	9.61	2.30	3.01	2.67
Change	0.63	4.43	2.58	3.55	17.27	10.43	3.42	18.26	10.82	0.57	4.62	2.58
Family workers 1995	1.79	2.58	2.20	0.28	1.28	0.78	0.57	0.84	0.70	0.90	1.25	1.07
Family workers 1960	5.01	4.28	4.64	2.68	1.37	2.01	2.45	0.12	1.27	6.22	0.43	3.19
Change	-3.22	-1.70	-2.44	-2.40	-0.09	-1.23	-1.88	0.72	-0.57	-5.32	0.82	-2.12
Own account 1995	18.49	5.51	11.84	9.32	4.00	6.64	9.12	3.30	6.20	16.08	11.24	13.66
Own account 1960	21.76	3.02	12.06	15.28	0.74	7.85	18.44	0.99	9.58	18.54	1.49	9.60
Change	-3.27	2.49	-0.22	-5.96	3.26	-1.21	-9.32	2.31	-3.38	-2.46	9.75	4.06
F/T employees 1995	34.83	12.00	23.13	56.40	17.20	36.64	54.97	28.45	41.67	43.48	29.75	36.62
F/T employees 1960	50.89	18.59	34.17	64.68	11.31	37.42	59.10	11.02	34.67	63.10	13.09	36.88
Change	-16.06	-6.59	-11.04	-8.28	5.89	-0.78	-4.13	17.43	7.00	-19.62	16.66	-0.26
All in employment 1995	64.85	33.45	48.76	74.40	50.41	62.31	79.62	66.98	73.28	63.79	50.52	57.16
All in employment 1960	80.07	28.46	53.35	87.50	24.08	55.10	86.37	24.88	55.13	91.97	18.27	53.34
Change	-15.22	4.99	-4.59	-13.10	26.33	7.21	-6.75	42.10	18.15	-28.18	32.25	3.82

	Spain			Sweden			Switzerland			UK		
	Male	Female	Total	Male	Female	Total	Male	Female	Total	Male	Female	Total
Domestic 1995	24.69	61.06	43.14	25.49	31.47	28.49	19.21	39.92	29.68	20.83	41.71	31.56
Domestic 1960	6.67	80.93	45.40	14.18	64.50	39.69	10.23	63.53	37.66	9.47	60.66	36.31
Change	**18.02**	**-19.87**	**-2.26**	**11.31**	**-33.03**	**-11.20**	**8.98**	**-23.61**	**-7.98**	**11.36**	**-18.95**	**-4.75**
Unemployed 1995	13.56	13.88	13.72	6.79	4.62	5.70	3.15	2.45	2.79	9.79	4.35	7.00
Unemployed 1960	0.91	0.19	0.54	0.48	0.23	0.35	0.12	0.09	0.10	2.86	1.02	1.89
Change	**12.65**	**13.69**	**13.18**	**6.31**	**4.39**	**5.35**	**3.03**	**2.36**	**2.69**	**6.93**	**3.33**	**5.11**
P/T employees 1995	1.79	5.10	3.47	4.54	15.02	9.79	6.68	26.68	16.78	3.61	20.77	12.42
P/T employees 1960	0.00	0.00	0.00	4.63	16.28	10.54	0.00	0.00	0.00	1.67	14.94	8.63
Change	**1.79**	**5.10**	**3.47**	**-0.09**	**-1.26**	**-0.75**	**6.68**	**26.68**	**16.78**	**1.94**	**5.83**	**3.79**
Family workers 1995	1.45	2.09	1.77	0.30	0.37	0.34	1.07	2.96	2.02	0.00	0.00	0.00
Family workers 1960	9.75	3.75	6.62	2.00	0.71	1.34	3.86	2.01	2.91	0.44	0.30	0.37
Change	**-8.30**	**-1.66**	**-4.85**	**-1.70**	**-0.34**	**-1.00**	**-2.79**	**0.95**	**-0.89**	**-0.44**	**-0.30**	**-0.37**
Own account 1995	14.21	5.14	9.61	10.35	3.68	7.01	12.37	5.66	8.98	11.33	1.98	6.53
Own account 1960	22.51	2.59	12.12	14.39	0.92	7.56	15.83	2.69	9.07	7.95	1.03	4.32
Change	**-8.30**	**2.55**	**-2.51**	**-4.04**	**2.76**	**-0.55**	**-3.46**	**2.97**	**-0.09**	**3.38**	**0.95**	**2.21**
F/T employees 1995	44.17	12.63	28.17	52.54	44.85	48.68	57.53	22.33	39.74	54.43	31.20	42.50
F/T employees 1960	60.15	12.54	35.32	64.32	17.36	40.52	69.96	31.69	50.26	77.61	22.04	48.48
Change	**-15.98**	**0.09**	**-7.15**	**-11.78**	**27.49**	**8.16**	**-12.43**	**-9.36**	**-10.52**	**-23.18**	**9.16**	**-5.98**
All in employment 1995	61.75	25.06	43.14	67.72	63.92	65.81	77.64	57.63	67.53	69.38	53.94	61.44
All in employment 1960	92.41	18.88	54.06	85.34	35.27	59.96	89.65	36.39	62.24	87.67	38.32	61.80
Change	**-30.66**	**6.18**	**-10.92**	**-17.62**	**28.65**	**5.85**	**-12.01**	**21.24**	**5.29**	**-18.29**	**15.62**	**-0.36**

Appendix Table A.3.1 *(continued)*

	Japan			USA		
	Male	Female	Total	Male	Female	Total
Domestic 1995	13.39	39.26	26.13	13.74	31.27	22.79
Domestic 1960	9.27	47.01	29.03	12.17	60.78	37.19
Change	**4.12**	**−7.75**	**−2.90**	**1.57**	**−29.51**	**−14.40**
Unemployed 1995	2.09	1.61	1.85	5.32	4.14	4.71
Unemployed 1960	0.77	0.34	0.54	4.47	2.17	3.29
Change	**1.32**	**1.27**	**1.31**	**0.85**	**1.97**	**1.42**
P/T employees 1995	10.99	22.29	16.56	6.23	12.34	9.38
P/T employees 1960	6.75	14.64	10.88	7.50	9.89	8.73
Change	**4.24**	**7.65**	**5.68**	**−1.27**	**2.45**	**0.65**
Family workers 1995	8.88	16.98	13.12	0.08	0.14	0.11
Family workers 1960				0.33	0.57	0.45
Change				**−0.25**	**−0.43**	**−0.34**
Own account 1995	22.95	5.11	13.61	8.47	4.55	6.45
Own account 1960				10.94	1.30	5.98
Change				**−2.47**	**3.25**	**0.47**
F/T employees 1995	51.37	15.91	32.81	65.82	47.19	56.20
F/T employees 1960				61.03	23.91	41.93
Change				**4.79**	**23.28**	**14.27**
All in employment 1995	84.52	59.13	72.02	80.94	64.59	69.39
All in employment 1960	89.96	52.65	70.43	83.36	37.04	59.52
Change	**−5.44**	**6.48**	**1.59**	**−2.42**	**27.55**	**9.87**

Source: As Appendix Tables A.2.1 and A.2.3.

Appendix Table A.4.1 Employment by sector and gender, 15 countries, c.1990

Sector etc.	Austria			Belgium			Denmark			Spain		
	Male	Female	Total	Male	Female	Total	Male	Female	Total	Male	Female	Total
Domestic	10.52	25.85	36.38	14.78	26.20	40.97	8.95	14.96	23.91	10.36	27.34	37.70
Unemployed	1.24	0.96	2.20	2.11	1.81	3.92	3.45	3.62	7.07	5.06	5.13	10.19
I	2.64	2.33	4.96	1.35	0.52	1.87	1.35	1.20	2.55	5.63	1.81	7.44
II	17.68	5.04	22.72	13.34	3.09	16.43	13.33	4.98	18.31	12.68	2.47	15.15
III	6.77	5.70	12.47	8.61	5.16	13.77	9.33	5.57	14.90	6.80	3.11	9.90
IV	1.99	1.96	3.95	2.59	1.92	4.51	3.31	2.94	6.25	1.52	0.51	2.03
V	5.22	6.47	11.70	8.05	10.48	18.53	7.08	14.96	22.04	1.96	2.39	4.34
VI	2.08	3.54	5.62	0.00	0.00	0.00	2.24	2.73	4.97	3.79	3.63	7.42
Unknown	0.00	0.00	0.00	0.00	0.00	0.00	0.00	0.00	0.00	2.60	3.22	5.82
TOTAL	48.15	51.85	100.00	50.82	49.18	100.00	49.05	50.95	100.00	50.39	49.61	100.00

Sector etc.	Finland			France			Germany			Greece		
	Male	Female	Total	Male	Female	Total	Male	Female	Total	Male	Female	Total
Domestic	12.16	20.00	32.16	12.52	22.60	35.12	11.36	27.12	38.48	11.68	29.34	41.02
Unemployed	6.45	3.97	10.42	2.65	3.42	6.07	1.94	1.87	3.81	1.85	2.77	4.62
I	2.23	2.93	5.16	2.34	1.17	3.50	1.57	0.88	2.45	7.71	2.70	10.41
II	14.62	6.77	21.39	13.25	4.33	17.57	17.00	5.62	22.62	9.99	2.76	12.75
III	4.68	7.67	12.35	6.37	4.47	10.84	5.61	6.36	11.97	8.54	2.79	11.33
IV	2.04	1.94	3.97	3.12	2.85	5.97	3.67	2.95	6.63	1.83	1.29	3.13
V	4.22	10.09	14.31	4.77	6.49	11.26	4.50	5.11	9.61	5.15	4.28	9.43
VI	0.00	0.00	0.00	4.05	5.61	9.66	1.43	3.00	4.43	2.52	1.66	4.17
Unknown	0.15	0.09	0.24	0.00	0.00	0.00	0.00	0.00	0.00	2.06	1.08	3.14
TOTAL	46.54	53.46	100.00	49.06	50.94	100.00	47.08	52.92	100.00	51.34	48.66	100.00

Appendix Table A.4.1 (continued)

Sector etc.	Ireland			Netherlands			Norway			Sweden		
	Male	Female	Total	Male	Female	Total	Male	Female	Total	Male	Female	Total
Domestic	7.79	28.61	36.39	12.31	27.34	39.64	10.20	16.98	27.18	13.26	15.76	29.02
Unemployed	6.94	2.31	9.25	2.17	2.53	4.70	2.49	1.59	4.08	2.05	1.26	3.31
I	7.68	0.55	8.23	1.83	0.48	2.31	3.64	1.34	4.98	1.62	0.60	2.22
II	13.63	2.75	16.38	12.33	2.25	14.59	13.36	3.45	16.81	14.62	4.40	19.02
III	7.04	3.55	10.59	8.25	4.03	12.29	8.72	6.90	15.62	7.36	5.40	12.76
IV	1.49	1.89	3.38	4.18	2.52	6.70	2.85	2.44	5.29	3.04	2.74	5.78
V	3.55	5.21	8.76	7.32	8.30	15.62	7.18	14.23	21.41	6.06	17.37	23.43
VI	3.40	3.61	7.01	1.73	1.90	3.63	1.87	2.76	4.63	1.66	1.85	3.52
Unknown	0.00	0.00	0.00	0.28	0.25	0.53	0.00	0.00	0.00	0.54	0.40	0.94
TOTAL	51.51	48.49	100.00	50.40	49.60	100.00	50.32	49.68	100.00	50.21	49.79	100.00

Sector etc.	UK			Japan			USA		
	Male	Female	Total	Male	Female	Total	Male	Female	Total
Domestic	9.24	20.83	30.07	4.99	23.13	28.12	7.70	17.66	25.35
Unemployed	4.13	1.29	5.42	1.01	0.74	1.74	3.16	2.35	5.51
I	1.53	0.36	1.89	3.02	2.44	5.46	1.84	0.46	2.30
II	15.34	4.83	20.18	17.70	7.83	25.53	12.55	4.41	16.96
III	7.93	5.72	13.64	11.54	7.10	18.64	11.01	8.02	19.03
IV	3.78	3.62	7.39	3.21	2.61	5.82	4.77	4.29	9.06
V	5.48	10.18	15.67	4.91	4.95	9.86	6.55	11.62	18.17
VI	1.76	3.40	5.16	1.41	3.42	4.83	1.34	2.29	3.62
Unknown	0.32	0.26	0.59	0.00	0.00	0.00	0.00	0.00	0.00
TOTAL	49.52	50.48	100.00	47.79	52.21	100.00	48.92	51.08	100.00

Note: Countries amalgamating Sector VI with III and V shown in italics.

Sources: National Censuses, unpublished documents and archives.

Appendix Table A.4.2 Employment by sector, gender, and educational level, 12 countries, c. 1990

Sector	Males						Females						All					
	1	2	3	4	5	Total	1	2	3	4	5	Total	1	2	3	4	5	Total
AUSTRIA (1990)																		
I	26.58	19.37	5.11	1.51	0.41	52.98	33.99	9.15	2.69	0.95	0.09	46.87	60.57	28.52	7.80	2.46	0.50	99.85
II	20.05	45.57	3.85	6.64	1.66	77.77	10.06	6.44	3.36	2.02	0.30	22.18	30.11	52.01	7.21	8.66	1.96	99.95
III	11.98	30.76	4.56	5.61	1.41	54.32	12.15	21.99	6.51	4.36	0.73	45.74	24.13	52.75	11.07	9.97	2.14	100.06
IV	3.92	13.63	7.85	14.02	10.86	50.28	8.33	9.55	15.47	13.23	3.12	49.70	12.25	23.18	23.32	27.25	13.98	99.98
V	5.11	14.37	3.65	7.73	13.79	44.65	11.52	9.69	12.30	10.49	11.33	55.33	16.63	24.06	15.95	18.22	25.12	99.98
VI	8.70	21.44	3.65	3.84	1.98	39.61	26.98	22.14	5.88	3.68	0.65	59.33	35.68	43.58	9.53	7.52	2.63	98.94
ALL	14.06	30.31	4.30	6.46	4.46	59.59	14.03	11.99	6.66	4.90	2.70	40.28	28.09	42.31	10.97	11.37	7.16	99.90

1 = Compulsory education only; 2 = Basic school-leaving qualification; 3 = Middle-level qualification; 4 = Non-university higher education; 5 = University

Sector	Males						Females						All					
	1	2	3	4	5	Total	1	2	3	4	5	Total	1	2	3	4	5	Total
BELGIUM (1991)																		
I	20.98	27.18	18.07	3.74	2.24	72.21	10.06	10.53	4.74	2.32	0.14	27.79	31.04	37.71	22.81	6.06	2.38	100.00
II	17.27	30.00	22.73	7.22	3.97	81.19	4.04	5.98	5.73	2.29	0.77	18.81	21.31	35.98	28.46	9.51	4.74	100.00
III (VI)	10.83	24.22	20.33	4.73	2.42	62.53	6.28	13.43	13.27	3.38	1.10	37.46	17.11	37.65	33.60	8.11	3.52	99.99
IV	2.07	6.76	18.61	16.62	13.26	57.32	1.82	6.33	19.03	10.30	5.20	42.68	3.89	13.09	37.64	26.92	18.46	100.00
V, VI	4.26	8.56	11.45	10.67	8.52	43.46	5.75	9.67	15.98	20.16	4.98	56.54	10.01	18.23	27.43	30.83	13.50	100.00
ALL	10.17	19.35	17.84	8.41	5.81	61.58	5.20	9.26	12.12	9.23	2.61	38.42	15.36	28.61	29.96	17.64	8.42	99.99

1 = Primary education only; 2 = Lower secondary; 3 = Upper secondary; 4 = Non-university tertiary; 5 = University

Sector	Males						Females						All					
	1	2	3	4	5	Total	1	2	3	4	5	Total	1	2	3	4	5	Total
DENMARK (1990)																		
I	47.07	27.58	75.62	9.14	4.52	163.94	97.13	8.36	24.59	7.71	1.05	138.84	144.20	35.95	100.21	16.85	5.57	302.78
II	27.25	4.36	33.58	6.04	1.60	72.83	14.58	2.51	8.36	1.41	0.31	27.17	41.83	6.87	41.94	7.46	1.91	100.00
III	26.30	4.07	27.46	3.61	1.17	62.62	4.64	3.79	3.04	2.00	0.41	13.88	30.95	7.86	30.50	5.61	1.58	76.50
IV	14.41	2.50	18.70	9.33	8.04	52.98	14.62	3.99	23.21	3.50	1.69	47.02	29.02	6.49	41.92	12.84	9.73	100.00
V	1.29	1.36	0.25	7.96	5.42	16.27	24.65	3.11	18.38	10.84	2.93	59.91	25.94	4.46	18.64	18.80	8.34	76.18
VI	20.74	2.76	17.76	2.48	1.36	45.10	31.01	5.17	14.70	3.12	0.91	54.90	51.75	7.93	32.45	5.60	2.26	100.00
ALL	19.22	5.77	21.35	8.59	3.29	58.22	20.03	0.78	14.74	4.90	1.33	41.78	39.25	6.55	36.09	13.49	4.62	100.00

1 = No vocational education; 2 = Basic vocational education; 3 = Full vocational education; 4 = Short and middle higher education; 5 = Long higher education

Appendix Table A.4.2 (continued)

Sector	Males						Females						All					
	1	2	3	4	5	Total	1	2	3	4	5	Total	1	2	3	4	5	Total
FRANCE (1990)																		
I	23.69	17.51	16.29	7.94	3.11	68.54	11.43	14.12	2.52	2.4	0.99	31.46	35.12	31.63	18.81	10.34	4.1	100.00
II	23.18	11.98	31.66	8.02	2.68	77.52	6.28	6.28	3.79	3.33	2.75	22.48	29.5	18.26	35.45	11.35	5.43	99.99
III	11.77	10.4	27.24	8.31	2.69	60.42	6.32	7.49	16.1	7.21	2.46	39.58	18.09	17.89	43.35	15.52	5.15	100.00
IV	7.61	4.25	9.8	11.91	17.3	50.87	5.75	4.96	13.0	12.5	12.96	49.13	13.36	9.21	22.76	24.42	30.26	100.01
V	5.69	4.17	12.89	7.56	12.07	42.39	8.43	7.29	15.4	11.9	14.64	57.61	14.12	11.46	28.28	19.43	26.71	100.00
VI	9.74	4.89	13.25	4.25	9.14	41.26	11.11	9.01	16.8	7.86	13.98	58.74	20.85	13.9	30.03	12.11	23.12	100.01
ALL	**13.59**	**8.42**	**20.73**	**7.71**	**7.20**	**57.64**	**7.83**	**7.52**	**11.56**	**7.46**	**7.99**	**42.36**	**21.42**	**15.94**	**32.29**	**15.17**	**15.18**	**100.00**

1 = No qualifications; 2 = Primary qualifications only; 3 = BEPC/CAP/HEP; 4 = BAC; 5 = Higher BAC or university diploma

Sector	Males						Females						All					
	1	2	3	4	5	Total	1	2	3	4	5	Total	1	2	3	4	5	Total
GERMANY (1987)																		
I	14.75	39.47	8.91	2.19	2.03	67.35	10.70	18.64	2.35	0.49	0.49	32.67	25.45	58.11	11.26	2.68	2.52	100.02
II	14.30	44.95	9.55	4.26	3.46	76.52	6.42	14.32	1.23	0.68	0.81	23.46	20.72	59.27	10.78	4.94	4.27	99.98
III	10.02	33.58	5.40	2.32	2.25	53.57	10.09	32.34	1.96	0.89	1.15	46.43	20.11	65.92	7.36	3.21	3.40	100.00
IV	7.21	21.70	5.06	6.20	10.91	51.08	10.61	29.59	2.56	2.15	4.03	48.94	17.82	51.29	7.62	8.35	14.94	100.02
V	6.68	16.54	3.53	4.05	10.22	41.02	10.61	28.75	6.96	3.57	9.09	58.98	17.29	45.29	10.49	7.62	19.31	100.00
VI	11.01	19.30	4.40	2.00	3.80	40.51	19.26	32.63	3.76	1.20	2.64	59.49	30.27	51.93	8.16	3.20	6.44	100.00
ALL	**10.55**	**31.03**	**6.34**	**3.79**	**5.70**	**57.41**	**9.70**	**24.60**	**3.19**	**1.64**	**3.45**	**42.58**	**20.25**	**55.63**	**9.53**	**5.43**	**9.15**	**99.99**

1 = No vocational qualification; 2 = vocational qualification only; 3 = Fachschule qualification; 4 = Fachhochschule qualification; 5 = university

Sector	Males						Females						All					
	1	2	3	4	5	Total	1	2	3	4	5	Total	1	2	3	4	5	Total
ITALY (1991)																		
I	7.86	30.58	19.78	5.69	0.78	64.69	5.21	16.69	10.29	2.79	0.33	35.31	13.07	47.27	30.07	8.48	1.11	100.00
II	2.34	22.46	34.08	14.34	1.91	75.13	0.47	6.13	11.90	5.88	0.51	24.89	2.81	28.59	45.98	20.22	2.42	100.02
III	1.17	16.93	30.94	17.38	1.63	68.05	0.45	6.37	13.28	10.96	0.88	31.94	1.62	23.30	44.22	28.34	2.51	99.99
IV	0.37	3.73	10.58	31.27	14.23	60.18	0.45	3.80	10.43	20.98	4.17	39.83	0.82	7.53	21.01	52.25	18.40	100.01
V	0.45	6.47	16.92	16.04	10.67	50.55	0.28	4.45	11.41	22.24	11.07	49.45	0.73	10.92	28.33	38.28	21.74	100.00
VI	1.44	13.63	25.18	9.16	0.65	50.06	2.08	16.96	22.69	7.75	0.48	49.96	3.52	30.59	47.87	16.91	1.13	100.02
ALL	**1.89**	**16.24**	**25.89**	**15.86**	**4.81**	**64.69**	**0.87**	**6.91**	**12.30**	**11.87**	**3.36**	**35.31**	**2.75**	**23.15**	**38.19**	**27.74**	**8.17**	**100.00**

1 = No qualifications; 2 = Primary qualifications only; 3 = Middle-school qualifications; 4 = Upper secondary qualifications; 5 = University

NETHERLANDS (1992)

	1	2	3	4	5	Sum	1	2	3	4	5	Sum	1	2	3	4	5	ALL
I	10.37	29.46	36.93	2.49	0.00	79.25	7.47	10.37	2.49	0.41	0.00	20.74	12.86	39.83	44.40	2.90	0.00	99.99
II	13.07	25.36	36.01	7.62	2.50	84.56	6.31	5.06	2.23	1.84	0.00	15.44	15.30	30.42	42.32	9.46	2.50	100.00
III	7.88	19.97	31.90	5.93	1.48	67.16	15.13	12.09	2.96	2.65	0.00	32.83	10.84	32.06	47.03	8.58	1.48	99.99
IV	1.57	6.87	26.04	15.45	12.45	62.38	17.60	7.15	1.72	7.73	3.43	37.63	3.29	14.02	43.64	23.18	15.88	100.01
V	1.53	5.46	16.99	13.25	9.63	46.86	23.93	7.55	2.21	15.15	4.29	53.13	3.74	13.01	40.92	28.40	13.92	99.99
VI	7.93	12.66	20.58	5.80	0.79	47.76	21.11	14.51	9.23	6.07	1.32	52.24	17.16	27.17	41.69	11.87	2.11	100.00
ALL	6.82	15.58	27.46	9.45	5.23	64.54	15.75	8.47	2.77	6.75	1.70	35.44	9.59	24.05	43.21	16.20	6.93	99.98

1 = First and second levels; 2 = Third level; 3 = Fourth level; 4 = Fifth level; 5 = Sixth level

NORWAY (1990)

	2	3	4	5	Sum	2	3	4	5	Sum	2	3	4	5	ALL
I	1.56	24.02	40.75	6.75	73.08	8.03	0.52	2.28	16.09	26.92	2.08	32.05	56.84	9.03	100.00
II	1.91	20.81	48.67	8.08	79.47	6.16	0.48	1.99	11.90	20.53	2.39	26.97	60.57	10.07	100.00
III	1.37	12.46	34.39	7.61	55.83	11.30	0.76	3.82	28.29	44.17	2.13	23.76	62.68	11.43	100.00
IV	1.54	3.77	24.86	23.76	53.94	4.92	0.77	9.85	30.53	46.07	2.31	8.69	55.39	33.61	100.01
V	0.95	2.91	12.75	16.91	33.52	11.11	1.42	23.10	30.85	66.48	2.37	14.02	43.60	40.01	100.00
VI	2.45	7.25	25.16	5.50	40.36	14.95	1.68	6.35	36.66	59.64	4.13	22.20	61.82	11.85	100.00
ALL	1.47	11.35	30.25	11.66	54.73	9.50	0.94	9.90	24.93	45.27	2.41	20.85	55.18	21.56	100.00

2 = Low educational level; 3 = Lower secondary; 4 = Upper secondary; 5 = Tertiary (NB: data available for four levels only)

PORTUGAL (1993)

	1	2	3	4	5	ALL
I	78.66	11.28	3.76	4.31	2.00	100.01
II	60.02	27.53	7.97	1.46	3.02	100.00
III	16.37	27.75	22.57	26.42	6.89	100.00
IV	13.88	14.13	24.70	31.40	15.90	100.01
V	44.70	14.13	12.19	12.95	16.03	100.00
VI	24.66	38.39	18.26	15.87	2.81	99.99
ALL	44.94	25.67	13.04	10.67	5.68	100.00

1 = Less than 6 years education; 2 = 6 Years; 3 = 9 Years; 4 = 11-12 Years; 5 = 14-17 Years

SPAIN (1987)

	1	2	3	4	5	Sum	1	2	3	4	5	Sum	1	2	3	4	5	ALL
I	21.59	41.29	11.73	0.58	0.47	75.66	2.79	13.67	7.68	0.14	0.08	24.36	29.27	54.96	14.52	0.72	0.55	100.02
II	9.46	47.58	23.00	2.16	1.51	83.71	7.57	6.85	1.24	0.33	0.29	16.28	10.70	54.43	30.57	2.49	1.80	99.99
III	5.15	35.54	24.51	1.73	1.57	68.50	13.61	13.26	2.98	0.77	0.75	31.37	8.13	48.80	38.12	2.50	2.32	99.87
IV	0.85	12.60	38.29	9.11	14.16	75.01	16.18	2.74	0.83	2.39	2.86	25.00	1.68	15.34	54.47	11.50	17.02	100.01
V	2.83	10.90	10.61	8.71	11.97	45.02	13.70	9.93	3.29	19.20	8.88	55.00	6.12	20.83	24.31	27.91	20.85	100.02
VI	3.40	22.40	18.95	2.21	4.05	51.01	17.44	20.98	7.36	1.79	1.41	48.98	10.76	43.38	36.39	4.00	5.46	99.99
ALL	8.51	34.98	20.37	2.74	3.30	69.90	10.63	11.69	3.80	2.49	1.46	30.07	12.31	46.67	31.00	5.23	4.76	99.97

1 = no education completed; 2 = primary only; 3 = middle-school only; 4 = pre-university qualification; 5 = university qualification

Appendix Table A.4.2 (continued)

Sector	Males						Females						All					
	1	2	3	4	5	Total	1	2	3	4	5	Total	1	2	3	4	5	Total
SWEDEN (1990)																		
I	41.64	19.39	5.75	4.32	1.63	72.73	15.36	7.08	2.47	1.54	0.82	27.27	57.00	26.47	8.22	5.86	2.45	100.00
II	36.23	34.54	11.75	0.11	3.51	86.14	6.79	1.46	2.99	1.67	0.95	13.86	43.02	36.00	14.74	1.78	4.46	100.00
III	9.00	11.76	12.34	6.14	3.69	42.94	24.52	18.59	8.63	3.80	1.53	42.83	33.52	30.35	20.97	9.94	5.22	100.00
IV	9.86	18.39	10.85	7.99	10.07	57.17	12.85	11.49	9.19	4.88	4.42	42.83	22.71	29.88	20.04	12.87	14.49	99.99
V	4.88	4.76	3.33	9.38	13.54	35.88	18.77	28.75	5.11	4.63	6.86	64.12	23.65	33.51	8.44	14.01	20.40	100.01
VI	18.43	14.30	7.00	3.63	2.93	46.29	21.93	15.24	9.38	3.57	3.59	53.71	40.36	29.54	16.38	7.20	6.52	100.00
ALL	16.60	16.48	8.04	5.57	7.76	54.46	16.03	16.37	5.74	3.60	3.80	45.54	32.63	32.85	13.78	9.17	11.56	99.99

1 = basic or people's school only; 2 = max. 2 years sec.; 3 = >2 years post-school; 4 = <3 years post-school; 5 = 3+ years post-school

Sector	Males						Females						All					
	1	2	3	4	5	Total	1	2	3	4	5	Total	1	2	3	4	5	Total
UNITED KINGDOM (1991)																		
I	31.20	17.85	21.28	2.34	5.77	78.44	10.78	5.67	3.69	0.71	0.71	21.56	41.98	23.52	24.97	3.05	6.48	100.00
II	19.60	13.91	32.80	4.56	5.30	76.17	9.05	9.46	3.65	0.62	1.05	23.83	28.65	23.37	36.45	5.18	6.35	100.00
III	17.03	18.94	21.53	1.88	3.16	62.54	10.30	12.05	12.09	1.14	1.88	37.46	27.33	30.99	33.62	3.02	5.04	100.00
IV	4.12	11.19	25.34	2.60	13.23	56.48	5.39	22.54	10.16	1.47	3.96	43.52	9.51	33.73	35.50	4.07	17.19	100.00
V	4.65	6.77	10.02	3.20	10.37	35.01	15.05	18.67	9.60	12.84	8.82	64.98	19.70	25.44	19.62	16.04	19.19	99.99
VI	9.79	7.90	12.10	1.19	3.15	34.13	24.25	20.35	16.33	2.36	2.58	65.87	34.04	28.25	28.43	3.55	5.73	100.00
ALL	13.12	12.59	22.11	3.13	7.04	57.99	11.70	14.87	8.71	4.01	3.63	42.92	24.82	27.46	30.82	7.14	10.67	100.91

1 = no qualifications; 2 = school-leaving qualification only; 3 = low vocational qualification only; 4 = high vocational qualification; 5 = university

Sources: As Appendix Table A.4.1.

Appendix Table A.4.3 Employment by sector, gender, and educational level, 12 countries, c.1990: deviations from national means of educational levels of gender sectors

Sectors	Males					Females					All				
	1	2	3	4	5	1	2	3	4	5	1	2	3	4	5
AUSTRIA (1990)															
I	22.08	-5.75	-1.32	-8.52	-6.39	44.43	-22.79	-5.23	-9.34	-6.97	32.57	-13.75	-3.16	-8.91	-6.66
II	-2.31	16.29	-6.02	-2.83	-5.03	17.27	-13.27	4.18	-2.26	-5.81	2.04	9.73	-3.76	-2.71	-5.20
III	-6.04	14.32	-2.58	-1.04	-4.56	-1.53	5.77	3.26	-1.84	-5.56	-3.97	10.41	0.09	-1.41	-5.02
IV	-20.29	-15.20	4.64	16.51	14.44	-11.33	-23.09	20.16	15.25	-0.88	-15.84	-19.13	12.35	15.89	6.82
V	-16.65	-10.13	-2.80	5.94	23.72	-7.27	-24.80	11.26	7.59	13.32	-11.46	-18.25	4.98	6.85	17.97
VI	-6.13	11.82	-1.76	-1.68	-2.16	17.38	-4.99	-1.06	-5.17	-6.06	7.97	1.74	-1.34	-3.77	-4.50
ALL	-4.50	8.55	-3.75	-0.53	0.32	6.74	-12.54	5.56	0.79	-0.46	0.03	0.04	0.01	0.01	0.01

1 = Compulsory education only; 2 = Basic school-leaving qualification; 3 = Middle-level qualification; 4 = Non-university higher education; 5 = University

Sectors	Males					Females					All				
	1	2	3	4	5	1	2	3	4	5	1	2	3	4	5
BELGIUM (1991)															
I	13.69	9.03	-4.94	-12.46	-5.32	20.84	9.28	-12.90	-9.29	-7.92	15.68	9.10	-7.15	-11.58	-6.04
II	5.91	8.34	-1.96	-8.75	-3.53	6.12	3.18	0.50	-5.47	-4.33	5.95	7.37	-1.50	-8.13	-3.68
III (VI)	1.96	10.12	2.55	-10.08	-4.55	1.40	7.24	5.46	-8.62	-5.48	1.75	9.04	3.64	-9.53	-4.90
IV	-11.75	-16.82	2.51	11.36	14.71	-11.10	-13.78	14.63	6.49	3.76	-11.47	-15.52	7.68	9.28	10.04
V, VI	-5.56	-8.91	-3.61	6.91	11.18	-5.19	-11.51	-1.70	18.02	0.39	-5.35	-10.38	-2.53	13.19	5.08
ALL	1.16	2.81	-0.99	-3.98	1.01	-1.83	-4.51	1.59	6.38	-1.63	0.00	0.00	0.00	0.00	0.00

1 = Primary education only; 2 = Lower secondary; 3 = Upper secondary; 4 = Non-university tertiary; 5 = University

Sectors	Males					Females					All				
	1	2	3	4	5	1	2	3	4	5	1	2	3	4	5
DENMARK (1990)															
I	-10.54	10.28	10.04	-7.91	-1.86	30.71	-0.52	-18.38	-7.94	-3.87	8.37	5.33	-2.99	-7.93	-2.78
II	-1.83	-0.57	10.02	-5.19	-2.43	4.35	7.71	-42.86	-5.48	-2.87	7.00	1.05	-0.28	-5.25	-2.51
III	2.74	-0.04	7.76	-7.72	-2.75	-5.78	20.74	-14.16	0.91	-1.70	1.20	3.73	3.79	-6.16	-2.56
IV	4.12	-8.97	2.73	-3.24	2.72	10.98	-5.10	17.19	-5.25	-23.49	1.85	-6.07	8.14	-12.01	8.54
V	2.86	3.35	2.82	-8.97	6.41	8.18	-0.56	-0.71	-7.91	1.01	10.29	1.98	-0.49	-7.92	3.85
VI	1.76	-1.72	3.28	-2.37	-9.96	-6.81	1.97	3.86	2.38	-0.01	2.87	-1.44	12.64	-11.12	-4.41
ALL	-7.61	2.95	-0.94	0.65	4.96	11.78	-4.56	1.46	-1.00	-7.68	0.00	0.00	0.00	0.00	0.00

1 = No vocational education; 2 = Basic vocational education; 3 = Full vocational education; 4 = Short and middle higher education; 5 = Long higher education

Appendix Table A.4.3 (continued)

Sectors	Males					Females					All				
	1	2	3	4	5	1	2	3	4	5	1	2	3	4	5
FRANCE (1990)															
I	13.14	9.61	-8.52	-3.59	-10.64	14.91	28.94	-24.28	-7.54	-12.03	13.70	15.69	-13.48	-4.83	-11.08
II	8.48	-0.49	8.55	-4.82	-11.72	6.69	12.00	-15.43	-0.36	-2.95	8.08	2.32	3.16	-3.82	-9.75
III	-1.94	1.27	12.79	-1.42	-10.73	-5.45	2.98	8.41	3.05	-8.96	-3.33	1.95	11.06	0.35	-10.03
IV	-6.46	-7.59	-13.03	8.24	18.83	-9.72	-5.84	-5.91	10.29	11.20	-8.06	-6.73	-9.53	9.25	15.08
V	-8.00	-6.10	-0.18	2.66	13.29	-6.79	-3.29	-5.58	5.43	10.23	-7.30	-4.48	-4.01	4.26	11.53
VI	2.19	-4.09	1.33	-4.87	6.97	-2.51	-0.60	-3.72	-1.79	8.62	-0.57	-2.04	-2.26	-3.06	7.94
ALL	2.16	-1.33	3.67	-1.79	-2.69	-2.94	1.81	-5.00	2.44	3.68	0.00	0.00	0.00	0.00	0.00

1 = No qualifications; 2 = Primary qualifications only; 3 = BEPC/CAP/HEP; 4 = BAC; 5 = Higher BAC or university diploma

Sectors	Males					Females					All				
	1	2	3	4	5	1	2	3	4	5	1	2	3	4	5
GERMANY (1987)															
I	1.65	2.97	3.70	-2.18	-6.14	12.50	1.43	-2.34	-3.93	-7.65	5.19	2.47	1.73	-2.75	-6.63
II	-1.56	3.11	2.95	0.14	-4.63	7.12	5.41	-4.29	-2.53	-5.70	0.47	3.65	1.25	-0.49	-4.88
III	-1.55	7.05	0.55	-1.10	-4.95	1.48	14.02	-5.31	-3.51	-6.67	-0.14	10.29	-2.17	-2.22	-5.75
IV	-6.13	-13.15	0.38	6.71	12.21	1.43	4.83	-4.30	-1.04	-0.92	-2.43	-4.35	-1.91	2.92	5.79
V	-3.97	-15.31	-0.92	4.44	15.76	-2.26	-6.88	2.27	0.62	6.26	-2.96	-10.34	0.96	2.19	10.16
VI	6.93	-7.99	1.33	-0.49	0.23	12.13	-0.78	-3.21	-3.41	-4.71	10.02	-3.70	-1.37	-2.23	-2.71
ALL	-1.87	-1.58	1.51	1.17	0.78	2.53	2.14	-2.04	-1.58	-1.05	0.00	0.01	0.00	0.00	0.00

1 = No vocational qualification; 2 = vocational qualification only; 3 = Fachschule qualification; 4 = Fachhochschule qualification; 5 = university degree

Sectors	Males					Females					All				
	1	2	3	4	5	1	2	3	4	5	1	2	3	4	5
ITALY (1991)															
I	9.40	24.12	-7.61	-18.94	-6.96	12.01	24.12	-9.05	-19.84	-7.24	10.32	24.12	-8.12	-19.26	-7.06
II	0.36	6.74	7.17	-8.65	-5.63	-0.86	1.48	9.62	-4.12	-6.12	0.06	5.43	7.78	-7.52	-5.75
III	-1.03	1.73	7.28	-2.20	-5.77	-1.34	-3.21	3.39	6.57	-5.41	-1.13	0.15	6.03	0.60	-5.66
IV	-2.14	-16.95	-20.61	24.22	15.48	-1.62	-13.61	-12.00	24.93	2.30	-1.93	-15.62	-17.18	24.50	10.23
V	-1.86	-10.35	-4.72	3.99	12.94	-2.18	-14.15	-15.12	17.23	14.22	-2.02	-12.23	-9.86	10.54	13.57
VI	0.13	4.08	12.11	-9.44	-6.87	1.41	10.80	7.23	-12.23	-7.21	0.77	7.43	9.67	-10.83	-7.04
ALL	0.17	1.95	1.83	-3.22	-0.73	-0.29	-3.58	-3.36	5.83	1.35	0.00	0.00	0.00	0.00	0.00

1 = No qualifications; 2 = Primary qualifications only; 3 = Middle-school qualifications; 4 = Upper secondary qualifications; 5 = University

NETHERLANDS (1992)

	1	2	3	4	5	1	2	3	4	5	1	2	3	4	5
I	3.50	13.12	3.39	-13.06	-6.93	2.42	25.95	-7.19	-14.22	-6.93	3.27	15.78	1.19	-13.30	-6.93
II	5.87	5.94	-0.62	-7.19	-3.97	4.85	8.72	-2.34	-4.28	-6.93	5.71	6.37	-0.89	-6.74	-4.43
III	2.14	5.68	4.29	-7.37	-4.73	-0.57	12.78	2.88	-8.13	-6.93	1.25	8.01	3.82	-7.62	-5.45
IV	-7.07	-13.04	-1.47	8.57	13.03	-5.02	-5.05	3.56	4.34	2.19	-6.30	-10.03	0.43	6.98	8.95
V	-6.32	-12.40	-6.95	12.08	13.62	-5.43	-9.84	1.83	12.31	1.14	-5.85	-11.04	-2.29	12.20	6.99
VI	7.01	2.46	-0.12	-4.06	-5.28	8.08	3.73	-2.80	-4.58	-4.40	7.57	3.12	-1.52	-4.33	-4.82
ALL	0.98	0.09	-0.66	-1.56	1.17	-1.77	-0.15	1.23	2.85	-2.13	0.00	0.00	0.01	0.00	0.00

1 = First and second levels; 2 = Third level; 3 = Fourth level; 4 = Fifth level; 5 = Sixth level

NORWAY (1990)

	2	3	4	5	2	3	4	5	2	3	4	5
I	-0.28	12.02	0.58	-12.32	-0.48	8.98	4.59	-13.09	-0.33	11.20	1.66	-12.53
II	-0.01	5.34	6.06	-11.39	-0.07	9.15	2.78	-11.87	-0.02	6.12	5.39	-11.49
III	0.04	1.47	6.42	-7.93	-0.69	4.73	8.87	-12.91	-0.28	2.91	7.50	-10.13
IV	0.45	-13.86	-9.09	22.49	-0.74	-10.17	11.09	-0.18	-0.10	-12.16	0.20	12.05
V	0.42	-12.17	-17.14	28.89	-0.27	-4.14	-8.78	13.19	-0.04	-6.83	-11.58	18.45
VI	3.66	-2.89	7.16	-7.93	0.41	4.22	6.29	-10.91	1.72	1.35	6.64	-9.71
ALL	0.28	-0.11	0.09	-0.26	-0.33	0.14	-0.11	0.31	0.00	0.00	0.00	0.00

2 = Low educational level; 3 = Lower secondary; 4 = Upper secondary; 5 = Tertiary (NB: data available for four levels only)

PORTUGAL (1993)

	1	2	3	4	5
I	33.71	-14.39	-9.28	-6.36	-3.68
II	15.08	1.86	-5.07	-9.21	-2.66
III	-28.57	2.08	9.53	15.75	1.21
IV	-31.06	-11.54	11.66	20.73	10.22
V	-0.24	-11.54	-0.85	2.28	10.35
VI	-20.28	12.72	5.22	5.20	-2.87
ALL	0.00	0.00	0.00	0.00	0.00

1 = Less than 6 years education; 2 = 6 Years; 3 = 9 Years; 4 = 11-12 Years; 5 = 14-17 Years

SPAIN (1987)

	1	2	3	4	5	1	2	3	4	5	1	2	3	4	5
I	16.23	7.90	-15.50	-4.46	-4.14	19.22	9.45	-19.55	-4.66	-4.43	16.95	8.28	-16.48	-4.51	-4.21
II	-1.01	10.17	-3.52	-2.65	-2.96	-4.69	-4.59	15.50	-3.20	-2.98	-1.61	7.77	-0.43	-2.74	-2.96
III	-4.79	5.21	4.78	-2.70	-2.47	-2.81	-4.40	12.39	-2.78	-2.37	-4.17	2.19	7.17	-2.73	-2.44
IV	-11.18	-29.87	20.05	6.92	14.12	-8.99	33.72	-35.71	4.33	6.68	-10.63	-31.33	23.46	6.27	12.26
V	-6.02	-22.46	-7.43	14.12	21.83	-6.33	-6.09	-28.62	29.68	11.39	-6.19	-25.84	-6.69	22.67	16.09
VI	-5.64	-2.76	6.15	-0.90	3.18	2.72	-3.84	4.61	-1.58	-1.88	-1.55	-3.29	5.39	-1.23	0.70
ALL	-0.14	3.37	-1.86	-1.31	-0.04	0.33	-7.79	4.35	3.05	0.10	0.00	0.01	0.01	0.00	0.00

1 = no education completed; 2 = primary only; 3 = middle-school only; 4 = pre-university qualification; 5 = university qualification

Appendix Table A.4.3 (continued)

Sectors	Males					Females					All				
	1	2	3	4	5	1	2	3	4	5	1	2	3	4	5
SWEDEN (1990)															
I	24.62	-6.19	-5.87	-3.23	-9.32	23.70	-6.89	-4.72	-3.52	-8.55	24.37	-6.38	-5.56	-3.31	-9.11
II	9.43	7.25	-0.14	-9.04	-7.49	16.36	-22.32	7.79	2.88	-4.71	10.39	3.15	0.96	-7.39	-7.10
III	-11.67	-5.46	14.96	5.13	-2.97	24.62	10.55	6.37	-0.30	-7.99	0.89	-2.50	7.19	0.77	-6.34
IV	-15.38	-0.68	5.20	4.81	6.05	-2.63	-6.02	7.68	2.22	-1.24	-9.92	-2.97	6.26	3.70	2.93
V	-19.03	-19.58	-4.50	16.97	26.18	-3.36	11.99	-5.81	-1.95	-0.86	-8.98	0.66	-5.34	4.84	8.84
VI	7.18	-1.96	1.34	-1.33	-5.23	8.20	-4.48	3.68	-2.52	-4.88	7.73	-3.31	2.60	-1.97	-5.04
ALL	-2.15	-2.59	0.98	1.06	2.69	2.57	3.10	-1.18	-1.26	-3.22	0.00	0.00	0.00	0.00	0.00
UNITED KINGDOM (1991)															
I	14.96	-4.70	-3.69	-4.16	-3.31	25.18	-1.16	-13.70	-3.85	-7.33	17.16	-3.94	-5.85	-4.09	-4.19
II	0.91	-9.20	12.24	-1.15	-3.71	13.16	12.24	-15.50	-4.54	-6.26	3.83	-4.09	5.63	-1.96	-4.32
III	2.41	2.82	3.61	-4.13	-5.62	2.68	4.71	1.45	-4.10	-5.65	2.51	3.53	2.80	-4.12	-5.63
IV	-17.53	-7.65	14.05	-2.54	12.75	-12.43	24.33	-7.47	-3.76	-1.57	-15.31	6.27	4.68	-3.07	6.52
V	-11.54	-8.12	-2.20	2.00	18.95	-1.66	1.27	-16.05	12.62	2.90	-5.12	-2.02	-11.20	8.90	8.52
VI	3.86	-4.31	4.63	-3.65	-1.44	11.99	3.43	-6.03	-3.56	-6.75	9.22	0.79	-2.39	-3.59	-4.94
ALL	-2.20	-5.75	7.31	-1.74	1.47	2.44	7.19	-10.53	2.20	-2.21	-0.22	-0.25	-0.28	-0.06	-0.10

1 = basic or people's school only; 2 = max. 2 years sec.; 3 = >2 years sec.; 4 = <3 years post-school; 5 = 3+ years post-school

1 = no qualifications; 2 = school-leaving qualification only; 3 = low vocational qualification only; 4 = high vocational qualification; 5 = university

Appendix Table A.5.1 Occupational classes by gender, 18 countries, 1960 and c.1995, ILO definitions

	Occupational class categories, 1960						Occupational class categories, c.1995					
	A	B	C	D	E	Total	A	B	C	D	E	Total
Austria												
All	6.88	3.50	15.35	23.03	51.24	100.00	8.42	11.65	33.21	8.38	38.34	100.00
Males	4.11	2.51	6.37	10.78	35.99	59.76	6.41	6.14	14.59	4.24	25.05	56.43
Females	2.77	0.99	8.98	12.25	15.24	40.23	2.01	5.51	18.62	4.14	13.29	43.57
Belgium[a]												
All	8.49	2.79	23.59	7.82	57.30	99.99	22.52	3.85	28.33	3.09	42.21	100.00
Males	4.91	2.55	13.52	6.58	44.97	72.53	11.15	3.13	12.79	2.11	31.46	60.64
Females	3.59	0.24	10.08	1.24	12.33	27.48	11.37	0.73	15.54	0.98	10.75	39.37
Denmark												
All	8.15	1.74	19.30	18.35	52.46	100.00	8.84	15.71	37.29	3.66	34.51	100.01
Males	4.14	1.53	9.95	16.66	36.03	68.31	6.75	9.64	13.66	3.04	19.23	52.32
Females	4.01	0.21	9.35	1.70	16.43	31.70	2.09	6.07	23.63	0.62	15.28	47.69
Finland												
All	8.12	1.63	11.97	34.81	43.48	100.01	29.40	4.82	23.52	7.18	35.08	100.00
Males	4.22	1.46	3.76	22.48	29.13	61.05	11.28	3.57	8.43	4.77	24.19	52.24
Females	3.90	0.17	8.20	12.33	14.35	38.95	18.12	1.25	15.08	2.41	10.89	47.75
France												
All	9.35	3.17	17.00	20.34	50.15	100.01						
Males	5.32	2.51	7.01	13.68	34.42	62.94						
Females	4.03	0.66	9.99	6.66	15.73	37.07						
Germany[b]												
All	7.92	3.25	20.24	14.11	54.48	100.00	16.71	3.84	30.31	3.96	45.18	100.00
Males	5.30	2.60	9.31	6.46	40.16	63.83	9.68	3.16	12.29	2.26	33.85	61.24
Females	2.62	0.65	10.93	7.65	14.31	36.16	7.03	0.69	18.02	1.71	11.33	38.78

Appendix Table A.5.1 (continued)

	Occupational class categories, 1960						Occupational class categories, c.1995					
	A	B	C	D	E	Total	A	B	C	D	E	Total
Greece												
All	3.42	0.77	9.74	57.78	28.30	100.01	11.95	13.08	18.56	23.28	33.13	100.00
Males	2.22	0.72	7.88	31.73	21.79	64.34	9.24	7.17	9.24	13.50	23.36	62.51
Females	1.20	0.05	1.86	26.05	6.51	35.67	2.71	5.91	9.32	9.78	9.77	37.48
Ireland[b]												
All	7.18	1.22	16.10	35.99	39.52	100.01	17.11	3.43	25.72	15.53	38.20	99.99
Males	3.43	1.13	8.50	32.15	28.73	73.94	9.12	2.93	12.45	14.42	28.41	67.33
Females	3.75	0.09	7.60	3.83	10.79	26.06	7.99	0.50	13.27	1.11	9.79	32.66
Italy												
All	5.38	1.28	14.83	29.06	49.44	99.99	1.17	9.81	28.08	4.49	56.45	100.00
Males	3.11	0.91	10.49	21.37	39.17	75.05	0.96	4.54	16.18	3.11	40.01	64.80
Females	2.27	0.36	4.34	7.70	10.28	24.95	0.21	5.27	11.90	1.38	16.44	35.20
Netherlands												
All	9.46	3.20	22.53	11.12	53.70	100.01	25.46	4.52	29.78	4.17	36.06	99.99
Males	5.76	3.06	14.35	10.15	43.73	77.05	14.06	3.76	13.48	3.21	25.13	59.64
Females	3.71	0.13	8.18	0.97	9.97	22.96	11.40	0.76	16.30	0.97	10.94	40.37
Norway												
All	8.13	3.19	14.66	19.56	54.46	100.00	27.46	7.20	20.56	5.14	39.65	100.01
Males	5.11	2.98	7.11	18.65	43.09	76.94	11.40	4.99	7.59	3.82	25.60	53.40
Females	3.02	0.21	7.55	0.91	11.37	23.06	16.05	2.20	12.97	1.32	14.05	46.59
Portugal[c]												
All	2.73	1.31	10.94	43.57	41.44	99.99	9.62	2.05	23.97	17.85	46.51	100.00
Males	1.35	1.23	9.15	40.38	29.38	81.49	4.35	1.67	12.22	8.84	29.14	56.22
Females	1.39	0.08	1.79	3.20	12.06	18.52	5.28	0.38	11.75	9.01	17.37	43.79

	A	B	C	D	E	Total	A	B	C	D	E	Total
Spain												
All	4.24		13.34	40.94	41.48	100.00	11.24	14.74	24.25	8.66	41.12	100.01
Males							7.63	7.55	13.01	6.36	29.51	64.06
Females							3.61	7.19	11.24	2.29	11.61	35.94
Sweden												
All	12.82	2.12	17.92	13.46	53.68	100.00	35.62		26.04	3.21	35.12	99.99
Males	7.93	1.96	7.76	12.34	40.35	70.34	12.77		11.52	2.43	24.96	51.68
Females	4.90	0.16	10.16	1.12	13.33	29.67	22.85		14.53	0.78	10.16	48.32
Switzerland												
All	8.98	1.23	20.35	11.43	58.01	100.00	5.04	14.99	34.85	5.02	40.10	100.00
Males	6.15	0.64	11.28	10.48	41.31	69.86	4.01	10.98	15.79	3.54	24.68	59.00
Females	2.83	0.58	9.08	0.95	16.69	30.13	1.03	4.01	19.06	1.48	15.42	41.00
UK[d]												
All	8.83	2.72	23.05	4.40	60.99	99.99	19.20	15.64	23.46	8.81	32.89	100.00
Males	5.45	2.55	10.34	4.01	44.92	67.27	10.81	10.48	6.54	4.21	22.77	54.81
Females	3.38	0.17	12.71	0.38	16.08	32.72	8.39	5.16	16.92	4.60	10.12	45.19
Japan												
All	4.89	2.33	20.99	32.63	39.16	100.00	12.45	3.72	34.01	5.44	44.38	100.00
Males	3.16	2.23	12.74	15.76	27.02	60.91	6.97	3.38	16.64	2.97	29.52	59.48
Females	1.73	0.10	8.25	16.87	12.14	39.09	5.48	0.34	17.38	2.46	14.85	40.51
USA												
All	11.69	8.51	22.06	6.60	51.15	100.01	17.90	14.01	26.64	2.81	38.64	100.00
Males	7.04	7.27	9.84	6.00	37.30	67.45	8.39	7.88	9.17	2.28	26.11	53.83
Females	4.65	1.23	12.22	0.60	13.84	32.54	9.51	6.13	17.47	0.53	12.53	46.17

A = professional and technical; B = administrative and managerial; C = junior non-manual; D = agricultural; E = manual

a 1995 figure is for 1992
b 1995 figure is for 1989
c 1995 figure is for 1991
d 1995 figure is for 1993

Source: ILO *Yearbooks* (various years).

Appendix Table A.5.2 Occupational classes by gender sector, 13 countries, c.1995, national definitions

Austria

	Males				Females			
	X	NM	SM	UM	X	NM	SM	UM
II	4.09	15.84	32.54	25.34	1.08	8.96	1.68	10.47
III	6.29	30.61	4.78	12.61	4.43	34.58	1.76	4.94
IV	8.19	37.87	1.08	1.95	5.11	42.20	0.09	3.51
V	2.25	37.18	2.47	2.73	1.11	46.22	0.52	7.52
VI	10.88	9.56	8.75	8.16	10.19	13.34	8.44	30.69

Belgium

	Males					Females				
	P	MGR	MNM	JNM	M	P	MGR	MNM	JNM	M
II	8.03	3.11	6.71	3.59	59.75	1.25	0.41	6.25	0.94	9.95
III (VI)	3.78	3.54	12.47	11.53	31.21	1.98	1.07	10.51	15.18	8.72
IV	18.46	6.09	21.36	6.51	4.90	6.02	2.02	29.44	2.71	2.49
V, VI	19.75	2.03	6.70	0.35	12.82	30.37	0.93	11.69	0.23	15.12

Denmark

	Males						Females					
	X	SNM	MNM	JNM	SM	UM	X	SNM	MNM	JNM	SM	UM
II	4.65	6.66	7.78	4.79	29.58	21.32	1.35	0.73	1.48	9.06	1.45	11.13
III	8.08	7.89	7.96	15.99	9.53	15.19	4.01	1.17	1.85	22.91	0.71	4.70
IV	7.94	17.60	9.67	12.14	3.21	3.27	2.76	4.12	4.01	32.15	0.29	2.85
V	0.80	8.19	7.52	9.66	1.86	3.85	0.42	3.84	18.65	24.31	0.29	20.61
VI	12.82	3.71	4.44	6.40	12.00	8.79	11.13	1.61	4.10	14.44	6.14	14.42

Finland

	Males				Females			
	P&E	MNM	JNM	M	P&E	MNM	JNM	M
II	10.95	3.23	2.64	53.38	2.61	0.44	7.48	19.27
III (VI)	5.05	8.34	6.37	25.79	3.84	1.63	26.95	22.02
IV	19.91	7.11	11.69	12.57	9.50	1.46	26.84	10.93
V, VI	23.35	3.87	1.99	5.14	57.48	1.72	2.25	4.20

France

	Males						Females					
	X	P&E	MNM	JNM	SM	UM	X	P&E	MNM	JNM	SM	UM
II	6.02	5.98	11.71	2.06	27.67	18.51	1.33	0.74	2.08	11.40	2.55	9.95
III	2.93	11.87	10.85	10.10	18.23	6.86	1.37	7.06	4.88	22.30	0.96	2.58
IV	0.52	19.68	12.36	13.46	4.12	2.78	0.08	5.35	7.28	31.71	0.29	2.36
V	0.02	8.84	14.02	13.93	5.23	3.14	0.00	5.33	17.97	30.29	0.67	0.57
VI	3.60	11.16	6.96	7.63	9.15	4.55	2.16	7.49	12.54	29.97	1.25	3.53

Germany

	Males						Females					
	X	SNM	MNM	JNM	SM	UM	X	SNM	MNM	JNM	SM	UM
II	4.77	2.70	16.41	2.82	38.79	9.68	0.99	0.32	3.84	7.91	5.17	6.60
III	7.13	2.87	11.57	6.87	14.31	4.10	4.10	0.97	7.13	34.27	3.28	3.40
IV	10.97	5.79	24.61	4.05	7.27	2.74	3.26	2.85	14.67	16.46	1.54	5.79
V	2.15	9.39	20.92	7.21	5.63	1.49	0.90	2.74	28.82	16.15	1.13	3.48
VI	9.54	2.36	6.41	5.49	5.95	2.56	9.95	1.03	7.74	22.67	9.90	16.41

Greece

	P&E	C	T&S	M	P&E	C	T&S	M
II	6.03	3.16	0.68	67.69	0.92	3.04	0.50	17.97
III (VI)	5.26	7.44	27.17	29.45	1.00	5.63	16.68	7.37
IV	28.61	20.20	7.33	4.02	12.49	22.04	2.12	3.20
V, VI	22.86	9.63	0.36	19.08	24.30	11.84	0.04	11.88

Netherlands

	P	MGR	JNM	M	P	MGR	JNM	M
II	10.03	6.28	9.42	57.29	1.48	0.43	9.48	5.60
III (VI)	4.25	3.44	31.02	23.20	1.69	0.50	33.90	2.00
IV	26.13	7.01	24.96	4.23	6.42	1.02	29.05	1.17
V, VI	21.23	2.25	12.68	4.68	27.36	1.22	29.84	0.75

Spain

	P	MGR	JNM	M	P	MGR	JNM	M
II	1.66	2.22	5.45	71.48	0.30	0.21	3.24	15.43
III (VI)	1.57	0.38	25.77	40.06	0.68	0.03	21.87	9.64
IV	18.07	9.56	40.51	6.87	3.78	0.05	18.63	2.54
V, VI	15.05	0.70	7.87	19.19	18.49	0.06	8.28	30.36

Sweden

	X	P&E	MNM	JNM	SM	UM	X	P&E	MNM	JNM	SM	UM
II	2.98	5.68	12.33	3.73	31.62	20.68	0.56	1.02	2.05	6.84	2.83	9.69
III	6.42	4.89	6.57	10.03	7.12	22.61	2.43	1.69	2.82	13.30	1.18	20.92
IV	2.13	12.32	16.34	6.60	4.38	6.50	1.21	10.43	13.45	21.36	0.59	4.70
V	0.22	8.39	6.72	3.53	2.24	4.30	0.20	7.36	18.66	10.82	12.25	25.29
VI	6.56	3.75	7.58	6.61	13.23	9.35	4.94	3.73	5.88	11.65	9.92	16.79

UK

	P&E	MNM	JNM	SM	SSM	UM	P&E	MNM	JNM	SM	SSM	UM
II	5.05	13.75	4.60	38.38	10.46	3.36	0.44	3.29	8.94	4.02	7.00	0.71
III	1.30	16.44	9.35	19.58	7.00	2.27	0.54	7.85	28.92	2.13	3.76	0.85
IV	11.18	21.76	10.72	3.83	2.98	0.58	2.63	11.04	32.99	0.46	0.66	1.17
V	5.82	13.40	6.54	3.91	2.70	1.81	3.82	28.17	13.88	3.60	8.84	7.51
VI	0.44	11.49	5.40	13.91	7.53	1.69	0.25	9.31	11.76	9.86	19.61	8.75

Japan

	P	MGR	JNM	M	P	MGR	JNM	M
II	5.56	4.37	9.68	49.56	0.47	0.37	9.30	20.67
III (VI)	0.83	3.75	28.50	25.65	0.53	0.45	27.65	12.57
IV	1.63	7.71	38.99	2.87	0.31	0.94	45.65	1.88
V, VI	17.96	2.99	12.73	20.05	17.20	0.31	14.36	14.38

USA

	MGR	P&T	JNM	SM	UM	MGR	P&T	JNM	SM	UM
II	9.68	7.71	4.72	26.06	25.37	3.02	2.13	7.87	2.49	10.96
III (VI)	5.68	2.73	19.93	7.65	21.50	3.89	1.56	25.76	0.79	10.51
IV	13.04	2.27	19.80	1.99	3.82	13.08	2.20	42.55	0.14	1.11
V, VI	6.12	15.39	2.73	3.22	9.67	6.31	23.42	16.79	0.32	16.04

C = clerical; JNM = junior non-manual; M = manual; MGR = managerial; MNM = middle-ranking non-manual; NM = non-manual; P = professional; P&E = professional and managerial; P&T = professional and technical; SM = skilled manual; SNM = senior non-manual; SSM = semi-skilled manual; T&S = trade and sales; UM = unskilled manual; X = self-employed and family workers

Sources: As Appendix Table A.4.1.

Appendix Table A.7.1   Family characteristics, 18 countries, c.1960

	A	B	C	D	E	F
Austria	42.45	21.60	42.60	2.65	5.00	13.00
Belgium	72.84	23.40	49.90	2.58	2.00	2.10
Denmark	59.79	22.90	54.40	2.54	6.00	7.80
Finland	49.18		44.70	2.71	4.10	4.00
France	61.77	23.50	43.30	2.73	2.80	6.10
Germany	55.78	23.70	53.30	2.37	3.40	6.30
Greece	61.77	24.40	49.90	2.27	1.50	1.20
Ireland	65.32	27.10	30.60	3.76	0.00	1.60
Italy	70.93	24.80	47.80	2.41	0.00	2.40
Netherlands	75.67	24.30	60.90	3.12	2.20	1.40
Norway	74.77	23.50	46.40	2.83	2.80	3.70
Portugal	81.68	24.80	50.20	3.01	0.40	9.10
Spain	80.93	26.10	45.90	2.86	0.00	2.30
Sweden	64.50	23.70	43.50	2.17	4.90	11.30
Switzerland	63.53		43.80	2.44	3.90	3.80
UK	60.66	23.30	51.00	2.66	2.20	5.20
Japan	45.29		59.40	2.01	3.70	
USA	60.78	20.30	73.50	3.61	9.40	5.30
Mean	63.76	23.83	49.51	2.71	3.02	5.09
.5SD	5.60	0.90	4.48	0.27	1.22	1.75
High = >	69.36	24.73	53.99	2.98	4.24	6.84
Low = <	58.16	22.93	45.03	2.44	1.80	3.34

A = % of all women not in paid employment (from Table A.2.1)
B = mean age of women at first marriage
C = marriage rate for women (%)
D = fertility rate (TFR)
E = crude divorce rates (%)
F = % of live births out of wedlock

Sources: Boh *et al.* 1989; Chesnais 1992; Coleman 1996*a*; national census data.

Appendix Table A.7.2 Family characteristics, 18 countries, c.1990

	A	B	C	D	E	F
Austria	45.67	25.70	50.10	1.48	8.50	25.20
Belgium	51.35	24.70	66.10	1.56	8.40	8.90
Denmark	33.13	27.90	38.50	1.75	13.10	46.50
Finland	31.93	26.60	38.00	1.81	9.60	27.40
France	40.22	26.00	38.50	1.65	8.40	27.50
Germany	47.77	26.50	48.50	1.39	8.80	11.10
Greece	59.72	24.10	92.80	1.34	2.60	2.40
Ireland	51.58	25.90	41.40	1.93	0.00	18.00
Italy	60.16	25.60	54.70	1.25	2.10	6.70
Netherlands	44.74	26.60	45.70	1.57	8.10	12.50
Norway	29.78	26.40	34.30	1.86	9.90	42.90
Portugal	46.02	24.50	81.00	1.52	2.80	16.10
Spain	61.06	25.30	52.40	1.26	2.10	9.60
Sweden	31.47	27.80	31.30	2.00	11.10	49.50
Switzerland	39.92	27.30	49.00	1.51	8.00	6.70
UK	41.71	24.80	50.30	1.79	12.30	30.80
Japan	41.29		57.70	1.50	3.60	
USA	31.27	23.70	68.00	2.07	20.90	26.00
Mean	43.82	25.85	52.13	1.62	7.79	21.64
.5SD	5.09	0.82	8.14	0.19	2.49	7.28
High = >	48.91	26.67	60.27	1.81	10.28	28.92
Low = <	38.73	25.03	43.99	1.43	5.30	14.36

A = % of all women not in paid employment (from Table A.2.3)
B = mean age of women at first marriage
C = marriage rate for women (%)
D = fertility rate (TFR)
E = crude divorce rates (%)
F = % of live births out of wedlock

Sources: Chesnais 1992; Coleman 1996*a*; national census data.

Appendix Table A.9.1 Religious adherence by type of faith, 17 countries, c.1960 (% total adult population)

	RC	L	R[a]	A	OP[b]	O	J	I	H	B	S	Other[c]	None or not known
Austria	89.00	6.00	0.20		0.40		0.20					0.40	3.80
Belgium	96.00												5.00
Denmark		95.00											
Finland		92.40				1.40							6.20
France	90.00		1.60			0.30		0.60				0.20	7.90
Germany	44.10	50.50			3.10		1.00	1.40				1.30	0.90
Greece (1951)	0.40				0.20	97.90	0.10						0.00
Ireland	94.86			3.69	0.91		0.12					0.19	0.24
Netherlands	40.40		37.60		2.70							3.60	18.40
Norway	0.20	96.20			2.70							0.60	0.20
Spain	99.90												0.10
Sweden		98.25			2.00								
Switzerland	45.40		52.70		0.50		0.40						1.00
UK (members) (1975)	5.83		3.80	5.32	3.11	0.46	0.93	0.93	0.69			2.08	76.85
UK (total community) (1960)	12.00		4.40	66.60	7.41	0.93	0.93	0.93	0.69			2.08	6.12
Japan[d]					0.79					74.93	82.40	8.77	
USA	25.70	7.05	5.58	2.80	48.60	2.13	3.24					1.29	3.61

RC = Roman Catholic   R = Reformed   S = Shinto
L = Lutheran   A = Anglican

OP = Other Protestant   J = Jewish   H = Hindu
O = Orthodox   I = Islamic   B = Buddhist

[a] Members of the Protestant churches stemming largely from the teachings of Calvin, Zwingli, and others. In the Dutch data they include the strongly Calvinist 'Reformed Reformed' Church as well as the official Reformed Church; in Swiss data the figure includes Lutherans, who are not distinguished as such in the national statistics; in Scotland the church indicated is the Church of Scotland.

[b] Including the main eighteenth- and nineteenth-century non-conformist Protestant churches (Methodists, Baptists, Congregationalists), but also smaller and mainly twentieth-century sects.

[c] May sometimes include some of the faiths specifically listed in earlier columns, where insufficient detail is given in national statistics.

[d] It is possible to be simultaneously a member of the Buddhist and Shinto faiths.

Sources: Certain national censuses; also Bogensberger and Zulehner 1972; Thorgaard 1972; Seppänen 1972; Isambert 1972; Kehrer 1972; Martin 1972; Highet 1972; Laeyendecker 1972; Vogt 1972; Almerich 1972; Gustafsson 1972; Campiche 1972; Moberg 1972; Mol 1972.

Appendix Table A.9.2 Religious adherence by type of faith, 17 countries, c.1990 (% total adult population)

	RC	L	R[a]	A	OP[b]	O	J	I	H	B	S	Other[c]	None
Austria	78.01	4.99										4.91	8.62
Belgium	65.00												
Denmark	0.62	87.40			0.97		0.07					0.03	10.91
Finland		88.00											
France	67.00		1.70			5.19	1.56	7.79		0.78		2.00	8.00
Germany	41.60	42.90			0.60		0.10	2.70				0.58	
Greece						99.42	0.04						0.02
Ireland	91.57			0.67	0.52							1.00	6.00
Italy (1981)	93.00												6.00
Netherlands	32.00		22.00		6.60			3.70	0.50				35.20
Norway	0.74	95.31			0.99		0.02	0.51					0.05
Spain	86.00											1.00	13.00
Sweden	1.75	86.47			1.75								0.46
Switzerland	40.00		46.10		2.10		0.30	2.20				0.40	7.40
UK (members) (1975)	4.28		2.60	3.78	2.82	0.58	0.63	2.30	0.84			3.97	
UK (total community) (1975)	11.72		3.14	55.86	6.90	1.05	0.63	2.30	0.84			3.97	
Japan[d]					1.24					72.35	94.06	9.10	
USA	30.39	4.24	2.31	1.27	40.96	1.31	2.44					6.00	11.00

RC = Roman Catholic   OP = Other Protestant   J = Jewish   H = Hindu   S = Shinto
L = Lutheran   O = Orthodox   I = Islamic   B = Buddhist
R = Reformed   A = Anglican

[a] Members of the Protestant churches stemming largely from the teachings of Calvin, Zwingli, and others. In the Dutch data they include the strongly Calvinist 'Reformed Reformed' Church as well as the official Reformed Church; in Swiss data the figure includes Lutherans, who are not distinguished as such in the national statistics; in Scotland the church indicated is the Church of Scotland.

[b] Including the main eighteenth- and nineteenth-century non-conformist Protestant churches (Methodists, Baptists, Congregationalists), but also smaller and mainly twentieth-century sects.

[c] May sometimes include some of the faiths specifically listed in earlier columns, where insufficient detail is given in national statistics.

[d] It is possible to be simultaneously a member of the Buddhist and Shinto faiths.

Sources: Certain national censuses; Albert-Lorca 1994; Campiche 1994; François 1994; Kokosalakis 1994; Pace 1994; Riis 1994; Voyé 1994; Willaime 1994.

Appendix Table A.10.1 Home, foreign, and ethnic minority populations, 13 countries, c.1990

Origins	Austria		Belgium		Denmark	
	number	%	number	%	number	%
ALL	3,753,989		10,038,661	98.71	5,233,000	
Home national	3,460,828	92.19	9,226,865	90.73	5,102,714	97.51
Other	293,161	7.81	811,796	7.98	130,286	2.49
ALL EUROPE			575,276	5.66	81,046	1.55
Western Europe			553,861	5.45	41,497	0.79
Scandinavia						
Denmark						
Finland						
Central West			220,179	2.17		
France			93,361	0.92		
Netherlands			65,294	0.64		
Germany	27,248	0.73				
South			328,434	3.23		
Greece						
Italy			240,127	2.36		
Portugal						
Spain						
Eastern Europe						
Poland						
ex-Yugoslavia	112,553	3.00				
Other or all						
MEDITERRANEAN			244,409	2.40		
Turkey	70,790	1.89	85,303	0.84	34,967	0.67
Middle East						
Near East			159,106	1.56		
Algeria						
Morroco			142,098	1.40		
Other or general						
ALL AFRICA						
(sometimes includes						
Middle East)						
South of Sahara						
ALL ASIA						
(sometimes includes						
Middle East)					47,045	0.90
Indian sub-continent and Iran						
India						
Pakistan and Bangladesh						
Indo-China and Korea						
Thailand						
China						
Japan						
Pacific islands						
Indonesia						
OCEANIA						
(sometimes includes Pacific)						
ALL AMERICA						
North America						
Hispanic America						
Caribbean						
Surinam						
ALL OTHER NON-WHITE						

Finland		France		Germany		Netherlands	
number	%	number	%	number	%	number	%
5,077,912		56,577,000		65,534,000		15,239,182	
4,983,271	98.14	52,417,541	92.65	60,191,500	91.85	13,863,182	90.97
94,641	1.86	4,159,459	7.35	5,342,500	8.15	1,376,000	9.03
37,288	0.73	2,026,631	3.58	2,343,700	3.58		
		1,694,431	2.99	1,439,000	2.20		
						135,000	0.89
		1,585,579	2.80	1,093,600	1.67		
				320,200	0.49		
		523,080	0.92	552,400	0.84		
		649,714	1.15				
		412,785	0.73				
24,072	0.47			904,700	1.38		
				662,700	1.01		
				1,694,600	2.59		
		1,393,195	2.46				
		614,207	1.09				
		572,652	1.01			178,000	1.17
						227,000	1.49
						188,000	1.23
						172,000	1.13

Appendix Table A.10.1 (continued)

Origins	Norway		Portugal		Spain	
	number	%	number	%	number	%
ALL	4,247,546		9,912,200		39,433,942	
Home national	4,041,355	95.15	9,780,607	98.67	38,972,573	98.83
Other	206,191	4.85	131,593	1.33	461,369	1.17
ALL EUROPE	94,565	2.23				
Western Europe	78,714	1.85				
Scandinavia	45,721	1.08				
Denmark	20,487	0.48				
Finland						
Central West	30,272	0.71				
France						
Netherlands						
Germany						
South						
Greece						
Italy						
Portugal						
Spain						
Eastern Europe						
Poland						
ex-Yugoslavia						
Other or all						
MEDITERRANEAN						
Turkey						
Middle East						
Near East						
Algeria						
Morroco						
Other or general						
ALL AFRICA						
(sometimes includes						
Middle East)					85,559	0.22
South of Sahara			55,786	0.56		
ALL ASIA						
(sometimes includes						
Middle East)	59,534	1.40				
Indian sub-continent and Iran	29,850	0.70				
India						
Pakistan and Bangladesh						
Indo-China and Korea						
Thailand						
China						
Japan						
Pacific islands						
Indonesia						
OCEANIA						
(sometimes includes Pacific)						
ALL AMERICA						
North America						
Hispanic America					87,677	0.22
Caribbean						
Surinam						
ALL OTHER NON-WHITE						

Source: National censuses.

Sweden		Switzerland		UK	
number	%	number	%	number	%
8,816,381		6,751,000		58,395,000	
7,801,081	88.48	5,459,238	80.87	55,189,000	94.51
1,015,300	11.52	1,291,762	19.13	3,206,000	5.49
538,077	6.10	1,102,277	16.33		
336,657	3.82	816,290	12.09	768,000	1.32
236,079	2.68				
74,935	0.85				
		208,793	3.09		
		53,418	0.79		
		88,168	1.31		
		607,497	9.00		
		370,699	5.49		
		122,068	1.81		
		106,853	1.58		
192,186	2.18	252,589	3.74		
40,695	0.46				
91,080	1.03	247,049	3.66		
		76,592	1.13		
57,269	0.65				
48,157	0.55				
		50,736	0.75		
72,297	0.82			1,569,000	2.69
				844,000	1.45
				725,000	1.24
54,084	0.61				
47,896	0.54				
				869,000	1.49
				773,000	1.32

Appendix Table A.10.2 Immigrant populations and remembered ancestry, USA, c.1990

	Immigrant population		Remembered ancestry	
	number	**%**	**number**	**%**
ALL	248,710,000	100.00	248,710,000	100.00
EUROPE			**210,452,000**	**84.62**
Europe (Western)			**187,752,000**	**75.49**
Scandinavia			**6,842,000**	2.75
Danish			1,635,000	0.66
Norwegian			3,869,000	1.56
Southern			**18,952,000**	7.62
Greek			1,110,000	0.45
Italian			14,665,000	5.90
Portuguese			1,153,000	0.46
Spanish			2,024,000	0.81
Western			**161,958,000**	65.12
French			10,321,000	4.15
German			57,947,000	23.30
Irish			38,736,000	15.57
Dutch			6,227,000	2.50
UK			**46,817,000**	18.82
British			1,119,000	0.45
English			32,652,000	13.13
Scottish			11,012,000	4.43
Welsh			2,034,000	0.82
Europe (Eastern)			**22,233,000**	**8.94**
Czech			5,977,000	2.40
Hungarian			1,582,000	0.64
Polish			9,366,000	3.77
ex-USSR			2,953,000	1.19
ASIA	**7,062,000**	**2.84**		
China	1,645,000	0.66	1,505,000	0.61
Indo-China	**1,505,000**	**0.61**		
Pacific	1,387,928	0.56		
Philippines	1,407,000	0.57	1,451,000	0.58
AMERICA				
North			**48,910,000**	**19.67**
Canadian			2,717,000	1.09
US			13,040,000	5.24
Native	1,959,000	0.79	8,708,000	3.50
Afro-American			23,777,000	9.56
Hispanic	**22,354,000**	**8.99**	**16,520,000**	**6.64**
Mexico	13,496,000	5.43	11,587,000	4.66
Puerto Rico	2,728,000	1.10	1,955,000	0.79
WHITE	199,686,000	80.29	1,800,000	0.72
BLACK	29,986,000	12.06		
ALL OTHER NON-WHITE	9,805,000	3.94		

Source: US National Census.

Appendix Table A.11.1 Party allegiances of certain social groups, c.1960–1970[a]

Country/ Party	ALL 1960–4	Manual workers	Jnr non-manual workers	Agri-cultural workers	Men	Women	Regular churchgoers	Small towns, etc.	Large towns
A 1969[b]									
SPÖ	44.00	50.00	24.20	7.30					
ÖVP	45.40	15.70	30.60	64.20					
FPÖ	7.00	3.10	6.00	1.70					
B 1968									
CVP/PSC	44.40	35.00	38.00	70.00	35.00	42.00	59.00	51.00	33.00
PSB/BSP	36.70	45.00	26.00	5.00	29.00	27.00	12.00	22.00	30.00
PLB	12.30	9.00	18.00	18.00	17.00	18.00	15.00	15.00	21.00
DK 1963[b]								A	B
SD	42.00	73.00	58.00	6.00	40.00	44.00		33.00	45.00
V	21.00	2.00	3.00	78.00	14.00	11.00		26.00	3.00
SF	6.00	10.00	6.00	0.00	9.00	10.00		5.00	19.00
KF	21.90	5.00	21.00	5.00	7.00	8.00		5.00	9.00
RV	7.50	7.00	8.00	7.00	7.00	6.00		4.00	7.00
								16.00	8.00

A = rural; B = capital

Country/ Party	ALL 1960–4	Manual workers	Jnr non-manual workers	Agri-cultural workers	Men	Women	Regular churchgoers	Small towns, etc.	Large towns
SF 1966				A				B	C
SDP	19.50	42.00	29.00	8+45	29.00	28.00		21.40	34.30
KESK	23.00	6.00	8.00	60+24	22.00	20.00		35.80	4.60
KOK	14.60	6.00	28.00	7+10	12.00	15.00		9.50	17.90
SKDL	22.00	34.00	6.00	9+25	21.00	20.00		20.20	22.70
LKP	6.40	5.00	15.00	2+6	5.00	7.00		3.50	9.70
SFP	6.40	3.00	9.00	10+0	7.00	5.00		5.30	6.80

A = farmers+farm workers; B = rural; C = urban

Country/ Party	ALL 1960–4	Manual workers	Jnr non-manual workers	Agri-cultural workers	Men	Women	Regular churchgoers	Small towns, etc.	Large towns
F 1967									
Majorité	45.80	30.00	35.00	45.00			35.00		
MRP	8.90						13.00		
Socialists	12.70	18.00	22.00	14.00			8.00		
PCF	21.08	31.00	18.00	13.00			1.00		
Centre dem	7.60	11.00	15.00	19.00			20.00		

Appendix Table A.11.1 (continued)

Country/Party	ALL 1960-4	Manual workers	Jnr non-manual workers	Agri-cultural workers	Men	Women	Regular churchgoers	Small towns, etc.	Large towns
D 1961									
CDU/CSU	45.30	33.00	45.00		40.40	49.60		52.60	45.40
SPD	36.20	49.00	34.00		39.70	32.90		24.60	39.20
FDP	12.80	1.00	4.00		13.60	12.20		7.80	7.90
GR									
Conservatives	41.80								
Liberals	44.00								
KKE	13.60								
IRL 1970									
FF	45.30	51.00	41.00	45.00				49.30	39.50
FG	32.00	12.00	29.00	30.00				25.90	18.00
Lab	12.00	16.00	6.00	0.00				5.80	19.90

I 1963 — Vote by ecological characteristics of area

	ALL 1960-4	A	B	C	D	E	F	G	H	I
DC	38.20	34.80	32.10	41.20	50.00	30.00				41.50
PCI	25.30	24.40	24.70	28.50			20.00	36.80	36.00	20.00
PSI+PSDI	19.90	25.30	21.60	18.20	10.00	9.10		11.00		
MSI	5.10	14.80	21.00	11.80			2.70	2.90	2.90	5.60
PLI+PRI	8.40									

A = industrial; B = tertiary; C = rural; D = small towns; E = large towns; F = northwest; G = north/central: zona bianca; H = north/central: zona rossa; I = south

NL 1967

	ALL 1960-4	Manual workers	Jnr non-manual workers	Men	Women	A	B	C	D	E
							overall identification			
PvdA	28.00	38.00	22.00	33.00	26.00	5.00	15.00	2.00	18.90	28.50
KVP	26.50	26.00	17.00	16.00	27.00	77.00	0.00	0.00	29.30	20.20
VVD	10.30	4.00	14.00	10.00	9.00	2.00	5.00	2.00	9.10	12.20
ARP	9.90	11.00	16.00	10.00	14.00	1.00	20.00	80.00	13.50	7.70
CHU	8.10	6.00	11.00	8.00	9.00	1.00	52.00	2.00	11.50	5.30

A = Roman Catholic; B = Calvinist; C = Reformed; D = rural; E = urban

N 1965

				A	
DNA	46.80	68.00	48.00	10+39	21.00
Høyre	20.00	6.00	22.00	9+14	14.00
SP	9.40	4.00	4.00	64+30	15.00
KrF	9.60	6.00	4.00	9+4	35.00
V	8.80	8.00	15.00	7+11	1.00

A = farmers+farm workers

S 1960

					A			
SAP	47.60	77.00	42.00	54.00	7.00	26.00	30.00	59.00
Höjere	15.70	3.00	20.00	9.00	17.00	16.00	12.00	10.00
CP	13.60	6.00	6.00	19.00	70.00	25.00	47.00	9.00
FP	17.50	10.00	31.00	13.00	5.00	25.00	8.00	16.00
V	4.90	3.00	1.00	2.00	1.00	9.00	1.00	1.00

CH 1975

							identification			
							A	B		
SPS	26.60	44.00	36.20	9.20	35.70	32.10	25.70	39.90	28.50	43.90
FDP	32.90	16.20	28.50	10.80	24.60	22.30	14.00	31.50	21.30	23.20
CDV	25.00	23.60	19.20	32.30	20.20	27.30	50.00	2.30	31.60	15.20
SVP	11.40	8.50	5.40	46.20	10.00	11.60	4.00	16.70	13.70	4.30

A = Roman Catholic; B = Calvinist

UK 1964

						overall identification						
						A	B	C	D	E	F	G
Cons.	43.40	26.30	57.20	40.20	43.10	47.30	45.20	26.30	31.50	47.40	42.00	27.00
Lab.	44.10	65.60	27.70	47.40	46.50	38.60	44.30	64.60	53.10	37.60	53.00	54.00
Lib.	11.20	7.70	14.20	11.70	9.80	13.80	9.70	9.10	15.50	14.50	4.30	14.20

A = all; B = Church of England; C = Roman Catholic; D = Non-C; E = South; F = Scotland; G = Wales

JAP 1958

LDP	55.80	41.00	43.00	70.00	57.00	56.00
All Socialist	36.20	58.00	56.00	30.00	42.00	42.00

USA 1960

						overall identification							
						A	B	C	D	E	F	G	H
Dem.	55.50	63.00	43.00	47.00	52.00	47.00	37.00	83.00	89.00	47.00	44.00	60.00	48.00	71.00
Rep.	44.00	37.00	57.00	53.00	48.00	53.00	63.00	17.00	11.00	53.00	56.00	40.00	52.00	29.00

A = Protestant; B = Roman Catholic; C = Jewish; D = rural; E = suburban; F = cities; G = White; H = Black

(notes follow overleaf)

Appendix Table A.11.1 (continued)

[a] The overall voting figures (ALL) relate to the average of elections in the period 1960–4. The demographic breakdown data relate to the election closest to 1960 for which analytical statistics are available; in some cases this is considerably later than 1960.

[b] Evidence based on mid-term opinion polls, not surveys based on a general election.

Abbreviations of party names:

Austria: SPÖ: Sozialistische Partei Österreich; ÖVP: Österreichische Volkspartei; FPÖ: Freiheitliche Partei Österreichs; LIF: Liberales Forum

Belgium: CVP/PSC: Christelijke Volkspartij/Parti Social Chrétien; BSP/PSB: Belgische Socialistische Partie/Partie Socialiste Belge; PLB: Parti Libéral Belge

Denmark: SD: Socialdemokratiet; V: Venstre; KF: Konservative Folkeparti; SF: Socialistisk Folkeparti; FRP: Fremskridtspartiet; RV: Radikale Venstre

Finland: SDP: Sosialdemokraattinen Puolue; KESK: Suomen Keskuste; KOK: Kansallinen Kokoomus; SKDL: Suomen Kansan Demokraattinen Litto; LKP: Liberaalinen Kansanpuolue; SFP: Svenska Folkpartiet

France: MRP: Mouvement Républicain Populaire; PCF: Parti Communiste Français

Germany: CDU/CSU: Christliche Demokratische Union/Christliche Soziale Union; SPD: Sozialdemokratische Partei Deutschland; FDP: Freie Demokratische Partei

Greece: KKE: Communist Party of Greece

Ireland: FF: Fianna Fáil; FG Fine Gael; Lab: Labour Party

Italy: DC: Democrazia Cristiana; PCI: Partito Comunista Italiano; PSI: Partito Socialista Italiano; PSDI: Partito Socialista Democratico Italiano; MSI: Movimento Sociale Italiano; PLI: Partito Liberale Italiano; PRI: Partito Repubblicano Italiano

Netherlands: PvdA: Partij van der Arbeid; KVP: Katholieke Volkspartij; VVD: Volkspartij voor Vreiheid en Demokratie; ARP: Anti-Revolutionaire Partij; CHU: Christelijk-Historische Unie

Norway: DNA: Det Norske Arbeidparti; SP: Senterpartiet; KrF: Kristeligt Folkeparti; V: Venstreparti

Sweden: SAP: Socialdemokratiska Arbetarpartiet; CP: Centerpartiet; FP: Folkpartiet; V: Vänsterpartiet MP: Miljöpartiet de Gröna

Switzerland: FDP: Freisinnig-demokratische Partei; CVP: Christlichdemokratische Volkspartei; SPS: Sozialdemokratische Partei der Schweiz SVP: Schweizerische Volkspartei

United Kingdom: Cons.: Conservative Party; Lab.: Labour Party; Lib.: Liberal Party

Japan: LDP: Liberal Democratic Party

USA: Dem.: Democratic Party; Rep.: Republican Party

Sources: *General:* Lane, McKay, and Newton 1997; *Austria:* Haerpfer 1983; *Belgium:* Delruelle *et al.* 1970; *Denmark:* Berglund and Lindström 1978; Glans 1977; *Finland:* Martikainen and Yrjönen 1994; *France:* Braud 1973; CEVF 1971; Frears 1977; *Germany:* Ritter and Niehuss 1991; *Ireland:* Carty 1981; Gallagher 1976; Sinnott 1995; *Italy:* Capecchi 1968; Caciogli and Spreafico 1990; *Netherlands:* Lijphart 1974; *Norway:* Sweden: Korpi 1983; *Switzerland:* Kerr 1987; *UK:* Heath 1991; *Japan:* Watanuki 1991; *USA:* Miller and Traugott 1989.

Appendix Table A.11.2 Social composition of support for parties, c.1960–1970[a]

Country/Party	Manual workers	Jnr non-manual workers	Agri-cultural workers	Men	Women	Regular churchgoers	Communities: Small	Large	
A 1969[b]									
SPÖ	68.00	25.00	5.00			23.00			
ÖVP	23.00	29.00	35.00			67.00			
FPÖ	26.00	40.00	23.00			21.00			
							A	B	C
B 1968									
CVP/PSC	32.60	24.50		44.40	55.60	87.00	68.00	22.00	10.00
PSB/BSP	58.30	23.00		50.50	49.50	24.20	41.00	49.00	10.00
PLB	17.90	25.20		48.60	51.40	48.10	36.00	43.00	21.00
Totals	38.00	26.00	9.00			58.00	53.00	34.00	13.00
							A	B	
DK 1977									
SD	56.00	36.00	1.00	45.00	55.00		27.00	30.00	
V	16.00	26.00	50.00	51.00	49.00		71.00	6.00	
SF	38.00	45.00	1.00	47.00	53.00		17.00	52.00	
KF	4.00	46.00	8.00	43.00	57.00		25.00	34.00	
RV	19.00	58.00	3.00	50.00	50.00		22.00	32.00	
Totals	37.00	39.00	11.00	47.00	53.00		35.00	28.00	
			A				B	C	
SF 1966									
SDP	70.00	16.00	7+4				10.80	26.40	
KESK	15.00	6.00	72+3				28.30	6.50	
KOK	20.00	33.00	12+0				10.60	26.70	
SKDL	79.00	5.00	11+3				20.80	21.30	
LKP	35.00	36.00	7+2						
SFP	22.00	23.00	43+0						

A = Flanders; B = Wallonia; C = Brussels

A = rural; B = capital

A = farmers+agricultural workers; B = north (1975 data); C = capital (1975 data)

Appendix Table A.11.2 (continued)

Country/Party	Manual workers	Jnr non-manual workers	Agri-cultural workers	Men	Women	Regular churchgoers	Communities: Small	Large	C	D
F 1977										
RPR	20.00	19.00	12.00	50.00	50.00	53.00	34.00	19.00		
PR	16.00	17.00	10.00	46.00	54.00					
PCF	46.00	19.00	4.00	52.00	48.00	4.00				
non-Comm. left	31.00	24.00	8.00	51.00	49.00	8.00				
Centre	11.00	18.00	13.00	57.00	43.00	35.00				
D 1967[c]										
CDU/CSU	31.00	31.00	8.00							
SPD	49.40	25.90	0.00							
FDP	11.70	35.60	?							
IRL 1969							A	B		
FF	28.00		10.90				58.00	21.50		
FG	14.00		15.60				65.60	21.10		
Lab	44.00		0.00				32.00	51.00		

A = rural; B = Dublin

Country/Party	Manual workers	Jnr non-manual workers	Agri-cultural workers	Men	Women	Regular churchgoers	Communities: A	B	C	D
I 1963[d]										
DC						86.00	67.00		33.00	38.00
PCI						29.00	24.00	8.00	30.00	38.00
PSI						41.00				
MSI						56.00	19.30	8.60	14.20	57.90

A = northwest; B = north/central: zona bianca; C = north/central: zona rossa; D = south

Country/Party	Manual workers	Jnr non-manual workers	Agri-cultural workers	Men	Women	Regular churchgoers	Communities: Small	Large
I 1976								
DC	62.90			38.60			65.50	48.20
PCI	67.40			50.50			13.40	30.70
PSI	53.70			53.00			25.70	28.70
PSDI	35.60			62.50			36.20	56.20
PRI	30.40			67.40			20.00	8.70
PLI	25.90			56.70			43.30	10.00
MSI	48.40			61.40			19.40	23.90
Totals	58.80			48.60			36.60	34.20

N 1965

DNA	64.00	22.00
Hoyre	14.00	52.00
SP	26.00	25.00

S 1960

					A	B	C
SAP	78.00		52.00	48.00	7.00	5.00	65.00
Höjere	13.00		47.00	53.00	22.00	9.00	57.00
CP	22.00	17.00	57.00	43.00	20.00	23.00	31.00
FP	33.00	57.00	49.00	51.00	26.00	5.00	69.00
V	88.00				0.00		

CH 1975

					A	B	C	D
SPS	49.00	58.80	2.30	43.70	34.60	65.40	30.20	26.30
FDP	55.50	58.70	3.80	41.30	26.80	73.20	32.60	20.00
CDV	40.20	48.70	12.40	51.30	94.30	5.40	49.20	13.40
SVP	22.90	52.30	36.10	47.70	16.50	83.50	46.50	8.10
Totals	46.50	56.20	8.50	43.80	45.00	54.00	36.20	20.40

A = Roman Catholic; B = Calvinist; C = rural; D = urban

JAP 1976

LDP	15.00	23.00	27.00
JSP	30.00	48.00	9.00

USA 1960

	A	B	C	D	E	F
Dem	27.00	17.00	7.00	15.00	22.00	7.00
Rep	17.00	11.00	1.00	42.00	18.00	2.00

A = TU; B = Roman Catholic; C = Jewish; D = White Anglo-Saxon Protestant; E = Southern White; F = Black

[a] Data are given for the election closest to 1960 for which analytical statistics are available; in some cases this is considerably later than 1960.
[b] Evidence based on opinion polls, not surveys based on a general election.
[c] CDU figures are from a 1965 survey.
[d] Statistics on church-going are 1968.

For party abbreviations, see Appendix Table A.11.1, except for: *France*: RPR: Rassemblement pour la République; PR: Parti Républicain; *Japan*: JSP: Japan Socialist Party.

Sources: *Austria*: Gerlich 1987; *Belgium*: Mommsen-Reindle 1980; *Denmark*: Delruelle *et al.* 1970; *Denmark*: Pedersen 1987; *Finland*: Martikainen and Yrjönen 1994; *France*: Frears 1977; *Germany*: Merkl 1980; *Ireland*: Carty 1981; *Italy*: Caciogli and Spreafico 1990; Zariski 1980; *Netherlands*: Lijphart 1974; *Norway*: Andersen and Björklund 1994; *Sweden*: Korpi 1983; *Switzerland*: Kerr 1987; *Japan*: Watanuki 1991; *USA*: Nie, Verba and Petrocik 1979

Appendix Table A.11.3 Party allegiances of certain social groups, 1990s

Country/ Party	All	Manual workers	Jnr non-manual workers	Agri-cultural workers	Men	Women	Regular churchgoers	Small towns, etc.	Large towns	
									A	B
A 1995										
SPÖ	34.92	41.00	32.00		35.00	40.00	22.00	31.10	45.00	32.50
ÖVP	27.67	13.00	28.00		26.00	29.00	61.00	41.90	19.10	28.50
FPÖ	22.50	34.00	22.00		27.00	16.00	10.00	19.40	22.40	21.80
Grünen	7.31	4.00	8.00		5.00	6.00		3.00	6.80	8.80
LIF	5.97	3.00	7.00		4.00	5.00		3.30	5.10	6.80

A = working class; B = *bourgeoisie*

B 1995		
CVP	16.70	
PSB	13.60	
BSP	12.00	
PVV	11.90	
PRL	8.20	
PSC	7.80	
VB	6.60	
VU	5.90	
ECOCO	5.10	
AGALEV	4.90	
DK 1994		
SD	34.60	
V	23.30	
KF	15.00	
SF	7.30	
FRP	6.40	
RV	4.60	
SF 1995		
SDP	28.30	
KESK	19.90	
KOK	17.90	
LKP	11.20	
VIHR	6.50	
SVP	5.50	

F 1997

RPR/UDF	33.50	20.00	21.00	54.00	31.00	36.00	62.00
PS	26.00	28.00	32.00	29.00	26.00	26.00	14.00
FN	15.00	24.00	17.00	4.00	18.00	12.00	7.00
Verts	7.00	8.00	10.00	0.00	6.00	8.00	6.00
PCF	10.00	15.00	6.00	3.00	11.00	9.00	2.00

D 1994[a]

							A	B
CDU/CSU	44.30	37.20	38.60		41.10	42.60	49.50	37.40
SPD	35.70	55.90	39.40		39.80	41.40	31.90	49.20
FDP	10.60	1.10	8.00		6.00	6.90	7.80	4.20
Grünen	4.80	3.60	12.70		10.00	8.20	9.00	7.90

A = Roman Catholic; B = Protestant

GR 1996

PASOK	41.40
ND	38.10
KKE	5.60

IRL 1992

FF	39.10	36.00	34.00	42.00	37.00	37.00
FG	24.50	15.00	19.00	25.00	20.00	20.00
Lab	19.30	19.00	18.00	8.00	16.00	13.00
PD	4.70	5.00	7.00	3.00	6.00	5.00

I 1995

PDS	21.10
FI	20.60
AN	15.70
PPI	6.80
Rif	8.60
Lega Nord	10.10
CCD/CDU	5.80

1994	A	B	C	D
	19.20	42.70	28.30	16.70
	24.80	16.80	19.60	33.30
	7.40	11.40	20.40	13.90
	15.40	14.80	16.40	13.90

A = north; B = Reg. Rosse; C = mezzogiorno; D = Sicily

NL 1994

PvdA	24.00
CDA	22.20
VVD	19.90
D66	15.50
SGP	4.80

Appendix Table A.11.3 (continued)

Country/ Party	All	Manual workers	Jnr non-manual workers	Agri-cultural workers	Men	Women	Regular churchgoers	Small towns, etc.	Large towns
N 1997									
DNA	35.00								
Høyre	14.30								
SP	7.90								
KrF	13.70								
SV	6.00								
FRP	15.30								
P 1995									
PSD	34.10								
PSP	43.80								
CDS	8.60								
PP	9.10								
E									
PSOE	37.50								
PP/AP	38.80								
IU	10.60								
CiU	4.60								
S 1994									
SAP	45.40								
M	22.30								
CP	7.70								
FP	7.20								
V	6.20								
MP	5.00								
CH 1995									
FDP	16.80								
CVP	16.80								
SPS	21.80								
SVP	14.90								

UK 1997

						1992 A	1992 B	1992 C	1992 D
Cons.	31.00	24.00	37.00	31.00	32.00	45.30	54.50	33.40	35.70
Lab.	45.00	57.00	37.00	46.00	45.00	37.10	20.70	50.60	39.00
Lib. Dem.	17.00	13.00	20.00	17.00	18.00	15.10	23.40	15.60	21.50
Nat.									13.10

A = London; B = South-east; C = North; D = Scotland

JAP 1986

LDP	17.20		50.80	28.90	27.60
JSP		17.20			

USA 1992

			A	B	C	1992 A	1992 B	1992 C	D	E	F
Dem.	43.00	41.00	45.00			36.00	44.00	80.00	39.00	83.00	61.00
Rep.	38.00	38.00	38.00			46.00	36.00	11.00	41.00	10.00	25.00
Perot	19.00	21.00	17.00			18.00	20.00	9.00	20.00	7.00	14.00

A = Protestant; B = Roman Catholic; C = Jewish; D = White; E = Black; G = Hispanic

---

ª Territory of former western Federal Republic only

Abbreviations of party names:

Austria: SPÖ: Sozialistische Partei Österreich; ÖVP: Österreichische Volkspartei; FPÖ: Freiheitliche Partei Österreichs; LIF: Liberales Forum

Belgium: CVP: Christelijke Volkspartij; PSB: Partie Socialiste Belge; BSP: Belgische Socialistische Partij; PVV: Partij voor Vrijheid en Vooruitgang; PRL: Parti Réformateur Libéral; PSC: Parti Social Chrétien; VB: Vlaamse Blok; VU: Volksunie

Denmark: SD: Socialdemokratiet; V: Venstre; KF: Konservative Folkeparti; SF: Socialistisk Folkeparti; FRP: Fremskridtspartiet; RV: Radikale Venstre

Finland: SDP: Sosialidemokraattinen Puolue; KESK: Suomen Keskuste; KOK: Kansallinen Kokoomus; LKP: Liberaalinen Kansanpuolue; VIHR: Vihreä Liitto; SFP: Svenska Folkpartiet

France: UDF: Union Française Démocratique; RPR: Rassemblement pour la République; PS: Parti Socialiste; FN: Front National; PCF: Parti Communiste Français

Germany: CDU/CSU: Christliche Demokratische Union/Christliche Soziale Union; SPD: Sozialdemokratische Partei Deutschland; FDP: Freie Demokratische Partei

Greece: PASOK: Pan-Hellenic Socialist Movement; ND: New Democracy; KKE: Communist Party of Greece

Ireland: FF: Fianna Fáil; FG Fine Gael; Lab: Labour Party; PD: Progressive Democrats

Italy: PDS: Partito Democratico della Sinistra; Fl: Forza Italia; AN: Alleanza Nazionale; PPI: Partito Popolare Italiano; Rif: Rifondazione Comunista

Netherlands: PvdA: Partij van der Arbeid; CDA: Christen Demokratisch Appel; VVD: Volkspartij voor Vreiheid en Demokratie; D66: Demokraten '66; SGP: Staatkundig Gereformeerde Partij

Norway: DNA: Det Norske Arbeidparti; SP: Senterpartiet; KrF: Kristeligt Folkeparti; SV: Sosialistisk Venstreparti; FRP: Fremskritspartiet

Portugal: PSD: Partido Social Democrata; PSP: Partido Socialista Portuguesa; CDS: Partido do Centro Democratico Social; PP: Partido Popular

Spain: PSOE: Partido Socialista Obrero Español; PP/AP: Partido Popular/Alianza Popular; IU: Izquerda Unida; CiU: Convergencia y Unio

Sweden: SAP: Socialdemokratiska Arbetarpartiet; M: Moderata Samlingspartiet; CP: Centerpartiet; FP: Folkpartiet; V: Vänsterpartiet; MP: Miljöpartiet de Gröna

Switzerland: FDP: Freisinnig-demokratische Partei; CVP: Christlichdemokratische Volkspartei; SPS: Sozialdemokratische Partei der Schweiz; SVP: Schweizerische Volkspartei; GPS: Grüne Partei der Schweiz

United Kingdom: Cons.: Conservative Party; Lab.: Labour Party; Lib. Dem.: Liberal Democratic Party; Nat. various Nationalist parties

Japan: LDP: Liberal Democratic Party; JSP: Japanese Socialist Party

USA: Dem.: Democratic Party; Rep: Republican Party

Appendix Table A.11.4 Social composition of support for parties, 1990s

Country/Party	Manual workers	Jnr non-manual workers	Agri-cultural workers	Men	Women	Regular churchgoers	Small towns, etc.	Large towns
A 1995								
SPÖ	24.00	18.00		45.00	55.00			
ÖVP	10.00	21.00		46.00	54.00			
FPÖ	35.00	22.00		41.00	38.00			
Grünen	17.00	33.00		62.00	61.00			
LIF	15.00	34.00		39.00	59.00			
DK 1994								
SD	47.00	51.00						
V	32.00	63.00						
KF	15.00	67.00						
SF								
FRP	46.00	39.00						
RV								
SF 1995			A					
SDP	52.00	43.00	4.00					
KESK	27.00	38.00	35.00					
KOK	13.00	77.00	10.00					
LKP								
VIHR								
SVP								

A = farm workers

					A	B	A	B
D 1994[a]								
CDU/CSU	28.00	44.00	46.00	54.00	53.00	39.00	34.00	19.00
SPD	43.00	46.00	46.00	54.00	35.00	52.00	28.00	27.00
FDP	6.00	58.00	44.00	56.00	54.00	29.00	27.00	25.00
Grünen	13.00	46.00	52.00	48.00	44.00	37.00	16.00	28.00

A = Roman Catholic; B = Protestant

N 1993								
DNA	48.00	37.00						
Høyre	20.00	61.00						
SP	27.00	42.00						
KrF		57.00						
SV	33.00							
FRP	44.00	39.00						

JAP 1986								
LDP	18.00	30.00	28.00	28.90				
JSP	28.00	51.00	9.00	27.60				

					A	B	A	B
USA 1992								
Dem.	39.00						83.00	61.00
Rep.	41.00						10.00	25.00
Perot	20.00						7.00	14.00

A = Black; B = Hispanic

[a] Territory of former western Federal Republic only

For party abbreviations, see Appendix Table A.11.3.

Appendix Table A.13.1 Public spending on welfare, 18 countries, 1960–1995

	Year	Government final consumption (less defence) as % of GDP	Social security spending as % of GDP	(1) + (2) as % of GDP
		(1)	**(2)**	
Austria	1960			
	1965	12.17	10.66	22.83
	1970	13.61	11.53	25.14
	1975	16.13	12.30	28.43
	1980	16.82	19.03	35.85
	1985	17.67	20.38	38.05
	1990	16.80	19.87	36.66
	1994	18.10	22.03	40.12
Belgium	1960	9.43	11.35	20.78
	1965	10.15	12.41	22.56
	1970	11.18	14.08	25.25
	1975	14.07	15.98	30.05
	1980	15.07	21.79	36.86
	1985	14.35	25.26	39.60
	1990	11.76	22.90	34.66
	1995			
Denmark	1970			
	1975			
	1980	24.11	16.63	40.74
	1985	23.14	16.32	39.46
	1990	23.20	18.36	41.56
	1995	23.42	21.55	44.96
Finland	1960	11.17	5.81	16.98
	1965	12.90	7.02	19.92
	1970	14.37	7.40	21.77
	1975	17.06	8.78	25.85
	1980	16.70	8.73	25.44
	1985	18.82	10.81	29.63
	1990	21.15	15.44	36.59
	1995	20.28	23.69	43.96
France	1970	10.44	17.04	27.48
	1975	11.42	15.95	27.36
	1980	15.13	14.49	29.62
	1985	16.17	22.07	38.24
	1990	14.96	21.31	36.27
	1995	16.41	23.22	39.63
Germany	1960	10.34	12.06	22.40
	1965	11.33	12.31	23.64
	1970	13.00	12.20	25.20
	1975	17.71	16.28	34.00
	1980	17.50	16.61	34.11
	1985	17.24	16.14	33.38
	1990	16.20	15.22	31.42
	1994	16.02	16.19	32.21

Government final consumption as % of GDP				Total spending as % of GDP			
education	health	welfare	housing	education	health	welfare	housing
2.67	3.35	12.24	0.42				
3.49	4.07	13.37	0.43				
3.80	4.53	20.10	0.35				
4.16	4.44	23.86	0.03				
3.97	4.60	23.12	−0.02				
4.31	5.15	25.34	−0.04				
5.23		14.91					
6.74		19.86					
7.15		25.00					
6.12	0.46	26.21	0.22	7.68	6.08	20.91	1.30
6.03	5.49	21.97	0.36	8.08	5.79	21.28	1.56
5.47	4.89	21.76	0.33	6.75	5.20	21.28	0.92
5.37	4.84	24.22	0.18	6.90	5.12	23.26	0.81
5.60	4.99	28.26	0.19	7.29	5.27	27.48	1.02
5.01	3.81	10.83	0.66				
4.78	3.86	11.04	0.63				
5.05	4.57	13.94	0.71				
5.20	4.68	18.94	0.67				
5.97	4.70	27.10	0.53				
4.98	3.19	23.64	1.15	5.60	9.87	18.08	3.49
4.63	3.06	22.71	1.14	5.34	7.30	19.55	3.18
5.16	3.44	26.66	1.36				
2.86	3.89	13.40	0.35	3.99	4.22	15.21	1.17
3.94	6.10	17.91	0.41	5.37	6.55	20.47	1.27
4.09	6.12	18.33	0.39	5.15	6.57	19.26	1.45
3.95	6.00	18.17	0.31	4.54	6.36	19.03	1.10
3.54	5.62	17.33	0.30	4.12	5.96	17.77	1.13

Appendix Table A.13.1 (continued)

	Year	Government final consumption (less defence) as % of GDP (1)	Social security spending as % of GDP (2)	(1) + (2) as % of GDP
Greece	1960	7.26	5.59	12.85
	1965	8.15	7.03	15.17
	1970	8.00	7.97	15.96
	1975	8.42	7.43	15.85
	1980	10.63	9.21	19.84
	1985	14.12	14.85	28.97
	1990	15.78	14.83	30.61
	1994	*14.71*	13.53	28.24
Ireland	1970	14.79	9.27	24.06
	1975	19.00	13.14	32.15
	1980	19.87	12.60	32.48
	1985	18.55	16.49	35.05
	1990	15.73	14.08	29.81
	1994	15.48	14.58	30.06
Italy	1960	*10.17*	13.30	23.47
	1965	*12.50*	14.83	27.33
	1970	10.66	15.11	25.77
	1975	11.70	20.21	31.91
	1980	13.05	14.11	27.16
	1985	14.37	17.16	31.53
	1990	15.51	18.15	33.66
	1995	14.58	3.21	17.79
Netherlands	1960	9.51	8.60	18.11
	1965	11.68	11.55	23.23
	1970	12.94	14.62	27.56
	1975	15.13	19.06	34.19
	1980			
	1985			
	1990	*11.46*	19.62	31.08
	1995	*11.32*	19.68	31.00
Norway	1970	11.82	13.84	25.66
	1975	13.71	18.37	32.08
	1980	42.24	14.37	56.61
	1985	16.88	14.76	31.63
	1990	19.36	19.53	38.89
	1995	*17.58*	15.79	33.37
Portugal	1960	6.76	2.95	9.71
	1965	5.54	3.97	9.51
	1970	7.05	3.11	10.16
	1975	10.96	8.57	19.53
	1980	19.40	6.64	26.04
	1985	28.04	6.81	34.85
	1990	12.57	10.95	23.52
	1993	16.18	14.17	30.35

Government final consumption as % of GDP				Total spending as % of GDP			
education	health	welfare	housing	education	health	welfare	housing
1.89	1.01	8.13	0.80				
1.93	1.14	7.58	0.63				
2.18	1.66	9.43	0.33				
2.98	2.02	15.18	0.12				
3.29	2.50	15.14	0.07				
3.85	3.08	0.89	0.37				
4.40	3.73	1.03	0.45				
4.27	3.14	0.58	0.41	4.91	5.24	13.19	1.10
4.63	3.08	0.72	0.52	5.08	5.42	15.98	1.88
4.91	3.50	0.75	0.49	5.33	6.30	16.63	1.41
4.25	3.18	0.68	0.51	4.67	5.41	17.88	1.17
4.86	2.41	0.86	0.17				
5.35	3.59	1.42	0.07				
5.04	4.05	1.64	−0.01	6.43	6.53	13.87	1.51
4.81	4.30	1.63	−0.04	5.90	6.22	14.47	0.53
5.41	4.73	2.10	−0.10	7.00	7.08	19.23	0.69
2.15	1.62	0.55	0.17	2.79	2.67	6.22	0.89
2.92	2.65	0.56	0.21	3.44	2.99	7.99	1.38
4.59	2.86	0.66	0.31	5.83	4.29	10.08	0.91
5.42	3.36	0.63	0.48	7.01	5.11	12.40	1.21

Appendix Table A.13.1 (continued)

	Year	Government final consumption (less defence) as % of GDP (1)	Social security spending as % of GDP (2)	(1) + (2) as % of GDP
Spain	1970	8.91	5.59	14.49
	1975	9.94	7.50	17.44
	1980			
	1985	12.76	15.96	28.72
	1990	14.06	15.88	29.93
	1995	16.61	17.34	33.95
Sweden	1965	13.60	9.18	22.78
	1970	17.92	11.24	29.16
	1975	21.20	15.81	37.01
	1980	26.07	17.60	43.68
	1985	24.96	18.22	43.18
	1990	24.58	19.98	44.57
	1994	25.21	24.77	49.98
Switzerland	1960	8.84	3.85	12.70
	1965	10.49	5.07	15.56
	1970	10.48	6.25	16.74
	1975	12.62	10.14	22.75
	1980	12.73	12.67	25.40
	1985	13.35	13.75	27.09
	1990	13.44	13.55	26.99
	1995	15.03	19.45	34.48
UK	1960	10.26	6.92	17.18
	1965	11.00	7.57	18.57
	1970	12.90	8.71	21.61
	1975	17.40	10.25	27.65
	1980	19.03	13.67	32.69
	1985	15.72	13.90	29.62
	1990	15.99	12.21	28.19
	1995	17.36	14.67	32.03
Japan	1965	*7.57*	4.79	12.36
	1970	*6.51*	4.61	11.12
	1975	*9.06*	7.71	16.77
	1980	9.18	10.07	19.25
	1985	8.76	10.90	19.66
	1990	8.38	11.50	4.45
	1995	9.02	13.38	8.82
USA	1960	8.57	5.25	13.82
	1965	9.69	5.42	15.11
	1970	11.53	7.41	19.45
	1975	13.22	11.54	24.76
	1980	*11.59*	10.83	22.42
	1985	*12.12*	10.86	22.98
	1990	*11.85*	11.26	23.11
	1995	*10.02*	13.08	23.10

Note: Figures in italics are provisional.

Government final consumption as % of GDP				Total spending as % of GDP			
education	health	welfare	housing	education	health	welfare	housing
1.15	0.71	1.49	0.35				
1.37	1.26	1.31	0.34				
2.63	3.47	1.61	0.86	3.75	4.67	14.78	2.02
2.98	3.71	1.66	0.90	4.17	5.11	14.86	2.29
5.32	4.83	2.32	0.50				
5.38	6.11	3.14	0.51				
5.90	7.30	4.81	0.57				
5.65	6.66	4.70	0.33				
5.23	6.55	5.24	0.49				
5.32	4.82	5.97	0.48				
4.98	5.55	1.59	0.80	6.45	5.88	14.48	3.63
3.80	4.71	1.44	0.67	4.85	5.02	14.73	2.08
3.67	4.71	1.52	0.60	4.87	5.04	13.06	2.05
4.48	5.72	1.88	0.61	5.35	5.81	16.64	1.63
2.82	0.35	0.30	0.29				
3.86	0.42	0.49	0.53				
3.76	0.38	0.50	0.58				
3.51	0.38	0.54	0.56				
3.23	0.40	0.55	0.57				
3.25	0.45	0.66	0.68				
4.57	0.92	0.37	0.48				
5.20	1.19	0.56	0.58				
4.56	1.06	0.60	0.54				

Source: OECD *National Income and Expenditures* (various years).

REFERENCES

Abbalea, F. (1992), 'Les Failles de la protection sociale en Europe: Problématique générale', *Recherche Sociale*, 121: 3–11.

Abercrombie, N. (1970), 'Superstition and Religion: The God of the Gaps', in D. A. Martin (ed.), *A Sociological Yearbook of Religion in Britain*, Vol. 3 (London: SCM Press), 93–129.

Acquaviva, S. (1972), 'Italy', in Mol (1972), q.v.

Alba, R., Handl, J., and Müller, W. (1994), 'Ethnischer Ungleichheit im deutschen Bildungssystem', *Kölner Zeitschrift für Soziologie und Sozialpsychologie*, 46/2: 209–38.

Albert, M. (1991), *Capitalisme contre capitalisme* (Paris: Seuil).

Albert-Lorca, M. (1994), 'Renouveau de la religion locale en Espagne', in Davie and Hervieu-Léger (1994), q.v.

Allmendinger, J., and Hinz, T. (1997), 'Mobilität und Lebenslauf', in Hradil and Immerfall (1997*b*), q.v., 248–85.

Almerich, P. (1972), 'Spain', in Mol (1972), q.v.

Altieri, G., and Villa, P. (1991), *La Position des femmes sur le marché du travail en Italie: Evolution entre 1983 et 1989* (Brussels: Equal Opportunities Unit of the European Commission).

Alund, A., and Schierup, C.-U. (1991), *Paradoxes of Multiculturalism* (Aldershot: Avebury).

Alwin, D. F., Bruan, M., and Scott, J. (1992), 'The Separation of Work and the Family: Attitudes towards Women's Labour-Force Participation in Germany, Great Britain, and the United States', *European Sociological Review*, 8/1: 13–37.

Amin, A., and Thrift, N. (eds.) (1994), *Globalization, Institutions, and Regional Development in Europe* (Oxford: Clarendon Press).

Amsden, J. (1972), *Collective Bargaining and Class Conflict in Spain* (London: LSE and Weidenfeld & Nicolson).

Andersen, J. G., and Bjørklund, T. (1994), 'Strukturische Wandel, neue Konfliktlinien und die Parteien', in Pappi and Schmitt (1994), q.v.

Anderson, B. (1983, 1991), *Imagined Communities*, 2nd edn. 1991 (London: Verso).

Anderson, M., Bechhofer, F., and Gershuny, J. (eds.) (1994), *The Social and Political Economy of the Household* (Oxford: Oxford University Press).

—— —— and Kendrick, S. (1994), 'Individual and Household Strategies', in M. Anderson, Bechhofer, and Gershuny (1994), q.v.

Aoki, M., and Dore, R. (1994), *The Japanese Firm* (Oxford: Clarendon Press).

Appelbaum, E., and Albin, P. (1990), 'Differential Characteristics of Employment Growth in Service Industries', in Appelbaum and Schettkat (1990), q.v.

—— and Schettkat, R. (eds.) (1990), *Labour Market Adjustments to Structural Change and Technological Progress* (New York: Praeger).

Arcq, E. (1997), 'Les Relations collectives du travail en Belgique', in Observatoire Social Européen, *Vers un pacte social européen?* (Brussels: Observatoire Social Européen).

Ariès, P. (1980), 'Two Successive Motivations for Declining Birth Rates in the West', *Population and Development Review*, 6: 645–50.

Ariza, J. (1976), *Comisiones Obreras* (Barcelona: Avance).

Armingeon, K. (1987), 'Gewerkschaften in der Bundesrepublik Deutschland 1950–1985: Mitglieder, Organisation und Aussenbeziehungen', *Politische Vierteljahresschrift*, 28/15.

Armingeon, K. (1988), *Die Entwicklung der westdeutschen Gewerkschaften, 1950–1985* (Frankfurt am Main: Campus).

Arts, W., and Hermkens, P. (1994), 'De eerlijke verdeling van huishoudelijketaken: percepties en oordelen', *Mens en Maatschappij*, 69/2.

Assimakopoulou, Z. (1998), 'The Development of Small Business Policy in Britain 1970–1990', Ph.D. thesis (Florence: European University Institute).

Atkinson, A. B. (1996), 'Income Distribution in Europe and the United States', *Oxford Review of Economic Policy*, 12/1: 15–28.

—— Rainwater, L., and Smeeding, T. (1995), *Income Distribution in European Countries*, Working Paper 9535 (Cambridge: University of Cambridge, Department of Applied Economics).

Austria (1994), *Österreichisches Statistisches Jahrbuch 1994* (Vienna: Austrian Government Publications).

Ayala, L. (1994), 'Social Needs, Inequality and the Welfare State in Spain: Trends and Prospects', *Journal of European Social Policy*, 4/3: 159–79.

Bagnasco, A. (1977), *Tre Italie: la problematica territoriale dello sviluo italiano* (Bologna: Il Mulino).

—— (1988), *La costruzione soziale del mercato* (Bologna: Il Mulino).

—— (1990), 'The Informal Economy', *Current Sociology*, 38: 157–74.

Barou, J. (1994), *Le Processus de ségrégation* (Paris).

Barreto, J. (1998), 'Portugal: Industrial Relations under Democracy', in Ferner and Hyman (1998), q.v., 395–425.

Bartolini, S. (forthcoming), *The Class Cleavage: The Political Mobilisation of the European Left, 1860–1980* (Cambridge: Cambridge University Press).

Baumol, W. (1967), 'Macroeconomics of Unbalanced Growth', *American Economic Review*, 57/3: 415–26.

Bax, E. (1990), *Modernization and Cleavage in Dutch Society* (Aldershot: Avebury).

Becattini, G. (ed.) (1987), *Mercato e forze locali: il distretto industriale* (Bologna: Il Mulino).

Beck, U. (1986), *Risikogesellschaft: Auf dem Weg in eine andere Moderne* (Frankfurt am Main: Suhrkamp).

—— Giddens, A., and Lash, S. (1994), *Reflexive Modernization: Politics, Tradition and Aesthetics in the Modern Social Order* (Cambridge: Polity).

Becker, G. S. (1974, 1981), *A Treatise on the Family* (Cambridge, Mass.: Harvard University Press).

Beckford, J. A., and Luckmann, T. (eds.) (1989), *The Changing Face of Religion* (London: Sage).

Beets, G., Liefbroer, A., and de Jong Giervekd, J. (1994), 'Het combineren van ouderschap en betaald werk: een longitudinale studie naar intensites en gedrag', *Mens en Maatschappij*, 69/2.

Bell, D. (1974), *The Coming of Post-Industrial Society: A Venture in Social Forecasting* (London: Heinemann).

—— (1976), *The Cultural Contradictions of Capitalism* (London: Heinemann).

Bendix, R. (1956), *Work and Authority in Industry: Ideologies of Management in the Course of Industrialization* (New York: Wiley).

—— (1977), *Nation Building and Citizenship: Studies of our Changing Social Order*, 2nd edn. (Berkeley: University of California Press).

Berger, J. (1990), 'Market and State in Advanced Capitalist Societies', *Current Sociology*, 38/2–3: 103–32.

Berger, P. (1989), 'Ungleichheitssemantiken. Graduelle Unterschiede und kategoriale Exklusivitäten', *Archives européennes de sociologie*, 30: 48–60.

Berger, S. and Dore, R. (eds.) (1996), *National Diversity and Global Capitalism* (Ithaca, NY: Cornell University Press).

—— and Piore, M. J. (1980), *Dualism and Discontinuity in Industrial Societies* (Cambridge: Cambridge University Press).

Berggren, C. (1991), *Von Ford zu Volvo: Automobilherstellung in Schweden* (Berlin: Springerverlag).

Berglund, S., and Lindström, U. (1978), *The Scandinavian Party System(S): A Comparative Study* (Lund: Student-Litteratur).

Bergmann, J. (1985), 'Gewerkschaften—Organisationstruktur und Mitgliederinteressen', in Endruweit *et al.* (1985), q.v.

Bernhardt, E. M. (1993), 'Changing Family Ties, Women's Position, and Low Fertility', in Federici, Mason, and Sogner (1993), q.v.

Bernstein, B. (1970), *Language and Social Classes: Socio-Linguistic Codes and Social Control* (London: RKP).

Bertaux, D., and Delcroix, C. (1992), 'Where Have All the Daddies Gone?', in Björnberg (1992*c*), q.v.

Bertilsson, M. (1990), 'The Welfare State, the Professions and Citizens', in Torstendahl and Burrage (1990), q.v.

Best, M. (1990), *The New Competition* (Oxford: Polity).

Beveridge, W. (1942), *Full Employment in a Free Society: A Report* (London: HMSO).

Bianchi, P. (1995), 'Italy: The Crisis of an Introvert State', in Hayward (1995), q.v.

—— and Giordani, M. (1993), 'Innovation Policy at the Local and National Levels: The Case of Emilia-Romagna', *European Planning Studies*, 1: 25–41.

—— and Gualtieri, G. (1990), 'Emilia-Romagna and its Industrial Districts: The Evolution of a Model', in R. Leonardi and R. Nanetti (eds.), *The Regions and European Integration: The Case of Emilia-Romagna* (London: Pinter).

Bimbi, F. (1992), 'Parenting in Italy: Asymmetric Relationships and Family Affection', in Björnberg (1992*c*), q.v.

Bishop, J. A., Chow, K. V., and Formby, J. P. (1993), *The Redistributive Effect of Direct Taxes: An International Comparison of Six Luxembourg Income Study Countries*, Working Paper 93 (Luxembourg: Luxembourg Income Study).

Björnberg, U. (1992*a*), 'Parenting in Transition: An Introduction and a Summary', in Björnberg (1992*c*), q.v.

—— (1992*b*), 'Parents' Ideals and their Strategies in Daily Swedish Life', in Björnberg (1992*c*), q.v.

—— (ed.) (1992*c*), *European Parents in the 1990s* (New Brunswick: Transactions).

Black, A. (1984), *Guilds and Civil Society in European Political Thought from the Twelfth Century to the Present* (London: Methuen).

Black, D. (1982), *Inequalities in Health*, ed. P. Townsend and N. Davidson (Harmondsworth: Penguin).

Blackburn, R., and Marsh, C. (1991), 'Education and Social Class: Revisiting the 1944 Education Act with Fixed Marginals', *British Journal of Sociology*, 42: 213–47.

Blanchet, D., and Ekert-Jaffé, O. (1997), 'The Demographic Impact of Family Benefits: Evidence from a Micro-Model and from Macro-Data', in Ermisch and Ogawa (1997), q.v.

Blossfeld, H.-P. (1993), 'Changes in Educational Opportunities in the Federal Republic of Germany: A Longitudinal Study of Cohorts Born between 1916 and 1965', in Shavit and Blossfeld (1993), q.v.

—— and Hakim, K. (eds.) (1997), *Between Equalization and Marginalization: Women Working Part-Time in Europe and the United States of America* (Oxford: Clarendon Press).

—— and Jänichen, U. (1990), 'Educational Expansion and Changes in Women's Entry into Marriage and Motherhood in the Federal Republic of Germany', EUI Working Papers in political and social sciences, SPS 90/2 (Florence: EUI).

—— and Shavit, Y. (1993), 'Persisting Barriers: Change in Educational Opportunities in Thirteen Countries', in Shavit and Blossfeld (1993), q.v.

—— Giannelli, G., and Mayer, K. U. (1993), 'Is There a New Service Proletariat? The Tertiary Sector and Social Inequality in Germany', in Esping-Andersen (1993*b*), q.v.

Blossfeld, H.-P., De Rose, A., Hoem, J. M., and Rohwer, G. (1995), 'Education, Modernization, and the Risk of Marriage Disruption in Sweden, West Germany and Italy', in Mason and Jensen (1995), q.v.

Böckler, S. (1991), *Kapitalismus und Moderne: Zur Theorie fordistischer Modernisierung* (Opladen: Westdeutscher Verlag).

Boegenhold, D., and Staber, U. (1991), 'The Decline and Rise of Self-Employment', *Work, Employment and Society*, 5/2: 223–39.

Bogensberger, H., and Zulehner, P. (1972), 'Austria', in Mol (1972), q.v.

Boh, K. (1989), 'European Family Patterns—a Reappraisal', in Boh *et al.* (1989), q.v.

—— Bak, M., Clason, C., Pankratova, M., Qvortrup, J., Sgritta, G. B., and Waerness, K. (eds.) (1989), *Changing Patterns of European Family Life* (London: Routledge).

Bourdieu, P. (1979), *La Distinction: Critique sociale du jugement* (Paris: Editions de Minuit).

—— (1993), 'Deux impérialismes de l'universel', in C. Fauré and T. Bishop (eds.), *L'Améreique des Français* (Paris: François Bourin).

—— and Passeron, J.-C. (1964), *Les Héritiers: Les Étudiants et la culture* (Paris: Editions de Minuit).

—— —— (1970), *La Reproduction: Les Fonctions du système d'enseignement* (Paris: Editions du Minuit).

Bouverne de Bie, M. (1994), 'Overheid, Ouders, Kinderen en Jongeren', *Tijdschrift voor Sociale Wetenschappen*, 39/3: 263–75.

Bowles, S., and Gintis, H. (1976), *Schooling in Capitalist America* (London: Routledge).

Boyer, R. (1984), *Wage Labor, Capital Accumulation and the Crisis, 1968–1982* (Paris: CEPREMAP).

—— (1988), *The Search for Labour Market Flexibility* (Oxford: Clarendon Press).

—— (1991), *New Directions in Management Practices and Work Organization* (Paris: CEPREMAP).

—— (1992), 'Le Capitalism français et ses concurrents: 1945–1991: Du miracle au blocage', in idem, *L'État de la France 1993–94* (Paris: La Découverte).

—— (1997), 'French Statism at the Crossroads', in Crouch and Streeck (1997), q.v.

—— and Hollingsworth, J. R. (eds.) (1997), *Contemporary Capitalism: The Embeddedness of Institutions* (Cambridge: Cambridge University Press).

—— and Saillard, Y. (1995), *Théorie de la régulation: L'État des savoirs* (Paris: La Découverte).

Bozon, M. (1990), 'Mariage et mobilité sociale en France', *Population*, 7: 171–90.

—— (1991), 'Les Enjeux des relations entre générations à la fin de l'adolescence', *Population*, 6.

Bradbury, M. (1993), *Male Pre- and Post-Tax Wage Inequality*, Working Paper 90 (Luxembourg: Luxembourg Income Study).

Brande, A. Van Den (1973), 'Voluntary Associations in the Belgian Political System', *Res Publica*, 15/2: 329–56.

Braud, P. (1973), *Le Comportement electoral en France* (Paris: Presses Universitaires de France).

Braverman, H. (1974), *Labor and Monopoly Capital* (New York: Monthly Review Press).

Breen, R., and Whelan, C. P. (1992), 'Social Class, Class Origins and Political Partisanship in the Republic of Ireland', *European Journal of Political Research*, 26/2: 117–33.

—— —— (1993), 'From Ascription to Achievement? Origins, Education and Entry to the Labour Force in the Republic of Ireland during the Twentieth Century', *Acta Sociologica*, 36: 3–18.

Breitschneider, J. *et al.* (1988), *Handbuch einkommens-, vermögens- und sozialpolitischer Daten* (Cologne: Bachem).

Brizay, B. (1975), *Le Patronat: Histoire, structure, stratégie* (Paris: Seuil).

Brown, C. G. (1992), 'A Revisionist Approach to Religious Change', in Bruce (1992), q.v.

Bruce, S. (ed.) (1992), *Religion and Modernization: Sociologists and Historians Debate the Secularization Thesis* (Oxford: Clarendon Press).

Brusco, S. (1992), 'Small Firms and the Provision of Real Services', in Pyke and Sengenberger, (1992), q.v.

Buchmann, M., Charles, M., with Sacchi, S. (1993), 'The Lifelong Shadow: Social Origins and Educational Opportunities in Switzerland', in Shavit and Blossfeld (1993), q.v.

Büchtemann, C., and Quack, S. (1989), 'Bridges or Traps? Non-Standard Employment in the Federal Republic of Germany', WZB Discussion Paper FIS 89: 6 (Berlin: WZB).

Bull, M. J. (1988), 'From Pluralism to Pluralism: Italy and the Corporatism Debate', in A. Cox and N. O'Sullivan (eds.), *The Corporate State* (Aldershot: Elgar).

Burchell, B. J., Dale, A., and Joshi, H. (1997), 'Part-Time Work among British Women', in Blossfeld and Hakim (1997), q.v., 210–46.

Burgalassi, S., Martelli, S., and Prandi, C. (1992), *Immagini della religiosità in Italia* (Milan: Angeli).

Burrage, M. (1990), 'The Professions in Society and History', in Burrage and Torstendahl (1990), q.v.

—— and Torstendahl, R. (eds.) (1990), *Professions in Theory and History* (London: Sage).

Caciagli, M., and Spreafico, A. (eds.) (1990), *Vent'anni di elezioni in Italia: 1968–1987* (Bologna: Liviana).

Calmfors, L., and Driffill, J. (1988), 'Bargaining Structure, Corporatism and Macroeconomic Performance', *Economic Policy*, 6.

Campiche, R. J. (1972), 'Switzerland', in Mol (1972), q.v.

—— (1994), 'Dilution ou recomposition? Confession en Suisse', in Davie and Hervieu-Léger (1994), q.v.

Capecchi, V. (1968), *Il Comportamento elletorale in Italia* (Bologna: Il Mulino).

Carty, R. K. (1981), *Party and Parish Pump: Electoral Politics in Ireland* (Waterloo: Wilfrid Laurier).

Cassis, Y. (1997), *Big Business: The European Experience in the Twentieth Century* (Oxford: Oxford University Press).

Castells, M. (1996), *The Rise of Network Society* (Oxford: Blackwell).

Castillo, J. J. (1990), 'Informatización, trabajo, y empleo en las pequeñas empresas españolas', *Revista Española de Investigaciones Sociológicas*, 49: 161–89.

—— and Victoria Jiménez, M. (1991), 'Nuevas formas de organización del trabajo y de implicación directa en España', *Revista Española de Investigaciones Sociológicas*, 56: 115–41.

Castles, F. G., and Flood, M. (1993a), 'Why Divorce Rates Differ: Law, Religious Belief and Modernity', in Castles and Flood (1993b), q.v.

—— —— (eds.) (1993b), *Families of Nations: Patterns of Public Policy in Western Democracies* (Aldershot: Dartmouth).

—— and Mitchell, D. (1991), *Three Worlds of Welfare Capitalism or Four?*, Working Paper 63 (Luxembourg: Luxembourg Income Study).

—— —— (1993), 'Worlds of Welfare and Families of Nations', in Castles and Flood (1993b), q.v.

Castles, S., and Miller, M. J. (1993), *The Age of Migration* (London: Macmillan).

Cavalli, A., and de Lillo, A. (1993), *Giovani anni 90* (Bologna: Il Mulino).

Cawson, A. (1986), *Corporatism and Political Theory* (Oxford: Blackwell).

CBS (Centraal Bureau voor de Statistiek) (1993), 'Sociale Kerncijfer', *Mens en Maatschappij*, 68/2: 186–90.

CEVF (Centre d'Étude de la Vie Française) (1971), *Les Élections législatives de mars 1967* (Paris: Colin).

Chadwick, B. A., Gauthier, M., Hourmant, L., and Wörndl, B. (1994), 'Trends in Religion and Secularization', in Langlois (1994), q.v.

Chafetz, J. S. (1995), 'Chicken or Egg? A Theory of the Relationship between Feminist Movements and Family Change', in Mason and Jensen (1995), q.v.

Chagas Lopes, M., Ferreira, C., and Perista, H. (1991), *La Position des femmes sur le marché du travail au*

Portugal: Evolution entre 1983 et 1989 (Brussels: Equal Opportunities Unit of the European Commission).

Chandler, A. (1977), *The Visible Hand: The Managerial Revolution in American Business* (Cambridge, Mass.: Harvard University Press).

Chapman, M. (ed.) (1993), *Social and Biological Aspects of Ethnicity* (Oxford: Oxford University Press).

Charles, M., and Höpflinger, F. (1992), 'Gender, Culture and the Division of Household Labor: A Replication of US Studies for the Case of Switzerland', *Journal of Comparative Family Studies*, 23/3: 375–88.

Chesnais, J.-C. (1992), *The Demographic Transition* (Oxford: Clarendon Press).

Chew, D. H. (ed.) (1997), *Studies in International Corporate Finance and Governance Systems: A Comparison of the U.S., Japan, & Europe* (Oxford: Oxford University Press).

Cigno, A. J. (1997), 'Economic Considerations in the Timing of Births: Theory and Evidence', in Ermisch and Ogawa (1997), q.v.

Cipriani, R. (1989), ' "Diffused Religion" and New Values in Italy', in Beckford and Luckmann (1989), q.v.

Clark, C. (1940), *The Conditions of Economic Progress* (London: Macmillan).

Clarke, L. (1992), 'Children's Family Circumstances: Recent Trends in Great Britain', *European Journal of Population*, 8/4: 309–40.

—— and Henwood, M. (1997), 'Great Britain: The Lone Parent as the New Norm?', in Kaufmann *et al.* (1997), q.v., 155–94.

Clayton, R., and Pontusson, J. (1998), 'The New Politics of the Welfare State Revisited: Welfare Reforms, Public-Sector Restructuring and Inegalitarian Trends in Advanced Capitalist Societies', EUI Working Papers of the Robert Schuman Centre; RSC 98/26 (Florence: European University Institute).

Clegg, H. A. (1972), *The System of Industrial Relations in Great Britain* (Oxford: Blackwell).

—— (1975), 'Pluralism in Industrial Relations', *British Journal of Industrial Relations*, 13/3.

—— (1979), *The Changing System of Industrial Relations in Great Britain* (Oxford: Blackwell).

Coase, R. (1937), 'The Nature of the Firm', *Economica*, 4: 386–405.

Cobalti, A., and Schizzerotto, A. (1993), 'Inequality of Educational Opportunity in Italy', in Shavit and Blossfeld (1993), q.v.

Coen, D. (1996), 'The Large Firm as a Political Actor in the European Union', Ph.D. thesis (Florence: European University Institute).

Cohen, E. (1995), 'France: National Champions in Search of a Mission', in Hayward (1995), q.v.

Coleman, D. (1996a), 'New Patterns and Trends in European Fertility: International and Sub-National Comparisons', in Coleman (1996b), q.v.

—— (ed.) (1996b), *Europe's Population in the 1990s* (Oxford: Oxford University Press).

Collidà, A. (1972), 'L'Intersind', in Collidà (ed.), *La Patronata Italiana* (Bari: Laterza).

Collins, R. (1979), *The Credential Society* (New York: Academic Press).

—— (1990a), 'Market Closure and the Conflict Theory of the Professions', in Burrage and Torstendahl (1990), q.v.

—— (1990b), 'Changing Conceptions of the Sociology of the Professions', in Torstendahl and Burrage (1990), q.v.

Comte, A. (1844), *Discours sur l'esprit positif* (Paris: Carilian-Goeury).

Contini, G. (1985), 'Politics, Law and Shop-Floor Bargaining in Post-War Italy', in S. Tolliday and J. Zeitlin (eds.), *Shopfloor Bargaining and the State* (Cambridge: Cambridge University Press).

Cooke, P., and Morgan, K. (1994), 'Growth Regions under Duress: Renewal Strategies in Baden-Württemberg and Emilia-Romagna', in Amin and Thrift (1994), q.v.

—— —— (1998), *The Associational Economy: Firms, Regions, and Innovation* (Oxford: Oxford University Press).

Coriat, B. (1979), *L'Atelier et le chronomètre* (Paris: Christian Bourgois).

Cotts Watkins, S. (1991), *From Provinces into Nations: Demographic Integration in Western Europe 1870–1960* (Princeton: Princeton University Press).

Coutrot, L., Fournier, I., Kieffer, A., and Lelièvre, E. (1997), 'The Family Cycle and the Growth of Part-Time Female Employment in France: Boon or Doom?', in Blossfeld and Hakim (1997), q.v., 133–63.

Crompton, R., and Jones, G. (1984), *White-Collar Proletariat: Deskilling and Gender in Clerical Work* (London: Macmillan).

Crouch, C. (1977), *Class Conflict and the Industrial Relations Crisis* (London: Heinemann).

—— (1990), 'Trade Unions in the Exposed Sector: Their Influence on Neo-Corporatist Behaviour', in R. Brunetta and C. Dell'Aringa (eds.), *Labour Relations and Economic Performance* (London: Macmillan and International Economics Association), 68–91.

—— (1993), *Industrial Relations and European State Traditions* (Oxford: Clarendon Press).

—— (1994), 'Incomes Policies, Institutions and Markets: An Overview of Recent Developments', in R. Dore, R. Boyer, and Z. Mars (eds.), *The Return of Incomes Policy* (London: Pinter).

—— (1996), 'The Social Contract and the Problem of the Firm', EUI Working Paper RSC No 96/46 (Florence: EUI).

—— (1998), 'Labour Market Regulations, Social Policy and Job Creation', in J. Gual (ed.), *Job Creation: The Role of Labour Market Institutions* (London: Elgar).

—— (2000*a*), 'National Wage Determination and European Monetary Union', in Crouch (2000*b*), q.v.

—— (ed.) (2000*b*), *After the Euro: Shaping Institutions for Governance in the Wake of European Monetary Union* (Oxford: Oxford University Press).

—— and Pizzorno, A. (eds.) (1978), *The Resurgence of Class Conflict in Western Europe since 1968* Vol I: *National Studies* and Vol II: *Comparative Analyses* (London: Macmillan).

—— and Streeck, W. (eds.) (1997), *Political Economy of Modern Capitalism: Mapping Convergence and Diversity* (London: Sage).

—— and Traxler, F. (eds.) (1995), *Organized Industrial Relations in Europe: What Future?* (Aldershot: Avebury).

—— Finegold, D., and Sako, M. (1999), *Are Skills the Answer? The Political Economy of Skill Creation in Advanced Industrial Countries* (Oxford: Oxford Univiersity Press).

Cully, M., O'Reilly, A., Millward, N., and Forth, J. (1998), *The 1998 Workplace Industrial Relations Survey: First Findings* (London: Department of Trade and Industry).

Currie, R. (1979), *Industrial Politics* (Oxford: Clarendon Press).

Cyba, S. (1987), 'Arbeitsbedingungen und berufliche Wertorientierungen', in Haller and Holm (1987), q.v., 37–80.

Daalder, H. (1971), 'On Building Consociational Nations: The Cases of the Netherlands and Switzerland', *International Social Science Journal*, 23/3: 355–70

—— (1974), 'The Consociational Democracy Theme', *World Politics*, 26/4: 604–21.

—— (ed.) (1987), *Party Systems in Denmark, Austria, Switzerland, the Netherlands, Belgium* (London: Pinter).

Dahl, R. A. (1961), *Who Governs? Democracy and Power in an American City* (New Haven: Yale University Press).

Dahlström, E. (1989), 'Theories and Ideologies of Family Functions, Gender Relations and Human Reproduction', in Boh *et al.* (1989), q.v.

Dahrendorf, R. (1957, 1959), *Soziale Klassen und Klassenkonflikt in der industriellen Gesellschaft*; in English (1959) as *Class and Class Conflict in an Industrial Society* (London: Routledge).

—— (1988), *The Modern Social Conflict: An Essay on the Politics of Liberty* (London: Weidenfeld & Nicolson).

Dalton, R. J., and Kuechler, M. (eds.) (1990), *Challenging the Political Order: New Social Movements in Western Democracies* (Cambridge: Polity).

Daly, M. (1996), 'The Gender Division of Welfare: The British and German Welfare States Compared', Ph.D. thesis (Florence: European University Institute).

Davie, G. (1994), 'Contrastes dans l'héritage religieux de l'Europe', in Davie and Hervieu-Léger (1994), q.v.

—— and Hervieu-Léger, D. (eds.) (1994), *Identités religieuses en Europe* (Paris: La Découverte).

Davies, N. (1997), *Europe: A History* (Oxford: Oxford University Press).

De Carlini, L. (1972), 'La Confindustria', in A. Collidà (ed.), *La Politica del padronato italiano* (Bari: De Donato).

Déchaux, J.-H. (1994), 'Les Trois Composants de l'économie cachée de la parenté: L'Exemple français', *Recherches Sociologiques*, 25/3: 37–52.

De Deken, J. (1995), 'The Politics of Solidarity and the Structuration of Social Policy Regimes in Postwar Europe', Ph.D. thesis (Florence: European University Institute).

Defourny, J. (1994), 'L'Associatif au carrefour des économies formelle et informelle', *Recherches Sociologiques*, 25/3: 109–30.

De Graaf, P., and Ganzeboom, H. (1990), 'Intergenerational Education Mobility in the Netherlands for Birth Cohorts from 1891 through 1960', *Netherlands Journal of Social Sciences*, 26/1: 35–50.

—— —— (1993), 'Family Background and Educational Attainment in the Netherlands for the 1891–1960 Birth Cohorts', in Shavit and Blossfeld (1993), q.v.

De Hoog, K. (1994), 'Le Travail informel, l'État-providence et les femmes: Le Cas des Pays-Bas', *Recherches Sociologiques*, 25/3: 53–65.

De Jong, J., Liefbroer, A., and Beekink, E. (1991), The Effect of Parental Resources on Patterns of Leaving Home among Young Adults in the Netherlands', *European Sociological Review*, 7/1.

Delanty, G. (1998), 'Social Theory and European Transformation: Is There a European Society?', *Sociological Research Online*, 3/1.

Delgado, M. (1993), 'Cambios recientes en el proceso de formación de la familia', *Revista Española de Investigaciones Sociológicas*, 64: 123–53.

De Lima, A. V. (1991), 'Velhos e novos agricultores em Portugal', *Análise Social*, 26/3: 335–59.

De Lima, M. P. (1991), 'Relações de Trabajo, Estratégias Sindicais e Emprego (1974–1990)', *Análise Social*, 26/5: 905–43.

Delivanis-Negreponti, M. (1981), *I Helliniki Oikonomia* (Thessaloniki: Paratiritis).

Dell'Aringa, C. (1990), 'Industrial Relations and the Role of the State in EEC Countries', in Commission des Communautés Européennes, DG V, and London School of Economics and Political Science, *Salaires et intégration européenne* (Brussels: European Commission, V/908/90).

Delruelle, N., Evalenko, R., and Fraeys, W. (1970), *Le Comportement politique des electeurs belges: Enquête de sociologie électorale* (Bruxelles: Université Libre de Bruxelles).

Delsen, L. (1998), 'When Do Men Work Part-Time?, in O'Reilly and Fagan (1998), q.v.

De Lucena, M., and Gaspar, C. (1991), 'Metamorfoses Corporativas?—Associções de Interesses Económicos e Institucionalização da Democracia em Portugal (I)', *Análise Social*, 26/5: 847–903.

Denmark (1995), *Statistisk Årbog 1995* (Copenhagen: Danish Statistical Service).

Dent, M. (1993), 'Professionalism, Educated Labour and the State: Hospital Medicine and the New Managerialism', *Sociological Review*, 41/2: 244–73.

Denver, D. (1998), 'The British Electorate in the 1990s', *West European Politics*, 21/1: 197–217.

De Rose, A. (1992), 'Socio-Economic Factors and Family Size as Determinants of Marital Dissolution in Italy', *European Sociological Review*, 8/1.

De Sousa Santos, B. (1994), 'État, rapports salariaux et protection sociale à la semi-périphérie—cas du Portugal', *Peuples Méditerranéens*, 66: 23–66.

Deutsch, K. (1966), *Nations and Social Communication* (Cambridge, Mass.: MIT Press).

Dex, S. (1985), *The Sexual Division of Work: Conceptual Revolutions in the Social Sciences* (Brighton: Wheatsheaf).

Diekmann, A. (1990), 'Der Einfluß schulischer Bildung und die Auswirkungen der Bildungsexpansion auf das Heiratsverhalten', *Zeitschrift für Soziologie*, 19/4, 265–77.

Dierickx, G. (1994), 'Christian Democracy and its Ideological Rivals', in D. Hanley (ed.), *Christian Democracy in Europe: A Comparative Perspective* (London: Pinter).

Di Luzio, G. (1999), 'Gleichberechtigung und Leistungsprinzip', Ph.D. thesis (Florence: European University Institute).

D'Iribarne, P. (1992), *La Logique de l'honneur: Gestion des entreprises et traditions nationales*, 2nd edn. (Paris: Le Seuil).

Dirn, L. (1991), *La Société française en tendances* (Paris: Presses Universitaires de France).

Dittgen, A. (1994), 'Disparités régionales du mariage civil en Europe du sud', *Population*, 49/2: 339–68.

Dobbelaere, K. (1981), *Secularization: A Multi-Dimensional Concept* (London: Sage).

Dølvik, J. E., and Stokke, T. A. (1998), 'Norway: The Revival of Centralized Concertation', in Ferner and Hyman (1998), q.v.

Dore, R. (1972), *British Factory–Japanese Factory: The Origins of National Diversity in Industrial Relations* (London: Allen and Unwin).

—— (1986), *Flexible Rigidities: Industrial Policy and Structural Adjustment in the Japanese Economy (1970–80)* (London: Athlone Press).

—— and Sako, M. (1998), revised edition, *How the Japanese Learn to Work* (London: Routledge).

Drain, M. (1994), 'L'Agriculture portugaise, évolution et perspectives', *Peuples Méditerranéens*, 66: 103–20.

Drewes Nielsen, L. (1991), 'Flexibility, Gender and Local Labour Markets—Some Examples from Denmark', *International Journal of Urban and Regional Research*, 15/1: 42–54.

Dubbins, S. (1999), 'European Collective Bargaining', Ph.D. thesis (Florence: European University Institute).

Due, J., Madsen, J. S., and Jensen, C. S. (1991), 'The Social Dimension: Convergence or Diversification of Industrial Relations in the Single European Market?', *Industrial Relations Journal*, 22/2: 85–102.

—— —— —— (1994), *The Survival of the Danish Model* (Copenhagen: DJØF).

Dunlop, J. (1958), *Industrial Relations Systems* (New York: Rinehart and Winston).

Duru-Bellat, M., Jarousse, J.-P., and Mingat, A. (1993), 'Les Scolarités de la maternelle au lycée: Étapes et processus dans la production des inégalités sociales', *Revue Française de Sociologie*, 34/1: 43–54.

Eder, K. (1993), *The New Politics of Class: Social Movements and Cultural Dynamics in Advanced Societies* (London: Sage).

Edwards, P., Hall, M., Hyman, R., Marginson, P., Sisson, K., Waddington, J., and Winchester, D. (1998), 'Great Britain: From Partial Collectivism to Neo-liberalism to Where?', in Ferner and Hyman (1998), q.v., 1–54.

Elvander, N. (1974a), 'The Role of the State in the Settlement of Labor Disputes in the Nordic Countries: A Comparative Analysis', *European Journal of Political Research*, 5: 363–85.

Elvander, N. (1974b), 'Collective Bargaining and Incomes Policies in the Nordic Countries: A Comparative Analysis', *British Journal of Industrial Relations*, 3: 417–37.

Endruweit, G., Gaugler, E., Staehle, W. H., and Wilpert, B. (eds.) (1985), *Handbuch der Arbeitsbeziehungen: Deutschland, Österreich, Schweiz* (Berlin: de Gruyter).

Erikson, R., and Goldthorpe, J. H. (1985), 'Are American Rates of Social Mobility Exceptionally High?', *European Sociological Review*, 1.

—— —— (1992), *The Constant Flux* (Oxford: Clarendon Press).

Ermisch, J. (1988), 'Economic Influences on Birth Rates', *National Institute Economic Review*, November: 71–81.

—— (1996), 'The Economic Environment for Family Formation', in Coleman (1996b), q.v.

—— and Ogawa, N. (eds.) (1997), *The Family, the Market, and the State in Ageing Societies* (Oxford: Clarendon Press).

Esping-Andersen, G. (1990), *The Three Worlds of Welfare Capitalism* (Cambridge: Polity Press).

—— (1993a), 'Post-Industrial Class Structures: An Analytical Framework' in Esping-Andersen (1993b), q.v.

—— (ed.) (1993b), *Changing Classes: Stratification and Mobility in Post-Industrial Societies* (London: Sage).

—— (1996a), 'Welfare States without Work: The Impasse of Labour Shedding and Familialism in Continental European Social Policy', in Esping-Andersen (1996b), q.v.

—— (ed.) (1996b), *Welfare States in Transition: National Adaptations in Global Economies* (London: Sage).

—— (1999), *Social Foundations of Post-Industrial Economies* (Oxford: Oxford University Press).

—— Assimakopoulou, Z., and van Kersbergen, K. (1993), 'Trends in Contemporary Class Structuration: A Six-Nation Comparison', in Esping-Andersen (1993b), q.v.

Etienne, B. (1988), 'Le Cas de Marseille', *Pouvoirs*, 47: 115–22.

Eurobarometer (1991), *Young Europeans*, 34:2 (Luxembourg: European Commission).

European Values Group (1992), *The European Values Study 1981–1990: Summary Report* (Aberdeen: Gordon Cook Foundation).

Eurostat (1990), *Structure and Activity of Industry* (Luxembourg: Commission of the European Communities).

Evans, G. (1992), 'Testing the Validity of the Goldthorpe Class Schema', *European Sociological Review*, 8: 211–32.

Faist, T. (1993), 'Ein- und Ausgliederung von Immigration', *Soziale Welt*, 44/2: 275–97.

Fassmann, H., and Münz, R. (1994), 'European East–West Migration', *International Migration Review*, 3: 520–38.

Featherman, D. L., Jones, F. L., and Hauser, R. M. (1975), 'Assumptions of Social Mobility Research in the US: The Case of Occupational Status', *Social Science Research*, 4.

Federici, N., Mason, K. O., and Sogner, S. (eds.) (1993), *Women's Position and Demographic Change* (Oxford: Clarendon Press).

Federkeil, G. (1997), 'The Federal Republic of Germany: Polarization of Family Structure', in Kaufmann *et al.* (1997), q.v., 77–113.

Feinstein, C. (1996), 'The Equalizing of Wealth in Britain since the Second World War', *Oxford Review of Economic Policy*, 12/1: 96–105.

Ferner, A., and Hyman, R. (eds.) (1998), *Changing Industrial Relations in Europe* (Oxford: Blackwell).

Ferrera, M. (1996), *A New Social Contract*, Robert Schuman Centre Working Paper 96/36 (Florence: European University Institute).

—— (1997), *Le trappole del welfare* (Bologna: Il Mulino).

Finke, R. (1992), 'An Unsecular America', in Bruce (1992), q.v.

Fischer, W. (1964), *Unternehmerschaft, Selbstverwaltung und Staat* (Berlin: Dunkcer und Humblot).

Fishman, J. A. (1985), *The Rise and Fall of the Ethnic Revival* (New York: Mouton).

Flaquer i Vilardebó, L., and Soler Serratosa, J. (1990), *Permanancia y cambio en la familia española* (Madrid: Centro de Investigaciones Sociologicas).

Flora, P. (ed.) (1985), *State, Economy and Society in Western Europe 1815–1975*, Vol. 2: *Politics and Government* (Frankfurt am Main: Campus).

Fluder, R., and Hotz-Hart, B. (1998), 'Switzerland: Still as Smooth as Clockwork?', in Ferner and Hyman (1998), q.v., 262–82.

FORSA (1987), *Ungeschätzte und statusgeminderte Arbeitsverhältnisse* (Dortmund: FORSA).

Forsé, M., Jaslin, J. P., Lemel, Y., Mendras, H., Stoclet, D., and Déchaux, J.-H. (1993), *Recent Social Trends in France 1960–1990* (Frankfurt am Main: Campus).

Fox, A. (1985), *History and Heritage* (London: Allen and Unwin).

France (1993), *Annuaire Statistique de la France 1993* (Paris: INSEE).

François, E. (1994), 'L'Allemagne du XVIe au XXe siècle', in Davie and Hervieu-Léger (1994), q.v.

Franks, J., and Mayer, C. (1997), 'Corporate Ownership and Control in U.K., Germany, and France', in Chew (1997), q.v.

Frears, J. R. (1977), *Political Parties in the French Fifth Republic* (London: Hurst).

Freedland, M. (1999), 'The Marketization of Public Services', in K. Eder, C. Crouch, and D. Tambini (eds.), *Citizens, Markets and the State* (Oxford: Oxford University Press).

Freedman, L. (ed.) (1995), *Military Intervention in European Conflicts* (Oxford: Blackwell).

Fritzell, J. (1993), 'Income Inequality Trends in the 1980s: A Five-Country Comparison', *Acta Sociologica*, 36: 47–62.

Fux, B. (1997), 'Switzerland: The Family Life Neglected by the State', in Kaufmann *et al.* (1997), q.v., 348–93.

Gallagher, M. (1976), *Electoral Support for Irish Political Parties, 1927–73* (Beverly Hills, Calif.: Sage).

Gallie, D. (1994), 'Patterns of Skill Change: Upskilling, Deskilling, or Polarization?', in Penn, Rose, and Rubery (1994), q.v.

—— White, M., Cheng, Y., and Tomlinson, M. (1998), *Restructuring the Employment Relationship* (Oxford: Oxford University Press).

Ganne, B. (1992), 'Industrial Development and Local Industrial Systems in Post-War France: Political Economy of a Transformation', in M. Storper and A. Scott (eds.), *Pathways to Industrialization and Regional Development* (London: Routledge).

Garnier, M., Hage, J., and Fuller, B. (1989), 'The Strong State, Social Class, and Controlled School Expansion in France 1881–1975', *American Journal of Sociology*, 95/2: 279–306.

Geißler, R. (1994a), 'Soziale Schichtung und Teilnahme an Herrschaft', in Geißler (1994c), q.v.

—— (1994b), 'Soziale Schichtung und Bildungschancen', in Geißler (1994c), q.v.

—— (ed.) (1994c), *Soziale Schichtung und Lebenschancen in Deutschland* (Stuttgart: Enke).

Gellner, E. (1965), *Thought and Change* (London: Weidenfeld and Nicolson).

—— (1982), *Nationalism and the Two Forms of Cohesion in Complex Societies* (London: British Academy).

—— (1983), *Nations and Nationalism* (Oxford: Blackwell).

—— (1994), *Encounters with Nationalism* (Oxford: Blackwell).

Genov, N. B. (1997), 'Four Global Trends: Rise and Limitations', *International Sociology*, 12/4: 409–28.

Gerlich, P. (1987), 'From Consociationism to Competitition: The Austrian Party System since 1945', in Daalder (1987), q.v.

Germany (1988), *Fachserie 1* (Wiesbaden: Statistisches Bundesamt).

—— (1994 and various years), *Statistisches Jahrbuch für die Bundesrepublik Deutschland* (Wiesbaden: Statistisches Bundesamt).

Gershuny, J. (1978), *After Industrial Society: The Emerging Self-Servicing Economy* (London: Macmillan).

—— (1993), 'Post-Industrial Career Structures in Britain', in Esping-Andersen (1993*b*), q.v.

—— Godwin, M., and Jones, S. (1994), 'The Domestic Labour Revolution: A Process of Lagged Adaptation', in M. Anderson, Bechhofer, and Gershuny (1994), q.v.

Gevers, P. (1983), 'Arbeidsverhoudingen in Belgie', *Tijdschrift voor Sociologie*, 4/1–2: 68–79.

Giddens, A. (1980), *The Class Structure of the Advanced Societies*, 2nd edn. (London: Hutchinson).

—— (1990), *The Consequences of Modernity* (Cambridge: Polity Press).

—— (1994), *Beyond Left and Right* (Cambridge: Polity Press).

—— (1998), *The Third Way: The Renewal of Social Democracy* (Cambridge: Polity Press).

Gill, R. (1992), 'Secularization and Census Data', in Bruce (1992), q.v.

Giner, S. (1994), 'The Advent of a European Society', *International Journal of Sociology*, 24/1: 11–30.

Ginn, J., and Arber, S. (1991), 'Gender, Class and Income Inequalities in Later Life', *British Journal of Sociology*, 42/3: 369–96.

Gitlin, T. (1995), *The Twilight of Common Dreams: Why America is Wracked by Cultural Wars* (New York: Metropolitan Books).

Glans, I. (1977), *Partier och ujäbare i Danmark* (Copenhagen: Politica).

Glasmeier, A. (1994), 'Flexible Districts, Flexible Regions? The Institutional and Cultural Limits to Districts in an Era of Globalization and Technological Paradigm Shifts', in Amin and Thrift (1994), q.v.

Glatzer, W., Hondrich, K. O., Noll, H.-H., Stiehr, K., and Wörndl, B. (1992), *Recent Social Trends in West Germany 1960–1990* (Frankfurt am Main: Campus).

Glazer, N. (1996), 'Multiculturalism and American Exceptionalism', European Forum 1995–96 (Florence: European University Institute).

Goetschy, J. (1998), 'France: The Limits of Reform', in Ferner and Hyman (1998), q.v., 357–94.

Goldey, D. (1998), 'The French General Election of 25 May–1 June 1997', *Election Studies*, 17/4: 536–50.

Goldthorpe, J. H. (1983), 'Women and Class Analysis: In Defence of the Conventional View', *Sociology*, 17: 465–88.

—— and Hope, K. (1974), *The Social Grading of Occupations: A New Approach and Scale* (Oxford: Clarendon Press).

Gorz, A. (1980), *Adieu au prolétariat* (Paris: Galilée).

Gough, I. (1979), *The Political Economy of the Welfare State* (London: Macmillan).

—— Bradshaw, J., Ditch, J., Eardley, T., and Whiteford, P. (1997), 'Social Assistance in OECD Countries', *Journal of European Social Policy*, 7/1: 17–43.

Gran, B. (n.d.), *Three Worlds of Old-Age Decommodification*, Working Paper 104 (Luxembourg: Luxembourg Income Study).

Grant, W., and Marsh, P. (1977), *The CBI* (London: Hodder and Stoughton).

Greece (1993), *Monthly Statistical Bulletin*, December.

Gregg, P., Machin, S., and Szymanski, S. (1993), 'The Disappearing Relationship between Directors' Pay and Corporate Performance', *British Journal of Industrial Relations*, 31/1: 1–9.

Grote, J. (1998), 'The Political Economy of Regionalism: State–Society Relations in Nine European Regions', Ph.D. thesis (Florence: European University Institute).

Grundy, E. (1996), 'Population Ageing in Europe', in Coleman (1996*b*), q.v.

Guerrero, T. (1999), 'Why do Spanish Young People Stay Longer at Home than the French', Ph.D. thesis (Florence: European University Institute).

Guillén, A. M. (1992), 'Social Policy in Spain: From Dictatorship to Democracy (1939–1982)', in

Z. Ferge and J. E. Kolberg (eds.), *Social Policy in a Changing Europe* (Frankfurt am Main: Campus/ Westview).

Guiraudon, V. (1998), 'Citizenship Rights for Non-Citizens: France, Germany, the Netherlands', in Joppke (1998*b*), q.v.

Gustafsson, B. (1972), 'Sweden', in Mol (1972), q.v.

—— and Lindblom, M. (1993), 'Poverty Lines and Poverty in Seven European Countries, Australia, Canada and the USA', *Journal of European Social Policy*, 3/1: 21–38.

Habermas, J. (1985), *Der philosophische Diskurs der Moderne: Zwölf Vorlesungen* (Frankfurt am Main: Suhrkampf).

—— (1998), *Die postnationale Konstellation: Politische essays* (Frankfurt am Main: Suhrkamp).

Hadenius, A. (1976), *Facklig organisationsutveckling* (Uppsala: Raben and Sjögren).

Hadjimichalis, C., and Vaiou, D. (1990), 'Flexible Labour Markets and Regional Development in Northern Greece', *International Journal of Urban and Regional Research*, 14/1: 1–24.

Haerpfer, C. (1983), 'Nationalratswahle und Wahlverhalten 1945–80', in P. Gerlich and W. C. Müller (eds.), *Zwischen Koalition und Konkurrenz: Österreichs Parteien seit 1945* (Vienna: Braumüller).

Hajnal, J. (1965), 'European Marriage Patterns in Perspective', in D. V. Glass and D. E. C. Eversley (eds.), *Population in History: Essays in Historical Demography* (London: Routledge).

Hakim, K. (1997), 'A Sociological Perspective on Part-Time Work', in Blossfeld and Hakim (1997), q.v., 22–70.

Hall, P. (1986), *Governing the Economy: The Politics of State Intervention in Britain and France* (Oxford: Polity).

—— and Franzese, Jr, R. J. (1998), 'Mixed Signals: Central Bank Independence, Co-ordinated Wage-Bargaining, and European Monetary Union', *International Organization*, 52/3: 505–36.

Haller, M. (1989), *Klassenstrukturen und Mobilität in fortgeschrittenen Gesellschaften: Eine vergleichende Analyse der Bundesrepublik Deutschland, Österreichs, Frankreichs und der Vereinigten Staaten von Amerika* (Frankfurt am Main: Campus).

—— (1994), 'European as a New Nation or a Community of Nations?', *International Journal of Sociology*, 24/3: 166–212.

—— (1997), 'Klassenstruktur und Arbeitslosigkeit—Die Entwicklung zwischen 1960 und 1990', in Hradil and Immerfall (1997*b*), q.v.

—— and Holm, K. (eds.) (1987), *Werthaltungen und Lebensformen in Österreich* (Vienna: Verlag für Geschichte und Politik).

Halman, L. (1994), 'Individualism in Europe and North America', XIII World Congress of Sociology, Bielefeld (Barcelona: International Sociological Association).

—— and Pettersson, T. (1994), 'Individualization and Value Fragmentation', XIII World Congress of Sociology, Bielefeld (Barcelona: International Sociological Association).

Halsey, A. H., Heath, A. F., and Ridge, J. M. (1980), *Origins and Destinations: Family, Class, and Education in Modern Britain* (Oxford: Clarendon Press).

Hamberg, G. (1990), *Studies in the Prevalence of Religious Beliefs and Religious Practices in Contemporary Sweden* (Uppsala: S. Academiae Ubsaliensis).

Hannan, M. T., Schömann, K., and Blossfeld, H.-P. (1990), 'Sex and Sector Differences in the Dynamics of Wage Growth in the Federal Republic of Germany', *American Sociological Review*, 55: 694–713.

Hansen, E. J. (1993), 'The Female Factor in the Changing Living Condition in Denmark', *International Journal of Sociology*, 23/2: 139–52.

Hansen, S. A., and Henriksen, I. (1980), *Velfærdsstaten 1940–1978* (Copenhagen: Gyldendal).

Hantrais, L. (1985), 'Leisure Lifestyles and the Synchronization of Family Schedules: A Franco-British Comparative Perspective', *World Leisure and Recreation,* April: 18–24.

Hardiman, N. (1992), 'The State and Economic Interests: Ireland in Comparative Perspective', in J. H. Goldthorpe and C. T. Whelan (eds.), *The Development of Industrial Society in Ireland* (Oxford: Oxford University Press).

Hartmann, M. (1993), 'Informatiker zwischen Professionalisierung und Proletarisierung: Zur Standardisierung beruflichen Wissens im EDV-Bereich', *Soziale Welt*, 44/3: 392–419.

Hausner, R., and Neumann, U. (1992), 'Armut in der Bundesrepublik Deutschland', *Kölner Zeitschrift für Soziologie und Sozialpsychologie*, 32, Sonderheft für Armut im Wohlfahrtstaat, 237–71.

Hayward, J. E. S. (1966), *Private Interests and Public Policy: The Experience of the French Economic and Social Council* (New York: Barnes and Noble).

—— (1983), *Governing France: The One and Indivisible Republic*, 2nd edn. (London: Weidenfeld and Nicolson).

—— (1986), *The State and the Market Economy: Industrial Patriotism and Economic Intervention in France* (Brighton: Wheatsheaf).

—— (ed.) (1995), *Industrial Enterprise and European Integration: From National to International Champions in Western Europe* (Oxford: Oxford University Press).

Heath, A. (1991), *Understanding Political Change* (Oxford: Pergamon Press).

Heidenreich, M. (1997), 'Arbeit und Management in den westeuropäischen Kommunikationsgesellschaften', in Hradil and Immerfall (1997b), q.v.

Hemerijck, A. (1992), 'The Historical Contingencies of Dutch Corporatism', D.Phil. thesis (University of Oxford).

—— and Bakker, W. (1995), 'A Pendulum Swing in Conceptions of the Welfare State', in B. Unger and H. Van Warden (eds.), *Convergence and Diversity* (Aldershot: Avebury), 144–81.

—— and Kloostermans, R. C. (1995), 'Der postindustrielle Umbau des korporistischen Sozialstaats in den Niederländern', in W. Fricke (ed.), *Jahrbuch Arbeit und Technik* 1995, 287–96.

Hendrickx, J., Schreuder, O., and Ultee, W. (1994), 'Die konfessionelle Mischehe in Deutschland (1901–1986) und den Niederländern (1914–1986)', *Kölner Zeitschrift für Soziologie und Sozialpsychologie*, 46/4: 619–45.

Herrigel, G. (1989), 'Industrial Order and the Politics of Industrial Change', in P. Katzenstein (ed.), *Industry and Politics in West Germany: Towards the Third Republic* (Ithaca, NY: Cornell University Press).

Hervieu-Léger, D. (1994), 'La Religion des européens: Modernité, religion, sécularisation', in Davie and Hervieu-Léger (1994), q.v.

Highet, J. (1972), 'Scotland', in Mol (1972), q.v.

Hirdmann, Y. (1988), 'Genussystemet—reflexioner kring kvinnors sociala underordning', *Kvinnovetenskaplig Tidskrift*, 3: 49–63.

Hirsch, F. (1977), *Social Limits to Growth* (London: Routledge and Kegan Paul).

Hirsch, J. (1966), *Die Öffentlichen Funktionen der Gewerkschaften* (Stuttgart: Ernst Klett Verlag).

Hirst, P., and Zeitlin, J. (1990), 'Flexible Specialization versus Post-Fordism: Theory, Evidence and Policy Implications', Birkbeck Public Policy Centre Working Paper (London: Birkbeck College).

Hochet, A. (1988), 'L'Immigration dans le débat politique français de 1981 à 1988', *Pouvoirs*, 47: 23–30.

Hoem, B. (1993), 'The Compatibility of Employment and Childbearing in Contemporary Sweden', *Acta Sociologica*, 36: 139–66.

—— and Hoem, J. M. (1987), 'The Swedish Family: Aspects of Contemporary Developments', Stockholm Research Papers in Demography 43 (Stockholm: University of Stockholm).

Hoem, J. (1991), 'La Standardisation indirecte améliorée et son application à la divortialité en Suède (1971–1989)', *Population*, 46/6: 1551–68.

Hofrichter, J., and Klein, M. (1994), 'Festung Europa. Das Ausmaß der Abneigung gegenüber Immigranten in der Europäischen Gemeinschaft zu Beginn der 90er Jahre', *Informationen zur Raumentwicklung*, 5/6.

Hollinger, D. A. (1995), *Postethnic America: Beyond Multiculturalism* (New York: Basic Books).

Hollingsworth, J. R., and Lindberg, L. N. (1985), *The Governance of the American Economy: The Role of Markets, Clans, Hierarchies and Associate Behavior*, WZB Discussion Papers 85–8 (Berlin: Wissenschaftszentrum Berlin).

—— and Streeck, W. (1994), 'Countries and Sectors', in Hollingsworth, Schmitter, and Streeck (1994), q.v.

—— Schmitter, P., and Streeck, W. (eds.) (1994), *Governing Capitalist Economies* (New York: Oxford University Press).

Höpflinger, F. (1976), *Industriegewerkschaften in der Schweiz* (Zurich: Limmat Verlag).

—— (1997), 'Haushalts- und Familienstrukturen im intereuropäischen Vergleich', in Hradil and Immerfall (1997*b*), q.v., 97–138.

Hornsby-Smith, M. P. (1992), 'Recent Transformations in English Catholicism: Evidence of Secularization?', in Bruce (1992), q.v.

Hornung-Draus, R. (1989), 'Das Vermögen der privaten Haushalte in der BRD: Bestand, Entwicklung und Verteilung', *Jahrbücher für National-ökonomie und -Statistik*, 206/1: 18–47.

Horrell, S. (1994), 'Household Time Allocation and Women's Labour Force Participation', in M. Anderson, Bechhofer, and Gershuny (1994), q.v.

—— Rubery, J., and Burchell, B. (1994), 'Working-Time Patterns, Constraints, and Preferences', in M. Anderson, Bechhofer, and Gershuny (1994), q.v.

Hout, M. (1989), *Following in Father's Footsteps: Social Mobility in Ireland* (Cambridge, Mass.: Harvard University Press).

—— Raftery, A. E., and Bell, E. O. (1993), 'Making the Grade: Educational Stratification in the USA, 1925–1989', in Shavit and Blossfeld (1993), q.v.

Houtart, F. (1972), 'Belgium', in Mol (1972), q.v.

Hradil, S. (1994), 'Soziale Schichtung und Arbeitssituation', in Geißler (1994*c*), q.v.

—— (1997), 'Soziale Ungleichheiten, Milieus und Lebensstile in den Ländern der Europäischen Union', in Hradil and Immerfall (1997*b*), q.v.

—— and Immerfall, S. (1997*a*), 'Modernisierung und Vielfalt in Europa', in Hradil and Immerfall (1997*b*), q.v., 11–26.

—— —— (eds.) (1997*b*), *Die Westeuropäischen Gesellschaften im Vergleich* (Opladen: Leske and Budrich).

Huber, E., Ragin, C., and Stephens, J. D. (1993), 'Social Democracy, Christian Democracy, Constitutional Structure and the Welfare State', *American Journal of Sociology*, 99/3: 711–49.

Huinink, J., and Mayer, K. U. (1995), 'Gender, Social Inequality, and Family Formation in West Germany', in Mason and Jensen (1995), q.v.

Humphries, J., and Rubery, J. (1991), *La Position des femmes sur le marché du travail au Royaume Uni: Evolution entre 1983 et 1989* (Brussels: Equal Opportunities Unit of the European Commission).

ILO (1998 and various years), *ILO Yearbook* (Geneva: ILO).

Inglehart, R. (1977), *The Silent Revolution: Changing Values and Political Styles among Western Publics* (Princeton: Princeton University Press).

—— (1984), 'The Changing Structure of Political Cleavages in Western Society', in R. Dalton (ed.), *Electoral Change in Advanced Industrial Democracies* (Princeton: Princeton University Press).

—— (1990), *Modernization and Post-Modernization: Cultural, Economic and Political Change in 43 Countries* (Princeton: Princeton University Press).

Inglehart, R. (1997), *Culture Shift in Advanced Industrial Society* (Princeton: Princeton University Press).

Isambert, F. A. (1972), 'France', in Mol (1972), q.v.

Ishida, H. (1993), *Social Mobility in Contemporary Japan: Educational Credentials, Class and the Labor Market in a Cross-National Perspective* (Basingstoke: Macmillan).

ISSP (1986), *Social Network and Support System* (Cologne: University of Cologne, Zentralarchiv für Empirische Sozialforschung).

Jacobi, O., Keller, B., and Müller-Jentsch, W. (1998), 'Germany: Facing New Challenges', in Ferner and Hyman (1998), q.v., 190–238.

Jacobs, H. (1989), 'Stability and Flexibility: The Determinant Factors' Changing Influence through Time', in Molle and van Mourik (1989*b*), q.v.

Jallinoja, R. (1989), 'Women between the Family and Employment', in Boh *et al.* (1989), q.v.

Janssen, J., and Ultee, W. (1994), 'De cultuur of de centen . . .', *Mens en Maatschappij*, 69/December.

Jäntti, M. (1993), *Changing Inequality in Five Countries: The Role of Markets, Transfers and Taxes*, Working Paper 91 (Luxembourg: Luxembourg Income Study).

Japan (1994), *Statistical Yearbook of Japan* (Tokyo: Government Statistical Service).

Jarausch, K. H. (1990), *The Unfree Professions: German Lawyers, Teachers and Engineers, 1900–1950* (New York: Oxford University Press).

Jensen, A.-M. (1995), 'Gender Gaps in Relationships with Children: Closing or Widening?', in Mason and Jensen (1995), q.v.

Jessop, B., Kastendiek, H., Nielsen, K., and Pedersen, O. K. (eds.) (1991), *The Politics of Flexibility: Restructuring State and Industry in Britain, Germany and Scandinavia* (Aldershot: Elgar).

Johnson, B., and Lundvall, B.-Å. (1991), 'Flexibility and Institutional Learning', in Jessop *et al.* (1991), q.v.

Johnson, P. (1996), 'The Assessment: Inequality', *Oxford Review of Economic Policy*, 12/1: 1–14.

Jonsson, J. O. (1993), 'Persisting Inequality in Sweden', in Shavit and Blossfeld (1993), q.v.

—— and Mills, C. (1993*a*), 'Social Class and Educational Attainment in Historical Perspective: A Swedish–English Comparison Part I', *British Journal of Sociology*, 44/2: 213–47.

—— —— (1993*b*), 'Social Class and Educational Attainment in Historical Perspective: A Swedish–English Comparison Part II', *British Journal of Sociology*, 44/3: 403–28.

Joppke, C. (1998*a*), 'Immigration Challenges the Nation State', in Joppke (1998*b*), q.v.

—— (1998*b*), *Challenges to the Nation State: Immigration in Western Europe and the United States* (Oxford: Oxford University Press).

—— (1999), *Immigration and the Nation State* (Oxford: Oxford University Press).

Jowell, R., Brook, L., Dowds, L., and Ahrendt, D. (eds.) (1993), *International Social Attitudes: The 10th Bsa Report* (Aldershot: Dartmouth).

Julémont, G. (1993), 'The Status of Women and the Position of Children', in Federici, Mason, and Sogner (1993), q.v.

Jurado Guerrero, T., and Naldini, M. (1996), *Is the South so Different? Italian and Spanish Families in Comparative Perspective*, MZES Arbeitpapier (Mannheim: University of Mannheim, mimeo).

Jürgens, U., Malsch, T., and Dohse, K. (1989), *Moderne Zeiten in der Automobilfabrik: Strategien der Produktionsmodernisierung und Arbeitsregulation im Länder- und Konzernvergleich* (Berlin: Springer-verlag).

Kaelble, H. (1987), *Auf dem Weg zu einer europäischern Gesellschaft* (Munich: C. H. Beck).

—— (1997), 'Europäische Vielfalt und der Weg zu einer europäischen Gesellschaft', in Hradil and Immerfall (1997*b*), q.v., 27–68.

Kalleberg, A., and Rosenfeld, R. (1990), 'Work in the Family and in the Labor Market: A Cross-National, Reciprocal Analysis', *Journal of Marriage and the Family*, 52/2: 331–46.

Kaplan, S. N. (1997), 'Corporate Governance and Corporate Performance: A Comparison of Germany, Japan, and the U.S.', in Chew (1997), q.v.

Kappelhoff, P., and Techenberg, W. (1987), 'Integration and Career Mobility in the Federal Republic and the United States', in Techenberg (1987), q.v.

Karpik, L. (1990), 'Technical and Political Knowledge: The Relationship of Lawyers and Other Legal Professions to the Market and the State in France', in Torstendahl and Burrage (1990), q.v.

Katzenstein, P. J. (1984), *Corporatism and Change: Austria, Switzerland, and the Politics of Industry* (Ithaca, NY: Cornell University Press).

Katzovien, M. A. (1970), 'The Development of the Services Sector: A New Approach', *Oxford Economic Papers*, 22: 362–82.

Kaufmann, F.-X. (1990), *Zukunft der Familie* (Munich: C. H. Beck).

—— Kuijsten, A., Schulze, H. J., and Strohmeier, K. P. (eds.) (1997), *Family Life and Family Policies in Europe*, i. *Structures and Trends in the 1980s* (Oxford: Clarendon Press).

Kaufmann, J.-C. (1994*a*), 'Les Ménages d'une personne en Europe', *Population*, 49.

—— (1994*b*), 'Nuptialité ou conjugalité? Critique d'un indicateur et état des évolutions conjugales en Europe', *Archives Européenes de Sociologie*, 35/1: 3–20.

Kecskes, R. and Wolf, C. (1993), 'Christliche Religiosität: Konzepte, Indikatoren, Messinstrumente', *Kölner Zeitschrift für Soziologie und Sozialpsychologie*, 45/2: 270–87.

Keeler, J. T. S. (1987), *The Politics of Neo-corporatism in France: Farmers, the State and Agriculture* (Oxford University Press).

Kehrer, G. (1972), 'Germany', in Mol (1972), q.v.

Kellerhals, J., and Montandon, C. (1991), *Les Stratégies éducatives des familles* (Geneva: Delachaux et Niestlé).

Kennedy, F., and McCormack, K. (1997), 'Ireland: Marriage Loses Popularity', in F.-X. Kaufmann *et al.* (1997), q.v., 195–224.

Kenworthy, L. (1995), *In Search of National Economic Success: Balancing Competition and Cooperation* (Beverly Hills and London: Sage).

Kerckhoff, A. C., and Trott, J. M. (1993), 'Educational Attainment in a Changing Education System: The Case of England and Wales', in Shavit and Blossfeld (1993), q.v.

Kern, H., and Schumann, M. (1987), 'Limits of the Division of Labour: New Production and Employment Concepts in West German Industry', *Economic and Industrial Democracy*, 8: 151–70.

Kerr, C. (1983), *The Future of Industrial Societies* (Cambridge, Mass.: Harvard University Press).

—— Dunlop, J. T., Harbison, F., and Myers, C. A. (1960), *Industrialism and Industrial Man* (Cambridge, Mass.: Harvard University Press).

Kerr, H. H. (1987), 'The Swiss Party System: Steadfast and Changing', in Daalder (1987), q.v.

Kester, C. (1997), 'Governance, Contracting, and Investment Horizons: A Look at Japan and Germany', in Chew (1997), q.v.

Kiely, G., and O'Raw, E. (1994), 'The Informal Economy in Ireland', *Recherches Sociologiques*, 25/3: 95–107.

Kiernan, K. E. (1992), 'The Respective Roles of Men and Women in Tomorrow's Europe', in *Proceedings of Eurostat Conference on Human Resources in Europe: At the Dawn of the 21st Century* (Luxembourg: Eurostat).

—— (1996), 'Partnership Behaviour in Europe: Recent Trends and Issues', in Coleman (1996*b*), q.v.

Kitschelt, H. (1990), 'New Social Movements and the Decline of Party Organization', in Dalton and Kuechler (1990), q.v.

Kjellberg, A. (1990), 'The Swedish Trade Union System: Centralization and Decentralization', XII World Congress of Sociology, Madrid Barcelona: International Sociological Association).

—— (1998), 'Sweden: Restoring the Model?', in Ferner and Hyman (1998), q.v., 74–117.

Klandermans, P. B. (1990), 'Linking the "Old" and "New" Movement Networks in the Netherlands', in Dalton and Kuechler (1990), q.v.

Klein, T., and Lauterbach, W. (1994), 'Bildungseinflüße auf Heirat, die Geburt des ersten Kindes und die Erwerbsunterbrechung von Frauen: Eine empirischer Analyse familienökonomischer Erklärungsmuster', *Kölner Zeitschrift für Soziologie und Sozialpsychologie*, 46/2: 279–98.

Klijzing, E. (1992), ' "Weeding" in the Netherlands: First-Union Disruption among Men and Women Born between 1928 and 1965', *European Sociological Review*, 8/1.

Knoellinger, C. E. (1960), *Labor in Finland* (Cambridge, Mass.: Harvard University Press).

Knudsen, L. B. (1997), 'Denmark: The Land of the Vanishing Housewife', in F.-X. Kaufmann *et al.* (1997), q.v., 12–48.

Knudsen, R. (1991), *La Position des femmes sur le marché du travail au Danemark: Evolution entre 1983 et 1989* (Brussels: Equal Opportunities Unit of the European Commission).

Kochan, T. A., Katz, H., and McKersie, R. B. (1986), *The Transformation of American Industrial Relations* (New York: Basic Books).

Kocka, J. (1981), *Die Angestellten in der deutschen Geschichte 1850–1980: Vom Privatbeamten zum angestellten Arbeitnehmer* (Göttingen: Vandenhoeck und Ruprecht).

—— (1990), ' "Bürgertum" and Professions in the Late 19th Century: Two Alternative Approaches', in Burrage and Torstendahl (1990), q.v.

Kogut, B. (ed.) (1993), *Country Competitiveness: Technology and the Organizing of Work* (New York: Oxford University Press).

Kohl, J. (1992), 'Armut im internationalen Vergleich', *Kölner Zeitschrift für Soziologie und Sozialpsychologie*, 32, Sonderheft für Armut im Wohlfahrtstaat, 272–99.

Kokosalakis, N. (1994), 'Orthodoxie grecque, modernité et politique', in Davie and Hervieu-Léger (1994), q.v.

König, W. (1987), 'Employment and Career Mobility of Women in France and the Federal Republic', in Techenberg (1987), q.v.

Koppen, J. K. (1991), 'Het wetenschappelijk onderwijs: egalitar of utilitar?', *Mens en Maatschhappij*, 66/2.

Korpi, W. (1978), *The Working Class in Welfare Capitalism* (London: Routledge).

—— (1983), *The Democratic Class Struggle* (London: RKP).

Kosonen, P. (1994), *European Integration: A Welfare State Perspective* (Helsinki: Yliopistopaino).

Kotthof, H. (1985), 'Betriebliche Interessenvertretung durch Mitbestimmung des Beirats', in Endruweit *et al.* (1985), q.v.

—— and Reindle, J. (1990), *Die soziale Welt kleiner Betriebe* (Göttingen: Verlag Otto Schwartz).

Kreckel, R. (1992), *Politische Soziologie der sozialer Ungleichheit* (Frankfurt am Main: Campus).

Kriesi, H.-P. (1986), 'Rahmbedingungen verbändlicher Handeln', in P. Farago and H.-P. Kriesi (eds.), *Wirtschaftsverbände in der Schweiz* (Grüsch: Verlag Rüegger).

—— (1989), 'New Social Movements and the New Class in the Netherlands', *American Journal of Sociology*, 94: 1078–117.

Kristensen, P. H. (1992), 'Industrial Districts in West Jutland', in Pyke and Sengenberger (1992), q.v.

Kruijt, J. P. (1958), *Verzuiling* (Heynis: Zaandijk).

Krulic, J. (1988), 'L'Immigration et l'identité de la France: Mythes et réalités', *Pouvoirs*, 47: 31–43.

Kuijsten, A. and Schulze, H.-J. (1997), 'The Netherlands: The Latent Family', in F.-X. Kaufmann *et al.* (1997), q.v., 253–301.

—— and Strohmeier, K. P. (1997), 'Ten Countries in Europe: An Overview', in F.-X. Kaufmann *et al.* (1997), q.v., 394–423.

Kvavik, R. B. (1976), *Interest Groups in Norway* (Oslo: Universitetsforlaget).

Laeyendecker, L. (1972), 'The Netherlands', in Mol (1972), q.v.

Lakemann, U. (1984), *Die Aktivitätsspektrum privater Haushalte in der Bundesrepublik Deutschland 1950–1980* (Berlin: WZB).

Lambert, Y. (1989), 'From Parish to Transcendant Humanism in France', in Beckford and Luckmann (1989), q.v.

—— (1993), 'Ages, générations et christianisme en France et en Europe', *Revue Française de Sociologie*, 34/4: 525–55.

Lane, C. (1991), 'Industrial Reorganization in Europe: Patterns of Convergence and Divergence in Germany, France and Britain', *Work, Employment and Society*, 5/4: 515–39.

Lane, J.-E., and Ersson, S. O. (1987, 1999), first and fourth editions, *Politics and Society in Western Europe* (London: Sage).

—— McKay, D., and Newton, K. (1997), *Politics Data Handbook: OECD Countries*, 2nd edn. (Oxford: Oxford University Press).

Lang, W. (1978), *Kooperative Gewerkschaften und Einkommenspolitik: das Beispiel Österreichs* (Frankfurt am Main: Peter Lang Verlag).

Lange, P., and Garrett, G. (1985), 'The Politics of Growth: Strategic Interaction and Economic Performance in the Advanced Industrial Democracies', *Journal of Politics*, 47/3: 792–828.

Langlois, P., with Caplow, T., Mendras, H., and Glatzer, W. (eds.) (1994), *Convergence or Divergence? Comparing Recent Social Trends in Industrial Societies* (Frankfurt am Main: Campus).

LaPalombara, J. (1964), *Interest Groups in Italian Politics* (Princeton: Princeton University Press).

Lapeyronnie, D. (1993), *L'Individu et les minorités: La France et la Grande Bretagne face à leurs minorités* (Paris: Presses Universitaires de France).

Lash, S. (ed.) (1991), *Post-Structuralist and Post-Modernist Sociology* (Aldershot: Elgar).

—— and Bagguley, P. (1988), 'Labour Relations in Disorganized Capitalism: A Five-Nation Comparison', *Environment and Planning D: Society and Space*, 6: 321–38.

—— and Urry, J. (1987), *The End of Organized Capitalism* (Oxford: Polity).

Leborgne, D., and Lipietz, A. (1988), 'L'Après-fordisme et son espace', *Les Temps Modernes*, 43/501: 75–114.

Lee, J. J. (1989), *Ireland 1912–1985: Politics and Society* (Cambridge: Cambridge University Press).

Lefranc, C., and Thave, S. (1994), 'L'Evolution de l'environnement familial des enfants', *Population*, 6.

Lefranc, G. (1976), *Les Organisations patronales en France* (Paris: Payot).

Le Galès, P. (1993), *Politique urbain et dévellopement local, une comparaison France–Grande Bretagne* (Paris: L'Harmattan).

Leggewie, C. O. (1994), 'Ethnizität, Nationalismus und multikulturelle Gesellschaft', in H. Berding (ed.), *Nationales Bewußtsein und kollektive Identität* (Frankfurt am Main: Suhrkamp).

—— (1996), 'What Europe can Learn from the United States: Multiculturalism Compared. Theories, Concepts and Policies in Germany and the United States', European Forum 1995–96 (Florence: European University Institute).

Le Grand, C. (1991), 'Explaining the Male–Female Wage Gap: Job Segregation and Solidarity Wage Bargaining in Sweden', *Acta Sociologica*, 34: 261–78.

Leicht, R., and Stockmann, R. (1993), 'Die Kleinen ganz groß? Der Wandel der Betriebsgrößenstruktur im Branchenvergleich', *Soziale Welt*, 44/2: 243–74.

Lelièvre, E. (1994), 'Formation des couples et fécondité hors mariage en Grande-Bretagne: Divergences et similitudes avec la situation française', *Population*, 49/1: 61–90.

Leminsky, G. (1965), *Der Arbeitnehmereinfluß in englischen und französischen Unternehmen: ein Vergleich mit der Mitbestimmung* (Cologne: Bund Verlag).

Lesthaeghe, R. (1995), 'The Second Demographic Transition in Western Countries: An Interpretation', in Mason and Jensen (1995), q.v.

—— and Moors, G. (1996), 'Living Arrangements, Socio-Economic Position, and Values among Young Adults: A Pattern Description for France, West Germany, Belgium, and the Netherlands, 1990', in Coleman (1996*b*), q.v.

Leveau, R., and Withol de Wenden, C. (1988), 'La Deuxième Génération', *Pouvoirs*, 47: 61–73.

Lewis, J. (ed.) (1993), *Women and Social Policies in Europe: Work, Family and the State* (Cheltenham: Elgar).

Lijphart, A. (1968), *Verzuiling, pacificatie en kentering in de Nederlandse politiek* (Amsterdam: De Bussy); published in English as *The Politics of Accommodation: Pluralism and Democracy in the Netherlands* (Berkeley: University of California Press).

—— (1974), 'The Netherlands: Continuity and Change in Voting Behaviour', in Rose (1974), q.v.

Lilja, K. (1998), 'Finland: Continuity and Modest Moves towards Company-Level Corporatism', in Ferner and Hyman (1998), q.v., 171–89.

Limousin, A. (1988), 'L'Histoire de l'immigration en France: Une histoire impossible', *Pouvoirs*, 47: 5–21.

Linz, J. (1981), 'A Century of Interests and Politics in Spain', in S. Berger (ed.), *Organizing Interests in Western Europe* (Cambridge: Cambridge University Press).

Lipset, S. M., and Rokkan, S. (1967), 'Cleavage Structures, Party Systems and Voter Alignments', in Lipset and Rokkan (eds.), *Party Systems and Voter Alignments* (New York: Free Press).

Lockwood, D. (1989), *The Blackcoated Worker*, 2nd edn. (Oxford: Clarendon Press).

Lopes, P. (1994), 'Valeur d'échange, valeur d'usage et valeur symbolique de l'économie informelle dans une situation de transition', *Recherches Sociologiques*, 25/3: 67–83.

Ludwig-Mayerhofer, W. (1992), 'Arbeitslosigkeit, Erwerbsarbeit und Armut', *Kölner Zeitschrift für Soziologie und Sozialpsychologie*, 32, Sonderheft für Armut im Wohlfahrtstaat, 380–402.

Lüschen, G. (1988), 'Familial-verwandtschaftliche Netzwerke', in Nave-Herz (1988*b*), q.v.

Lüscher, K., and Schultheis, F. (1988), 'Die Entwicklung von Familienpolitik—Soziologische Überlegungen anhand eines regionalen Beispiels', in Nave-Herz (1988*b*), q.v.

Lutz, W., Wils, A., and Nieminen, M. (1991), 'The Demographic Dimension of Divorce: The Case of Finland', *Population Studies*, 45/3: 437–53.

Lyons, B., and Sembenelli, A. (1996), 'EU Manufacturing Firms in Context', in S. Davies and B. Lyons (eds.), *Industrial Organization in the European Union* (Oxford: Oxford University Press), 12–33.

McCarthy, C. (1977), *Trade Unions in Ireland, 1894–1960* (Dublin).

McClelland, C. E. (1990), 'Escape from Freedom? Reflections on German Professionalization, 1870–1933', in Torstendahl and Burrage (1990), q.v.

McCrone, D. (1994), 'Getting By and Making Out in Kirkcaldy', in M. Anderson, Bechhofer, and Gershuny (1994), q.v.

McLeod, H. (1992), 'Secular Cities? Berlin, London and New York in the Later 19th and Early 20th Centuries', in Bruce (1992), q.v.

—— (1997), *Religion and the Peoples of Western Europe 1789–1989*, 2nd edn. (Oxford: Oxford University Press).

Maier, H. (1987), *Das Modell Baden-Württemberg* (Berlin: IIM).

Mair, P. (1997), *Party System Change: Approaches and Interpretations* (Oxford: Clarendon Press).

Majone, G. (1993), *Deregulation or Re-regulation? Policymaking in the European Community since the Single Act*, Working Paper SPS 93/2 (Florence: European University Institute).

—— (1994), *Understanding Regulatory Growth in the European Community*, Working Paper SPS 94/17 (Florence: European University Institute).

Mann, K. (1992), *The Making of an English 'Underclass'?* (Milton Keynes: Open University Press).

Mansner, A. (1989), *Suomalaista Yhtaiskuntaa Rakentamassa: STK 1907–1982*, iii. *1956–1982* (Helsinki: STK) (Swedish summary by C. Makkonen, 'Fran General strejken till den Inkomstpolitiska Eran').

Maravall, J. M. (1997), *Regimes, Politics and Markets: Democratization and Economic Change in Southern and Eastern Europe* (Oxford: Oxford University Press).

Marie, C.-V. (1988), 'Entre économie et politique: Le "Clandestin", une figure sociale à géometrie variable', *Pouvoirs*, 47: 75–92.

Marin, B. (1982), *Die paritätische Kommission: Aufgeklärter Technokorporatismus in Österreich* (Vienna: Internationale Publikationen).

—— (1990), 'Generalized Political Exchange: Preliminary Considerations', in B. Marin (ed.), *Generalized Political Exchange* (Frankfurt am Main: Campus).

Markovits, A. (1988), 'The Other "American Exceptionalism": Why Is There No Soccer in the United States?', *Praxis International*, 8/2: 125–50.

Marks, G., Scharpf, F. W., Schmitter, P. C., and Streeck, W. (eds.) (1996), *Governance in the European Union* (London: Sage).

Marshall, A. (1912), *Industry and Trade* (London: Macmillan).

Marshall, G. (1997), *Repositioning Class: Social Inequality in Industrial Societies* (London: Sage).

—— and Rose, D. (1990), 'Out-Classed by Our Critics?', *Sociology*, 24.

—— Newby, H., Rose, D., and Vogler, C. (1988), 'Distributional Struggle and Moral Order in a Market Society', *Sociology*, 21.

—— Vogler, C., Rose, D., and Newby, H. (1987), *Social Class in Modern Britain* (London: Hutchinson).

—— Roberts, S., Burgoyne, C., Swift, A., and Routh, D. (1995), 'Class, Gender, and the Asymmetry Hypothesis', *European Sociological Review*, 11.

Marshall, T. H. (1963), *Sociology at the Crossroads and Other Essays* (London: RKP).

Martikainen, T., and Yrjönen, R. (1994), 'Die Parteibindungen der finnischen Wähler im sozialen Wandel', in Pappi and Schmitt (1994), q.v.

Martin, D. (1965), 'Towards Eliminating the Concept of Secularization', in J. Gould (ed.), *Penguin Survey of the Social Sciences* (Harmondsworth: Penguin).

—— (1972), 'England', in Mol (1972), q.v.

—— (1978), *A General Theory of Secularization* (Oxford: Blackwell).

—— (1994), 'Remise en question de la théorie de la sécularisation', in Davie and Hervieu-Léger (1994), q.v.

Martinelli, A. (1980), 'Organized Business and Italian Politics: Confindustria and the Christian Democrats in the Post-war Period', in P. Lange and S. Tarrow (eds.), *Italy in Transition* (London: Frank Cass).

—— and Treu, T. (1984), 'Employers' Organisations in Italy', in Windmuller and Gladstone (1984), q.v.

Martínez Lucio, M. (1998), 'Spain: Regulating Employment and Social Fragmentation', in Ferner and Hyman (1998), q.v., 426–58.

Mason, K. O., and Jensen, A.-M. (eds.) (1995), *Gender and Family Change in Industrialized Societies* (Oxford: Clarendon Press).

Mastekaasa, Arne (1994), 'Marital Status, Distress, and Well-Being: An International Comparison', *Journal of Comparative Family Studies*, 25/2: 183–207.

Mathews, J. (1989), *Age of Democracy: The Politics of Post-Fordism* (Melbourne: Oxford University Press).

Matthiesen, P. C. (1993), 'Family Formation in Denmark', *International Journal of Sociology*, 23/2–3: 107–14.

Matzner, E., and Streeck, W. (1991), *Beyond Keynesianism: The Socio-Economics of Production and Full Employment* (Aldershot: Elgar).

Maurice, M., and Sorge, A. (1989), *Dynamique industrielle et capacité d'innovation de l'industrie de la machine-outil en France et en RFA* (Aix en Provence: Laboratoire d'économie et de sociologie du travail).

—— Sellier, F., and Silvestre, J.-J. (1982), *Politique d'éducation et organisation industrielle en France et en Allemande* (Paris: Presses Universitaires de France).

Mayer, C., and Alexander, I. (1990), *Banks and Securities Markets: Corporate Financing in Germany and the UK* (London: Centre for Economic Policy Research).

Mayer, K. U., and Blossfeld, H.-P. (1990), 'Die gesellschaftliche Konstruktion sozialer Ungleichheit im Lebensverlauf', in P. A. Berger and S. Hradil (eds.), *Lebenslagen, Lebensläufe, Lebensstile. Sonderband 7 der Sozialen Welt*.

Meager, N. (1993), *Self-Employment and Labour Market Policy in the European Community*, WZB Discussion Paper FIS 93: 201 (Berlin: WZB).

—— Kaiser, M., and Dietrich, H. (1992), *Self-Employment in the UK and Germany* (London: Anglo-German Foundation).

Meisaari-Polsa, T. (1997), 'Sweden: A Case of Solidarity and Equality', in F.-X. Kaufmann *et al.* (1997), q.v., 302–47.

Mendras, H. (1988), *La Seconde Révolution française, 1965–1984* (Paris: Gallimard).

—— (with Cole, A.) (1991), *Social Change in Modern France: Towards a Cultural Anthropology of the Fifth Republic* (Cambridge: Cambridge University Press).

Menniti, A., Palomba, R., and Sabbadini, L. L. (1997), 'Italy: Changing the Family from within', in F.-X. Kaufmann *et al.* (1997), q.v., 225–52.

Merkl, P. H. (1980*a*), 'The Sociology of European Parties: Members, Voters and Social Groups', in Merkl (1980*b*), q.v.

—— (ed.) (1980*b*), *Western European Party Systems* (New York: Free Press).

Merz, J., and Wolff, K. (1986), *Eigenarbeit und Erwerbsarbeit im Haupt- und Nebenerwerb* (Frankfurt am Main: Unius).

Meulders, D., Plasman, R., and Vander Stricht, V. (1993), *Position of Women on the Labour Market in the European Community* (Aldershot: Dartmouth).

Mevissen, J. W., and Renooy, P. H. (1987), 'The Economy of Daily Life: The Meaning of Social Networking for the Informal Economy', *Tijdschrift voor Arbeidsvraagstukken*, 3: 5–16.

Meyer, T. (1993), 'Der Monopolverlust der Familie', *Kölner Zeitschrift für Soziologie und Sozialpsychologie*, 45/1: 23–40.

Michel, A. (1989), 'The Impact of Marriage and Children on the Division of Gender Roles', in Boh *et al.* (1989), q.v.

Michelat, G. (1990), 'L'Identité catholique des français: II. Appartenances et socialisation', *Revue Française de Sociologie*, 30/3: 355–88.

Micheletti, M. (1984), 'The Involvement of Swedish Labour Market Organisations in the Swedish Political Process' (Stockholm: Studieförebundet Näringsliv og Samhälle, mimeo).

Michie, J., and Grieve Smith, J. (eds.) (1995), *Managing the Global Economy* (Oxford: Clarendon Press).

Middlemas, K. (1979), *Politics in Industrial Society* (London: Andre Deutsch).

—— (1990), *Power, Competition and the State*, ii. *Threats to the Postwar Settlement: Britain, 1961–74* (London: Macmillan).

Miller, W. E., and Traugott, S. (1989), *American National Election Studies Data Sourcebook 1952–86* (Cambridge, Mass.: Harvard University Press).

Milza, P. (1988), 'L'Intégration des Italiens en France: "Miracle" ou vertus de la longue durée?', *Pouvoirs*, 47: 103–13.

Mingione, E. (1991), *Fragmented Societies: A Sociology of Economic Life beyond the Market Paradigm* (Oxford: Blackwell).

Mitterauer, M., and Sieder, R. (1982), *The European Family* (Oxford: Blackwell).

Moberg, D. (1972), 'The USA', in Mol (1972), q.v.

Mol, H. (ed.) (1972), *Western Religion: A Country by Country Sociological Inquiry* (The Hague: Mouton).

Molle, W., and van Mourik, A. (1989*a*), 'Introduction', in Molle and van Mourik (1989*b*), q.v.

—— —— (eds.) (1989*b*), *Wage Differentials in the European Community* (Aldershot: Avebury).

Mommsen-Reindl, M. (1980), 'Austria', in Merkl (1980*b*), q.v.

Morais, A. M. (1993), 'A orientação no contexto de socialização primária—implicações no (in) sucesso escolar', *Análise Social*, 121/2: 267–307.

Morishima, M. (1982), *Why Has Japan 'Succeeded'?: Western Technology and the Japanese Ethos* (Cambridge: Cambridge University Press).

Morris, L. (1994), 'Informal Aspects of Social Divisions', *International Journal of Urban and Regional Research*, 18/1: 112–26.

Müller, W. (1994), 'Bildung und soziale Plazierung in Deutschland, England und Frankreich', in H.-F. Peisert and W. Zapf (eds.), *Gesellschaft, Demokratie und Lebenschancen* (Stuttgart: Deutsche Verlags-Anstalt).

—— and Haun, D. (1994), 'Bildungsgleichheit im sozialen Wandel', *Kölner Zeitschrift für Soziologie und Sozialpsychologie*, 46/1: 1–42.

—— and Karle, W. (1993), 'Social Selection in Educational Systems in Europe', *European Sociological Review*, 9/1: 1–23.

—— and Shavit, Y. (eds.) (1998), *From School to Work* (Oxford: Clarendon Press).

—— Steinmann, S., and Schneider, R. (1997), 'Bildung in Europa', in Hradil and Immerfall (1997*b*), q.v., 177–245.

—— Lüttinger, P., König, W., and Karle, W. (1989), 'Class and Education in Industrial Nations', *International Journal of Sociology*, 19/3: 3–19.

Muller-Escoda, B., and Vogt, U. (1997), 'France: The Institutionalization of Plurality', in F.-X. Kaufmann *et al.* (1997), q.v., 49–76.

Müller-Wichmann, C. (1987), *Von wegen Freizeit* (Frankfurt am Main: IG Metall).

Münz, R. (1996), 'Migrants, Aliens, Citizens: European Migration and Its Consequences', European Forum 1995–96 (Florence: European University Institute).

Murray, C. (1990), *The Emerging British Underclass* (London: Institute of Economic Affairs).

Myrdal, G. (1944), *An American Dilemma* (New York: Harper).

Nave-Herz, R. (1988*a*), 'Kontinuität und Wandel in der Bedeutung, in der Struktur und Stabilität von Ehe und Familie in der Bundesrepublik Deutschland', in Nave-Herz (1988*b*), q.v.

—— (ed.) (1988*b*),*Wandel und Kontinuität der Familie in der BRD* (Stuttgart: Enke).

—— (1989), 'Tensions between Paid Working Hours and Family Life', in Boh *et al.* (1989), q.v.

Nesti, A. (1985), *Il religioso implicito* (Rome: Editrice Ianua).

Nie, N. H., Verba, S., and Petrocik, J. R. (1979), *The Changing American Voter*, enlarged edition (Cambridge, Mass.: Harvard University Press).

Nielsen, K. (1991), 'Learning to Manage the Supply-Side: Flexibility and Stability in Denmark', in Jessop *et al.* (1991), q.v.

Noiriel, G. (1988), *Le Creuset français* (Paris: Seuil).

Noll, H.-H. (1997), 'Wohlstand, Lebensqualität und Wohlbefinden in den Ländern der Europäischen Union', in Hradil and Immerfall (1997*b*), q.v.

Noll, H.-H., and Langlois, S. (1994), 'Employment and Labour Market Change: Two Models of Growth', in Langlois *et al.* (1994), q.v.

Nordic Council (1995), *Nordic Statistical Yearbook* (Copenhagen: Nordic Council).

Norway (1982), *Maktutredningen: Sluttrapport* 3, 93–100 (Oslo: Universitetsforlaget).

—— (1992), *Statistisk Årbok 1992* (Oslo: NOU).

—— (1995), *Statistisk Årsbok 1995* (Oslo: NOU).

Nousiainen, J. (1971), *The Finnish Political System* (Cambridge, Mass.: Harvard University Press).

Nurminen, E., and Roos, P. J. (1992), 'Models of Parenting: Between Generations and Classes', in Björnberg (1992*c*), q.v.

O'Connor, J. (1973), *The Fiscal Crisis of the State* (New York: St Martin's Press).

OECD (1993), *Employment Outlook* (Paris: OECD).

—— (1994*a*), *The OECD Jobs Study: Part I Evidence and Evaluations* (Paris: OECD).

—— (1994*b*), *Employment Outlook* (Paris: OECD).

—— (1995), *Income Distribution in OECD Countries: Evidence from the Luxembourg Income Study*, Social Policy Studies No. 18 (Paris: OECD).

—— (1996), *Employment Outlook* (Paris: OECD).

—— (1997), *Employment Outlook* (Paris: OECD).

—— (various years), *Education at a Glance* (Paris: OECD).

—— (various years), *National Income and Expenditures* (Paris: OECD).

Offe, C. (1985), *Disorganized Capitalism* (Cambridge: Polity).

—— (1990), 'Reflections on the Institutional Self-Transformation of Movement Politics', in Dalton and Kuechler (1990), q.v.

—— and Wiesenthal, H. (1980), 'Two Logics of Collective Action: Theoretical Notes on Social Class and Organizational Form', *Political Power and Social Theory*, 1.

Olsen, J. P. (1983), *Organized Democracy* (Bergen: Universitetsforlaget).

Olson, M. (1982), *The Rise and Decline of Nations: Economic Growth, Stagflation and Social Rigidities* (New Haven: Yale University Press).

Olsson, A. S. (1991), *The Swedish Wage Negotiation System* (Aldershot: Dartmouth).

Oppenheimer, V. (1988), 'A Theory of Marriage Timing', *American Journal of Sociology*, 94: 563–91.

O'Reilly, J. (1992), 'Banking on Flexibility: A Comparison of the Use of Flexible Employment Strategies in the Retail Banking Sector in Britain and France', *International Journal of Human Resource Management*, 3/1.

—— (1994), 'You can't always get what you want: Employers' and Employees' Preferences for Part-Time Work in Britain and France', *Gender, Work and Organisations*, 1/3.

—— and Fagan, C. (eds.) (1998), *Part-Time Prospects: An International Comparison of Part-Time Work in Europe, North America and the Pacific Rim* (London: Routledge).

Pace, E. (1994), 'Désenchantement religieux en Italie', in Davie and Hervieu-Léger (1994), q.v.

Paci, M. (1997), *Welfare State* (Rome: Ediesse).

Pahl, R. E. (1988), 'Some Remarks on Informal Work, Social Polarisation and the Social Structure', *International Journal of Urban and Regional Research*, 12: 247–67.

Pappi, F. U., and Schmitt, H. (eds.) (1994), *Parteien, Parlamente und Wahlen in Skandinavien* (Frankfurt am Main: Campus).

Parri, L. (1987*a*), 'Staat und Gewerkschaft in der Schweiz 1873–1981', *Politische Vierteljahresschrift*, 28/1.

—— (1987*b*), 'Neo-corporatist Arrangements: "Konkordanz" and Direct Democracy in the Swiss Experience', in Scholten (1987*b*), q.v.

Parsons, T., and Bales, R. F. (1955), *Family, Socialization and Interaction Process* (New York: Free Press).

Pavelle, M. (1994), 'Le Travail "informel" de la femme rurale en Grèce: Une occupation qui n'a pas de nom', *Recherches Sociologiques*, 25/3: 85–94.

Pedersen, M. N. (1987), 'The Danish Working Multiparty System: Breakdown or Adaptation?', in Daalder (1987), q.v.

Penn, R. (1990), *Class, Power and Technology: Skilled Workers in Britain and America* (Cambridge: Polity).

—— Rose, M., and Rubery, J. (eds.) (1994), *Skill and Occupational Change* (Oxford: Oxford University Press).

Peron, R. (1991), 'Les Commerçants dans la modernisation de la distribution', *Revue Française de Sociologie*, 32: 179–207.

Pestoff, V. A. (1991), *The Demise of the Swedish Model and the Resurgence of Organized Business as a Major Political Actor* (Stockholm: University of Stockholm, Department of Business Administration).

—— (1994), 'Employer Organizations: Their Changing Structures and Strategies in Nine OECD Countries', mimeo, Stockholm University.

—— (1995), 'Towards a New Swedish Model of Collective Bargaining and Politics', in Crouch and Traxler (1995), q.v.

Petit, P. (1990), 'Structural Change, Information Technology, and Europe: The Case of France', in Appelbaum and Schettkat (1990), q.v.

—— and Ward, T. (1995), 'The Implications for Employment in Europe of the Changing Pattern of Trade and Production in the Global Economy', Round Tables on the Social Dialogue (Brussels: European Commission).

Peuckert, R. (1996), *Familienformen im sozialen Wandel*, 2nd edn. (Opladen: Leske and Budrich).

Pfaff, A. B. (1992), 'Feminisierung der Armut durch den Sozialstaat?', *Kölner Zeitschrift für Soziologie und Sozialpsychologie*, 32, Sonderheft für Armut im Wohlfahrtstaat, 421–45.

Pfau-Effinger, B. (1993), 'Modernisation, Culture and Part-Time Employment: The Example of Finland and West Germany', *Work, Employment and Society*, 7/3: 383–410.

—— (1998), 'Culture or Structure as Explanations for Differences in Part-Time Work in Germany, Finland and the Netherlands?', in O'Reilly and Fagan (1998), q.v.

Phelps Brown, [E.] H. (1968), *A Century of Pay* (London: Macmillan).

—— (1977), *The Inequality of Pay* (Oxford: Oxford University Press).

—— and Hopkins, S. V. (1955), 'Seven Centuries of Building Wages', *Economica*, 22/87: 195–206.

—— —— (1956), 'Seven Centuries of the Prices of Consumables, Compared with Builders' Wage Rates', *Economica*, 23/92: 296–314.

Pinnelli, A. (1995), 'Women's Condition, Low Fertility, and Emerging Union Patterns in Europe', in Mason and Jensen (1995), q.v.

Piore, M., and Sabel, C. (1984), *The Second Industrial Divide* (New York: Free Press).

Pirenne, H. (1927), *Les Villes du moyen age* (Paris: Presses Universitaires de France).

Plantenga, J. (1991), *La Position des femmes sur le marché du travail aux Pays-Bas: Evolution entre 1983 et 1989* (Brussels: Equal Opportunities Unit of the European Commission).

Pochet, P. (1998), 'Les Pactes sociaux en Europe dans les années 1990', *Sociologie du Travail*, 2/98: 173–90.

—— and Van Lerde, A. (eds.) (1998), *UEM et enjeux sociaux* (Paris: Presses interuniversitaires).

Polanyi, K. (1957), *The Great Transformation: The Political and Economic Origins of our Time* (Boston: Beacon Press).

Pontusson, J. (1997), 'Between Neo-Liberalism and the German Model: Swedish Capitalism in Transition', in Crouch and Streeck (1997), q.v.

Portugal (Direcção geral da Família) (1988), *Tempo para o trabalho tempo para a Familia* (Lisbon: Direcção geral da Família).

—— (Commissão para o ano internacional da família) (1994), *Relatório situação actual da Familia Portuguesa* (Lisbon: Direcção geral da Família).

Prais, S. J. (1981), 'Vocational Qualifications of the Labour Force in Britain and Germany', *National Institute Economic Review*, 98.

Presvelou, C. (1994), 'Crise et économie informelle: Acquis et interrogations', *Recherches Sociologiques*, 25/3: 7–36.

Pyke F., and Sengenberger, W. (eds.) (1992), *Industrial Districts and Local Economic Regeneration* (Geneva: IILS).

Querido, A. (1972), 'Portugal', in Mol (1972), q.v.

Raftery, A. E., and Hout, M. (1989), *Inequality and Opportunity in Irish Education 1925–1980* (Stanford, Calif.: Stanford University Press).

Rainwater, L. (1992), 'Ökonomische versus soziale Armut in den USA', *Kölner Zeitschrift für Soziologie und Sozialpsychologie*, 32, Sonderheft für Armut im Wohlfahrtstaat, 3195–220.

—— (1997), *Inequality and Poverty in Comparative Perspective*, Estudio 1997/110 (Madrid: Instituto Juan March).

—— and Smeeding, T. (1994), 'Le Bien-être économique des enfants européens: Une perspective comparative', *Population*, 6.

Rasmussen, E. J. (1985), '25 Years of Labour Government and Incomes Policy', Ph.D. thesis (Florence: European University Institute).

Regalia, I. (ed.) (1997), *Le relazioni industriali al livello regionale* (Milan: FrancoAngeli).

—— and Regini, M. (1998), 'Italy: The Dual Character of Industrial Relations', in Ferner and Hyman (1998), q.v.

Regini, M., and Regalia, I. (1996), *Italia anni '90: Rinasce la concertazione* (Milan: IRES).

Requena Santos, F. (1994), 'Redes de Amistad, Felicidad y Familia', *Revista Española de Investigaciones Sociológicas*, 66: 73–89.

Reynaud, J.-D. (1975), *Les Syndicats en France*, Tome I (Paris: Seuil).

—— and Grafmeyer, Y. (eds.) (1981), *Français, qui êtes-vous?* (Paris: La Documentation Française).

Reynolds, S. (1997), *Kingdoms and Communities in Western Europe 900–1300* (Oxford: Oxford University Press).

Richards, A., and García de Polavieja, J. (1997), *Trade Unions, Unemployment and Working Class Fragmentation in Spain*, Estudio 1997/112 (Madrid: Instituto Juan March).

Riis, O. (1994), 'Religion et identité nationale au Danmarque', in Davie and Hervieu-Léger (1994), q.v.

Ritter, G. A., and Niehuss, M. (1991), *Wahlen in Deutschland 1946–91* (Beck: Munich).

Ritzer, G. (1993), *The McDonaldization of Society* (Thousand Oaks: Pine Forge).

Robertson, R. (1989), 'Globalization, Politics, and Religion', in Beckford and Luckmann (1989), q.v.

Rochon, T. R. (1990), 'The West European Peace Movement and the Theory of New Social Movements', in Dalton and Kuechler (1990), q.v.

Room, G. (ed.) (1990), *New Poverty in the European Community* (London: Macmillan).

Rose, R. (ed.) (1974), *Electoral Behaviour: A Comparative Handbook* (New York: Free Press).

Rosenbaum, J. E., and Kariya, T. (1989), 'From High School to Work: Market and Institutional Mechanisms in Japan', *American Journal of Sociology*, 94: 1334–65.

Rothstein, B. (1985), 'The Success of the Swedish Labour Market Policy: the Organisational Connection to Policy', *European Journal of Political Research*, 13, 153–65.

Ryner, M. (1998), 'Political Trade Unionism Facing the EMU: Economic Restructuring and

Responses in Sweden and Germany', paper presented at conference of Society for the Advancement of Socio-Economics, Vienna, July 1998, mimeo.

Sabel, C., Herrigel, G., Deeg, R., and Kazis, R. (1989), 'Regional Prosperities Compared: Massachusetts and Baden-Württemberg in the 1980s', *Economy and Society*, 18: 374–404.

Sackmann, R., and Häussermann, H. (1994), 'Do Regions Matter? Regional Differences in Female Labour-Market Participation in Germany', *Environment and Planning A*, 26: 1377–96.

Sako, M. (1988), *Partnership between Small and Large Firms: The Case of Japan* (Luxembourg: Commission of the European Communities).

—— (1992), *Prices, Quality and Trust: Inter-Firm Relations in Britain and Japan* (Cambridge: Cambridge University Press).

—— (1996), 'Suppliers' Associations in the Japanese Automobile Industry: Collective Action for Technology Diffusion', *Cambridge Journal of Economics*, 20: 651–71.

—— and Helper, S. (1998), 'Determinants of Trust in Sulier Relations: Evidence from the Automotive Industry in Japan and the United States', *Journal of Economic Behavior and Organization*, 34: 387–417.

Samouco, A. (1995), 'O estado-providencia e a sociedade rural. Revaloizacão der recursos e re-orendamento de estrategias num novo contexto: a agricultura de pluriactividade', *Análise Social*, 121: 391–408.

Sanders, K. (1993), 'Intrede op de arbeidsmarkt. Generatieen sekseverschillen jaar voor Nederland, West-Duitsland en de Verenigde Staten', *Sociale Wetenschappen*, 36/1: 24–44.

Sandwijk, P., and Van Waveren, B. (1987), *Tinkering with the Neighbourhood: Research into the Relationship between Neighbourhood, the Informal Economy and Urban Renewal* (Rotterdam: Stichting BOOG).

Sawyer, M. (1976), 'Income Distribution in OECD Countries', *OECD Economic Outlook* (Paris: OECD).

Schäfer, W. (ed.) (1984), *Schattenökonomie* (Göttingen: Vandenhoech und Ruprecht).

Schäfers, B. (1990), *Gesellschaftlicher Wandel in Deutschland* (Stuttgart: Enke).

Schain, M. A. (1985), 'Immigration and Politics in France', in J. Ambler (ed.), *The French Socialist Experiment* (Philadelphia: ISHI Press).

—— (1996), 'Minorities and Immigrant Incorporation in France: The State and the Dynamics of Multiculturalism', European Forum 1995–96 (Florence: European University Institute).

Scharpf, F. W. (1996), 'Negative and Positive Integration in the Political Economy of European Welfare States', in Marks (1996).

—— (1999), *Governing in Europe: Effective and Democratic?* (Oxford: Oxford University Press).

Schierup, C.-U. (1998), 'Multipoverty Europe: Perspectives on Migration, Citizenship and Social Exclusion in the European Union and the United States', in J. Gundara and S. Jacobs (eds.), *Interculturalism in Europe: Cultural Diversity and Social Policy in the European Union* (Aldershot: Arena).

Schmidt, M. G. (1993), 'Gendered Labour Force Participation', in F. G. Castles and Flood (1993*b*), q.v.

Schmitter, P. C. (1974), 'Still the Century of Corporatism?', *Review of Politics*, January.

—— and Grote, J. (1997), *The Corporatist Sisyphus: Past, Present and Future*, Working Paper SPS 97/4 (Florence: European University Institute).

Schnapper, D. (1991), *La France de l'Intégration* (Paris: Gallimard).

Scholten, I. (1987*a*), 'Corporatism and the Neo-Liberal Backlash in the Netherlands', in Scholten (1987*b*), q.v.

—— (ed.) (1987*b*), *Political Stability and Neo-Corporatism* (Beverly Hills and London: Sage).

Schütze, Y. (1988), 'Zur Veränderung im Eltern-Kind-Verhältnis seit der Nachkriegszeit', in Nave-Herz (1988*b*), q.v.

Schütze, Y., and Lang, F. R. (1993), 'Freundschaft, Alter und Geschlecht', *Zeitschrift für Soziologie*, 22/3: 209–20.

Scott, J. (1986), *Capitalist Property and Financial Power* (Hassocks: Wheatsheaf).

—— (1990), 'Corporate Capital and Corporate Rule: Britain in an International Perspective', *British Journal of Sociology*, 41.

—— (1997), *Corporate Business and Capitalist Classes* (Oxford: Oxford University Press).

Seccombe, W. (1992), *A Millennium of Family Change* (London: Verso).

Seppänen, P. (1972), 'Finland', in Mol (1972), q.v.

Sgritta, G. B. (1989), 'Towards a New Paradigm: Family in the Welfare State Crisis', in Boh *et al.* (1989), q.v.

Shavit, Y., and Blossfeld, H.-P. (eds.) (1993), *Persistent Inequality: Changing Educational Attainment in Thirteen Countries* (Boulder, Colo.: Westview).

Shonfield, A. (1964), *Modern Capitalism* (Oxford: Oxford University Press).

Simmel, G. (1900), *Philosophie des Geldes* (Leipzig: Duncker und Humblot).

Simon, W. (1976), *Macht und Herrschaft der Unternehmerverbände BDI, BDA und DIHT im ökonomishen und politischen System der BRD* (Cologne: Pahli Rugenstein Verlag).

Singelmann, J. (1978), *From Agriculture to Services: The Transformation of Industrial Employment* (Beverly Hills, Calif.: Sage).

Singer, P. (1971), 'Força de trabalho e emprego Brasil 1920–1969', *Cadernos CEBRAPS*, 3.

Sinnott, R. (1995), *Irish Voters Decide* (Manchester: Manchester University Press).

Smeeding, T. M., and Coder, J. (1993), *Income Inequality in Rich Countries during the 1980s*, Luxembourg Income Study Working Paper 88 (Luxembourg: Luxembourg Income Study).

Smith, A. (1986), *The Ethnic Origins of Nations* (Oxford: Blackwell).

Sogner, S. (1993), 'Historical Features of Women's Position in Society'. in Federici, Mason, and Sogner (1993), q.v.

Sørensen, Aage (1991), 'On the Usefulness of Class Analysis in Research on Social Mobility and Socioeconomic Inequality', *Acta Sociologica*, 34: 71–88.

Sørensen, Annemette (1992), 'Zur geschlechtsspezifischen Struktur von Armut', *Kölner Zeitschrift für Soziologie und Sozialpsychologie*, 32, Sonderheft für Armut im Wohlfahrtstaat, 345–66.

Soskice, D. (1990), 'Wage Determination: The Changing Role of Institutions in Advanced Industrialized Economies', *Oxford Review of Economic Policy*, 4.

Soysal, Y. N. (1994), *Limits of Citizenship: Migrants and Postnational Membership in Europe* (Chicago: University of Chicago Press).

Spain (1994), *Annuarios Estatisticos 1994* (Madrid: Institute Nacional de Estadistica).

Spånt, R. (1979), *Den svenska förmögensförderningens utveckling* (Stockholm: SOU).

Spencer, H. (1864), *Illustrations of Universal Progress* (London: Appleton).

Spitaels, G. (1967), *Le Mouvement Syndical en Belgique* (Brussels: Université Libre de Bruxelles).

Starrin, B., and Svensson, P.-G. (1992), 'Gesundheit und Soziale Ungleichheit', *Kölner Zeitschrift für Soziologie und Sozialpsychologie*, 32, Sonderheft für Armut im Wohlfahrtstaat, 403–18.

Steedman, H., Mason, G., and Wagner, K. (1991), 'Intermediate Skills in the Workplace: Deployment, Standards and Supply in Britain, France and Germany', *National Institute Economic Review*, 136: 60–76.

Stephens, J. D. (1996), 'The Scandinavian Welfare States: Achievements, Crisis, and Prospects', in Esping-Andersen (1996b), q.v.

Stille, F. (1990), 'Structural Change in the Federal Republic of Germany: The Case of Services', in Appelbaum and Schettkat (1990), q.v.

Story, J. (2000), 'The Political Economy of EU Financial Integration: The Battle of the Systems', in Crouch (2000*b*), q.v.

Streeck, W. (1983), 'Zwischen Markt und Staat: Interessenverbände als Träger öffentlicher Politik', in F. W. Scharpf and M. Brockmann (eds.), *Institutionelle Bedingungen der Arbeitsmarkt- und Beschäftigungspolitik* (Frankfurt am Main: Campus).

—— (1987), 'Industrial Relations and Industrial Change: The Restructuring of the World Automobile Industry in the 1970s', *Economic and Industrial Democracy*, 8: 437–62.

—— (1992), *Social Institutions and Economic Performance* (London: Sage).

—— (1993), 'The Social Dimension of the European Economy', in D. Mayes, W. Hager, A. Knight, and W. Streeck, *Public Interests and Market Pressures* (London: Macmillan).

—— (1994), 'Pay Restraint Without Incomes Policy: Institutionalized Monetarism and Industrial Unionism in Germany', in R. Dore, R. Boyer, and Z. Mars (eds.), *The Return to Incomes Policy* (London: Pinter).

—— (1997), 'German Capitalism: Does it Exist? Can It Survive?', in Crouch and Streeck (1997), q.v.

—— and Schmitter, P. C. (1985), 'Community, Market, State—Association?' in Streeck and Schmitter (eds.), *Private Interest Government: Beyond Market and State* (Beverly Hills, Calif. and London: Sage).

Strohmeier, K. P., and Kuijsten, A. (1997), 'Family Life and Family Policies in Europe: An Introduction', in F.-X. Kaufmann *et al.* (1997), q.v., 1–11.

Swann, G. M., Prevezer, M., and Stout, D. (1998), *The Dynamics of Industrial Clustering: International Comparisons in Computing and Biotechnology* (Oxford: Oxford University Press).

Sweden (1994 and 1997), *Statistisk Årsbok* (Stockholm: Statistika Centralbyrån).

Sweet, J. A., and Bumpass, L. (1987), *American Families and Households* (New York: Russell Sage Foundation).

Switzerland (1995 and 1996), *Statistisches Jahrbuch der Schweiz 1996* (Zurich: Neue Zürcher Zeitung).

Tåhlin, M. (1993), 'Class Inequality and Post-Industrial Employment in Sweden', in Esping-Andersen (1993*b*), q.v.

Talos, E. (1981), *Staatliche Sozialpolitik in Österreich* (Vienna: Verlag für Gesellschaftskritik).

Techenberg, W. (ed.) (1987), *Comparative Studies of Social Stratification* (Armonk, NY: Sharpe).

Therborn, G. (1993), 'The Politics of Childhood: The Rights of Children in Modern Times', in F. G. Castles and Flood (1993*b*), q.v.

—— (1995), *European Modernity and Beyond: The Trajectory of European Societies 1945–2000* (London: Sage).

—— (1996), 'Más allá de la ciudadanía: ¿Democracia post-liberal o liberalismo post-democrático?', in J. Felix Tezanos (ed.), *La democracia post-liberal* (Madrid: Editorial Sistema), 331–51.

—— (1997), 'Europas künftige Stellung—Das Skandinavien der Welt?', in Hradil and Immerfall (1997*b*), q.v.

Thorgaard, J. (1972), 'Denmark', in Mol (1972), q.v.

Thurley, K., and Lam, A. (1990), *Skill Formation of Electronics Engineers: Comparing the Learning Behaviour of British and Japanese Engineers* (London: London School of Economics and Political Science).

Titmuss, R. M. (1970), *The Gift Relationship: From Human Blood to Social Policy* (London: Allen & Unwin).

Tödtling, F. (1994), 'The Uneven Landscape of Innovation Poles: Local Embeddedness and Global Networks', in Amin and Thrift (1994), q.v.

Tönnies, F. (1887), *Gemeinschaft und Gesellschaft: Grundbegriffe der reinen Soziologie* (1991 edition: Darmstadt: Wissenschaftliche Buchgesellschaft).

Torcal Loriente, M. (1992), 'Análisis dimensional y estudio de valores: el cambio cultural en España', *Revista Española de Investigaciones Sociológicas*, 58: 97–122.

Torstendahl, R. (1990), 'Essential Properties, Strategic Aims and Historical Development: Three Approaches to Theories of Professionalism', in Burrage and Torstendahl (1990), q.v.

—— and Burrage, M. (eds.) (1990), *The Formation of Professions* (London: Sage).

Toulemon, L. (1994), 'La Place des enfants dans l'histoire des couples', *Population*, 6.

Touraine, A. (1969), *La Société post-industrielle* (Paris: Denoël).

—— (1992), *Critique de la Modernité* (Paris: Fayard).

Traxler, F. (1982), *Evolution Gewerkschaftlicher Interessenvertretung* (Vienna: Braumüller).

—— (1986), *Interessenverbände der Unternehmer: Konstitutionsbedingungen und Steuerungskapazitäten, analysiert am Beispiel Österreichs* (Frankfurt am Main: Campus).

—— (1993), 'Business Associations and Labor Unions in Comparison: Theoretical Perspectives and Empirical Findings on Social Class, Collective Action and Associational Organizability', *British Journal of Sociology*, 44/4: 673–91.

—— (1995), 'Farewell to Labour Market Associations? Organized versus Disorganized Decentralization as a Map for Industrial Relations', in Crouch and Traxler (1995), q.v.

—— (1996), 'Collective Bargaining and Industrial Change: A Case of Disorganization? A Comparative Analysis of Eighteen OECD Countries', *European Sociological Review*, 12/3: 271–87.

—— (1997), 'Collective Bargaining in the OECD: Developments, Preconditions and Effects', mimeo, European Sociological Association Conference, Colchester.

Treiman, D. J. (1970), 'Industrialisation and Social Stratification', in E. O. Laumann (ed.), *Social Stratification: Research and Theory for the 1970s* (Indianapolis: Bobbs Merrill).

—— and Yamaguchi, K. (1993), 'Trends in Educational Attainment in Japan', in Shavit and Blossfeld (1993), q.v.

—— and Yip, K.-B. (1989), 'Educational and Occupational Attainment in 21 Countries', in M. L. Kohn (ed.), *Cross-National Research in Sociology* (Beverly Hills, Calif.: Sage).

Tribalat, M. (1995), *Faire France: Une enquête sur les immigrés et leurs enfants* (Paris: La Découverte).

Trigilia, C. (1986), 'Small-Firm Development and Political Sub-Cultures in Italy', *European Sociological Review*, 2/3: 161–75.

—— (1991), 'The Paradox of the Region: Economic Regulation and the Representation of Interests', *Economy and Society*, 20/3: 306–27.

Tsoukalis, L. (1997), *The New European Economy Revisited* (Oxford: Oxford University Press).

Turone, S. (1981), *Storia del Sindacato in Italia 1943–1980* (Bari: Laterza).

United Kingdom (Royal Commission on the Distribution of Income and Wealth) (1975), *Report No. 1: Initial Report on the Standing Reference*, Cmnd. 6171 (London: HMSO).

—— (1995), *Annual Abstract of Statistics* (London: HMSO).

USA (1994), *US Statistical Yearbook* (Washington, DC: Government Printer).

Van de Kerckhove, J. (1979), 'De Opstelling van de Vakbeweging op de Achtergrond van de Industrielle Ontwikkeling in Belgie: Politisiering en Professionisiering', Antwerp: Vlaams-Nederlands Sociologencongres, mimeo.

Van den Bosch, K. (1996), *Trends in Financial Poverty in Western Capitalist Countries*, Robert Schuman Centre Working Paper 96/40 (Florence: European University Institute).

Van der Lippe, T., Van Doorne-Huiskes, A., and Siegers, J. J. (1993), 'Het aandeel van mannen in huishoudelijk werk', *Mens en Maatschappij*, 68/2: 133–52.

Van der Ploeg, S. W. (1992), 'Expansie van het voorgezet en hoger onderwijs: effecten van verandringen op de arbeidsmarkt, in gezinnen en in het onderwijssysteem', *Mens en Maatschappij*, 67/2: 156–76.

Van Deth, J. W., and Janssen, J. I. H. (1994), 'Party Attachments and Political Fragmentation in Europe', *European Journal of Political Research*, 25: 87–109.

Van Kersbergen, K. (1996), *Social Capitalism: A Study of Christian Democracy and the Welfare State* (London: Routledge).

Van Praag, C. S. (1991), 'Het bijzondere van Nederland: de landenvergelijking in het Sociaal en Cultureel Rapport', *Mens en Maatschappij*, 66/4: 343–64.

Van Well, F. (1994), ' "I Count My Parents among my Best Friends": Youths' Bonds with Parents and Friends in the Netherlands', *Journal of Marriage and the Family*, 56/4.

Vassille, L. (1989a), 'Similarity among Countries: An International Comparison Based on Data from the 1978/79 EC Survey', in Molle and van Mourik (1989b), q.v.

——(1989b), 'Industries: The Role of Productivity, Skill and Other Factors', in Molle and van Mourik (1989b), q.v.

Vester, M. (1989), 'Neue soziale Bewegungen und soziale Schichten', in U. C. Wasmuht (ed.), *Alternative zur alten Politik? Neue soziale Bewegungen in der Diskussion* (Darmstadt: Wissenschaftliche Buchgesellschaft).

Vielle, P. (1997), 'Le Coût indirect des responsabilités familiales', Ph.D. thesis (Florence: European University Institute).

Vilrokx, J., and Van Leemput, J. (1998), 'Belgium: The Great Transformation', in Ferner and Hyman (1998), q.v., 315–47.

Visser, J. (1990), *In Search of Inclusive Unionism* (Deventer: Kluwer).

——(1996), 'Trends and Variations in European Collective Bargaining', mimeo (Amsterdam: CESAR, University of Amsterdam).

——and Hemerijck, A. (1997), *A Dutch 'Miracle'* (Amsterdam: Amsterdam University Press).

Voelzkow, H. (1990), *Mehr Technik in die Region: Neue Ansätze zur regionalen Technikförderung in Nordrhein-Westfalen* (Wiesbaden: DUV).

——and Glassmann, U. (1998), 'The Governance of Local Economies in Germany', Cologne: Max Planck Institut für Gesellschaftsforschung, mimeo.

Vogt, E. V. (1972), 'Norway', in Mol (1972), q.v.

Von Trotha, T. (1990), 'Zum Wandel der Familie', *Kölner Zeitschrift für Soziologie und Sozialpsychologie*, 42/3: 452–73.

Voyé, L. (1994), 'Belgique: Crise de la civilisation parossiale et recomposition de la croire', in Davie and Hervieu-Léger (1994), q.v.

Waerness, K. (1989), 'Caring', in Boh *et al.* (1989), q.v.

Wagner, G., Ott, N., and Hoffmann-Nowotny, H.-J. (eds.) (1989), *Familienbildung und Erwerbsbeteilung im demografischen Wandel* (Berlin: Springer).

Wall, R., Robin, J., and Laslett, P. (eds.) (1983), *Family Forms in Historical Europe* (Cambridge: Cambridge University Press).

Wallis, R., and Bruce, S. (1992), 'Secularization: The Orthodox Model', in Bruce (1992), q.v.

Ward, C. K. (1972), 'Ireland', in Mol (1972), q.v.

Watanuki, J. (1991), *Social Structure and Voting Behaviour in Japan* (New Haven: Yale University Press).

Waters, M. (1990), *Ethnic Options: Choosing Identities in America* (Berkeley: University of California Press).

Weber, I. (1994), 'Soziale Schichtung und Gesundheit', in Geißler (1994c), q.v.

Weber, M. (1922), *Wirtschaft und Gesellschaft* (Tübingen: Mohr).

Weiss, L., (1988), *Creating Capitalism* (Oxford: Blackwell).

Wiegand, E. (1992), *Zunahme der Ausländerfeindlichkeit? Einstellung zu Fremden in Deutschland und Europa* (Mannheim: ZUMA).

Wieviorka, M. (1996), 'Cultural Differences and Democracy: United States and France', European Forum 1995–96 (Florence: European University Institute).

Wilensky, H. (1975), *The Welfare State and Equity* (Berkeley: University of California Press).

—— (1976), *The 'New Corporatism', Centralization, and the Welfare State* (Beverly Hills, Calif.: Sage).

Willaime, J.-P. (1994), in 'Laïcité et religion en France', in Davie and Hervieu-Léger (1994), q.v.

Williamson, O. (1975), *Markets and Hierarchies* (New York: Free Press).

—— (1985), *The Economic Institutions of Capitalism* (New York: Free Press).

Williamson, P. J. (1985), *Varieties of Corporatism* (Cambridge: Cambridge University Press).

Willis, R. J., and Michael, R. T. (1997), 'Innovation in Family Formation: Evidence on Cohabitation in the United States', in Ermisch and Ogawa (1997), q.v.

Wilson, B. (1966), *Religion in Secular Society* (London: Watts).

Wilthagen, T. (ed.) (1998), *Advancing Theory in Labour Law and Industrial Relations in a Global Context* (Amsterdam: North Holland).

Windolf, P. (1992), 'Zyklen der Bildungsexpansion 1870–1990', *Zeitschrift für Soziologie*, 21/2: 110–25.

—— and Beyer, J. (1996), 'Co-operative Capitalism: Corporate Networks in Germany and Britain', *British Journal of Sociology*, 47/2: 205–31.

Windmuller, J. P. (1969), *Labor Relations in the Netherlands* (Ithaca, NY: Cornell University Press).

—— and Gladstone, A. (eds.) (1984), *Employer Associations and Industrial Relations: A Comparative Study* (Oxford: Oxford University Press).

Withol de Wenden, C. (1988), 'Les Pays européens face à l'immigration', *Pouvoirs*, 47: 133–44.

Wright, E. O. (1979), *Class Structure and Income Determination* (New York: Academic Press).

—— (1985), *Classes* (London: Verso).

—— (1997), *Class Counts* (Cambridge: Cambridge University Press).

Young, M., and Wilmott, P. (1973), *The Symmetrical Family* (London: RKP).

Zariski, R. (1980), 'Italy', in Merkl (1980*b*), q.v.

Zysman, J. (1983), *Governments, Markets, and Growth: Financial Systems and the Politics of Industrial Change* (Ithaca, NY: Cornell University Press).

INDEX